A Dictionary

of

Words and Phrases

Used in

Ancient and Modern

Law

BY

ARTHUR ENGLISH

OF THE NEW YORK BAR, FORMERLY ASSISTANT
ATTORNEY DEPARTMENT OF INTERIOR,
WASHINGTON, D. C.

In Two Volumes
Volume I

BeardBooks
Washington, D.C.

A Dictionary
of
Words and Phrases
Used in
Ancient and Modern
Law

Washington, D. C. :

Washington Law Book Co.

Entered according to the Act of Congress, in the year 1898,

by

Arthur English

in the office of the Librarian of Congress, at Washington, D. C.

Reprinted 2000 by Beard Books, Washington, D.C.

ISBN 1-58798-066-5

Printed in the United States of America

EXPLANATORY STATEMENT.

A dictionary proper should be confined to words, and the definitions of those words. It should be neither a digest nor a collection of essays or briefs. It should also contain all the words ancient and modern that a student or lawyer might come across in his readings. No dictionary is complete without the ancient words or terms, any more than it would be without the modern words.

In this work the effort has been to make the definitions as short as possible, yet so clear that a man without legal education can understand them. Purely statutory and judicial definitions have been avoided because these are continually being changed, to meet changed conditions. As from 15,000 to 20,000 cases are annually decided in the United States by the Supreme Courts alone, decisions given in a book of this kind would be worthless, particularly when digests and reports are issued monthly, quarterly and annually. Further, citations do not belong in a dictionary, but in a digest.

Essays or long discussions of subjects have been avoided because few have time to read such, and fewer care to, while those who have time prefer to investigate for themselves.

In most cases the definition has been placed under the principal word either in singular or plural. All kinds of estates are either under estate or estates ; all courts under court or courts ; all evidence under evidence ; all bills under bill or bills ; all laws under law or laws, &c.

Of old writs most are under Breve, Capias, or begin with De. A complete system of cross-references will be found in all except leading subjects, such as those mentioned above, in which case it was not deemed necessary. Maxims have been purposely excluded, as have phrases which are not names, as neither is properly part of a dictionary, but belong in a different work. An Appendix is added, in which will be found the Constitution of the U. S., Magna Charta of 9 Hen. III., as confirmed by Edward I., the English regnal years, and abbreviated titles of reports and works on law.

THE AUTHOR.

NEW YORK CITY, \
June, 1890.

A DICTIONARY

OF

WORDS AND PHRASES

USED IN

ANCIENT AND MODERN LAW.

A.

A. In Roman law, the letter on a juror's ballot meaning absolvo; in elections, antiquo. In Law French, of ; at ; to ; for ; in ; with ; from. In Latin, from ; by ; at ; on ; if ; of. The brand placed upon a convicted adulteress by the New England Puritans of 1658–1785.

A. 1. First-class ; of the highest class.

A. D. Anno Domini ; in the year of our Lord.

A. G. Attorney-General.

A. J. Assistant, or associate judge or justice.

A. J. J. Associate judges or justices.

A. L. J. Associate law judge or justice.

A. R. Anno Regni (in the year of the reign.)

A aver et tener. To have and to hold.

A cancellis. A chancellor.

A consiliis. Of counsel. Counsellor.

A cueillette. In French law, the taking of freight on condition that the whole cargo be completed from other sources.

A dato. Same as A DATU.

A datu. From the date.

A die datus. From the day of the date.

A forfait et sans garantie. A French expression equal to " without recourse."

A fortiori. By a stronger reason.

A latere. From the side. Collateral, without right. See LEGALE A LATERE.

A libellis. An officer having charge of petitions addressed to the sovereign. A chancellor.

A me. A tenure direct from a superior lord. Detaining unjustly from one. To withhold unjustly from another.

A mensa et thoro. From table and bed. From bed and board.

A nativitate. From birth ; as a disability a nativitate.

A palatio. Palatine.

A posteriori. An argument based on observation. An argument which demonstrates cause from facts taken as an effect.

A prendre. To take. See PROFIT A PRENDRE.

A priori. An argument on analogy. Argument demonstrating effects from facts taken as a cause.

A quo. From which.

A rendre. That which is to be rendered or paid.

A responsis. One whose duty was to give answers.

A rubro ad nigrum. From the red to the black. From the title, which was anciently in red, to the body of a statute, which was in black.

A saver. Same as A SAVOIR.

A savoir. To know ; to wit.

A secretis. A chancellor.

A sociis. From its associates ; from the context ; from its surroundings.

A tort. Of or by wrong ; wrongfully.

A vinculo matrimonii. From the tie or bond of marriage.

(1)

Ab. From ; away from ; out of ; down from ; since ; after ; by ; at ; in ; on.

Ab actus. An officer who entered the proceedings of a court. A clerk of a court.

Ab epistolis. A secretary or one having charge of the correspondence of another.

Ab initio. From the beginning.

Ab irato action. See ACTION AB IRATO.

Ab vinculis matrimonii. From the bonds of matrimony.

Abacot. A cap worn by ancient kings.

Abactor. A cattle stealer.

Abactores. Same as ABACTORS.

Abactors. Stealers and drivers away of cattle.

Abacus. Meaning arithmetic. (From abacus, a table on which the ancients made figures).

Abacy. A religious house governed by an abbot.

Abalienate. To alienate or estrange one. To transfer the ownership to another.

Abalienation. A transfer of property by sale or other alienation ; the complete transfer of a thing.

Abalieno. Abalienate.

Abamita. A sister of one's great great grandfather.

Abadengo. In Spanish law, lands or towns within the jurisdiction of an abbot. Land owned by a religious corporation.

Abandon. To give up ; to forsake ; to desert ; to leave ; to relinquish ; to renounce; to resign ; to abdicate ; to surrender ; to forego.

Abandonee. One to whom property is relinquished or abandoned. An insurer of property which has become a total loss.

Abandonment. Desertion ; surrender; relinquishment of property. See ABANDON.

Abandonment for torts. In Civil law, the abandoning by the master, of a slave or animal that had committed a tort.

Abandum. A thing sequestered, proscribed, or abandoned.

Abandun. Same as ABANDUM.

Abante. From before.

Abarnare. To discover and disclose a crime to a magistrate.

Abasista. An arithmetician.

Abatamentum. Abatement (which see).

Abatare. To abate ; to overthrow, demolish.

Abatavit. He or she abated.

Abate. To break down or destroy ; to step in between a former possessor and his heirs.

Abatement. A making less ; a destroying ; suspension ; removal. The term applied to a plea praying that the suit may abate. An entry by interposition.

Abatement of a freehold. Where a stranger makes entry and gets possession of the freehold before the heir enters. See INTRUSION.

Abatement of an estate. Same as ABATEMENT OF A FREEHOLD.

Abatement of a legacy. Where a legacy is reduced in order to pay all debts and other legacies.

Abatement of a nuisance. The removal of a nuisance.

Abatement of a writ. Where it is quashed or set aside on account of some defect.

Abatement of litigation. Where an action is terminated by the death of a party or change of interest during the litigation.

Abatement, Plea in. A plea which defeats a particular action without affecting the right ; one which suspends the right to sue.

Abater. Same as ABATOR.

Abatist. Beat down, quashed, defeated, interposed.

Abator. He who removes a nuisance. He who steps in between a former possessor and his heirs. The cause in effecting an abatement. See INTRUSION.

Abatre. To abate, throw down, or destroy.

Abatu. Wood cut, or fallen.

Abatuda. Anything diminished.

Abatuda, Moneta. Money clipped.

Abatude. Same as ABATUDA.

Abatus. Beaten or thrown down.

Abavia,. In Civil law, a great great grandmother.

Abavita. A great great grandfather's sister.

Abavunculus. In Civil law, a great great grandmother's brother.

Abavunculus magnus. Same as ABAVUNCULUS.

Abavunculus maximus. Same as ABAVUNCULUS.

Abaty (s'Abaty). Entered by abatement ; interposed.

Abaudissent. To give themselves up to.

Abavus. Forefather ; ancestor ; great great grandfather.

Abbaiaunce. Abeyance.

Abbaizance. Abeyance.

Abbas. An Abbat.

Abbat. (or Abbot). A spiritual governor of a religious house.

Abbatis. A hostler or steward of the stables.

Abbatissa. An Abbess.

Abbetare. To abet ; an abettor.

Abbetator. An abbetor.

Abbetor. An accomplice ; one who aids, abets, or encourages a crime.

Abbetum. Abatement.

Abbot. See ABBAT.

Abbreviamentum. An abridgement ; a summary.

Abbreviare. To abridge ; to make shorter.

Abbreviate of adjudication. In Scotch law, an abstract of the adjudication, the amount of debt and the land adjudged.

Abbreviatio. An abbreviation.

Abbreviatio placitorum. An abstract of pleadings previous to the Year Books.

Abbreviation. A name, word or term which is shortened so that a part stands for the whole.

Abbreviators. Officers who draft the the Pope's briefs and preface papal bulls.

Abbreviature. A short draft.

Abbrevoir. A watering place.

Abbroach. To forestall a market. See ABBROCHEMENT.

Abbrocamentum. Abbrochement.

Abbroche. Same as ABBROACH.

Abbrochement. The buying up of goods by wholesale before they are brought to market and selling at retail ; forestalling a market or fair. See FORESTALLING.

Abbuttals (or Abutals). The buttings or boundaries of lands.

Abcariare. To carry away.

Abdicate. To renounce or refuse anything, particularly the throne or government. In Roman law, to disinherit.

Abdication. A renunciation ; the voluntary relinquishment of an office (not in favor of another), before the term has expired.

Abdico. To renounce a thing.

Abditorium. A hiding place for relics, plate, or money.

Abditus. Hidden, concealed.

Abducere. To carry away a human being.

Abduco. To abduct. To alienate. To entice.

Abduction. The offense of taking away or detention of a man's wife, child or ward, either by violence or fraud or persuasion.

Abduxit. He led or carried away.

Abearance. Deportment, conduct, or behavior.

Abeched. Satisfied.

Aberemurder. Murder as distinguished from manslaughter and chance-medley.

Abesse. To be absent. To be out of one's possession. To be out of existence.

Abet. To encourage, incite, promote or procure a crime.

Abettans. Abetting.

Abettare. To abet ; an abettor.

Abbettator. An abbettor.

Abbettor. One who aids, abets, encourages, or incites a crime ; an accomplice.

Abeyance. In expectation, remembrance and intendment of law. (An estate is in abeyance when present in no man, but belonging to him who is next to enjoy it).

Abiaticus. A grandson.

Abide. To dwell ; to sojourn. To await ; to support ; to suffer.

Abide by. To obey, to conform to.

Abiding by. In Scotch law, the judicial declaration of a party that he abides by a deed which has been attacked as forged, at his peril.

Abiding conviction. The settled conviction of guilt which may follow a thorough examination of all the evidence in a cause.

Abigeat. The crime of stealing cattle by driving them away in herds.

Abigeator. A cattle stealer.

Abigeatus. The offense of cattle stealing.

Abigei. Persons who stole cattle.

Abigere. In Civil and Scotch law, to drive away ; applied to cattle stealing.

Abigere. To drive out. To produce abortion.

Abigeus. A cattle stealer.

Abigo. To drive away. (Applied to abigeators).

Ability. Capacity. State of being able ; power to do anything. Legal capacity.

Abitio. A going away.

Abishering. Same as ABISHERSING.

Abishersing. Immunity from, being quit of, amerciaments.

Abjectire. To lose a cause by default or neglect to prosecute.

Abjudicare. To deprive of a thing by the decision of a court.

Abjudicate. To give away by judgment.

Abjudicatio. Depriving by judgment.

Abjudication. The depriving of a thing by the judgment of a court, Rejection.

Abjudicatus. Forejudged.

Abjudico. To give sentence against one.

Abjurare. To forswear ; to renounce or abandon upon oath.

Abjuratio. Abjuration.

Abjuratio Regni. Abjuration of the Realm.

Abjuration. A renunciation upon oath.

Abjuration of allegiance. The renunciation of allegiance to one sovereign preparatory to taking the oath of allegiance to another.

Abjuration of the Realm. An oath taken to forsake the realm forever. (Anciently a person accused of any crime, except treason or sacrilege, who took refuge in a church or other sanctuary, might save his life by confessing his offense and swearing to forsake the realm).

Abjure. To deny anything on oath.

Abjuro. To abjure.

Able-bodied. Absence of defects which incapacitate to the performance of a certain duty.

Ablegate. To send out. An envoy of the Pope.

Ablegatus. Same as ABLEGATE.

Ablocation. In Roman law, a hiring out for money.

Abmatertera. A great great grandmother's sister.

Abnepos. A great great grandson.

Abneptis. A great great granddaughter.

Abnormal. Irregular ; departing from a fixed rule. A term applied to law affecting persons not under natural relations or conditions, as if insane or under age.

Abnormis. Abnormal.

Abode. Habitation, dwelling place.

Abolition. Annulling ; effacing ; abrogating ; an amnesty ; leave given by a judge to desist from prosecution.

Abolitor. One who takes away a thing.

Abordage. In French law, collision of vessels.

Abortion. A miscarriage, or the premature expulsion of the fœtus. The foetus when brought forth before the term of gestation is completed.

Abortive trial. See TRIAL, ABORTIVE.

Abortus. A child delivered before the proper time.

About. Around, close to, near, in the proximity of.

Aboutissement. An abutment or abuttal.

Above. Higher, upper, superior.

Above, court. The appellate court to which a cause is removed.

Above, defendant. The defendant before an appellate court.

Above mentioned. Quoted above. The expression arose from writing or scrolls where everything written before was necessarily above.

Above par. See PAR, ABOVE.

Above, plaintiff. The plaintiff in an appellate court.

Abpatruus. A great great grandfather's brother.

Abrado. To rub off ; to erase.

Abrasio. Erasing in a writ.

Abridge. To shorten, condense, diminish. To make a declaration or count shorter in substance. To deprive of.

Abridgement. A compendium ; epitome. A digest of the law. The reduction of a demand. The condensation of the work of an author.

Abridgement of damages. The right which a court has in certain cases to reduce damages.

Abroad. In another country ; beyond the seas.

Abroachment. Same as ABBROCHEMENT.

Abroceur. A broker.

Abrogate. To set aside or appeal. To annul ; to abolish : to repeal.

Abrogation. The legal annulling or a repeal of a law. The act of abrogating.

Abrogation, express. Repeal by express words.

Abrogation, implied. An abrogation implied by law from facts or in a statute or treaty from terms of a subsequent one.

Abrogo. To take away anything ; to abrogate it ; to repeal.

Abs. The form of a or ab (from) in composition.

Abs-cedo. To depart from some place; to withdraw an action.

Abscessio. Abscession.

Abscession. A separating.

Abscessus. Departure. Absence.

Abscond. To disappear ; to hide one's self with intent to avoid legal process.

Absconding debtor. One who goes beyond the jurisdiction or conceals himself from his creditors.

Absconditor. One who hides. A debtor who secretes himself.

Absconditus. Hidden.

Abscondo. To conceal carefully ; to keep out of view.

Absence. Non-appearance.

Absence beyond seas. Out of England ; out of a State, or the United States.

Absence cum dolo et culpa. Absence to avoid a writ, subpœna, citation, arrest, or to defeat creditors.

Absence, entirely voluntary. That on account of business or trade.

Absence, necessary. Where a person is banished, transported, or confined in a penitentiary or prison.

Absence, necessary and voluntary. Absence in public service.

Absence, probable. That of students or scientists in study or investigation.

Absens. Absenting.

Absent. Not present. Laboring under legal disability.

Absente. Being absent.

Absentee. One who has departed from the State he lived in without leaving any one to represent him. One who never had a fixed residence in the State and resides abroad.

Absentees. Owners of land in Ireland who do not live upon it. A Parliament held in Dublin on May 10th, in the eighth year of Henry VIII.

Absentia. Not present. Laboring under some legal disability ; absent.

Absents. Remains away.

Absoile. To absolve, to pardon.

Absoluta. Absolute, complete.

Absolute. Unconditional ; complete in itself ; not relative ; final.

Absolute acquittal. A decree whereby an accused is declared innocent.

Absolute allegiance. See ALLEGIANCE, ABSOLUTE.

Absolute alienation. See ALIENATION, ABSOLUTE.

Absolute conveyance. One without condition or qualification.

Absolute covenant. See COVENANT, ABSOLUTE.

Absolute delivery. See DELIVERY, ABSOLUTE.

Absolute estate. One subject to no condition.

Absolute guaranty. See GUARANTY, ABSOLUTE.

Absolute interest. See INTEREST, ABSOLUTE.

Absolute law. See LAW, ABSOLUTE.

Absolute pardon. See PARDON, ABSOLUTE.

Absolute property. See PROPERTY, ABSOLUTE.

Absolute rights. See RIGHTS, ABSOLUTE.

Absolute rule. See RULE, ABSOLUTE.

Absolute sale. A perfected sale.

Absolute title. See TITLE, ABSOLUTE.

Absolute warrandice. In Scotch law, warranty against all the world.

Absolute warranty. See WARRANTY, ABSOLUTE.

Absolutely. Completely ; without condition or qualification.

Absolutio acquittal. Same as ACQUITTAL, ABSOLUTE.

Absolution. Legal acquittal of the penalty of excommunication. In French law, dismissal of a charge.

Absolutism. A government in which a person or class governs without any limitation or restraint.

Absolutorium. A means of deliverance from.

Absolutorius. Pertaining to acquittal.

Absolutus. Complete, perfect ; absolute.

Absolve. To set free ; to declare innocent ; to deliver from excommunication.

Absolvo. I acquit.

Absolvitur. In Scotch law, an acquittal. A decree in favor of a defendant.

Absoniare. To shun or avoid. (A word used in the Saxon oath of fealty).

Absque. Without ; out of ; far from ; contrary to.

Absque aliquo inde redendo. (Without rendering therefrom). A grant from the sovereign without a reservation of rent.

Absque consideratione curiæ. Without the consideration of the court.

Absque hoc. Without that. The formal words of a traverse in Latin.

Absque impetitione vasti. Without impeachment of waste. A clause in a lease releasing the lessee from liability for waste.

Absque tali causa. (Without such

cause). Words used in the replication de injuria.

Abstention. Preventing an heir from obtaining possession. The tacit renouncing, by an heir, of a succession.

Abstract. To take from ; to separate ; to remove; to take away. A concise abridgement ; an epitome, summary.

Abstract of fine. See FINE, ABSTRACT OF.

Abstract of Pleas. A short statement of pleas intended to be pleaded.

Abstract of Title. See TITLE, ABSTRACT OF.

Abstracted multures. See ACTION OF ABSTRACTED MULTURES.

Absurde. Absurdly ; discordantly.

Abundans. Abundant.

Abundant. Plentiful ; more than necessary.

Ab-undo. To overflow ; to abound; to be unnecessary.

Abuse. Excess of ordinary use. Violation. Departure from right. Legal though unjust action.

Abuse of a female child. Injury to the organs of generation in an unsuccessful attempt at sexual intercourse.

Abuse of distress. Where an animal that has been distrained is made use of, which makes the distrainer liable for a conversion.

Abuse of process. Obtaining an advantage over an opponent by the improper use of some regular legal proceeding.

Abusus. Abuse.

Abut. To touch ends. See ADJOINS.

Abbutare. To abut. To touch. To take a new direction. To bound upon.

Abutment. A mass of masonry at the end of a bridge ; the part which touches the land.

Abbuttals. The bounds of lands.

Abbutter. One whose land is contiguous to or abuts that of another.

Abutting. Bounding upon ; adjoining ; in contact with.

Ac. And.

Ac etiam. And also. Words used in introducing the real cause of an action where it was necessary to allege a fictitious cause to give the court jurisdiction. See BILL OF MIDDLESEX.

Ac si. As if.

Academy. A society of men associated for the promotion of some art ; a grammar school ; a seminary of learning.

Acapte. A feudal relief payable on every change of tenant by an emphyteusis.

Acate. A purchase, contract, or bargain.

Acc., Accord. Abbreviations of Accordant.

Accapitare. To pay homage or relief to lords of manors.

Accapitum. Money paid on admission to a feud ; relief due the chief lord.

Accedas ad curiam. (Go to the court). A Chancery writ directing the removal of a replevin suit from a hundred court or court baron to a superior court.

Accedas ad vice comitem. (Go to the sheriff). A writ to a coroner commanding him to deliver a writ to a sheriff directing the latter to make return on a writ which he had refused or neglected to return.

Accedens. Adding to ; joining ; increasing ; advancing.

Accedo. To approach. To fall to one's share. To befall. To rise or advance.

Accelerate. To hasten the time when an interest or estate is to vest in possession or enjoyment.

Acceleration. The shortening of the period, by extinguishment, surrender, or merger, within which the possession of an expectant estate is vested.

Accept. To acknowledge the sufficiency or validity of. To agree to pay a bill of exchange when due. To assent to the terms of. To receive with approval.

Accord and satisfaction. See SATIS-FACTION, ACCORD AND.

Accordant. Agreeing.

According. In accordance with, in agreement with.

According to law. As the law would cause or compel a thing to be done. In accordance with the provisions of law.

Accouchement. The act of being delivered of a child.

Accoucheur. A male assistant in child-birth.

Accoucheuse. A midwife ; a female assistant in child-birth.

Account. A computation ; a bill. Money had and received by defendant for plaintiff's use. A writ or action against a bailiff or receiver, to render account. A business relation in which debts and credits are created. A statement of debts and credits. A record of receipts and expenditures.

Account, action of. See ACTION OF ACCOUNT.

Account, book. See BOOK-ACCOUNT.

Account book. See BOOK, ACCOUNT.

Account current. An open account to which items are added at intervals ; one open to further charges.

Account, deposit. See DEPOSIT ACCOUNT.

Account, final. The completing account ; one which makes further action unnecessary.

Account, first. One made prior to all others.

Account in bank. Same as BANK ACCOUNT.

Account, liquidated. See LIQUIDATED ACCOUNT.

Account, open. An account with one or more items unsettled ; one to which items are added at intervals.

Account, partial. An incomplete account. Involving but a part.

Account-render. See ACTION OF ACCOUNT-RENDER.

Account rendered. An account delivered to the debtor, showing the creditor's demand.

Account, running. See RUNNING ACCOUNT.

Account, stated. An account rendered and admitted as correct by the debtor.

Accountant. One who receives money to the use of another. A man employed in accounts.

Accountable. Liable to account ; liable to be called to account ; under obligation to render an account of money invested or held in trust for another.

Accountable receipt. An acknowledgement in writing of the receipt of money or property, and a promise to account to some person for all or a part of the same.

Accountant. A man employed in accounts. One who makes a written statement regarding trust property committed to his charge. One who receives anything for which he has to account to another.

Accountant-General. An officer in Chancery to receive money lodged in Court.

Accountants to the Crown. Persons and officers accountable to the Crown for moneys received by them.

Accounting. Making up and rendering an account.

Accounts, merchant's. See MERCHANT'S ACCOUNTS.

Accounts, mutual. Accounts kept between merchants ; those based on a course of dealing wherein each party has given credit to the other.

Accounts, public. The public accounts of the Kingdom or Government.

Accouple. To marry. To unite.

Accredit. To receive an envoy and credit him with the authority with which he comes. To send an envoy or agent with proper credentials.

Accreditulare. To purge one self of an offense by oath.

Accredulitare. Same as ACCREDITULARE.

Accrescere. To grow to ; to accrue.

Accresco. Same as ACCRESCERE.

Accretion. Increment ; a growing to ; the increase of land by natural causes.

Accroach. To attempt the exercise of sovereign power.

Accroche. To encroach. To delay.

Accrocher. In French law, to delay.

Accrocher un process. To stay the proceedings in a suit.

Accrual. The vesting of a right in a person without his act.

Accrue. To accede to; to become added to; to append to ; to fall due.

Accrued. Due and payable.

Accruer. The act of accruing. Increase.

Accruer, clause of. A clause in a deed to tenants in common, providing that the survivor shall receive the share of the other tenants on the latters' decease.

Accruing. Becoming, falling, but not yet due.

Accruing costs. See COSTS, ACCRUING.

Accumulated surplus. See SURPLUS, ACCUMULATED.

Accumulation. Collecting or adding to ; a gathering in quantity.

Accumulative. Cumulative ; heaping up ; additional.

Accumulative judgment. A judgment rendered after another judgment has already been rendered against the same person.

Accumulative sentence. A sentence passed before the expiration of the first one, which will take effect as soon as the first one ends.

Accusare. To charge ; to accuse.

Accusation. An indictment; the charging any person with a crime ; censure.

Accusator. Any kind of an accuser.

Accuse. To charge with a crime or offense.

Accuser. One who makes an accusation.

Accuso. To accuse.

Accustomed. Usual. Made customary by use.

Accustumatus. Accustomed.

Acephali. Levellers in the reign of Henry I. who acknowledged no superior.

Acequia. A canal or ditch.

Achat. Same as ACHATE.

Achate. A purchase or bargain.

Achate arere. Bought back.

Achators. Buyers. Contractors.

Achatours. Purveyors to the King.

Acherset. An ancient measure of corn, about eight bushels.

Acholite. A church servant next under a sub-deacon.

Acknowledge. To admit. To admit the validity of. To avow as one's act.

Acknowledgment. Confession; avowal ; admission ; owning to. The act of a party to an instrument writing, in declaring before the proper officer, that the instrument is his free act and deed. The official certificate of an officer before whom such a declaration is made.

Acknowledgment money. Sum paid by copyhold tenants to new landlords.

Acolothist. Same as ACHOLITE.

Acolyte. See ACHOLITE.

Acquainted. Familiar with ; well-known ; (as where one swears he is well acquainted with an applicant for naturalization, etc.) Having a substantial knowledge of the subject-matter, as in the matter of documents, etc.

Ac-quesco. To become physically quiet. To assent to an assertion.

Acquest. An estate newly acquired or acquired by purchase. Acquisition.

Acquets. Property acquired by purchase. Profits of property between husband and wife.

Acquiesce. To consent by silence, or neglect to dissent.

Acquiescence. Compliance ; assent ; a tacit approval or encouragement of an act done. A keeping quiet.

Acquietabimus. We will acquit.

Acquietancia. An acquittance ; an instrument by which the discharge of a debt is effected. Exemption from service or duty.

Acquietandas plegiis. A justice's writ to compel a creditor to acquit a surety after debt satisfied.

Acquietantia. An acquittance ; a release.

Acquietare. To acquit ; to pay ; to be clear of a debt or criminal charge.

Acquietatus. Acquitted ; pronounced innocent by a jury.

Acquietatus inde. Therefore he is discharged or acquitted.

Acquire. To gain ; to come to ; to attain ; to obtain.

Acquired. Obtained ; procured. Obtained from an ancestor in any way other than by gift, devise, or descent.

Acquired allegiance. See ALLEGIANCE, ACQUIRED.

Acquiro. To acquire ; to acquire by some rule of law.

Acquisition. An increase or accession; the act of making a thing one's own. Procuring property ; the property itself.

Acquisition, original. That which is obtained by one's own effort, and not derived from the act of another or the act of law.

Acquisition, derivative. That which is obtained by the operation of law or the act of another.

Acquisitive prescription. See PRESCRIPTION, ACQUISITIVE.

Acquisitum. A purchase. Newly acquired feudal rights.

Acquit. To set free ; to clear from a charge or accusation ; to discharge ; to absolve.

Acquit a caution. In French law, a certificate stating that security had been given that freight loaded on a ship would not be exported.

Acquittal. Setting free ; the act of a jury in finding a person not guilty who has been accused of a crime.

Acquittal, absolute. See ABSOLUTE ACQUITTAL.

Acquittal, former. An acquittal in a former prosecution.

Acquittal in fact. A verdict of not guilty.

Acquittal in law. A discharge by operation of law.

Acquittance. A written discharge of a debt.

Acquitted. Released from a debt, duty, charge or obligation. Exonerated ; freed from legal custody ; judicially discharged from an accusation.

Acre. An open ground or field. A surface of land containing in England and the United States 43,560 square feet.

Acre-fight. A duel by single combatants, with sword and lance.

Across. From one side to the side opposite.

Act. A thing done or performed. The exercise of power. An effect produced by power exerted. A law made by a legislative body.

Act, adopted. An act for a certain locality which does not come into effect until adopted by the people of that locality.

Act, authentic. See AUTHENTIC ACT.

Act book. See BOOK, ACT.

Act, bubble. See BUBBLE ACT.

Act, collateral. See COLLATERAL ACT.

Act, felony. See FELONY ACT.

Act in pais. An act out of court.

Act, judicial. One performed by a court or person having discretionary power to determine a question.

Act, ministerial. See MINISTERIAL ACT.

Act, municipal corporation. Stat. 5 and 6 Wm. IV. c. 75.

Act of adjournal. In Scotch law, an order of the court of justiciary entered on its minutes.

Act of attainder. An act of a legislature declaring a person attainted.

Act of bankruptcy. An act which exposes a debtor to proceedings in a court of bankruptcy.

Act of curatory. The order of a court by which a curator or guardian is appointed.

Act of faith. See AUTO DE FE.

Act of God. An accident which results from natural causes.

Act of grace. A Scotch act passed in 1696, providing for the maintenance of debtors imprisoned by their creditors. An executive or legislative act pardoning offenders.

Act of honor. Acceptance of protested paper to save someone's credit. See ACCEPTANCE SUPRA PROTEST.

Act of indemnity. An enactment for the protection or relief of one who has committed some illegal act which subjects him to a penalty.

Act of Parliament. An act of the legislature of Great Britain.

Act of insolvency. Such an act as shows a person or corporation insolvent or unable to meet obligations, or in the case of a bank, of doing that required by law to sustain its credit.

Act of State. An act done by a State official within the scope of his authority.

Act of the law. Operation of the law.

Act of settlement. The 12 and 13 William III., c. 2, by which the Crown of England was limited to the present royal family.

Act of supremacy. Statute 1st Elizabeth, c. 1, by which the supremacy of the Crown in matters ecclesiastical was established.

Act of uniformity. Statute 1 Elizabeth, c. 2, and 13 and 14 Charles II, c. 4, by which the public worship of the Church of England is regulated.

Act of warding. A warrant to imprison a debtor.

Act on petition. A summary method to obtain the adjudication of a question in divorce, probate, or ecclesiastical matters.

Act, overt. See OVERT ACT.

Act, preliminary. See PRELIMINARY ACT.

Act, private. An act which affects only certain persons or corporations.

Act, public. A statute which affects the public at large.

Act, special. Same as ACT, PRIVATE.

Act, Tenterden's. See TENTERDEN'S ACT.

Act, test. See TEST ACT.

Act, Thellusson. See THELLUSSON ACT.

Acta. The acts or proceedings of magistrates and public officers, or courts of record. Records ; actions ; the acts of individuals.

Acta diurna. Daily acts,

Acta in toga. Acts in the gown.

Acta publica. The register of public acts.

Acte. In French law, a writing attesting the performance of an act or the happening of an event.

Acte authentique. In French law, a deed executed before a public officer in accordance with law.

Acte de francisation. In French law, a certificate attesting to the registration of a ship.

Acte d'heritier. In French law, act of inheritance. An act indicating the intention of an heir to accept an inheritance.

Acte extra-judiciaire. In French law, a document served by one party upon another without legal proceedings.

Actes de noissance. In French law, certificates of birth.

Actes de mariage. In French law, certificates of marriage.

Actes de deces. In French law, certificates of death.

Actes de l'etat civil. In French law, public documents.

Actilia. Armour. Military utensils.

Acting. Performing the duties of an office which belongs to another ; as, acting partner, executor, &c,

Actio. An action. A suit.

Actio ab irato. Doing an act through anger. An action to set aside a will, testament, or devise against an heir.

Actio accrevit. An action has accrued.

Actio ad exhibendum. An action to exhibit. In Civil law, an action to compel the production of a thing with the cause of detaining it.

Actio æstimatoria. In Civil law, an action by a buyer to reduce a contract price.

Actio arbitraria. In Civil law, an action depending on the discretion of a judge.

Actio bonæ fidei. Action of good faith.

Actio calumniæ. In Civil law, an action to prohibit a defendant from prosecuting a groundless action.

Actio civilis. A civil action.

Actio commodati. In Civil law, an action to enforce the obligation of borrowing or lending.

Actio commodati directa. An action brought to recover a thing loaned, and not returned.

Actio commodati contraria. Actions brought to compel the execution of a contract.

Actio communi dividundo. In Civil law, an action to secure a division of joint property.

Actio condictio indebiti. An action to recover a sum of money paid by mistake.

Actio confessoria. In Civil law, an action for the enforcement of a servitude which the plaintiff claims in the land of another.

Actio contraria. A cross-action.

Actio damni injuria. In Civil law, a class of actions for damages.

Actio de dolo malo. Action of fraud.

Actio de pecunia constituta. In Civil law, an action against one who had engaged to pay money.

Actio de peculio. In the Roman law, an action to which fathers and masters were liable on the contracts of their children and servants to the extent of their separate estate.

Actio depositi contraria. An action to compel a depositor to fulfill his contract.

Actio depositi directa. An action brought to get back something deposited.

Actio directa. A direct or strict law action as distinguished from equity.

Actio empti. In Civil law, an action to compel a seller to perform or compensate for failure so to do. See ACTIO VENDITI.

Actio ex conducto. One to compel a bailee to deliver the thing hired.

Actio ex contractu. An action based on contract.

Actio ex delicto. One based on tort.

Actio ex empto. An action of purchase ; brought by the buyer to obtain possession of the thing bought.

Actio exercitoria. An action against the owner of a ship on contracts made by the owner's slave while the latter was navigating the ship.

Actio ex vendito. An action of sale ; brought by the seller to recover the price of the article sold and delivered.

Actio ex locatio. In Civil law, an action against one who hired an article.

Actio ex stipulatu. In Civil law, an action to enforce a stipulation.

Actio familiæ erciscundæ. In Civil law, an action for apportioning an inheritance.

Actio finium regundorum. A mixed action for division and regulation of boundaries.

Actio furti. Action of theft.

Actio honoraria. In Civil law, an honorary or prætorian action.

Actio indirecta. Any action not included in actio directa.

Actio in factum. In Civil law, an action on a particular state of facts.

Actio in personam. An action against the person.

Actio in rem. Same as ACTION IN REM.

Actio in simplum. An action for the single value of a thing.

Actio institoria. In Civil law, an action against the owner of a shop, on contracts made by his slave, while the latter was in charge of the shop.

Actio judicati. In Civil law, an action after judgment in which a judicial warrant was issued to seize first the movables, which were sold, then the immovables, which were delivered to creditors. If the land did not satisfy the debts they likewise were sold.

Actio legis. An action at law.

Actio legis aquiliæ. An action to recover damages for maliciously injuring, killing, or wounding anything belonging to another.

Actio mandati. In Civil law, an action to enforce a contract of mandate.

Actio mixta. A mixed action. See ACTION, MIXED.

Actio negatoria. In Civil law, an action to resist a claim of servitude.

Actio negotiorum, gestorum. In Civil law, an action between principal and agent.

Actio non accrevit infra sex annos. A plea of the statute of limitations to the effect that plaintiff's claim had not accrued within six years.

Actio nominata. A named action; one where there was a writ de cursu before statute Westminster II.

Actio non. Abbreviation of actio non habere debet. (He ought not to have his action).

Actio non ulterius. The clause in the new plea to the further maintenance of the action, introduced in place of the plea puis darrein continuance, that the plaintiff ought not further to have or maintain his action.

Actio noxalis. A noxal action ; an action on account of an injury done by a slave.

Actio personalis. A personal action.

Actio pignoratitia. In Civil law, an action based on an action of pledge.

Actio præjudicialis. In Civil law, a preparatory action.

Actio præscriptis verbis. In Civil law, an action based on the unwritten law.

Actio prætoria. In Civil law, a prætorian action, or one introduced by the Prætor, as distinguished from the more ancient form of civil action.

Actio pro socio. An action brought by one partner to compel the other partners to fulfill their contract.

Actio publiciana. In Civil law, a prætorian action for the restoration of a thing in which one had obtained possession, but which had not yet ripened into a right of property.

Actio quanti minores. Same as ACTIO ÆSTIMATORIA.

Actio realis. A real action.

Actio redhibitoria. Same as ACTION, REDHIBITORY.

Actio rerum amotarum. In Civil law, an action for things taken away.

Actio rescissoria. In Civil law, an action for the recovery of a thing which has been lost by prescription but under such circumstances as would warrant a restoration.

Actio sequitur. An action lies (or is sustainable).

Actio serviana. In Civil law, an action to recover goods pledged for the rent of a farm.

Actio stricti juris. In Civil law, an action of strict right. Actions determined in accordance with the strict letter of the law.

Actio super casum. An action on the case.

Actio transitoria. An action, the cause of which might have arisen in one county as well as another. All personal actions whether ex contractu or ex delicto.

Actio (or interdictum), unde vi. To recover possession of land taken by force ; similar to the modern action of ejectment.

Actio utilis. An action against a principal on the contract of his agent.

Actio venditi. In Civil law, an action to compel a buyer to perform his obligation. See ACTIO EMPTI.

Actio vi bonorum raptorum. An action for goods forcibly taken, and to recover a penalty triple their value.

Actio vulgaris. In Civil law, a common action. A legal action.

Action. A civil or criminal proceeding in a court of justice for the determination of some issue of fact or law. A legal demand of a right. A proceeding in a court of law, which at one time ended with the judgment and did not include execution. See SUIT.

Action, accessory. In Scotch law, an action accessory or incident to another.

Action, amicable. An action brought to settle a doubtful point of law, by the consent of both parties.

Action, ancestral. One brought to recover land, based on the seizin of the ancestor.

Action, bailable. One which requires the defendant to furnish bail for his appearance.

Action, civil. The form of a suit for the recovery of that which is due.

Action, common law. An action allowed at common law and to bring which statutory authority is not necessary.

Action, criminal. An action for the punishment of a violator of public law.

Action, consistorial. In Scotch law, matrimonial cause.

Action, croft. See CROFT ACTION.

Action, declaratory. In Scotch law, one in which the right of the plaintiff is requested to be declared but nothing claimed by the defendant.

Action, droitural. An action brought to determine a right to the title, as distinguished from a possessory action.

Action emulationem vicini. An action brought merely to distress or injure another.

Action, ex-contractu. Action for a breach of contract. (As assumpsit, debt, covenant and detinue).

Action, ex-delicto. Action for wrong not connected with a contract. (As case, trover, replevin and trespass vi et armis).

Action, exercitory. See EXERCITORY ACTION.

Action, false. Same as ACTION, FICTITIOUS.

Action, feigned. Same as ACTION, FICTITIOUS.

Action, feodal. Real action.

Action, fictitious. One brought to settle a point of law, there being in fact no controversy.

Action for mesne profits. See ACTION OF MESNE PROFITS.

Action for real poinding. See POINDING, REAL.

Action, formed. One for which a set of words is prescribed. See ACTIO NOMINATA.

Action, honorary. Same as ACTIO PRÆTORIA.

Action in rem. An action for the recovery of a thing against the one possessing it, by the one to whom it belongs.

Action, joinder of. See JOINDER OF ACTION.

Action, joint. See JOINT ACTION.

Action, local. One which must be brought in a particular place.

Action, mixed. A suit for the thing and against the person who has it. An action partaking of the nature of both a real and personal action, as for the restitution of real property and damages from the one who committed a wrong in connection with it.

Action, noxal. In Roman law, an action on account of an injury done by a slave.

Action of a writ. A term applied to the plea by defendant that the plaintiff had no right to the writ sued upon although he might be entitled to another writ for the same matter.

Action of abstracted multures. An action for tolls against those who, being bound to grind their corn at a certain mill, neglected so to do.

Action of account. An action to compel the defendant to render an account and pay the balance, if any, to the plaintiff.

Action of account-render. An action against one having money for some purpose, where the jury determines the item in dispute.

Action of adherence. In Scotch law, an action for the restitution of conjugal rights.

Action of book debt. An action for the recovery of a debt evidenced by a book account.

Action of contravention. See CONTRAVENTION, ACTION OF.

Action of debt. An action for the recovery of money due on a contract whether expressed or implied, verbal or written, for a sum certain or which can be reduced to a certainty.

Action of deceit. See DECEIT.

Action of declarator. Same as DECLARATORY ACTION.

Action of jactitation. In Louisiana an action for slander of title.

(2)

Action of mesne profits. An action to recover rents, profits, and the value of waste or dilapidations committed by one who wrongfully held it from the other.

Action of proper improbation. In Scotch law, one brought to declare a writing false or forged.

Action of reduction. In Scotch law, one brought for the production of a writing to have it set aside, or its effect ascertained, or if not produced, that it shall be declared false or forged.

Action of seduction. An action for the loss of society and services of a wife or daughter, because of having been seduced.

Action of sett. See SETT, ACTION OF.

Action of simple reduction. In Scotch law, an action to have a writing called for declared null, until produced.

Action of tort. See TORT, ACTION OF.

Action of transumpt. See TRANSUMPT, ACTION OF.

Action of trespass. An action for damages for injuries resulting immediately from an act of force. If not the immediate result of the forcible act, the proper form of action is case. See ACTION UPON THE CASE.

Action of trespass on the case. Same as ACTION UPON THE CASE.

Action on account. Same as ACTION OF ACCOUNT.

Action on the case. See ACTION UPON THE CASE.

Action, ordinary. In Scotch law, an action not recissory.

Action, penal. A suit for some penalty or punishment on the parties sued. Action for the recovery of a penalty.

Action, personal. A suit on any contract or account, or for an offense or trespass; one brought to recover personal property.

Action, petitory. See PETITORY ACTION.

Action, popular. One for a breach of a penal statute.

Action, possessory. One brought to recover possession, without determining the right.

Action, prætorian. See ACTIO PRÆ-TORIA.

Action, preparatory. An action brought to determine a preliminary matter on which another matter depends, or to determine some question involved in another action.

Action qui tam. One brought on behalf of the King and the informer.

Action, real. One for the recovery of real property.

Action, recissory. One to avoid a deed or instrument writing. In Scotch law, an action of proper improbation, action of reduction, action of simple reduction. See those Titles.

Action, redhibitory. In Civil law, an action to set aside a sale because of defect in the thing sold.

Action, statutory. An action which can be brought by authority of some statute.

Action, transitory. One which may be brought in any county.

Action upon the case. An action for damages for injuries resulting indirectly from some act of force. See ACTION OF TRESPASS.

Actionable. That which furnishes ground for an action.

Actionare. To prosecute one in a suit at law.

Actionary. A shareholder.

Actiones nominatæ. Writs for which precedents existed. See REGISTER OF WRITS.

Actiones legis. Law suits.

Actions, consolidation of. See CONSOLIDATION OF ACTIONS.

Active. That which is in active existence.

Active debt. One drawing interest.

Active trust. One which requires action on the part of the trustee.

Acto. A coat of mail.

Acton Burnel. The statute of 11 Ed. I. A. D., 1283, ordaining the Statute Merchant.

Actor. The proctor or advocate in civil courts or causes. A plaintiff.

Actor dominicus. The lord's bailiff or attorney.

Actor ecclesiæ. The advocate or pleading patron of a church.

Actor in rem suam. An agent or attorney in his own business.

Actor villæ. The steward or head bailiff of a town or village.

Actores fabulæ. Fabulous or fictitious plaintiffs.

Actores provinciarum. Tax gatherers, treasurers or managers of the public debt.

Actornay. In Scotch law, an attorney.

Actrix. A female actor or plaintiff.

Acts, bread. English statutes providing for the sustenance of those in prison for debt.

Acts, confiscation. See CONFISCATION ACTS.

Acts, joint debtor. See JOINT DEBTOR ACTS.

Acts of court. The memoranda of the nature of pleas, particularly in an Admiralty Court.

Acts of Sederunt. Statutes of Scotland made by Lords of Session, by virtue of Act of Parliament of James V. The general rules and orders of the Scotch Court of Sessions.

Acts of Union. Between England and Wales, 27 Henry VIII., c. 27, and 34 and 35 Henry VIII., c. 26 ; between England and Scotland, 5 Anne, c. 8 ; and 6 Anne, cc. 6 and 23 ; between England and Ireland, 39 and 40 George III., c. 67.

Acts, recording. See RECORDING ACTS.

Acts, six. See SIX ACTS.

Acts, tenure of office. See TENURE OF OFFICE ACTS.

Actual. Existing in fact.

Actual breaking and entering. See BREAKING AND ENTERING, ACTUAL.

Actual cash value. The amount of cash which goods will bring in the market.

Actual continuance. See CONTINUANCE, ACTUAL.

Actual cost. See COST, ACTUAL.

Actual delivery. See DELIVERY, ACTUAL.

Actual fraud. See FRAUD, ACTUAL.

Actual loss. An actual destruction.

Actual malice. See MALICE, ACTUAL.

Actual notice. See NOTICE, ACTUAL.

Actual occupation. See OCCUPATION, ACTUAL.

Actual ouster. See OUSTER, ACTUAL.

Actual possession. Actual occupation.

Actual sale. See SALE, ACTUAL.

Actual total loss. See LOSS, ACTUAL TOTAL.

Actual use. See USE, ACTUAL.

Actuarius. An actuary.

Actuary. A short-hand writer. A copyist. A clerk who registered the acts of the convocation. A secretary of a public body or ecclesiastical court. The manager of a stock company. An adviser on matters of calculation. One skilled in the principles of annuities and insurance calculations.

Actum. An act. A public transaction in a legislative body, before the people, before a public official, or in a court. A thing done.

Actus. An act. The right of driving cattle through a place. A way between fields. The performing of a thing; public performance. An act of Parliament ; a statute.

Actus geminus. A two-fold act.

Actus Parliamenti. An act of Parliament.

Actutum. Immediately.

Ad. To; for; at; until; by; near; on; on account of; upon; toward; in relation to; about; concerning.

Ad admittendum clericum. (For admitting a clerk). A writ given a successful plaintiff in quare impedit commanding the bishop to admit his clerk.

Ad barras. Old term for a barrister.

Ad colligendum bona defuncti. To collect the goods of the deceased. See LETTERS AD COLLIGENDUM.

Ad communem legem. An old writ of entry brought by reversioners for the recovery of lands wrongfully alienated by a life-tenant.

Ad exhæreditationem. To the injury of the inheritance. Words in ancient writs of waste.

Ad factum præstandum. In Scotch law, obligations of such a character that one under them could not claim the act of grace, sanctuary, or cessio bonorum.

Ad filum aquæ. To the thread of the stream.

Ad filum viæ. To the middle of the way.

Ad inquirendum. To enquire. A judicial writ directing inquiry into a matter material to a cause pending.

Ad jura legis. For the rights of the law.

Ad jura regis. For (preserving) the rights of the Crown. A writ brought by the King's clerk against those who would eject him from a living.

Ad litem. For the suit ; with reference to the suit; for the purpose of prosecuting or defending a suit.

Ad longum. At length.

Ad melius inquirendum. A writ to a coroner directing him to hold a second inquest.

Ad nocumentum. To the nuisance. Words used in ancient assize of nuisance.

Ad ostium ecclesiæ. At the door of the church. A species of dower. See DOWER.

Ad quem. To which.

Ad quod damnum. To what damage. A writ directing the sheriff to inquire what damage if any will result if a specified act be done.

Ad quod non fuit responsum. To which there was no answer. A phrase used in old English reports signifying that a point raised was not noticed by the court or answered by the other side, or that an objection was met by the court and not again referred to by the counsel who made it.

Ad rationem ponere. To place at the bar and interrogate. To arraign on trial.

Ad recognoscendum. To recognize.

Ad referendum. To be referred. To be considered. Subject to the action of another.

Ad respondendum. See CAPIAS AD RESPONDENDUM.

Ad satisfaciendum. See CAPIAS AD SATISFACIENDUM.

Ad sectam. At the suit of.

Ad sectam index. See INDEX AD SECTAM.

Ad terminum qui præteriit. For a term which has passed; for an expired term. A writ of entry for lessor or his heirs where lands are withheld.

Ad tunc et ibidem. The clause of an indictment containing the statement of a matter "then and there being found."

Ad valorem duty. See DUTY, AD VALOREM.

Ad ventrem inspiciendum. See WRIT DE VENTRE INSPICIENDO.

Ad vitam. For life.

Ad waractum. To fallow.

Ad æquare. To make equal to; to level with.

Ad-æquatio. To make equal to; an adjusting; an adapting.

Ad-æque. In like manner, equally so.

Adæratio. An estimating in money.

Ad-æro. To estimate in money. To appraise; to reckon.

Adagium. An adage. A common saying. A maxim.

Adalat. Justice. Equity. Court of Justice.

Adawlut. A corruption of Adalat.

Adawlut, Dewanny. See DEWANNY ADAWLUT.

Adawlut, Foujdarry. See FOUJDARRY ADAWLUT.

Adcordabilis denarii. Money paid to a lord by his vassal upon the selling or exchanging of a feud.

Adcredulitare. To purge one's self of an offense by oath.

Ad-dicere. To award or adjudge anything to one. To sentence; to condemn. To give assent to a thing.

Addictio. The adjudging of goods and their possession to one.

Addicticius. Added, annexed, additional.

Addition. The estate, degree, occupation, and place of abode given one beside his name. In English law, estate, degree, or names of dignity, trade, mystery or occupation, place of residence.

Additional. Added to; joined to; given with some other. The title a person bears in addition to his name.

Additionales. Additional terms to be added to a previous contract.

Ad-do. To add. To give, bring, put, carry, place, lay, apply, &c., a person or thing to another. To bring near to; to add to or give; to join or annex to.

Address. An appeal. A petition. A consignment. The drawee's name and residence in a bill of exchange. That part of a bill in equity describing the court.

Address for service. The address of plaintiff or defendant where notice of proceedings may be served on him.

Adduce. To allege as relevant for proof.

Adeem. To take away; to revoke.

Adelantado. In Spanish law, a governor of a province. A presiding judge. A judge with jurisdiction over a part or the whole of a kingdom.

Adelgiare. To purge one's self of crime by oath.

Adeling. A title of honor belonging to a King's children. Also used by the Saxons to denote nobles in general.

Adempted. Taken away. See ADEMPTION.

Ademptio. A taking away; a seizure; a revocation of a legacy.

Ademptio bonorum. An ademption of goods.

Ademptio civitatis. A taking away the rights of citizenship.

Ademption. The disposal by a testator of property devised or bequeathed by his will or testament so that the devise or bequest is destroyed. The act by which this is done.

Adeo. So; as; so far; as far; so much.

Adeprimes. At first; for the first time; in the first place.

Adequate. Equal to; proportionate; sufficient. (Where there is an adequate remedy at law for redress of an injury, the parties cannot resort to a court of equity).

Adequate cause. See CAUSE, ADEQUATE.

Adequate consideration. See CONSIDERATION, ADEQUATE.

Adequate remedy. See REMEDY, ADEQUATE.

Aderere. In arrear; behind.

Adesouth. Under. Beneath.

Adespota. Without an owner or master. Things which have no owner or claimant.

Ad-esse. To be present. To advocate. To defend in law. To undertake a legal cause, as an attorney.

Adfatimi. Act of adoption.

Adferruminatio. In Civil law, welding iron.

Adfines. Affines.

Adfixus. Affixus.

Adgnatus. Same as AGNATUS.

Adhere. In Scotch law, to affirm a previous decision; to restore a conjugal right.

Adherence. In Scotch law, an action by either party for the restitution of conjugal rights.

Adhering. Attaching one's self to.

Adhibere. To bring one thing to another; to bring one to a place.

Adieu. Without day. Final dismissal from court.

Adiratus. Strayed or lost.

Adit. A horizontal entry to a mine.

Additus. A right of going through another's field to one's own; a public road; a carriage way.

Adjacens. Adjacent.

Adjacent. Lying near to, or in the neighborhood of.

Adjacentes. The sides on the breadth of land.

Adjectio. An adding to; annexation.

Adjective law. See LAW, ADJECTIVE.

Adjoin. To lie side by side; to be contiguous to.

Adjoining. Contiguous; touching; in contact with.

Adjourn. To put off; to delay; to postpone to a day certain.

Adjournal. In Scotch law, the business of a single day of the Court of Judiciary. Postponement.

Adjornare. To adjourn.

Adjournatur. It is adjourned.

Adjourned summons. See SUMMONS, ADJOURNED.

Adjourned term. See TERM, ADJOURNED.

Adjourner. To adjourn.

Adjournment. Putting off until another time or another time and place.

Adjournment day. A future day appointed for the trial of issues not then ready to be tried.

Adjournment day in error. A day set in English practice on which to finish matters left unfinished on affirmance day.

Adjournment day in eyre. The day when justices of eyre will again sit.

Adjudge. To pass a sentence; to decree; to decide judicially.

Adjudger. In Scotch law, one to whom property of a debtor is judicially transferred to satisfy a debt.

Adjudicata. Adjudged; decided; settled.

Adjudicataire. In Canadian law, one who buys at a sale made by order of court. In Scotch law, a judicial sale or process for transferring a debtor's estate to his creditor.

Adjudicate. To adjudge; to sentence; to determine.

Adjudicated. Sentenced; adjudged; determined.

Adjudicatio. An adjudication or award. One of the legal modes of obtaining property among the ancient Romans.

Adjudication. Judgment; d e c r e e; award.

Adjudication, articulate. See ARTICULATE ADJUDICATION.

Adjudication, former. A previous judicial determination of a matter without which a verdict could not have been rendered.

Adjudication in implement. In Scotch law, a grantee's action against a grantor who refuses to complete his title.

Adjudico. To adjudge or award a thing to one.

Adjudicatus. Same as ADJUDICATA.

Adjunctio. A joining to. An addition. Adjunction (which see).

Adjunctio verborum. A union of words.

Adjunction. A method of accession, or gaining property, when one man's property is materially affixed to that of another.

Adjuncts. Additional judges. Additional judges to the English High Court of Delegates.

Adjunctum. Common appurtenant. An incident. An adjunct.

Adjunctum accessorium. An accessory or appurtenance.

Adjusted. Determined the amount due as indemnity for a loss, or injury.

Adjustment. Regulation; settlement of rights, claims, etc. The termination, division, and settlement of a loss under a marine or other insurance policy.

Adjust. To regulate; to put in order; to determine what is due; to settle. To ascertain and apportion.

Adjuster. He who adjusts or determines the amount of a claim.

Adlegiare. To purge one's self of a crime by oath.

Adluvio. Same as ALLUVIO.

Admallare. To sue.

Admanuensis. One who lays his hand on the testament when he makes oath.

Admeasurement. An assignment by measure; reducing to measure. A writ against persons who usurp more than their share.

Admeasurement of dower. See ADMEASUREMENT, WRIT OF.

Admeasurement of pasture. See ADMEASUREMENT, WRIT OF.

Admeasurement, writ of. A writ allowed against a widow who withheld from an heir more than she was entitled to as dower; and against one who placed more cattle on a common than he was entitled to place there.

Admensuratio. Admeasurement.

Admininicle. Aid or support. Whatever pertains to judicial proceedings. Cumulative or corroborative testimony. Evidence introduced to prove a lost deed.

Adminicular. Auxiliary to. In aid or support of.

Adminicular evidence. Evidence in support of other evidence.

Adminiculate. To give adminicular evidence.

Adminiculator. One who supports. An officer in the Roman Catholic Church who administers to the necessities of widows, orphans, and poor and sick persons.

Adminiculum. Same as ADMINICLE.

Administer. To manage, take care of. To supply. To measure out. To perform the duties of administrator.

Administered. See ADMINISTER.

Administrable. Capable of being administered.

Administratio ad colligendum. Administration for the purpose of collecting and preserving goods about to perish.

Administratio cum testamento annexo. Administration with the will annexed.

Administratio de bonis non, vel de bonis non administratis. Administration of the goods not administered.

Administratio de son tort. Administration in his own wrong.

Administratio durante absentia. Administration during absence (of the executor).

Administratio durante m i n o r e ætate. Administration during minority of an executor.

Administratio pendente lite. Administration granted pending a suit about a will.

Administration. Aid or assistance. Management of property or public affairs. The service rendered in the settlement of a decedent's estate.

Administration ad colligendum. See ADMINISTRATIO AD COLLIGENDUM.

Administration, ancillary. See ANCILLARY ADMINISTRATION.

Administration cœterorum. Of the rest of the goods which cannot be administered under a limited power given.

Administration cum testamento annexo. Administration with the will annexed.

Administration de bonis non. Concerning goods not disposed of.

Administration de bonis non, cum testamento annexo. Upon goods not administered and with the will annexed to the letters.

Administration, foreign. Administration in another State or country.

Administration, letters of. Letters given by the probate court or officer to the person selected to administer upon an estate.

Administration, limited. See LIMITED ADMINISTRATION.

Administration, public. Administration by a public officer, usually where there are no relatives.

Administration, special. Limited in time or power.

Administration suit. A suit brought in chancery, in English practice, by any one interested, for administration of a decedent's estate, when there is doubt as to its solvency.

Administrator. One who assists in the care and direction of a thing or matter. He to whom the goods of the intestate are committed by a court.

Administrator at law. In Scotch law, the father.

Administrator, domestic. One appointed at the domicile of the deceased.

Administrator, foreign. One appointed by a jurisdiction foreign to that within which the deceased had his domicile, or in which he left property.

Administrator pendente lite. One who serves as an administrator while a suit is pending to test the validity of the will.

Administrator, public. A public officer who administers property, usually when there are no relatives.

Administrator with the will annexed. One appointed where the will names no executor or the one appointed will not or cannot serve.

Administratrix. A female administrator.

Admiral. Formerly an officer governing the King's Navy and Judge of the Admiralty Court. The title was not used in England until Ed. I.; prior to that he was styled Marinariorum Capitaneus. Commander of a naval fleet. Abolished in U. S. in 1891. See MARINARIORUM CAPITANEUS ; also ADMIRAL, REAR.

Admiral, Lord High. The chief officer of the English navy, and theoretical head of the Courts of Admiralty.

Admiral of the Port of London. A title of the Lord Mayor of London.

Admiral, Port. See PORT ADMIRAL.

Admiral, Rear. The highest grade of a naval commander in the U. S.

Admiral, Vice. A grade of naval commander in the U. S., abolished in 1890.

Admiralitas. Admiralty or Court of Admiralty. The Court of the Admiral.

Admiralty. See LAW, ADMIRALTY.

Admiralty, droit of. See DROIT OF ADMIRALTY.

Admiralty droits. See DROITS, ADMIRALTY.

Admiralty, High Court of. See COURT OF ADMIRALTY, HIGH.

Admiralty jurisdiction. See JURISDICTION, ADMIRALTY.

Admiralty territorial jurisdiction. Jurisdiction extending to all matters arising from navigation on navigable waters.

Admissible. Worthy of being entertained. Capable of being admitted.

Admissibility. The quality of being admissible.

Admission. The act of admitting.

Admission and institution. Admitting a clergyman into a church.

Admission, direct. Same as ADMISSION, EXPRESS.

Admission, express. One made openly and directly.

Admission, implied. One inferred from an act or the conduct of the party.

Admission, incidental. An admission made in connection with another matter, or in the admission of another fact.

Admission in pleading or evidence. Same as ADMISSION, JUDICIAL.

Admission, judicial. One made in pleadings or during the progress of a trial.

Admission, partial. In equity practice, a qualified, or uncertain admission.

Admission, plenary. Without any qualification.

Admission, solemn. Same as ADMISSION, JUDICIAL.

Admissionalis. An usher.

Admit. To permit. To take. To receive. To allow one to enter. To license. To give possession to.

Admittance. The entrance of a copyholder upon his estate.

Admittendo clerico. Admitting a clerk. A writ directed to a bishop requiring him to admit a clerk to a benefice.

Admittendo in socium. A writ for associating persons with judges in assize.

Admixtio. A mingling; admixture.

Admixture. Intermixture of the goods of different owners so that they are indistinguishable.

Ad-modum. Wholly, quite, just, exactly, completely.

Admonitio trina. The three warnings given to a prisoner standing mute before subjecting him to the peine forte et dure.

Admonition. A judicial reprimand. An ecclesiastical censure.

Admortization. The act of reducing to mortmain.

Adnepos. The son of a great great grandson.

Adneptis. The daughter of a great great granddaughter.

Adnichiled. Annulled, cancelled or made void.

Adnichiler. Same as ADNICHILED.

Adnihil. To annul.

Adnihilare. To annul.

Adnihilo. To reduce to nothing.

Adnotatio. The subscription of a name or signature to an instrument.

Adolescentia. The age between puberty and majority.

Adolescence. The age between childhood and manhood or womanhood; from twelve to twenty-one in females, fourteen to twenty-one in males.

Adonque. Then.

Adonques. Then.

Adopt. To receive as one's own. To take as a son or daughter the child of another.

Adoptator. One who adopts another; an adopter.

Adoptio testamentaria. Adopted by will.

Adoption. The taking or choosing of another's child as one's own.

Adoptive act. See ACT, ADOPTIVE.

Adoptivus. Pertaining to adoption; made or acquired by adoption; adoptive.

Adoun. Then.

Ad-promissor. One who is security for another, bail.

Adquieto. Payment.

Adquirere. Same as ACQUIRERE.

Adrahmare. To pledge solemnly.

Adrectare. To do right, satisfy, or make amends.

Adrhamire. Same as ADRAHMARE.

Adrift. Floating on the water and not deposited on the shore.

Adrogate. To adopt an impubes. See ADROGATIO; also IMPUBES.

Adrogatio. In Roman law, the adoption of a boy under fourteen, or a girl under twelve. See IMPUBES.

Ads., Adsm., Ats. Abbreviations or contractions of AD SECTAM.

Adsallire. To assail.

Adrogation. Same as ADROGATIO.

Adscendentes. Ascendants.

Adscititious. Additional. Supplemental. Not essential.

Adscribo. To add in writing or by writing, as by a codicil. To add one's name to an instrument as a witness. To annex or to bind to in writing.

Adscript. Written after. Attached. A serf attached to an estate. A villain regardant.

Adscripti. Annexed by writing. Ascribed; set apart.

Adscripti glebæ. Annexed to the soil. Slaves of the Middle Ages, who were sold with the land.

Adscription. The attachment of one to land so that neither is transferred without the other.

Adscriptitii glebæ. Quasi-freemen, annexed or adstricted to the soil; persons employed in cultivating the soil and in performing other rural services for the owner. See ADSCRIPTI GLEBÆ.

Adscriptitius. Limited, annexed, or bound to.

Adscriptive. Attached to the land.

Adscriptus. Added, joined, or annexed or bound by or in writing; enrolled, registered; united, joined, annexed, bound to, generally.

Adscriptus, fundus. See FUNDUS ADSCRIPTUS.

Adscriptus glebæ. Annexed to the soil; belonging to or attached to the soil.

Adscriptus, servus colonæ. See SERVUS COLONÆ ADSCRIPTUS.

Adsecurare. To make secure; as by giving pledges.

Adsecuratio. Assurance; insurance.

Adsertor. One who (formally) asserts that another is free or a slave. A freer, protector, deliverer, advocate.

Adsertores. The friends who came forward on behalf of the man held in servitude, who could do nothing for himself.

Adsessor. Assessor. Judge.

Adsessores. In Roman law, side judges; assistants to the regular judges.

Adsignare. To affix a seal to an instrument; to seal it; to seal it in company with others. To assign; to designate for a specific purpose.

Adstipulator. In Roman law, one who received the same promise as his principal and could exact fulfillment from the promisor, even if his principal were dead.

Adtractus. A purchase.

Adtunc. Then.

Adtunc existens. Then being.

Adult. In Civil law, a person who has reached the age of fourteen if a male, or twelve if female. In Common law, a person aged twenty-one.

Adulter. One who corrupts. A man who has illicit intercourse with another man's wife; an adulterer or adulteress.

Adulter solidorum. An adulterator of metals; a counterfeiter.

Adultera. A woman who commits adultery.

Adulterare rationes. To forge accounts.

Adulterated. Corrupted; made impure.

Adulteration. The mixing of inferior substances with other substances to be sold as pure and genuine.

Adulterator. A forger; a corrupter; a counterfeiter.

Adulteratores monetæ. Counterfeiters of money.

Adulteress. A woman who commits adultery.

Adulterina moneta. Counterfeit money.

Adulterine. The issue of adulterous intercourse. Illegal; unauthorized; adulterated.

Adulterine castle. A castle erected by a feudal lord without authority from the king.

Adulterine gild. One organized without a charter.

Adulterinus. Adulterous. Not full blooded, not genuine.

Adulterium. Adultery; the violation of another's bed, the crime of corrupting a married woman, or the wife of another. A fine anciently imposed for adultery or fornication.

Adulterium testamentum. A forged will.

Adulterous. Spurious; guilty of adultery.

Adulterous bastard. See BASTARD, ADULTEROUS.

Adultery. Incontinence between two married persons. Sexual intercourse between two persons, one of whom is married to another. A marriage not approved by ecclesiastical authorities. Intrusion into a benefice while the incumbent is living.

Adultery, double. Adultery where each party is married to another.

Adultery, incestuous. Adultery by persons related within the prohibited degrees of marriage.

Adunque. Then.

Ad-usque. To, quite, or even to ; all the way to.

Adv. Abbreviation of ADVERSUS, (against).

Advance. To move forward. To propose. To offer. To make earlier. To pay during the performance of an act but before it is completed. To pay beforehand. To give on credit. To raise the market price of. Anything supplied beforehand.

Advance, further. See FURTHER ADVANCE.

Advance note. See NOTE, ADVANCE.

Advanceamentum. Advancement, (which see).

Advancement. The act of advancing. Portion of settlement in life. A settlement of real estate made in advance by a parent to or for a child; also that received in that way.

Advances. Money advanced before earned or due. Money lent or given.

Advantage. Benefit; profit; aid.

Advantagium. An advantage.

Advena. One who comes to a place; a new comer, a foreigner, stranger or alien.

Advent. The month preceding the Nativity.

Adventicia dos. Foreign or strange dower (that which is given by some friend other than the father).

Adventicia casus. From or by an unusual, extraordinary, or accidental case or event.

Adventicia pecunia. Money obtained, not from one's possessions, but by inheritance, usury, presents, &c.

Adventicia cœna. A banquet given on one's arrival.

Adventicius. That is present by coming, coming from abroad; strange, foreign.

Adventitia bona. Adventitious goods; goods which fall to one otherwise than by inheritance.

Adventitia dos. Same as ADVENTICIA DOS.

Adventitious. Not inherent, but that which comes from without.

Adventitius. Coming from without; foreign.

Adventura. An adventure, (which see).

Adventuræ maris. Adventures of the sea.

Adventure. A peril. A chance or accident; a risk or hazard; an enterprise; a thing sent to sea at the risk of the person sending it, to be sold at the best advantage by the supercargo. A partnership for one transaction.

Adventure, bill of. See BILL OF ADVENTURE.

Adversa. Adverse; unfavorable; opposite; afflictive.

Adversa fortuna. Adverse fortune.

Adversa valetudo. Ill health.

Adversaria. Rough memoranda.

Adversarius. An antagonist, opponent, adversary, rival.

Adversary. An antagonist, opponent, rival.

Adversary proceeding. See PROCEEDING, ADVERSARY.

Adverse. Opposed to; conflicting with.

Adverse claim. See CLAIM, ADVERSE.

Adverse enjoyment. See ENJOYMENT, ADVERSE.

Adverse possession. See POSSESSION, ADVERSE.

Adverse title. See TITLE, ADVERSE.

Adverse user. See USER, ADVERSE.

Adverse witness. See WITNESS, ADVERSE.

Adversus. Opposite to; against.

Advertisement. Information by printing in a newspaper or posting.

Advertisement, official. One made in pursuance of law.

Advice. Legal counsel. Opinion.

Advice, as per. Words on bill of exchange which prevent payment until receipt of letter of advice.

Advisamentum. Advisement; advice.

Advisare. To advise.

Advisari. To be advised; to examine; to deliberate.

Advise. To give advice; to suggest; to take counsel. To consult, as a court does after the argument and before the decision of a cause.

Advisable. Agreeing with sound advice. Expedient.

Advised. Prepared to give judgment.

Advisement. Advice. The deliberation or consultation of a court, etc., before delivering an opinion.

Adviser. One who gives advice; one who gives information.

Advisory. Containing a suggestion.

Advocare. To call to, or upon; to call in aid; to call upon to warrant another's title; to vouch.

Advocare filium. To acknowledge as a child.

Advocassie. The office of an advocate.

Advocata. A woman who had the right of presentation to a church.

Advocate. The patron of a cause in civil and ecclesiastical law. A person privileged to plead for another in court. The patron of a living.

Advocate, Devil's. A person in the Roman Catholic Church, whose business is to raise objections to a candidate for enrollment in the calendar of saints.

Advocate-General. In England, the military and naval adviser of the Crown.

Advocate, Judge. See JUDGE ADVOCATE.

Advocate, Lord. The chief Crown lawyer and public prosecutor in Scotland.

Advocate, Queen's. In English law, a member of the Advocate's College and legal adviser and counsel for the Queen.

Advocates, faculty of. The bar of Scotland, in Edinburg.

Advocati. Patrons; pleaders; speakers; advocates.

Advocati ecclesiæ. Patrons, advocates of the church.

Advocati fisci. Advocates of the fisc or revenue; fiscal advocates.

Advocatia. The functions, duty or privileges of an advocate.

Advocation. In Scotch law, a process for removing a cause from an inferior to a superior court before judgment.

Advocatione decimarum. A writ for tithes.

Advocator. An advocate; one who called on or vouched another to warrant his title.

Advocatus. An advocate.

Advocatus Diaboli. The Devil's Advocate. See ADVOCATE, DEVIL'S.

Advocatus ecclesiæ. The patron of a church or living.

Advocatus fisci. Advocate of the fisc or treasury; a fiscal advocate.

Advoutry. Same as ADVOWTRY.

Advow. To justify or maintain an act formerly done. To call upon or produce.

Advowee. He who holds an advowson.

Advowee paramount. The highest patron ; the sovereign.

Advowson. The right of presentation to a church or ecclesiastical benefice.

Advowson appendant. One annexed to a manor.

Advowson, donative. When the patron could place his clerk without presentation, institution, or introduction.

Advowson, collative. An advowson held by a bishop, in which case presentation is not necessary.

Advowson in gross. One distinct from the manor.

Advowson presentative. When the patron presents to the bishop.

Advowterer. Adultery, adulterer.

Advowtry. Continuing, by a married woman, to live with a man with whom she had committed adultery.

Ædes. A building for habitation; a dwelling for men.

Ædes ædificiaque. Houses and buildings.

Ædicta magistratum. The edicts of the magistrates.

Ædicta prætorum. The edicts of the prætors.

Ædificare. To erect a building.

Ædificium. A building or edifice of any kind, even though not suitable for a dwelling.

Ædifico. To build, construct, raise, erect, or establish anything.

Ædile. In ancient Rome, a magistrate who had the supervision of buildings, streets, markets, provisions, sewers, taverns, temples, baths, etc.

Ædilitum edictum. In Roman law, an edict which provided against fraud in sales.

Ædis. Same as ÆDES.

Æfesn. Money paid to a property owner for the privilege of feeding swine in his woods.

Æg deme. "I judge."

Ægroto. To be sick; being sick or indisposed.

Ægylde. Unavenged; unpaid.

Æl. A grandfather.

Ælmesse. Same as ALMS.

Æneas. Same as ANECIUS.

Æqualitas. Equality, similarity, uniformity.

Æque. In like manner.

Æquitas. Equity.

Æquivocum. Of various or doubtful meaning.

Æquus. Equal; fair; just.

Æraria. A mine; a smelting or refining place.

Ærarium. The public treasure or finances.

Ærerer. To plough.

Ærolite. (Air stone). A mass which falls from an unknown place upon the earth. Under the doctrine of accretion it belongs to the person on whose property it falls.

Æs. Money. Any crude metal dug out of the earth, except gold and silver.

Æs alienum. The money of another; another's money or property; a debt.

Æs suum. One's own money; that which is due us.

Æsnecia. Esnecy, the right or privilege of the eldest born; the privilege allowed the eldest daughter of drawing first, in the partition of lands by lot.

Æsnecius. Same as ANECIUS.

Æsnetia. Same as ÆSNECIA.

Æstimatio. A valuation.

Æstimatio capitis. Estimating the number of persons by counting the number of heads. The value of a man in money. See CAPITIS ESTIMATIO.

Æstimatio frumenti. The estimation of the value of the fruit. How much real money one should pay instead of the corn which he was to furnish.

Æstimatio possessionem. An estimation of the value of possessions.

Ætas. Age. The period of life.

Ætas infantiæ proxima. The age next to infancy.

Ætas legitima. In Civil law, lawful age, which was twenty-five.

Ætas perfecta. Same as ÆTAS LEGITIMA.

Ætas pubertati proxima. The age next to manhood.

Ætas prima. In Civil law, the first age.

Ætate probanda. Same as ÆTATI PROBANDA.

Ætati probanda. (For proving the age). An obsolete writ that laid to enquire whether the King's tenant by chivalry was of proper age to receive the land.

Ætatis precatio. A praying of age, or for the allowance of a privilege or indulgence on account of age.

Ætheling. Same as ADELING.

Affaire. To do, make; to be made or taken.

Affairs. Business interests and transactions.

Affatimi. Same as ADFATIMI.

Affect. To act upon; to concern. To attaint with crime.

Affection. Attachment. A feeling towards a person. Love.

Affectus. Intention. Disposition. Impulse.

Affeer. To assess a tax; to fix, liquidate, or reduce to a precise sum; to moderate, mitigate or regulate.

Affeere. Same as AFFEER.

Affeerement. The assessment, liquidation, moderation, or mitigation of an amercement.

Affeerers. Same as AFFEERORS.

Affeerors. Persons chosen at court leet and baron, and sworn to affeer amercements imposed on offenders. See AFFEER.

Afferatores. Same as AFFEERORS.

Affermer. To establish. To confirm. To let to farm.

Affert. It belongs; it behooves.

Affiance. An agreement by man and woman to marry.

Affiant. A person making an affidavit.

Affidara. Same as AFFIDARE.

Affidare. To swear to. To swear fealty. To pledge one's faith.

Affidari. To be mustered and enrolled for soldiers.

Affidatio. A plighting or pledging of faith; an affiance.

Affidatio dominorum. An oath taken by the lords in Parliament.

Affidatus. A tenant by fealty.

Affidavit. A declaration in writing, sworn to before a person competent to administer the oath.

Affidavit, counter, One filed in opposition to the statements made in another affidavit.

Affidavit of cause of action. One which avers that a just cause of action exists.

Affidavit of claim. One verifying the statement of facts upon which a claim is made.

Affidavit of defence. One which states the correctness of the facts upon which the defendant relies for defence.

Affidavit of increase. See INCREASE, AFFIDAVIT OF.

Affidavit of merits. A formal statement under oath that the defendant has good grounds of defense.

Affidavit of service. An affidavit that a writ, notice, or other paper has been served upon a person.

Affidavit of script. See SCRIPT, AFFIDAVIT OF.

Affidavit, poverty. See POVERTY AFFIDAVIT.

Affidavit, supplemental. One containing statements upon the same subject-matter as a previous affidavit, and intended to remedy a defect in the former one.

Affidavit to hold to bail. One which states that the cause of action is valid.

Affiert. It belongs, it behooves.

Affilare. To file ; to put on record.

Affilari. To file or affile ; to put on record.

Affilatum. Affiled.

Affile. To put on file.

Affiletur. Let it be filed.

Affiliation The assignment of a child to a parent by legal authority; the adjudging of a man to be the father of an illegimate child.

Affinage. Refining of metal.

Affinatas. The state or condition of affinis; relationship by marriage.

Affines. Those connected by marriage.

Affinis. One related by marriage.

Affinitas. The relationship between the respective kindred of a married couple.

Affinitatis. Same as AFFINITAS.

Affinitis. Same as AFFINITAS.

Affinity. Same as AFFINITAS.

Affirm. To confirm a former law or judgment. To confirm a voidable contract. To make a statement as a witness in court without taking oath.

Affirmance. The confirmation of a former law, contract, or judgment. A statement as a witness not under oath.

Affirmance day, general. A day appointed in English Court of Exchequer for the general affirmance or reversal of judgments.

Affirmance, express. Where the party declares his determination of fulfilling the contract.

Affirmance, implied. One arising out of and grounded upon the acts of the party without any direct and express declaration.

Affirmant. One who affirms without taking oath.

Affirmare. To affirm; confirm; assert; ratify; state in pleading; to give evidence not under oath.

Affirmare jurejurando. To affirm a thing by an oath; to make a solemn asseveration in the form or nature of an oath. To aver, state, or declare a thing in a pleading.

Affirmare opinionem. To ratify, confirm, or sanction a former law or judgment. To ratify or confirm a voidable act of the party.

Affirmatim. In the affirm; affirmatively.

Affirmation. An unsworn declaration to tell the truth. Asseveration or averment of a fact or assertion.

Affirmative. That which declares a thing to be true.

Affirmative and negative. Affirming a thing by one party and denying it by the other. (Necessary in pleading to make up an issue).

Affirmative averment. See AVERMENT, AFFIRMATIVE.

Affirmative, pregnant. An allegation in the affirmative which implies a negative.

Affirmative statute. See STATUTE, AFFIRMATIVE.

Affirmatively. Positively; by positive testimony, not inferential. On the affirmative side.

Affirmator. One who affirms or asserts a thing.

Affirming gun. Same as SEMONCE.

Affirmo. To present or represent a thing (a fact or assertion) as fixed, firm, certain, true.

Affix. To attach; to append; to fasten to.

Affixio. A joining, fixing, or fastening to.

Affixus. Affixed, fixed, or fastened to.

Affonage. In French law, the right to take necessary firewood from a forest.

Afforare. To set a value or price on anything.

Afforatus. Appraised or valued.

Afforce. To strengthen, add to, increase. To compel. To ravish.

Afforcement. A strengthening, adding to; increase.

Afforcer. To afforce; to add; to increase; to strengthen.

Afforciament. Same as AFFORCEMENT.

Afforciamentum. An afforcement.

Afforciamentum curiæ. An afforcement of a court.

Afforcing the assize. To obtain a verdict by adding jurors until some twelve of the jury agreed; or, later, by keeping the jury without food and drink till a verdict be reached.

Afforciare. To add, increase, or make stronger.

Afforest. To turn ground into a forest.

Afforestare. Same as AFFOREST.

Affranchir. To affranchise; to make free.

Affranchise. To make free.

Affray. The fighting of two or more in a public place, where a stroke is given or offered, or a weapon drawn. If the fighting be in private, it is no affray, but an assault.

Affrayer. To terrify.

Affrectamentum. An affreightment, or freightment.

Affreight. To charter.

Affreightment. The freight of a ship. The contract for the use of a vessel.

Affreightment, contract of. The contract for the hire of a ship.

Affretement. In French law, the hiring of a vessel.

Affri. Bullocks or horses or beasts of the plow.

Affri carucæ. Beasts of the plow.

Afiert. Same as AFFIERT.

Aforciamentum. Same as AFFORCEMENT.

Aforciamentum districtiones. Afforcement of a distress.

Aforciamentum plegiorum. Afforcement of pledges.

Afore. Before.

Aforesaid. As before mentioned. (An expression used to avoid repetition).

Aforethought. Premeditated; prepense.

Aforethought, malice. See MALICE AFORETHOUGHT.

African. A negro.

After. Succeeding; subsequent; exclusive of; subject to.

After-acquired. Obtained after some event.

After-discovered. Something disclosed after an event or occurrence, as after-discovered evidence, etc.

Aftermath. The second crop.

Afternoon. That part of the day between noon and sunset.

Ag. Against; agreeing.

Against. In opposition to; contrary; in contradiction to.

Against the form of the statute. In violation of a statute. (Essential words in indictments and declarations on penal statutes).

Against the peace. A term used to charge a breach of the peace.

Against the will. Not voluntarily. Words used to charge violence.

Agait. Waiting; in wait.

Agalma. The impression of anything on a seal.

Agard. Award.

Agarder. To award; to condemn.

Age. The part of time wherein men live. The period at which persons are qualified to perform certain acts. The period of existence of persons or things.

Age. Water.

Age, full. One-and-twenty; majority.

Age, lawful. The period in life when one may legally perform certain acts.

Age, non. Under the age when certain acts can be legally performed. Under the age when one can be held criminally responsible.

Age of consent. See CONSENT, AGE OF.

Agency. Activity. The relation of an agent to a principal. The means of acting.

Agency, collecting. See COLLECTING AGENCY.

Agency, commercial. A person or association whose business is collecting information for others regarding the credit of those engaged in trade or commerce.

Agency, Indian. An office where an Indian agent transacts business.

Agenda. Things to be done.

Agenfrida. The true lord or owner of anything.

Agenhine. A domestic or inmate; one of the household.

Agens. One who acts or does an act; an actor or doer; an agent.

Agens in extremis. An actor in extremity. A plaintiff; one who brings a suit. A conductor or manager of affairs.

Agent. One employed to act for another. Acting.

Agent and Consul-General. A consul-general who also acts as commercial agent.

Agent and patient. Where the same person is the doer of a thing and the party to whom it is done. (As an executor who is a creditor of the deceased and pays himself out of the estate).

Agent, commercial. See COMMERCIAL AGENT.

Agent, consular. The agent of a consul.

Agent, diplomatic. Same as DIPLOMAT.

Agent, fiscal. An agent having charge of the financial matters of another, particularly of a government.

Agent, general. An agent authorized to perform certain acts, or employed as practising a certain trade or profession.

Agent, innocent. One who is caused to perform a part in a crime through another without intention or knowledge of the effect of his act.

Agent, managing. See MANAGING AGENT.

Agent, public. A person exercising a power of government, and upon whom such power has been specifically conferred.

Agent, special. A person employed for a special purpose; as to do a single act or transaction.

Agent, sub. A person employed by another agent to do all or a part of his duties.

Agent, universal. One who has the power to do all the acts his principal can do.

Agent, vice. See VICE-AGENT.

Agent, vice commercial. One who acts in the place of a commercial agent in his absence.

Agential. Relating to an agent or agency.

Agents, parliamentary. See PARLIAMENTARY AGENTS.

Age-prayer. Same as AGE-PRIER.

Age-prier. A motion by a minor that a suit against him be stayed until he be of age. Where a defendant prayed in aid of the King or another. See AID, PRAYER.

Ager. Territory, district, domain; the whole of a soil belonging to a community. Improved or productive land; a field, whether pasture, arable, nursery ground, or anything of the kind. The open country, fields—as distinguished from the town. Land generally. An ancient German measure of land.

Ager peregrinus. Foreign territory.

Agere. To act, to do.

Agetur. Suit is brought.

Agger. In Civil law, a dam; a bank; a mound.

Aggravated. Made worse; increased in severity.

Aggravated assault. See ASSAULT, AGGRAVATED.

Aggravation. A making worse; more injurious; tending to increase the amount of damages claimed; tending to enhance the enormity of a crime or the injury of a wrong. In Church law, a curse against an obstinate offender.

Aggravation, matter of. That which is ground for increasing the damages awarded for an injury. See EXEMPLARY DAMAGES.

Aggreamentum. Agreement.

Aggregate. To bring together in one mass or body; to make as a whole. The complete whole.

Aggregatio mentium. A union of minds; a mutual agreement.

Aggregation. Collection; accumulation.

Aggrego. To add or join to something.

Aggressor. One who begins a dispute or quarrel; either by contumelious language, or by threatening or striking another.

Aggrieved. Subjected to an injury or erroneous judgment.

Aggrieved party. See PARTY, AGGRIEVED.

Agild. Free from penalties; not subject to the customary fine.

Agiler. An observer or informer.

Agillarius. A sworn keeper of cattle in a common field. (There are two kinds; one of the town and the other of the lord of the manor).

Agiller. Same as AGILER.

Agio. The term used in commerce to express the difference in value between one kind of currency and another.

Agiotage. Speculation on the price of public securities.

Agisant. Lying.

Agisements. Cattle of others which are fed for pay.

Agiser. To lie.

Agist. To put, place, assign, apportion. To feed the cattle of strangers in the King's forests; to take in cattle to feed or pasture at a certain rate of compensation.

Agistamentum. The feeding of cattle at a certain rate per week, especially in the King's forests; also the profit thereof.

Agistare. To adjust, assign, apportion, assess; to assign or apportion cattle, or other animals, to a feeding ground.

Agistator. The bailee in assignments of cattle; the officer of the forest who took account of cattle there agisted.

Agisted. Fed; applied to cattle of strangers fed in theKing's forest.

Agister. One who takes other men's cattle to feed at a certain compensation.

Agistment. Where other men's cattle are fed at a rate per week. The profit of feeding the cattle of others.

Agistment of sea-banks. Where lands are charged with a tribute to keep out the sea.

Agistor. Same as AGISTARE.

Agitatio. The state of being in motion.

Agium. A termination placed on words to signify service, or duty.

Agius. Holy.

Agnasci. To be born to one; to be born in addition to; to have issue after making a will.

Agnates. Same as AGNATI.

Agnati. Relatives of the father; agnates.

Agnaticius. Pertaining to the agnati.

Agnaticius jus. The right of the agnati to enter upon an inheritance.

Agnatic. Derived from or through males.

Agnatio. The condition of the agnatus; consanguinity on the father's side.

Agnation. Same as AGNATIO.

Agnatus. Born to or connected with by birth. (By usage, limited to relations on the father's side).

Agnatus proximus. The next or nearest agnate.

Agnitio. An acknowledgment, admission, acceptance.

Agnomen. A surname; an additional name.

Agnomination. An additional name.

Agnosco. To acknowledge as one's own.

Agnostic. One who believes in the theory that God is unknown or unknowable.

Agnus. A lamb, usually for sacrifice.

Agnus Dei. The Lamb of God. An oval piece of white wax, stamped with the figure of a lamb, and consecrated by the Pope. (Prohibited by Stat. 13 Eliz., from being brought into England).

Ago. Agere (which see).

Agraria via. A way through the fields; a private way.

Agrariæ leges. The Agrarian laws.

Agarian. Relating to land, or the division or distribution of land.

Agrarian law. A law of ancient Rome, to distribute and regulate the public land. Among its provisions was one which prevented any man from holding over 330 acres of the public land. It originated in 367 B. C., became obsolete, but was revived by Tiberius Gracchus in 134 B. C.

Agrarii. Those who urged the Agrarian laws, and sought the possession of the public lands.

Agrarium. A tax upon land.

Agrarius. Pertaining to the fields or lands.

Agraticum. A revenue from land; a land tax.

Agreamentum. Agreement.

Agreare. To agree.

Agreavit. He agreed.

Agree. To be in concord; to grant; to yield; to settle amicably; to concur.

Agree. In French law, a commercial lawyer or one who manages commercial cases only.

Agreeance. In Scotch law, an agreement.

Agreed. Contracted. Established by agreement.

Agreed balance. One which has received the assent of both parties to an account.

Agreed statement of facts. A statement of facts which the parties to a cause agree shall be submitted to a court for judgment.

Agreement. A joining together of two or more more minds in anything done or to be done. The effect of the joint consent of two or more parties to a contract. (To be legal, the parties must be capable of contracting).

Agreement, articles of. See ARTICLES OF AGREEMTNT.

Agreement, conditional. One which depends on the happening of an event, the performance of a condition, or the existence of a state of facts.

Agreement, executed. An agreement where nothing further has to be done.

Agreement, executory. One to be performed.

Agreement, express. Such as are in express terms.

Agreement, implied. One implied from facts.

Agreer. In French marine law, to equip a vessel.

Agri. Arable land in common fields.

Agri limitati. In Roman law, lands belonging to the State which were obtained by conquest.

Agri limitrophi. The lands set apart to furnish subsistence to the troops stationed on the frontiers.

Agricola. A cultivator of land.

Agricultor. Agriculturist, farmer, husbandman.

Agriculture. The cultivation of the ground for the purpose of raising fruit, vegetables, grain and other crops for the consumption of man and beast. Tillage; husbandry.

Agriculture, Department of. See DEPARTMENT OF AGRICULTURE.

Agrum hereditarii. A grant of hereditary land.

Agusadura. A fee for sharpening plows due a lord from his vassal.

Ahteid. One bound by oath. An ancient Bavarian oath.

Aid. Help, assistance. Originally the obligation upon the feudal tenant to assist his lord in defence of the feud or feudal society. Afterwards, understood to import an obligation to contribute to the private necessities of the lord. (Aids were not of direct feudal obligation, and were various and uncertain, but became established renders of duty. The three most frequent aids in Normandy were, to make the lord's eldest son a knight, to marry his oldest daughter and to ransom his person).

Aid and abet. To assist, encourage. To assist another in accomplishing some design or purpose.

Aid and comfort. An act of benefit to an enemy which would have subjected the doer to punishment for treason by his own country.

Aid bonds. See BONDS, AID.

Aid of the King. Where the King's tenant prays in aid of the King on account of rent demanded of him by others. (The prayer acts as a stay until the King's counsel can be heard).

Aid, municipal. The assistance rendered by a township or county toward internal improvements.

Aid, prayer. A petition to call in help from another person who has interest in the thing contested. See AID-PRIER.

Aid-prier. A prayer by which one having a limited interest in lands, for which he was sued, sought suspense of action until he could obtain aid of the lord or reversioner.

Aid pur faire l'eigne fitz chevaler. Aid to make the eldest son a knight.

Aid, reasonable. See REASONABLE AID.

Aid pur l'eigne file marier. Aid to marry the eldest daughter.

Aid society. Same as BENEFIT SOCIETY.

Aide. See AID.

Aider. Same as ABBETOR.

Aider by verdict. Where a defect or error in pleading which might have been objected to is, after verdict, no longer open to objection.

Aiding and abetting. Being present and doing something to aid a person in the commission of a crime without sharing directly in the deed.

Aids. Extraordinary grants to the Crown by the Commons. See AID.

Aids pur faire fitz chevaler and file marier. Aid to make the eldest son a knight and to marry the eldest daughter. See AID.

Aie. I have.

Aiee. A grandfather. See AILE.

Aiet. He shall have.

Aielesse. A grandmother.

Aieul. A grandfather. Same as AILE (which see).

Aile. A grandfather. A writ against a stranger who dispossesses a grandson heir.

Ailours. Elsewhere; besides.

Ainesse. Esnecy; the right of the eldest born.

Ainsi. Then; so; even so; after the same manner; so that; unless.

Air, right of. See RIGHT OF AIR.

Aire. In Scotch law, an itinerant court similar to the English Eyre.

Aireau. A plow.

Airer. To plow.

Airt and pairt. In Scotch law, an accessary.

Air-way. An air passage to a mine.

Aisiamentum. An easement or privilege.

Aisne. Eldest or first born.

Aisne fitz. Eldest son.

Aisne file. Eldest daughter.

Aisneesse. The right or privilege of the eldest or first born; esnecy.

Aisnecia. Same as AISNETIA.

Aisnetia. Eldership.

Aive. Water.

Ajant. Having.

Ajournement. In French law, a writ for acquiring jurisdiction, similar to a summons.

Ajourner. To summon; to adjourn.

Ajuar. In Spanish law, the articles, such as furniture and jewels, of a wife.

Ajuge. Adjudged.

Ajuger. To adjudge, award.

Ajutage. A tube for carrying water from an aperture.

Akin. Of kin.

Al. At; at the; to; to the; with.

Al. A syllable at the beginning of a name of a place denoting antiquity.

Al fine. At last; at the end.

Ala. Goes; gone; went.

Alæ ecclesiæ. The side aisles of a church.

Alaneradius. Same as ALANERARIUS.

Alanerarius. A keeper of dogs for hawking.

Alant. Going.

Alaric, Breviary of. See BREVIARY OF ALARIC.

Alarm list. A list containing the names of those liable to military watch.

Alast. Goes; went; gone.

Alba. A white precious stone; the pearl. One of the six garments worn by a priest.

Alba firma. White farm or rent; blanch farm; money-rent. Rent payable in silver, or white money, as distinguished from corn or provisions called black mail, or black rent. To hold by white farm is to hold freely in socage. A species of tenure or ground rent.

Albanage. The state or condition of an alien or foreigner; alienage.

Albanagium. The state of being an alien.

Albanus. A new comer. A stranger. A foreigner. An alien. (Opposite to Indigena.)

Albergellum. A defence for the neck. A habergeon.

Albinagii Jus. The right of albanage. See ALBINATUS JUS.

Albinatus. The state or condition of an alien.

Albinatus jus. The right of the King at the death of an alien to receive all he is worth, unless he has exemption. The right of albanage.

Albinus. Same as ALBANUS.

Album. A whitened tablet on which anything is inscribed. The tables on which the Pontifex Maximus registered the principal events of the year, called the Annales Maximi. The tablets of the Prætor, on which his edicts were written, and which were posted up in some public place, where they might be seen by all.

Album. White ; blank ; not written upon.

Album argentum. Silver without mark or stamp ; silver uncoined ; white money.

Album breve. A blank writ.

Album Senatorium. The roll of the Senators.

Albus. White. Favorable, fortunate, propitious.

Albus Liber. The white book, or book containing the customs and laws of England.

Alcabala. In Spanish law, a duty paid on the transfer of property.

Alcalde. An office in Spain and some places originally Spanish, with duties similar to those of a mayor or justice of the peace.

Alcedo. The king-fisher.

Alcyon. Same as ALCEDO.

Ald. Same as AL.

Alder. The first.

Alderman. Originally a senator or senior. An associate to the magistrate of a city or town corporate. A degree of nobility among the Saxons signifying an earl. Literally an elder. A member of a city or town legislature.

Aldermannus. An alderman.

Aldermannus civitatis vel burgi, The alderman of a city, or borough.

Aldermannus comitatus. The alderman of a county.

Aldermannus hundredi. The alderman of the hundred, created by Henry I.

Aldermannus hundredi sive wappentachii. An alderman of a hundred or wapentake.

Aldermannus regis. The King's alderman.

Aldermannus totius Angliæ. The alderman of all England. An office in the nature of a Lord Chief Justice of England.

Aldermanria. Aldermanship; the office of an alderman.

Ale. Gone. A malt liquor.

Ale house. A house where ale is sold to be drunk on the premises.

Alea. In Civil law, a game of chance. Gain or loss of a contract.

Aleator. In Civil law, a gambler.

Aleatory. Hazardous; uncertain.

Aleatory contract. A hazardous contract; a contract of risk; a contract of insurance.

Alecenarium. A species of hawk, called a lanner.

Ale-conners. Officers who were appointed to test ale and beer in London.

Aler. To go.

Aler a Dieu. (To go to God). To be acquitted.

Aler sans jour. To go without day.

Alera. He shall go.

Ale-silver. An annual rent paid the Lord Mayor of London by those who sell ale there.

Alestake. A stake with a sign on that ale is sold there; used by country people.

Ale-taster. A sworn officer of a court leet to testify to the quality of ale sold within the lordship.

Aleu. An allodial estate.

Alfet. A cauldron wherein the boiling water was put for a criminal to put his arms, in the ordeal.

Algo. In Spanish law, property.

Alia. In another way; in a different manner.

Alia enormia. (Other wrongs). A general statement of injuries at the end of a declaration in trespass, under which matters of aggravation may be given in evidence.

Aliamenta. Such right of way as necessary for a tenant's convenience.

Alias. Otherwise; at another; at another time; at other times; on another occasion; formerly; before. A second or further writ, issued after a capias is sued out without effect.

Alias capias. Another or second capias.

Alias ca. sa. Another writ to take (the person); to make satisfaction.

Alias dictus. Otherwise called. The manner of description of a defendant when sued on a specialty.

Alias scire facias. That you again come to be informed. A second writ of scire facias.

Alias writ. A second writ, issued after a previous one has been issued without effect.

Alibi. In or at another place; elsewhere.

Alien. One born in a foreign country, not naturalized. An allodial estate as distinguished from a fief. See ALLEN and ALLIEN.

Alien ami. See ALIEN AMY.

Alien amy. Alien friend; a subject of a foreign nation in friendship with our own.

Alien and sedition laws. See LAWS, ALIEN AND SEDITION.

Alien born. A naturalized citizen or subject.

Alien enemy. A subject of a foreign nation at war with our own.

Alien friend. See ALIEN AMY.

Alienable. That which can be transferred from one person to another.

Alienage. The condition or status (legal) of an alien.

Alienare. To alien or alienate; to make another's; to transfer to another.

Alienate. Same as ALIENARE.

Alienatio mentis. Loss of consciousness; deprivation of reason.

Alienation. A transferring the property of one thing to another; conveyance, especially of real property. Changing from ecclesiastical to secular ownership.

Alienation, absolute. An unconditional and unqualified transfer of real property.

Alienation, conditional. An alienation depending on the happening of some event or the performing of some act.

Alienation office. An English office for obtaining fines upon writs of entry and covenant.

Aliene. Same as ALIENARE.

Alienee. One to whom property is transferred.

Aliener. Same as ALIENARE.

Alieni. Another; other.

Alieni generis. Of another kind.

Alieni juris. Under another's authority.

Alieni res. Another's property.

Alienigena. Foreign alien; a foreigner, an alien, a stranger. Produced from different materials; heterogeneous.

Alien-nee. An alien born.

Alienism. Same as ALIENAGE.

Alienor. He who transfers realty.

Alienum. Same as ALIENUS.

Alienum puerum. The child of another.

Alienus. That which pertains to another person, place, object, etc., belongs to another; the property of another; foreign, alien.

Alienus homo. Another's man or slave. Not belonging to one, alien from, not related or allied, not friendly.

Alike. With resemblance; equal.

Aliment. In Scotch law, to give support to a person unable to support himself.

Alimenta. In Civil law, aliments.

Alimentarius. Aliment; nourishment.

Alimentarius lex. A law relating to the apportionment of provisions to the poor.

Alimentarius res. Things pertaining to sustenance.

Aliments. In Civil law, and Scotch law, necessary support.

Alimentum. Foods, provisions, aliment.

Alimonia. Nourishment ; sustenance ; alimony.

Alimonia naturalis. Natural sustenance.

Alimonium. Alimony.

Alimony. Nourishment or maintenance. The allowance given a married woman upon separation from her husband.

Alimony pendente lite. Alimony allowed while a cause is pending.

Alimony, permanent. Alimony payable so long as both parties live.

Alio. To another person or thing; to another place; elsewhere.

Alio intuitu. With a different intent than that given.

Alioqui successuri. Those who would have otherwise succeeded.

Alios. Other persons.

Aliqualis. Such as it is; any sort of.

Aliqualis probatio. Proof such as it is; any sort of proof.

Aliqualiter. In any way.

Aliquid. Something; somewhat; some; any; many; in some degree; to some extent.

Aliquis. Any one.

Aliter. Otherwise; in another manner; in other respects.

Aliud. Another; one thing; another thing.

Aliud examen. A different or foreign mode of trial.

Aliunde. From another person, place, or thing; from elsewhere.

Alius. Another; other.

Alive. Not dead. (The law presumes that an animal stolen is "alive," but if dead when stolen, it must be so stated in the indictment).

All. Each and every one ; everything.

All faults. See FAULTS, WITH, ALL.

All-fours. Entirely alike. (A metaphorical expression, applied to decisions and cases which are alike in the material points).

All rights reserved. An expression used by authors as notice that they reserve all rights given by law, such as right of translation, dramatization.

Allaunds. Harehounds.

Allay. Same as ALLOY (which see).

Allegans. Alleging.

Allegare. To allege; to state.

Allegata. Matters alleged; allegations.

Allegata et probata. (Alleged and proved). Allegations made in a cause and what is proved.

Allegation. Statement or pleading. Positive assertion.

Allegation, defensive. See DEFENSIVE ALLEGATION.

Allegation, disjunctive. An allegation which states a thing alternatively, or with the use of " or."

Allegation, immaterial. One not necessary to the claim or defence. One which requires no answer.

Allegation, material. One necessary to sustain the claim or defence. Such an allegation as requires explanation or denial.

Allegation of faculties. A statement of a husband's property made by a wife praying alimony.

Allegation, rejoining. The reply made by the complainant to a defensive allegation.

Allegation, responsive. Same as DEFENSIVE ALLEGATION.

Allegatum. Alleged.

Allege. To affirm; to declare; to plead.

Alleged. Affirmed; declared; pleaded.

Allegiance. The lawful obedience which a subject owes his country.

Allegiance, absolute. See ALLEGIANCE, NATURAL.

Allegiance, acquired. The allegiance due from a naturalized citizen.

Allegiance, local. That due from an alien or stranger during the time he remains in a country.

Allegiance, natural. The allegiance a man owes the country he was born in from the time of his birth until he leaves it and becomes a citizen of another country. (Also called absolute and permanent allegiance).

Allegiance, permanent. See ALLEGIANCE, NATURAL.

Allegiare. To defend or justify one's self by course of law.

Alleging diminution. The alleging of some error in a subordinate part of the nisi prius record.

Allego. To send one away with a commission of charge; to dispatch.

Allen. Same as ALLIEN.

Allenarly. In Scotch law, alone, only, merely; used to limit an estate.

Aller. To go.

Alleviare. To levy or pay an accustomed fine or composition. To redeem by such payment.

Alley. A narrow street in common use.

Alliance. A union between States for some common purpose.

Alliance, defensive. One between two nations in which each agrees to defend the other in case of attack.

Alliance, offensive. One between two nations in which each agrees to aid the other in a war against another.

Allien. An allodial estate as distinguished from a fief. See ALLEN and ALIEN.

Alligeantia. Allegiance.

Allision. The striking of a stationary body by a moving body. Injuries from one vessel rubbing against another or against a wharf.

Allocare. To allow. An allowance made upon an account in the English Exchequer.

Allocate. To apportion. To assign.

Allocation. A placing or adding to a thing. An allowance made on account in the exchequer. The act of setting apart. The allowance of an item in an account. The item allowed.

Allocatione facienda. Making an allowance. A writ allowing an accountant money he has lawfully expended in his office; it is directed to the Lord Treasurer and Barons of the Exchequer.

Allocato comitatu. A new writ of exigent before another county court on the former writ not being served or complied with.

Allocatur. It is allowed. The endorsement on a request for a writ or order. The writ requested. A certificate that costs taxed are allowed.

Allocatur exigent. An ancient writ issued on the return of an exigent in outlawry proceedings.

Allocatur, non. It is not allowed.

Allocatur, special. The allowance of the special writ required.

Allocatus. The demand, by a court, of a convicted prisoner, whether the latter has anything to say why sentence should not be pronounced.

Allodarii. Plural of ALLODARIUS. Those who hold allodial lands. Those who hold an estate as large as a subject can have. See ALLODIAL.

Allodarius. He who holds allodial lands. See ALODARII.

Allodial. That which is not held of any superior; an estate held free (the opposite of feudal).

Allodialis. Allodial.

Allodium. Free, absolute, independent ownership; an estate held in absolute dominion, without owing any rent, fealty, service or duty to any superior on account thereof. Land is not held in allodium either in England or United States. In U. S. it is held subject to the right of the State to take when it decides the land is required for public purpose. The land is also held only on the payment of a sum of money or any service the State sees fit to impose; on failure to pay or perform the service the State can forfeit the land or hold for its own use or benefit, or grant to another.

Allodum. Lands held in absolute dominion. See ALLODIUM.

Allograph. A document written by another than any of the parties thereto. (The opposite of autograph).

Alloigner. To eloign; remove to a distance; delay.

Allonge. A piece of paper annexed to a bill or note, for the purpose of making further indorsements, where no room is left for that purpose on the instrument itself.

Allopathy. The common practice of medicine as opposed to homeopathy. The art of curing diseases by inducing different symptoms from those of the primary disease.

Allot. To assign; to apportion; to distribute. To set apart a portion of a thing or things for a person as his or her share.

Allotment. A share; the part appropriated.

Allotment note. An assignment by a seaman of a part of his wages to a near relative.

Allottee. The person to whom something is allotted.

Allow. To permit; to grant; to yield; to sanction; to make provision for.

Allowance. Sanction; license; permission; a grant or stipend. That portion or amount allowed by a court for any purpose.

Alloy. A mixture of other metals with silver or gold.

Alloynour. One who carries away anything secretly.

Alluminor. One who anciently painted on paper or parchment, particularly letters on deeds and charters.

Alluvies. A pool of water occasioned by the overflowing of the sea or a river. Land formed by alluvion.

Alluvio. Alluvion.

Alluvio maris. The washing up of the sea; formation of soil or land from the sea.

Alluvion. The imperceptible increase or gain of land from the flooding of a stream or the sea, and washing sand, slubb, earth, etc., so as in time to form land where none existed before.

Alluvionis, jure. By right of alluvion. See ALLUVION.

Alluvius. Added to the land by the wash of water; alluvial.

Ally. One who co-operates with or assists another in time of war.

Alm. Soul.

Alma mater. Benign mother; a foster mother. A term applied to the college or university where one has graduated. (It is said to have been first applied to Cambridge).

Almanac. A publication stating the days of the week, month and year and other matters incidental thereto. Part of the law of England of which the courts must take notice.

Almaria. The archives or muniments of a church or library,

Alme. Soul.

Almer. Same as ALMONER.

Almes. Alms; anything given in charity, as money, food, clothing, etc.; a charitable donation.

Almesfesh. A Saxon word for alms-money.

Almoign. Alms.

Almoin. Alms.

Almoner. The distributor of the King's daily alms; usually a bishop.

Almoxarifazgo. In Spanish law, duties, both customs and excise.

Alms. See ALMES.

Almsfeoh. Alms money or Peter pence.

Alms-house. A house appropriated for the reception and support of the poor.

Almutium. A cap of goat's or lamb's skin.

Alnage. Ell measure; the measuring with an ell. A duty for measuring cloth.

Alnager. A sworn officer of the King, who examines and measures cloths made in the country, and puts seals on them; and also collects the duty or alnage for every cloth so sealed.

Alnetum. A place where alders grow.

Aloarius. The holder of an allodium.

Alode. Same as ALLODIUM.

Alodes. Allodium.

Alodiones. Owners of an undivided inheritance.

Alodis. Allodium.

Alodium. See ALLODIUM.

Alone. For the exclusive use of; exclusively.

Along. Lengthwise of; by the side of, as distinguished from across.

Alors. Then; there.

Aloverium. A purse.

Aloyner. Same as ALLOIGN.

Als. A contraction of ALIAS and ALIOS (others).

Alsatia. A name applied to White-friars (which see).

Also. Moreover; in addition to. Besides; as well as.

Alt. An abbreviation of ALTA.

Alt al ewe. Let him go to the water (ordeal).

Alta. High.

Alta proditio. High treason.

Alta tenure. The highest tenure; in capite, or by military service.

Alta via. A highway; the highway.

Alta via regia. The King's highway; "the King's high street."

Altarage. The offerings made upon the altar. The voluntary contributions of worshippers at the altar. Priest's profits. Tithes.

Alter. The one; the other of two; the one of two; another; a second.

Alter ego. Another's self; another like me in appearance or behavior.

Alteration. The changing of a thing.

Alteration, colorable. One without substantial change, but made merely to evade the copyright law.

Alteration, immaterial. One which does not materially alter the intention of the parties.

Alteration, material. One which essentially changes the meaning of an instrument writing.

Alteration, suspicious. Such an alteration in an instrument writing as would cause suspicion that it would have a different effect than that first intended.

Altercation. A strife or contest in words; a dispute, debate, either with or without passion.

Altercator. An orator who strives to conquer his antagonist by interrogatories; a disputant.

Altercor. To have a discussion or debate with any one. To strive to gain the victory over an opponent, in a court, by putting questions for him to answer.

Alterfoits. At another time; formerly

Alternat. The practice of assigning the first place to a nation in a draft of a treaty which is given to it.

Alternatim. Interchangeably.

Alternative. Giving an option in two things; as, to do an act or show cause, like a writ of mandamus.

Alternative obligation. See OBLIGATION, ALTERNATIVE.

Alternative writ. An order of Court directing a person to do a stated thing or show cause why he does not do it.

Alterno. To do anything by turns; to interchange with something; to alternate.

Altius non tollendi. In the Civil law, a servitude due by the owner of a house, by which he is restrained from building beyond a certain height.

Altius tollendi. In the Civil law, a servitude which consists in the right, to him who is entitled to it, to build his house as high as he may think proper.

Alto et basso. High and low. The absolute submission of all differences. (When a matter is submitted in alto and basso).

Altre. Another.

Altrei. Another.

Altum mare. The open ocean outside of the fauces terræ as distinguished from arms of the sea (brachium maris). The waters of the ocean without the boundaries of any country.

Alturnare. Same as ATTORNARE.

Altus. High, deep.

Alumna. A foster-daughter, a pupil.

Alumni. The foster children of a college; (those who have received their education at a college).

Alumni fluminum. The occupants of a river.

Alumnus. That which is nourished, brought up. A nursling, a pupil, a scholar; foster-son.

Alveus. A river bed; the channel or bed of a river or stream.

Alveus derelictus. A deserted channel; the dry bed of a stream.

Always, provided. See PROVIDED ALWAYS.

Am. Abbreviation for AMENDED, also AMERICAN.

Amabyr, vel Amvabyr. A custom in honor of Clun, belonging to the Earls of Arundel. This custom, Henry, Earl of Arundel, released to his tenants.

Amalfitan Code. See Code AMALFITAN.

Amalgamate. To combine mercury with other metals. To unite or merge into one. See CONSOLIDATION.

Amalgamation. Same as CONSOLIDATION.

Amalphitan code. Same as CODE AMALFITAN.

Amalphitan table. The sea laws of Amalphi. See Code, AMALFITAN.

Amand. A penalty or fine.

Amanuensis. One who writes at the dictation of another.

Ambactus. A servant or client.

Ambasciator. An ambassador.

Ambassador. A diplomatic agent. A person sent by one sovereign power to another, with authority to treat on affairs of state.

Ambassiator. An ambassador.

Ambaxiator. An ambassador.

Amber. An old English measure of four bushels.

Ambideux. Both.

Ambidexter. One who uses both hands. One who plays on both sides. He that, when a matter is in suit between men, takes money on the one side and of the other, either to labor the suit or such like; or if he be of the jury, to give his verdict.

Ambidextrous. Having the use of both hands.

Ambiguitas. Ambiguity.

Ambiguitas latens. Latent or hidden ambiguity. See AMBIGUITY, LATENT.

Ambiguitas patens. Patent, open or apparent ambiguity. See AMBIGUITY, PATENT.

Ambiguitas verbi. Ambiguity of a word. Ambiguity, uncertainty of expression.

Ambiguity. Uncertainty of meaning in the words of a written instrument.

Ambiguity, apparent. Same as PATENT.

Ambiguity, hidden. Same as LATENT.

Ambiguity, latent. Where the instrument itself is, upon the face of it, intelligible enough, but a doubt arises as to the subject-matter to which it applies.

Ambiguity, open. Same as PATENT.

Ambiguity, patent. One which appears to be ambiguous upon the face of the deed or instrument itself, and renders it obscure and unteligible.

Ambiguum placitum. An ambiguous (or doubtful) plea. A plea for delay.

Ambit. A boundary line, as going around a place; an exterior or inclosing line or limit.

Ambitus. The procuring of a public office by money or gifts; the unlawful buying or selling of a public office.

Ambodexter. Same as AMBIDEXTER.

Ambra. Same as AMBER.

Ambry. A pantry. The place where the arms and everything pertaining to housekeeping were anciently kept.

Ambula in jus. A going into court; coming before a judge; going to law.

Ambulare. To walk about.

Ambulatoria voluntas. A movable or changeable will. (As long as a man lives he has the power to alter his will or testament.)

Ambulatorius. Ambulatory or movable; admitting of alteration or revocation; not fixed.

Ambulatory. Same as AMBULATORIUS.

Ambush. A place where troops lie in wait for the purpose of attacking the enemy. An ambuscade. The act of attacking an enemy from a concealed place.

Ameliorations. Betterments.

Amenable. To bring or lead unto. Tractable. Subject to answer in a court. (Applied to a woman who is governable by her husband).

Amend. To make better.

Amende honorable. A satisfactory apology. A punishment by disgrace, or by having to do an humble act. In French law, a punishment for violators of public decency.

Amendment. The correction of an error in any part of the record of a case. An improvement or addition.

Amendment, material. A change that materially varies the party's case, and causes surprise to the other side.

Amends. Reparation; satisfaction.

Amends, tender of. Such a tender of satisfaction as statute makes a defence to an action for damages.

Amentia. Insanity, idiocy.

Ameralius. A Roman commander of a war vessel.

Amerce. To punish or fine at the discretion of the court. See AMERCIAMENT.

Amercement. Same as AMERCIAMENT.

Amerciament. The pecuniary punishment imposed upon an offender against law. (Amerciaments differ from fines; fines are fixed by statute; amerciaments are arbitrarily imposed. No court can fine but a court of record, other courts can only amerce).

Amerciamentum. An amerciament, or amercement.

Amerciare. To amerce.

American. A name especially applied to the natives of the United States. A descendant of Europeans born in the United States. One born on one of the American continents or near-by islands.

American clause. A clause in a policy of insurance that the insurer shall be liable for the full amount mentioned in the policy despite any subsequent insurance of the same subject by others.

Amesnable. Same as AMENABLE.

Amesner. To lead, drive; to cite; to bring the body of a party into court.

Amesse. Same as AMICUS.

Ameublissement. In French law, an agreement in relation to immovable articles which considers them as chattels.

Ami. Same as AMY.

Ami, prochein. See PROCHEIN AMY.

Amica. A female friend. A concubine, mistress, courtesan.

Amicable. Friendly, agreed.

Amicable action, See ACTION, AMICABLE.

Amicable composition. See COMPOSITION, AMICABLE.

Amicable compounder. COMPOUNDER, AMICABLE.

Amicable suit. See SUIT, AMICABLE.

Amicia. Same as ALMUTIUM.

Amictus. The uppermost of the six garments worn by a priest. The others are the alba, cingulum, stola, manipulus and planeta.

Amicus. A friend.

Amicus curiæ. A friend of the court. One who gives his advice, or suggests something for the assistance and information of the court when not counsel in the cause. A bystander who informs a doubting or mistaken judge in matter of law.

Amiral. In French law, an admiral.

Amissa, lex. See LEX AMISSA.

Amita. An aunt on the paternal side.

Amita major. A great great aunt on the father's side.

Amita maxima. A great great grandfather's sister.

Amitinus. A cousin.

Amittere. In Civil law, to lose.

Amittere curiam. To lose the court; to be deprived of the privilege of attending the court.

Amittere, legem. See LEGEM AMITTERE.

Amittere legem terræ. To lose the law of the land; to be deprived of the liberty of swearing in any court; to lose the capacity of being a juryman, or being sworn as a witness in a cause; to be no longer ''othesworthe.''

Amittere liberam legem. To lose one's frank-law, i. e., to become infamous, and not to be accounted a free and lawful man.

Ammobragium. Same as CHEVEAGE.

Amnery. An almshouse.

Amnestia. An amnesty.

Amnesty. An act of pardon or oblivion.

Among. Intermingled with.

Amont. Upwards; above.

Amortir. Same as AMORTIS.

Amortis. To alien lands in mortmain.

Amortise. Same as AMORTIS.

Amortisement. Same as AMORTIZATION.

Amortization. Extinguishing a debt through a sinking fund. An alienation of lands or tenements in mortmain (to any corporation or fraternity, and their successors, &c.)

Amortize. To alienate in mortmain. To extinguish by means of a sinking fund. See AMORTIZATION.

Amortizement. Same as AMORTIZATION.

Amotion. A putting or turning. Dispossession of lands. The wrongful taking of personal chattels. The removal of an officer or member of a corporation.

Amount. To arise to. The aggregate; the sum total. Above.

Amount covered. The amount an insurer is liable for.

Amount of loss. The amount the insurer loses if the subject-matter of the insurance be injured or destroyed.

Amour. Grace; favor.

Amoveas manus. That you remove the hands. See OUSTER-LE-MAIN.

Amoveo. To remove; to put out of office. To remove a judicial proceeding, as a plaint.

Amparo. A certificate given in Spanish-American countries to one claiming land to protect him until the regular evidence of title can be issued.

Ampliare. To enlarge; to extend.

Ampliare jurisdictionem. To extend the jurisdiction.

Ampliare justitiam. To enlarge or extend the right.

Ampliation. An enlargement. The granting of further time for the trial of a cause. A deferring of judgment till the cause is further examined. In French law, a duplicate of an acquittance or other instrument.

Amplio. More; more completely; more absolutely.

Amplius. In Roman law, more. Further time. A word used by a prætor signifying that decree be delayed until further consideration.

Amputation of right hand. A punishment anciently inflicted for assaulting a judge in court.

Amtita. Possession of lands.

Amy. A friend. See PROCHEIN AMY.

An. A year.

An assurance by matter of record. A fine of lands.

An, jour et waste. Year, day, and waste (which see).

Anacrisis. In Civil law, inquiry into a matter by any means, usually torture.

Anagraph. A register. An inventory. A commentary.

Analogia. Analogy.

Analogous. A likeness in effects, when the things are otherwise entirely different. Corresponding or resembling in certain respects.

Analogous case. A case which is analogous. See ANALOGOUS; also ANALOGY.

Analogy. An argument or guide in forming legal judgments, and very commonly a ground for such judgments. Reasoning in which from certain resemblances others are inferred.

Analyst. One who analyzes. See ANALYZE.

Analyze. To find the ingredients or component parts of substances. To resolve into first principles or elements; to decompose.

Anarchist. A promoter of anarchy.

Anarchy. Lack of government; disorder; the state of being without law or a governing power.

Anathema. The ban, the curse of excommunication, pronounced with religious solemnity by ecclesiastical authority, and accompanied by excommunication.

Anatocism. Taking interest on interest; receiving compound interest.

Anatocismus. Anatocism; taking interest on interest.

Anatocismus conjunctus. Compound interest added to the principal.

Anatocismus separatus. Interest considered separately; compound interest as new capital.

Ancestor. One who has gone before in a family. One from whom an estate is inherited. (A predecessor only applies to a body politic, an ancestor to a natural person.) See PREDECESSOR.

Ancestors, collateral. See COLLATERAL ANCESTORS.

Ancestral. That which relates to, or has been done by one's ancestors.

Ancestral action. See ACTION, ANCESTRAL.

Ancestral homage. See HOMAGE, ANCESTRAL.

Ancestral writs. Writs of ayle, befayle, trefayle, nuper obiit, &c., limited for abatement to collateral relatives of the fourth degree, but were without limit in lineal ascent.

Anchor. A measure for liquids containing ten gallons. A weight to fasten a ship to the bottom of a sea or river. To fasten with an anchor.

Anchorage. A duty collected from ships, for the use of the haven where they cast anchor.

Ancient. Old, not modern; antique. Being so old as to have acquired some right or privilege accorded in view of long continuance. See ANCIENT HOUSE.

Ancient deeds. See ANCIENT WRITINGS.

Ancient demesne. A tenure by which all the manors in the days of Edward the Confessor and William the Conqueror were held.

Ancient house. One which has stood long enough to acquire an easement of support against the adjoining land; in England, twenty years.

Ancient lights. Windows which have had continuous light for twenty years or more.

Ancient messuage. A dwelling erected before the time of legal memory, (the reign of Richard I.)

Ancient readings. Lectures upon old English statutes.

Ancient records. See ANCIENT WRITINGS.

Ancient rent. See RENT, ANCIENT.

Ancient serjeant. The oldest of the Queen's serjeants.

Ancient wall. See WALL, ANCIENT.

Ancient writings. Deeds and other documents more than thirty years old, which do not require preliminary proof if coming from the person who naturally might possess them.

Ancients. Gentlemen of the Inns of Court. Those who have gone through their course of reading in the inner temple. (Inns of Chancery consist of ancients and students; Gray's Inn, of benchers, ancients, barristers and students).

Ancienty. Eldership or seniority.

Ancienty of light. The right of having light remain unobstructed.

Ancillaris. Attendant upon; subservient to; auxiliary; subordinate; dependent.

Ancillary. Attendant upon; auxiliary; subordinate.

Ancillary administration. Subordinate to another administration. An administration granted of the assets of deceased in a jurisdiction other than that in which deceased was domiciled at time of death.

Ancipitis usus. Of doubtful use. In International law, applied to that which may be either hostile or peaceful.

And. Added to. Together with. Sometimes construed to mean " or." See OR.

And therefore he brings his suit. See SUIT, AND THEREFORE HE BRINGS HIS.

Andena. A swath in mowing. As much ground as a person can stride over at once.

Androchia. A milkmaid.

Androgynus. An hermaphrodite.

Androlepsia. The taking of a man. In Athens, the making men prisoners. By Attic law, if a man had been by forcible assault killed by a stranger, the next of kin had a right to take any three men prisoners, but no more, and to detain them until the murderer was either punished, or delivered up to be punished.

Andromania. Morbid or excessive sexual desire in females. It is also often associated with, or becomes a form of, insanity. Also termed hysteromania, nymphomania, and furor uterinus.

Aneantir. Same as ANIENTER.

Anecius. The eldest born.

Anelacius. A short knife or dagger.

Anfealtible. Same as ANFELDTYHDE.

Anfeldtyhde. A simple accusation. Among the Saxons, a simplex accusation was when the oath of the criminal and two more, was sufficient to discharge him, and a triplex, when the oath of five others was sufficient to discharge him.

Angaria. Personal service. Service exacted by a government or by a lord of his tenant. Impressing of ships.

Angariate. To exact forced service.

Angariation. Exaction of service. Toil.

Angary, right of. The right of a belligerent to use or destroy the property of neutrals within belligerent territory.

Angel. An ancient English coin valued at ten shillings.

Angeld. Single value of a thing.

Angelica vestis. The garment of a monk which laymen put on before death.

Angild. The bare single valuation or compensation of a criminal.

Anglia. England.

Anglice. English. A word one time used in pleading as introduction to the English translation of matter described in Latin.

Anglicus. English; an Englishman.

Anglischeria. Englishery; the fact of being an Englishman.

Anglo-Indian. An Englishman who inhabits British territory in India.

Angylde. The price fixed by the Saxons as the value of a man. The value placed upon cattle and chattels.

Anhlote. A single tribute or tax.

Anichiler. To avoid, annul.

Aniens. Void; of no force or effect.

Anient. Void; of no force or effect; annulled.

Aniente. Same as ANIENT.

Anienter. To make void or annul; to bar.

Anientir. Same as ANIENTER.

Anientisement. Destruction; waste.

Anima legis. The life of the law; the vital principle of the law.

Animal. Any living creature which can move at will, other than human.

Animalia domitæ naturæ. Animals of a tame nature. Domestic animals.

Animalia feræ naturæ. Animals of a wild nature.

Animalia otiosa. Such animals as were not used for working, as distinguished from averia carucæ, beasts of the plow; called also averia otiosa and catalla otiosa.

Animals, domestic. Tame animals used for work and those which contribute to man's needs, as cows, sheep, &c.

Animals of a base nature. Such as are not fit for food.

Animo. With the intention or design.

Animus. The mind, disposition, will, inclination, intention, purpose.

Animus furandi. The intention to steal.

Animus revertendi. The intention of returning.

Ann. A year. In Scotch law, the half year's pay due the widow or heir of a deceased clergyman.

Annales. Yearlings; cattle of the first year. Annuals. The Year Books.

Annaly. In Scotch law, to alienate. To transfer.

Annats. First fruits.

Annates. First fruits.

Annex. To attach; to unite to at the end; to add; to join. To connect with permanently.

Annex incidents. See INCIDENTS, ANNEX.

Annexation. The union of one thing to another; the fastening of chattels to the freeholds, or letting them into it, which gives them the quality of fixtures.

Annexation, actual. One existing in fact; as, fixtures to a freehold.

Annexation, constructive. One implied by law.

Anni. Years.

Anni et tempora. Years and terms. An old title of the Year Books.

Anni nobiles. Noble years. The age at which a girl becomes by law fit for marriage (the age of twelve).

Anni nubiles. Marriageable years; the age of twelve in the female, and fourteen in the male.

Anniculus. A year old; a yearling. Of one year's age; a child a year old.

Anniented. Abrogated; frustrated or brought to nothing.

Anniversarius. Annually; yearly.

Anniversary days. Days appointed in commemoration of the death or birth of persons or the happening of events.

Anno. Year.

Anno Christi. In the year of Christ.

Anno Domini. In the year of our Lord. The computation of time from the birth of Christ. (The Romans computed from the building of Rome; the Greeks from the Olympiad).

Anno Mundi. In the year of the world.

Anno Regni. In the year of the reign.

Anno Reipublicæ Conditæ. In the year of the foundation of the Republic.

Annoisance. Nuisance.

Annona. Corn or grain; whatever is laid up for a year's subsistence. Anything contributed by one person for the support of another.

Annona frumentum hordeo admixtum. Annual corn mixed in barley; (corn and barley mixed).

Annona panis. Annual produce of bread; (bread without reference to the amount).

Annonæ civiles. Yearly rents from certain lands payable to certain monasteries.

(4)

Annonarius. Of, or pertaining to provisions.

Annotatio. In Civil law, the sign manual of an Emperor. A rescript over the Emperor's own signature.

Annotation. A written comment. A note. In Civil law, annotatio. The designation of a place of deportation. Summoning an absentee.

Annoto. To enter or register an absent among the accused. To note or designate one already condemned to punishment. To mark upon; to designate. To designate a place of deportation. To give notice to a defendant or accused person, to appear in order to make his defense.

Annoyance. That which annoys; a nuisance.

Annoysance. A nuisance.

Annua pensione. An ancient writ for providing the King's chaplain, unpreferred, with a pension.

Annual assay. The trial, yearly, of the gold and silver coins of the U. S. to determine whether the law is complied with as to weight and fineness.

Annual income. That which is received annually from any property or investment.

Annual message. See MESSAGE, ANNUAL.

Annual pension. See PENSION, ANNUAL.

Annual rent. See RENT, ANNUAL.

Annual rent right. In Scotch law, a rent granted out of land, in lieu of interest, taking of the latter being forbidden by law prior to the reformation.

Annuale. A yearly sum assigned to a priest for celebrating an anniversary of masses for a year.

Annualia. Same as ANNUALE.

Annually. Yearly. At the end of each year during a certain period.

Annuitant. One who is entitled to an annuity.

Annuities, consolidated. See CON-SOLIDATED ANNUITIES.

Annuities of teinds. In Scotch law, annuities allowed the crown, yearly, out of tithes not set apart for pious purposes or paid to the bishop.

Annuity. A yearly payment of a certain sum of money, granted to another for life, for years, or in fee, and chargeable on the person of the grantor. See RENT CHARGE.

Annuity, certain. One payable for a definite number of years.

Annuity, contingent. One continued through a period uncertain, or which has no fixed time within which to be paid.

Annuity, deferred. Same as DEFERRED ANNUITY.

Annuity in fee. A perpetual annuity which may, however, be limited to a man's heirs or executors.

Annuity, life. An annuity payable during the life of the beneficiary.

Annuity, perpetual. A yearly sum granted to another in fee.

Annuity, reversionary. An annuity that begins after a certain time or event.

Annuity table. A table based upon statistics and used by insurance companies, &c., showing the probable longevity of a person at any particular age.

Annuity tax. See TAX, ANNUITY.

Annuity, terminable. One limited by a given term.

Annul. To abolish; to abrogate; to repeal; to make void.

Annulus. A ring. The ring of a door.

Annulus et baculus. The ring and staff, or crozier. (These were symbols anciently used in making feudal investiture. A spear was sometimes used).

Annus. A year.

Annus deliberandi. A year of deliberation. In Scotch law, the year allowed by law to the heir to deliberate whether he will enter and represent his ancestor. (Now shortened to six months).

Annus, dies, et vastum. Year, day, and waste.

Annus et dies. A year and a day.

Annus gratiæ. A year of grace or favor.

Annus luctus. A year of mourning. In Roman law, the year following a husband's death, during which his widow was required to remain unmarried.

Annus mirabilis. A wonderful year. The year A. D. 1066 in English history when William, the Bastard, of Normandy, assumed the kingship by title of conquest.

Annus utilis. An available year, One during which a right could be exercised or a prescription grow.

Annuus redditus. A yearly rent or payment; an annuity.

Annuus reditus. Same as ANNUUS REDDITUS.

Anomalous plea. See PLEA, ANOMALOUS.

Anon. Abbreviation of Anonymous.

Anonymous. Wanting a name; nameless. (Applied to a case reported where the names of the parties are not given).

Another. One other; not the same; one more; any other.

Anoysance. A nuisance.

Anoyer. To trouble, annoy.

Anscot. A tax or tribute to be paid, according to the custom of the country.

Ansel. Same as AUNSEL.

Ansul. Same as AUNSEL.

Answer. To make reply to a charge; to make a statement in writing in defence of a complaint, declaration, bill, libel, etc.

Answer, foreign. See FOREIGN ANSWER.

Answer, supplemental. See SUPPLEMENTAL ANSWER.

Antapocha. A writing showing acquittance of a debt. In Roman law, a transcript or counter-part of the instrument called apocha, signed by the debtor and delivered to the creditor.

Ante. Before, in front, forward.

Ante exhibitionem billæ. (Before the exhibition of the bill). Before the commencement of the suit.

Ante litem contestatem. Before the suit be contested.

Ante litem motam. Before litigation commenced.

Ante nuptias donatio. A gift before the nuptials.

Ante solutionem. Before payment.

Antea. Formerly.

Antecedent. Being or occurring before. That which exists or occurs before. Presumptive.

Antecessor. A predecessor in office (opposite to successor). A law teacher, a professor of law. An ancestor.

Ante-date. Before date. Applied to the dating of documents before the day of their execution, such as bills, notes, cheques, etc.

Ante-factum. Done before. A thing done before.

Ante-gestum. Same as ANTE-FAC-TUM.

Ante-juramentum. A preliminary or preparatory oath. An oath taken before trial or purgation by the accuser that he would prosecute, and by the accused (the oath to be taken on the day of the ordeal) that he was innocent.

Ante-nati. Those born before; persons born before a particular period or event. See POST-NATI.

Ante-natus. Born before. See NATUS, ANTE.

Ante-nuptial. Before marriage.

Ante-nuptial contract. See CONTRACT, ANTE-NUPTIAL.

Ante-nuptialis donatio. Same as ANTE NUPTIAS DONATIO.

Antestatus. A witness.

Anti. Against.

Anti manifesto. A published statement made by a nation at war showing that it is on the defensive.

Antic. Old time, of old; antique.

Antichresis. A mortgage in which the debtor transfers the thing or estate to the creditor, who is entitled to retain the use and profits in lieu of interest; the one receiving the property giving the grantor a counter-letter. See MORTGAGE, WELSH.

Anticipation. A taking before; using an income before it is due. The granting by a married woman, having a separate estate, of the anticipated income from the same. Protest against the issuance of a patent on the ground that the subject-matter is already known to the public.

Antient. Same as ANCIENT.

Anti-graphus. In Roman law, an officer whose duty it was to keep an eye over the money which the tax gatherers collected for the use of the State.

Antigraphy. A copy of a deed.

Antimony. An apparent or real conflict between two propositions or authorities. an opposition, contradiction or inconsistency of laws.

Anti-nomia. Antimony.

Antinomias. Antimony.

Antiqua costuma. Ancient custom.

Antiquæ custumæ. Ancient customs. Customs upon woolfels and leather, granted to Edw. I., by Parliament, in the third year of his reign.

Antiqua statuta. Ancient statutes. The Acts of Parliament from Richard I. to Edward III.

Antiquare. In Roman law, to reject a new law or restore an old one.

Antiquo. To restore a former law or practice; to reject or vote against a new law; to prefer the old law.

Antiquatio. An abrogating, annulling, repealing.

Antiquatio pœnarum. An annulling or repealing of penalties or punishments.

Antiquissimarum gentium. The archives of the ancient nations.

Antiquum dominicum. Ancient demesne. A species of villien socage; the tenants being the same with glebæ ascripticii. A species of copyhold tenure existing in certain manors, which were actually in the hands of the crown in the time of Edward the Confessor and William the Conqueror.

Antiquum mollendinum. An ancient mill.

Anti-rent. Against the payment of land rent.

Anti-rent party. A party organized in 1844 in New York State in opposition to paying land rents under leases from patroons.

Anti-renter. One opposed to the payment of rent.

Anti-rentism. The principles of the anti-rent party.

Antistitium. A monastery.

Antithetarius. A term applied to one who endeavored to discharge himself of a fact of which he was accused, by recriminating, or charging his accuser with the same fact.

Anti-trust law. Act of Congress, July 2, 1890, entitled " To protect trade and commerce against unlawful restraints and monopolies.''

Antrustio. A confidential feudal vassal. A follower of the ancient Frank and German chiefs.

Anuels Livres. The Year Books.

Anulus. A ring, especially for the finger; a signet ring. (In the time of the Roman Republic, the right to wear a gold ring was possessed only by the knights).

Any. Every; whoever; whatsoever.

Any term of years. A period of time not less than two years.

Anyent. Same as ANIENT.

Aore. Now.

Apanage. In French law, the provision made for the support of the younger members of a royal family from the public revenues. See APPANAGIUM.

Apanago. Persons without a father; spurious children.

Apartment. A room in a house or other building; lodgings.

Apatisatio. An agreement.

Aperio. In Civil law, to open, as a will or codicil. To open, as a way or road. In feudal law, to escheat, or revert to the lord.

Aperire locum. To lay open a place; to disclose something unknown; to reveal, unfold; to prove; to explain.

Aperta brevia. Open writs, unsealed.

Aperta rapina. Open rapine.

Aperta, vel patentes brevia. Open or patent writs.

Apertum. Open or apparent.

Apertum factum. An overt act; an apparent, open act.

Apertum murdrum. Plain or apparent murder; open killing.

Apertura testamenti. In Civil law, the proof of a will by the acknowledgement of witnesses, who sealed it.

Apertus. Same as APERTUM.

Apex. The extreme end of a thing; the point; the summit.

Apex juris. The summit of the law. A stricter application of the rules of law even than required by simple justice.

Apex justi pretii. The summit of a just or lawful price.

Apices juris. Subtleties or extreme points of law, etc.

Apices litigandi. Subtleties of litigation; sharp technical points or captious objections in pleading or practice.

Apierge. It appears.

Apocæ. Same as APOCHA.

Apocha. In Civil law, the receipt of the creditor acknowledging the payment of a debt.

Apochæ oneratione. Bills of lading.

Apocrisarius. A messenger. An ambassador.

Apocrisarius cancellarius. In Civil law, one who had charge of the royal seal and signed royal documents.

Apocrisiarius. Same as APOCRISARIUS.

Apograph. An inventory. A copy, not an autograph.

Apographia. Same as APOGRAPH.

Aporiare. To bring to poverty. To shun, or avoid.

Apostacy. A renunciation by a Christian, of that religion. See APOSTATE.

Apostare. To violate; to wilfully break or transgress.

Apostasia. A falling away from religion.

Apostata. An apostate.

Apostata capiendo. A writ for the apprehension of one who, having entered a religious order, abandoned the same, and was acting contrary to the rules of the order.

Apostata, lex. See LEX APOSTATA.

Apostare. Same as LEX APOSTATA.

Apostate. A deserter from the faith; one who renounces the Christian faith. One who has forsaken the faith, principles, party or sect to which he before adhered.

Apostille. An addition; a marginal note.

Apostles. In Civil law, short dimissory letters granted one who appealed from a decree and containing a statement of the cause and that the record would be sent up. Papers sent up in admiralty on appeal.

Apostoli. In Civil law, a certificate from an inferior to a superior judge on the removal or appeal of a cause.

Apostolus. A messenger, ambassador, legate, or nuncio.

Apostyle. Same as APOSTILLE.

Apotheca. A place of deposit.

Apothecary. One who keeps a store or building where medicines are sold; a compounder of medicines according to physicians' prescriptions. (In England, an apothecary has a license to practice medicine).

Appanage. Same as APPANAGIUM.

Appanagium. A provision for the support of younger sons; also an allowance made to younger branches of a sovereign house out of the revenues of the country, generally together with a grant of public domains. See APANAGE.

Apparator. One who prepares. A provider. A messenger of the ecclesiastical courts. See APPARATOR COMITATUS.

Apparator comitatus. An officer of the spiritual court, sometimes a sheriff. A sheriff, in England, was styled apparator comitatus, as having charge of certain county arrangements and expenditures; and for which yearly sums were sometimes allowed him in that capacity. See APPARITOR.

Apparatrix. She who prepares.

Apparel money. Pin money.

Apparel, wearing. See WEARING APPAREL.

Apparent. Manifest; evident; proved.

Apparent ambiguity. Same as AMBIGUITY, PATENT.

Apparent danger. Such conduct or actions on the part of another as would lead a person to believe his life was in danger and makes killing an apparent necessity. See HOMICIDE, JUSTIFIABLE.

Apparent defects. See DEFECTS, APPARENT.

Apparent easement. See EASEMENT, APPARENT.

Apparent heir. One whose right of inheritance is indefeasible, provided he outlive the ancestor.

Apparent maturity. The date when a negotiable instrument is due.

Apparent title. See TITLE, APPARENT.

Apparentia. An appearance; appearance. The coming into court of either of the parties to an action. The coming into court of a defendant; or party proceeded against.

Appareo. To appear; to be regularly before a court.

Apparere. To appear.

Apparitio. Appearance; an appearance.

Apparitio in judicio. An appearance in court.

Apparitionem, post. After appearance.

Apparitor. In Civil law, an officer who waited upon a magistrate or superior officer and executed his commands. In ecclesiastical law, one who cites or summons to appear; a summoner; a messenger who cites offenders in a spiritual court, and serves the process of the court.

Apparlement. In like manner.

Apparura. Furniture, implements tackle, etc.

Apparura carucarum. Plow tackle.

Appeal. The accusation by a private subject against another of some crime. The removal of an equity, admiralty, or ecclesiastical cause from an inferior to a superior court. (A law case is not removable by appeal, but by writ of error, which is issued by the superior court).

Appeal bond. A bond given to pay the costs and judgment below, if the appeal be not prosecuted with success.

Appeal, cross. See CROSS-APPEAL.

Appeal of false judgment. An old procedure by which an accused charged his peers of giving malicious or false judgment and challenged them to combat.

Appeals, Court of. See COURT OF APPEALS.

Appear. To come before a court, either in person or by an attorney.

Appearance. To respond to the process of a court. Coming into court as party to a cause.

Appearance bail. See BAIL, APPEARANCE.

Appearance, compulsory. One compelled by services of process or attachment.

Appearance, conditional. One to be made upon certain conditions.

Appearance day. See DAY, APPEARANCE.

Appearance de bene esse. One which is to be an appearance except in a certain event.

Appearance docket. A book which shows in brief all the proceedings had in a cause.

Appearance, general. An unconditional submission to the jurisdiction of a court.

Appearance, gratis. One made without requiring or receiving notice.

Appearance, optional. One made when only required to protect a right.

Appearance, special. One made for a special purpose.

Appearance, subsequent. An appearance after one had already been entered.

Appearance, voluntary. That made without process.

Appearand heir. See HEIR, APPEARAND.

Appel. An appeal; a challenge.

Appeler. Same as APPELLER.

Appellans. One who appeals or prosecutes an appeal; an appellant; an accuser or challenger.

Appellant. He who takes an appeal. See PLAINTIFF IN ERROR.

Appellare de facto. To appeal one of fact (as principal).

Appelare de forcia. To appeal one of force (as an accessory).

Appellate. Relating to appeals and the review of proceedings of other tribunals.

Appellate jurisdiction. See JURISDICTION, APPELLATE.

Appellatio. An appeal.

Appellatio ad populum. An appeal to the people.

Appellator. One who appeals; an appellant.

Appellatoria tempora. The time within which an appeal is allowed.

Appellatorius. Relating to an appellant.

Appellatus. An appellee; one who is appealed or against whom any appeal is made; the person accused by an appeal.

Appellatus de facto. One who is appealed, or accused of the fact, or act.

Appellatus de forcia. One who is appealed or accused of the force.

Appellee. The party against whom an appeal is made; the party answering to or opposing an appeal.

Appeller. To call; to summon before a judge; to appeal or accuse.

Appello. To complain of; to accuse; to summon before a court. To appeal from the sentence or decision of an inferior judge or court to a superior.

Appellor. A criminal who accuses his accomplice. One who challenges a jury.

Appellum. An appeal.

Appenage. The portion of the King's younger children, in France. See APPANA-GIUM; also APANAGE.

Appenagium. Same as APPANAGIUM.

Appendage. Something added to, belonging to, or annexed to another thing.

Appendagium. Same as APPENDAGE.

Appendant. A thing of inheritance belonging to another thing of inheritance more worthy. Annexed to anything and going with it. (Like appurtenant, except that rights appendant to land cannot be created by grant).

Appendant advowson. See ADVOW-SON, APPENDANT.

Appendant and appurtenant. Things that by time of prescription have belonged, appertained, and are joined to another principal thing, by which they pass and go as accessory to the same principal thing, as lands, advowsons, commons, piscaries, ways, courts, and divers such like, to a manor, house, office, or such others. See APPENDANT.

Appenditia. The appurtenances or appendages to an estate, etc.

Appenditia domi. The appendages or pertinences of a house.

Appendix. A printed record of the papers, proceedings, and evidence in a cause, used in an appeal to the English House of Lords.

Appensura. Payment by weight instead of by tale.

Appertain. To belong to; d e p e n d upon.

Appertaining. Belonging to. Use; occupation.

Applicable. Capable of being applied. Suitable. Relevant.

Applicare. To apply. To fasten to. To moor.

Application. A request in writing.

Application of payments. The appropriation of money paid by a debtor, to some particular debt.

Applico. To fasten to; to moor a vessel.

Appodiare. To lean against or prop up anything.

Appoint. To nominate or constitute; to designate; to decide upon; to fix, establish, or ordain. To provide with necessary equipments. To use the appointing power.

Appointee. One in whose favor a power of appointment is executed. One selected for some particular purpose.

Appointive judiciary. See JUDIC-IARY, APPOINTIVE.

Appointment. The act of appointing. The state of being appointed, or that which is appointed.

Appointment, general. An appointment which allows the donee to name any one he pleases as appointee. See POWER OF APPOINTMENT.

Appointment, illusory. One which has no substantial interest, being merely nominal.

Appointment, power of. See POWER OF APPOINTMENT.

Appointment, special. One by which the donee is restricted to naming only particular persons as appointees. See POWER OF APPOINTMENT.

Appointor. The donee; the one who executes the power of appointment. (He who confers the power is the donor).

Apponare. To apportion corody.

Apponere. To pledge or pawn.

Apponere decem tales. See DECEM TALES.

Appono. To place, put, or set to. To put in or set up.

Apport. Tax. Tribute. Expenses. Charge. Imposition. Payment.

Apportion. To divide, assign, or distribute proportionately.

Apportionment. The dividing of a thing, other than land, into parts. A distribution according to a certain proportion. A distribution of a common fund or entire subject-matter among all those who have a title to a portion of it. Equitable allotment. The arrangement on the basis of population. See PARTITION.

Apportionment of a condition. Waiver of a partial breach of it.

Apportionment of common. A division of common among those entitled to the same.

Apportionment of contract. The performance in part by subsequent agreement of the parties.

Apportionment of rent. A division among two or more in proportion to their interests.

Apportionare. To apportion.

Apportionatæ. Apportioned, assessed.

Apports en nature. In French law, that contributed by a partner to the partnership other than cash.

Apportum. The revenue or profit a thing brings the owner. A pension, annuity, etc.; a corody.

Apposal of sheriff. The charging a sheriff with money received upon accounts in the exchequer.

Appose. To interrogate or question.

Apposer. An officer in the English Exchequer, whose business it was to examine the sheriff's estreats with the record, and to ask (appose) the sheriff what he could say to every particular sum therein; (usually termed the foreign apposer).

Appostille. In French law, an addition or annotation made in the margin of any writing.

Appraisal. A valuation of property by one who is authorized; the act of appraising.

Appraise. To value; to set a price upon, by authority of law.

Appraisement. Same as APPRAISAL.

Appraiser. One authorized to appraise or set a value on articles of property.

Appraiser, Government. An officer selected by a collector of customs whose duty is to value dutiable merchandise.

Appraiser, mercantile. An officer whose duty is to regulate the tax and license fees paid by merchants, in accordance with the amount of business done by them.

Appraiser, merchant. An appraiser who acts with a government appraiser in the interests of the importer.

Appraiser, Re. See RE-APPRAISER.

Appreciare. To appraise or estimate. To set a value on; to estimate the worth of.

Appreciatæ. Appraised.

Appreciatio. Appraisement.

Apprehend. To grasp mentally or physically. To seize. To arrest. To believe. To conceive. To fear. To dread.

Apprehension. A taking hold of a person or thing; the seizure or capture of a person.

Apprendre. To apprehend; to learn.

Apprentice. A person bound by indenture to a tradesman or artificer, to be taught in his trade.

Apprentice, parish. See PARISH APPRENTICE.

Apprenticeship. The condition of one bound to another as apprentice. The relation between master and apprentice.

Apprenticii ad legem. Apprentices at law; an ancient term for barristers

Apprenticius. An apprentice.

Apprenticius ad legem. An apprentice or student at law; a learner in the law.

Apprenticius legis. An apprentice or learner of the law.

Apprenticius ad barras. An apprentice at the bars or bar of the court.

Apprentise. Same as APPRENTICIUS.

Apprentise en la ley. An apprentice of or in law.

Apprentitii ad legem. Same as APPRENTICII AD LEGEM.

Apprest. Prepared, ready.

Apprester. To prepare.

Apprestes. Payments; loans.

Appretio. To value or estimate at a price; to appraise, tax. To purchase.

Apprimes. First.

Appris. Learned or skilled.

Apprise. Learned or skilled.

Apprising. In Scotch law, taking possession of the estate of a debtor in payment of debt.

Apprizal. Same as APPRAISAL.

Approach. The entrance to a bridge. The right of one ship to visit another upon the open sea to ascertain the latter's nationality.

Approbare. To improve, to cultivate and enclose waste land. To test, to try; to prove good.

Approbate. To approve. To license to preach.

Approbate and reprobate. To approve and reject; to take advantage of one part and reject the rest. The doctrine of election.

Approbator. An approver.

Appromissor. One who is security for another.

Appropriare communiam. Same as APPROPRIARE ET INCLUDERE COMMUNIAM.

Appropriare et includere cummuniam. To approve, or separate and enclose a common; to discommon it.

Appropriate. To set apart; to annex; to take for one's self; to take as one's own. Fit, proper, suitable, adapted to the purpose.

Appropriation. Reserving for a particular purpose. The application of a sum paid by a debtor to a creditor to the payment of a particular debt. Annexing perpetually a benefice to a religious corporation of which the latter is the patron.

Appropriation of payments. See APPROPRIATION.

Appropriator. A religious corporation with right to profits of a benefice.

Approprio. To appropriate.

Approuamentum. An approvement or improvement; inclosure; the enclosing part of a common or waste ground, leaving sufficient common with egress and regress for the commoners.

Approuare. To approve or improve land.

Approuator. An approver of lands.

Approval. Sanction. Commendation. The act of regarding or receiving with favor.

Approve. To augment to the utmost. To declare in favor of. To accuse. To improve. See APPROVER; also APPROVEMENT.

Approveamentum. Same as APPROUAMENTUM.

Approved endorsed notes. See NOTES, APPROVED ENDORSED.

Approvement. The profit of lands; lands newly improved; the making of an enclosure by a lord, of part of a waste, leaving some common with outlet to commoners. The confession made by an approver.

Approver. To vouch. To approve. To prove. One guilty of a crime who confesses and accuses another of equal guilt. If the latter were acquitted the approver was hanged on his own confession. In modern times, a guilty person who gives evidence against a principal or accessary.

Approvers. Plural of Approver. Bailiffs of lords ; those having the letting of the King's demesnes in small manors. (Sheriffs are the King's approvers). Persons sent out in counties to increase the rent of the farms of hundreds held by sheriffs.

Appruare. To take to one's own use or profit.

Appulus. In Civil law, driving to.

Appurtenances. Things belonging, appertaining or appurtenant to another thing as to a principal; (a right of way, or other easement to land; a right of common to a pasture; out-buildings, etc., to a dwelling-house or messuage, etc., all of which pass as incident or appurtenant to the principal thing).

Appurtenant. Belonging to; accessory or incident to.

Appurtenantia. Appurtenances.

Appuye. The point to lean on; the defence.

Apres. After; afterwards.

Apris. Learned.

Apt time. See TIME, APT.

Apt words. See WORDS, APT.

Apta viro. Marriageable. Fit for a husband. A woman of an age to be married.

Apud. At, by, with, close by, near, before, into, among.

Apud acta. Among the acts. In Civil law, oral appeals taken before the judge.

Aqua. Water.

Aqua calida. Boiling water.

Aqua currens. Running water.

Aqua dulcis. Fresh water.

Aqua fervida. Boiling water.

Aqua fontanæ. Spring water.

Aqua frigida. Cold water.

Aqua salsa. Salt water.

Aquæ. Waters; streams.

Aquae cursus. Water course; a running stream of water; a body of running water; a natural stream, including rivers and rivulets.

Aquæ ductus. The right of conducting water through the land of another.

Aquæ profluens. Flowing water.

Aquæ haustus. In the Civil law ; the right of drawing water from another's spring or well.

Aquæ immittendæ. Of water to be cast or thrown. In the Civil law, a servitude which occurs where the owner of a house so surrounded with other buildings, that it has no outlet for its water, has to cast water from his roof, or out of his windows, on his neighbor's roof, court or land. At the Common law it was known as an easement of drip (servitus stillicidii).

Aquagangium. A passage for water.

Aquage. A water-course; toll paid for water carriage; ewage.

Aquaguagium. A water-gage; a mark placed on the banks of streams to show where the water rose to a certain point.

Aquagium. A water course; a duct or passage for water; a canal, ditch, or trench for leading off water, especially for marshy grounds.

Aquatic rights. See RIGHTS, AQUATIC.

Aquatiles. Water fowls, as mallard, heron, etc.

Aquatilis. Living, growing or found in, by, or near water; aquatic.

Arabant. They ploughed. (Applied to vassals who held their lands by plough service).

Arabilis. Arable land.

Arace. To rase, or erase.

Arage and carriage. Same as AR-RIAGE and CARRIAGE.

Araho. To make oath in a church or holy place.

Aralia. Plow-lands.

Aranare. Same as ARRAINARE.

Arare. To ear, to plow.

Aratia. Arable grounds; plow-lands.

Aratio. A plowing; and in general the cultivation of the ground. Agriculture.

Arator. One who plows; a plowman.

Aratrifaber. A plow-wright.

Aratrum terræ. Same as ARATUM TERRÆ.

Aratum terræ. A plow-land, as much as can be tilled by one plow.

Aratura terræ. The plowing of land; the service which the tenant was to do for his lord in plowing his land.

Araturia. Arable land.

Arbiter. A judge; umpire of the contest; an arbitrator.

Arbiter compromissarius. An arbiter by mutual agreement.

Arbitrament. An award in arbitration.

Arbitrament and award. A plea that the matter has been referred to arbitration, and a decision given.

Arbitramentum. The judgment, decision or award of arbitrators, upon the questions before them.

Arbitrary. Bound by no law; not fixed by statute; discretionary; despotic.

Arbitrary punishment. See PUNISH-MENT, ARBITRARY.

Arbitratio. The judgment, will. Arbitration.

Arbitration. Examination and determination by arbitrators of a matter in dispute between two or more persons.

Arbitration by rule of court. An arbitration under the direction and by the order of a court.

Arbitration, compulsory. Where a party to a controversy is compelled by law to have the same determined by arbitrators.

Arbitration in pais. Arbitration out of court by agreement of the parties.

Arbitration, International. The submission to arbitration by nations of matters in dispute between them.

Arbitration of exchange. The converting of the money of one country into that of another through the use of another medium.

Arbitration, voluntary. One consented to by both parties.

Arbitrator. One to whose decision matters in dispute are submitted by mutual consent.

Arbitrement. An award in arbitration.

Arbitrium. Same as ARBITREMENT.

Arbor. A tree; a tree growing, as distinguished from wood cut, or dead wood.

Arbor civilis. A civil tree. A figure or table, in the shape of a tree, showing the degrees of relationship between persons and the course of descent from one to another.

Arbor consanguinitatis. A tree of consanguinity. A tree-shaped table, showing the genealogy and descent of a family. (The Romans called it arbor juris, the tree of right).

Arbor finalis. A tree used for marking a boundary line. A tree used as a boundary of lands; a tree from which the boundary lines are drawn.

Arbor juris. See ARBOR CONSAN-GUINITATIS.

Arbor terminalis. Terminal or boundary tree.

Arbores terminales. Terminal or boundary trees.

Arbores coupes et importes. Trees cut and carried away.

Arca. A chest or coffer; a place for keeping money. A place for keeping public money, state treasures, revenues.

Arca chirographica Judeorum. The charter chest of the Jews. This was a common chest with three locks and keys, kept by certain Christians and Jews, wherein by order of Richard I., all the contracts, mortgages and obligations belonging to the Jews were kept, to prevent fraud.

Arcana cælestia. Heavenly secrets.

Arcana imperii. State secrets; mysteries of government.

Arcanum imperii. The secret of the empire; the secret of the state.

Arcarius. A controller of public revenues; a keeper of public money; a cashier.

Archaionomia. The chief or principal laws. The title of a collection of Saxon laws made by Mr. Lambard in the time of Queen Elizabeth, in the Saxon language, and to which additions were made by Doctor Wilkins.

Archbishop. The chief of the clergy in his province.

Archbishop of Canterbury. See CANTERBURY, ARCHBISHOP OF.

Arch-deacon. Originally one having superintendence over all the parochial clergy in a deanery. His jurisdiction is but such as conferred by the bishop whose substitute he is.

Archeota. A keeper of the archives; a recorder.

Archery. A service of keeping a bow to defend the lord's cattle.

Archetype. The original of which any copy or resemblance is made; a model.

Archicapellanus. A chief or high chancellor.

Archidiaconus. An archdeacon.

Archiepiscopus. An archbishop.

Archirum. Same as ARCHIUM.

Archium. The archives. The rolls; any place where records, charters, and other public papers and evidences are kept.

Archives. The rolls. Any place where records, charters, and evidences belonging to the Government are kept.

Archievesque. Archbishop.

Archivist. The keeper of the archives.

Archon. A ruler, magistrate. The chief magistrate of Athens. One of the nine chief magistrates of Athens after 583 B. C.

Arddelio. Same as ARTHEL.

Ardhel. Same as ARTHEL.

Ardent spirits. Alcoholic distilled liquors.

Arder. To burn.

Ardour. A burner; an incendiary.

Ardours de mesons. Burners of houses.

Are. In the metric system the unit measure of capacity equal to 0.908 quarts dry, or 1.0567 quarts, liquid measure.

Area. A broad piece of ground; a vacant place.

Arenales. In Spanish law, sandy beaches.

Arentare. To rent out, or let at a certain rent.

Arer. To plow.

Arer et semer. To plow and sow.

Arer et seymer. To plow and sow.

Arer les prees. To plow the meadows.

Arere. Behind; in arrear. Back; again.

Areriesment. Surprise; affrightment.

Aretro. Behind; in arrear.

Arg. Abbreviation of Arguendo.

Argentarii. Money lenders.

Argentarium. In Roman law, the written evidence of a loan.

Argentarius. In Roman law, a money lender.

Argentarius miles. A servant who carried money from one part to the other of a treasury, or the English Exchequer, to be tested.

Argentifodina. A silver mine.

Argentum. Silver plate; silver bullion or uncoined silver; money paid by weight; money generally; money paid by tale, or counted; goods generally.

Argentum album. Silver coin or bullion passed as money. Plain or blank silver.

Argentum annumerare. To put money to one's account.

Argentum Dei. God's money; earnest money. Money given by way of earnest upon the making of a bargain.

Argentum factum. Silver wrought or worked; (wrought into articles of various kinds).

Argentum infectum. Silver unwrought or in the mass.

Argentum non signatum. Silver not marked or stamped; uncoined silver; bullion; common silver coin.

Argentum que expositum in ædibus. Silver publicly set out in money.

Argil. Clay, lime, gravel. The lees of wine hardened.

Argoil. Same as ARGIL.

Arguendo. In asserting, proving, arguing; in the course of argument. (Frequently abbreviated Arg.)

Argument. An address, or the reasoning used to sustain a proposition.

Argument list. A list of causes or issues set down for argument before a court.

Argument, re. See RE-ARGUMENT.

Argumentative. Indirect, inferential. (Used of a plea, the important part of which is stated by implication only).

Argumentor. To adduce proof of a thing. To make a conclusion; to conclude.

Argumentosus. Ingenious.

Argumentum ad invidiam. An argument or appeal to low passions or reasoning.

Argumentum ad judicium. An argument to the judgment; an appeal made to proofs drawn from any of the foundations of knowledge.

Argumentum ad verecundiam. An argument or appeal to the modesty; an appeal to the decency of an opponent or person to whom is made an address.

Argumentum baculinum. The argument of the staff; an appeal to force; club law.

Aribannum. A feudal fine for not joining the army in answer to the King's summons.

Arierban. The edict of French and German feudal kings calling tenants to arms.

Arierisment. Surprise; affright.

Arietum levantio. A sportive exercise. Same as QUINTAIN.

Arimanni. The title of a class of freemen in the Middle Ages, who possessed some independent property of their own, employing themselves in agriculture. They rented lands, also, from the neighboring lords, paying beside the stipulated rent, certain services of labor for their landlord, as harvesting, or ploughing.

Aristo-democracy. A form of government where the power is divided between the great men of the nation and the people. A form of government composed of nobles and commonalty.

Aristocracy. A form of government in which the supreme power is vested in a council composed of select members, or nobles, or in a privileged order, without a monarch and exclusively of the people. The nobility or chief persons in a state. A privileged class of the persons or political party in the state.

Arles. Earnest.

Arles-penny. See EARLE-PENNY.

Arm of the law. Instrumentality of the law.

Arm of the sea. See SEA, ARM OF.

Arma. A sword; armor; implements of war; arms; both of offence and defence.

Arma capere. To be made a knight.

Arma dare. To dub or make a knight.

Arma libera. Free arms. A sword and lance given a servant with his freedom.

Arma moluta. Weapons that cut, as distinguished from those that break or bruise.

Arma reversata. Reversed arms; one of the punishments inflicted upon knights convicted of treason or felony.

Armalia. Arable grounds.

Armaria. Same as ALMARIA.

Armata vis. In Civil law, an armed force.

Armed. Provided with weapons. Applied to a ship, provided with cannon and ammunition for the same.

Armed neutrality. The condition of a neutral nation which is prepared for war.

Armed peace. See PEACE, ARMED.

Armed rebellion. A rebellion carried on with arms of war.

Armig. Same as ARMIGER.

Armiger. An esquire. One who bears arms; an armor-bearer or shield-bearer. A title of gentlemen who bore arms. (The term Armiger was also formerly applied to the higher servants in convents).

Armigeri natalitii. Descendants of an armiger.

Armiscara. A punishment. A punishment of carrying a saddle on back in token of subjection.

Armiscaria. Same as ARMISCARA.

Armistice. Cessation of hostilities between nations at war.

Armor. That worn in defence.

Armour. Same as ARMOR.

Arms. Weapons of offence and defence. See ARMS, COAT OF.

Arms, coat of. The insignia anciently stamped on a knight's coat of mail; now used on carriages, stationery, &c. A badge painted on a shield to distinguish armed knights; they were not hereditary until Richard I.

Arms, law of. See LAW OF ARMS.

Armum. A weapon.

Armum molutum. A sharp weapon.

Army. A body of men legally organized and prepared for war.

Arnaldia. A disease causing loss of hair.

Aro. To plow; to till; to cultivate land.

Aromatarius. A grocer.

Arpen. Same as ARPENT.

Arpent. According to Domesday 100 perches. In U. S., particularly Louisiana, Arkansas and Missouri, an area of land containing 37,056¼ square feet. If square, 192 ft. 6 in. x 192 ft. 6 in.

Arpentator. A measurer or surveyor of land.

Arquebuss. A short hand gun. A pistol or caliver.

Arra. Same as ARRHA.

Arrack. A spirit procured by distillation from the cocoa tree, or rice. An English duty payable for arrack from the East Indies.

Arræ. Same as ARRHA.

Arracher. To erase.

Arraiamentum. An arranging or array; the array.

Arraiare. To array; to sit in order.

Arraiatio peditum. An arraying of foot soldiers.

Arraiatores. Arraiers or arrayers; commissioners of array. See ARRAIERS.

Arraiatus. Arrayed.

Arraiers. Commissioners whose duty was to see that soldiers were properly accoutred. Officers who had charge of soldiers armor.

Arraign. To call a person to answer in law. To call one to the bar of a court to answer the matter charged against him in an indictment. Also applied to the old criminal proceedings by appeal.

Arraignment. The act of arraigning. See ARRAIGN.

Arrainare. To arraign; to order, or sit in order; to conduct in an orderly manner; to prosecute, institute or bring. In Criminal law, to call a man to answer in form of law.

Arrameur. Title given by the Normans to officers employed to load vessels.

Arranare. Same as ARRAINARE.

Arrangement. Setting in order.

Arrangement, deed of. See DEED OF ARRANGEMENT.

Arras. In Spanish law, the gift of property by a husband to a wife on account of marriage.

Arratura terræ. Same as ARATURA TERRÆ.

Array. The whole body of jurors summoned to attend court. The list of jurymen, arranged in the panel.

Arrearages. Money not paid when due. The remainder due on account.

Arrears. Same as ARREARAGES.

Arrect. To accuse; accused.

Arrectati. Persons accused or suspected.

Arrectatus. One suspected of any crime.

Arrendamiento. In Spanish law, the contract of leasing or hiring land.

Arrentare. To rate or assess; to let at a certain sum or rent; to rent.

Arrentatus. Accused.

Arrentation. A renting or rent. In Forest law, the licensing an owner of lands in a forest to enclose them with a low hedge and a small ditch, under a yearly rent.

Arrer. Same a ARARE.

Arrere. Same as ARARE.

Arrest. Restraint of one's person by a lawful warrant.

Arrest, double. Holding a defendant twice to bail for the same cause (only allowed under special circumstances).

Arrest, false. Depriving a person of liberty without lawful cause; false imprisonment.

Arrest, malicious. One made without probable cause.

Arrest of judgment. The staying of the judgment in a cause after verdict for error apparent on the record.

Arrest of inquest. The staying of an inquest. A plea to stay an inquest.

Arrest parol. See PAROL ARREST.

Arrestandis bonis ne dissipentur. A writ for arresting or attaching goods lest they shall be dissipated, or squandered.

Arrestando ipsum qui pecuniam recepit. A writ for the arresting of one who, having received prest money or bounty, does not enlist.

Arrestare. To arrest; to take or seize a person. Also written Arestare.

Arrestare bona. To arrest the goods.

Arrestari et imprisonari. To be arrested and imprisoned.

Arrestatio. Arrest.

Arrested. In admiralty practice, the seizure of a ship by the service of a writ in an action in rem.

Arrestee. In Scotch law, a judgment debtor against whom an arrestment has been issued. See ARRESTMENT.

Arrester. To arrest, to take into legal custody. In Scotch law, a judgment creditor. See ARRESTEE.

Arrestment. Arrest. In Scotch law, a process of attachment or garnishment.

Arresto facto super bonis mercatorum alienagenorum. For making arrest or seizure of the goods of foreign merchants. The name of a writ for seizure of the goods of aliens found within the kingdom, as indemnity for goods taken from a denizen in a foreign country after a denial of restitution.

Arrestum jurisdictionis fundandæ causa. An arrestment for the sake of establishing or founding jurisdiction.

Arret. In Canada and Louisiana, the judgment or decree of a court in a matter of which it has jurisdiction.

Arret, saisie. Attachment of property in the hands of a third person.

Arrettare. To accuse.

Arreted. Imputed to.

Arretter. To accuse.

Arrha. The money given to ratify a contract; earnest money; a part of the purchase money; a pledge.

Arrhæ. Same as ARRHA.

Arrhabo. Same as ARRHA.

Arriage and carriage. Indefinite services formerly exacted from tenants.

Arrierban. Same as ARIERBAN.

Arriere fieffs. Fees granted by the King's feudatories to others.

Arrier vassal. The vassal of a vassal.

Arrival. Applied to a vessel means coming into a port on business.

Arrive. To reach a place of destination by going toward it. To reach the point in a harbor to which a ship is destined.

Arrogation. In civil law, the adoption of one sui juris, or of age.

Arrondissement. One of the subdivisions of a French department.

Arrura. A day's plowing.

Ars. Burnt. Skill; trade; art.

Arsæ et pensatæ. Burnt and weighed; applied to money tested by fire and weighed.

Arsenal. A public place for the manufacture or storage of arms and military stores.

Arser in le main. Same as ARSURE EN LE MAIN.

Arsion. Burning; arson.

Arson. The malicious and felonious burning of the house or out-house of another.

Arsure en le main. Burning in the hand. Burning with a hot iron on the brawn of the left thumb; a punishment formerly inflicted upon lay offenders who were allowed the benefit of clergy, to distinguish their persons and prevent them claiming the privilege a second time.

Arsura. The trial of money by fire after being coined.

Art. Skill in the use of rules or principles. A principle put into practice. In Patent law, a useful art or manufacture.

Art and part. Applied to one who is the deviser and perpetrator of a crime.

Art, useful. The process, operation, or principle of producing something useful. The application of knowledge in such a way that something useful will be produced.

Art, words of. Technical words.

Arthel. A vouchee. To vouch for.

Article. A species of pleading in the English ecclesiastical courts. The divisions or paragraph of a document.

Article, proprietary. See PROPRIETARY, ARTICLE.

Articled clerk. A person bound to serve with some practicing attorney for his instruction until admitted to practice.

Articles. A system of rules. The specification of matters agreed upon or established by authority. A statute with subject-matters under distinct heads. An instrument writing setting forth matters agreed upon between parties thereto.

Articles, approbatory. In Scotch law, the answer to articles improbatory.

Articles, improbatory. In Scotch law, averments setting forth facts relied upon to sustain a cause.

Articles, Lords of. A committee of Scotch Parliament appointed with a view to enabling the crown to defeat any measure before debate. It was abolished in 1690.

Articles of Agreement. Instruments writing containing the terms of an agreement.

Articles of Association. Articles of agreement signed by parties to a proposed joint stock company or corporation as a basis for the granting of a charter.

Articles of Confederation. The articles which united the thirteen colonies, afterwards called the thirteen original States. They were reported July 12, 1776, ratified July 9, 1778, by eight States and by the last State March 1, 1781. They gave way to the Constitution, March 4, 1789.

Articles of Faith. A statement of the faith of the Church of England, formed by Cranmer, and revised by the convocation of 1562; it consisted of thirty-nine points of doctrine. See ARTICLES, THE THIRTY-NINE.

Articles of Impeachment. The indictment or accusation found by the House of Representatives in the U. S. against an official for violation of law, or malfeasance in office.

Articles of Magna Charta. See ARTICULI MAGNÆ CHARTÆ.

Articles of Partnership. Articles setting forth the terms of the agreement between partners.

Articles of Peace. See PEACE, ARTICLES OF.

Articles of Religion. Same as ARTICLES OF FAITH.

Articles of Roup. In Scotch law, conditions of sale.

Articles of Set. In Scotch law, an agreement for a lease.

Articles of the Clergy. Same as ARTICULI CLERI.

Articles of the Navy. A set of rules established by law for the regulation of the Navy.

Articles of the Peace. See PEACE, ARTICLES OF THE.

Articles of Union. The twenty-five articles agreed to by England and Scotland in 1707 for the union of the two kingdoms.

Articles of War. Regulations of the Army and Navy of the United States.

Articles, shipping. See SHIPPING ARTICLES.

Articles, The Thirty-nine. The thirty-nine points of doctrine adopted at a convocation of the church of England, held in London, 1562-63. See ARTICLES OF FAITH.

Articulate adjudication. In Scotch law, a separate adjudication for each of several claims.

(5)

Articulately. Distinctly, separately. In Civil law practice, by distinct allegations.

Articuli. Articles. Statutes. Treatises.

Articuli ad Novas Narrationes. A treatise on pleadings added to the Novæ Narrationes.

Articuli cleri. Articles of the clergy. The title of a statute passed 9 Edw. II., for the purpose of settling the great questions of cognizance then existing between the ecclesiastical and temporal courts.

Articuli de moneta. Articles concerning money, or the currency.

Articuli Magnæ Chartæ. Articles of Magna Charta. The original articles or heads of agreement (consisting of forty-nine heads), at the Congress of Runimede or Runingmede, upon which the charter of King John was founded. The document was entitled Articuli Magnæ Carti Liberatatum sub sigillo Regis Johannis—articles of the Great Charter of Liberty under the seal of King John.

Articuli super chartas. Articles upon the charters. A statute passing 28 Edw. 1. st. 3, c. 19, confirming or enlarging many particulars of Magna Charta, and the Charta de Foresta.

Articulo mortis. In the articles of death; at the point of death.

Articulus. An article or complaint in a religious court.

Artificer. One who with his own hands creates an artificial article. One who by his own artifice creates an article from raw material. See MANUFACTURERS.

Artificial. Not natural; technical; made by art; pertaining to an art, trade or profession. Constructed in a technical manner.

Artificial boundary. See BOUNDARY, ARTIFICIAL.

Artificial fruits. See FRUITS, ARTIFICIAL.

Artificial person. See PERSON, ARTIFICIAL.

Artificial presumptions. See PRE-SUMPTIONS, ARTIFICIAL.

Artificially. By art, not naturally; made by human law.

Artium Magister. A Master of Arts. The highest college or university degree in arts. Abbreviated A. M.

Artium Baccalaureus. Bachelor of Arts. Abbreviated A. B.

Arundel. An ancient honor in England. See HONOR.

Arundinetum. A place where reeds grow.

Arura. A ploughing; a day's work at ploughing.

Arvil. Burial rights.

Arvil supper. A feast at a funeral.

As. A unit; unity. In Civil law, a pound in weight. A sum subject to division; applied to the whole of an inheritance. A coin, divided into twelve parts used to denote rates of interest. See UNCIÆ.

As per advice. See ADVICE, AS PER.

As usuarius. A pound lent upon usury (or interest).

Asaver. To wit; to say; to be understood.

Ascavoir. Same as ASAVER.

Ascend. To pass in an ascending line.

Ascendants. Ancestors in a direct line.

Ascendentientes. In Spanish law, heirs in the ascending line.

Ascending line. The line of ancestry which ascends through ancestors; as father, grandfather, great grandfather and so on.

Ascent. Passing upwards. Passing of an estate to an heir in the ascending line.

Ascertain. To learn by investigation. To make certain; to establish.

Ascesterium. A monastery.

Ascient. Knowing; knowingly.

Ascripticii. Same as ASCRIPTITII.

Ascriptitii. A species of soke-man, or tenant in ancient demesne.

Ascriptitii glebæ. Slaves of the Middle Ages. See ADSCRIPTI GLEBÆ; also ADSCRIPTITII GLEBÆ.

Ascriptitius. In Roman law, a foreigner naturalized in the colony where he lives.

Ascun. Any; any one; some.

Aside. See SET ASIDE; also STAND ASIDE.

Asoyne. Same as ESSOIN.

Aspect. A selected view of a proposition.

Asportare. To carry away.

Asportation. The carrying away of goods; required to constitute larceny.

Asportator. One who carries away stolen goods.

Asportavit. He carried away.

Asporto. To bear, carry or take something away.

Ass. Abbreviation of Assisa, an assize.

Assach. An old Welsh purgation by the oaths of three hundred men. (Abolished by Henry V.)

Assaia. An assay or examination.

Assaia mensurum et ponderum. The assay of measures and weights.

Assaie. An essay, an examination or trial.

Assalire. To assault.

Assaltus. An assault. In the Feudists, written also Assultus. In the old Common Law, written Insultus.

Assart. To make plain. To clear land of timber. The offence of removing the trees and coverts for deer in a forest.

Assartare. To assart, or remove by the roots; to clear land.

Assarted. Cleared of trees, brush, &c.

Assartum. Assart; land cleared of its wood and converted to tillage.

Assartatum. Asserted or cleared.

Assassin. One who commits murder for pay. A member of an oriental band of hashish or Indian hemp eaters who committed murder for hire. It originated in Persia in 1190, immigrated to Syria, was headed by the Old Man of the Mountain, was prominent during the Crusades and was suppressed in 1272 by the Sultan Bibars of Egypt.

Assassination. Murder for pay. See ASSASSIN.

Assath. Same as ASSACH.

Assault. To attempt to hurt another by striking at him. See BATTERY.

Assault, aggravated. An assault with intention to commit another crime.

Assault, simple. One without intent to commit any other injury or act.

Assay. The examination of weights and measures. To learn the elements of which an article is composed.

Assay office. See OFFICE, ASSAY.

Assaya. Same as ASSAIA.

Assayator. An assayer.

Assayator regis. The King's assayer.

Assaye. An assay.

Assayer. To assay, try. A person who separates gold and silver from other metals and substances to determine the quantity of.

Assayers. Those who assay.

Assayiare. To associate as a judge.

Assecurare. To make secure by pledges. See ASSECURO.

Assecuro. To make secure; to assure or secure by pledges, or any solemn interposition of faith. To confirm or establish.

Assecuratio. In the Law of Contracts, assurance. In old Maritime law, assurance or insurance of a vessel or cargo. A contract for the safe transportation of things for a certain premium. A voyage insured.

Assecuration. Same as ASSECURATIO.

Assecurator. In Maritime law, an insurer.

Assedare. To tax equally.

Assedation. A Scotch name for lease.

Assembly. A number of persons gathered together for some specific purpose. A congregation; a convocation; a convention.

Assembly, civil. One where people meet for amusement, worship, trade, etc.

Assembly, general. A name given in some of the U. S. to the State legislature.

Assembly, lawful. One held in accordance with the law of the place it is in.

Assembly, political. One required by law for public purposes.

Assembly, popular. A meeting of the people or their direct representatives.

Assembly, unlawful. The meeting of three or more persons to do an unlawful act.

Assemblage. An aggregation of persons or things collected together.

Assemblyman. A member of a State legislature, in some of the United States.

Assensu patris. See DOWER EX ASSENSU PATRIS.

Assent. Consent; agreement and approval.

Assent, constructive. See CONSTRUCTIVE ASSENT.

Assent, express. One expressly given in words.

Assent, implied. That implied from facts.

Assent, mutual. An assent by both parties. The agreement of two minds to a contract.

Assertare. To assart. See ASSART.

Assertatum. Assarted. See ASSART.

Assertory covenant. A promise under seal affirming something.

Assertory oath. See OATH, ASSERTORY.

Assess. To tax; to rate; to determine the proportion each is to pay of a tax.

Assessed taxes. Taxes on certain articles, as carriages, houses, etc.

Assessment. An estimate or proceeding by which a sum required for public or other purpose is determined. The sum itself. The determination of the degree of or the extent of.

Assessment of damages. See DAMAGES, ASSESSMENT OF.

Assessment, political. A demand made upon a member of a political party for a contribution of money to be used in the expenses of the campaign.

Assessor, nautical. A person familiar with practical maritime matters who acts as friend to an admiralty court.

Assessors. Those who fix the value of taxable property. Advisers to a court.

Assets. Property which can be used to satisfy debts.

Assets entre mains. Assets in hand (personal assets).

Assets, equitable. Those which creditors can reach only through a court of equity.

Assets, legal. Those in the hands of the executor or administrator, which may be reached in an action at law.

Assets, marshalling. See MARSHALLING ASSETS.

Assets per descent. Real assets. See ASSETS, REAL.

Assets, personal. Personal property.

Assets, real. Land in the hands of an heir chargeable with the payment of the debts of the ancestor.

Asseveration. An affirmation. A positive assertion.

Assewiare. To drawn or drain water from marsh grounds.

Assez. Enough.

Assideo. To assess; to fix, settle, define, determine, reduce to a certainty, either in point of time, number, amount, quantity, quality, etc.

Assidere. To tax equally.

Assign. To make over to another. To point out (as assign error.) One to whom an assignment is made. One appointed by the act of a party to perform an act or enjoy a benefit.

Assignable. Capable of being lawfully transferred.

Assignatio dotis. Assignment of dower (which see).

Assignation. In Scotch law, an assignment.

Assignatis. An assignee or assign; a person assigned or appointed to a particular duty.

Assignay. In Scotch law, an assignee.

Assignee. An assign. See ASSIGNS.

Assignee in fact. One made an assignee by another.

Assignee in law. One created by operation of law.

Assignee, official. An assignee appointed by court to assist other assignees in administering the estate of an insolvent.

Assignee, provisional. One to whom the assets of an insolvent are temporarily conveyed pending the appointment of a permanent assignment.

Assignees. Same as ASSIGNS.

Assignment. A grant of personal property. The written evidence of such grant. The transferring of an interest from one to another. The transfer of one's interest in land. See SUBLET.

Assignment, compulsory. One made in pursuance to the requirements of law.

Assignment, domestic. One made at a person's domicile.

Assignment, equitable. See EQUITABLE ASSIGNMENT.

Assignment, foreign. One made in another jurisdiction.

Assignment, legal. An assignment of property or a right enforceable by a court of law.

Assignment, new. See NEW ASSIGNMENT.

Assignment, novel. See NOVEL ASSIGNMENT.

Assignment of dower. Setting out dower according to the establishment. See ESTABLISHMENT OF DOWER.

Assignment of errors. See ERROR, ASSIGNMENT OF.

Assignment preferential. One made in favor of a particular creditor or creditors.

Assignment, voluntary. One made voluntarily without compulsion of any kind.

Assignor. He who assigns or makes over property to another.

Assigns. Those to whom assignments are made. Those appointed by act of party to do an act or enjoy a benefit.

Assimulare. To join highways.

Assinitas. Affinity by marriage.

Assis. Situated; fixed; assessed.

Assisa. An assise, a session. In old English and Scotch law, a species of jury on inquest; a certain number of men, usually twelve, summoned to try a cause, and who sat together for that purpose. A species of writ or real action. The proceedings in court upon a writ of assise. The verdict or finding of the jury in a writ of assise. A court or sittings of a court. A statute, ordinance or law. A tribute or tax or mulct. The term has been employed for so many different purposes that it has been termed nomen equivocum.

Assisa armorum. Assise of arms. A statute or ordinance requiring the keeping of arms for the common defence.

Assisa cadere. To fail in an assise; to be non-suited.

Assisa cadit in juratum. The assise falls into a jury. To submit a question to a jury.

Assisa continuando. For continuing the assise. The name of a writ addressed to the justices of the assise for the continuation of a cause, when certain words alleged could not have been proved in time by the party having occasion for them.

Assisa de Clarendon. The assise of Clarendon.

Assisa de mensuris. Assise of measures (a common rule for weights and measures established 8 Richard I.)

Assisa de nocumento. An assise of or concerning a nuisance. An assise or writ which lay to remove a nuisance, and to recover damages. The writ commanded the sheriff to summon an assise, that is a jury, to view the premises, and have them at the next commission of assises, that justice might be done therein. It has long been superseded by the action on the case, and was expressly abolished in England.

Assisa de forestæ. Assise of the forest. A statute regulating actions in the King's forest.

Assisa et assaia panis. The assise and essay of bread.

Assisa forestæ. Assise of the forest. A statute regulating actions in the King's forest.

Assisa friscæ fortia. Assise of fresh force.

Assisa generalis. The general assise or court (the Parliament).

Assisa mortis antecessoris. Assise of mort d'ancestor (death of the ancestor). See ASSISE OF MORT D'ANCESTOR.

Assisa novæ disseysinæ. Assise of novel disseisin. A writ of action which lay where a tenant in fee-simple, fee-tail, or for life, was disseised of his lands, tenements or hereditaments. (Superseded by the action of ejectment, before its express abolition by the statute 3 and 4 Will. IV. c. 27).

Assisa panis et cerevisiæ. Assise of bread and ale or beer. A statute 51 Henry III., regulating the sale of bread and ale.

Assisa proroganda. A writ to justices of assise staying a cause.

Assisa ultimæ presentationis. Assise of darrein presentment. This action is now entirely disused, being superseded by the action of quare impedit. See ASSISE OF DARREIN PRESENTMENT.

Assisa utrum. Assise of utrum; otherwise called a writ of juris utrum.

Assisa venalium. The assise of saleable commodities exposed for sale. The regulation of the sale of certain articles (usually the common necessaries of life), by public authority; defining or fixing the quantity, weight, quality, etc., to be sold for a certain price.

Assisatum. Fixed or established.

Assise. (From Assideo, to sit together). Originally an assembly of knights and justices at a time and place certain. A circuit court. The court, time, or place, where writs and processes of assise are taken. An ordinance or statute; a tribute; a tax; a real action, an action at law; a writ; an adjustment or measure. See ASSISA.

Assise at large. An action brought by an infant to enquire of a disseisin as to whether his ancestor were competent when he made the deed pleaded.

Assise de utrum. A writ to enquire whether tenements are in frankalmoign or the lay fee of the tenant. See JURIS UTRUM; also ASSISE UTRUM.

Assise, grand. See GRAND ASSISE.

Assise in point of assise. Where a tenant pleads no wrong, no disseisin, to the defendant's action.

Assise of bread. An old English statute regulating the price of bread.

Assise of Clarendon. The council held at Clarendon, A. D. 1164, in the reign of Henry II., at which statutes termed Constitutions of Clarendon were adopted. See CONSTITUTIONS OF CLARENDON.

Assise of darrein presentment. A writ granted against a stranger who has disturbed a clerk in a benefice. See ASSISA ULTIMÆ PRESENTATIONIS.

Assise of fresh force. A writ for one disseised of lands and tenements allowed by custom in some English boroughs or cities.

Assise of novel disseisin. Same as ASSISA NOVÆ DISSEYSINÆ.

Assise of nuisance. A writ of assise for abatement of a nuisance or for damages.

Assise of mort d'ancestor. Assise of the death of the ancestor. A writ granted a natural heir against a stranger who has abated.

Assise of right of damages. Where the tenant confesses an ouster, is adjudged wrong, and the demandant is awarded a writ for damages.

Assise of the forest. A statute regulating actions in the King's forest.

Assise of the King. Statute 18 Edw. II., of frank-pledge.

Assise out of the point of assise. Where the tenant pleads something by exception, as a foreign release.

Assise rents. See RENTS, ASSISE.

Assiser. A juror. An assessor. A supervisor of weights and measures.

Assisores. Persons who settled assises or imposed taxes.

Assisors. In Scotch law, jurors.

Assistance. Help; aid. A writ issued by chancery to execute a decree for the possession of lands.

Assistance, court of. See COURT OF ASSISTANCE.

Assistance, writ of. A writ out of the exchequer authorizing a public officer to seize goods prohibited or not having paid duty. A writ issued from a Court of Equity to aid the carrying out of its judgment. A writ issued by a Colonial Court before the Revolution, authorizing officers to call assistance in searching premises for contraband.

Assistant. In the United States army, the second in rank in the staff branches, as assistant quartermaster, etc. In the English army, the third in rank. In New England colonies, a member of the Governor's Council. The chief judge of Seville, Spain.

Assistants, court of. See COURT OF ASSISTANCE.

Assisus. Fixed or certain.

Assisus reditus. A fixed, certain, set or standing rent. Called rent of assise.

Assithment. A weregild. A compensation for killing a man.

Assiza et recognitio. The assise and recognizance.

Assises de Jerusalem. A code prepared by an assembly of barons and lords after the conquest of Jerusalem in 1099.

Assize. Same as ASSISE. Also to fix, to regulate, to assess; as assizing of men for arms. In Scotch law, a jury or inquest.

Assizors. Those who hold the assizes, or lay on the taxes.

Associate. One acting or connected with another in any affair.

Associate attorney (or counsel). One who is associated with another attorney.

Associate in crime. One associated with another in the commission of a crime.

Associate justice (or judge). One associated with another or other judges, not the chief justice.

Association. The act of being joined with another or others in interests. An organization without charter; any society or body which is not incorporated. A patent sent by the king to the justices appointed to take the assise; or of oyer and terminer, to have other persons associated with them to take the assise.

Association, articles of. See ARTICLES OF ASSOCIATION.

Association, co-operative. A joint stock association for the benefit of its members, usually in creating and maintaining a store or lending money to its members.

Association loan. See BUILDING AND LOAN ASSOCIATION.

Association, stock. See STOCK ASSOCIATION.

Association, voluntary. See VOLUNTARY ASSOCIATION.

Associations, building and loan. See BUILDING AND LOAN ASSOCIATIONS.

Associations, consolidation of. See CONSOLIDATION OF ASSOCIATIONS.

Assoile. To absolve; to deliver from excommunication. To free or absolve from guilt, or its consequences; to pardon, to forgive.

Assoiler. Same as ASSOILE.

Assoilzie. To acquit, absolve; to deliver from excommunication.

Assouth. Quit, free, discharged.

Assultus. An assault.

Assume. To claim or accept benefits or obligations.

Assumpsit. He undertook or promised. An express or implied promise to perform or pay something to another for consideration. The name of an action on the case, which lies for the party injured by the non-performance of a parol contract. If the contract or promise be express, the action is called special assumpsit; if implied by law, indebitatus assumpsit or general assumpsit.

Assumpsit, express. A promise made verbally or by writing not sealed.

Assumpsit, general. See ASSUMPSIT.

Assumpsit, indebitatus. See ASSUMPSIT.

Assumpsit, implied. A promise implied by law from the facts or act of the party.

Assumpsit, non. See NON ASSUMPSIT.

Assumpsit, special. See ASSUMPSIT.

Assumption. The day of the death of a saint, so-called.

Assurance. Insurance. An instrument used as evidence of the title to land. Warranty; certainty; indemnity.

Assurance, collateral. One made as incidental or additional to another.

Assurance, common. The evidence of a conveyance of property.

Assurance, disentailing. Same as DISENTAILING DEED.

Assurance, further. See FURTHER ASSURANCE.

Assurance, future. One to be made in the future.

Assurance of lands. Where lands or tenements are conveyed by deed.

Assurantia. An assurance. Insurance. A deed or instrument of conveyancing.

Assuare. To assure. To make sure or secure; to confirm or establish; to insure. To convey.

Assure. To insure,

Assured. One who is insured.

Assurer. An underwriter; one who insures others.

Assysers. Same as ASSISORS.

Assythement. In Scotch law, damages awarded the relatives of one murdered, against a murderer who has neither been convicted nor punished.

Aster. A man who is a resident. A contemptuous diminutive, as politicaster, an inferior politician.

Astipulation. An agreement. A witness or record.

Astipulator. Same as ADSTIPULATOR.

Astitrarius hæres. Same as ASTRARIUS HÆRES.

Astitution. To place or set in order, one by another. (An arraignment was formerly so called).

Astrarius. The occupant of a hearth, or house; a person in actual possession.

Astrarius hæres. Where an ancestor gives his heir or family a house during his lifetime. A son who lived in his father's family.

Astrarii in atrio sive in astro. Those who are domiciled together in the hall and on the hearth.

Astre. A hearth; a fire-place. A house.

Astrer. A householder, or occupant of a house or hearth.

Astrict. To bind.

Astriction. A power of contracting; a stringency. In Scotch law, a binding. A servitude by which the grain growing on certain lands is required to be carried to a certain mill to be ground.

Astriction to a mill. A right to compel those having grain in or brought within a certain locality, to have it ground at a certain mill at a certain price. See ACTION OF ABSTRACTED MULTURES.

Astrihiltet. A penalty of double the damage for breach of the King's peace.

Astronomical month. See MONTH, ASTRONOMICAL.

Astrum. A hearth or dwelling place; a dwelling house or place of habitation.

Astute, not. Applied to a court means not inclined.

Asysa. Same as ASSISE.

Asyle. Asylum.

Asylum. A sanctuary. A place of refuge. A place for the confinement of lunatics, or orphans.

At. Hath; and; in; within; or near.

At a premium. See PREMIUM, AT A.

At arm's length. Out of another's undue influence or control.

At bar. Before the court.

At chambers. See CHAMBERS, AT.

At discretion. Without restriction.

At interest. See INTEREST, AT.

At large. Not limited to any particular matter, place, or person; not under physical restraint. Not from any particular district. From the whole. Applicable to the whole. In general.

At law. According to law, as distinguished from equity or admiralty. See IN LAW.

At least. At the lowest estimate.

At length. In full.

At liberty. Free from restraint.

At maturity. The date of payment.

At once. Immediately; at the same time.

At par. At the value indicated on its face.

At sea. On a voyage. Without the limits of a port or harbor. On the sea. Outside of the jurisdiction of a country.

At sight. When presented. When seen.

Atamita. In Civil law, a great great great grandfather's sister.

Atavia. In Civil law, a great grandmother's grandmother.

Atavunculus. The brother of a great grandfather's grandmother.

Atavus. A fourth grandfather.

Ategar. A hand dart used by the Saxons.

Atha. An oath. The power to administer or exact an oath.

Athe. The privilege of administering an oath.

Atheist. One who does not believe in a God.

Atheling. Same as ADELING.

Atia. Malice; hatred. A writ of inquiry as to whether one should be committed on suspicion.

Atilium. Tackle; rigging.

Atillia. Utensils or country implements.

Atlantic Ocean. The ocean which separates the American continents from Europe and Africa, exclusive of the Gulf of Mexico.

Atmatertera. A great grandfather's grandmother's sister.

Atmatertera agna. Same as ATMATERTERA.

Atpatruus. The brother of a great grandfather's grandfather.

Atrium. A court yard; a church yard.

Ats. At suit of. Same as ADS., AT SECTAM.

Attacar. To tie or bind.

Attach. To fasten to; to annex; to affix. To seize or arrest by judicial process. To take a person or goods by commandment of a writ or precept and keep for presentment in court.

Attache. Attached to; connected with. One attached to the suite of an ambassador; a person attached to a foreign legation.

Attachiamentum. An attachment.

Attachiamentum bonorum. Attachment of goods (which see).

Attachiamentum de spinis et boscis. An attachment of the thorns and wood. An attachment or privilege granted to the officers of a forest to take to their own use, thorns, bushes and windfalls, within their precincts.

Attachiamentum. A foreign attachment (which see).

Attachiare. To attach.

Attachment. Taking a person or property already within the jurisdiction of the Court. A writ for such purpose.

Attachment, Court of. The Woodmote of the Forest. See WOODMOTE.

Attachment, domestic. One against a resident.

Attachment, execution. See EXECUTION-ATTACHMENT.

Attachment, foreign. A process used to attach the goods of a foreign or absent debtor, found within some liberty or city, to satisfy creditors.

Attachment of privilege. The summoning of one before a tribunal in which another had a special privilege of litigating. The power to arrest in a privileged place.

Attachment of property. Attachment of real or personal property.

Attachment of the forest. The Court of Attachment (which see).

Attachment of vessel. The seizure of a vessel after libel filed.

Attachment, personal. One issued against the person only.

Attack collaterally. To question in an independent proceeding.

Attainder. In English criminal law, the stain, forfeiture, and corruption of blood which followed on being condemned for certain crimes. That extinction of civil rights and capacities which takes place whenever a person who has committed treason or felony receives sentence of death for his crime. (He is no longer of any credit or reputation; he cannot be a witness in any court, neither is he capable of performing the functions of a man, for, by anticipation of his punishment, he is already dead in law). The consequences of attainder are forfeiture of property and corruption of blood. In American law, attainder is scarcely known, and is expressly prohibited by Constitution U. S., Art. I, sect. XI.

Attainder, Act of. See ACT OF ATTAINDER.

Attainder, Bill of. A law declaring a person attainted and his blood so corrupted that he could not inherit or transmit property.

Attainder by confession. Attainder arising from confession before a coroner in sanctuary, or by pleading guilty in court.

Attainder by outlawry. Same as ATTAINDER BY PROCESS.

Attainder by process. When the accused flees from justice and is outlawed.

Attainder by verdict. Where the accused is found guilty by the verdict of a jury.

Attaint. To make impure. A writ to enquire if a jury gave a false verdict; the action was tried by a jury of twenty-four men; and if the first verdict were found false, the twelve men of the first jury were adjudged infamous.

Attaint d'une cause. In French law, the gain of a suit.

Attainted. Had judgment of death pronounced upon him for felony or treason.

Attainture. Legal censure.

Attal sarisin. A deserted mine.

Attegia. A little house.

Atteindre. To reach to; to overtake or come to. To attaint, convict.

Attempt. To endeavor. To perform some act toward committing an offence. See INTENT.

Attendant. One who owes a service to another.

Attendant terms. See TERM, ATTENDANT.

Attentare. To attempt.

Attentat. (He attempts). A wrong motion or act in a cause made by the judge a quo pending an appeal.

Atterminare. To put off to a succeeding term. To prolong the time of payment of a debt.

Atterminer. Same as ATTERMINARE.

Attermining. Granting further time for payment of a debt. Same as ATTERMINARE.

Attermoiement. A composition; as with creditors.

Attest. To witness. To certify to.

Attestatio. An attesting; attestation; testimony.

Attestation. Evidence. Testimony. The act of witnessing an instrument in writing at the request of the party making the same, and subscribing it as a witness.

Attestation clause. The sentence in an instrument writing signed by the witnesses to its execution.

Attested copy. A copy of a document which has been verified.

Attesting witness. See WITNESS, ATTESTING.

Attestment. Attestation; testimony.

Attestor. One who attests.

Attestor of a cautioner. In Scotch law, one who certifies to the sufficiency of a cautioner and agrees to become subsidiary liable for the debt.

Atteynte. Attaint.

Attilamentum. Tackling or tackle; rigging; furniture, equipment.

Attilatus. Harnessed, tackled.

Attilatus equus. A horse with his gear or harness on.

Attile. Tackle of a ship.

Attilia. The rigging or tackle of ships.

Attilium. The rigging or tackle of a ship.

Attincta. An attaint, stain, or blackening; a conviction or finding guilty of some offence.

Attinctus. Stained or blackened. Attainted.

Atting. Same as ATTINGENT.

Attingent. They amount to, attain.

Attingentia. Amounting to; attaining.

Attingere. To amount to; to touch.

Attingo. To touch; to come in contact with; to reach to; to be allied to; to be united or connected with.

Attingunt se. They amount to.

Attorn. To consent to a transfer; to put in one's place; to make attornment.

Attornamentum. Attornment.

Attornare. To turn; to exchange; to give one thing in place of another. To attorn; to transfer or turn over.

Attornare rem. To turn or attorn over a thing, as money and goods (to assign or appropriate them to some particular use and service).

Attornare homagium et servitium tenentis. To attorn the homage and service of a tenant.

Attornato faciendo vel recipiendo. A writ commanding a sheriff of a county or hundred court to admit an attorney.

Attornatio. An attornment.

Attornati et apprenticii. Attorneys and apprentices.

Attornatus. One who is attorned, or put in the place of another; a substitute; an attorney.

Attornatus vel procurator. An attorney or procurator (proctor).

Attornatus generalis. A general attorney; one who is authorized to appear in all suits and causes, and in all courts; or in all suits at a particular circuit, or for a specified time.

Attornatus Regis (or Reginæ). The attorney of the King or Queen. The Attorney-General.

Attorne. An attorney.

Attorney. One appointed by another to act for him; a lawyer. An agent.

Attorney, associate. See ASSOCIATE ATTORNEY.

Attorney at large. Anciently an attorney-at-law who practiced in all the courts.

Attorney-at-law. One who has the authority to act for another in court.

Attorney, district. See DISTRICT ATTORNEY.

Attorney-General. The attorney for the Government.

Attorney in fact. An agent for the doing of some fact specified in an instrument writing.

Attorney, letter of. A power of attorney.

Attorney of the wards and liveries. The third officer of the English duchy court.

Attorney, power of. See POWER OF ATTORNEY.

Attorney, warrant of. An authority to an attorney-at-law to appear on behalf of a party to an action and allow the other side to take judgment by default.

Attorney's certificate. In England, a certificate that a specified attorney had paid his annual tax.

Attorneyship. The office of an attorney.

Attornment. A transferring or turning over. The consent of the tenant to accept the grant of the seignory. The transferring by a tenant of his land or services.

Au. At, to, for, until, in case of.

Au besoin. In case of need. In French law, words employed in the direction of bills of exchange, pointing out certain persons, who, in case of a refusal or failure of the drawee, are to be applied to, that they may honor and pay the bill; it is the nature of an acceptance supra protest (which see).

Aubaine. See Droit d'Aubaine.

Auceps syllabarum. (A catcher of syllables). A quibbler.

Auction. A public sale to the highest bidder.

Auctionariæ. Catalogues of goods to be sold at auction.

Auctionarii. Brokers. See Auctionarius.

Auctionarius. A broker, or person who loaned money. An auctioneer, in the modern sense. See Auctioneer.

Auctionarius qui emit. An auctioneer who buys.

Auctioneer. One who solicits bids at an auction. One who conducts an auction or public sale.

Auctor. A plaintiff; a principal; a vendor.

Auctor in rem suam. A judge, an adviser, a principal in his own affairs.

Auctores in rem suam. The phrase, auctor in rem suam, when applied to several.

Auctoritas. In Civil law, authority. A royal charter. A diploma.

Auctoritas populi. The authority of the people. The popular will or decision.

Aucun. Some; some one; any one.

Aucunement. Somewhat.

Aucupium. Catching at, or taking advantage of, or laying stress upon trivial mistakes or oversights.

Audience. A hearing. An interview with the ruler or chief executive of a nation.

Audience Court. See Court, Audience.

Audience of leave. The audience with a foreign representative after he has been recalled.

Audire. To hear.

Audiendo et terminando. Same as Oyer and Terminer.

Audit. A hearing; to hear. To examine, adjust and settle accounts.

Audita querela. (The complaint having been heard). A writ to be delivered from an unjust judgment or execution by setting it aside for some injustice which could not be pleaded in bar to the action. It lay for some matter occurring after judgment, amounting to a discharge, which could not have been taken advantage of otherwise.

Auditor. One who hears. An officer appointed to examine, verify, and approve the accounts of those handling money or supplies.

Auditor compotæ. The auditor of the account.

Auditor of the receipts. An officer of the English Exchequer.

Auditors of the imprest. Former officers of the English Exchequer who audited the customs, naval and military expense accounts.

Auditus. Hearing; the hearing.

Augea. A cistern for water.

Augmentation. The increase to the crown of revenues by the confiscation of religious institutions under Stat. 27, Hen. VIII. The court established to settle disputes relative to such institutions, and the land thereof.

Augmentation, process of. In Scotch law, one secured by a clergyman to obtain an increase in salary.

Augur. A particular college of priests at Rome, who pretended to foretell the future by observing the lighting, the flight or note of birds, &c.

Adjourd'huy. To-day.

Aula. A hall or court; the court of a baron or manor; a court baron. A hall or chief mansion house; the usual appendage of a manor.

Aula ecclesiæ. The nave of a church, anciently used by temporal courts.

Aulæ Regiæ Janitor Primarius. Same as Groom Porter.

Aula Regis. The King's hall or palace. (Also called Curia Regis, the King's Court). It was the Supreme Court of the kingdom, and was composed of the King's great officers of State, resident in his palace, and usually attendant on his person. Eventually the Aula Regis was dissolved, and its jurisdiction and authority resolved into several courts: King's Bench, Common Bench, Exchequer, and Chancery.

Aulnage. Same as ALNAGE.

Aulnager. Same as ALNAGER.

Aumone. Lands given to a church in return for prayers offered for repose of the donor's soul.

Aumone, service in. Prayers for the repose of the soul of a donor of lands who granted them in consideration thereof.

Auncel. A stilliard or steel yard. See STILLIARD.

Auncel weight. Same as AUNCEL.

Aunciatus. Antiquated.

Aupres. Near; nigh; about.

Aures. Cutting off the ears. A punishment inflicted by the Saxons for theft.

Auricular witness. See WITNESS, AURICULAR.

Auricularum scissio. Cutting or cropping off the ears.

Aurum Reginæ. Queen's gold; the gold of the Queen.

Auscultare. The instruction of monks for public reading.

Aussi. Also; in this manner.

Australian ballot. A term applied in U. S. to a ballot on ticket used in the election of different officials, which is in some features similar to that used in Australia. The system is different in different States, but the underlying principle is to enable one to vote secretly and to have no ballots used except those printed by authority of law.

Austurcus. A goshawk.

Aut. Either; or.

Autant. As much; so much; like as.

Auter. Another, other.

Auter action pendant. (Another action pending). A plea in abatement stating that a prior suit has been begun for the same cause.

Auter droit. In the right of another.

Auter vie. The life of another.

Auterfoits acquit. A former acquittal of the same charge.

Auterfoits convict. A former conviction of the same offence.

Auterment. Otherwise.

Auters. Others.

Authentic. Legally correct.

Authentic act. An act which has been legally executed and certified to by the proper officer.

Authentication. A certificate by the proper officer of a thing done, or, of the authority in one to do a thing.

Authentics. A collection of Justinian's Novellæ Constitutiones by an unknown author.

Authenticum. In Civil law, the original of an instrument writing.

Author. One who creates something new in itself.

Authorities. Those who have the execution of public law. Principles, decisions of judges, and statements of law writers, cited to sustain a legal proposition.

Authorities, constituted. Officers provided for in a constitution.

Authorities, constituting. Those who appoint constitutional officers.

Authorities, ecclesiastical. In England, the clergy and others having authority in the church.

Authorities, lawful. Persons given power by law to perform some act.

Authority. A power to do something; legal power; force; rule; influence. A rule, principle, interpretation or act cited to maintain a proposition.

Authority by law. Authority created by statute or operation of law.

Authority coupled with an interest. An authority for which the agent has given consideration, or which is given as partia al security.

Authority, delegation of. The giving or conferring of authority.

Authority, executive. Authority to execute the law.

Authority, express. That given in express terms.

Authority, general. Authority to perform all acts of a certain character.

Authority, implied. That implied from the facts or acts of the principal.

Authority, judicial. The authority of a judge.

Authority, legislative. Power of a legislature.

Authority, limited. That confined within certain limits.

Authority, naked. Authority wholly for the benefit of another.

Authority, special. Authority to do a particular act only.

Authority, unlimited. An authority where the agent is allowed to use his own discretion.

Authorize. To give power to.

Auto. Act.

Auto accordado. In Spanish law, an order emanating from some superior tribunal, promulgated in the name and by the authority of the sovereign.

Auto da fe. Same as AUTO DE FE.

Auto de fe. (Act of Faith). The judicial announcement, with its execution, of the sentence of the Inquisition, and the ceremonies attending the announcement.

Autocracy. An independent or self-derived power. A government where the power of the monarch is supreme, unlimited, uncontrolled by law.

Automobile. (Act of moving). Capable of being propelled by a motor.

Automobiles. All motor traction vehicles capable of being propelled on ordinary roads. Specifically, horseless carriages.

Autonomy. Subject to one's own law. One's power to give law to himself. The power or right of self-government. The state of absolute freedom, independence. The right of a people to establish the form of government they deem best without interference from others.

Autopsy. The examination of a dead body to discover the cause of death.

Autre. Other, another.

Autre action pendante. Same as AUTER ACTION PENDANT.

Autre action pendente. Same as AUTER ACTION PENDANT.

Autre vie. Another's life.

Autrefois. At another time; formerly, before, heretofore.

Autrefois convict. Formerly acquitted. A plea so called, by a criminal to an indictment, that he has been formerly acquitted on an indictment for the same offence.

Autrefois attaint. Formerly attainted. A plea of former attainder in bar to an indictment.

Autrefois acquit. Formerly convicted. A plea by a criminal, in bar to an indictment, that he was formerly convicted of the same identical crime.

Autrefoits. Same as AUTREFOIS.

Autrofoitz. Same as AUTREFOIS.

Autresint. Likewise.

Autumnale æquinoctium. Autumnal equinox.

Autumnalia. Fruits which ripen in the autumn.

Auxi. Also; in like manner; in addition to; too, further, likewise.

Auxibien. As well.

Auxiliary. One who or that which aids.

Auxilii petitio. A beseeching of aid; a prayer in or for aid. A petition to the court by a tenant in real actions, for the aid of another person interested in the property demanded, to help him defend the action; otherwise called aid prayer (which see).

Auxilium. Aid; a kind of tribute or service paid by the vassal to his lord, being one of the incidents of the tenure by knight's service. Aid or help to commit a crime.

Auxilium ad filium primogenitum militem faciendum, vel ad filiam primogenitam maritandam. Aid to make the eldest son a knight, or to marry the eldest daughter. An ancient writ which was addressed to the sheriff to levy compulsorily an aid toward the knighting of a son and the marrying of a daughter of the tenants in capite of the crown.

Auxilium ad filium militem faciendum et filiam maritandam. Same as preceding AUXILIUM AD FILIUM, &c.

Auxilium curæ. Aid, assistance of the court. An order or precept of the court citing and convening a party, at the suit and request of another, to appear and warrant something.

Auxilium Regis. The aid, assistance of the King; the King's aid. Money levied for the royal use and the public service, as taxes granted by Parliament.

Auxilium vicecomiti. Assistance or support of the sheriff; a customary aid or duty payable to the sheriffs out of certain manors for the better support of their offices.

Auxionarius. Same as AUCTIONARIUS.

Auxy. Same as AUXI.

Auxybien. As well.

Avage. A payment by tenants for allowing pigs to run in the lord's woods.

Avail. To be of use, or advantage. To profit; to promote; to benefit. Proceeds or profits from labor, sales, etc.

Avail of marriage. In Scotch law, value of marriage; a sum paid by a vassal to his lord when he (the vassal) married. The right of the lord or guardian to give an infant ward in marriage.

Available. That which can be readily utilized. That which is suitable under the circumstances.

Availe. Same as AVAILS.

Avails. Profits; proceeds; funds.

Aval. In French law, undertaking; guaranty; surety for payment. The guaranty or suretyship (avalage) of a bill of exchange; so called because usually placed at the foot or bottom (a val) of the bill.

Avalage. Suretyship.

Avaler. To descend; lower; put down; swallow.

Avallum. A written guarantee. (Also written Avalum).

Avant. Before.

Avant propos. Preliminary matter; preface.

Avantagium. Advantage; profit.

Avanture. Chance; hazard; mischance.

Avaria. Average or contribution.

Avaria carucæ. Beasts of the plow.

Avarie. Average. Loss or injury in navigation.

Avaunt. Before; forthcoming.

Avec. With.

Avec baraterie. Barratrously. Fraudulently.

Avecques. With.

Aveigner. To come, become; happen.

Avenage. Oats paid as rent or in lieu of services. See AVENAGIUM.

Avenagium. A certain quantity of oats paid to a landlord in lieu of some other duties. See AVENAGE.

Avener. To come, become; happen.

Avenor. An officer of the King's stables who provides oats for the horses.

Aventura. A mischance or accident by which the death of a man is suddenly occasioned without felony.

Aventure. Chance; mischance; aventura.

Aventuræ. Trials of skill at arms. Military exercises on horseback.

Aventurous. Casual; contingent.

Aver. A working animal.

Aver. To state; to plead; to verify. To have.

Aver corn. A rent in corn paid a religious house. Corn drawn to the lord's granary.

Aver et tener. To have and to hold.

Aver land. Lands plowed or manured for use of a monastery.

Aver penny. Money paid toward the King's carriages, by rent from land, instead of services by beasts in kind.

Aver silver. A rent so named.

Avera. A day's work for a plowman; valued in Domesday, at 8 pence.

Average. Horse or carriage service. Proportion borne by merchants whose goods are lost at sea. A duty paid for goods on ship above the freight. A medium, mean.

Average charges. See CHARGES, AVERAGE.

Average, general. The apportionment in general among the proprietors or their underwriters of the loss of part of a ship's cargo occasioned by being destroyed or injured to save the ship.

Average, gross. Same as AVERAGE, GENERAL.

Average loss. See LOSS, AVERAGE.

Average of corn fields. The stubble.

Average particular. Partial loss or damage to goods which must be borne by the owner, and is settled by the underwriters according to the ratio which the goods lost bore to the whole goods insured. (Also called Average or Partial Loss).

Average, petty. Small charges paid by the master for the benefit of the ship and cargo, such as pilotage, towage, anchorage, etc.

Average prices. See PRICES, AVERAGE.

Averagium. Average.

Averdupois. See AVOIRDUPOIS.

Averia. Cattle; working cattle. Property, goods, chattels, etc.

Averia caracuæ. Beasts of the plow; draft cattle. At common law these were privileged over other cattle.

Averia elongata. Cattle eloigned (carried to places unknown).

Averia otiosa. Idle, unemployed beasts, cattle.

Averiis captis in Withernam. Beasts, cattle taken in Withernam. A writ to take cattle in exchange for those unlawfully distrained and driven out of the country.

Averium. A beast; a working animal.

Averium ponderis. A live beast of full weight. Property, goods, chattels, etc., of full weight.

Averment. An offer to justify an exception pleaded in abatement. The ending part of a plea in confession and avoidance. The statement of a fact.

Averment, affirmative. A positive allegation that a fact is true.

Averment of notice. See NOTICE, AVERMENT OF.

Averment, negative. An allegation of some fact in negative form.

Averments, general. Averments made in general terms.

Averments, immaterial. Averments not material to the issue.

Averments, impertinent. Same as AVERMENTS, IMMATERIAL.

Averments, particular. The allegation of particular facts.

Averments, unnecessary. Allegations not necessary to a determination of the issue.

Averrare. To carry goods on horses or in a wagon.

Avers. Cattle, beasts.

Aversio. In Civil law, turning away. An averting. In bulk, not in portions. As a whole, not in part.

Aversio periculi. The fear of danger. An averting or turning away of peril. A name given to the contract of insurance (Assecuratio) because one of the parties undertakes to avert the peril of the other on the seas, or takes it upon himself.

Aversionem, sale per. Sale by bulk.

Averum. Goods, property, substance, treasures. A beast of burden.

Avet. In Scotch law, to assist; to abet.

Avia. In Civil law, a grandmother.

Aviaticus. In Civil law, a grandson.

Avisamentum. Advice, counsel.

Avisare. To advise.

Avisement. Advisement; consideration; consultation.

Aviser. To advise; to deliberate; to consult.

Avitious. Left by one's ancestors.

Avizandum. Advisement; deliberation.

Avocat. Advocat. An advocate.

Avocation. Business; employment.

Avoid. To evade. To escape. To make of no force or effect. To make vacant.

Avoidable accident. See ACCIDENT, AVOIDABLE.

Avoidance. A making void; an evading or escaping; the state of being vacant. A benefice void of an incumbent. See PLENARTY.

Avoidance, matter of. New matter alleged to avoid the legal effect of admitting the facts pleaded by an opponent. See CONFESSION and ADVOIDANCE.

Avoir. To possess. Property, estate, wealth, money, substance, means, ability, effects, goods, chattels; having those or either of them.

Avoirdupois. The name of a system of weights the unit of which is sixteen ounces or 7000 grains.

(6)

Avoucher. The calling upon a warrantor to fulfil his undertaking. The calling or summoning into court by a tenant, of a person bound to him to warranty, that is, either to defend the right against the demandant, or to yield him other lands, etc., in value.

Avoue. In French law, an attorney; an advocate.

Avouterie. Adultery.

Avow. To declare openly to justify an act. See ADVOW.

Avowant. One who makes an avowry. See AVOWRY.

Avowee. The holder of an advowson.

Avowrie. Same as AVOWRY.

Avowry. A pleading in an action of replevin, by which the defendant avows, that is, acknowledges the taking where he took it in his own right, and sets forth the reason for so doing.

Avowterer. An adulterer, with whom a married woman continues in adultery. The crime is called avowtry.

Avowtry. See AVOWTERER.

Avowy. The justification of a distress.

Avulsion. A taking away by tearing loose; tearing away anything. The sudden removal of soil from one man's estate to another's by the immediate and manifest power of a stream.

Avunculus. An uncle by the mother's side.

Avus. A grandfather.

Await. Waylaying; lying in wait to commit a wrong,

Award. The judgment or decision made and given by referees, or an arbitrator, or arbitrators, or an umpire, respecting any matter in dispute submitted to him or them. To adjudge entitled to. To give; to grant.

Award, Geneva. See GENEVA AWARD.

Award, no. See NO AWARD.

Award, Paris. See PARIS AWARD.

Awarda. An award.

Awardum. An award.

Away-going crop. A crop sown during the last year of a tenancy, but not ripe till the end of the term.

Awe. Water.

Awenhine. Same as AGENHINE.

Awm. A measure of wine containing forty gallons.

Awame. In Rhenish, 50 gallons. In Antwerp, 35 gallons.

Awnhinde. A domestic servant.

Axis. A board or table such as Solon's laws were written upon at Athens.

Ay. In the beginning of French words, same as AI.

Ayant cause. In French law, an assignee; a successor to property; a representative as distinguished from an heir, who acquires the right by inheritance.

Ayd. Aid.

Ayde. Aid.

Ayd-pryer. A prayer in aid or for aid. See AID PRAYER, also AID-PRIER.

Ayel. The name of a writ.

Ayle. Grandfather; a grandfather.

Ayle, pere et fitz. Grandfather, father and son.

Ayle, or de avo. A writ against a stranger who abates the heir on the death of his grandfather or grandmother.

Ayuntamiento. In Spanish law, a congress. A municipal legislature.

Aylours. Besides; otherwise; elsewhere.

Ayre. Same as EYRE.

Aysiamentum. Easement.

Azaldus. A poor horse.

B.

B. As an abbreviation denotes Bene, Bonus, Bona, Bachelor, Bail, Bankruptcy, Baron, Bench, Bill, Bond, Book. In Colonial times, a person convicted of burglary was branded on the cheek with B. in indelible ink.

B. B. Bail bond.

B. C. Bail court; bankruptcy cases. Before Christ.

B. E. Baron of the Court of Exchequer.

B. F. Bonum factum, (a proper thing).

B. R. Bancus Regis (King's Bench). Bancus Reginæ (Queen's Bench). Bankruptcy reports, also Bill of Rights.

B. S. Bancus superior, upper bench.

Baca. A hook or link of iron; a staple.

Bacbarende. Bearing or carrying upon the back, or about the person; an open or manifest robber or thief. See BACKBERINDE.

Bacberende. Same as BACBARENDE.

Bacheleria. The yeomanry as distinguished from the baronage.

Bachelor. A simple knight and not Knight of the Bath. Anciently applied to an admiral if under the degree of baron. A man who has never been married. One upon whom a college or university has conferred the first degree.

Bachelors, knight. See KNIGHT BACHELORS.

Back. To endorse on the back of a legal paper.

Backadation. Same as BACKWARDATION.

Backbear. Carrying on the back. Applied in old forest law, to one caught with a deer on his back and which warranted his arrest.

Backberend. Same as BACKBERINDE.

Backberinde. Bearing upon the back or about the person. Where a person is found with stolen goods upon him. See BACKBEAR; STABLE STAND; DOG DRAW; BLOODY HAND.

Backberynde. Same as BACKBERINDE.

Back-bond. In Scotch law, a declaration of trust.

Backing. Indorsement.

Backing a warrant. Where a justice of the peace indorses a warrant issued in another county, thus enabling it to be served in the county he belongs in.

Backside. The rear; a yard in the rear of a house.

Backverinde. Same as BACKBERINDE.

Backwardation. A sum paid a seller for deferring the delivery of stock until the next account day.

Backwards, forwards and. See FORWARDS AND BACKWARDS.

Bacinnium. A vessel to hold water to wash the hands.

Bacinis. A service of holding the basin on the day of the King's coronation.

Baco. A bacon hog.

Bactile. A candle stick of wood.

Baculo et annulo. With staff and ring. The insignia of a Roman Catholic bishop.

Baculum. A staff, rod or wand, anciently used in the ceremony of making livery of seisin, where there was no building on the land.

Baculus. Same as BACULUS NUNCIATORIUS.

Baculus nunciatorius. "The proclaiming staff or wand." A white stick or wand, by erecting which on the grounds of a defendant in real actions, he was anciently warned or summoned to appear in court at the return of the original writ.

Bad. The technical word for unsoundness in pleading. When applied to a person, means one who violates moral or municipal law habitually.

Bad faith. Unlawful intention. Intent to defraud.

Bad plea. See PLEA BAD.

Badge. A mark of identification. A device worn by an officer as an emblem of authority.

Badge of Fraud. An act which causes a transaction to be suspected as fraudulent.

Badger. One who buys corn or victuals in one place and carries to another to sell. To pester; to worry.

Bag. An uncertain quantity of goods; a sack for holding and measuring goods.

Baga. A bag or purse.

Bagagier. A carrier of goods.

Bagavel. A franchise granted the citizens of Exeter, by Ed. I. to collect toll on articles brought into that city.

Baggage. That which a passenger carries for personal use. As to what is, is a question of law to be determined by the facts in each particular case.

Bahadum. A chest or coffer.

Baiement. A hedge fence.

Bajardour. A bearer of a weight or burden.

Bail. Delivery, custody, guardianship. Delivery of land; livery. The setting at liberty of one arrested or imprisoned on surety taken for his appearance when wanted. A bond given that a person will be produced when wanted. In Canadian law, a lease. Also those who become sureties. See MAINPERNOR, and MAINPRIZE.

Bail a cheptel. In French law, a contract by which one person agrees to feed and care for the cattle of another and bear half the losses in return for half the profits.

Bail a ferme. Same as BAILER A FERME.

Bail a loyer. In French law, a contract for the letting of a house.

Bail a rente. In French law, a contract partaking of both a sale and a lease of property.

Bail above (or to the action). Same as BAIL TO THE ACTION.

Bail absolute. Bail given to pay a specified sum if another, entrusted with money, fails to account for the same at the proper time.

Bail appearance. Same as BAIL BELOW OR TO THE SHERIFF.

Bail below (or to the sheriff). A bail bond given to the sheriff as surety for the appearance of some one arrested on mesne process.

Bail bond. See BOND, BAIL.

Bail, civil. Bail given in civil actions.

Bail common (or straw bail). Where the sureties are merely fictitious and used only for entering an appearance.

Bail court. See COURT, BAIL.

Bail de la seisine. Livery of seisin. Bail, as embracing both delivery and keeping.

Bail emphyteutique. In Canadian law, a lease for an unlimited number of years.

Bail, excessive. Bail unreasonably large in amount.

Bail, fixing. Making the liability of a special bail absolute by judgment or some other procedure.

Bail in error. Bail given to stay an execution until an alleged error can be passed upon.

Bail, jump. See JUMP BAIL.

Bail, justifying. Ascertaining the sufficiency of bail.

Bail piece. See BAILPIECE.

Bail, special. Where the sureties giving bail are bona fide responsible. See BAIL, COMMON.

Bail, straw. See BAIL, COMMON.

Bail to the action. Bail stipulating that if the defendant does not satisfy the judgment or give himself up, the sureties will so do.

Bail to the sheriff. See BAIL, BELOW.

Bailable. Requiring bail; admitting of bail.

Bailable action. See ACTION, BAILABLE.

Bailable process. Same as PROCESS, BAILABLE.

Bailable offence. See OFFENCE, BAILABLE.

Bailage. A former customs duty of the city of London levied on certain exports and imports at that city. It was bought by the government, act of William IV. 3 and 4.

Bail-bond. The instrument writing executed by a surety.

Baile. Same as BAIL.

Bailee. A person who receives a thing in trust upon a contract that the trust will be executed; the one to whom a bailment is made.

Bailer. To put into the hands of; to deliver, commit, or intrust getting; to lease; to send. See BAILOR.

Bailer a ferme. In French law, to let to farm; to let on a lease.

Bailey. An outer wall about a feudal castle. The outer court of a castle. A court. A fortress.

Bailey, Old. See OLD BAILEY.

Bailie. In Scotch law, a bailiff; an alderman; a magistrate.

Bailiff. An officer of the hundred, of liberties, of manors, of husbandry, &c. A keeper; a steward; a subordinate magistrate. A Sheriff's officer or deputy. A tipstaff.

Bailiff, bound. A bailiff who gives the sheriff security against liability for his actions; commonly called bum-bailiff.

Bailiff errant. A bailiff's deputy.

Bailiff, special. Same as BAILIFF, BOUND.

Bailiff, water. See WATER BAILIFF.

Bailiffs of franchises. Officers who perform the duties of sheriffs within certain liberties or privileged jurisdictions, in which formerly the king's writ could not be executed by the sheriff.

Bailiffs of hundreds. Officers appointed hundreds by the sheriffs to collect fines therein and summon juries; to attend the judges and justices of the assizes and quarter sessions; and also to execute writs and process in the several hundreds.

Bailivia. Same as BAILIWICK.

Bailiwick. That over which a bailiff exercises certain powers. The jurisdiction of a bailiff or sheriff. A liberty exempted from a sheriff's jurisdiction; a county.

Baillee. Same as BAIL.

Bailler. Same as BAILER.

Bailleur de fonds. A money lender. A dormant, or sleeping partner. In Canadian law, the unpaid vendor of real estate.

Bailli. One on whom judicial power was conferred.

Baillie. A bailiff. A Bailie, which see.

Bailment. A delivery of goods in trust upon a contract that the trust will be faithfully executed by the bailee.

Bailment gratuitous. The receiving and undertaking to do some act with respect to an article, without reward.

Bailor. The one who makes a bailment. See BAILMENT.

Bailpiece. A certificate that certain persons became bail in a cause mentioned to a certain amount.

Baillivus. Same as BALLIVUS.

Bailly. A bailiff.

Bailly. Care, guardianship, government. A bailiff.

Bailor. One who delivers a thing to a bailee.

Bailour. A surety; a bailor.

Bair-man. In Scotch law, an insolvent and naked debtor not worth more than five shillings and five pence.

Bairns. In Scotch law, one's children.

Bairn's part. In Scotch law, children's part.

Bait. To lure from home by means of food. To harass a confined animal.

Baiting animals. Having them worried by dogs.

Balæna. One of the royal fish (piscis regalis), the head of which belonged to the King and the tail to the Queen.

Balance. The excess of one account over the other. That which remains after a part has been disposed of; the residue.

Balance, agreed. See AGREED BALANCE.

Balance, final. Balance remaining on a final settlement.

Balance, net. Balance after deduction of charges.

Balance of trade. See TRADE, BALANCE OF.

Balance-order. An order to pay up the balance of a call due, served on a contributory to a company.

Balance, partial. Balance existing on a partial settlement.

Balance sheet. A sheet upon which are placed the balance of a merchant's accounts.

Balcanifer. A standard bearer.

Balcony. A railed platform projecting from a wall.

Baldakinifer. Same as BALCANIFER.

Baldio. In Spanish law, waste land.

Bale. A quantity of goods fastened together.

Balena. Same as BALÆNA.

Balenger. A barge or water vessel. A man-of-war.

Baleuga. A territory or precinct.

Balia. A bailiwick; the district, territory or jurisdiction of a bailiff.

Balise. In French law, a buoy.

Balistarius. A ballister or cross-bowman.

Balium. Bail.

Balius. In Civil law, a teacher; a tutor; a guardian.

Baliva. A bailiwick or jurisdiction. See BALLIVA.

Balivo amovendo. A writ to remove a bailiff from his office.

Balivus. Same as BALLIVUS.

Balkers. Persons standing on a raised surface to give notice of something to others.

Ballare. To dance.

Ballast. Weight used to keep ships balanced.

Ballastage. Toll paid for the privilege of taking ballast from the bottom of a harbor or port.

Ballena. Same as BALÆNA.

Ballia. Same as BALIA.

Balliare. To bail; to set free from arrest or custody, and deliver to the keeping of other persons.

Ballium. Bail. A fortress or bulwark.

Balliva. A bailiwick; the territory or district under the jurisdiction of a sheriff; a sheriff's county; a district or place of jurisdiction.

Ballivi errantes, seu itinerantes. Bailiffs errant, or itinerant. Same as BAILIFFS OF FRANCHISES.

Ballivi franchesiarum. Bailiffs of franchises.

Ballivi hundredorum. Bailiffs of hundreds.

Ballivia. Same as BAILIWICK.

Ballivo amovendo. Same as BALIVO AMOVENDO.

Ballivus. A bailiff, baily or baillie.

Ballot. To vote. To express one's will by a ticket or ball embodying or indicating the same. The ticket or ball so used. The aggregate of votes cast. The act of voting.

Ballot, Australian. See AUSTRALIAN BALLOT.

Ballot box. A box in which ballots are placed when voting.

Ballot, marked. A ballot so marked as to indicate for whom it is cast.

Balnearii. A term applied to thieves who stole the clothes of bathers in the public baths of Rome.

Balnearii fures. Bath thieves. See BALNEARII.

Ban. A proclamation or public notice. An edict. A curse or denunciation. See BANN; also BANNS.

Banal. Relating to a ban or place privileged from the service of process. Having privileges.

Banal mill. One at which the lord may require his tenants to have their grain ground.

Banality. In Canadian law, the right by which a lord compels his tenants to do something to his profit, as grind at his mill, bake at his oven, &c.

Banc. A seat or bench of judgment.

Banc, sittings in. The sittings of a superior court in full, as distinguished from the sittings of the judges at nisi prius or on circuit.

Bancale. A covering of ease or ornament for a bench or seat.

Banci narratores. Countors of the Bench—otherwise called sergeant countors; advocates or pleaders.

Banco. In the Bench.

Banco regis. On the King's Bench.

Bancus. A bench or seat in the King's hall or palace. A bench. A table. A stall. A counter on which goods are offered for sale. A seat of judgment or tribunal for the administration of justice; the ancient and original name of the Court of Common Pleas, or Communis Bancus.

Bancus apud Westmonasterium. The Bench at Westminster.

Bancus, Communis. The Common Bench; the English Court of Common Pleas. See COURT OF COMMON PLEAS.

Bancus Reginæ. The Queen's Bench.

Bancus Regis. The King's Bench; supposed to be always held before the King himself. Hence the term, in Banco Regis, in the King's Bench. Abbreviated B. R.

Bancus ruptus. A broken bench. See BANKRUPT.

Bancus superior. The upper bench. During the Protectorate the King's Bench was so called.

Band. In Scotch law, a proclamation calling for soldiers.

Bandit. An outlaw; a man under the ban of the law.

Bane. Destruction, injury or overthrow. A malefactor. A denunciation of a malefactor by hue and cry. See LE BANE.

Baneret. A knight made in the field, of a degree next below a baron. See KNIGHT BANNERET.

Bani. Deodands.

Banishment. A civil death inflicted on an offender compelling him to leave the country.

Bank. A bench; the bench of justice. (An official meeting of all the judges of a common law court is called "sitting in bank" (or banc). The expression is used of a court sitting to determine questions of law, as distinguished from nisi prius sittings to determine questions of fact). A place where money is deposited. To deposit money in bank. A corporation engaged in the banking business.

Bank account. The fund one has in bank. The statement of the fund as to amounts deposited and drawn out.

Bank cashier. The officer of a bank who executes its financial operations.

Bank check. See BANK CHEQUE.

Bank cheque. An order to a bank to pay on demand from the funds of the drawer on deposit, a specified sum of money to either the bearer or a person mentioned.

Bank credits. Accommodations allowed by a bank to one who deposits security.

Bank le Roy. The King's Bench.

Bank, national. A bank organized by authority of and in accordance with the Federal banking laws of the United States.

Bank note. Same as BANK BILL.

Bank, savings. A bank established to receive and safe keep small deposits of money.

Bank, state. A bank established by virtue of State laws.

Bankable. That which will be accepted by a bank as equal to cash.

Bank bill. A promissory note payable to bearer on demand, issued by a bank and intended to circulate as money.

Bankers. Originally, moneyed goldsmiths. Private persons in whose hands money is deposited for safety. Those who make a business of banking.

Banker's note. See NOTE, BANKER'S.

Bankerout. Bankrupt.

Banking. The business of receiving, lending, issuing or dealing in money and discounting commercial paper.

Banking association, national. Same as BANK, NATIONAL.

Bank note. Same as BANK BILL.

Bankrupt. Originally, one who attempted to defraud his creditors. Now, defined by statute, but the term is generally applied to one without sufficient means to meet his pecuniary obligations. Also one who has filed, or against whom has been filed a petition in bankruptcy, or who has been adjudged a bankrupt.

Bankrupt, cessionary. One who surrenders his goods to his creditors.

Bankrupt, involuntary. One against whom a petition in bankruptcy has been filed without his consent.

Bankrupt law. See LAW, BANKRUPT.

Bankrupt, notour. See NOTOUR BANKRUPT.

Bankrupt system. The law and proceedings relating to bankruptcy.

Bankrupt, voluntary. One who voluntary files a petition in bankruptcy.

Bankruptcy. The condition of a bankrupt. That division of law by virtue of which a debtor's assets are divided among his creditors and he is thereafter discharged of all existing indebtedness.

Bankruptcy, act of. An act to establish a uniform system of bankruptcy. in the U. S., the act of July 1st, 1898.

Bankruptcy, contemplation of. The expectation of and making provision for bankruptcy.

Bankruptcy courts. See COURTS, BANKRUPTCY.

Bankruptcy, date of. In U. S. bankrupt law of 1898, the date when the petition is filed. See BANKRUPT.

Bankruptcy, fraudulent. Bankruptcy where the debtor endeavors to defraud his creditors.

Bankruptcy, composition in. See COMPOSITION IN BANKRUPTCY.

Bankruptcy, compulsory. See BANKRUPT, INVOLUNTARY.

Bankruptcy, time of. Same as BANKRUPTCY, DATE OF.

Banleuca. Same as BANLEUGA.

Banleuga. The limits of a manor or town.

Banlieu. Same as BANLEUGA.

Banlieue. Same as BANLEUGA.

Bann. The right of certain lords to announce the time to mow, reap, and pick grapes. An extent of territory. An enclosed place. The boundary of such a place. An area privileged from process. A military standard or banner. Calling a military force. The force called. A national army called for service.

Banneret. Same as BANERET.

Banni. Same as BANNITUS.

Banniare. To proclaim; to declare or decree publicly; to publish an edict, decree or proclamation. To summon; to call out by edict either to court or to military service; to summon to a standard, bannum or banner. To prescribe; to confiscate. To banish; to expel from a bannum or certain territory.

Banniatus. Same as BANNITUS.

Bannimus. We ban or expel. The form of public proclamation expelling a member from the University of Oxford.

Banni nuptiarum. The nuptial banns; the banns of matrimony.

Banning. Exclamation against or cursing of another.

Bannire. For a judge to cite one to appear in court.

Bannire ad placita, ad molendinum. To summon tenants to the lord's court and to bring corn to his mill to be ground.

Bannitus. Banished; outlawed. An outlaw, or banished man.

Banns. The announcement in church of an intended marriage.

Bannum. A ban. The limits of a manor or town.

Bannum. Same as BANNUS.

Bannum solvat. He shall pay a ban or fine.

Bannus. An edict, statute, or public ordinance; a ban. In old European law, a fine or penalty. A tribute. Banishment or exile; proscription; confiscation. An anathema or curse. A proclamation or publication—as the proclamation of marriage contract in a church. A field or territory; the limit or precinct of a town.

Bannus Regis. The King's ban, or proclamation.

Banque. A bench. A table. A counter.

Banque route. A broken bench or counter.

Bans of matrimony. A public announcement of a contemplated marriage.

Banyan. A Hindu merchant. A Hindu who acts as agent and interpreter for a European.

Bar. Any obstacle which obstructs, hinders, or defends; a barrier. The railing that encloses the place which counsel occupy in courts of justice. The place in court where prisoners are stationed. A plea sufficient to destroy the plaintiff's action. Members of the legal profession.

Bar associations. Associations of lawyers.

Bar, blank. See BLANK-BAR.

Bar fee. Money formerly paid a sheriff or gaoler by an acquitted prisoner.

Bar, perpetual. A plea which overthrows the plaintiff's action forever.

Bar, plea in. A plea which bars or defeats an action. A plea which alleges ground for barring an action.

Bar, special. A plea which sets up some special circumstance of fact.

Bar, temporary. A plea good for the present, but which may afterwards fail.

Bar to a common intendment. An ordinary plea, generally to the declaration.

Bar, trial at. Trial before a quorum of judges of a superior court.

Baragaria. A concubine.

Barataria. Same as BARRATRIA.

Baratarius. A barrator; one who encourages barratry.

Baratria. The crime committed by a judge who is induced by a bribe to pronounce a judgment.

Barbanus. In the old law of the Lombards, an uncle.

Barbarian Code. See CODE BARBARIAN.

Barbican. A watch-tower.

Barbicanage. Money given for the maintenance of a barbican, or toward repairing a bulwark.

Barca. A barque.

Barcaria. See BARCARIUM.

Barcarium. A sheep cote; a sheep walk.

Bard wool. To cut the head and neck from the rest of the sheep's fleece.

Bare. Same as NAKED.

Bare possession. Same as POSSESSION, NAKED.

Bare (or dry) trustee. One whose active duties are at an end and who can be compelled to convey the property according to the directions of his cestui que trust.

Barectator. A barrettor.

Baret. A wrangling suit. A brawl or quarrel.

Bargain. An agreement of one party to buy and another to sell real or personal property.

Bargain and sale. At one time the contract for conveyance of land without actual transfer. A contract for the sale and conveyance of land. The delivery of personalty followed by actual sale.

Bargain, time. See TIME BARGAIN.

Bargainee. One who is to receive property under a bargain. A grantee.

Bargainer. One who makes a bargain.

Bargainor. One who is to deliver something under contract.

Barge. A flat-bottomed boat without means of propulsion, used for the transportation of large quantities of merchandise, cars, &c., by being towed. Also, a similar boat used for pleasure.

Bark. The letter of a statute or instrument writing as distinguished from its meaning.

Barkary. A tan-house or place to keep tan bark.

Barleycorn. One third of an inch. A nominal rent or consideration.

Barmote. The Court of Berghmote, in Derbyshire, England. See BERGHMOTE.

Barnard's Inn. An English Chancery Inn.

Barnesiam. The tackle of a ship.

Baro. A man. A freeman, or freedman. A strong able-bodied man who serves for hire. A warrior or chief; a baron. A vassal, a freeholder who held immediately of the king. A man of dignity and rank; a baron, lord, or nobleman.

Baron. The lowest rank of nobility in England, next below a viscount. The governor of a province or seignory. A freeholder who held directly of the King. A husband. A freeman. A judge of the Court of Exchequer.

Baron and feme. Same as BARON ET FEME.

Baron, cursitor. See CURSITOR BARON.

Baron et feme. Man and woman; husband and wife.

Baronage. Same as BARONAGIUM.

Baronagium. The whole body of the barons. The baronage of the King's Court. The retinue, attendants, or following of a baron.

Baronatus. Same as BARONIA.

Barones majores. Greater barons.

Barones minores. Inferior barons.

Barones quinque portuum. Barons of the cinque ports.

Barones Scaccarii. Barons of the Exchequer during reign of Henry I., in England. The six judges of the Court of Exchequer in England of whom one is styled the chief baron.

Barones Scaccario. Same as BARONES SCACCARII.

Baronet. A dignity originally created in 1611, descendible to male issue, and taking precedence of all knights. See BARONETTUS.

Baronettus. A baronet; a little baron. It is an hereditary dignity created by letters patent and usually descendible to the issue, male, but is not a title of nobility. See BARONET.

Baronia. A barony. The dignity, territory, patrimony or fee of a baron. A manor or the territory of a manor. A part of a county; a hundred. A house of a certain kind in London.

Baronissa. A baroness; the wife of a baron.

Barons by letters patent. Those created by deed.

Barons by office. Those ex-officio barons.

Barons by prescription. Those whose ancestors have been barons out of memory.

Barons of the Cinque Ports. Members of Parliament from the Cinque Ports.

Barons of the Exchequer. The six judges of the English Exchequer.

Barony. The honor and territory which gives title to a baron. An old name for a manor.

Barony of land. Fifteen acres of land. A subdivision of a county in Ireland.

Barr. Same as BAR.

Barra. A bar. Same as BAR (which see).

Barraster. Same as BARRISTER.

Barrasterius. A barrister; a pleader at the bar.

Barrasyer. A barrister; a counsellor learned in the law and admitted to plead for others in a court.

Barratare. To cheat, defraud, embezzle.

Barrator. One who commits barratry.

Barratrare. Same as BARRATARE.

Barratria. Barratry; fraud, deceit, criminal fault, embezzlement, &c. In the Italian law, barratria has the sense of fraud or deceit committed in contracts and sales.

Barratrie. Same as BARRATRY.

Barratrous. Having the quality or character of barratry; fraudulent.

Barratry. An act by the master or sailor of a ship which is grossly negligent, or criminal, which benefits the actor to the injury and without the consent of the owner. Every species of fraud, knavery or criminal conduct in the master or mariners of a ship by which the owners or freighters are injured. In Scotch law, the crime of a judge who receives a bribe to pronounce a judgment. Fraud, deceit, criminal fault, embezzlement, &c. See BARRETRY.

Barratta. A contention; a quarrel.

Barre. Bar; the bar of a court. The bar, that is, the members of the legal profession practicing in a particular court. Bar; a plea in bar.

Barrector. See BARRETTOR.

Barrel. A measure of wine, ale, oil, &c. A measure of quantity in the U. S. holding 31 gallons of wine; 196 pounds of flour; or 2¾ bushels of apples.

Barren money. See MONEY, BARREN.

Barren rent. See RENT, BARREN.

Barrenness. A condition which prevents conception.

Barretta. A contention; a quarrel; a wrangling suit, etc.

Barreter. See BARRETTOR.

Barreterius. See BARRETOR.

Barretor. See BARRETTOR.

Barretor, common. See COMMON BARRETOR.

Barretry. The offence of disturbing the peace by the maintenance and bringing of numerous suits at law. See difference between this and BARRATRY.

Barretour. See BARRETTOR.

Barrettor. A common mover of suits and quarrels in disturbance of the peace. Barretor, Barretour, Barrector, Barectator, Barreterius and Barreteur, all have the same meaning.

Barreteur. See BARRETTOR.

Barr-fee. Same as BAR FEE.

Barrier. A wall of coal which separates two adjoining mines.

Barriers. A martial exercise with short swords. Places of defence on the frontiers. Obstructions.

Barrister. An English term for a pleader at the bar; a counsellor learned in the law and admitted to plead for others in a court.

Barrister, inner. In England, a Queen's counsel who is entitled to plead within the bar.

Barrister, outer. In England, one who pleads outside the bar.

Barrister, utter. Same as BARRISTER, OUTER.

Barrister, vacation. In England, a barrister recently admitted to the bar required to attend the sessions of the House for several vacations.

Barrmote. Same as BERGHMOTE.

Barrows. Hillocks in England said to be sepulchers of the Roman dead.

Barter. To exchange one commodity for another.

Barton. The demesne lands of a manor; a manor house. Out-houses. A farm, distinct from a mansion.

Barus. Same as BARO.

Bas. Low; base; inferior.

Bas chevaliers. Inferior knights by tenure of military fee. Bachelors.

Bas court. Any inferior court not of record, as a court baron.

Bas cur. Same as BAS COURT.

Bas estat. Base estate (the estate of a base tenant).

Bas ville. Same as BASE VILLE.

Bascinet. A basin-shaped helmet.

Base animals. Those which cannot be used for food.

Base coin. Debased coin.

Base court. Same as BAS COURT.

Base estate. An estate held by a base service.

Base fee. A tenure at the will of the lord. Same as FEE, QUALIFIED.

Base-infeftment. Same as RIGHTS, BASE.

Base justice. Same as BASSA JUSTITIA.

Base rights. See RIGHTS, BASE.

Base services. The lowest menial labor.

Base tenant. One bound to perform base services.

Base tenure. A tenure by base services, as villenage or customary services.

Base ville. The suburbs or inferior town.

Baselard. A poinard or dagger.

Basels. A coin abolished by Henry II. in 1158.

Basenet. A basin-shaped helmet.

Basileus. King; Emperor. The title given to the Emperor Justinian in some of his novels. A title given to the King of England, in charters before the conquest, in imitation of that assumed by the Emperors of the East and West.

Basilica. A compilation of Roman and Greek law, supposed to have been made during the latter part of the ninth and beginning of the tenth centuries. It was published as a code, A. D. 887.

Basils. Same as BASELS.

Basin. In marine insurance, a portion of the sea enclosed within rocks.

Basket tenure. Same as CANESTELLUS.

Basnetum. A helmet.

Bassa. Low.

Bassa haia. A low hedge.

Bassa justitia. Low justice. In Feudal law, the right of a feudal lord to try persons accused of petty offences or trespasses.

Bassa tenura. A base tenure. A holding by villenage or other customary service; the opposite of Alta Tenure.

Bassilland. A poniard or dagger.

Bassinet. A skin anciently used by soldiers to cover themselves with. A basin-shaped helmet.

Basso. Low. (Also written Bassa and Bassus).

Bassus. Low. (Also written Basso; Bassa).

Bastard. One born out of wedlock. Under old English law and in the U. S., unless changed by statute, the marriage of his parents did not legitimize, but under Canon and Civil law it did. See BASTARDUS.

Bastard, adulterous. One produced by persons one or both of whom are married to another when the child was conceived.

Bastard eigne. Bastard elder; an older bastard son. The child of two unmarried persons who afterward intermarry and have another and legitimate son, who is known in law as filius mulieratus or mulier puisny, the first or bastard son being the bastard eigne.

Bastard, special. One made legitimate by the subsequent marriage of its parents.

Bastard, William the. See CONQUEROR, WILLIAM THE.

Bastarda. A female bastard.

Bastardia. Bastardy; the state or condition of a bastard. See BASTARDY.

Bastardize. To show to be a bastard.

Bastardus. Bastard; of spurious origin, base or low-born. One that is not only begotten but born out of wedlock. Though as an individual the public laws protect his life and property. See BASTARD.

Bastardy. Begetting an i l l e g i m a t e child. The condition of being a bastard. The plea or objection of illegitimacy.

Bastardy bond. A bond given by the father of a bastard to pay a fixed sum periodically for the support of the child for a specified length of time, to prevent his becoming a public charge.

Bastardy process. The proceeding against a putative father of a bastard for the maintenance of a child to prevent it becoming a public charge.

Bastardy, incestuous. The issue begotten by those not married but related within the prohibited degrees of marriage.

Bastart. A bastard.

Baston. A staff or club. An officer, tipstaff. See BASTONS.

Bastons. Officers of the wardens of the fleet; so called from their red staffs.

Bastonicum. Close custody.

Basus. To take toll by strike or bushel and not by heap. See STRYKE.

Batable ground. Land between England and Scotland when distinct kingdoms. Ground that is in controversy.

Bataille. Battel; the trial by combat or duellum.

Bataile. Same as BATAILLE.

Batalare. To handle or brandish weapons; to fight.

Batalia. A battle or combat.

Batchelor. A bachelor. See BACH-ELOR.

Batella. A boat.

Batellus. A little boat; a skiff. A ferry-boat.

Bateria. Same as BATTERIA.

Bath, Knights of the. An order of knighthood instituted by Richard II.

Batiment. In French law, a vessel or ship.

Batitoria. A fulling mill; being a mill where cloth is shrunk.

Batus. A boat.

Battel. A trial by combat; the last three occurred in England in 1571, 1631 and 1638, respectively. Abolished 59 Geo. III. § 46. See BATTEL, WAGER OF.

Battel, wager of. A practice which prevailed in the courts of chivalry of trial by personal combat. In some cases the parties might fight by champions. If the appellee were vanquished he was hanged; if he killed the appellant or fought a certain length of time, he was acquitted. If the appellant cried craven, the appellee recovered damages, but the appellant lost his liberam legem and became infamous. See BATTEL; also CRAVEN.

Battere. To beat or strike with a stick or club. To beat another unlawfully, whether with club, stick or fist, or otherwise.

Batteria. Battery (which see).

Battery. The unlawful beating of another; the least touching of another's person, willfully or in anger. Every battery, a fortiori, includes an assault. See ASSAULT.

Batture. A bottom of sand, a species of alluvion rising toward, or up to, or above the surface of a river.

Baubella. Jewels or precious stones.

Baudekin. Cloth of gold; brocade.

Bautboys. High timber as distinguished from underbrush.

Bawd. A procurer.

Bawdy-house. A house of ill-fame. A house in which two or more women reside and engage in illegitimate sexual intercourse for money.

Bay. A pond of deep water to turn a mill wheel. A harbor.

Bayle. Same as BAILEE.

Bayler. Same as BAILER.

Bayley. A bailiff.

Baylment. Same as BAILMENT.

Bayly, A bailiff.

Bayou. A creek or stream peculiar to Louisiana and Texas. An outlet from a swamp, pond or lagoon, to a river or the sea.

Beach. Same as SHORE.

Beacon. A fire or light maintained as a signal.

Beaconage. Money paid to maintain a beacon.

Bead. A prayer; first used by the poor in lieu of books.

Beadle. An officer to execute process for the forest courts.

Beam. That part of a stag's head where the horns grow. A balance of weights. A support for floors and roofs.

Bear. To carry; to hold. To have expressed upon it, as the date or rate of interest. One who speculates for a fall in prices, in the Stock Exchange.

Bearer. One who bears anything.

Bearers. Those who oppress others. Maintainers.

Bearing date. Having date. Being dated.

Beast. A four-footed animal used for labor, food, or sport.

Beastgate. Land sufficient to feed one beast.

Beasts of the chase. In England, the doe, marten, buck, fox, and roe. See FERÆ CAMPESTRES.

Beasts of the forest. In England, the hind, hart, boar and wolf. See FERÆ SIL-VESTRES.

Beasts of the plow. Animals used in cultivating the soil.

Beasts and fowls of warren. In England, the hare, coney, pheasant and partridge.

Beasts of the contest. Those which contested with gladiators and criminals in the arena at Rome.

Beat. To unlawfully lay hands upon.

Beating the bounds. Perambulation, (which see).

Beau-pleader. Fair pleading; apt or correct pleading; or the fair or favorable hearing of a plea or suit. Lord Coke considers it a fine imposed for the privilege of pleading fairly, by way of amendment, after a former vicious plea. A writ prohibiting a fine for inapt pleading, given by statute of Marl. 52, Hy. III., c 11.

Beberches. Services by a tenant, at the bidding of the lord.

Bed. The right to sexual intercourse. That part of the land under a lake, river or bay, which is rarely exposed, but usually covered with water.

Bedel. A crier or messenger of a court. An apparitor. A collector of the King's rents.

Bedelary. The jurisdiction of a bedel.

Bederepe. A service requiring the tenant to reap the landlord's corn.

Bedeweri. Profligate persons.

Beef. An animal fit for beef.

Beerhouse. In England, a place where beer sold can be drunk either on or off the premises. See BEERSHOP.

Beershop. In England, a place where beer is sold, but can only be drunk off the premises. See BEERHOUSE.

Beeves. Bulls, oxen, steers, or cows, slaughtered for food.

Befail. Same as BEFAYLE.

Befayle. A writ where the heir was abated on death of his great grandfather or great grandmother.

Before. Exclusive of the day mentioned. Prior to. In the presence of.

Before the Court. Within the jurisdiction and control of a court for consideration.

Before trial. After the institution of a suit, but before the issue is placed before the court or jury for determination.

Bega. In India, a land measure equal to about a third of an acre.

Beggar. One who lives by soliciting alms.

Begging. Soliciting the gift of money or articles.

Begin. To institute; to initiate. To first operate upon or become subject to.

Begin, right to. The right of the party upon whom the burden of proof rests; the right of the one who affirms.

Begins to run. When a cause of action first arises, or is subject to the operation of law.

Begotten. Procreated.

Begum. In India, a woman of high rank.

Behalf. Advantage. Benefit. Defence.

Behalf of, in. See IN BEHALF OF.

Behavior. Demeanor with respect to law.

Behavior, disorderly. Behavior in violation of law or the proceedings of a court or legally constituted body.

Behavior, good. Conformity to law.

Behetria. In Spanish law, lands occupied by those who could select their own lords.

Behoof. Use; benefit; advantage.

Being. Existing.

Belgæ. Inhabitants of Somersetshire, Wiltshire and Hampshire, in England.

Belief. Conviction drawn from facts known, but where the believer knows that other facts might exist which would change his opinion if known. See KNOWLEDGE.

Bellagines. Same as BILLAGINES.

Bellator. A warrior, a soldier.

Bellatoris campus. The field of battle.

Bellatorius. Warlike, martial; useful in warlike expeditions.

Belli imperator. War chief or general.

Belligerency. The state of a nation or peoples who are at war with another.

Belligerent. One who is at war with another.

Bello. To carry on war; to war; to make war.

Bellum. War; an armed contest between nations.

Bellum internecinum. An internecine war, that is, a war of mutual destruction.

Bellum intestinum. An intestine war; a civil war.

Bellum lethale. A deadly war.

Below. Inferior; subordinate.

Below par. See PAR, BELOW.

Bench. A tribunal of justice; a seat of judgment; the court; the body of judges, as distinguished from the bar.

Bench, King's. Formerly the highest court of Common law in England during the reign of a King.

Bench, Queen's. Formerly the highest court of Common law in England during the reign of a Queen.

Bench warrant. See WARRANT, BENCH.

Benchers. Members of the English Inns of Court who are charged with its management.

Bene. Well; legally; sufficiently; in due form.

Benefice. An ecclesiastical living or promotion. Formerly portions of land given by lords to their followers for maintenance. See BENEFICIA.

Beneficia. Estates held by feudal tenure, being originally gifts from the lord. From this arose the word Benefice, as applied to the care of the souls of a parish.

Beneficial. Benefitting; tending to benefit; yielding a benefit to.

Beneficial enjoyment. The enjoyment one has in an estate for his own benefit and not for another.

Beneficial interest. Interest in an estate which arises from other than ownership.

Beneficial power. See POWER, BENEFICIAL.

Beneficiare. One in whose favor a bill of exchange is drawn or contract is made.

Beneficiary. One who derives a benefit from anything. He who is in possession of a benefice. A cestui que trust. See BENEFICE; also CESTUY QUE TRUST.

Beneficio primo ecclesiastico habendo. For having the privilege or benefice in the first church. An ancient writ from the King to the Lord Chancellor to bestow the first vacant benefice upon a particular person.

Beneficium. A privilege, a favor, right; any particular privilege. Originally an estate held for life, only, given to military men. An estate received from a superior.

Beneficium abstinendi. The privilege of abstaining applied to the power of an heir to abstain from accepting the inheritance.

Beneficium cedendarum actionem. The benefit of making over actions. In the Civil law, the privilege by which a surety could, before paying the creditor, compel him to make over to him the right of action.

Beneficium clericale. The clerical privilege; the privilege of clergy. (Abolished by Stat. 7 and 8, Geo. IV., c. 28). See BENEFIT OF CLERGY.

Beneficium competentiæ. In Roman law, the right of being exempt from any judgment which would deprive a man of necessities.

Beneficium divisionis. In Roman law, the right of a co-surety to be exempt from contribution beyond his share.

Beneficium inventarii. In Roman law, the privilege of an heir to have the testator's property inventoried before he took possession that he might know whether the assets exceded the liabilities or not.

Beneficium ordinis, excussionis, or discussionis. In Roman law, same as Discussion in Scotch law.

Beneficium separationis. In Roman law, the right granted a creditor to have the property of a testator separated from that of an insolvent heir.

Benefit. Profit. Advantage.

Benefit building societies. Those societies intended to assist their members in the purchase of land and the erecting of buildings thereon.

Benefit of cession. In Civil law, the exemption of a debtor from future imprisonment on surrendering his property to his creditors.

Benefit of clergy. The exemption from punishment of those who were clergymen; afterwards extended to all those who could read. (Abolished by Stat. 7 and 8, Geo. IV., c. 28). See ARSURE EN LE MAIN.

Benefit·of discussion. See DISCUSSION.

Benefit of division. Same as BENEFICIUM DIVISIONIS.

Benefit of inventory. Same as BENEFICIUM INVENTARII.

Benefit society. One created and maintained for the purpose of assisting its members or their relatives.

Bene-placitum. Good pleasure; good will.

Benerth. An ancient service rendered the lord with plow and cart.

Benevolence. A voluntary gratuity and sometimes extorted sum given by tenants to a lord, or subjects to the King.

Benevolent. Kind; charitable.

Benevolentia regis habenda. The form of purchasing the King's pardon and restoration to an estate.

Beora. A grove of trees on the top of a hill.

Bequeath. To leave personal property by will or testament.

Bequeathe. Same as BEQUEATH.

Bequest. A gift of personalty by testament. It is an inchoate property until the executor delivers possession. See LEGACY, TESTAMENT, WILL.

Bequest, executory. The bequest of a contingent, or future interest in personal property.

Bequest, residuary. The bequest of all of the remainder of a testator's property after debts, legacies, &c., have been paid.

Bequest, specific. A bequest of property of a particular kind.

Berbiage. A rent paid for the depasturing of sheep.

Berbica. An ewe.

Berbicaria. A sheep down or ground on which to feed sheep.

Berbicus. A ram.

Bercaria. An enclosure for the keeping of sheep; a sheep-fold. A place where bark was tanned.

Bercarius. A shepherd.

Bercator. A shepherd.

Bereafodon. They bereaved.

Berefellarii. A name applied to seven churchmen of St. John's Church of Beverly, England.

Berefreid. A large wooden tower.

Berefreit. Same as BEREFREID.

Berenica. A manor; villages or hamlets belonging to some town or manor.

Berewicha. Same as BERENICA.

Berghmaster. An officer among Derbyshire (England) miners who acts as a coroner. A mountaineer or miner.

Berghmayster. Same as BERGMASTER.

Berghmote. Anciently an assembly or court on a hill to decide controversies among miners of Derbyshire, England.

Berghmoth. Same as BERGHMOTE.

Beria. A large flat open field. A burgh; a manor.

Bering Sea dispute. The dispute between the U. S. and England which arose, originally, through the objection of the U. S. to the killing by Canadians in Bering Sea, of female seals during pregnancy or while caring for their young. The question was submitted to a board of arbitration which made an award in Paris in 1893. See PELAGIC SEALING.

Bernet. Incendiarism. Any capital offence.

Bernita. Same as BERENICA.

Berquiarium. Same as BERCARIA.

Berra. A plain open heath. To grub up barren heaths.

Berry. The habitation of a nobleman. A dwelling-house. A sanctuary.

Bersa. A limit or bound. A park paling.

Bersare. To hunt or shoot.

Bersarii. Those who hunted the wolf.

Besayel. Same as BESAILE.

Berselet. A hound.

Berton. Same as BARTON.

Bertonarii. Farmers who held bartons at the will of the lord. See BARTON.

Berwica. Same as BEREWICHA.

Bery. Anciently a sanctuary. The seat of habitation or mansion of a nobleman.

Bes. In Roman law, eight unciæ or two-thirds of an As. Two-thirds of an inheritance. Eight per cent. interest. See As.

Besaiel. A great grandfather. A writ based on the seisin of a great grandfather.

Besaile. The father of the grandfather. A writ against a stranger who dispossed the heir of a great grandfather. See AILE, also MORT D'ANCESTOR.

Besantine. Same as BISANTIUM.

Besayle. Same as BESAILE.

Bescha. A spade or shovel. A piece of land turned up with a spade; as much land as a man can dig with a spade in a day.

(7)

Best. That which excels all others. That which is most beneficial or advantageous under the circumstances.

Bestes. Beasts; cattle.

Bestes des charues. Beasts of the plow.

Bestiæ carucæ. Beasts of the plow.

Bestiality. Carnal intercourse with the lower animals. See BUGGERY.

Bestials. Beasts or cattle of any sort. Cattle purveyed for the King's provision.

Bet. A wager.

Betaches. Laymen using glebe lands.

Betrothment. An agreement between a man and woman to marry at a future time.

Better. Legally or equitably superior.

Better equity. See EQUITY, BETTER.

Betterment. An improvement which substantially increases the value of land. The increased value of land through public improvements.

Betterment acts. Legislative acts which protect an innocent purchaser to the extent of improvements he may have made on land.

Betting. An agreement between two or more persons that a sum of money, to which each has contributed, shall become the property of one or more on the happening of an event.

Between. Intervening. Among. Involving joint action of two or more.

Beverage. A liquor drunk for pleasure, as distinguished from one drunk for health.

Beverches. Same as BEBERCHES.

Bewared. Expended.

Beyond sea. Out of the kingdom of Great Britain and Ireland. In U. S. it means out of the State, or out of the United States.

Beyond the four seas. Same as BEYOND SEA.

Bezant. Same as BISANTIUM.

Bi. Two; twice.

Bias. A mental inclination.

Bible, family. See FAMILY BIBLE.

Bibliotheca. A library.

Bicycle. A vehicle of two wheels, propelled by the person who rides the same.

Bid. To make an offer on something offered for sale. The offer itself. The amount for which a contractor proposes to do certain work.

Bid off. To bid successfully at an auction.

Bid, upset. A local term applied in parts of the United States to a higher offer than that received for property previously sold at auction by order of court, in order to have the auction sale disapproved. See UPSET PRICE.

Bidale. An invitation to drink ale at the house of a poor person who expects charitable contribution in return.

Bidall. Same as BIDALE.

Bidder. One who offers a certain price for an article at an auction.

Bidding, by. Fraudulent bidding of a puffer to cause bona fide bidders to offer a higher price.

Biddings. Offers of money for property sold at auction.

Bidentes. Two yearlings or sheep of the second year.

Bielbrief. In maritime law, a written statement furnished an owner by a ship builder of a vessel's measurement and dimensions. In Danish law, a contract of bottomry.

Bidviana. Fasting for two days.

Bien. Well; advisable; good in law.

Biennially. Once in every two years.

Biennium. The period of two years.

Biens. Goods; chattels; personal property. In the Common law, the term biens includes all chattels, as well real as personal. In the United States, the term goods has been held to include money, banknotes and coin, promissory notes, and the stock or shares of an incorporated company.

Biens et chateux. Goods and chattels. A common term employed to designate personal property.

Biens immovables. Immovable goods.

Biens meubles et immeubles. Goods movable and immovable.

Biens movables. Movable goods.

Bifanga. Possessions of land.

Biga. Anciently a wagon; a cart or chariot drawn by two horses side by side.

Bigamia. Bigamy; a second marriage.

Bigamus. A person twice married. A bigamist. See BIGAMY.

Bigamy. Originally meant being twice married. Now, marrying a second time while the first marriage is still in force.

Bigata. Same as BIGA.

Bigener. Descended from two different races; hybrid.

Bigenera. Same as BIGENER.

Bigenerum. Same as BIGENER.

Bigot. A name at one time applied to Rollo and the Normans. An intolerant adherent to a creed, system, or opinion.

Bilagæ. Billagines.

Bilagines. By-laws of corporations. See BILLAGINES.

Bilan. A balance sheet.

Bilanche deferends. A writ directing that wool be weighed by the corporation transporting it.

Bilanche deferendis. Same as BILANCHE DEFERENDS.

Bi-lateral. Two-sided.

Bi-lateral contract. See CONTRACT, BI-LATERAL.

Bilaw. A fine for not repairing banks, ditches, on a certain day.

Bilboes. A punishment inflicted at sea with a device similar to the stocks.

Bilge. The flat part of a ship's bottom. To stave in the bilge of a ship so it leaks.

Biline. Collateral.

Bilinguis. Two-tongued; double-tongued. One who can speak two languages. A jury de medietate linguæ or one composed of two nationalities.

Bilinguis fabula. A deceitful narration; having a double meaning; allegorical.

Bill. A declaration or complaint in writing; a proposed indictment placed before a grand jury for its action. A proposed law. A common engagement for money. A single bond without condition. A w r i t t e n statement of an indebtedness.

Bill, accommodation. See ACCOMMODATION BILL.

Bill book. A book in which an account of promissory notes and bills of exchange are kept.

Bill chamber. In Scotch law, a department of the Court of Session, always open for the hearing of petitions, the issuance of injunctions and interdicts.

Bill, creditor's. A bill to enforce a debt or judgment out of property not subject in law to execution. A bill to set aside a fraudulent conveyance, and subject the property to the payment of a debt or judgment.

Bill, cross. One filed by the defendant against the plaintiff or by another against both parties in relation to the subject-matter of the original bill. A bill of exchange or promissory note given in consideration of another bill or note.

Bill, deficiency. A legislative bill for supplying a deficiency in a previous appropriation of money. A loan to the English government by the Bank of England, to supply a temporary deficiency.

Bill, Dingley. See DINGLEY, BILL.

Bill fee. See FEE, BILL.

Bill, fishing. A bill in equity which seeks discovery on allegations loosely or unintelligibly made.

Bill for a new trial. A bill in equity to enjoin a judgment at law and praying for a new trial.

Bill for cancellation. One brought to destroy evidence which at some future time might injure the plaintiff.

Bill for foreclosure. A bill in equity filed by a mortgagee for the sale of the mortgaged property and satisfaction of the debt, interest and costs. See FORECLOSE.

Bill, foreign. A bill of exchange drawn or payable in a foreign country.

Bill in chancery. A statement of the facts in proper form, addressed to the Chancellor of a Court of Chancery, which are the ground for requesting the relief.

Bill in equity. Same as BILL OF EQUITY.

Bill in the nature of a bill of review. A bill in equity filed by one not a party to a proceeding to have the same re-examined and the decree reversed.

Bill in the nature of a bill of revivor. A bill in equity filed to revive a suit where a bill of revivor is insufficient to supply the defect or remedy the abatement.

Bill in the nature of a supplemental bill. A bill introducing new parties and new interests in a cause already commenced. It is distinguished from a supplemental bill, as in the latter, the parties or the interests are the same as those of the original bill.

Bill, not a true. See NOT A TRUE BILL.

Bill, not original. A bill which is filed after the original bill, but relating to the same matter and parties.

Bill, obligatory. A written acknowledgement of an indebtedness under seal.

Bill of adventure. A writing made by a shipper of goods or common carrier showing that the shipment is the venture of another person and that the shipper or carrier is not responsible for anything but delivery as consigned. See ADVENTURE.

Bill of advocation. In Scotch law, a bill bringing the judgment of an inferior court before a superior court for review.

Bill of attainder. See ATTAINDER, BILL OF.

Bill of certiorari. A bill in equity to remove a cause to a superior court. See CERTIORARI.

Bill of conformity. A bill in equity filed by an executor or administrator praying that the court direct the administration of the estate for the benefit of the creditors and enter a decree determining the order of payment.

Bill of costs. An account rendered of the costs taxed against the parties to a suit.

Bill of credit. A writing requesting one to give credit to the bearer on the guarantee of payment by the writer. A document issued by a State, and designed to circulate as money, promising to pay a certain sum. United States Constitution prohibits bills of credit being issued by a State.

Bill of debt. Same as DEBT, BILL OF.

Bill of discovery. A petition in equity praying for an order requiring a party to disclose certain facts within his knowledge.

Bill of divorce. A petition praying for a divorce.

Bill of entry. A memorandum entered at the Custom House of goods imported or for export.

Bill of equity. A written or printed statement of a plaintiff's case addressed to a court of equity.

Bill of exceptions. A statement in writing of the exceptions to the rulings of the court.

Bill of exchange. A written order from one person to another for the payment of money to a third person.

Bill of exchange, domestic. A bill drawn on a person living in the same State or country with the drawer.

Bill of exchange, foreign. Same as FOREIGN BILL.

Bill of exchange, parties to. The drawer, drawee, acceptor, payee, also in case of transfer, the indorser, indorsee and holder.

Bill of exchequer. See EXCHEQUER, BILL OF.

Bill of gross adventure. In French law, an instrument writing evidencing a contract of bottomry or other maritime loan.

Bill of health, A consular or other official certificate given to a ship's master, at the time of sailing stating the sanitary conditions and general health of ship and crew.

Bill of health, clean. See HEALTH, CLEAN BILL OF.

Bill of indemnity. An act, passed by Parliament every session, for the relief of those who for any reason have not taken the necessary oaths of office. ·

Bill of indictment. A formal written accusation presented by a grand jury in court.

Bill of information. A bill in equity filed on behalf of the State to obtain that due it or damages.

Bill of interpleader. A petition in equity by the holder of a fund in the proceeding by interpleader.

Bill of lading. A written acknowledgment by a carrier of the receipt of goods for transportation.

Bill of Middlesex. A process by which the Court of King's Bench sitting in Middlesex, obtained jurisdiction of a person without obtaining an original writ. The method was to allege a fictitious trespass in the county of which the court always had jurisdiction, and further state the real cause of action. On return that the defendant was not in the county a latitat was issued to the sheriff of the county where he was. This also alleged the fictitious trespass and the real cause of action.

Bill of mortality. An official record and report of the number of deaths and their causes in a given place within a stated time.

Bill of pains and penalties. A special statute imposing punishment upon a person charged with treason or other high crime without his being convicted thereof by judicial proceedings. (Forbidden by the U. S. Constitution).

Bill of parcels. An invoice or statement of the articles composing a parcel or package of goods; usually sent to the purchaser with the articles.

Bill of particulars. A written exhibit of items constituting a demand for which suit is brought, or facts upon which indictment or charge is founded.

Bill of peace. A petition in equity filed to consolidate actions in order to prevent multiplicity of suits concerning the same matter.

Bill of privilege. An old English mode of procedure against persons privileged from arrest.

Bill of proof. Proceedings to establish his title, by one who claims to be the real owner of goods sought to be attached.

Bill of review. A bill to review a judgment in chancery, when there is error or some new evidence.

Bill of revivor. A bill filed to revive an abated suit.

Bill of revivor and supplement. A bill in equity which is both a bill of revivor and a supplemental bill.

Bill of Rights. See RIGHTS, BILL OF.

Bill of sale. An instrument writing by which the transfer of title to personal property is declared and established. An instrument writing in the nature of a mortgage for the transfer of title to personal property, as security for a debt.

Bill of sale, grand. See GRAND BILL OF SALE.

Bill of sight. A written description of imported goods given to the customs officials when the exact quality or quantity of the goods is not known, so they may be landed and examined.

Bill of stores. A custom-house license to a merchant vessel to carry stores for the voyage free of duty.

Bill of sufferance. A license allowing merchants to carry goods from port to port within the same country without paying duty.

Bill, original. A bill stating a ground for relief never before in litigation between the same parties.

Bill payable. A bill of exchange, promissory note, or other written agreement to pay money.

Bill penal. A bill of debt with a penalty in case of default.

Bill, private. A legislative bill for the benefit of a private individual as distinguished from one for the public welfare.

Bill, public. A legislative bill for the benefit of the public at large as distinguished from a private bill.

Bill quia timet. (Because he fears). A bill to prevent apprehended injury to property.

Bill receivable. A promissory note, bill of exchange, or acceptance held by a person to whom it is payable.

Bill rendered. The written statement of a claim for money owed.

Bill, ship's. See SHIP'S BILL.

Bill, single. A bill obligatory without a condition or penalty.

Bill, supplemental. A bill filed to supply some omission or defect in the original bill which could not be cured by amendment.

Bill taken pro confesso. See PRO CONFESSO, BILL TAKEN.

Bill to carry a decree into execution. A bill filed to obtain a decree which is required before a previous decree can be carried into execution.

Bill to perpetuate testimony. A bill to obtain the testimony of persons whose testimony may be required regarding a matter not yet, but which may be, in litigation.

Bill to quiet title and possession. Same as BILL TO REMOVE CLOUD UPON TITLE.

Bill to remove cloud upon title. A bill brought to settle and confirm a title which is really good, so that the possessor cannot be annoyed in the future by another person who holds evidences or deeds, but has not brought action.

Bill to suspend a decree, A bill for the suspension of a decree because of a particular state of facts.

Bill to take testimony. A bill filed for permission to take the testimony of a witness liable to die or leave the country. See PERPETUATING TESTIMONY.

Bill to take testimony de bene esse. Same as BILL TO TAKE TESTIMONY.

Bill, true. The indorsement made on a bill of indictment by a grand jury, when they found it sufficiently sustained by evidence.

Billa. Bill; a bill. A formal statement or declaration of the facts of the case, as the ground of the action. A formal written statement of complaint to a court of justice.

Billa cassatur. That the bill be quashed. The form of judgment rendered for defendant on plea of abatement to a bill.

Billa escambium. Bill of exchange (which see).

Billa excambii. A bill of exchange. A written order or request by one person to another, for the payment of money absolutely and in all events.

Billa exonerationis. A bill of or on account of the lading of freight.

Billa vera. A true bill. The indorsement made on a bill of indictment by a grand jury, when they found it sufficiently sustained by evidence.

Billæ nundinales. Fair or market bills.

Billagines. By-laws; the laws of towns; municipal laws. The private laws or regulations made by any corporation for its own government, which are binding upon it if made in conformity with the general law, otherwise they are void.

Bille. Bill; a bill; a bill of exceptions.

Billet. To place or quarter soldiers. A soldier's quarters in a civilian's house.

Billet a ordre. A bill payable to order.

Billet a vue. A bill payable at sight.

Billet de change. A billet or letter of exchange. In French law, the Billet de change is given when the party with whom the contract is made is not at present prepared to give the bill of exchange agreed on, and merely gives a billet, by which he engages hereafter to furnish one.

Billet de complaisance. An accommodation bill.

Billeta. A bill or petition exhibited in Parliament.

Billet wood. Fire wood; fixed by statute 43 Elizabeth, at three feet four inches long and seven inches in compass; under this size was forfeited to the poor.

Billet of gold. Wedges or ingots of gold.

Billetum. A billet, bill or memorandum. Such as was allowed to parties to require of the sheriff or under sheriff to whom a writ was delivered.

Billingsgate. A fishmarket in England. Abusive and vulgar epithets.

Billio. Bullion.

Billo. Bullion.

Billos. A bill.

Bills, inland. Domestic bills of exchange.

Billus. A bill, stick or staff. A watchman.

Bills, money. See MONEY BILLS.

Bi-metallic. Relating to or composed of two metals. (Applied to money).

Bi-metalism. The use of two metals as money at a fixed ratio. The doctrine of such a monetary system.

Bind. To obligate.

Binding. Making obligatory.

Binding instruction. See INSTRUCTION, BINDING.

Binding out. Obligating to perform certain labor for a certain time.

Binding over. Obligating to keep the peace or appear as a witness.

Biothanetus. One who deserves to come to an untimely end.

Bi-partite. Of two parts; divided in two. An indenture, where there were two parties, and two parts of the deed. Tripartite (of three parts) and quadripartite (of four parts), are also used.

Birauban. To rob.

Biraubodedun. They robbed.

Biretum. A cap or coif of a judge or sergeant at law; a thin cap fitting the head closely.

Biretus. Same as BIRETUM.

Birrettum. Same as BIRETUM.

Birth. The act of being born.

Bis. Twice; in two days; in a two-fold manner.

Bis petitum. A thing twice demanded.

Bisacutus. A double-edged iron weapon.

Bisaile. A great grandfather.

Bisantium. An ancient gold and silver coin, first coined at Bizantium or Constantinople, and at one time current in England.

Bi-scot. A fine of two shillings for not repairing ditches, banks, etc., after having once been notified and time extended. See BILAW.

Bi-sextiles. Containing an intercalary day.

Bisextilis annus. A bisextile year. Leap Year. The bissextile year has one more day than the other years and happens every fourth year; it was ordained by the statute de Anno Bissextili, 21 Hen. III., that the day increasing in the Leap Year, and the day next before, should be accounted but one day.

Bi-sextum. An intercalary day.

Bi-sextus. Same as BI-SEXTUM.

Bishop. Chief of the clergy in his diocese.

Bishop, arch. See ARCHBISHOP.

Bishop's court. See COURT, BISHOP'S.

Bishopric. The diocese of a bishop.

Bissa. A hind.

Bissextile. Leap Year. See BISEXTILUS ANNUS.

Bisus. Brown bread; a brown loaf.

Black acre and white acre. Terms anciently applied to pieces of land to distinguish them.

Black Act. The statute of Geo. I., cap. 22, against persons committing crimes with blackened faces.

Black Acts. Old Scotch statutes enacted prior to 1587 and printed in black letters.

Black Act, Waltham. See WALTHAM BLACK ACT.

Black Book. One of several books so named because of the black binding. A record of commissioners under Henry VIII., detailing alleged practices in monasteries.

Black Book of the Admiralty. An ancient repository of Admiralty law, containing the laws of Oleron with many ordinances and commentaries.

Black Book of the Exchequer. A book in the Exchequer of England, containing ancient charters, conventions, etc.

Black Code. See CODE BLACK.

Black game. Heath grouse, as distinguished from the heath fowl or red grouse.

Blackleg. A professional swindler, especially by the use of games of chance.

Black-mail. A certain rent in money, consisting of corn or base money. A tribute formerly paid the border chiefs by those living in the northern counties of England, to secure protection from the border thieves and moss troopers. A contribution to prevent the carrying out of a threat. To obtain money by threats. Hush money.

Black Maria. The wagon in which prisoners are carried between a court and a jail.

Black rent. See RENT, BLACK.

Black rod. Chief usher to the King and custodian of all peers when first committed for crime.

Black rod, gentleman usher of. Same as BLACK ROD.

Blacks. Negroes; persons of African descent.

Blackstone, Sir William. The author of the compilation of English common and statute law, known as Blackstone's Commentaries, first delivered as lectures at Oxford College, England, and published in 1765–69.

Black-ward. A sub-vassal.

Blada. (Plural of Bladum). Corn or grain.

Blada a solo separata. Grain separated from the soil; grain after it has been harvested.

Blada crescentia. Corn or grain growing.

Blada nondum a solo separata. Crops not yet severed from the soil.

Blada in garbis. Grain in swaths or straw.

Blada vel alia catalla. Grain or other chattels.

Bladarius. A corn monger; a retailer of corn.

Blade. Fruit, corn, hemp, flax, herbs, &c.

Bladier. An engrosser of corn or grain.

Blanc. White, blank, smooth.

Blanc seign. A blank paper signed and delivered to one to fill in at discretion.

Blanch ferme. White farm, or white rent; rent payable in silver and not in cattle.

Blanch furines. Rent paid in base coin.

Blanch holding. A Scotch tenure, similar to free and common socage; the duty payable being in general, trifling.

Blanch rents. Same as BLANCH FERME.

Blanche. Same as BLANC.

Blancus. Same as BLANC.

Bland-Allison Act. An act of Congress dated Feb. 28, 1878, directing the Secretary of the Treasury to purchase not less than two nor more than four million dollars worth of silver bullion per month and coin the same into standard silver dollars of 412½ grains each. See SHERMAN COINAGE ACT; also COINAGE REPEAL ACT OF 1893.

Blanhornum. A little bell.

Blank. A space in a document left free from writing or print that it may be filled with appropriate words or marks when required. Also the document with such unfilled spaces.

Blank acceptance. An acceptance written before the bill is made.

Blank-bar. A plea in bar in trespass obliging plaintiff to assign the certain place where trespass was committed.

Blank bond, See BOND, BLANK.

Blank indorsement. See INDORSEMENT, BLANK.

Blanket mortgage. See MORTGAGE, BLANKET.

Blanket policy. See POLICY, BLANKET.

Blanks. White money coined by Henry V. in part of France subject to England, value 8d. Vacant spaces in a declaration which at one time were good cause of demurrer.

Blasarius. An incendiary.

Blasphemare. Blasphemy.

Blasphemia. Blasphemy.

Blasphemous libel. See LIBEL, BLASPHEMOUS.

Blasphemy. Denying what is deemed to be due the God of the Christian religion. It was an offence at common law.

Ble. Sight; color. Corn.

Bleat. Peat or earth dried for burning.

Blees. Corn, grain.

Blees scies. Grain cut.

Blench holding. Same as BLANCH HOLDING.

Blended fund. The proceeds from the sale of both real and personal property. (Usually applied to the estate of deceased person).

Blinks. Boughs broken from trees and thrown where deer are likely to pass.

Blissom. Copulation between ram and ewe.

Blocade de facto. A blockade in fact but without notice to neutrals.

Blockade. The cutting off of communication or commerce from a port by force.

Blockade, paper. One proclaimed but not made effective by force.

Blockade, public. That established by proclamation and in fact.

Blockade, simple. That established by a naval officer without the direction of his government.

Blodeous. Deep red color.

Blood. Kin; of the same stock; having a common ancestor.

Blood, cold. See COLD BLOOD.

Blood, full. See FULL BLOOD.

Blood, half. Where persons have the same father but different mothers.

Blood money. Money anciently paid by a man slayer as compensation to the next of kin; the amount varying with the rank of the killed.

Blood, whole. Where persons have the same parents or ancestors.

Bloodwit. A fine for shedding blood. To be quit of (exempt from) amercements assessed for blood shedding. In Scotch law, a riot in which blood is shed. See WERE.

Bloodwite. Same as BLOODWIT.

Bloody hand. In the act. In Forest law, being found with bloody hands which fact warranted an arrest, the presumption being that the person so caught had killed game unlawfully.

Blue laws. See LAWS, BLUE.

Board. A table. That which is given on a table as food. A body of persons charged with some duty (as a board of directors).

Board, canvassing. A number of persons appointed or elected to examine and count the votes cast at an election.

Board, light-house. See LIGHT-HOUSE BOARD.

Board of Control. An English board of privy councillors who at one time governed the British possessions in India.

Board of Directors. See DIRECTORS, BOARD OF.

Board of Green Cloth. Same as COURT OF GREEN CLOTH.

Board of Health. See HEALTH, BOARD OF.

Board of Supervisors. A board of county officials in some of the U. S., who have charge of the county moneys and other matters relating to county government.

Board of Trade. In England, a committee on commerce, selected from the privy council. In U. S. an association of merchants for the promotion of business interests.

Board of Works. A board of officers in some cities having charge of the streets, sewers, public property, and reservations.

Board on Geographic Names. A board organized Sept. 4, 1890, to determine the correct geographic nomenclature and orthography for various maps, charts and publications issued by the executive departments of the U. S. government.

Board wages. A money allowance in lieu of board. Board and lodging also as pay for service.

Boarder. One who is fed or fed and lodged in the house of another under a contract for a certain period at a certain price. As to whether one is a guest or a boarder, the facts of each case must determine.

Boarding-house. A house where boarders are habitually and voluntarily received, and which is made known publicly as a boarding-house.

Bob veal. See VEAL, BOB.

Boc. A writing; a book; a charter. Land bocs, or other evidences of title corresponding to modern deeds.

Boceras. A Saxon notary, scribe or chancellor.

Boc-hord. A place where books, evidences, or writings were kept.

Bock-hord. Same as BOC-HORD.

Bockland. A possession or inheritance held by evidence in writing. Lands held by charter in allodium descendible to all the sons and called gavelkind and devisable only by will and termed terræ testamentales.

Boc-land. Same as BOCKLAND.

Boddemerey. Bottomry.

Boddemerie. Bottomry.

Bodmerie. Bottomry.

Body. A human being. The principal part of a thing. An artificial organization. A number taken collectively.

Body, corporate. A corporation.

Body, deliberative. A body existing for careful consideration or legislative deliberation.

Body, heirs of the. See HEIRS OF THE BODY.

Body of a county. A county considered as a whole.

Body of an instrument. The material part.

Body of laws. See LAWS, BODY OF.

Body politic. A State. A corporation.

Body - snatching. Taking a human body from a grave without legal authority.

Boia. Chains or fetters.

Boilary. A place for boiling. Water from a salt well belonging to other than the owner.

Bois. Underwood. Timber.

Bolt. A long narrow piece or package of material, as cloth. A piece of canvas of thirty-eight yards. To withdraw from a political party. The withdrawal from a political convention while in session.

Boldagium. Same as BOLTAGIUM.

Bolhagium. Same as BOLTAGIUM.

Boltagium. A little house or cottage.

Bolter. A sieve for separating flour from bran.

Bolting. The private arguing of a case by law students.

Bon. Good; sufficient in law.

Bona. Goods; personal chattels; movable property; chattels real as well as personal.

Bona caduca. Fallen possessions or those which fall back or escheat. Goods without an heir.

Bona civium. The citizen's goods.

Bona confiscata. Confiscated or forfeited goods.

Bona et catalla. Goods and chattels.

Bona et merchandisæ. Goods and merchandise.

Bona felonum. Goods of felons; the goods of those convicted of felony.

Bona fide. Good faith; without fraud or deceit.

Bona fide emptor. A purchaser in good faith; a bona fide purchaser.

Bona fide possessor. A possessor in good faith.

Bona fide præscriptio. A prescription in good faith.

Bona fide purchaser. A purchaser in good faith.

Bona fides. Good faith; (the opposite of mala fides).

Bona forisfacta. Forfeited goods.

Bona fugitivorum. The goods of one who had fled for felony, forfeited to the King.

Bona gestura. Good behavior; good abearing.

Bona gratia. By or through kind favor; with good grace; by mutual good will or consent. Applied in the Civil law, to a species of divorce where the parties separated by mutual consent.

Bona immobilia. Immovable goods.

Bona mobilia. Movable goods.

Bona notabilia. Notable goods; extraordinary goods. In English Ecclesiastical law, goods worthy of notice, or of value sufficient to be considered.

Bona paraphernalia. Goods which the wife has for her own separate use, such as rings for her fingers, ear-rings, and other personal ornaments.

Bona patria. Good country. An assise or jury of good neighbors.

Bona peritura. Perishable goods.

Bona utlagatorum. Goods of outlaws.

Bona vacantia. Vacant, unoccupied or ownerless goods.

Bona waiviata. Goods stolen and waived. In England, they went to the sovereign; in the U. S., they may be reclaimed by the owner. See WAIVED.

Bonæ fidei. Of or in good faith.

Bonæ fidei actio. An action of good faith.

Bonæ fidei contractus. A contract of good faith.

Bonæ fidei emptor. A purchaser in good faith.

Bonæ fidei possessor. A possessor in good faith.

Bonaght. A tax in Ireland to support Bonaghti, a class of war knights.

Bonaghty. Same as BONAGHT.

Boncha. A bunch.

Bond. To secure by bond. To place goods in a bonded warehouse. To encumber with a debt. A deed in which the obligor agrees to pay a certain sum at a day appointed. In a servile state; captive. An interest-bearing certificate. In Scotch law, a bondman.

Bond and disposition in security. In Scotch law, a mortgage of land.

Bond and mortgage. A bond for the payment of money and a mortgage of realty as security for the performance of the bond.

Bond, appeal. See APPEAL BOND.

Bond, average. A bond given to the captain of a vessel by the consignee of a cargo, that he will pay his share of the general average.

Bond, back. A bond given to indemnify a surety.

Bond, bail. An instrument under seal by which a defendant and usually two sureties are bound to pay a sum to the sheriff if defendant do not appear and answer to the action in which he has been arrested.

Bond, bastardy. See BASTARDY BOND.

Bond, blank. A Scotch security in which the creditor's name was not, but could be, inserted at any time, by the holder of the bond. (Such a bond was subsequently declared invalid).

Bond, bottomry. See BOTTOMRY BOND.

Bond, cautionary. In Scotch law, a bond given as security for the performance of some obligation.

Bond, claim. One given by the plaintiffs in replevin.

Bond, claim property. Same as BOND, CLAIM.

Bond, claimant's. Same as BOND, CLAIM.

Bond, convertible. A bond of a stock company convertible into stock at the option of the holder.

Bond, cost. A bond conditioned that the party or his bondsman will pay all costs which may be taxed against the former in a particular action.

Bond, counter. A bond given against another bond, as where a bond is given to protect one seizing goods and the holder of the goods gives a bond to hold them pending a determination of the ownership.

Bond, coupon. See COUPON BOND.

Bond, debenture. See DEBENTURE.

Bond, delivery. A bond that goods or their value will be delivered up at a certain time or upon certain conditions.

Bond, double. In Scotch law, a bond with a penalty.

Bond, dormant. One on which no payment has been made for twenty years.

Bond, forthcoming. A bond that property will be delivered up if wanted or the court so decrees.

Bond, heritable. See HERITABLE BOND.

Bond, hypothecation. A bottomry bond.

Bond, income. A bond payable from net earnings or a percentage of such earnings. A bond which pledges the income of a corporation for the payment of certain obligations.

Bond, joint. See JOINT BOND.

Bond, joint and several. A bond in which the obligors bind themselves jointly and severally.

Bond of corroboration. In Scotch law, an additional obligation which strengthens or confirms the original bond.

Bond, general mortgage. A bond secured by a mortgage upon the whole of the corporate property, even though parts of the property are already mortgaged.

Bond, land. See LAND BOND.

Bond, municipal. See BOND, PUBLIC.

Bond, official. One given by a public officer that he will faithfully discharge the duties of his office.

Bond, penal. A bond to pay a sum on failure to perform a certain act.

Bond, property. Same as BOND, CLAIM.

Bond, public. One issued by a government either National, State, or a political division thereof, for public purposes.

Bond, refunding. A bond stipulating that money paid for any purpose will be repaid if it subsequently appear that the payment should not have been paid.

Bond, registered. A bond for the payment of money registered in the owner's name.

Bond, replevin. A bond given by a claimant of property delivered to him under writ of replevin, that he will return the property if he does not show that its detention by the defendant was unlawful.

Bond servant. A slave.

Bond, single. See SINGLE BOND.

Bond, straw. A bond in which the obligors are not responsible for the payment if forfeited, or in which the sureties are fictitious.

Bond tenants. Copy-holders; customary tenants; those holding at the will of the lord according to the custom of his manor.

Bonda. Same as BUNDA.

Bondage. Slavery.

Bondager. One who does bond service. In Scotch law, a female farm laborer supplied a lord by a tenant as a consideration of the tenancy.

Bondagium. Bondage; v i l l e n a g e; slavery or servitude.

Bond-book. A book in which bonds are executed and preserved.

Bond-creditor. A creditor whose debt is secured by bond.

Bonded warehouse. See WAREHOUSE, BONDED.

Bondholder. One who owns bonds.

Bondi. Bondmen or villains.

Bonds, aid. Bonds issued to aid the construction of a railway or other work.

Bonds, Confederate. Bonds issued by the Confederate States during their war with the U. S.

Bonds, Lloyd's. See LLOYD'S BONDS.

Bondsman. A surety. One bound by some obligation.

Bondus. A bondman; a slave.

Bones gents. Good men (of the jury); persons qualified to act as jurors.

Boni homines. Good men; lawful men; good men and true.

Boni et legales homines. Good and lawful men.

Bonis credere. In Civil law, to surrender property as to a creditor.

Bonis non amovendis. (The goods not to be removed). A writ directing the sheriff not to allow one bringing writ of error to move his goods until the errors assigned are determined.

Bonitarian right. Right of possession.

Bonitarian ownership. In Roman law, an equitable title to things as distinguished from one acquired by law.

Bonne foi. Good faith.

Bono et malo. See DE BONO ET MALO.

Bonorum forisfactura. A forfeiture of goods.

Bonum. Same as BONA.

Bonum factum. A proper thing.

Bonum publicum. The public weal; public advantage; the public or common good.

Bonus. Good; good in law. A premium paid for a loan or the use of one's credit, or for a special favor, or for an extraordinary service, or for a grant or privilege. A premium paid to a grantor or vendor. An extra dividend out of profits of a stock company. A sum of money paid to an agent in addition to the agreed compensation.

Bonus gestus. Good abearing (or abearance). The good behavior of a subject to the King and his liege people for which men were sometimes anciently compelled to give pledges.

Book. One or more printed sheets bound with a cover. As to what comes within the word is a matter for judicial determination.

Book-account. An account kept in a book regularly used for that purpose.

Book, account. A book in which business transactions are entered by a merchant or trader.

Book, act. In Scotch law, the book in which the minutes of a court are entered.

Book, cost. See COST BOOK.

Book, demurrer. A record of a cause at issue on a demurrer, for use of the court or counsel.

Book entries. Entries in an original book, of goods sold and delivered and work performed.

Book of accounts. Same as BOOK, ACCOUNT.

Book of acts. Records of a surrogate's office.

Book of adjournal. In Scotch law, records of criminal trials in the justiciary.

Book of original entries. The book containing the first entries of facts relating to any contract or article bought, sold, or exchanged.

Book of rates. A statement of duties authorized by English Parliament.

Book of responses. In Scotch law, a record of non-entries and relief duties payable by heirs who took precepts from Chancers.

Book, order. See ORDER BOOK.

Book, paper. See PAPER BOOK.

Book-land. Free socage land. Tenemental land held by deed under certain rents and free services. See FOLK LAND.

Books, The. Reports of decisions of English courts.

Boom. An enclosure in a stream made to hold floating logs.

Boom company. See COMPANY, BOOM.

Boon days. Certain days, occurring once a year, upon which copyhold tenants performed base services for their lord.

Boot. Something additional. Same as BOTE.

Boothage. Same as BOTHAGIUM.

Booting-corn. Rent corn; rent paid in corn in return for leases.

Booty. The spoil of war, captured on land. Goods taken by robbery.

Booty of war. Property captured by an army.

Bordage. A service of carrying timber from the woods for the lord; also of finding the lord in provisions. See BORDAGIUM; also BORDLANDS.

Bordagium. A species of base tenure by which certain lands, known as bord lands were anciently held in England, the tenants being termed bordarii. See BORDAGE.

Bordaria. A cottage.

Bordarii. Boors, husbandmen, or cottagers; the inhabitants of the bordlands. See BORDAGIUM; also BORDLANDS; also BORDLODE and BORDAGE.

Bord-brigch. Same as BURGH-BRECH.

Border warrant. A warrant issued by a judge on one side of the border between England and Scotland for the purpose of arresting a person or the effects of a person living on the other side.

Bord-halfpenny. A toll paid for setting up booths in the market.

Bordimanni. Same as BORDARII.

Bordlands. Lands for the maintenance of the board or table. Lands held in bordage. See BORDAGE; BORDAGIUM; BORDARII.

Bordlode. A service of carrying timber from the woods for the lord. The quantity of food paid by the Bordarii for their land.

Bord-service. A tenure by which bordlands were held.

Borel-folk. Country people.

Borg. Same as BORGH.

Borgbriche. Same as BURGBRECH.

Borgesmon. The head of each family in a tithing.

Borgh. A pledge; a surety. The contract for surety. The head of a tithing or decennary who was surety for the members.

Borgh of Hamhald. In Scotch law, a pledge given to a buyer of goods by the seller that the goods will be forthcoming, that the seller's title is good and that the latter will warrant the same.

Borghbrech. Same as BURGH-BRECH.

Born. Brought into being. Issued from a woman's womb.

Borough. A place of safety; a town having a wall or enclosure. A town that sends burgesses to Parliament; a corporation town. A part of a township with a municipal charter.

Borough courts. See COURTS, BOROUGH.

Borough English. A custom of certain boroughs that the land shall descend to the youngest son or youngest brother. This custom existed in the reign of Henry II. (1154–1189).

Borough fund. The revenues from rents and produce of land, &c., belonging to a municipal borough in its corporate capacity; also a borough rate which is sometimes added to it.

Borough, Parliamentary. A town which sends one or more representatives to Parliament.

Borough sessions. Courts established in English boroughs by the Municipal Corporation Act, with limited criminal jurisdiction.

Borough, third. Same as HEADBOROUGH.

Borough-heads. Borough holders; borsholders.

Borough-reeve. The chief municipal officer in an incorporated English town before the Municipal Corporation Act.

Borrow. To obtain under a contract to return.

Borrowe. In Scotch law, a pledge.

Borrowhead. Same as HEADBOROUGH.

Borsholder. Same as HEADBOROUGH.

Bortmagad. A house maid.

Boscage. The food wood and trees yield to cattle. See BOSCAGIUM.

Boscagium. Boscage; browse-wood; the food which wood and trees yield to cattle; mast, etc. An ancient duty of windfallen wood in the forest.

Boscaria. Wood houses or ox houses.

Boscus. All manner of wood.

Bosinnus. A rustic pipe.

Bostar. A recompense or satisfaction.

Bote. Compensation; reparation; an estover; an allowance.

Boteler. One who provides the King's wine. Same as BUTLER (which see).

Boteless. One who commits sacrilege of which no compensation can acquit him. Without emendation.

Botellaria. A wine cellar.

Botes. Wood cut off a farm by the tenant for necessary repairs; this the common law allows him without any previous agreement.

Botha. A booth or stall in a fair or market.

Bothagium. Toll for keeping a stand or booth in a fair or market.

Bothena. A barony or lordship.

Bothna. A park where cattle are enclosed and fed.

Boting-corn. Rent corn; rent paid in corn in return for leases.

Bottomage. Bottomry.

Bottomry. The lending of money to the owner of a ship and taking a mortgage on the ship as security.

Bottomry bond. The instrument writing containing the provisions of a bottomry contract.

Bouche. A mouth. An allowance of provision to those attending the king or nobleman on a military expedition.

Bouche of court. An allowance of provisions to the knights and servants who attended the King on a military expedition.

Bough. Giving a bough of a tree in conveying land to hold in capite.

Bought and sold note. A memorandum of a sale given by a broker to both the buyer and seller of merchandise. See NOTE, BOUGHT; also NOTE, SOLD.

Bought note. See NOTE, BOUGHT.

Boulevard. A rampart. A walk along a fort. An ornamental reservation containing a driveway.

Bound. The utmost limits of land. Charged with the performance of some legal duty.

Bound bailiff. See BAILIFF, BOUND.

Boundary. The line between two estates or territories.

Boundary, artificial. An object placed by man to indicate the boundary line, as a fence.

Boundary line. A dividing line or mark. In ship building the line where the hull meets the stem, keel and stern post.

Boundary, natural. A natural object on the boundary line.

Bounded tree. Same as BOUND TREE.

Bounders. Marks indicating the distances or courses of a survey.

Bounds. The legal line separating lands or jurisdictions.

Bounds, metes and. See METES AND BOUNDS.

Bound tree. A tree used for marking a boundary line; a tree used as a boundary of lands; a tree from which the boundary lines are drawn. See ARBOR FINALIS.

Boulter bread. Bread made of wheat or corn without the bran or boultel left in.

Bounty. An inducement, either money, property, or some right offered for the performance of some act. Anything given or offered to a man to enlist in the military or naval service. Compensation paid to or a benefit conferred upon a person or class of persons.

Bounty land warrants. Warrants given as a bounty and entitling the holder or a specified person to a certain quantity of land.

Bounty lands. Lands given as a bounty.

Bounty lands, military. See MILITARY BOUNTY LANDS.

Bounty, Queen Anne's. See QUEEN ANNE'S BOUNTY.

Bourgh. A market town; a borough, town or village; a corporate town; a town that is not a city. In French law, an assemblage of houses surrounded with walls; a fortified town or village. Originally, any aggregation of houses from the greatest city to the smallest hamlet.

Bourgeois. The inhabitant of a bourg. A person entitled to the privilege of a municipal corporation; a burgess.

Bourgeoisie. In old French law, the citizens of a bourg, spoken of collectively. In later French law, the privilege or franchise of being a burgess; citizenship.

Bourse. An exchange or meeting place for merchants.

Bourse de commerce. In French law, an association in each city having a bourse, of merchants and others interested in commerce, together with two persons appointed by the government.

Bout. An end; a butt; the end of a piece of land; a line limiting at the end.

Bouts. Butts; ends. Leather bottles.

Bouts et cotes. Ends and sides; butts and bounds.

Bouwerye. In old New York Dutch, a farm. A farm upon which the farmer and his family resided.

Bouwmeester. In old New York Dutch, a farmer.

Bovata terræ. As much land as an ox can plow. See BOVE DE TERRE.

Bove de terre. An ancient measure of land; as much as an ox could till or go over; called by some fifteen acres. In Scotch law, called an oxgang or oxengang; oxgate or oxengate of land, equal to twelve acres.

Boveria. An ox house.

Boverium. An ox house.

Boves. Oxen, bullocks.

Bovettus. A steer or castrated bullock.

Bovicula. A heifer or young cow.

Bow-bearer. An under officer of the forest who reported any violation of the forest laws.

Bowyers. Persons in London anciently compelled to keep a certain number of bows for sale, under a penalty.

Boycott. To refuse to deal or associate with a person. Abstaining from association or dealings with a person.

Boycotting. Refusing to have business relations with a person or corporation until a request is complied with.

Box-days. In Scotch law, days appointed by the court of session in which to lodge necessary papers during vacation.

Bozero. In Spanish law, an advocate either for himself or others.

Brace de la mer. An arm of the sea. A portion of the sea where the tide flows and reflows.

Bracelets. Beagle hounds.

Bracenarius. A master of the hounds.

Bracetus. A female beagle.

Brachium maris. An arm of the sea.

Bracinum. A brewing.

Bracton. The writer of the treatise De Legibus et Consuetudinibus Angliæ (which see).

Brahman. Same as BRAHMIN.

Brahmin. A Hindu priest. The first of the Hindu castes.

Bramin. Same as BRAHMAN.

Branch. A separate part of a class of persons descended from a common ancestor. A stream tributary to another.

Brand. To stamp. To impress with a red-hot iron. To mark. The mark thus impressed.

Branding. Placing a brand on a person or thing. A punishment for certain offences after being allowed benefit of clergy so the person could not obtain the exemption a second time.

Brangwyn. A name signifying a white crow, given to the stat. 4 Henry IV., c. 4.

Branks. A scold's bridle or contrivance fastened to the head with a piece of iron to restrain the movement of the tongue.

Brasiator. A brewer; a malster.

Brasium. Malt.

Brawl. A noisy quarrel; a noisy disturbance of the peace.

Brawling. In England, the offence of quarreling or creating a disturbance in a churchyard.

Breach. Breaking. Violation. The part of a declaration which charges breach of contract.

Breach, continuing. Continuous violations of law or contract.

Breach of close. Unlawful entry on another's land.

Breach of contract. Neglect to perform its conditions.

Breach of covenant. Violation of the terms of a deed in which certain things were agreed to be done or not done; it is a civil injury.

Breach of duty. Neglect to perform a duty in a proper manner.

Breach of peace. See PEACE, BREACH OF.

Breach of pound. The breaking a pound or place where cattle which have been distrained are placed with a view to rescuing them.

Breach of prison. An escape of one lawfully confined in prison.

Breach of privilege. Violation of the privilege of a legislature.

Breach of promise. The breaking or violation of an agreement or undertaking. Violation of a promise to marry.

Breach of trust. Deviation from the provisions of a trust. Appropriating a thing entrusted to a wrong purpose.

Breach of warranty. The breaking of any of the covenants of warranty.

Bread acts. See ACTS, BREAD.

Bread and beer. Name of an English statute fixing the quality of bread and beer.

(8)

Bread and water. A punishment inflicted at one time for certain offences in the province of Pennsylvania.

Break. To sever by force. To violate. To prove the invalidity of.

Break bulk. To commence unloading a cargo. To open a package or parcel of anything and use it; which prevents the buyer from objecting to it and returning it to the seller.

Break doors. To open doors by force.

Break jail. To escape when legally confined.

Break seals. To remove or break the seals placed on articles by authority of law.

Breaking a case. See CASE, BREAKING A.

Breaking and entering, actual. The removal of any part or fastening of a house by force and entering therein.

Breaking and entering, constructive. The obtaining of an entrance into a house by fraud, threats, or conspiracy, with intent to commit a felony.

Breaking of arrestment. In Scotch law, one who disregards an arrestment and delivers the money or goods to the debtor.

Breast of the court. Discretion of the court.

Brecca. A breach or decay.

Brecuia. A brew house.

Brede. Broad. Deceit.

Bredwite. A fine for not complying with the regulations relating to weight and quantity of bread.

Breed-bate. A barretor. See BARRATRY.

Bref. A writ.

Bref a prendre la terre. A writ to take the land.

Bref de entree. A writ of entry.

Brefe d'annuite. A writ of annuity.

Brefe d'entre. A writ of entry.

Brefe de droit. A writ of right.

Brefe d'errour. A writ of error.

Brehon. An ancient hereditary Irish judge.

Brehon laws. The unwritten laws of the Brehons which prevailed in Ireland, before its occupation by the English; so called from brehon, a judge. Abolished by 40 Edw. III. See BREHON.

Breihovin. Brehon.

Breisua. Wether sheep.

Brenagium. A payment in bran to feed the lord's hounds.

Brephotrophi. Persons charged with the care of houses for foundlings.

Brethren. Brothers. Members of an association. When applied to an individual family includes sisters.

Brethren, elder. See ELDER BRETHREN.

Brethren of Trinity House. SEE ELDER BRETHREN.

Bretoise. The law of the Marches of Wales, in force among ancient Britons.

Bretoyse. Same as BRETOISE.

Bretts and Scotts, Law of the. See LAW OF THE BRETTS AND SCOTTS.

Brettwalda. A ruler of the Saxon heptarchy.

Breve. A writ; an original writ by which all actions in the Superior Courts of England were commenced; no one was permitted to sue without a writ. Any writ of the King under seal, whereby he commanded anything to be done for the furtherance of justice. A commission to a judge or justice of a Superior Court in the form of a breve. In Roman law, brevia were in the form of letters.

Breve ad admittendum clericum. A writ for admitting a clergyman, clerk or priest.

Breve ad inquirendum. A writ to enquire; a writ of inquiry. A judicial writ, commanding inquiry to be made of any thing relating to a cause pending.

Breve ad quod damnum. A writ as to what damage. A writ commanding the sheriff to inquire by the oaths of jurors as to the damage, etc., before the crown will grant certain liberties, for changing of ancient highways, etc. In American law, in certain cases, to inquire, etc., where lands and tenements are appropriated for public use.

Breve casu proviso. A writ in the case provided. A writ of entry given by the stat. Gloucester, c. 7. for a reversioner against a tenant in dower who alienated in fee, or for life, etc.

Breve clausum. A writ close.

Breve de admensuratione dotis. A writ for the admeasurement of dower. Allowed a widow who received more land as dower than belonged to her.

Breve de admensuratione pasturæ. A writ for the admeasurement of pasture. A writ for those that had common of pasture, in cases where any one or more of them surcharged the common with cattle.

Breve de ætate probanda. A writ for proving age. An ancient writ which lay to the escheator or sheriff of a county, to summon a jury to enquire whether the heir of a tenant in capite, claiming his estate on the ground of full age, was, in fact, of age or not.

Breve de allocatione facienda. A writ for making an allowance. A writ directed to the lord of the treasury and barons of the Exchequer to allow certain officers credit for payments made by them.

Breve de anno pensione. A writ for an annual pension. The name of an ancient writ directing the abbot or prior to pay a yearly pension due to the King out of an abbey or priory, to the person named in the writ.

Breve de anno redditu. A writ for annuity. The name of a writ for the recovery of an annuity.

Breve de apostata capiendo. A writ for taking an apostate. The name of an ancient writ commanding the sheriff to apprehend an apostate and bring him back to his abbot or prior.

Breve de arrestandis bonis ne dissipentur. A writ to arrest goods that they may not be dissipated. A writ to seize the cattle and goods in the hands of a party, and hold them to prevent their being made away with pending a suit.

Breve de arrestando ipsum qui pecuniam recepit. A writ for the apprehension of one who has taken prest money. An old writ for apprehending one who had taken such money and then hid himself when he should go.

Breve de assisa continuanda. A writ to continue an assise.

Breve de assisa proroganda. A writ for proroguing an assise. Writ issued where one of the parties, in consequence of being employed in the King's service, could not attend; it directed justices to prorogue or postpone an assise to a certain day.

Breve de attornate recipiendo. A writ for receiving an attorney. An ancient writ to the judges of a court, requiring them to receive and admit an attorney of a party.

Breve de audiendo et terminando. A writ for hearing and determining; or to hear and determine. An old writ, to certain justices, to hear and determine cases of treason, felonies, heinous misdemeanor, trespass, riotous breach of the peace, etc.

Breve de averiis captis in withernamium. A writ for taking cattle in withernam. An old writ on return to a writ of replevin, that the cattle or goods, were carried away, concealed or otherwise withheld, directing the sheriff to take other cattle or goods of the defendant in withernam and detain them until he could replevy the first mentioned cattle.

Breve de averiis replegiandis. A writ for replevying beasts. A writ brought by one whose cattle were distrained or put in the pound, directing the sheriff, to cause the beasts or chattels, etc., which had had been so taken to be replevied.

Breve de avo. A writ of ayle or ayel. A writ for an heir to recover the possessions of lands of which a grandfather or grandmother was seized in fee-simple on the day of his or her death, from a stranger who had had abated.

Breve de bonis non amovendis. A writ for not removing goods. An old writ directing the sheriffs of London, in cases where a writ of error was brought by a defendant against whom a judgment was recovered, to see that his goods and chattels were safely kept while the error remained undetermined.

Breve de calceto reparando. A writ for repairing a causeway. An ancient writ directing the sheriff to distrain the inhabitants of a place to repair and maintain a causeway.

Breve de cartis (or chartis) reddendis. A writ for rendering or redelivering charters or deeds.

Breve de catallis reddendis. A writ for rendering chattels. A writ to compel the delivery of a specific chattel unjustly detained from the owner.

Breve de cautione admittenda. A writ to take security. An ancient writ directing a bishop who held an excommunicated person in prison for his contempt, notwithstanding he had offered sufficient security to obey the commands of the church; to take such security and release the prisoner.

Breve de certificando. A writ for certifying; or requiring a thing to be certified.

Breve de certiorando. A writ for certifying or informing. A writ directed to the sheriff, commanding him to certify to a particular fact.

Breve de champertia. A writ of or in relation to champerty. A writ directed to the justices of the bench, commanding the enforcement of the statute of Champertores. (33 Edw. III).

Breve de chimino. A writ of way. The name of a writ for the enforcement of a right of way. See QUOD PERMITTAT.

Breve de clamia admittenda in itinere per attornatum. A writ in eyre, to admit a person's claim by attorney. An ancient writ directing the justices in eyre, to admit a person's claim by attorney, who could not come in person, in consequence of being employed in the King's service.

Breve de clerico admittendo. A writ for admitting a clerk. The writ of execution in a quare impedit, directed to the bishop and commanding him to admit the plaintiff's clerk.

Breve de clerico convicto commisso gaolæ in defectu ordinarii deliberando. A writ for discharging a clerk under conviction, from imprisonment in jail, by the default of his ordinary.

Breve de clerico infra sacros ordines constituto non eligendo in officium. A writ concerning a clerk established in holy orders, for not choosing to serve in office. A writ directing the bailiffs, to release a person in holy orders who had been compelled to accept the office of bailiff or beadle.

Breve de clerico capto per statutum mercatorium deliberando. A writ for delivering a clerk arrested on a statute merchant.

Breve de communi pastura admensuranda. A writ to admeasure common of pasture.

Breve de communi pastura admensuare. A writ to admeasure common of pasture.

Breve de computo. A writ of account. An action against one who by reason of his office ought to render an account to another, but refuses so to do. An action of account.

Breve de consanguineo. A writ of consanguinity. An ancestral writ allowed where a man's great great grandfather or collateral relative beyond certain degrees, was seized of lands, etc., in fee on the day of his death, and a stranger abated the heir.

Breve de conspiratione. A writ concerning a conspiracy. A writ allowed where two or more persons conspired to indict a person falsely, and the latter was acquitted.

Breve de consuetudinibus et servitiis. A writ of customs and services. A writ for the lord against a tenant who withheld from him the rents and services due by custom or tenure for his land.

Breve de contumace capiendo. A writ for taking a contumacious person. A writ out of Chancery in cases where a person has been pronounced by an ecclesiastical court to be contumacious and in contempt.

Breve de conventione. A writ of covenant.

Breve de continuando assisam. A writ to continue an assise.

Breve de contributione facienda. A writ for making contribution. A writ founded on the statute of Marlbridge, c. 9, to compel coparceners or tenants in common, to aid the eldest in performing the services due by them ; or to make contribution.

Breve de copia libella deliberanda. A writ for delivering a copy of the libel. An ancient writ directing the judge of a spiritual court, to deliver to a defendant a copy of the libel filed against him in such court.

Breve de coronatore eligendo. A writ for electing a coroner. Writ to the sheriff commanding him to proceed to the election of a coroner.

Breve de coronatore exonerando. A writ for discharging or removing a coroner for some cause mentioned therein.

Breve de corrodio habendo. A writ for having a corody or to exact a corody from a religious house.

Breve de curia claudenda. A writ for closing a court. A writ to compel a party to close or inclose his court or land about his house, where it was left open.

Breve de cursu. A writ of course, or in ordinary course. A writ which issued in ordinary cases, and of course, which it was the duty of a cursitor to make out.

Breve de custodia terræ et hæredis. A writ for the wardship of the land and heir. A writ of ward or writ of right of ward. A writ allowed a guardian in knight's service or socage, to recover the possessions and custody of the ward.

Breve de custode admittendo. A writ for admitting a guardian.

Breve de custode amovendo. A writ for removing a guardian.

Breve de debito. A writ of debt; a writ for the debt. A writ in an action of debt.

Breve de deceptione. A writ of or on account of deceit. A writ, and the action founded upon it, to recover damages for a wrong or injury committed deceitfully. Also a judicial writ to recover lands which had been lost by the default of the tenant in a real action, without his fault.

Breve de detentione. Same as BREVE VEL ACTIO DE DETENTIONE.

Brevo de domo reparando. A writ for repairing a house. A writ to compel a man to repair his house when it threatened to fall, to the injury of another's freehold.

Erevo de dote assignanda. A writ for assigning dower. A writ for a widow of a tenant in capite, commanding the King's escheator to cause her dower to be assigned to her.

Breve de dote, unde nihil habet. A writ of dower whereof she has nothing. Otherwise called "a writ of dower unde nihil habet." A writ for a widow where no part of her dower has been assigned her, commanding the tenant or person deforcing her to assign her reasonable dower.

Breve de ejectione custodiæ. A writ of ejectment of wardship granted where a guardian had been forcibly ejected from his wardship.

Breve de ejectione custodiæ terræ et heredis. A writ concerning the ejectment of the wardship of the land and the heir. A special writ which lay for a guardian in socage to recover the wardship of the land and the heir.

Breve de ejectione firmæ. A writ of ejectment or ejection of farm. Allowed where lands or tenements were let for a term of years and afterward the lessee was ousted of his term. Originally it was a writ for the recovery of damages for such ouster, but was afterwards used as a remedy for the recovery of the term itself, with damages and costs for withholding the same. It is the foundation of the present action of ejectment.

Breve de errore. A writ of error.

Breve de errore corrigendo. A writ for correcting error.

Breve de escæta. A writ of escheat. A writ anciently allowed the lord where his tenant died without heir, to recover possession of lands that had escheated to him.

Breve de escambio monetæ. A writ for the exchange of money. An ancient writ to authorize a merchant to make a bill of exchange.

Breve de essendo quietum de theolonio. A writ of being quit of toll.

Breve de essonio de malo lecti. A writ of essoin of infirmity or sickness of bed. A writ to examine whether the party was in fact sick or not.

Breve de estoveriis habendis. A writ for having estovers. Allowed a wife divorced a mensa et thoro, to recover her alimony or estovers.

Breve de estrepamento. A writ of or concerning estrepement. Writ to stop or prevent the commission of waste in lands by a tenant, during the pendency of a suit against him for their recovery.

Breve de excommunicato capiendo. A writ for taking an excommunicated person. A writ commanding the sheriff to take an excommunicated person and imprison him in the county goal, until he was reconciled to the church.

Breve de excommunicato deliberando. A writ for delivering an excommunicated person from prison. Allowed when he made satisfaction to the church.

Breve de excommunicato recapiendo. A writ for retaking an excommunicated person. Allowed where he had been liberated from prison without making satisfaction to the church, or giving security that he would so do.

Breve de executione facienda in withernamium. A writ for making execution in withernam.

Breve de executione judicii. A writ of execution of judgment. A writ commanding the sheriff to do execution upon a judgment.

Breve de exemplificatione. A writ of exemplification. Allowed for the exemplification of an original.

Breve de exoneratione sectæ. A writ of exoneration of suit. A writ for the King's ward to be exempt from all suits to the county court, hundred, leet, or court baron, during the time of wardship.

Breve de expensis militum levandis. A writ for levying the expenses of knights. Directing the sheriff to levy the allowance for knights of the shire for attendance in Parliament.

Breve de expensis militum non levandis. A writ to abstain from levying the expenses of knights.

Breve de extento. A writ of extent.

Breve de falso judicio. A writ concerning a false judgment. A writ to the courts at Westminster to reverse the judgment of some inferior court not of record.

Breve de fine capiendo pro terris. A writ for a juror who had been attainted for giving a false verdict, to obtain the release of his person, lands and goods, on payment of a certain fine to the King.

Breve de fine non capiendo pro pulchre placitando. A writ prohibiting the taking of fines for fair pleading.

Breve de fine pro redisseisina capiendo. A writ for taking a fine for a redisseizin. A writ to release one imprisoned for a redisseizin, on his paying a fine.

Breve forisfactura maritagii. A writ of forfeiture of marriage.

Breve de forma donationis. A writ concerning the form of the gift. A writ formerly used to recover entailed property.

Breve de hærede deliberando illi qui habet custodiam terræ. A writ for delivering an heir to him who has wardship of the land.

Breve de hærede rapto et abducto. A writ concerning an heir ravished and carried away. The writ for a lord who, having by right the wardship of his tenant under age, could not obtain his body, the same having been carried away.

Breve de hæretico comburendo. A writ for burning a heretic.

Breve de homagio respectuando. A writ for respiting or postponing homage.

Breve de homine capto (capiendo) in withernamium. A writ for taking a man in withernam. A writ to take in withernam one that had taken and led out of the country any bondman or woman so that he or she could not be replevied according to law.

Breve de homine replegiando. A writ for replevying a man. The writ to replevy a man out of prison, or out of the custody of any private person upon giving security to the sheriff that the man shall be forthcoming to answer any charge against him. In England, the writ is not now used, but in some of the United States it is still in force.

Breve de idemptitate nominis. A writ respecting the identity of name. An ancient writ for one who was taken and arrested in any personal action, and committed to prison for another of the same name.

Breve de identitate nominis. Same as BREVE DE IDEMPTITATE NOMINIS.

Breve de idiota inquirendo vel examinando. A writ to inquire as to whether a man be an idiot or not.

Breve de ingressu. A writ of entry.

Breve de inquirendo. A writ for inquiring; a writ of inquiry.

Breve de intrusione. A writ respecting an intrusion. Allowed for a reversioner, where tenant for life, or in dower, or by the courtesy, died seized, etc., and after death a stranger intruded upon the land.

Breve de leproso amovendo. A writ for removing a leper.

Breve de libera falda. Writ of free fold.

Breve de libera piscaria. A writ of free fishery.

Breve de liberati allocanda. A writ for a free allowance.

Breve de libero passagio. A writ of free passage.

Breve de libertati probanda. A writ for proving freedom. Allowed for such as, being demanded for villeins or viefs, offered to prove themselves free.

Breve de libertatibus allocandis. A writ for allowing liberties. The name of several writs allowed for a citizen or burgess entitled to certain liberties to have them allowed him.

Breve de licentia transfretandi. A writ of permission to cross the sea. Directing wardens of certain ports, to permit the persons named in the writ to cross the sea from such port, on certain conditions.

Breve de lunatico inquirendo. A writ for inquiring about a lunatic or lunacy. A writ, or commission in the nature of a writ, to inquire into a person's state of mind, and whether the party be a lunatic or not; also called a commission of lunacy.

Breve de magna assisa eligenda. A writ of or for choosing the grand assise.

Breve de manucaptione. A writ of manucaption or mainprise. Allowed one imprisoned on a charge of felony, who had offered bail which had been refused. It directed the sheriff to discharge him on his finding sufficient mainpernors or bail.

Breve de manutenendo. A writ of maintenance. Issued against a person for the offence of maintenance.

Breve de medio. A writ of mesne, or middle. A writ in the nature of a writ of right. Allowed an undertenant against the mesne lord, where the mesne allowed his under tenant, or tenant paravail to be distrained by the lord paramount for the rent due the latter from the mesne lord.

Breve de minis. A writ against threats. A writ allowed where a person was threatened with personal violence, or the destruction of his property, to compel the offender to keep the peace.

Breve de mittendo tenorum recordi, etc. A writ to send the tenor of a record, or to exemplify it under the great seal.

Breve de moderata misericordia capienda. A writ for taking a moderate amercement. Allowed for one who was excessively amerced in a court not of record, directing the lord of the court, or his bailiff, to take a moderate amercement of the party or to mitigate that taken.

Breve de nativo habendo. A writ for having one's villein. A writ directing the sheriff, to apprehend the villein who had fled from his lord, and restore him, with all his chattels, to the lord.

Breve de non procedendo ad assisam rege inconsulto. A writ for not taking an assise, without the King's advice.

Breve de non residentia clerici regis. A writ of non-residence of clerk or servant of the King. An ancient writ to excuse one employed in the royal service of non-residence.

Breve de odio et atia. A writ of hatred and malice, or ill-will. An ancient writ for a person committed to prison on a charge of homicide, without bail. It directed the sheriff to make inquiry by the oaths of lawful men, whether the party in prison was committed upon just cause of suspicion, or was charged through hatred and malice. In Magna Charta it is called breve inquisitionis —a writ of inquisition—which should issue gratis, and never be refused.

Breve de onerando pro rata portione. A writ for charging according to a ratable proportion.

Breve de onorando secundum ratum portionis. A writ for charging according to the rate of proportion. A writ for a joint tenant, or tenant in common, distrained for more rent than his proportion of the land come to, to compel others to pay proportionately with him.

Breve de parco fracto. A writ of pound breach. Issued against one who violently broke a pound, and took from it beasts which were lawfully impounded.

Breve de partitione facienda. A writ for making partition.

Breve de perambulatione facienda. A writ for making perambulation. A writ sued out with the assent of both parties, when they were in doubt of the bounds of their lands, their lordships or manors, or of their towns.

Breve de pipa vini carianda. A writ for carrying a pipe of wine. A writ of trespass for carrying a pipe of wine so carelessly that it was stove and the contents lost.

Breve de plegiis acquietandis. A writ for acquitting or releasing pledges.

Breve de pone. A writ of pone.

Breve de ponendo sigillum ad exceptionem. A writ for putting a seal to an exception. It commanded the justices to put their seals to exceptions taken by a party in a suit.

Breve de post disseisina. A writ of post disseisin.

Breve de procedendo ad judicium. A writ for proceeding to judgment. A writ allowed where the judges of any subordinate court would not give judgment either on one side or the other, when they ought so to do.

Breve de procedendo in assissa. A writ for proceeding in an assise. The writ directing the justices of assise to proceed in an assise, where the proceedings had been stayed.

Breve de proparte. A writ of partition. An ancient writ established as the mode for procuring a partition of an estate.

Breve de proprietate probanda. A writ for proving property.

Breve de protectione. A writ of protection. A writ by which the King might privilege a defendant from all personal and many real suits for one year at a time, and no longer, because of his being engaged in royal service out of the realm.

Breve de quarantina habenda. A writ for having quarantine.

Breve de rationabili parte. A writ for a reasonable part.

Breve de rationabili parte bonorum. A writ for a reasonable share of goods. Allowed a wife and children of a deceased person against executors, to recover their reasonable share of goods after debts and funeral expenses paid.

Breve de rationabilibus divisis. A writ for reasonable boundaries. A writ to settle the boundaries between the lands of persons in different towns or hamlets, when they do not know the boundaries.

Breve de recordo et processu mittendis. A writ to send the record and process. A species of writ of error requiring the record and process in a cause to be sent to a Superior Court.

Breve de recto. A writ of right or license to sue for possession of an estate.

Breve de recto patens. A writ of right patent; an open writ of right.

Breve de recto de dote. A writ of right concerning dower.

Breve de recto de advocatione. A writ of right of advowson. A writ for one who had an estate in an advowson to him and his heirs in fee-simple, to prevent disturbance.

Breve de recto de rationabili parte. A writ of right or reasonable part.

Breve de redisseisina. A writ of re-disseisin.

Breve de reparatione facienda. Writ for making reparation. The writ lay to compel the repairing of a house, mill, bridge, etc.

Breve de replegiare. A writ of re-plevin.

Breve de replegiare de averiis. Same as BREVE DE AVERIIS REPLEGIANDIS.

Breve de recussu. A writ of rescue or rescous. The writ allowed where cattle distrained or persons arrested were rescued from those taking them.

Breve de retorno habendo. Writ for having a return. The writ issued upon a judgment for the defendant in an action of replevin, awarding him a return of the goods or property replevied.

Breve de salva gardia. A writ of safeguard. A writ granted strangers seeking their right by course of law in England, and apprehending violence or injury from others.

Breve de salvo conducto. A writ of safe conduct. A license granted to a foreigner to come into, remain in, go through and depart from the kingdom without being molested.

Breve de scutagio habendo. A writ for having escuage or scutage. An ancient writ against tenants by knight service to compel them to serve in the King's wars or send substitutes or pay escuage.

Breve de secta ad molendinum. A writ of suit at mill. A writ given as a remedy for the withdrawal of the customary service of doing suit to another's mill.

Breve de secunda deliberatione. A writ of second deliverance. Allowed a plaintiff in replevin, where the defendant has obtained judgment for the return of the goods by default or non-suit, in order to have the same distress again delivered to him on giving the same security as before.

Breve de secunda superoneratione. A writ of second surcharge. A writ allowed where admeasurement of pasture had been made, and one who had surcharged the common did it a second time after such admeasurement.

Breve de securitate pacis. A writ of security of the peace. A writ for one who was in fear of some bodily harm from another.

Breve de servitiis et consuetudinibus. Same as BREVE DE CONSUETUDINIBUS ET SERVITIIS.

Breve de statuto mercatorio. A writ of statute merchant. A writ for imprisoning one who had forfeited a statute-merchant bond until the debt was satisfied.

Breve de statuto stapulæ. A writ of statute staple. A writ to take the body to prison and seize upon the lands and goods of one who had forfeited the bond known as the statute-staple bond.

Breve de superoneratione pasturæ. A writ of surcharge of pasture. A judicial writ for one who was impleaded in the county court, for surcharging a common with his cattle, where he had been formerly impleaded in the same court, and the cause removed into one of the courts at Westminster.

Breve de supersedendo. A writ of supersedeas.

Breve de sylva cædua. A writ concerning coppice wood, a wood which could be cut without injury.

Breve de theolonio. A writ of toll. A writ of trespass in favor of one who was prevented from taking toll.

Breve de transcripto pedis finis levati mittendo. A writ for sending the transcript of the foot of a fine levied.

Breve de transgressione. A writ of trespass or transgression.

Breve de transgressione, ad audiendum et terminandum. A writ for hearing and determining concerning a transgression. A writ or commission directing the judges to hear and determine any outrage or misdemeanor.

Breve de uxore rapta et abducta. A writ of or in relation to a wife ravished and carried away.

Breve de vasto. A writ of waste. A writ given as a remedy for waste in lands, houses, etc.

Breve de ventre inspiciendo. A writ of or for inspecting the abdomen. A writ allowed a presumptive heir to examine a widow suspected of feigning herself pregnant (with a view to produce a supposititious heir to the estate), in order to ascertain whether she be with child or not. Also a writ issued where a woman sentenced to be executed pleaded pregnancy.

Breve de vi laica amovenda. A writ of or for removing lay force.

Breve de viridario eligendo. A writ to elect a verderor.

Breve de warrantia chartæ. A writ of warranty of charter. A writ for one who was enfeoffed, with a clause of warranty in the charter of feoffment, and afterward impleaded in an assise or other action, in which he could not vouch or call to warranty. The writ issued against the feoffer, or his heir, to compel them to warrant the land unto him.

Breve de warrantia diei. A writ of warranty of day. An ancient writ allowed one directed personally to appear in court to an action, who had been, in the meantime, employed in the King's service.

Breve innominatum. A writ containing a general complaint without stating the particulars of the plaintiff's cause.

Breve inquisitionis. A writ of inquisition. See BREVE DE ODIO ET ATIA.

Breve judiciale. A judicial writ. A writ issued after a suit has commenced.

Breve ne injuste vexes. A writ that you do not unjustly oppress.

Breve nominatum. A writ having the facts named. A nominate writ.

Breve originale. An original writ.

Breve patens. A patent or open writ; one not closed or sealed up.

Breve reparatione facienda. A writ for making repairs. A writ allowed one to compel another to repair a house, mill, bridge, etc.

Breve replegiare de averiis. A writ of replevin of cattle.

Breve testatum. An attested brief; a brief memorandum in writing attested by witnesses.

Breve vel actio de detentione. A writ of action for detention. Commonly known as the action of detinue, a personal action ex delicto, to recover the possession of a specific chattel personal wrongfully detained from another, or its value and damages, where the possession was acquired lawfully by the defendant.

Brevet. A patent, commission, warrant. In French law, a warrant or commission granted by government authorizing the exercise of some right. In English law, a royal warrant, granting a favor, privilege, title, or dignity. In Military law, a commission in the army, at large, conferring a degree of rank specified in the commission without the compensation of such rank.

Brevet d'importation A patent or license for importation.

Brevet de perfectionment. A patent for improvement.

Brevia. Writs.

Brevia adversaria. Adversary writs. Writs brought by an adversary to recover land.

Brevia amicabilia. Amicable writs. Writs by agreement of friends.

Brevia anticipantia. Writs in anticipation or for prevention.

Brevia clausa. Writs closed ; close writs.

Brevia de transgressione. Writs of trespass.

Brevia de videndo mulierem. Writs to examine a woman.

Brevia formata. Ancient forms of writs, upon which Fitzherbert's Natura Brevium is a comment. See REGISTER OF WRITS.

Brevia formata or de cursu. Writs formed or of course. Original writs, the form of which was fixed. SEE B R E V I A FORMATA.

Brevia judicialia. Judicial w r i t s. Writs which followed after the original writs, and during the progress of an action, which varied according to the varieties of actions.

Brevia magistralia. Magisterial writs. Writs to suit the nature of the action and the facts of each case.

Brevia testata. Brief memoranda attested by witnesses. A form used in feudal times from which the modern deed has developed.

Breviarium Alaricianum. The breviary or abridgement of Alaric. The name of a code of laws, compiled under the direction of Alaric II., King of the Visigoths, for the use of the Romans living in his empire, published A. D. 506. See CODE BARBARIAN.

Breviarium Aniani. A name sometimes applied to the Breviary of Alaric, because Anian, Alaric's Chancellor, certified to the copies of the breviary. See BREVIARY ALARICIANUM.

Breviarium. A summary, abridgement, abstract, epitome.

Breviarius. Abridged.

Breviary of Alaric. See CODE BARBARIAN; also BREVIARIUM ALARICIANUM. Also BREVIARIUM ANIANI.

Breviate. An abstract or epitome ; a brief.

Brevibus et rotulis liberandis. A mandate directing the sheriff to deliver his office to his successor.

Brewers. Those who brew malt liquors.

Bribe. Anything of value given or promised to induce one to violate his duty while acting in a public capacity.

Bribery. Offering a reward to influence a person's action.

Bribour. One who pilfers the goods of others.

Bricolis. Ancient engines for beating down walls.

Bridewell. A house of correction.

Bridge. A structure erected over water for the passage of persons or vehicles.

Bridge, county. See COUNTY BRIDGE.

Bridge, free. One for travelling over which no toll is charged.

Bridge over. See OVER, BRIDGE.

Bridge, private. One erected for the use of the owners.

Bridge, public. One which is a public highway, whether a free or toll bridge.

Bridge, toll. One for travelling over which toll is charged.

Bridgebote. Same as BRIGBOTE.

Bridge-masters. Those having the care of a bridge.

Bridle road. A narrow street for pedestrians and those on horseback, and not for general use by wagons or carriages.

Brief. A writ. A papal rescript sealed with wax. An abridged statement of a person's case. A citation of the authorities relied upon to maintain a legal proposition or proportions. A legal argument.

Brief al'evesque. A writ allowed a bishop to remove an incumbent unless he obtained a judgment in quare impedit or was meanwhile presented.

Brief, mess. See MESS BRIEF.

Brief of title. An abridged and orderly statement of all matters affecting title to a piece of real property. A chain of title.

Brief out of the Chancery. In Scotch law, a writ relating to the matters of minors, lunatics, widows, &c.

Brief, papal. A letter on discipline by the Pope.

Brief, sea. Same as LETTER, SEA.

Brief statement. See STATEMENT, BRIEF.

Brief statement, counter. See STATEMENT, COUNTER BRIEF.

Briefe. A writ.

Briefe de droit. A writ of right.

Briefe de recto clauso. A writ of right close.

Brieffe. A writ.

Briefve. A writ.

Brieve. A writ.

Briga. Contention, litigation, strife, controversy.

Brigand. A lawless fellow, a robber, freebooter.

Brigandine. A pointed coat of mail.

Brigbote. Contribution toward the repair of bridges.

Bringing money into court. Depositing money with a court clerk or marshal to satisfy a debt, or await the determination of an interpleader.

Bris. In French law, breaking. A wreck caused by dashing against a rock or the coast.

Britton. A work on English law, founded on Bracton and Fleta, written during reign of Edw. I. The authorship is not definitely known.

Broach. A barrel.

Brocage. The compensation of a broker.

Brocagium. Brocage or brokerage. The business or occupation of a broker. The fee or commission for transacting business as a broker.

Brocards. Law maxims.

Brocarius. In Scotch law, a broker, or brocker, negotiator, mediator, or middleman, in any transaction or contract.

Brocator. A broker, a mediator, a middleman.

Broccarius. Same as BROCARIUS.

Broccator. Same as BROCATOR.

Brocciator. Same as BROCATOR.

Brocella. A wood; a thicket.

Brocha. An awl.

Broche. A spit.

Brochia. A large can or pitcher.

Brocker. A broker.

Broggers. Same as BROKERS.

Brok. An old sword or dagger.

Broken on the wheel. A species of torture by which the victim was placed upon a wheel and his bones broken by being struck with an iron bar.

Broken stowage. That space in a ship not filled by any part of the cargo.

Broker. A person employed to make contracts for others. See different kinds of BROKER.

Broker, commercial. One who negotiates sales or purchases of articles of commerce, or the transportation of the same, for others.

Broker, custom house. See CUSTOM HOUSE BROKER.

Broker, discount. One who discounts notes and bills, and lends money on securities.

Broker, exchange. One who negotiates the sale or purchase of bills of exchange.

Broker, insurance. An insurance agent.

Broker, merchandise. One who negotiates sales for another without having possession of the property he has for sale.

Broker, money. One who deals in money. A money changer.

Broker, note. One who negotiates the sale of commercial paper.

Broker, pawn. See PAWNBROKER.

Broker, produce. One who buys and sells farm products.

Broker, real estate. One who negotiates the sale or purchase of real estate for others.

Broker, ship. One who negotiates the sale or purchase of ships and ship furniture.

Broker, stock. One who negotiates the sale or purchase of the stocks of corporations.

Brokerage. The occupation of a broker. The compensation of a broker.

Brossus. Bruised or injured by blows.

Brothel. The common habitation of prostitutes.

Brother of the half blood. One who has the same mother but a different father with another, or the same father and a different mother.

Brother of the whole blood. One who has the same mother and father with another.

Brotherhood. Those of the same occupation or profession. A society.

Brothers, consanguine. Two who descend from different mothers but have the same father.

Brothers, germane. Brothers having the same father and mother.

Brothers, uterine. Two who descend from the same mother but have different fathers.

Brought. Begun; instituted.

Browbeat. To intimidate by look or action.

Bruarium. A heath ground.

Bruera. A heath or heathy ground.

Bruere. Same as BRUERA.

Brueria. Briars. Heather.

Brugbote. Same as BRIGBOTE.

Bruillus. A wood or grove.

Bruiletus. A small wood.

Bruise. A contusion. An injury without breaking the skin.

Brukbarn. In Swedish law, the child of a struggle, or one begotten in rape.

Bruneta. Same as BURNETA.

Bruscia. Brushwood.

Brusula. Brushwood.

Brutum fulmen. A harmless thunderbolt; a noisy but ineffectual menace; a law neither respected nor obeyed.

Bubble Act. An English Act of Parliament passed in 1720 to prevent fraudulent speculations. It was repealed in 1825.

Bubbles. Speculative schemes; wildcat speculations.

Bucket shop. A place where people gamble in futures after the form and on the prices quoted by the large stock exchanges.

Bucklarium. A buckler.

Buckler. A shield.

Buckstall. A trap for catching deer.

Bucinus. An ancient military weapon for a footman.

Budget. The annual statement of the English Chancellor of the Exchequer which contains the estimates of the receipts and expenditures of the government.

Buers. Same as BALKERS or CONDORS.

Buggery. Carnal copulation by man or woman with a beast, or a man with a man, or with woman unnaturally.

Builder. One who contracts to construct buildings and other structures.

Builder's rent. See RENT, BUILDER'S.

Builder's risk. See RISK, BUILDER'S.

Building. An enclosed edifice for residence or business purposes.

Building and loan associations. Associations for accumulating money by contributions from the members and for lending the same to such members on receiving real estate as security.

Building lease. A lease of land for a long term of years containing an agreement by the lessee to build thereon.

Building, out. A building appurtenant to a main building.

Building societies, benefit. See BENEFIT BUILDING SOCIETIES.

Buildings, public. Those owned or used by the government.

Bulio salis. As much salt as is made at one boiling. A measure of salt of about twelve gallons.

Bulk. The part of a building which projects beyond the foundation. The principal part of anything. The whole of a ship's hold.

Bulk, break. See BREAK BULK.

Bulk, in. In a loose mass, not in packages.

Bull. A brief or mandate from the Pope or Bishop at Rome. One who speculates in the stock exchange for a rise in the market.

Bull and boar. A custom which once existed in parts of England requiring a parson to keep a bull and boar for use of his parishioners in return for tithes of calves and pigs.

Bulla. A Roman seal which was either gold, silver, wax, or lead.

Bullaria. A place for boiling.

Bullaria aquæ salsæ. A boilary of salt water; a salt pit or salt house where salt is boiled.

Bulldoze. To intimidate by threats, or threatening manner.

Bulletin. An official announcement of public matters. In France, the registry of laws.

Bullion. Gold or silver in bulk before being coined.

Bullion fund. Money appropriated for the purchase of bullion for coinage.

Bullito salis. A boiling of salt; as much brine or salt as was made from one boiling.

Bultel. The refuse from wheat or corn making flour.

Bulwer-Clayton Treaty. See CLAYTON-BULWER TREATY.

Bum-bailiff. Same as BAILIFF, BOUND.

Bummaree. Bottomry.

Bunda. A hill or hillock. A bound, boundary, border or limit.

Bundesrath. The Federal Council of Germany, which shares the legislative power with the Reichstag. The Federal Council of Switzerland.

Bundle. For a man and woman to lie together on the same bed without undressing; once a custom of lovers and engaged couples in Wales, and parts of New England and Pennsylvania. The Pennsylvania courts have passed on this practice, in connection with suits for seduction, holding that a father cannot recover where he allows his daughter to bundle.

Bundles. The records of Chancery lying in the rolls.

Bundling. Same as BUNDLE (which see).

Bungalow. An East Indian country house.

Burbreach. A fine imposed on a city or borough for breach of the peace. Also an exemption from such fine. See BURGHBRECHE.

Burchea. An ancient gun used in the forests.

Burcifer regis. Keeper of the King's private purse.

Burdare. To jest or trifle.

Burden. An obligation; duty; charge.

Burden of proof. The obligation resting upon a party to a cause to establish the truth of a proposition.

Burden, real. In Scotch law, a money condition upon an estate which has a preference right of payment over both heir and creditors.

Burden sack. A sack full of provender.

Burdensome. Oppressive.

Bureau. A division of a department of public service.

Bureau of American Republics. A bureau with headquarters at Washington, D. C., to collect and distribute commercial information concerning the American Republics. It is supported by contribution from the various republics.

Bureau of Engraving and Printing. A bureau of the Treasury Department of the U. S. which designs, engraves, prints and finishes all government notes, bonds, certificates, national bank notes, stamps, drafts, cheques, licenses, &c.

Bureau of Equipment. A bureau of the U. S. Navy Department charged with everything relating to the equipment of vessels of the navy.

Bureau of Immigration. A bureau of the U. S. Treasury Department charged with the administration and enforcement of the immigration and alien contract labor laws.

Bureau of Labor. See LABOR, BUREAU OF.

Bureau of Navigation. A bureau of the U. S. Navy, charged with the promulgation, record and enforcement of the Secretary's orders to the fleets and officers of the navy, and having charge of signal and cipher codes and regulations and the enforcement thereof, and various other matters connected with the movement of the war ships, their officers and men.

Bureau of Ordinance. A bureau of the U. S. Navy Department charged with all that relates to the manufacture and purchase of offensive and defensive arms and apparatus required by war vessels.

Bureau of Statistics. A bureau under the U. S. Treasury Department charged with the collection and publication of statistics relating to commerce, immigration and navigation.

Bureau of Yards and Docks. A bureau of the U. S. Navy, charged with everything relating to the planning, construction and maintenance of all docks, walls and buildings within the Navy Yards and Naval Home, and the general administration of the navy yards and everything used and connected therewith.

Bureau of Veritas. An association of maritime underwriters in Brussels, established for the rating and inspection of vessels of all nationalities.

Bureaucracy. Government by bureaus. Undue authority by bureaus. The officials collectively in the executive departments of a government.

Burg. Same as BURGUS.

Burga latrocinium. Burglary; robbery from a castle or mansion house.

Burgage. A dwelling house in a borough. Land held by burgage tenure. A tenure by which houses or lands, formerly the site of houses, in ancient boroughs, are held of the King or other lord of the borough at a certain yearly rent called burgage tenure. See BURGAGE TENURE.

Burgage holding. In Scotland, one by which lands are held of the sovereign in royal boroughs. See BURGAGE; also BURGAGE TENURE.

Burgage tenure. A species of socage tenure by which tenements in a borough are held by an annual rent in money or a service relating to trade.

Burgagium. Burgage; the tenure of burgage.

Burgarii. Inhabitants of a castle or fortress; defenders, etc. Burgers or burgesses; inhabitants of a borough or walled town.

Burgarius. A burgess; a citizen of a city. An inhabitant or freeman of a borough (burgus); a person duly and legally admitted a member of a municipal corporation.

Burgator. One who broke into and robbed a burgus; a burglar or house breaker. One who breaks into houses or enclosed places, as distinguished from one who committed robbery in the open country.

Burgbote. A tribute levied or a contribution made toward the building or repairing of castles or walls of a city.

Burgemote. Same as BURGHMOTE.

Burg-English. Borough English.

Burgenses. Inhabitants of a borough.

Burgeristh. Breach of the peace in a town.

Burgess roll. A list of those entitled to certain rights under act 5 and 6 Wm. IV. c. 74.

Burgesses. Men of trade or the inhabitants of a walled town. Those who represent a borough in Parliament. Magistrates or chief officers of boroughs.

Burgh. A borough.

Burghbote. Same as BURGHBOTE.

Burgh-breche. Breach or violation of pledge. The offence of violating the pledge given by the inhabitants of a tithing to keep the peace; breach of the peace. A fine imposed on a town for breach of the peace.

Burgh-brich. Same as BURGH-BRECH.

Burghmails. Annual payments to the Scotch crown.

Burgh-mote. A court of a borough. A court held in burghs or towns three times a year, at which the earldorman or alderman presided.

Burgh engloyse. Borough English.

Burghware. A citizen or burgess.

Burgi latrocinium. Theft or larceny from a castle or mansion house.

Burglar. One who breaks and enters an apartment, dwelling house, church or public building in the night time with intent to commit a felony. See BURGLARY.

Burglaria. Burglary.

Burglarious. With intention to commit burglary.

Burglariously. A word required by the common law to be used in an indictment for burglary.

Burglary. Breaking and entering the house, room or apartment of another, or a public building, or a church, in the night, with intent to commit felony. (Statute has enlarged the meaning of the word). See DAY; also NIGHT.

Burglariter. Burglariously.

Burglator. A burglar.

Burgomaster. The chief executive officer of a German city, town, or borough.

Burgundian, Code. See CODE BURGUNDIAN.

Burgundian, law. See CODE BURGUNDIAN.

Burgus. A castle, fort, fortress; a burg or bourg. An ancient town. An incorporated town or village.

Burgwhar. A burgess.

Buri. Husbandmen.

Burking. Murder for the purpose of selling the bodies for dissection.

Burkism. Same as BURKING.

Burlaw Courts. See COURTS, BURLAW.

Burn. To consume by fire. To injure or destroy by fire.

Burneta. Cloth made of dyed wool.

Burning. Injuring or destroying by fire. Marking by red-hot iron.

Burning in the hand. The old practice of burning on the thumb those given benefit of clergy. See CAUTERIZETUR IN MANU; also BRANDING,

Burrochium. A burrock or weir over a river where wheels are laid for taking fish.

Burrock. Same as BURROCHIUM.

Bursa. A purse; a bag.

Bursar. The treasurer of a college; a charity student.

Bursaria. The bursery of a convent or college.

Bursarii. Persons who receive and pay out money at a college. Stipendiary students of a college.

Bursary. The place for receiving and paying money at a college.

Burrough mailles. Burrow-meals. In Scotch law, rents paid to the King by the burgesses, or inhabitants of a borough or burrow, and which went to the King's private treasury.

Burrow mailles. Same as BURROUGH MAILLES.

Burrow mealis. Same as BURROUGH MAILLES.

Burrow-meals. See BURROUGH MAILLES.

Bursarum scissores. Cutters of purses; cut-purses.

Burse. Same as BOURSE.

Bursee. A purse.

Bury. Same as BERRY.

Burying alive. The ancient English punishment of those who made contracts with Jews; also of those found guilty of sodomy.

Buscarle. A Saxon domestic servant.

Business. Occupation; that by which one earns a living.

Business, contentious. See CONTENTIOUS BUSINESS.

Business corporation. See CORPORATION BUSINESS.

Business hours. The hours during which the community usually transacts business.

Business, in course of. In accordance with business methods or usages.

Business paper. Commercial paper.

Business, place of. The place where one usually transacts his business.

Business, quasi public. One which is under the supervision of a government, as distilling.

Business usages. The customs usually observed in business circles or transactions.

Busones comitatus. Barons of the county.

Bussa. A ship; vessel used in herring fishing; a smack.

Bussellus. A bushel.

Bustard. A large game bird.

Buthna. Same as BOTHNA.

Buthscarle. Mariners or seamen.

Butler. One who provides the King's wine. See BUTLERAGE.

Butlerage. An old English duty of two shillings per tun paid by merchant strangers

(9)

in consideration of prisage being remitted. An imposition on imported wines for sale which the King's butler took from every ship. See PRISAGE.

Butler's ordinance. An ancient English ordinance (not statute) permitting an heir to punish waste during the life of his ancestor.

Butt. A measure of wine containing 126 gallons.

Buttals. Abuttals.

Butted and bounded. A phrase used in describing the end and side or circumscribing lines to a piece of land.

Butts. Anciently a place where archers met to compete in shooting. Short pieces or ends of land in arable ridges or furrows.

Butts and bounds. Same as ABUTTALS.

Butty. Things used in common. A deputy or associate.

Buy. To obtain for money.

Buy in. To buy one's own property at public auction.

Buyer. One who buys.

Buyer's option. A call. See CALL.

Buying title. Buying the right of a disseisee. It was not allowed by the common law, and it was made an offence in England by stat. 36 Henry VIII.

Buzonis. The shaft of an arrow before being feathered or sledged.

By. Near but not attached to. Beside; on, or before. Bordering on. Adjoining. By means of. To. Through. In accordance with.

By bill. A term anciently meaning, begin by bill, instead of by an original writ. Begun by capias ad respondendum.

By bill without writ. Same as BY BILL.

By estimation. A term equivalent to "more or less;" meaning that the quantity is by estimate and not by actual measurement.

By force of. By virtue of.

By God and my country. The old form of answer of an accused to the question "how wilt thou be tried?"

By law men. The chief men of a town who represent the others.

By the bye. Incidentally; w'thout special process. At one time applied to a declaration filed in a new cause against one in custody at the suit of another plaintiff.

By-bidding. Same as BIDDING, BY.

By-bil-wuffa. A Hindu mortgage, or conditional sale.

By-laws. Rules for the regulation of corporations or associations covering matters not reached by the general law. By-laws against public policy or Statute law are void.

By-road. A used road, recognized by law, but not laid out.

Bystanders. Persons present in court.

C.

C. As an abbreviation designates Cajus or Gajus or Gaius. As a numeral, centum (a hundred). Upon voting tablets it stood for condemno—I condemn (opposite to absolvo—I absolve, I declare innocent). The initial letter of Codex. In Colonial Rhode Island, the letter branded upon the foreheads of convicted counterfeiters.

C. A. Court of Appeals; Chancery appeals.

C. A. V. Curia advisari vult (which see).

C. B. Common Bench; chief baron.

C. C. Cepi corpus; civil code; county court; chief commissioner.

C. C. J. Circuit, county court, or city judge.

C. C. P. Court of Common Pleas; code of civil procedure.

C. D. Commissioner's decisions.

C. F. I. Cost, freight and insurance.

C. J. Chief justice; circuit judge.

C. J. B. Chief judge in bankruptcy.

C. L. Civil law; common law.

C. L. P. Common law procedure.

C. O. D. Collect on delivery.

C. P. Common pleas.

C. Q. T. Cestui que trust.

C. R. Chancery Reports; curia regis.

C. T. A. Cum testamento annexo (with the will attached).

Ca. Here.

Ca. Sa. See CAPIAS AD SATISFACIENDUM.

Cab. A closed public carriage used to transport persons for hire.

Cab stand. A place where cabs are permitted to stand to await passengers.

Cabal. A term applied to the ministry in reign of Chas. II., who sought to restore the power of the Pope. The initials of their names spelled the word. They were Clifford, Ashley, Buckingham, Arlington and Lauderdale.

Cabalist. In French law, a factor or broker.

Caballa. Belonging to a horse.

Caballaria. Relating to a horse. A tenure in which the service comprised furnishing a horseman in time of war, or when required by the lord.

Caballarius. A horseman.

Caballeria. In Spanish law, a portion of spoils taken or lands conquered in a war, granted to a horse soldier. An allotment of land being a lot one hundred feet front and two hundred feet deep.

Cabellero. In Spanish law, a knight.

Cabinet. Members of the Privy Council of England. It was established in 1693. In U. S. a Cabinet has no legal existence, but the term is applied to the chief officers of the branches of the executive department who are appointed to carry out the policy of the President in executing law.

Cabinet Council. In England, confidential advisers of the monarch on public matters.

Cable. To send a message by submarine cable. A rope or chain used to moor vessels. A large conductor of electricity composed of several wires.

Cable, submarine. An electric cable laid under the sea.

Cablis. Same as CABLISH.

Cablish. Brushwood; windfall wood.

Cachepalus. An inferior bailiff or sheriff's deputy.

Cacherellus. Same as CACHEPALUS.

Catchet, lettres de. See LETTRES DE CACHET.

Cacicazgos. Land vested by Spanish-American law, in the heads of Indian villages and successors.

Caciques. Heads of Spanish-American villages. See CACICAZGOS.

Cadastre. In Spanish law, a statement of the area and value of land in a certain district, obtained for taxation purposes.

Cadastur. In French law. Same as CADASTRE of Spanish law.

Cade. Six hundred herring.

Cadere. To fall; cease; fail; abate; end.

Cadere assisa. To be nonsuited.

Cadere in. To fall into, change into; become liable to.

Cadet. The younger son of an English gentleman. A volunteer in the army unassigned to any post. A student in a military or naval school.

Cadi. A civil magistrate in Turkey.

Cadit. It abates, falls, ceases.

Caduca. Escheats; escheated estates or lands.

Caduca bona. In the Civil law, fallen possessions; those possessions which do not go to the heir mentioned in a will because he is childless, but pass by descent to heirs who have children, or if there be none, to the Exchequer.

Caducæ. Escheated portions.

Caducary. Pertaining to escheat, or forfeiture.

Caduceator. In the Civil law, a herald sent to the enemy; an officer with a flag of truce. A servant to a priest.

Caducial clause. In Scotch law, that by which settled property is made to revert to the settlor or his heirs.

Cædua. Kept for cutting. In the Civil law, a forest kept for cutting.

Cæp gildum. Same as CEAPGILDE.

Cæsar. A name assumed in Rome by the successors of Julius.

Cæsarian operation. The unnatural delivery of a child by cutting an aperture in the woman's side. If the woman die before the child cries the husband does not become tenant in curtesy, even though the child be born alive.

Cæterorum. Administration granted as to the residue of an estate, which cannot be administered under the limited power already granted.

Cagia. A cage for birds.

Cahenslyism. A plan, for the Roman Catholic Church in the United States, which was suggested to Pope Leo XIII. by Peter Paul Cahensly, of the German Parliament, in 1891. Cahensly suggested that the bishops in U. S. be chosen so as to give foreign nationalities, who were Catholics, proportionate representation in the church.

Calamus. A pen; writing or penmanship.

Calamus legis. The pen of the law.

Calangium. A challenge; a claim or dispute.

Calcaria. Spurs.

Calcaria deaurata. Gilded sandals.

Calcea. A common highway; a causeway; a path or road raised with earth and paved.

Calceata. Same as CALCEA.

Calcetum. Same as CALCEA.

Calcagium. An ancient tax levied or contribution made toward the making and repairing of common roads.

Calcifurnium. An old European term for a lime-kiln.

Cale. In French law, a punishment for sailors. It consisted of hauling them under a ship. See KEELHAUL.

Calecarium operationes. Work and labor done by adjoining tenants.

Calefagium. A right to take f u e l yearly.

Calendar. A list of things arranged with details of information. A system of fixing the order, length and subdivisions of years and months. (England and the U. S. use that of Pope Gregory XIII., Russia and Greece, that of Julius Cæsar).

Calendar Amendement Act. An English statute passed in 1751 changing the first of the year from March 25, to January 1, and destroying the eleven days diference between the new and old style. See NEW STYLE.

Calendar, Gregorian. The calendar established by Gregory XIII which changed the Julian Calendar by making Oct. 5, 1582, Oct. 15, 1582, and then continuing regularly after that day. Gregory also made the last year of a century of 365 days duration except one divisible by four. Gregory's system is also called the New Style.

Calendar Julian. The calendar established by Julius Cæsar. By it every three years of 365 days is followed by a year of 366 days. It is twelve days behind the Gregorian Calendar.

Calendar Mohammedan. A calendar used in countries having the Moham-

medan religion. It reckons time from the Hegira July 16, A. D. 622. The year is twelve lunar months of 29 days, 12 hours and 44 minutes. See CYCLE.

Calendar Newgate. Same as MALEFACTOR'S BLOODY REGISTER (which see).

Calendar month. A month, the length of which is fixed by the calendar as distinguished from the lunar month which has 29 5-6 days.

Calendar of causes. A list of causes made by the clerks, containing the title, the form of action, the date of issue, and the names of the attorneys in each cause.

Calendar of prisoners. The names of prisoners and the judgment against each kept by a sheriff.

Calendarium. The calendar. See CALENDAR.

Calends. The first day of the Roman month. The first calend is the day before the first of the month mentioned, the second calend, the second day before, and so on.

Calends, Greek. Words meaning time never to come, as the Greeks had no Calends.

Caliburne. The famous sword of King Arthur.

Calida melleia. A sudden, or violent, affray.

Caliver. A pistol or hand gun.

Call. To summon. To drive (to call a plow). An assessment for payment of subscription of a stock company or to pay losses. A notice that bonds will be presented for payment. A contract conveying the privilege of demanding within a designated period, and agreeing to deliver on demand some article, on payment of the stipulated price. A natural object mentioned in the descriptive part of a deed. Money payable on demand is on call. See PUT; also STRADDLE.

Call a case. To announce that the court is ready to hear and determine a cause.

Call a docket. To announce the cases on the docket, and make inquiry of the parties as to whether they be ready for trial, argument or motion.

Call a jury. To select the names of those who are to serve, subject to challenge.

Call a list. Same as CALL A DOCKET.

Call a party. To call a party's name in open court and request his appearance.

Call a witness. To request his appearance in open court; to present him for examination.

Call day. In English law, the day law students are called to the bar.

Call of the House. A call of the names of a legislative body to determine who of the members is present.

Calling. Crying out to command attention. Usual occupation.

Calling the plaintiff. A formal nonsuiting when the plaintiff desires to abandon the case, effected by his non-appearance at the call of the crier.

Calling to the bar. Admitting to the practice of law.

Calling upon a prisoner. The inquiry of a prisoner of why judgment should not be passed upon him.

Callis. The King's highway.

Calpes. In Scotch law, a donation to the chief of a clan for protection and maintenance.

Calumnia. A claim or demand. A challenge. An objection. In Roman and Civil law, false accusation; vexatious litigation; a malicious prosecution.

Calumniæ judicium. An act of vexatious litigation.

Calumniæ juramentum. An oath, once required in Civil and Canon law of parties to a cause, that they were not actuated by malice in bringing or defending a suit.

Calumniæ jusjurandum. The same or nearly the same as CALUMNIÆ JURAMENTUM.

Calumniare. To claim or demand. To object to. To challenge.

Calumniata. Objected to.

Calumniator. In Roman and Civil law, a contriver of tricks or artifices; a pettifogger; a perverter of law; a chicaner, etc. One who accuses another of a crime without cause; one who brings a false accusation.

Calumny, oath of. In Scotch law, an oath taken by the parties to an action that the facts alleged by them were true. (Not used now except in consistorial actions). In Civil law, oath required of a plaintiff that he had good cause and was not actuated by malice.

Calumpnia. Challenge or claim. An objection or exception. Same as CALUMNIA.

Calumpniare. Same as CALUMNIARE.

Calumpniata. Same as CALUMNIATA.

Calumpniosus. That may be challenged or objected to; objectionable.

Calvin's case. A case in 7 Rep. 1, which decided that those born in Scotland after the accession of James I. to the crown of England were natural born English subjects.

Camara. In Spanish law, a treasury.

Cambellanus. A chamberlain.

Cambellarius. Same as CAMBELLANUS.

Cambiator. An exchanger; a cambist. A person skilled, expert in cambistry or exchanges; a trader or dealer in bills of exchange and promissory notes. A banker; one who deals in exchange, or is skilled in the science.

Cambiatores monetæ. Exchangers of money; money exchangers.

Cambitas. Exchange, trade.

Cambio. In Spanish law, exchange.

Cambi-partia. Champerty.

Cambi-particeps. A champertor.

Cambipartita. Champerty.

Cambipartitor. A champertor.

Cambist. A cambiator. A person skilled, expert in exchange. One who trades in notes and bills of exchange.

Cambitoria. Of or relating to exchange.

Cambium. Change or exchange. A bill of exchange.

Cambium reale. Real or manual exchange. Exchange of goods for goods.

Cambium manuale. Same as CAMBIUM REALE.

Cambium locale, mercantile, or trajectitum. Local, mercantile, or foreign exchange. Terms used to designate the modern mercantile contract or exchange, whereby a man agrees, in consideration of a sum of money paid to him in one place, to pay a like sum in another place.

Camera. A winding or crooked plat of ground. A chamber; a room in a dwelling house. A treasure chamber, or treasury. A judge's chamber or private place for the transaction of judicial business.

Camera regis. A chamber of the King. A place of certain commercial privileges, Applied to the city of London.

Camera scaccari. The chamber of the Exchequer.

Camera stellata. The Star Chamber.

Cameralistics. The science of obtaining and expending money for public purposes.

Camerarius. A chamberlain; a keeper of the treasure chamber; a keeper of the public money; a treasurer. An officer who had charge of the royal apartments, but was not a treasurer.

Camino. In Spanish law, a highway.

Camisia. A garment belonging to priests.

Camoca. A garment of silk.

Campana. A bell.

Campana bajula. A small hand-bell used in the ceremonies of the Roman Catholic and Protestant Church, by sextons and others.

Campanarium. A belfry, bell tower or steeple, a place where bells are hung.

Campanile. Same as CAMPANARIUM.

Campartum. Any part or portion of a large field or ground which would otherwise be in common. Champerty.

Campers. A share or division of land, or other thing.

Campertum. A corn field; a field of grain.

Campestres. The deities who preside over contests. Field birds—as partridges, quails, rails, etc.

Campfight. A duel or battle between two champions.

Campi partitio. The buying of a right to property on a condition that part of it, if obtained by suit, shall belong to the purchaser.

Campio. A champion, or one who fought in another's cause in trial by battle. One who fought in his own cause.

Campio conductivus. A hired champion. See BATTEL, WAGER OF.

Campio regis. Champion of the King. See CHAMPION OF THE KING.

Campipers. Same as CAMPERS.

Campum partire. To divide the field or land. To agree with a plaintiff or defendant to divide the subject-matter of a suit, between them, if the cause be won; the champerter, at his own cost and expense, to carry on the parties' suit.

Campum partive. Same as CAMPUM PARTIRE.

Campus. An assembly of the people. In Feudal and old English law, a field or plain. The field, marked out for the duel in the trial by battle. The combat itself; campfight.

Campus campiones. Field champions. The combatants in the trial by battle

Campus Maii. The field of May. An anniversary of the Saxons, held on May Day, when they assembled to consider the defence of the kingdom.

Campus Martii. The field of March; The national assembly of the Franks, held in the month of March.

Can. When a debtor promises to pay as soon as he can, the law construes it to mean within a reasonable time.

Canal. An artificial body of water confined between banks for the inland navigation of vessels.

Canal, Nicaragua. See NICARAGUA CANAL.

Cancel. To satisfy. To destroy, to make null by drawing lines across the face of an instrument in the manner of a lattice or cross. To strike out of existence.

Cancella. Chancery; the chancery; the Court of Chancery; a court of equity.

Cancellaria. Same as CANCELLA.

Cancellarius. A porter; a doorkeeper. A director of chancery; the head clerk in chancery; the chancellor.

Cancellarius de Scaccario. Chancellor of the Exchequer. An officer of the British crown, who formerly sat in the exchequer with the regular judges to watch the interests of the crown.

Cancellarius ducatus et comitatus palatini domini regis Lanc. Chancellor of the duchy and county palatine of Lancaster from the lord the King. The presiding officer, of the court of the duchy of Lancaster. He has a special equity jurisdiction of lands held of the King, in right of the duchy of Lancaster.

Cancellatim. Lattice formed; trellis-like.

Cancellation. Anciently the fixing of boundaries of land. The act of cancelling. See CANCEL.

Cancellatura. A cancelling.

Cancelli. Bars; lattice work. The bars enclosing the bar of a court of justice.

Candidate. One who offers himself for election to public office.

Candidati. In Roman law, candidates.

Candlemas-day. The second day of February. Set apart by the Roman Catholics in honor of the Virgin. (It was at one time no day in court).

Canestellus. A basket.

Canes operliæ. Dogs with whole feet (not lawed or with the toes or ball cut off). See EXPEDITATE.

Canfara. A trial by hot iron.

Canipulus. A short sword.

Canna. A rod or distance, in the measure of ground.

Canon. A rule, law, or ordinance; a standard of judgment; an ecclesiastical law or rule of the church. A member of a chapter. other than a dean, of a cathedral or college church. A person possessing a prebend.

Canon law. A body of ecclesiastical law, which originated in the Church of Rome, relating to matters of which it has jurisdiction. It is styled CORPUS JURIS CANONICI (which see).

Canon religiosorum. A book containing the rules of convent orders.

Canonica pensitationes. Relating to to annual payments, compensation; or expenditures.

Canonical. Relating to or conforming with the Canon law.

Canonical obedience. The obedience to the Canon law by a clergyman.

Canonical punishment. See PUNISHMENT, CANONICAL.

Canonicus. In the Civil law, of or relating to an annual tribute. In Ecclesiastical law, a spiritual person found in a list; a canon; a prebendary.

Canonist. A professor of Canon law.

Canonry. An ecclesiastical benefice, attached to the office of canon.

Canons of descent. The principles governing the transmission of property.

Canons of construction. Laws governing construction or interpretation.

Canons of inheritance. Same as CANONS OF DESCENT.

Cant. In Civil law, a method of dividing property held in common.

Cantel. A lump amount. That above the measure. A piece of anything.

Canterbury, Archbishop of. The chief dignitary in the English Church.

Cantle. Same as CANTEL.

Cantred. A hundred. In Wales, a hundred villages.

Canum. A tribute, usually something produced from the soil, due the lord from a feudal tenant.

Canvas. To examine and count votes at an election. The act of so doing.

Canvassing board. See BOARD, CANVASSING.

Cap of maintenance. In England, an ornament or regalia used by the sovereign; also one used by some provincial mayors.

Capacitas. Capacity. Ability or power given by law to take, dispose or to do certain acts.

Capacity. Competency to give or take an estate or thing, or to sue or be sued. See CAPACITAS.

Capax. Capable of; a taker or holder. Possessing capacity. Suitable.

Capax doli. Capable of doing wrong.

Capax negotii. Capable of negotiating.

Cape. Take; take thou. A writ judicial touching lands and tenements.

Cape ad valentiam. Take to the value; take equal to the value. A writ given a voucher against the lands of a vouchee who makes a default.

Cape, grand. See GRAND CAPE.

Cape magnum. A writ forfeiting land on default in demanding a view.

Cape parvum. A writ forfeiting land on default after appearance and prayer for view.

Capella. A chest in which religious relics were preserved. A small building in which relics were preserved. A chapel.

Capellanus. A chaplain or minister of a chapel.

Capellus. A covering for the head.

Capellus ferreus. A helmet or head piece. A steel cap.

Capellus militis. A military head piece.

Capere. To take.

Capers. Small war vessels owned by private parties.

Capias. You may take. A judicial writ in actions at Common law, so termed from the commanding words in the writ when in Latin. The general name applied to several kinds of writs of attachment or arrest.

Capias ad audiendum judicium. You take to hear judgment. A writ to bring in a defendant who was found guilty of a misdemeanor, to receive his judgment.

Capias ad computandum. You take (the defendant) to make a count.

Capias ad respondendum. You take to answer. An original writ, by which actions at law were frequently commenced. Later the writ only issued after the suit has been commenced by summons, where an arrest of the defendant is required.

Capias ad satisfaciendum. You take to satisfy. A writ after judgment to take the defendant and hold him to satisfy the plaintiff's debt and damages.

Capias ad satisfaciendum, ita quod habeas corpus ejus, etc. You take (the defendant) to satisfy, so that you may have his body, etc.

Capias ad valentiam. (You take to the value). A kind of grand cape allowed the defendant in a real action where the demandant recovered because the person called to warrant made default. It directed a sheriff to take land of vouchee to the value of the land recovered.

Capias exigi facias. You take to cause to be driven out, or expelled.

Capias in withernam. You take in withernam. A writ allowed where a distress is driven out of the county, or concealed and the sheriff, upon a replevin, cannot make deliverance to the party. A taking of other cattle or goods in lieu of those that were formerly unjustly taken away.

Capias in withernam de averiis. You take of the cattle in withernam.

Capias in withernam de homine. You take for a servant in withernam.

Capias pro fine, or misericordia. You take for the fine or in mercy. A writ for taking one condemned to pay a fine to the King, and to imprison him until he paid it.

Capias si laicus. That you take (defendant) if he be a layman.

Capias simul cum. You take together with. A writ directing the sheriff to take a certain defendant together with other defendants in the action.

Capias utlagatum. You take the outlaw. A writ to take the body of one outlawed and hold him to answer.

Capias utlagatum et inquiras de bonis et catallis. You take the outlaw and inquire concerning his goods and chattels.

Capiatur pro fine. Let him be taken for the fine. A clause in a judgment in debt; directing that the party be taken until he paid a fine, being a punishment for the public misdemeanor as well as the private injury.

Capiendo, apostata. See APOSTATA CAPIENDO.

Capio. To take, lay hold of, seize. To have a right of inheritance. To take, seize, or arrest. To take or receive judicially.

Capio dominio. A taking by right of ownership.

Capita. The heads. The entire body whether of men, or animals, or inanimate things.

Capita, distribution per. Same as CAPITA, DIVIDED PER.

Capita, divided per. A division where each heir inherits an equal portion whether the issue of an immediate heir or the immediate heir himself. If a man leave four sons and one of these sons die and leave two heirs and the estate of the ancestor is to be divided per capita, the two grandchildren share equally with their three uncles and do not, as in a division per stirpes, simply receive the share of their father. See STIRPES, DIVIDED PER.

Capita, per. By heads.

Capita legis. Heads or chapters of the law.

Capita libri. Heads or grand divisions of a book.

Capita, succession per. Where the claimants are next in degree to the ancestor, in their own right and not by right of representation.

Capitage. Same as CHEVAGE.

Capitagium. Capitage.

Capitagium vel capitale argentum. Capitage or head silver.

Capitaine. Captain, c o m m a n d e r, leader. Master of a vessel.

Capitaine flote. Commander of the fleet.

Capital. Principal. First of importance. Punishable by death. Relating to a death in consequence of crime. Available produce or assets. The money paid in by shareholders of a corporation. A sum of money invested. The seat of government of a State or nation.

Capital crime. A crime or felony punishable with death.

Capital felony. Same as CAPITAL CRIME.

Capital floating. See FLOATING CAPITAL.

Capital punishment. See PUNISHMEMT, CAPITAL.

Capital stock. See STOCK, CAPITAL.

Capitale. A thing which is stolen or the value of it. See CAPITAL.

Capitale messuagium. A chief messuage.

Capitale placitum. A principal plea.

Capitale vivens. Live cattle.

Capitales constabularii. High constables. Officers appointed in every hundred whose duty was to keep the peace, serve process, return lists of jurors, &c.

Capitalia. Plural of Capital.

Capitalis. The head, chief, or principal, as applied to persons, judicial proceedings, property, etc.

Capitalis baro. Chief baron.

Capitalis baro scaccarii domini regis. Chief baron of the King's Exchequer.

Capitalis custos. Chief warden or magistrate; mayor.

Capitalis debitor. A principal debtor, as distinguished from plegius, a surety.

Capitalis dominis. The chief lord. The immediate lord of the fee, to whom the obligation of the tenant is direct and personal.

Capitalis justiciarius. Chief justice; chief justice or justiciary. A title given the presiding justice in the Court of Aula Regis. It was not used after reign of Hen. III.

Capitalis justiciarius ad placita coram rege tenenda. Chief justice for holding pleas before the King. The title of the chief justice of the King's bench, first assumed in the latter part of the reign of Henry III.

Capitalis justiciarus banci or de banco. Chief justice of the bench or in the bench. The title of the English Court of Common Pleas.

Capitalis justiciarius in itinere. The chief justice in eyre; or chief itinerant judge.

Capitalis (or summus) justiciarius totius angliæ. Chief justice of all England.

Capitalis plegius. A chief pledge; a head-borrow; the head of a decenary.

Capitalis redditus. A chief rent.

Capitalis terra. A head-land. A piece of land lying at the head of other land.

Capitalism. A system of concentrating the capital or aggregate products of industry in the hands of few. The power of such a concentration.

Capitaneus. A leader; a captain. A naval commander. The commander of a ship or vessel. In Feudal law, one who held an estate or dignity in capite.

Capitaneus baro regis vel regni. A chief lord or baron of the King or kingdom.

Capitaneus et custos navis. Captain and warden of the sea (an old title given to a naval officer).

Capitare. To abut.

Capitatim. By the head; to each individual.

Capitatio. A poll tax. Capitation.

Capitation. A counting of heads. The act of assessing by heads. A poll tax; a tax imposed yearly on the head or person.

Capitation grant. Same as CAPITATION.

Capitation tax. See CAPITATION.

Capite. Of, from, by the head. The name of a tenure held directly from the King.

Capite minutus. In Civil law, one who had lost legal status.

Capite, tenure in. A tenure held directly of and created by the sovereign, and not one which the King obtained by escheat.

Capitilitium. Poll money; money individually, one by one.

Capitis. Of the head; of the person.

Capitis deminutio. In the Roman Civil law, the abatement or loss of a statute or civil qualification.

Capitis diminutio. Same as CAPITIS DEMINUTIO.

Capitis diminutio maxima. The change from full rights to none, as from freedom to slavery.

Capitis diminutio media. A loss of citizenship and family rights, but not freedom.

Capitis diminutio minima. The change of one's family relations only, as by arrogation.

Capitis æstimatio. Same as CAPITIS ESTIMATIO.

Capitis estimatio. The estimate of a man's value in money; a fine paid by the Saxons for murder, etc. Under Saxon law the King's value was thirty thousand thrymsæ or £500, and if killed half the were went to the people and half to the King's relatives. An Archbishop or Earl, fifteen thousand thrymsæ or £250.; a bishop or Earlderman, eight thousand thrymsæ or £133, 6s. 8d. A Belli Emperator or Summus Præfectus (highest chief, general, or governor) four thousand thrymsæ or £66, 13s. 4d. ; priest or thane two thousand thrymsæ or £33, 6s. 8d. A common person two hundred and sixty-seven thrymsæ or £4, 9s.

Capitus periculum adiri. To risk the peril of life; to risk one's life.

Capitis poena. Capital punishment.

Capititium. A covering for the head.

Capitula. A collection of laws, regulations or ordinances arranged under different heads. Chapters or assemblies of ecclesiastical persons.

Capitula coronæ. Chapters or schedules of the crown. Heads of inquiry similar to Chapters of the Eyre.

Capitula de Judæis. Chapters or articles concerning the Jews. Articles directing the justices itinerant in the reign of Richard I., to inquire and adjudge what revenue should be paid by the Jews to the King for protection, license to trade, etc.

Capitula itineris. Chapters of the Eyre (which see).

Capitula ruralia. Chapters or assemblies held by rural deans and parochial clergy.

Capitular. A statute, or body of statutes.

Capitularia. Chapters, etc. In Feudal law, a collection of laws, divided into short chapters, promulgated by Charlemagne and other Kings of the Franks.

Capitulary. A statute. A body of statutes. Relating to the chapter of a cathedral. A member of a chapter.

Capitulate. To yield on stipulations. To surrender by treaty.

Capitulation. Surrender. Reduction. A conditional surrender. The instrument stating the terms of surrender. A statement. A recapitulation. The declaration of rights sworn to by the Emperor of the Holy Roman Empire. An agreement, in Civil law, between the people and the prince, regarding the administration of the government.

Capitulations. The articles by which Turkey granted certain extra-territorial rights to foreigners residing in that country. A treaty between the Swiss and the Pope and nations regarding employment of Swiss mercenaries.

Capitulator. One who capitulates.

Capituli agri. Lands that lie at the head or upper end of the land or furrows.

Capitulum. A small head. A chapter. In Ecclesiastical law, an assembly of ecclesiastical persons.

Cappa. A cap. One of the ceremonies of creating an earl or marquis.

Cappa honoris. The cap of honor.

Captain. The commander of a company. He that commands but one band. An officer below a major and above a lieutenant in military rank. A naval officer who commands a man-of-war, ranking between a commodore and a commander.

Captation. In French law, the act by which one person influences the mind of another. An endeavor to obtain something by persuasion or appeals.

Captator. One who obtains anything through unfair methods.

Captio. A taking or seizure of a thing. The taking or arrest of a person. A holding of a court. A taking or receiving.

Captio assisæ. The taking of the assise.

Captio rei unius in alterius satisfactionem. A taking of one thing in satisfaction of another.

Caption. That part of an instrument writing which shows where, when, and by what authority it is taken, found or executed. The title or heading of a legal document.

Caption, letters of. See LETTERS OF CAPTION.

Caption process. In Scotch law, a warrant of imprisonment to force back a process.

Captives. Prisoners of war.

Captor. One who takes or seizes property in time of war; one who takes the property of an enemy; one who takes a prize at sea.

Capture. A taking or seizure of the goods of an enemy; a taking of prizes in time of war, particularly at sea. The taking of a prey. An arrest or seizure.

Captus. A taking or seizing.

Captus et in prisona detentus. Taken and detained in prison.

Capud. Head; the head.

Caput. In Feudal law, a chief; the head of the State. In old English law, upper end of a place. A principal place, house, or messuage. A beginning.

Caput anni. New Year's Day, on which anciently was held the feast of fools. See FESTUM STULTORUM.

Caput baroniæ. The head of a barony. The castle of a nobleman.

Caput comitatus. The head or chief of the county. The sheriff; the King. One of the ancient titles of the earl.

Caput feudi vel terræ. The head of the fee or land ; the chief lord of a fee.

Caput jejunii. Ash Wednesday, the first day of Lent.

Caput legis. A head or principal division of law.

Caput loci. The head or upper end of any place.

Cuput lupinum. A wolf's head. An outlawed felon who could be knocked on the head like a wolf by anyone without committing any crime. (In the reign of King Alfred, and until some time after the Conquest, no man could be outlawed but for felony, and then the outlawed person was said to have caput lupinum, because he might be put to death by any man, as a wolf might).

Caput mortuum. A dead head. A thing void.

Caput portus. The head of a port. The town to which a port belongs and which gives the denomination to the port, and is the head of it.

Caput, principium et finis. The head, origin and end. A term applied to the King as head of Parliament.

Caput terræ. The head of a piece of land. A piece of unplowed land left at end of a plowed field. Also called a butt.

Caput villæ. The head or upper end of a town.

Caputagium. Head or poll money or the payment of it. Same as CHEVAGE.

Caputium. A head of land; a headland.

Car (or Char). A place beginning with this prefix formerly meant a city.

Car tel est notre plaisir. For such is our pleasure. Words used by a King in an ordinance.

Carabus. A raft or boat.

Carat. See CARRAT.

Caravanna. A company of travellers associated for mutual protection.

Carcan. An instrument of punishment resembling a pillory. Sometimes the punishment itself.

Carcanum. A prison or workhouse.

Carcare. To unload; to unload a vesse'; to load a cart or wagon. To charge as in an account.

Carcare et discarcare. To load and unload.

Carcata. Freighted; loaded.

Carcatio. Lading.

Carcationes. Ladings.

Carcatus. Loading. A ship freighted.

Carcel-age. Prison-fees.

Carcer. An inclosing; an inclosed place. A prison, jail.

Cardinal. A Roman Catholic Church dignitary next in rank to the Pope.

Care. Attention. (The different degrees of care cannot be defined, except in a general way; the facts in each case where the question arises must govern).

Care, due. That which is proper and legal under the circumstances. See CARE.

Care, great. More than ordinary attention and diligence. See CARE.

Care, ordinary. That which a person of ordinary mind exercises over his own property. See CARE.

Care, reasonable. Same as CARE, DUE. See CARE.

Care, slight. A small degree of care. See CARE.

Carecta. A cart.

Carectarius. A carter.

Carectata. A cartload.

Carena. A period of forty days.

Careta. Same as CARECTA.

Caretorius. A carter.

Carga. In Spanish law, a charge or incumbrance.

Cargaison. In French law, a cargo.

Cargare. To charge.

Cargo. Merchandise carried by a vessel.

Cariagium. Carriage; the carrying of goods or other things for the King.

Cariare. To carry.

Cariare et recariare. To carry and recarry.

Cariavit. He carried.

Cariator. A carrier.

Cariatores. Carriers.

Caricature. An exaggerated picture or description calculated to produce ridicule or contempt.

Caristia. Dearth; scarcity.

Caritas. A grace-cup ; an allowance of best wine drunk in commemoration of religious or other festivals.

Cark. A quantity of wool which is a thirtieth part of a sarpler. See SARPLER.

Carle. See KARLE.

Carlisle tables. Life and annuity tables compiled in 1780 at Carlisle, England.

Carlist. A supporter of Charles X., of France and his line. A legitimist. An adherent of Don Carlos, son of Charles IV., of Spain, and his descendants.

Carmen. In the Roman law, a formula in religion or law; a formulary; a form of words used in various cases, as of divorce, etc.

Carmen necessarium. A necessary formula; an indispensable lesson.

Carnal. Fleshly.

Carnal knowledge. Sexual intercourse.

Carnalis. Fleshly, carnal. See CARNALITER COGNOVIT.

Carnalitis. Fleshliness; carnality. See CARNALITER COGNOVIT.

Carnaliter. Carnally. See CARNALITER COGNOVIT.

Carnaliter cognovit. Carnally knew. (Carnaliter cognovit, Carnalis, Carnalitas, and Carnaliter, were technical words in indictments, and once held essential to charge the defendant with the crime of rape).

Carnally knew. Had sexual connection, or at least penetration. See CARNALITER COGNOVIT.

Carnarium. A charnel house or repostory for the bones of the dead.

Carno. Immunity or privilege.

Caro verbicina. Mutton.

Caroome. A London, England, license to keep a cart.

Carpemeals. A coarse cloth.

Carr. A wheeled cart.

Carrack. Same as CARRICK.

Carracle. Same as CARRICLE.

Carrat. A weight or burden; a weight of four grains used in weighing diamonds.

Carrecta. Same as CARECTA.

Carrels. Private apartments (applied to places where monks retired to meditate or study).

Carrera. In Spanish law, a right of way for a carriage.

Carreta. A cartload.

Carreta fœni. A load of hay.

Carriage. The act of a carrier in transporting merchandise or persons. The vehicle of transportation.

Carrick. A ship of great burden.

Carricle. A large ship.

Carrier. One whose occupation is the transportation of persons or property for hire.

Carrier, common. One who makes it a business to carry persons or merchandise from one place to another for pay. One who holds himself out to the public as ready to carry for all alike for a compensation.

Carrier, private. One who carries merchandise or persons from one place to another in a particular instance. One who though carrying for hire in a special instance, does not carry for the public generally.

Carrier, special. Same as CARRIER, PRIVATE.

Carrum. A four-wheeled vehicle.

Carrus. A kind of four-wheeled wagon for transporting burdens.

Carry. To bear on one's person.

Carry away. To take at a distance from a place.

Carry costs. See COSTS, CARRY.

Carry on. To transact, as a business.

Carry stock. To hold stock or merchandise for another.

Carrying away. The act of removing articles (necessary to constitute larceny).

Cart. A vehicle of two wheels, as distinguished from a wagon or carriage which has four.

Cart bote. Wood or timber which a tenant is allowed by law to take from an estate, for the purpose of repairing carts and other instruments of husbandry.

Carta. A charter, deed or writing. In Spanish law, a deed; a letter; a power of attorney.

Carta partita de affrectamento. A charter party of affreightment.

Carta de foresta. The charter of the forest.

Carta de una parte. A charter or deed of one part.

Carta perdonationis. A charter of pardon.

Carta indentata (or indentura). A deed indented, or indenture. A deed executed in parts, or as many copies as there are parties, each indented like the teeth of a saw, or in a waved line, on the top or side, to correspond with the other.

Carte. In French Marine law, a chart.

Carte blanche. A white or blank sheet of paper. An authority to do any act relating to any affair. A blank sheet signed, given with authority to fill the space above.

Cartel. An agreement concerning the exchange of prisoners between two hostile States. A written challenge.

Cartel ship. A ship of truce, unarmed, used to exchange prisoners, carry messages, &c., between two hostile States.

Cartist. One who supports the Constitution of Spain or Portugal.

Cartman. A person who transports articles in a cart for hire.

Cartulary. A collection of charters, deeds or records. A copy of deeds or records. A copy of a register or record. An officer in charge of records.

Carua. Same as CARUCA.

Caruca. A plow. A plow land; as much land as one plow could cultivate.

Carucage. Same as CARUCAGIUM.

Carucagium. A tax or tribute anciently imposed upon every plow, for the public service.

Carucarium apparura. Plow tackle.

Carucarius. In the Civil law, the driver of a caruca. In old English law, a plowman.

Carucata. A plow land. A quantity of land containing as much as might be tilled by one plow in a year and a day. Said to be a plow land of one hundred acres. A soke.

Carucatarius. One who held land in socage or plow tenure.

Carucate. Same as CARUCATA.

Carue. A plow land.

Carvage. Same as CARUCAGIUM.

Carvagium. Same as CARUCAGIUM.

Carve. Same as CARUCAGIUM.

Cas. Case; the case; an event or occurrence.

Cas fortuit. A fortuitous event; an inevitable accident.

Casa. A house with land sufficient for the support of one family; otherwise called hida. A hide of land.

Casæ. A country estate; a farm.

Casamentum. The land held by a vassal or tenant.

Casata. Same as CASA.

Casatus. A feudal tenant having his own house and property.

Case. An occurrence. A question for determination. A controversy. A state of facts. A suit. A claim put in such form that a court can act upon it. An action at law, equity, or admiralty. A statement of facts for the determination of a court. See ACTION UPON THE CASE.

Case, action on the. Same as ACTION UPON THE CASE.

Case, action upon the. See ACTION UPON THE CASE.

Case, agreed. A statement of facts agreed to by both parties to a cause submitted for decision.

Case, analogous. See ANALOGOUS CASE; also ANALOGOUS.

Case, breaking a. The private discussion by judges of a case before them for determination.

Case, certified. A case certified from the judges of an inferior to a superior court, for a decision of a question arising in a case, where the inferior judges cannot agree.

Case for motion. A statement of the previous proceedings, the facts on which the motion is based.

Case, hypothetical. See HYPOTHETICAL CASE.

Case in judgment. The facts of a legal controversy, pending or decided.

Case law. Law which is established on the authority of court decisions alone.

Case, leading. See LEADING CASE.

Case, made. A statement of facts submitted to a court as basis for a motion.

Case of first impression. One in in which a point of law arises for the first time.

Case on appeal. A brief statement of the proceedings had below. It is usually connected and precedes the brief.

Case, reserved. A case wherein the jury find a verdict for plaintiff subject to the opinion of the court on a question of law.

Case, special. In English practice, a case made up by agreement of the parties without pleading. The parties agree on the facts and state the questions of law arising thereon for the opinion of the judge.

Case, stated. An agreed statement of facts submitted in writing to the court for decision.

Case system. A system of studying or teaching the science of law by means of court decisions on questions of law.

Case, Taltarum's. See TALTARUM'S CASE.

Case to move for new trial. Same as CASE FOR MOTION.

Case, Twyne's. See TWYNE'S CASE.

Case, Tyrrel's. See TYRREL'S CASE.

Cases and controversies. Claims brought before courts for hearing and determination.

Cases, criminal. See CRIMINAL CASES.

Cash. Lawful money.

Cash price. A price for cash as distinguished from one for credit.

Cashier. To dismiss by revoking a commission of office. One who has charge for another of money used in business. The chief executive officer of a bank. In French law, a petition for the redress of grievances stated, at one time presented to the deputies in the States General. See BANK CASHIER.

Cashlite. A mulct or fine.

Cask. An uncertain quantity of goods varying in size with the article.

Cassabitur. The writ shall be quashed.

Cassare. To quash or make void; to annul, to abate.

Cassarius. Of or belonging to a cottage; a dweller in a cottage; a cottager.

Cassata. Same as CASATA.

Cassatæ. Quashed.

Cassatio. A quashing, making void; an abatement.

Cassation. In French law, the act of reversing or annulling the validity of a judgment.

Cassation, court of. Same as COUR DE CASSATION.

Cassatum. Same as CASATA.

Cassatus. A vassal or feudal tenant possessing a casa.

Casser. Same as CASSARE.

Cassetur. Quashed.

Cassetur billa. That the bill be quashed. The form of the judgment for the defendant on a plea of abatement, where the action was commenced by bill.

Cassetur breve. That the writ be quashed. The form of the judgment for the defendant on a plea in abatement, where the action was commenced by original writ.

Cassidile. A small sack, purse or pocket.

Cassock. A garment worn by priests.

Cassula. A garment worn by priests; a cassock.

Cast. To defeat in a suit. Thrust upon. Vest with.

Cast an essoin. To put in an excuse for non-appearance in an action.

Cast-away. Applied to a vessel means lost or perished.

Caste. Chastely.

Castel. Same as CASTLE.

Castel guardum. Same as CASTELLI-GUARDIA.

Castellain. The land owner or captain of a castle. The constable of a fortified house; one who has the custody of the King's mansions. See CASTELLANUS.

Castellani. The occupants of a castle.

Castellania. The office of a castellain; the territory, precinct, or jurisdiction of a castle.

Castellanus. A castellain; the keeper, constable, or captain of a castle or fortified house, acting in the name or in the place of the owner. An officer of the forest.

Castellarium. The precinct or jurisdiction of a castle.

Castellatus. The jurisdiction of a castle.

Castelli-guardia. Guard of a castle; castle guard. An imposition laid upon such of the King's subjects as dwelt within a certain compass of any castle, to maintain such as watched the same. The district inhabited by those subject to such service.

Castellatio. Leave of the King to build a castle.

Castellorum operatio. Castle work; work on castles done by inferior tenants as a service.

Castellum. Same as CASTEL.

Caster. Suffix put by the Romans to places where castles were built.

Castigation. A correcting, chastising, punishment, correction, reproof, etc.

Castigatorium. A device for the punishment of female scolds. It was also called the tumbrel, tre-bucket, scolding stool, cucking stool, ducking stool, gogin stole, coke stole. It consisted of a stool fixed to the end of a long pole on which the scolding woman was seated and plunged in water.

Castigatory. A ducking stool for common scolds. See CASTIGATORIUM.

Casting. Offering; tendering.

Casting vote. See VOTE, CASTING.

Castle. A fortress in a town. A citadel; a stronghold. The mansion of a nobleman. (More than eleven hundred castles were demolished in England during the civil war).

Castle, adulterine. See ADULTERINE CASTLE.

Castle guard. Same as CASTELLIGUARDIA.

Castle-guard rents. Money paid toward the maintenance of a castle and those who guarded it.

Castleward. Same as CASTLE-GUARDIA.

Castle yard. Same as CASTELLIGUARDIA.

Castrate. To remove the testicles from a male animal.

Castration. The act of removing testicles.

Castrensis. In Roman law, relating to military service.

Castrum. A castle.

Casu. By chance, casually, by accident.

Casu consimili. In a like case. A writ of entry given a reversioner against the alienee of a tenant in courtesy, or a tenant for life.

(10)

Casu proviso. In the case provided for. A writ of entry given by the statute of Gloucester (6 Edw. I., c. 7), to a reversioner against the alienee of a tenant in dower.

Casual. That brought about without premeditation or design.

Casual ejector. The ostensible defendant in a common law action of ejectment.

Casual pauper. One assisted by law outside of his domicile.

Casual poor. Those not belonging to a community but thrown upon its charity by accident or necessity.

Casualis conditio. A condition depending upon chance.

Casualities of superiority. In Scotch law, payments other than rent from a tenant to his lord for matters uncertain which arise during the tenancy.

Casualities of wards. In Scotch law, that due the superior in ward holdings.

Casualty. Injury or destruction which happens by accident. See ACCIDENT.

Casum. A house.

Casus. A case. An event; a circumstance or combination of circumstances. A case at law; a cause for action. A chance; an accident or misfortune.

Casus, adventicia. See ADVENTICIA CASUS.

Casus belli. A cause of war; a cause for war.

Casus fœderis. The case of the treaty. A case or subject matter of a treaty; matter within the terms of a treaty. The end of the league; the end of the compact; a matter within the terms of a contract.

Casus fortuitus. An accidental case; an accident.

Casus isolatus. An isolated case; an unusual circumstance.

Casus major. An extraordinary casualty.

Casus omissi. Omitted cases ; casual omissions. (Plural of Casus Omissus).

Casus omissus. An omitted case; a case not provided for. Applied to failure to provide in a statute, contract or regulation for cases which may arise.

Cat. A whip with nine lashes used in the whipping of criminals.

Catalla. Goods and chattels.

Catalla felonum, vel fugitivum aut utlagatorum. The chattels of felons, or fugitives, or outlaws.

Catalla otiosa. Goods or chattels not in use as distinguished from animals which are worked. In Old English law, idle cattle (comprising horses, oxen, mules) not used for working.

Catallactics. Political economy.

Catallis captis nomine districtionis. You take the goods or chattels in the name of distress. An old English writ for rent of a house in a borough and which warranted the taking of doors, windows, etc.,

Catallis reddendis. An ancient writ of detinue. See BREVE DE CATALLIS REDDENDIS.

Catallum. A chattel.

Catals. Goods and chattels.

Cataneus. A tenant in capite.

Catapulta. A warlike engine to shoot darts. A cross-bow.

Catascopus. An archdeacon.

Catching a bargain. Securing an agreement to buy an expectant estate at a price below its value.

Catchings. Things caught and taken into the custody of the party.

Catchland. Land which was not known to belong to any particular parish, the tithes of which became the property of the minister first seizing them.

Catchpole. In old English law, a sheriff's officer, assistant, or bailiff, probably so called because he caught by the poll or head the party arrested.

Categorical. Direct. Unconditional.

Category. A class or description of things.

Cater cousin. A distant relation.

Cateux. Chattels.

Cathedra stercoris. A chair or seat of dung. A cucking stool. See CASTIGATORIUM.

Cathedral. The church of the bishop.

Cathedral preferments. All dignities and officials in a church below that of bishop.

Cathedratick. A sum of two shillings which was paid the bishop by inferior clergy.

Catholic creditor. In Scotch law, a creditor who has security for his debt on several parts of the debtor's property.

Catholic Emancipation Act. Stat. 10 Geo. IV., c. 7, which restored Roman Catholics to civil rights except the holding of ecclesiastical and certain other offices.

Catholicus. Universal. Relating to all. See DEFENDER OF THE FAITH.

Catonia regula. In Roman law, the rule that what is void at the beginning will not become valid by time.

Cattle. Among the early Saxons, any kind of wealth; later any live stock kept for profit. Now confined to domestic bovine animals such as oxen, bulls, cows and calves.

Cattle guard. An obstruction to prevent cattle going upon a railroad track.

Cattle, transient. See TRANSIENT CATTLE.

Cattle-gate. A right of pasturing cattle in another's land.

Catzurus. A hunting horse.

Caucus. A private meeting of persons to formulate plans, or policies or for other political purposes.

Cauda terræ. A land's end or bottom of a ridge or furrow in arable land.

Caudex. Same as CODEX.

Caulceis. Roads paved with flint or other stone.

Caupones. Innkeepers.

Cauponium. A tavern, an inn.

Caursines. Italian money-lenders expelled from England in the reign of Henry III. for extortion.

Causa. In the Civil law, by reason of; on account of. The consideration for making a contract.

Causa affinitatas. Because of affinity; a ground of divorce.

Causa cadere. To lose one's cause.

Causa causans. The cause causing ; that producing cause.

Causa causata. The cause caused, the immediate cause.

Causa cognita. A known c a u s e. Upon the cause being judicially examined.

Causa consanguinitatis. Because of consanguinity; a ground for divorce. See DIVORCE.

Causa constituere. To institute a cause; a lawsuit.

Causa exponere. To present a judicial process or cause.

Causa frigiditatis. On account of coldness, frigidity. In old English law, a cause for divorce a vinculo matrimonii.

Causa hospitandi. For the purpose of being entertained as a guest.

Causa impotentiæ seu frigiditatis. Because of impotency or frigidity. A ground for divorce. See DIVORCE.

Causa jactitationis maritagii. A suit of jactitation of marriage.

Causa jactitationis matrimonii. A suit for jactitation of marriage.

Causa matrimonialis. A matrimonial cause.

Causa matrimonii prælocuti. By reason of the marriage before treated of. A writ where a woman gives land in consideration of marriage and the man refuses to carry out his agreement.

Causa metus. Because of fear. In old English law, a ground for divorce. See DIVORCE.

Causa mortis. In prospect or expectation of death; in anticipation or contemplation of death.

Causa mortis donatio. See DONATIO CAUSA MORTIS.

Causa perpetua. A perpetual or permanent cause.

Causa pia. A pious or charitable cause.

Causa præcontractus. On account of precontract. A ground for divorce. See DIVORCE.

Causa proviso. A writ of entry brought by a reversioner against a tenant in dower who had alienated land for a greater estate than he had.

Causa proxima. The proximate cause. The nearest cause.

Causa remota. The remote cause. A cause producing an effect through another or other causes.

Causa sine qua non. A cause without which a thing cannot be or exist.

Causa turpis. An unlawful motion or purpose.

Causam agere. To move or prosecute a cause; to manage a lawsuit.

Causam dicere. To defend one's self; to make a defence (as an advocate).

Causam litigare. To litigate or cause a suit.

Causam nobis significes. (You signify to us the reason). A writ directing the mayor of a city or town to show cause why he neglected performing certain duties.

Causans. Causing.

Causare. To cause; to produce; to complain of; to show cause against; to object to. To manage a cause; to litigate.

Causata. Caused.

Causativum litis. A cause which gives jurisdiction.

Causator. A litigant; one who takes the part of another in a suit; one who litigates for another.

Cause. The motive, inducement, consideration for making a contract or performing an act. An action or suit at law. Any civil or criminal question contested before a court or tribunal. Reason, motive, consideration. Anything which produces an effect.

Cause, adequate. In Criminal law, such cause as prevents an ordinary mind from reflecting before committing an act.

Cause de remover plea. Cause to remove a plea.

Cause, for. Because of some legal disability. For good and sufficient reason.

Cause of action. The ground for an action.

Cause of collision. See COLLISION, CAUSE OF.

Cause, pecuniary. See PECUNIARY CAUSE.

Cause, probable. Such facts as would lead an ordinary mind to believe that further inquiry might prove guilt.

Cause, proximate. The nearest cause; the dominant cause. The result complained of.

Cause, reasonable. Probable cause. Facts that would influence an ordinary mind.

Cause, remote. See REMOTE CAUSE.

Cause, short. See SHORT CAUSE.

Causes celebres. Celebrated, famed, renowned cases. A book containing French decisions of importance during the 17th and 18th centuries.

Causes of instance. See INSTANCE, CAUSES OF.

Causeway. A raised road.

Causidicus. A pleader. In the Civil law, one who argues a cause ore tenus.

Causo reservatio. The right to receive a pension from another in return for land transferred.

Causor. To conduct a cause in law; to be an advocate; to make a defence.

Cautela. Caution.

Cautele. Caution.

Cauterizetur in manu. He may (shall) be burned in the hand. See BRANDING.

Cauterizo. To burn with a hot iron; to brand.

Cautio. A bond as surety. The surety. The ev dence of a contract.

Cautio fidejussoria. Security in the form of bonds of third parties.

Cautio juratorio. Security in the form of a party's oath.

Cautio pignoratitia. Security by the deposit of valuables.

Cautio pro expensis. Security for costs or expenses.

Cautio usufructuaria. Security given by tenants for life to preserve the property from waste.

Caution. To warn; a warning. Care to avcid injury. In Scotch law, security given for the performance of some obligation. The person who gives the security.

Caution, juratory. In Scotch law, security given by oath.

Caution money. (Scotch). Money deposited as security.

Caution, writ of. A caveat in relation to land titles filed with the registrar.

Cautionary. Conveying a warning. Constituting a security.

Cautionary order. See ORDER, CAUTIONARY.

Cautionary town. A town whose revenues are pledged as security for a loan.

Cautione admittenda. An ancient writ against a bishop who held an excommunicated person in jail after the latter had offered security that he would in the future obey the orders of the church.

Cautionement. In French law, becoming surety.

Cautioner. One who cautions. One who serves a writ of caution. One who stands security in a caution. See CAUTION, WRIT OF; also CAUTION.

Cautioner, attestor of. See ATTESTOR OF CAUTIONER.

Cautionry. The giving of bail.

Cautionry, extrajudicial. (Scotch). An obligation given to a creditor, either by the cautioner becoming a party in the original obligation, or by his entering into a separate bond of cautionry. See CAUTION; also CAUTIONRY.

Cavaliers. Adherents of Chas. I. and Chas. II., as opposed to members of Parliament and the Puritans or Roundheads.

Caveat. Let him beware; let him take heed. At one time process issued by an Ecclesiastical court, to prevent the proving of a will or the granting an administration. In old English law, a writ to prevent the granting of letters patent. A formal notice to a court, judge, or public officer, not to do a certain act. A process in the nature of an injunction, to prevent the granting of a patent for lands. A description of an incompleted patent filed in the U. S. Patent Office, which filing entitled the inventor to three months' protection.

Caveat actor. Let the doer beware.

Caveat emptor. Let the buyer beware. A purchaser of property must examine as to its title and quality before buying, otherwise he cannot complain, in the absence of fraud.

Caveat venditor. Let the seller take heed. A phrase of the Civil law, which implies that the seller must beware lest he make himself responsible for the quality of an article he sells. This is directly contrary to the Common law, where the seller is not bound except on giving an express warranty or practicing fraud.

Caveat viator. Let the traveller take care. A traveller, given permission to cross private land, does so at his own risk and must use reasonable care in avoiding defects in the road.

Caveatee. One on whom a caveat is served.

Caveator. One who files a caveat.

Cavena. The repository of the necessities of life.

Cavers. Offenders punishable in the Mote or Miner's Court.

Caya. A quay, kay or key, or wharf.

Cayagium. Cayage or kayage; a toll or duty anciently paid to the King for landing goods at a quay or wharf.

Ce. This, that.

Ceals. Those.

Ceans. Here within.

Ceap. A bargain. Something for sale. Cattle as a medium of exchange. Ceapgilde.

Ceapgilde. Payment or forfeiture of cattle.

Cease. End; stop; discontinuance.

Cecy. This, that.

Cede. To transfer; to pass the title to. Generally applied to the transfer of territory from one sovereignty to another.

Cedent. In Scotch law, an assignor.

Cedenter. By yielding.

Cedo. I grant.

Cedula. A schedule. In Spanish law, a circular letter or order; a bill or order. Notice to a fugitive criminal to appear in court affixed to the door of his house. An admission by a debtor, of a debt, and an agreement to pay the same, on a specified time.

Cedule. In French law, a note in writing.

Cel. This.

Celation. Concealment of pregnancy or delivery.

Celdra. A chaldron, a measure.

Celer lecti. The head of a bed.

Celibacy. The condition of one unmarried.

Cellarius. One who keeps provisions; a steward of a monastic institution; a cellarer or bursar.

Cellerarius. Same as CELLARIUS.

Celles. Those.

Celles que. Those who.

Celles que trusts. Persons entitled to the purchase-money, or the residue of any other property, after discharging the debts.

Celsus. P. Juventius Celsus. A writer on Roman law.

Celtæ. A brave and warlike nation, or tribe, who formerly possessed old Gaul. They included the Gadhelic and Cymric peoples.

Celui. He, him. He who.

Celuy. He, him. He who.

Cemetery. A burying ground apart from a church.

Cendulæ. Small pieces of wood laid like tiles to cover the roof of a house. Shingles.

Cenegild. Kin-money. A mulct or fine paid to relatives of the deceased by the one who killed him.

Cenninga. Notice given by the buyer to the seller that the thing sold was claimed by another, and to appear and justify the sale.

Cens. In French and Canadian law, a tax, tribute or payment imposed on a tenant. A quit-rent.

Censare. To ordain; to decree.

Censaria. A farm or house and land let at a standing rent.

Censarii. Farmers subject to a tax.

Censatario. One who grants or pays a censo.

Cense money. Money paid in some manors in England by those summoned to swear fealty to the lord. See CENSURE.

Censitaire. In Canadian law, a tenant by cens. See CENS.

Censo. An annuity. Ground rent. An agreement to settle an annuity on a person.

Censo reservatio. The right to receive a pension from another in return for land transferred.

Censor. A Roman magistrate who had supervision of public manners and morals and the register of property for taxation. In some countries an official who examines manuscripts with power to allow or permit the same to be published. A Chinese official who sees that decrees agree with ancient precedent. A college officer similar to a dean.

Censors. Those above sixteen who swore fealty to the lord.

Censive tenure. In Canadian law, tenure in which the tenant paid in kind as distinguished from military services.

Censuales. Those who paid a certain rent and performed certain services to obtain the protection of the church.

Censualisto. The recipient of a censo.

Censuere. They have decreed. In Roman law, applied to the decree of the Roman Senate.

Censumethidus. A dead rent. Mortmain.

Censumorthidus. A dead rent. Mortmain.

Censure. A custom in certain manors in England of citing all above the age of sixteen to swear fealty to the lord or pay a fine every year. The lightest form of ecclesiastical punishment.

Census. An enumeration. A valuation. Collection of statistics regarding persons and their possessions. A tax or tribute; a toll. A yearly payment of rent. A yearly income or revenue. In Scotch law, a subsidy or tax.

Census regalis. The royal revenue.

Centare. In Metric system, a measure of surface equal to 1,550 square inches.

Centena. A hundred. A district of one hundred freemen, established for military and civil purposes. A Saxon hundred. A hundred weight. See HUNDRED.

Cent. In U. S., and Canada and Hawaiian Islands, a coin valued at one hundredth part of a dollar.

Centena piscium. A hundred weight of fish.

Centenarii. Plural of Centenarius.

Centenarius. One of a centena or hundred; the head or chief of a centena. Among the Goths, Germans, Franks and Lombards, an inferior judge. In Anglo-Saxon law, a judicial magistrate; a centurio.

Centeni. A hundred men; among ancient Europeans, the number of men enrolled for military service from each district.

Centesima. In Roman law, the hundredth part.

Centesimatio. The punishing of every hundredth man. See DECIMATION.

Centesimæ. Interest at twelve per cent. per annum.

Centigram. In Metric system, 0.154 grains avoirdupois.

Centiliter. In Metric system, 0.6102 cubic inches dry or 0.338 fluid ounces liquid measure.

Centimeter. In Metric system, 0.3937 inches in length.

Central Criminal Court. See COURT, CENTRAL CRIMINAL.

Centralization. The bringing of control to a centre. The consideration of control under one power.

Centumviri. In Roman law, a court of a hundred and five judges or three from each of the thirty five Roman tribes.

Centuria. A division. A division into a hundred of a kind.

Centurio. The commander of a century. An officer with jurisdiction over a hundred friborgs or ten tithings; afterwards called bailiff or constable of the hundred.

Centurion. Same as CENTURIO.

Century. One hundred. A hundred men. A hundred years.

Ceo. This; that.

Ceola. A large ship.

Ceorl. A villein or inferior person among the Saxons next above a theow or slave. A Saxon freeman without land.

Cepi. I have taken or arrested.

Cepi corpus. I have taken the body. The return made by a sheriff to a capias that he has taken the body of the party.

Cepit. Took, he took. The emphatic word in a writ of trespass and replevin. When the action in replevin, is for the taking only, it is said to be ''in the cepit.''

Cepit et abcarriavit. He took and carried away.

Cepit et abduxit. He took and led away. The teste in writs of trespass, where the writ was for living things, either persons or animals.

Cepit et asportavit. He took and carried away. The teste in writs of trespass where the writ was for dead things.

Cepit in alio loco. He took in another place. A plea in replevin where the defendant took the goods or cattle in another place than that alleged, and he desires a return of the same.

Ceppagium. The stumps or roots of trees that remain in the ground after the tree is felled.

Cera. Wax. A writing tablet smeared over with wax. A seal of wax.

Cera impressa. Wax impressed; wax with an impression. A seal.

Ceragium. A contribution for the candles in a church.

Ceragrum. Same as CERAGIUM.

Cerevisia. Ale.

Cert money. Head money paid for the keeping of the court-leet, by tenants to the lords of manors.

Certa res. A certain thing; a thing determined, certain, sure.

Certain. Definite. Established. Known.

Certain intent in particular, To a. See TO A CERTAIN INTENT IN PARTICULAR.

Certain services. Such as were defined and fixed in quantity.

Certainty. That which is subject to one meaning or intention. Real state ; truth ; fact ; regularity.

Certainty, moral. Such an impression upon the mind that an allegation is true as causes one to accept it as true and act accordingly. A strong presumption drawn from facts.

Certainty to a common intent. The taking of words capable of artificial and natural sense, in their natural sense.

Certainty to a certain intent in general. That which upon a reasonable construction may be deemed certain without resorting to possible facts which do not appear.

Certainty to a certain intent in particular. The greatest technical accuracy.

Certificando de recognitione stapulæ. A writ directing the mayor of a staple to certify to the Lord Chancellor a statute staple taken before him where the party who obtained it, refuses to bring in the same.

Certificatio assisæ novæ disseisinæ. A certification of assise of novel disseisin.

Certificate. An instrument writing certifying to some fact or record.

Certificate de coutume. In French law, a statement by a foreign lawyer of the law of his country upon certain questions.

Certificate from a holder of property attached. A certificate stating the amount and character of the property and the defendant's interest therein.

Certificate, gold. Certificates issued by the U. S., as currency, redeemable in gold deposited for their redemption.

Certificate into Chancery. The written opinion of a common law court on a matter arising in a chancery suit.

Certificate of assise. A writ granting a retrial before justices of assise.

Certificate of costs. See COSTS, CERTIFICATE OF.

Certificate of deposit. See DEPOSIT, CERTIFICATE OF.

Certificate of registry. A copy or abstract of a ship's register.

Certificate, receiver's. See RECEIVER'S CERTIFICATE.

Certificate, scrip. See SCRIP CERTIFICATE.

Certificate, silver. Certificates issued by the U. S., as currency redeemable in silver deposited for their redemption.

Certificate of stock. See STOCK, CERTIFICATE OF.

Certificate, trial by. Where the point at issue is determined by the certificate of the only authority competent to decide.

Certification. In Scotch law, notice given to a party in a cause, of the course which will be followed in case he fails to appear.

Certified case. See CASE, CERTIFIED.

Certified check. A check upon which the cashier or bank teller has stamped and written words which indicate that there are funds to pay the same, and they will be held to meet that particular check.

Certified copy. See COPY, CERTIFIED.

Certiorari. To be informed of; to be certified of. A writ from a superior to an inferior court directing it to certify or send up the record of a cause. A mode of appeal from the judgment of a special tribunal or a court not of record.

Certiorari, bill of. See BILL OF CERTIORARI.

Certiorari, writ of. A writ to remove the record of a cause from a lower to a higher court. See CERTIORARI.

Certitudo. Certainty.

Cert-money. Head money paid yearly by the residents of a manor for certain holding of the leet. Sometimes paid to a hundred.

Certum. Certain, determined, resolved, sure, fixed.

Cerura. A mound, fence, or enclosure.

Certum letæ. Same as CERT-MONEY.

Cervisarii. Tenants who were required to contribute ale for the lord's table.

Cervisarius. A beer or ale brewer.

Cervisia. Ale.

Cervus. A deer.

Cesionario. In Spanish law, an assignee.

Cess. To cease. Determine. Stop. A tax or assessment. Anciently, in Ireland, it meant an exaction of victuals, at a certain rate, for soldiers.

Cessare. To cease; to stop.

Cessat. A ceasing.

Cessat executio. A writ staying execution.

Cessavit. He has ceased. A writ to recover land where a tenant ceases to pay rent or perform services for two years, or a religious house ceases to perform spiritual services.

Cessavit per biennium. He has ceased through two years. See CESSAVIT.

Cesse. An assessment or tax. In Ireland an exaction of victuals for soldiers in garrison.

Cesser. Neglect; omitting to do a thing. The termination of an estate.

Cesser provided for. The provision specifying on what events terms for years raised by settlement shall cease.

Cesset executio. The execution ceases; let execution stay. A stay of execution or an order for such stay; the entry of such stay on record.

Cesset processus. The process stays; let the process stay. A stay of proceedings entered on the record on an issue; the entry on record of a stay of the proceedings.

Cessio. A giving up, assigning, surrendering. Cession.

Cessio bonorum. A giving up, assigning, or cession of goods or property. The surrender of an insolvent's estate and effects to his creditors for their benefit. A process in Scotland similar to that in England in bankruptcy. In Roman law, this surrender of goods exempted the debtor from punishment, from infamy, and discharged his debts to the extent of the property relinquished.

Cessio in jure. In Roman law, a fictitious suit in which one party desiring an article claimed it, the possessor acknowledged the claim to be just, and the magistrate decreed the former to be the owner.

Cession. The act of ceding. A ceasing; a yielding up or giving over. The assigning by a debtor of his property to his creditors. The vacating of a benefice by accepting another not compatible.

Cession des biens. In French law, the surrender by a debtor of his goods to his creditors. It is both voluntary and compulsory.

Cession of goods. The surrender of goods by a debtor to his creditors.

Cessionary. In Scotch law, an assignee.

Cessionary bankrupt. See BANK-RUPT, CESSIONARY.

Cessment. An assessment.

Cessor. One who ceased or neglected so long to perform a duty that he incurred danger from the law.

Cessure. Ceasing; giving over or departing from. A bailiff.

C'est. It is.

C'est ascavoir. That is to say; to-wit.

Cest ascavoir. Same as C'EST AS-CAVOIR.

Cestascavoire. Same as C'EST AS-CAVOIR.

Cestui. He. (Also spelled Cestuy).

Cestui que trust. He in trust for whom, or for whose benefit another is enfeoffed or seized of lands or tenements, or is possessed of personal property. The beneficiary under a trust.

Cestui que use. He for whose use. He for whose benefit land is held by another.

Cestui que vie. He for whose life. He whose life is the measure of the duration of an estate.

Cestuis que trustent. They in trust for whom.

Cestuy. Same as CESTUI.

Cet. That.

Cettuy. That.

Ceu. This, that. (A corruption of Ceo).

Ceuls. Those.

Ceulx. Those.

Ceux. These, those.

Cf. Abbreviation of the Latin conferre, to compare.

Ch. Abbreviation of chapter, c h i e f, chancellor.

Chace. Same as CHACEA.

Chacea. A chase (which see).

Chaceable. That which may be chased, hunted.

Chaceare. To hunt.

Chacer. To chase. To hunt. To compel.

Chacurus. A horse or a hound for the chase.

Chafe. To heat.

Chafewax. An officer who fitted the wax for sealing writs, etc., in Chancery.

Chaffer. Same as CHAFE.

Chaffers. Wares or merchandise.

Chaffering. Bartering one thing for another.

Chaffery. Buying and selling.

Chain. A surveyor's measure 22 yards long.

Chain of title. A statement in regular order of the grantors and grantees of a particular piece of land with the dates of the conveyances and other facts briefly stated, relating to the title. See TITLE, ABSTRACT OF.

Chairman. One who presides over a meeting of any character.

Chalenger. Same as CHALLENGE.

Chalking. An impost on merchants of the staple.

Challenge. An exception against persons or things. An invitation to a contest of any kind. Act of a sentry in demanding the countersign from those who appear at his post. An exception against, or an exception to, a juror or voter.

Challenge for cause. A challenge upon cause or reason alleged.

Challenge for favor. A challenge because the juror is favorably inclined toward the other side.

Challenge, general. A challenge to a juror on the ground that he is incompetent to serve in any case.

Challenge peremptory. A challenge in a criminal case without alleging the cause.

Challenge principal. A challenge in a civil case alleging an exception, which if true, is allowed by law.

Challenge propter affectum. See PROPTER AFFECTUM.

Challenge propter defectum. See PROPTER DEFECTUM.

Challenge propter delictum. See PROPTER DELICTUM.

Challenge propter honoris respectum. See PROPTER HONORIS RESPECTUM.

Challenge to the array. A challenge to the whole jury or array in the panel.

Challenge to the poll. A challenge to particular persons in the array.

Chalunge. A claim.

Chamber. A court. A treasury. A room in a dwelling-house used for sleeping, for an office, or for a court.

Chamber, bill. See BILL CHAMBER.

Chamber deacons. Same as CHAMBERDEKINS.

Chamber of accounts. An old royal court in France charged with the duty of the King's revenue.

Chamber of commerce. A society of merchants in a city, organized to promote commerce.

Chamber survey. One not made on the land.

Chamber, widow's. See WIDOW'S CHAMBER.

Chamberdekins. Poor Irish scholars living under no rule in mean habit. Beggars banished England by 1 Hen. V., cap. 7, 8.

Chamberlain. An official who regulates the etiquette of a King's court. An official who had charge of the King's household except his bedchamber, which was in charge of a groom of the Stole. A steward of a municipal corporation. An official of the Pope who has charge of his revenues. Anciently an attendant at an inn. An officer of the Exchequer who kept the keys of the Treasury and the book of Domesday. In some of the United States, a treasurer.

Chambers, at. The sitting of a judge privately to hear and determine matters not required to be done in an open court.

Chambers of the King. The havens or ports or parts of the sea inside of a line drawn from one projecting point to another.

Chambium. Change or exchange. Same as CAMBIUM.

Chambre depinct. Painted chamber. Applied to St. Edward's Chamber.

Champ de Mai. Same as CAMPUS MAII.

Champ de Mars. Same as CAMPUS MARTII.

Champart. In French law, a share or division of the profits of land; a part of the crop annually due the landlord by bargain or custom.

Champartor. One who is guilty of the offence of champerty. One who by previous agreement is to receive part of land, debt, or anything sued for.

Champarty. A bargain with the plaintiff or defendant to receive part of the land, debt, or thing sued for in consideration of services performed or expense of suit being borne. See CHAMPERT; also see BUYING TITLE.

Champert. A share or division of land; champerty. An agreement to divide matter sued for, if the suit be successful the champertor is to carry on the party's suit at his own expense. In Scotch law, a gift or bribe taken by a judge.

Champertor. One who is guilty of champerty.

Champertous. Relating to champerty. Affected by champerty.

Champerty. Same as CHAMPARTY.

Champion. Those who anciently defended a cause in trial by battle.

Champion of the King. An officer who, at the coronation of an English King, proclaimed his readiness to defend the King's title.

Chance. An accident. An unlawful act committed without design. See ACCIDENT.

Chance-medley. A casual meeting or affray. The accidental killing of a man in self-defence upon a sudden encounter, or sudden quarrel. See CHAUD-MEDLEY.

Chancel. That part of a church where the communion table stands.

Chancellarie. Chancery.

Chancellary. Chancery.

Chancellor. The presiding judge in the Court of Chancery. The officer of the Exchequer who held the seal of the Court of Chancery. The President of the Federal Council in Germany. In France, the keeper of the Great Seal and President of the Councils. The keeper of the Great Seal under the Eastern Empire, a part of the Holy Roman Empire. In Scotch law, the foreman of a jury. In some of the United States, the chief officer of a court of equity. The chief officer of a university.

Chancellor, Lord High. The highest judicial officer of England, supreme in the Court of Chancery, keeper of the Great Seal, privy counsellor and prolocutor of the House of Lords.

Chancellor of the diocese. One who assists a bishop in law matters and holds his consistory court.

Chancellor of a university. The head officer of a university.

Chancellor of the Duchy of Lancaster. The one who presides over the Duchy Court.

Chancellor of the Exchequer. The principal financial officer of Great Britain. Formerly one who presided over the Court of Exchequer and also sat on the equity side.

Chancellor, vice. An equity judge whose decree is reviewable by the Chancellor. In Roman Catholic Church, the head Cardinal of the Chancery charged with the Pope's briefs and bulls.

Chancer. To adjust in an equitable manner. To tax, as costs.

Chancers. Formerly those who taxed costs.

Chancery. Equity; a court of extraordinary jurisdiction in cases of equity. See COURT OF CHANCERY.

Change. To alter. An alteration. An abbreviation of exchange.

Changer. An officer of the King's Mint whose duty is to exchange coin for bullion.

Changing order. See ORDER, CHANGING.

Channel. The bed of a stream. The deepest and principal part through which the water of a stream flows.

Chanter. To sing ; to declare aloud. To find a verdict. The chief singer in a cathedral choir.

Chantry. A church or altar in a cathedral endowed with lands or revenues.

Chapel of ease. A chapel built in aid of the original church.

Chapelry. The limits of a chapel precinct.

Chaperon. A hood or bonnet. An escutcheon on the foreheads of horses that drew a hearse.

Chapitre. A brief statement of matters to be enquired into by justices of the Eyre, of assise, or the peace. The matters presented to the inquest by the justice.

Chapitres de Eyre. Chapters of the Eyre (which see).

Chapitus. Under old English law, a summary of matters to be presented to the justices in Eyre, of assise, or of peace, at their session. Charge to a grand jury by a judge.

Chaplain. A clergyman attached to a King, ship, regiment, or institution to perform religious service.

Chapman. A pedlar.

Chapter. A division of a book. A distinct enactment where the legislation of a whole session is considered.

Chapters of the Eyre. Chapters or schedules of inquiry embracing different crimes delivered to the justices itinerant, on behalf of the crown and read to the juries from the various hundreds, at the opening of the Eyre.

Character. The natural qualities or habits of a person. See REPUTATION.

Character, general. The estimation of a person in the community where he lives. Reputation.

Character, good. Good reputation for one or more good qualities. Good natural qualities.

Chare. A Plow.

Charette. A cart.

Charge. To accuse of an offence. To instruct in the law. To impose an obligation to pay money. To enter in an account a memorandum of money due. To place one under an obligation of knowing some fact or duty. A thing done that binds him that does it. A tax. A lien. In Scotch law, a written command of the crown and the instrument containing it.

Charge and discharge. The exhibition by complainant and respondent of their accounts against each other before a master.

Charge and specification. The allegation of guilt with a statement of the particular overt acts.

Charge, average. Charges determined by dividing the receipts by the tonnage carried, and obtaining the charge per ton per mile.

Charge, collateral. An obligation which descends with an estate and binds the heir or executor.

Charge d'affaires. A person in charge of the affairs of an embassy. The title of an inferior diplomatic representative, or minister of the fourth-class.

Charge, further. See FURTHER CHARGE.

Charge, general. The instruction of a judge to a jury upon the entire case.

Charge, over. See OVERCHARGE.

Charge, special. A charge made to a jury at the request of counsel upon some special point.

Charge to enter heir. In Scotch law, a writ directing a person to enter an heir to the possessions of his ancestor.

Chargeable. Capable of or subject to charge.

Chargeant. Heavy; weighty.

Charge-sheet. The police blotter or daily record of arrests and charges against prisoners.

Charges. Entries of money due. Incumbrances on property. Allegations of wrong. Expense of settling an estate. Allegations denying or avoiding as a defence in equity.

Charges, outward. Charges against a vessel for pilotage on leaving port.

Charging order. See ORDER, CHARGING.

Charging part. In a bill in Chancery, the allegation intended to anticipate the answer.

Charitable corporation. See CORPORATION, CHARITABLE.

Charitable use. See USE, CHARITABLE.

Charity. Acts of kindness and humanity. Relief given the poor.

Charks. Charred pit coal.

Charre. A quantity of lead consisting of thirty pigs or 2100 lbs.

Chart. A plan used by mariners at sea.

Charta. A charter or deed.

Charta chirographata (or Communis). An indenture. See CHARTA COMMUNIS.

Charta communis. A common or mutual charter or deed. A deed or charter containing mutual obligations, and to which both parties could refer to establish their respective rights.

Charta de confirmatione. A charter of confirmation.

Charta de feoffmento. A charter or deed of feoffment.

Charta de foresta. The charter (laws) of the forest. Statute 9, Hen. III. and 34 Ed. I., of England.

Charta de una parte. A charter or deed of one party or executed by one party only.

Charta de quiete clamantia. A charter or deed of quit-claim.

Charta indentata. A charter or deed indented.

Charter libertatem regni. The charter of the nation's liberty. Applied to Magna Charta as the grantor of liberty.

Charta (or carta) pardonationis. A charter or deed of pardon. A charter under the great seal by which a man is forgiven a felony or other offence against the crown.

Charta pardonationis se defendendo. A charter or pardon for defending one's self. A form or pardon for one who killed another in self-defence.

Charta-partita. Charter-party (which see).

Charta perelegem terræ. The charter by the law of the land.

Charta regia. A royal charter or grant.

Charta seu libellus prædialis. A charter or deed of land.

Chartæ communes. Common or mutual charters.

Chartas, articuli super. See ARTICULI SUPER CHARTAS.

Charte. The organic law of the French monarchy established on the restoration of Louis XVIII., in 1814.

Chartel. A letter of defiance or challenge to a single combat. An instrument writing for settling the exchange of prisoners of war.

Charte-partie. A charter-party.

Charter. Written evidence of things done between man and man. A grant of privilege. An act of incorporation. A power to establish a branch of an organization. The lease of a vessel. The act of leasing a vessel. An exemption. To hire. To establish.

Charter colony government. One established under a royal charter.

Charter by progress. One renewing a grant in favor of an heir or successor of a vassal.

Charter land. Free socage land. Tenemental land held by deed under certain rents and free services.

Charter master. In England, a coal mining contractor.

Charter member. One of the incorporators or organizers of a society or corporation.

Charter Oak. An oak tree at Hartford, Conn., in which, November, 1687, the charter of Connecticut, granted by Chas. II., of England, was hidden when James II. sent Sir Edmund Andros to resume the colony charters.

Charter of incorporation. The instrument evidence of the creation of a corporation.

Charter of pardon. A pardon under the Great Seal of England.

Charter of the forest. Same as CHARTA DE FORESTA.

Charter, original. In Scotch law, one by which land is first granted.

Charter party. An instrument writing among merchants and sea-faring men, setting forth the covenants or agreement between them regarding merchandise and maritime affairs. It states the terms as to the condition of the cargo of the ship and the freight, and binds the master to deliver the cargo in good condition at the place of consignment (dangers of the sea excepted). It need not be under seal.

Charter rolls. English records of royal charters granted from 1199 to 1516.

Charterage. The business of chartering vessels.

Chartered ship. A ship which has been secured by charter party.

Charterer. A freeholder. One who charters vessels.

Charters, articles upon the. See ARTICULI SUPER CHARTAS.

Chartis reddendis. An ancient writ against one who refused to deliver charters of feoffment entrusted to his keeping.

Chartophylax. A keeper of archives. A keeper of records or public instruments; a chartulary; a registrar.

Chartre. A charter.

Chartula. A little paper; a small writing.

Chartularius. A keeper of the archives of court. A chartophylax.

Chartulary. Same as CHARTULARIUS. A record in a monastery of its property; the official who keeps it and the room where it is kept.

Charue. A plow.

Chase. A large extent of open woods, less than a forest, and larger than a park, used for hunting. See PARK; also FOREST.

Chasea. A chase (which see).

Chaste. Pure in conduct. Abstaining from unlawful sexual intercourse.

Chastell. A castle.

Chastity. Moral purity. Refraining from unlawful sexual intercourse.

Chastity, solicitation of. Soliciting another to have unlawful sexual intercourse.

Chateaux. Chattels.

Chateux. Chattels.

Chateux meuble. Personal chattels.

Chateux meuble et inmeuble. Chattels movable and immovable.

Chattel interest. An interest less than a freehold, in corporeal hereditaments.

Chattel mortgage. See MORTGAGE, CHATTEL.

Chattels. All movable or immovable goods except such as are part of the freehold.

Chattels, goods and. See GOODS AND CHATTELS.

Chattels, incorporeal. See INCORPOREAL CHATTELS.

Chattels personal. Movable personal goods. Property which can be moved from place to place, not permanently fastened to realty. The condition of the property in its present state determines whether it be a real or personal chattel. A growing tree is part of the realty, but when cut down becomes personal property. This is true of other things.

Chattels real. Such as are annexed to or issue out of the realty.

Chaud-medley. The killing of a person in an affray in the heat of blood and while under the influence of passion. Distinguished from Chance-medley (which see).

Chaud-melle. Same as CHAUD-MEDLEY.

Chaumpert. A species of tenure.

Chaunger. Same as CHANGER.

Chauntry. A church or altar in a cathedral endowed with lands or revenues.

Chauntry lands. Lands which had been given to support a church.

Chauntry rents. Rents paid to the Crown by the servants, or purchaser of chauntry lands.

Chaux. Those.

Chaye. Fallen.

Cheapingavel. Same as CHIPPINGAVEL.

Cheat. To defraud; one who defrauds.

Cheaters. Escheaters.

Cheaunce. An accident, chance.

Checir. To fall; to abate.

Check. An order on a bank to pay a specified sum to the bearer, or person mentioned or the latter's order. See CHEQUE.

Check. To control. To restrain. To verify.

Check, certified. See CERTIFIED CHECK.

Check, memorandum. One given as an evidence of indebtedness to be taken up by the maker and not presented at a bank.

Check, raised. One fraudulently increased in amount.

Checker. A Scotch abbreviation for exchequer.

Check-roll. A book containing the names of the King's or a nobleman's household servants.

Chef. A head; the head.

Chef de la societe. The chief or president of the company or firm or society.

Chefe. A head; the head.

Chefe del an. The head or beginning of the year.

Cheir. To fall.

Chelindra. An ancient ship.

Chemerage. The privilege of the eldest.

Chemier. The eldest born.

Chemin. A way, or right of way.

Chemis. In Scotch law, a dwelling-house.

Cheque. A written order on a bank to pay a specified sum of money. See CHECK.

Chescun. Every one; every.

Cheser. To fall.

Chester. Same as CASTER.

Chet. To fall.

Chevage. A money tribute paid those holding land by villenage to their lords. A sum paid a chief for protection. See CHEV-AGIUM.

Chevagium. Head money; chevage. A sum of money formerly paid by villeins to their lords in acknowledgement of their bondage. It was also exacted in England of the Jews annually at Easter. A sum of money annually given for protection, to a head chief.

Chevalier. A knight, a military dignity.

Chevalier d'industrie. A knight of industry.

Chevantia. An advance of money on credit.

Chevisance. Anciently, an unlawful bargain. A perfecting of a bargain; an agreement or composition; a making of a bargain.

Cheviscal. Same as CHEVITIÆ.

Chevitiæ. The heads at the ends of plowed land.

Cheze. A mansion house.

Chi apres. Hereinafter.

Chicane. Swindling.

Chief. Principal. Leading. One before or above others.

Chief Baron. The presiding judge in the Court of Exchequer.

Chief, declaration in. A declaration for the chief cause of action.

Chief, examination in. Same as EX-AMINATION, DIRECT.

Chief Executive. The head executive office of a State or government.

Chief Justice. The presiding Judge of an Appellate Court. The presiding justice.

Chief Justice of England. The chief justice of the King's (Queen's) Bench.

Chief justiciar. The presiding judge of the Aula Regis, who was also Minister of State, and guardian of the kingdom in the King's absence.

Chief, in. First; direct; opposed to second or cross.

Chief lord. The highest lord of the fee.

Chief-pledge. The head of a decenary; a head-borow.

Chief-rents. The rents of freeholders of manors; quit rents, because free of other services.

Chief, tenants in. Tenants in capite, those holding immediately under the King or chief lord.

Chief Warden of the Forest. See FOREST, CHIEF WARDEN OF.

Chiefage. Same as CHEVAGE.

Chiefrie. A small rent payable by a feudal tenant to the lord paramount.

Chievance. Usury.

Child. An infant. A minor. Legitimate offspring.

Childhood. The period between infancy and puberty.

Childwit. A fine on a bondwoman who has unlawfully begotten a child. A fine paid the lord by the reputed father of a bastard.

Children's part. Same as ORPHANAGE PART.

Childwite. Same as CHILDWIT.

Chiltern hundreds. The hundreds of Stoke, Desborough, and Bonenham, England, at one time the resort of robbers which a steward was appointed to suppress. The stewardship is a nominal office, and as a member of Parliament can not resign during his term, but acceptance of a civil office vacates his seat, it is usually given to a member of the House of Commons who desires to retire.

Chimin. The King's highway; a private way; a way, or right of way.

Chimin appendant. A right of way to and from a closed field or pasture.

Chiminage. A toll due by custom for having a way through a forest.

Chiminus reginæ. The Queen's highway.

Chimney corner survey. One not made on the land.

Chimney-money. Hearth money ; a duty paid to the Crown for every hearth in a house.

Chinese. Natives of China.

Chinese Exclusion Act. Act of U. S. Congress, approved Oct. 1, 1888, prohibiting the entering of Chinese laborers into the U. S.

Chinese Restriction Act. Act of U. S. Congress, May 6, 1882.

Chipp. When used as a prefix to an English town signified it was a market town.

Chippingavel. An old toll for buying and selling.

Chirchgemot. A meeting in a church.

Chirgemot. Same as CHIRCHGEMOT.

Chirograph. Hand-writing. The chirographum of the Saxons or charter of the Normans. A public instrument of conveyance. A word written between a bipartite deed through which the wavering or indented line was cut.

Chirographa. Hand-writings.

Chirographer. An officer of the Common Pleas who engrossed fines or agreements which put an end to suits over land. See FINE OF LANDS.

Chirographum. A chirograph. A deed executed in two parts with "chirographum" or certain other words written in the middle, and divided, through those words, into two parts. The written evidence of a debt, or obligation.

Chirographus or chirographarius finium et concordiarum. A chirographer of fines and agreements or acknowledgments.

(11)

Chirurgeon. An ancient name of a surgeon.

Chivage. Same as CHEVAGE.

Chivalry. A tenure by knight's service.

Chivalry common. Knight service to other than the King.

Chivalry regal. Knight service to the King.

Chocaunt. Lying down. Same as COUCHANT.

Chop church. An old term applied to those who exchanged benefices.

Chops. The mouth of a harbor.

Choral. One who was anciently allowed to sit in the choir of a church.

Chorepiscopus. A rural bishop, or bishop's vicar.

Chose. A thing. The word is joined to other words to express its meaning.

Chose in action. An incorporeal thing. A right in action. A right to demand by action.

Chose in possession. A right to possession and also the actual possession.

Chose local. A thing annexed to a place, as a mill.

Chose transitory. A thing which can be moved from place to place.

Chosen freeholder. See FREEHOLDER, CHOSEN.

Chrenecruda. The procedure, under Salic law, by a person unable to pay his debts or fines, of making a rich relative liable for the same. It comprised an application to the relative and the throwing of green herbs upon him. This latter was the completion of the contract and the relative was bound for the obligation.

Chrism. Oil and balsam used in baptism, confirmation, and ordination.

Chrismale. A cloth laid over a child's head in certain forms of baptism.

Chrismatis denarii. Money at one time paid a bishop by parochial clergy for a chrism consecrated.

Christian. One who is a member of the Christian religion.

Christian name. See NAME, CHRISTIAN.

Christiani-Judaizantes. Judaizing-Christians.

Christianissimus. See DEFENDER OF THE FAITH.

Christianitatis curia. The Court Christian or Ecclesiastical Court.

Christianity. The doctrines of the Christians.

Christmas day. The 25th of December.

Chronicon pretiosum. The title of a work showing the value of money at different periods in English history.

Church. A building consecrated by a bishop in which to hold divine worship; until consecrated, it is not legally a church. The clerical body as distinguished from the laity; ecclesiastical authority. The society which professes a religion.

Church-ale. A wake or feast in commemoration of the consecration of a church.

Church-rates. Those for the payment of the church expenses; at one time compulsory.

Church reeves. Same as CHURCH WARDENS.

Church wardens. Officers of the church. The legal representatives of a parish and a corporation by custom.

Churchesset. Corn paid to the church.

Churchscot. Oblation paid to a parish priest.

Churle. A ceorle; a carl; a tenant at will who held land for rent or services. There were two sorts; one hired tenementary estate, the other tilled and manured the demesnes, yielding work not rent. The latter were called Socmen.

Ci. So.

Ci dieu vous eyde (aide). So help you God.

Ci dieu moy eyde (aide). So help me God.

Cibatus. Victualled.

Ciens. Here; hitherto.

Cieus. Those; such.

Cil. He.

Cingulum. One of the six garments worn by a priest.

Cink. Five.

Cinque ports. (Five ports). Originally five (now seven) ports on the S. E. coast of England, nearest France, which received important privileges for furnishing a large number of warships and men-at-arms to the King. They are Romney, Dover, Sandwich, Hastings, Hythe, Winchelsea and Rye.

Cipher. Characters understood only by those who use them. A key to such characters.

Cippi. The stocks.

Cipps. The stocks.

Circa. About, concerning, respecting; in relation to.

Circa horam. About or within the hour. Formerly in stating an hour when a fact took place; "circa horam" was sufficient; but not so as to a day, which had to be stated with precision.

Circada. A tribute anciently paid a bishop or archdeacon for visiting a church.

Circuit Court. See COURT, CIRCUIT.

Circuit Court of Appeals of U. S. See COURT OF APPEALS OF U. S., CIRCUIT.

Circuit paper. A written statement of the time and place they will be held and other information relating to assises.

Circuits. Certain divisions of a country to which judges go to hold court.

Circuitus verborum. Circuity of words.

Circuity. Indirect method, course, or action.

Circuity of action. An indirect course of action.

Circular. Going around. A printed statement for general distribution.

Circular note. Same as LETTERS OF CREDIT.

Circulating medium. The medium of exchange, whether money or articles used as money.

Circulation. That which goes from one person to another. The act of going from one to another.

Circumduction. In Scotch law, the end of the time given to file papers or do any other act in a cause.

Circumduction of the term. In Scotch law, the announcement of a judge that the time within which proof should have been given has elapsed.

Circumspecte agatis. Act circumspectly, cautiously, considerately. The initial word or title of the statute 13 Edw. I. St. 4, A. D. 1285, prescribing to the judges some cases relating to prohibitions.

Circumstances. Facts. Incidental or subordinate facts. Means. Influences. A person's status.

Circum stantia (circumstantia). Facts standing around. A circumstance.

Circumstantial. Relating to facts. Made up of circumstances alone.

Circumstantial evidence. Evidence made up of circumstances other than direct testimony of witnesses.

Circumstantias. Circumstances.

Circumstantibus. Among the standers around, the bystanders. A word signifying the completion of a jury from qualified bystanders.

Circumstantibus, tales de. So many of the bystanders. A writ to the sheriff to make up from bystanders the number necessary to complete a jury.

Circumvention. Deceit, fraud, stratagem, imposition. Deceit practiced to induce one to perform some act.

Ciric-bryce. A violation of church privileges.

Ciric sceat. An ancient church contribution payable on the day of St. Martin, usually in corn.

Cirographum. A chirograph which see.

Cirographatum. Chirographed in the form of a chirograph.

Cista. A box or chest for containing charters, deeds, or other things.

Citacion. In Spanish law, a judicial summons to a defendant to appear and answer the allegations of a plaintiff.

Citatio. A citation or summons to court.

Citatio ad reassumendam causam. A citation for resuming or reviving a cause. The teste of a summons which issued when a party died pending a suit, against the heir of the defendant or plaintiff, as the case might be.

Citation. A judicial paper directed to an officer to be served by him. A judicial summons or order. An authority cited to sustain a proposition.

Citation, edictal. In Scotch law, a judicial citation made on a foreigner having lands in Scotland, or a Scotchman living abroad.

Cite. To summon. To notify to appear. To refer to in support of a proposition.

Citizen. One who is a legal subject of a government. In U. S. one born within the jurisdiction, or made a citizen by law. In Roman law, one who had the freedom of a city and the right to exercise civil and political rights. In England, an inhabitant of a city.

Citizen, complete. In Roman law, one having both civil and political rights.

Citizen, naturalized. One who has been made a citizen by law.

Citizen, partial. In Roman law, one having civil but not political rights.

Citizenship. The condition of a citizen.

Citra. Without.

Citra causæ cognitionem. Without a judicial examination or cognizance of the cause.

City. An incorporated town.

City officer. See OFFICER, CITY.

City purpose. For its improvement.

City warrant. See WARRANT, CITY.

Civic. Relating to a city or citizen.

Civics. The science which treats of the relations between citizens and the government.

Civil. Pertaining to a citizen and a State. Established by law. Opposed to criminal, military, ecclesiastical, political or natural. Occurring within a state or between citizens.

Civil action. An action or suit between private persons.

Civil assembly. See ASSEMBLY, CIVIL.

Civil cognation. See COGNATION, CIVIL.

Civil commotion. See COMMOTION, CIVIL.

Civil damage acts. Same as LAWS, CIVIL DAMAGE.

Civil damage laws. See LAWS, CIVIL DAMAGE.

Civil death. The extinction of a person's legal rights in consequence of being outlawed, or attainted, or entering a monastery, &c.

Civil disability. See DISABILITY, CIVIL.

Civil embargo. See EMBARGO, CIVIL.

Civil injury. A wrong which affects an individual as an individual. See INJURY, CIVIL.

Civil law. See LAW, CIVIL.

Civil liberty. Liberty of the individual to conduct his own affairs as he sees fit; subject only to the rights of others and the law of the land.

Civil life. See LIFE, CIVIL.

Civil list. The appropriation in the U. S. for the expenses of the government; in England, for the expenses of the royal household and establishment. The list of civil causes in a court.

Civil marriage. See MARRIAGE, CIVIL.

Civil month. See MONTH, CIVIL.

Civil obligation. Same as OBLIGATION LEGAL.

Civil office. See OFFICE, CIVIL.

Civil officer. See OFFICER, CIVIL.

Civil polity. The method and machinery of the government.

Civil possession. See POSSESSION, CIVIL.

Civil process. A writ or order in a civil suit.

Civil rebellion. See REBELLION, CIVIL.

Civil remedy. See REMEDY, CIVIL.

Civil responsibility. See RESPONSIBILITY, CIVIL.

Civil rights. See RIGHTS, CIVIL.

Civil Rights Acts. Acts of Congress creating and extending civil rights to all citizens without regard to race, color, or previous condition. These acts were based on the 14th Amendment of the Constitution.

Civil Rights cases. Cases before the Federal courts which arose under the 14th Amendment and the Civil Rights Acts.

Civil sanctuary. See SANCTUARY, CIVIL.

Civil service. See SERVICE, CIVIL.

Civil Service Commission. A commission appointed by the President of the U. S. to execute the Civil Service Law.

Civil Service Law. See LAW, CIVIL SERVICE.

Civil side. The civil jurisdiction of a court having both civil and criminal jurisdiction.

Civil state. The whole people organized under law and government.

Civil status. Condition with respect to being of age, married or unmarried, legitimate or illegitimate.

Civil war. See WAR, CIVIL.

Civilia placita. Civil pleas.

Civilian. One learned in the Civil law. One not belonging to the army or navy.

Civilis. Civil, as distinguished from criminal.

Civilis actio. A civil action.

Civilis causa. A civil cause.

Civilis injuriæ. Civil injuries.

Civilista. A civil lawyer or civilian.

Civiliter. Civilly.

Civiliter mortuus. Civilly dead; dead in law.

Civilization. A law or judgment which converts a criminal proceeding into a civil one. An improved condition of a people.

Civilize. To transfer to the civil from the military or criminal jurisdiction.

Civilly. In accordance with civil procedure, as distinguished from criminal and military.

Civis. In the Roman law, a citizen as distinguished from incola.

Civitas. Peoples living under the same laws. The law of a State. The civil law. Citizenship. In old English law, a city.

Civitatis jura. The laws of a city or State; civil law.

Claim. To demand as a right. A challenge of the ownership of property that one has not in possession, but which is detained by wrong. A demand as of right, or of anything due. A mechanic's or other lien. A tract of land taken up under the U. S. public land laws.

Claim, adverse. A claim in conflict with that of another. See POSSESSION, ADVERSE.

Claim, affidavit of. See AFFIDAVIT OF CLAIM.

Claim bond. See BOND, CLAIM.

Claim, continual. In old English law, a claim for land made at least once within each year and a day in the vicinity of the land, by one who was kept from entry thereon through force or threats.

Claim, counter. A contrary claim.

Claim, cross. See CROSS CLAIM.

Claim, non. Neglect to assert a claim within a legal time.

Claim, mining. See MINING CLAIM.

Claim of cognizance. Same as CLAIM OF CONUSANCE.

Claim of conusance. An ancient claim of jurisdiction over a cause which the plaintiff had begun out of the claimant's court.

Claim of liberty. A petition to the King in the Court of Exchequer to have liberties and franchises confirmed there by the Attorney-General.

Claim of title. A claim to the title of property. As to what is must be determined from the facts in the case.

Claim, placer. See PLACER CLAIM.

Claim, quit. See QUIT CLAIM.

Claimant. Anciently, the plaintiff in the action of ejectment. One who makes a claim.

Claimant, pre-emption. See PRE-EMPTION CLAIMANT.

Claimant's bond. Same as BOND, CLAIM.

Claims, municipal. See MUNICIPAL CLAIMS.

Clam. Hidden; secretly, covertly, clandestinely.

Clamantem et auditum infra quatuor parietes. Crying and being heard within the four walls. An expression applied where a man married a woman, seized in fee, and a child was born, which had been heard to cry. The mother being alive at the birth and the child being capable of inheriting, gave the father an inchoate right as tenant in courtesy.

Clamans. Claiming.

Clamantis. Of, from, or by claiming.

Clamare. To cry out; to claim.

Clamea. A claim.

Clamea admittenda in itinere per attornatum. An ancient writ directing the justices in Eyre to admit the claim of a person in King's service to appear by attorney.

Clameum. A claim.

Clameus. A claim.

Clamo. To claim; to demand or challenge; to assert a right to a thing.

Clamor. A claim or suit. A complaint; clamor. A cry or outcry. The cry of a newly born babe. A proclamation, an accusation.

Clamor de haro. The Norman expression for pursuit and cry after offenders.

Clamor patriæ. The cry of the country, "the hue and cry." See HUE AND CRY.

Clamor pro hutesios. A complaint by outcry.

Clamor popularis. The cry of the people.

Clare. Clearly, brightly, intelligibly, distinctly, illustriously.

Clare constat. In Scotch law, a precept for giving seizin of lands to an heir.

Claregarius armorum. A herald at arms.

Claremethen. In Scotch law, the warranty of stolen goods or cattle. The law relating to such warranty.

Clarendon, Constitutions of. See CONSTITUTIONS OF CLARENDON; also ASSISE OF CLARENDON.

Claretum. A liquor made of wine and honey. See HIPPOCRAS.

Clarificatio. A glorification. In old Scotch law, a making clear; the purging or clearing of an assise.

Clarificatio debiti. The clearness of a debt established.

Clarifico. To make illustrious or famous. In Scotch law, the same as CLARIFICATIO.

Clario. A trumpet.

Class. A body of persons with like characteristics, or in the same occupation, or having a common purpose, or in similar circumstances.

Classes, criminal. See CRIMINAL CLASSES.

Classiarius. A seaman or sea soldier.

Claud. A ditch.

Claudere. To enclose open fields. To close, finish or end.

Clause. Close. A sentence or part of a law, an instrument writing, or written or printed document.

Clause, American. See AMERICAN CLAUSE.

Clause, attestation. See ATTESTATION CLAUSE.

Clause, caducial. See CADUCIAL CLAUSE.

Clause, derogatory. See DEROGATORY CLAUSE.

Clause, guarantee. See GUARANTEE CLAUSE.

Clause, interpretation. See INTERPRETATION CLAUSE.

Clause, irritant. In Scotch law, that clause in a deed which declares void the acts contrary to the tenancy by which the estate is held.

Cause, memorandum. See MEMORANDUM CLAUSE; also MEMORANDUM ARTICLES.

Clause of accruer. See ACCRUER, CLAUSE OF.

Clause of forfeiture. The clause in a contract which provides that on default, a specified sum shall be paid as penalty. A clause which provides that a subject-matter of a deed or contract shall be forfeited on certain conditions.

Clause of novadamus. See NOVADAMUS, CLAUSE OF.

Clause, onerous. See ONEROUS CLAUSE.

Clause, overreaching. See OVERREACHING CLAUSE.

Clause, potestative. In French law, the clause in a contract in which one party reserves the right to annul it.

Clause, precatory. See PRECATORY CLAUSE.

Clause, residuary. The clause in a will, devise or testament which disposes of, or directs the disposition of, what remains after previous legacies have been satisfied.

Clause, resolutive. In Scotch law, that clause in a deed which extinguishes the right of a person committing an act prohibited by the irritant clause, or any act contrary to the conditions upon which the estate is granted.

Clause rolls. Same as CLOSE ROLLS.

Clause, rotten. A clause in a contract for insurance of a ship providing that, if the ship on inspection shall be found unseaworthy, because rotten, the insurers shall be released of the obligation.

Clause, saving. One which excludes or exempts from the operation of a law or instrument writing.

Clause, sharp. See SHARP CLAUSE.

Clause, shifting. See SHIFTING CLAUSE.

Clause, sue and labor. See SUE AND LABOR CLAUSE.

Clause, sweeping. See SWEEPING CLAUSE.

Claustura. An inclosure or that which bounds it; a barrier around a field. Brushwood for fences or hedges.

Clausula. A clause; sentence.

Clausula ancillaris. An ancillary, auxiliary, subservient clause.

Clausula de non obstante de futuro. A clause of notwithstanding the future.

Clausula derogatoria. A derogatory clause; a clause that derogates.

Clausula inutilis. A useless or inoperative clause.

Clausula non obstante. A clause notwithstanding.

Clausum. A close; an e n c l o s u r e. Close, as applied to writs, &c. See CLOSE.

Clausum fregit. He broke the close; a cause of action for breaking a close.

Clausum Paschæ. The close of Easter. The eighth day after the feast of Easter.

Clausura. An inclosure.

Clausura heyæ. The inclosure of a hedge.

Clausure. An inclosure.

Claves. Keys.

Claves curiæ. The keys of the court. In old Scotch law, a term applied to the officers of a court; the sergeant, clerk and dempster or doomster.

Claves insulæ. The keys of the island. Applied to twelve persons on the Isle of Man to whom weighty matters were referred.

Clavia. A club or mace.

Clavigeratus. A treasurer of a church.

Clawa. A small enclosure.

Clayton-Bulwer Treaty. A treaty between the U. S. and Great Britain, signed by their agents respectively, John M. Clayton and Henry Lytton Bulwer, dated April 19, 1850. It related to the proposed Nicaragua canal and stipulated among other things that neither country should ever obtain or maintain for itself any exclusive control over the said canal, and that neither should ever erect or maintain any fortifications commanding the same or in the vicinity thereof, or occupy, or fortify or colonize or assume or exercise any dominion over Nicaragua, Costa Rica, the Mosquito coast or any part of Central America.

Clean bill of health. See HEALTH, CLEAN BILL OF.

Clean hands. An expression meaning free from illegality, injustice, &c., in the matter of a claim.

Clear. To be free from. Beyond doubt.

Clear days. The days between and exclusive of the dates mentioned. When anything is to be done, in a certain number of clear days, the first day as well as the last day is included.

Clear land. To remove timber and underbrush, leaving the stumps.

Clearance. A certificate from the authorities that a vessel has complied with the law and has leave to sail. The granting of a clearance certificate.

Clearance certificate. One which permits a vessel to leave or clear from a port.

Clearing. The settlement between banks arising through interchange of checks, etc. A tract of forest land after the trees are removed.

Clearing House. An office established by the bankers of a city where their representatives meet daily to exchange checks, drafts, etc., and adjust balances.

Clearly. Without uncertainty or doubt.

Clementinæ constitutiones. Constitutions of Pope Clement.

Clementis Papæ Constitutiones. Constitutions of Pope Clement.

Clement's Inn. An English Chancery Inn.

Clenging. In Scotch law, a purging or clearing.

Clere. Clear, confident.

Clerement. Clearly.

Clergy. The body of ecclesiastics ; ministers of a religion as a body.

Clergy, benefit of. See BENEFIT OF CLERGY.

Clergyable. Relating to or admitting of benefit of clergy.

Cleri, articuli. See ARTICULI CLERI.

Clerical error. An error in writing.

Clerical tonsure. The shaving of the head; so-called from being once peculiar to all clerks and clergymen.

Clericale privilegium. The clerical privilege; the privilege or benefit of clergy. See BENEFIT OF CLERGY.

Clericalis. Clerical, priestly.

Clericatus. The clerical office.

Clerici. Clerks, clergymen.

Clerici de cancellaria. Clerks of the Chancery.

Clerici de cursu. Clerks of course, or in the usual course. Clerks whose business it was to make out the common writs or writs of course (de cursu). See CLERICI DE SECUNDA FORMA.

Clerici de majori gradu. Clerks of the higher grade.

Clerici de prima forma. Clerks of the first form or rank. The chief clerks of Chancery.

Clerici de primo gradu. Same as CLERICI DE PRIMA FORMA.

Clerici de secunda forma. Clerks of the second form or grade. Called in the Stat. Westm. II., Clerici de Cursu, and afterward Cursitores. They were charged with making out writs de cursu.

Clerici prænotarii. The six clerks in Chancery.

Clerici primi gradus. Clerks of the first grade.

Clericum admittendum. Admitting a clerk. See BREVE DE CLERICUM ADMITTENDUM.

Clericus. A clerk or priest. A person who could write. A clerk of a court; an officer who issued writs or enrolled pleas.

Clericus et custos rotulorum. Clerk and keeper of the rolls.

Clericus mercati. Clerk of the market.

Clericus mercati hospitii regis. The clerk of the market at the King's gate. An ancient official who had general supervision over markets at a time when they were located near the court of the King.

Clericus parochialis. A parish clerk.

Clericus parvæ bagæ, et custos rotulorum, et domus conversorum. Clerk of the petty bag, and keeper of the rolls, and of the house of the converts. Applied to the Master of the Rolls.

Clericus sacerdotis. The priest's clerk.

Clerimonia. Clergy, or the privilege of clergy.

Clerk. A secular priest. One who could read and write. A person employed to keep records. A person employed to do writing.

Clerk, articled. See ARTICLED CLERK

Clerk, district. See DISTRICT CLERK.

Clerk of Courts. In Pennsylvania, the chief clerk of Oyer and Terminer and Quarter Sessions.

Clerk of a Court. An officer of a court, whose duty comprised entering and keeping its records and seal, issuing summons and processes, certifying to copies, &c.

Clerk of the Crown. Chief official of the Crown office in Chancery. (Anciently, Clerk of the Hamper).

Clerk of the Estreats. The officer of Exchequer who received estreats for the Remembrancer's office and wrote them out to be served.

Clerk of the Hamper. An officer in Chancery who received all the fees due the King.

Clerk of the Hanaper. Same as CLERK OF THE HAMPER.

Clerk of the House of Commons. One of the chief officers of the lower House of Parliament.

Clerk of the Market. The superintendent of a public market. Anciently in England, he had certain judicial jurisdiction over controversies arising within the market.

Clerk of the Nihils. One who entered such sums as the sheriff returned nihil, &c., in Exchequer.

Clerk of the Parliaments. One of the chief officers of the House of Lords.

Clerk of the Peace. In England, an officer whose duties are to officiate at sessions of the peace, prepare indictments, &c.

Clerk of the Pell. An officer of exchequer, so called from his parchment roll, pellis receptorum.

Clerk of the Pleas. An officer in whose office persons filed their pleas.

Clerk of the Pipe. An officer of exchequer through whose custody were conveyed (as water through a pipe) all account and debts due the King.

Clerks of Assise. Officers who take the place of the associates or masters on the circuits, and also record the judicial proceedings.

Clerks of Records and Writs. English officers of the Court of Chancery. (The office is now abolished).

Clerks of Seats. Clerks who prepare the grants of probate and letters of administration in the principal registry of the probate division, England.

Clerks, six. See SIX CLERKS.

Clerkship. The time spent by a student at law in the office of an attorney before being eligible to examination for admission to the bar. At one time, the art of drawing pleadings and entering them in Latin in the court hand. An office where the duties are those of a clerk.

Cleronimus. An heir.

Cleronomy. An individual inheritance.

Cleruch. An Athenian who resided in conquered lands.

Clerus. The clergy.

Client. One receiving the protection of another. One for whom a lawyer acts professionally.

Clientage. Clients, as a body.

Clientela. The state of a client, clientship, protection, patronage, guardianship. Applied also to the relation of a church to its patrons.

Cliff. A Saxon word which when beginning or ending names signifies a rock.

Clifford's Inn. An English Inn of Chancery.

Clito. The son of a King. See CLITONES.

Clitones. The eldest and all the sons of Kings.

Clive. Same as CLIFF.

Cloaca. The worst part of a prison.

Cloacerius. An office imposed on an offending brother of a religious house.

Cloere. A prison or dungeon.

Close. To terminate. To fill. To obstruct. To bring together. To enclose. To shut up. To come to an agreement. Limited. Not public. A piece of land surrounded by a fence, or an invisible boundary existing in law only. A term applied to private or close writs and letters as distinguished from those that were open or patent.

Close copies. Copies of documents which were not required to be confined to any particular number of words to the page.

Close hauled. In Admiralty law, the arrangement of a vessel's sails, so she can sail in the direction from which the wind blows, by the shortest route.

Close port. See PORT, CLOSE.

Close rolls. The record of letters or writs of the King which were sealed and directed to particular persons as distinguished from open letters or patents.

Close writs. Private and sealed writs directed by the King to particular persons and not intended for the public. They are recorded in the Close rolls.

Closed sea. See SEA, CLOSED.

Closh. Skittles; at one time prohibited by English law.

Clothe. To invest.

Cloture. The method of closing debate in a deliberative body.

Cloud. A claim, whether good or bad.

Clough. A valley. An allowance to turn the scale.

Clove. A quantity of cheese weighing eight pounds.

Club law. Force used as a means of redress.

Clubs. Associations of persons for various purposes.

Cluta. Horse shoes. Iron coverings for tires.

Clypei prostrati. A noble family extinct.

Clypeus. A shield. One of a noble family.

Cnafa. A knave.

Cnyt. A knight.

Co. Abbreviation of company; also county. With; together; complete.

Co-adjutor. A fellow helper; an assistant.

Co-administrator. One who is administrator with another or others.

Co-adunatio. A uniting of persons together; a combination or conspiracy.

Coal note. A promissory note at one time used in London, Eng., containing the phrase "value received in coals."

Coalition. In French law, an agreement between two or more not to do a thing except on a condition agreed upon. A conspiracy.

Co-assignee. One of two or more assignees of the same matter.

Coast. The land on the edge of a country bordering on the sea.

Coast and Geodetic Survey. A bureau of the U. S. Government charged with the survey of the Atlantic, Gulf, and Pacific coasts of the U. S. and the survey of rivers to the head of tide water or navigation. Its work includes sounding and observations of temperature and currents.

Coasting trade. Trade carried on in navigable waters within the jurisdiction of one and the same government.

Coastwise. Along the coast.

Coastwise vessel. See VESSEL, COASTWISE.

Coat of arms. See ARMS, COAT OF.

Cocherings. A tribute in Ireland. See BONAGHT.

Cockbill. To put the yards of a ship at an angle with the deck.

Cocket. A seal belonging to the King's Custom House; a certificate that customs have been paid ; to give such certificate ; a place where imported goods are first entered. A kind of bread. A measure.

Cockettare. To Cocket.

Cockettari. To be cocketted; to be furnished with a certificate that goods are customed.

Cockettum. In old English law, a cocket. A seal belonging to the custom house. A piece of parchment, sealed and delivered by the officers of the custom house, to merchants, as a warranty that their merchan dises are customed.

Cockpit. The old name for the Judicial Committee of the Privy Council, so called because the room where it sat was on the site of the old cockpit of Whitehall.

Cocksetus. A boatman; a cockswain.

Cocula. A cup in the form of a boat.

Code. A system of law. A systematic body of law enacted by a legislature and intended to take the place of all other law within the jurisdiction. A system of signals. The explanation of a cipher. In Civil and Roman law, a classified collection of laws.

Code, Alfred's. An alleged compilation of laws made by Alfred the Great, A. D. 887.

Code, Amalfitan. The oldest existing code of Admiralty law, compiled in the 11th century by the merchants and magistrates of Amalfi, an Italian seaport.

Code, Black. The laws regulating the colored race in the South of the United States before their freedom. See CODE NOIR.

Code, Burgundian. A collection of Roman laws for the government of the Roman subjects of the Burgundians, compiled between 517 and 523 A. D.

Code, Civil. A code relating to civil rights and remedies. The Code Napoleon (which see).

Code, Criminal. A code defining crimes and fixing the punishment for the commission thereof.

Code de procedure civil. That part of the Code Napoleon which relates to the courts and the procedure therein.

Code, Eaton. A collection of laws made by Governor Eaton by authority of the General Court of New Haven Colony. First published in 1656 in London.

Code, Gregorian. A collection of Roman laws covering a period between 196 and 295 A. D.; compiled by Gregory about 300 A. D.

Code, Gentoo. The laws of the Hindus translated while Warren Hastings was Governor-General of India.

Code, Hermogenian. A code of Roman laws supposed to be from 287 to 304 A. D. named after Hermogenianus, a Roman jurist.

Code, Justinian. See CODEX JUSTINIANEUS.

Code, Ludlow's. Same as CODE OF 1650.

Code, Mosaic. See LAW, MOSAIC.

Code Napoleon. The civil code of France prepared by direction of Napoleon, I., 1803–10. It was the first of six codes, the last of which was compiled in 1827.

Code Noir. The edict of Louis XIX. of France, in 1685, regulating the West Indian colonies and the treatment of the negroes there.

Code of Frederick the Great. A codification of Prussian laws made by Frederick the Great in 1751.

Code of Honor. The rules of duellists.

Code of 1650. A complication of the early laws of New Haven colony also called Ludlow's Code.

Code, Papian. See CODES, BARBARIAN.

Code, penal. Same as CODE, CRIMINAL.

Code pleading. A method of pleading substituted for the common law pleading, used in several American States. It has no particular form and varies in different States.

Code, Rhodian. See LAWS, RHODIAN.

Code, The. Same as CODE OF HONOR.

Code, The New. See THE NEW CODE.

Code, The Old. See THE OLD CODE.

Code, Theodosian. A collection of Roman laws from the time of Constantine to that of Theodosius II. It comprises 16 books and was first published in 438 A. D.

Co-defendant. See DEFENDANT, CO.

Codes, Barbarian. The laws made by Gothic tribes on Roman territory. They comprised Breviary of Alaric, Papian Code and Edict of Theodoric.

Codes, Field. Codes compiled by a commission of which David Dudley Field of New York was a member and named for him. Some of the ideas of these codes have been adopted in other States.

Codex. The trunk of a tree, the stock, the stem. A book, a volume, a roll, a writing. A code of laws ; a body of laws ; a collection or compilation of laws by public authority.

Codex Gregorianus. See CODE, GREGORIAN.

Codex Hermogenianus. See CODE, HERMOGENIAN.

Codex Theodosianus. See CODE, THEODOSIAN.

Codex Justinianeus. The Code of Justinian. So called by Justinian himself to distinguish it from the Code of Theodosius. It is a collection of imperial constitutions in twelve books compiled by Tribonian and nine associates, under the direction of Justinian, A. D. 529. This code was the first of the four collections of laws which make up the Corpus Juris Civilis.

Codex Repetitæ Prælectionis. The New Code. The new edition of the Code of Justinian, issued A. D. 534. See CODEX JUSTINIANEUS.

Codex Vetus. The Old Code. The first edition of Codex Justinianeus (which see).

Codicil. A supplement to a will.

Codicilli. A writing of the Emperor, a diploma, a cabinet order. An individual, testamentary order ; an addition, appendix to a will ; a codicil.

Codicillus. A codicil.

Codification. The act of compiling a code of laws. The reducing of laws to a systematic form.

Codifier. One who compiles a code.

Codify. To compile a code.

Co-emptio. In Roman law, the sale of a wife to a husband.

Co-emption. The act of buying all of any community.

Co-emptores terrarum. Mutual purchasers of lands. Statute 18 Eliz. 1.

Cœna, adventicia. See ADVENTICIA CŒNA.

Coercion. Duress.

Coercion, direct. Same as COERCION, POSITIVE.

Coercion, implied. That cœrcion which the law implies from the relation of the parties, as a wife assisting her husband in an act.

Coercion, legal. Same as COERCION, IMPLIED.

Coercion, positive. Coercion by physical force.

Co-executor. One who is executor with another or others.

Cofra. A chest or trunk.

Cofrada. An organization for performing religious work.

Cofferer. An officer of the King's household next under the controller.

Coggle. A small fishing boat.

Cognates. In the Civil law, relations by the mother's side, or through females.

Cognati. In the Civil law, relations by the mother's side; cognates.

Cognatio. In the Canon law, consanguinity as distinguished from affinity. In the Common law, kindred by blood; consanguinity.

Cognatio a latere. Relationship from the side ; collateral consanguinity. Relationship which exists between persons who are descended from the same stock or ancestor, as between two brothers from the same father, or two cousins from the same grandfather, as distinguished from lineal consanguinity, in which the relatives are descended the one from the other.

Cognation. The relationship, in Civil law, between two persons of the same blood.

Cognation, civil. One which results from family ties only.

Cognation, mixed. One resulting from both family and blood ties.

Cognation, natural. That resulting from blood only.

Cognatione. A writ of cosenage. See COSENAGE.

Cognatus. Relation. A relation by the mother's side.

Cognisance. Same as COGNIZANCE.

Cognisee. He to whom a fine of lands was acknowledged.

Cognisor. He that acknowledged a fine of lands to another.

Cognitio. The acknowledgement of a fine; jurisdiction; cognizance.

Cognitio de famosis libellis. A judicial examination as to an infamous libel.

Cognitio inter patrem et filium. A judicial examination between father and son.

Cognitio placitum. Cognizance of pleas.

Cognitio placitorum. Jurisdiction of pleas. Judicial power of a court.

Cognitione. Ensigns and arms or a military coat mounted with arms.

Cognitionibus admittendis. For admitting cognitions or certifying the taking of fines. In old English law, a writ directing one who had taken fines and neglected to certify the same to the Court of Common Pleas, to so do.

Cognitionibus mittendis. A writ commanding a certification of a fine of lands.

Cognitionis causa. For cognizance or jurisdiction. For the purpose of investigating judicially.

Cognitor. One who acknowledges ; a cognizor, or conusor. In civil law, an advocate who appeared for another.

Cognitura. In Roman law, a fiscal agent, who searched for unknown debtors of the treasury. The attorneyship of the State.

Cognizance. An acknowledgement of a fine. An answer of a bailiff who has made a distress. An exclusive right to try causes ; a privilege granted to a city or town which may be pleaded to oust jurisdiction of another court ; jurisdiction ; judicial power.

Cognizance, claim of. See CLAIM OF COGNIZANCE.

Cognizatus. One to whom an ackowledgement is made ; a cognizee, or conusee.

Cognizee. The party to whom a fine was levied. The party plaintiff in the proceedings, to whom the acknowledgement of the other's right to the land in question was made.

Cognizor. The party levying a fine. The party who acknowledged the other party's right to the land in question ; the party defendant in the proceedings.

Cognomen. A surname.

Cognoscere. To acknowledge.

Cognosco. To acknowledge.

Cognovit. He has acknowledged.

Cognovit actionem. He has acknowledged the action ; a confession that the plaintiff's action is just.

Cogware. Coarse cloths.

Cohabit. To live with one. To live together as husband and wife. To occupy the same bed and have sexual intercourse.

Cohabitare. To cohabit.

Cohabitant ut vir et uxor. They were living together as man and wife.

Cohabitation. The living together after the manner of husband and wife. See COHABIT.

Cohæredes. Co-heirs.

Co-heres. A co-heir or joint-heir. (Co-parceners).

Co-hertio. Coertion. The coercive power of a court. Restraint without process of law.

Cohuogium. A tribute paid by those who met in a market or fair.

Coif. A title applied to sergeants at law. A lawn skull cap.

Coin. To stamp metal and make it money. A piece of metal made money by law.

Coin, debased. See DEBASED COIN.

Coinage. The power to coin money. The act of coining money. The money coined as a whole.

Coinage Act of 1873. The act of February 12, 1873, reversing and amending the laws relative to mints and assay offices and coinage.

Coinage Act, Sherman. See SHERMAN COINAGE ACT.

Coinage Repeal Act of 1893. An act approved November 1, 1893, which repealed that part of the Sherman Coinage Act, providing for the purchase of silver bullion. See SHERMAN COINAGE ACT.

Co-judices. Associate judges having equality of power with others.

Coke, Sir Edward. The greatest and most learned Common law lawyer who ever existed, either in ancient or modern times. Chief Justice of England during reign of James I., and author of Coke on Littleton, and other works, including the celebrated reports and the remainder of the Institutes, of which Coke on Littleton is the first.

Cokestate. A cucking stool.

Cold blood. See BLOOD, COLD.

Cold water ordeal. An ordeal by which persons condemned to it were cast into a river. If they sank until pulled up by the rope fastened to them they were acquitted, if they floated they were held guilty, it being claimed that the water rejected them because guilty. See ORDEAL.

Coliberts. Tenants in socage; villeins who were raised to a condition between servants and freemen.

Coliberti. Same as COLIBERTS and CO-LIBERTUS.

Co-libertus. One of the Coliberti, a class of inferior tenants mentioned in Domesday. See COLIBERTI and COLIBERTS.

Collagio bonorum. Collatio bonorum (which see).

Collapsio. A falling together; precipitation.

Collateral. On the side; not direct; an accompanying or subordinate fact on condition. Property hypothecated as security for a debt. Corroborative. Secondary.

Collateral Act. An act, other than payment of money, for the performance of which a bond was given.

Collateral ancestors. Ancestors on the side, as uncles, aunts, grand uncles, &c.

Collateral assurance. An assurance made by bond outside of the deed.

Collateral charge. See CHARGE, COLLATERAL.

Collateral consanguinity. See CONSANGUINITY, COLLATERAL.

Collateral deed. See DEED, COLLATERAL.

Collateral descent. See DESCENT IN A COLLATERAL LINE.

Collateral estoppel. See ESTOPPEL, COLLATERAL.

Collateral evidence. See EVIDENCE, COLLATERAL.

Collateral fact. See FACT, COLLATERAL.

Collateral heirs. See HEIRS, COLLATERAL.

Collateral impeachment. An attempt in a collateral proceeding, to destroy the effect of a judgment rendered in another action.

Collateral inheritance. See INHERITANCE COLLATERAL.

Collateral inheritance tax. See TAX, COLLATERAL INHERITANCE.

Collateral issue. See ISSUE, COLLATERAL.

Collateral kindred. See KINDRED, COLLATERAL.

Collateral limitation. A limitation which makes the duration of an estate depend on some other event than the life or blood of the grantee.

Collateral line, descent in. See DESCENT IN A COLLATERAL LINE.

Collateral promise. See PROMISE, COLLATERAL.

Collateral security. See SECURITY, COLLATERAL.

Collateral undertaking. An agreement to do an act or pay money because of another existing contract, debt or liability.

Collateral warranty. See WARRANTY, COLLATERAL.

Collaterales et socii. Assistants and associates (of the Chancellor). Applied to Masters in Chancery.

Collateralis. Collateral.

Collaterally. In a collateral manner. In an independent proceeding (as to attack a judgment collaterally). Indirectly.

Collaterally, attack. See ATTACK COLLATERALLY.

Collaterally, impeach. Same as ATTACK COLLATERALLY.

Collaterals. Collateral security or kin.

Collaticius. Brought together, contributed, mingled.

Collatio. A comparison of two things by putting them together. Contribution or average.

Collatio beneficii. A collation of a benefice. The presentation and institution taken together.

Collatio bonorum. A collection of goods or property. The bringing together of money advanced by a deceased father to a son or daughter, into a common fund ; to divide the common fund among all the children equally.

Collatio signorum or sigillorum. A comparison of marks (signs) or seals. The mode of testing the genuineness of a seal, etc., by comparing it with another known to be genuine.

Collation. A Civil law term synonymous with "hotchpot." The conferring of a benefice by a bishop where the bishop is the patron. See Collatio BENEFICII.

Collation of seals. When one seal was set on the back of the other.

Collation to a benefice. Same as COLLATIO BENEFICII (which see).

Collatione facta uni post mortem alterius. A writ commanding the justices of Common Pleas to direct the bishop to admit a clerk in the place of a deceased clerk who had been presented by the King.

Collatione heremitagii. A writ by which the King conferred a hermitage upon a clerk.

Collative advowson. One in which the bishop has the right of patronage.

Colleague. An associate of another in a legislative or other body, as a commission or board.

Collect. To bring together. To obtain money due.

Collect on delivery. To collect the money due the seller and the charges of carriage, on delivery of the goods.

Collecting agency. An agency organized to collect money due.

Collection. The act of obtaining payments of money.

Collection, for. An endorsement on a note or check, meaning that the endorser desires and gives authority to have it collected when due.

Collector. One to whom letters ad colligendum are granted. A custom or revenue officer charged with the enforcement of the Custom or Revenue law.

Collector of the Customs. A collector of custom duties at a port of entry.

Collector of the Port. Same as COLLECTOR OF THE CUSTOMS.

Collectores. Collectors; persons appointed to make collections for another.

Collega. In Civil law, one having joint and equal authority with another.

Collegatarius. In Civil law, a co-legatee.

Collegatory. One who receives a legacy in common with others.

College. A corporation, company, or society legally established for educational purposes. An association of persons living together.

College, Electoral. In the United States a body composed of the electors chosen by the people of each State who are charged with the election of a President and Vice-President.

College, Herald's. See HERALD'S COLLEGE.

College, Lawful. One created by law, or existing without violation of law.

College of Arms. Same as HERALD'S COLLEGE.

College, Unlawful. One existing without authority of law.

Collegia. A college.

Collegia illicita. Unlawful colleges, associations, etc.

Collegia licita. Lawful colleges, etc.

Collegialiter. In a corporate capacity.

Collegium. A college, guild, corporation, company, fraternity. An ecclesiastical body under control of the State.

Collegium admiralitatis. The college or society of the admiralty.

Collegium fabrorum. A company of workers in hard materials, as wood, stone or metal.

Collegium fecialium. The college of fetiales. (A Roman college of priests, who sanctioned treaties when concluded and performed the ceremonies attending a formal declaration of war).

Collegium fetialium. The college of fetiales. See COLLEGIUM FECIALIUM.

Collegium illicitum. an unlawful college or corporation. One not confirmed by special enactment or by the Emperor.

Collegium licitum. One confirmed by special enactment or imperial constitution.

Collegium vel universitas. A corporation or community.

Collibertus. Same as CO-LIBERTUS.

Colliery. Contiguous and connected veins of coal worked as one concern.

Colligenda bona defuncti. Collecting together the goods or property of the deceased.

Collision. A striking together of two bodies; applied to the running together of vessels. See ALLISION.

Collision and damage. A suit in admiralty for damages for injuries caused by collision.

Collision by inscrutable fault. Where it is impossible to determine through whose fault the collision occurred.

Collision by inevitable accident. Where the collision resulted by natural causes and not the fault of those in charge of either vessel.

Collision, cause of. Same as COLLISION AND DAMAGE.

Collision by mutual fault. Where the collision was due to the fault of those in charge of both vessels.

Collision, fortuitous. See FORTUITOUS COLLISION.

Collistrigium. A pillory. In old Scotch law, joggs.

Collitigant. A litigant.

Collocation. The arrangement or marshalling of the creditors of an estate in the order in which they are to be paid according to law.

Collocutio. Same as COLLOQUIUM.

Colloquium. A conversation, applied to the part of a declaration tn slander alleging that defendant spoke the words.

Collusion. An agreement between two or more for one to bring an action against another in order to defraud a third person; a secret agreement for unlawful purpose.

Colne. In old English law, an account.

Coloni partiarii. Farmers who paid to the landlords a portion of the crop instead of rent.

Colonia. A possession in land; a landed estate; a farm. Abode, dwelling in general. A colony, colonial town, settlement. A portion of land assigned to a single colonus for cultivation as a task. A country house with sufficient land for the support of a husbandman and his family.

Colonial. Relating to the U. S. when they were colonies of Great Britain.

Colonial laws. See LAWS, COLONIAL.

Colonial Office. An English department of State through which colonial governors are appointed and communicated with, and colonial matters transacted.

Colonius partiarius. A husbandman or farmer who gives a share to his landlord.

Colonicus. Relating to agriculture or husbandry, to a colony.

Colonist. A member of a colony.

Colonize. To establish a colony.

Colonus. In Roman law, one who hired a house in the country. A husbandman; an inferior tenant employed in cultivating the lord's land. A term corresponding with the Saxon word ceorl.

Colony. A settlement in a foreign land, but under control of the parent government. The territory so settled.

Colony, charter government. See CHARTER COLONY GOVERNMENT.

Colony, proprietary. See PROPRIETARY COLONY.

Color. Appearance of legality. Pretended legality. A plea to draw the issue from the jury to the judge by giving color to the plaintiff's title and thus raising a question of law. Having more than one-sixteenth African blood.

(12)

Color, express. Where the defence pleads feigned matter from which a good cause appeared to exist, but not in reality.

Color, give. To admit an apparent right to exist in an opponent.

Color, implied. That which is given by the character of the defendant's defence

Color of office. Pretended authority of office.

Color officii. Color of office. See COLOR OF OFFICE.

Color of law. Apparent legality.

Color of right. Semblance of right.

Color of title. That which purports to be title, but is not; as a deed from one having no interest to convey. (As to what is, the court must determine as a question of law drawn from facts).

Colorable. Not what it purports to be. An alteration of an article or thing to such an extent as to make it apparently something different, though to leave it substantially the same to evade the copyright law of infringement.

Colorable alteration. See ALTERATION COLORABLE.

Colorable imitation. Such an imitation as is likely to deceive.

Colorable plea. See PLEA, COLORABLE.

Colore. In a plausible manner. By color (of a supposed estate, right or authority).

Colore officii. Under color of office.

Colored person. One of African descent. One having more than one-sixteenth of African blood.

Colorless. Not indicated by qualities, motives, or partiality.

Colorless will. One which does not indicate the motives for its provisions.

Colpare. To lop off; to cut off.

Colpicium. Same as COPPICE.

Colpo. A small wax candle.

Columbiarum. A dove cote, a pigeon house.

Comaunder. To commit or send.

Combarones. Fellow barons or commonalty of the cinque ports. A fellow member of Parliament from the cinque ports.

Comba terræ. A valley or low place between two hills.

Combat. A duel. A battle between two or more.

Combe. A narrow valley.

Combination. A joining two by two; a union of persons or things. In Patent law, a union of two parts as of machines or machinery. See COMBINE; also ANTI-TRUST LAW.

Combine. To bring into close union. To associate for a purpose. In United States, a combination of persons to effect secretly, what open methods would not obtain. A conspiracy. A combination, in the form of a trust to raise prices or obstruct the ordinary course of trade.

Comburendo heretico. See BREVE DE COMBURENDO HERETICO.

Combustio. A burning, consuming. The punishment of burning.

Combustio domorum. The burning of houses; arson.

Combustio pecuniæ. Burning of money. The ancient mode of trying mixed and corrupt money, by melting it down to determine its quality.

Come. As; so; whereas.

Come. To appear in court. The form "comes" is used in pleading to indicate the appearance of defendant.

Comen. Common.

Comen counsel. Common counsel.

Comes. An official and honorary title of great antiquity and various application, originating under the Roman empire. It was applied to an attendant on a Roman official, and in England to an earl and other persons of authority.

Comes and defends. Words in pleading meaning appears and defends the action.

Comes mariscallus. Earl marshal. An English officer of State, who anciently presided in the court of chivalry.

Comes stabuli. The overseer of the stable; constable. A superintendent of the imperial stables, and master of all matters of chivalry and feats of arms on horseback.

Comitas. Comity.

Comitas gentium. Comity of nations.

Comitas inter communitates. Comity between communities or nations.

Comitas inter gentes vel communitates. Courtesy between nations or communities.

Comitatu commisso. A commission of a county. A writ authorizing a sheriff to enter upon the charge of a county.

Comitatu et castro commisso. A commission of a county and castle. A writ conferring the charge of a county, together with the keeping of a castle, upon a sheriff.

Comitatus. A county or shire. An earldom. A county court. A train, suite, following, attendance or household.

Comitatus palatinus. County palatine. See COUNTIES PALATINE.

Comites. Companions; followers; retainers; adherents; earls; counts. Persons attached to a public minister.

Comites paleys or palentynes. Counts or earls palatine. Those charged with the government of a county.

Comitia. In Roman law, an assembly.

Comitia centuriata. An assembly of the Roman centuries composed of both patricians and plebeians.

Comitia curiata vel calata. An assembly of the Roman curiæ composed of patricians.

Comitia tributa. An assembly of the Roman tribes, composed of plebeians only.

Comitissa. A countess; an earl's wife.

Comitiva. The dignity and office of a comes; afterwards called comitatus. A fellow traveller. A company of robbers.

Comity. Courtesy between nations or States.

Comity, judicial. The courtesy exhibited by different judicial jurisdictions each for the other.

Comity of Nations. The courtesy by which one nation recognizes or follows the law of another.

Comity of States. The comity of nations, applied in the United States by the different States.

Command. Order; power; rule. To govern; to order; to lead; to have the supreme authority.

Commandement. In French law, a writ notifying a judgment debtor or one who agreed to pay under notarial seal, that unless he pay, his property will be seized and sold.

Commander in Chief. One who has full control of the military of a country in time of war.

Commandery. A manor with lands and tenements belonging to the priory of St. John of Jerusalem, in England, during the time of the Knight Templars.

Commandite. A special or limited partnership.

Commanditaires. Special partners; dormant, sleeping partners.

Commandment. The offence of getting another to do an unlawful act. The mandate of a judge.

Commarchio. A boundary or border; a common boundary.

Commarchis. The confines or boundaries of a place; a common boundary.

Commence. Begin.

Commencement of a declaration. The names of the parties, the character in which they stand, the form of the action, and the method by which jurisdiction of the person is obtained.

Commencement of proceedings. In U. S. Bankrupt law, of 1898, the date when the petition was filed.

Commenda. A thing commended or intrusted; (a church). A benefice commended by the crown to the care of a clerk to hold till a proper pastor is provided for it. An association in which individuals are entrusted with capital.

Commenda quotuplex, et qualis. A four-fold commendam, and how constituted.

Commendam recipere. To take, receive a benefice or living.

Commendam. A void benefice commended to the care of a clerk until filled.

Commendam retinere. To hold a benefice until the proper pastor is provided for it.

Commendam semestris. A half-yearly living on benefice.

Commendare. To commend; commit or entrust one's self to the protection of another.

Commendatio. Praise; recommendation.

Commendation. Anciently, where the owner of land under the feudal law placed himself under the protection of a lord, thereby becoming his vassal. The giving of a benefice in commendam. See COMMENDATUS.

Commendators. Laymen to whom benefices were entrusted.

Commendatory. He who holds a void benefice in commendam.

Commendatory letters. See LETTERS, COMMENDATORY.

Commendatus. In Feudal system one who lived under the protection of a person of power. A person who voluntarily placed himself under the protection of a lord.

Commendo. To commit to one for preservation, or protection; to entrust to; to recommend. To deposit; to lend; to entrust a thing to another.

Commentarium. A brief. An abstract.

Commerce. An exchange of property of any kind between nations or individuals.

Commerce, Active. Imports and exports transported in ships of the nation referred to.

Commerce, Chamber of. See CHAMBER OF COMMERCE.

Commerce, Domestic. That carried on wholly within the limits of a State or country.

Commerce, Foreign. That carried on with a foreign State or country.

Commerce, International. That carried from one nation to another.

Commerce, Interstate. Commerce between the several States or persons living in different States.

Commercia belli. Stipulations or treaties of war; war contracts.

Commercial. Relating to commerce.

Commercial agency. See AGENCY, COMMERCIAL.

Commercial agent. A person living in a foreign country and having certain consular authority by appointment from his own government. A consul.

Commercial agent, vice. See AGENT, VICE COMMERCIAL.

Commercial broker. See BROKER, COMMERCIAL.

Commercial law. See LAW, COMMERCIAL.

Commercial marine. Facilities for carrying on trade on the ocean. Everything used in the transportation of commerce on the sea.

Commercial paper. See PAPER, COMMERCIAL.

Commercial traveller. One who travels in the interest of a mercantile house.

Commercium. Commercial intercourse, trade, traffic, commerce.

Commercium belli. A stipulation, contract or treaty of war.

Commessalis. A table companion; a mess-mate.

Comminalty. The commonalty. The people.

Comminatorium. (From Comminor, to threaten one with something). A clause one time added to writs, admonishing the sheriff to execute them faithfully.

Commise. Forfeiture. In old French law, the forfeiture of a fief; the penalty attached to the ingratitude of a vassal.

Commissariat. The department of an army having charge of supplies of food, &c. The officers of a Commissary Department. The supplies furnished an army. In Scotch law, the office or jurisdiction of a commissary.

Commissarius. A commissary; one who is entrusted with anything. The title of an officer who exercised certain spiritual jurisdiction in the bishop's diocese.

Commissary. One who exercises ecclesiastical jurisdiction in the out places of a diocese. One who takes charge of the supply and distribution of provisions for an army. In Scotch law, the judge of a Commissary Court.

Commission. The performance of an act. A written authority empowering or directing a person or persons named to perform some act or exercise certain jurisdiction or official duties. The persons appointed to exercise the jurisdiction or duties. In Civil law, a bailment without reward to perform some act in connection with the article bailed.

Commission Agent. One who sells goods for another on commission.

Commission, Civil Service. See CIVIL SERVICE COMMISSION.

Commission day. In England, the day the assise opened.

Commission del credere. See DEL CREDERE.

Commission, Fish. See FISH COMMISSION.

Commission, Interstate Commerce. A commission created by the Interstate Commerce Act of Feb. 4, 1887. It is composed of five commissioners and their jurisdiction is fixed by the act.

Commission Merchant. Same as COMMISSION AGENT.

Commission, Nicaragua Canal. A commission of three engineers appointed under Act of U. S. Congress, March 2, 1895, to report on the feasibility and cost of completing the canal. See NICARAGUA CANAL.

Commission of Anticipation. A commission under the Great Seal of England to collect a future tax or subsidy.

Commission of Appraisement. In Admiralty law, a commission to appraise property to be released on bail, the value of which is in dispute.

Commission of Appraisement and Sale. In Admiralty law, a commission appointed to appraise and sell property arrested and ordered to be sold by court.

Commission of Array. An officer's authority to muster and enlist persons for military duty.

Commission of Assise. In old English law, the commission from the crown appointing and directing two or more commissioners in England to go on a circuit about the kingdom to try, by a local jury, such matters then pending before Westminster Hall. These commissioners were called judges of Assise and Nisi Prius.

Commission of Association. A commission to associate two or more learned persons with the circuit judges.

Commission of Bankrupt. In England, a commission granted to some five persons called commissioners, by the Lord Chancellor, to examine into the affairs of bankrupts.

Commission of Charitable Uses. A commission out of chancery to enquire of and correct abuses in the distribution of the proceeds from lands given for charitable purposes.

Commission of Delegates. A commission under the Great Seal of England to certain persons, usually two lords, two bishops, and three law judges, to sit on an appeal to the King in Chancery where sentence has been given by an archbishop in an ecclesiastical cause.

Commission of Fish and Fisheries, U. S. A bureau established by Congress, February 9, 1891, charged with the propagation and distribution to suitable waters of food fishes, the study of fish and fish diseases, &c., and the collection of statistics relating thereto.

Commission of General Gaol Delivery. One of the English commissions directing the judges to sit at assises and try and deliver every prisoner in jail when the judges arrive whether under indictment or not.

Commission of Jail Delivery. See JAIL DELIVERY, COMMISSION OF.

Commission of Lunacy. A commission out of chancery to enquire into a person's sanity.

Commission of Nisi Prius. In old English law, a commission to the judges of Nisi Prius and Assise, to try questions of fact on which issue had been joined at Westminster.

Commission of Oyer and Terminer. In old English law, a commission which directed certain judges to enquire, hear and determine all treasons, felonies, and misdemeanors, within certain districts or circuits.

Commission of Peace. In old English law, a commission requiring all justices of peace and sheriff to be present at the sittings of the judge of Assise and Nisi Prius.

Commission of Rebellion. A writ of chancery to apprehend as a rebel one who refuses to appear after proclamation by the sheriff, to appear on pain of his allegiance.

Commission of unlivery. In English Admiralty law, a commission issued to the marshal to unload a vessel in order to have the cargo appraised.

Commission to take depositions. A written authority from a court to take testimony of witnesses without the jurisdiction of court, or unable to appear.

Commissioned officer. See OFFICER, COMMISSIONED.

Commissioner. One who holds a commission or is authorized by law to examine into any public matter or execute any public act. An officer appointed to assist a court in any particular. In Scotch law, one selected to manage the affairs of an unincorporated town.

Commissioner, County. See COUNTY COMMISSIONER.

Commissioner, Fish. See FISH COMMISSIONER ; also COMMISSION OF FISH AND FISHERIES, U. S.

Commissioner-General of Immigration. Chief officer of the U. S. Bureau of Immigration.

Commissioner, Jury. See JURY COMMISSIONER.

Commissioner, Interstate Commerce. A member of the Interstate Commerce Commission.

Commissioner of Bail. An officer having authority to take bail for appearance.

Commissioner of Education. An officer of the Interior Department at Washington, D. C., charged with the collection of statistics and other information relating to the progress and condition of education in the several States and Territories.

Commissioner of Indian Affairs. An officer of the Interior Department at Washington, D. C., charged with the administration of all laws relating to the different tribes of Indians in the several States and Territories.

Commissioner of Internal Revenue. An officer of the U. S. Treasury Department charged with the assessment and superintendence of the collection of internal revenue taxes and enforcement of internal revenue laws.

Commissioner of Labor. Chief of the U. S. Department of Labor.

Commissioner of Navigation. An officer of the U. S. charged with the general superintendance of the commercial marine and merchant seamen and the determination of all questions relating to the issue of registers, enrollments and licenses of vessels.

Commissioner of Patents. An officer of the Interior Department at Washington, D. C., charged with the administration of the Patent law, the issuing of letters patent for inventions, and the registration of trade-marks.

Commissioner of Pensions. An officer of the Interior Department at Washington, D. C., charged with the administration of the laws granting bounty lands or pensions on account of service or for injuries in any war in which the United States have been engaged.

Commissioner of Railroad, U. S. An officer of the United States at Washington, D. C., charged with an examination of the accounts and condition of railroads all or in part west, north or south of the Missouri river, to which the U. S. have granted subsidy, credit, or loan. He is required to make an annual report to the Secretary of the Interior regarding the same.

Commissioner of the General Land Office. An officer of the Interior Department at Washington, D. C., charged with the survey, management and sale of the public domain.

Commissioner, Shipping. See SHIPPING COMMISSIONER.

Commissioners, Ecclesiastical. A corporation created by 6 and 7 Wm. IV., to suggest measures for the welfare of the established Church of England.

Commissioners of Array. See ARRAIERS.

Commissioners of Bail. Officers charged with taking bail in civil causes.

Commissioners of Bankrupt. See COMMISSION OF BANKRUPT.

Commissioners of Deeds. Officers given power by a foreign State to take acknowledgments and oaths to be used in the foreign State.

Commissioners of Highways. County or township officers in many of the U. S. with certain power over the highways.

Commissioners, Railroad. See RAILROAD COMMISSIONERS.

Commissioners, United States. Officers appointed by U. S. Circuit Courts to take bail, recognizance, affidavits, &c., hold preliminary hearings and to some extent represent the judge in his absence.

Commissions. Compensation paid an agent or other as a percentage on the amount of money received or expended, or business transacted. See COMMISSION.

Commissions, Military. Courts convened for the trial of violations against martial law.

Commissive. Committing. See WASTE, COMMISSIVE.

Commissoria lex. Same as LEX COMMISSORIA.

Commit. To perpetrate. To be guilty of. To place in trust. To send to a place of confinement.

Commitment. An order in writing consigning a person to prison. The act of sending to a place of confinement.

Commitment, Warrant of. Authority in writing to place one in confinement. A mittimus. See MITTIMUS

Committee. Those to whom any matter is referred for execution or report. One to whom the care of an insane person is committed.

Committee, Joint. A committee composed of members of two separate organizations or of members from two houses of a legislature.

Committee of a Lunatic. One to whom the custody or property of a lunatic is committed.

Committee of Ways and Means. See WAYS AND MEANS, COMMITTEE OF.

Committitur. He is committed. An order or minute setting forth that the person named in it is committed to the custody of the sheriff. Generally employed on the surrender of a defendant by his bail, in which case it is a minute of the surrender and commitment.

Committitur-piece. An instrument in the form of a bail-piece, by which a defendant already in custody is charged in execution, at suit of the same or another plaintiff.

Committing Magistrate. One having authority to hear criminal charges and commit to jail or hold to bail for future action by a higher tribunal.

Committo. To commit. To entrust to; To commit; to be guilty of.

Commixtio. In Civil law, the mixing of dry or solid things belonging to different owners.

Commodate. In Scotch law, a loan for use.

Commodati actio. In Civil law, an action for a thing lent.

Commodato. In Spanish law, a loan to be returned in kind.

Commodatum. A thing lent to be returned in specie. See MUTUM ; also IN SPECIE.

Commodity. Merchandise. Anything subject to taxation. Privilege of carrying on a particular business.

Commodum. At a fit time ; seasonably ; a convenient or favorable condition ; accommodation ; convenience ; advantage.

Commoigne. A fellow monk; one who lives in the same convent.

Common. A right or privilege to take from or use another's property. Belonging equally to the public, to many, or to more than one.

Common appendant. A right of common, appendant to an estate established by presumption only. A right to feed commonable cattle on other lands of the same manor.

Common appurtenant. A right of common appended to an estate which may be established by grant or prescription. A right to feed cattle on the land of another; it may extend to cattle not commonable.

Common assurances. Evidences of title.

Common at large. Same as COMMON IN GROSS.

Common bail. See BAIL, COMMON.

Common bar. Blank bar (which see).

Common barratry. See BARRATRY; also COMMUNIS BARRECTATOR.

Common barretor. One who habitually causes suits and quarrels without ground for the same.

Common because of vicinage. Common because of neighborhood, as where inhabitants of two adjoining townships mutually permit their cattle to feed in either.

Common Bench. The bench, as distinguished from the King's Bench; the Court of Common Pleas.

Common carrier. See CARRIER, COMMON.

Common carriers of passengers. Such as make a business of carrying for hire all who apply for transportation.

Common Council. A city legislature. A branch of a city council.

Common counts. See COUNTS, COMMON.

Common days. The days in Common Bench on which writs were returnable. Ordinary days in the court.

Common debtor. In Scotch law, a garnishee. An arrester. A judgment creditor.

Common de schaack (or shack). A common which existed in the east of England by special custom allowing persons occupying lands lying together to turn in their cattle to feed, after harvest, on all the land.

Common error. An error of law which has many precedents.

Common erudition. Common learning; familiar law or doctrine.

Common, extinguishment of. Destruction or loss of the right of common.

Common fine. See FINE, COMMON.

Common fishery. Same as COMMON OF PISCARY.

Common form. The proof of a will on the oath of the executor, as distinguished from proof by witnesses.

Common gambler. See GAMBLER, COMMON.

Common highway. See HIGHWAY, COMMON.

Common House. The lower house of Parliament in England.

Common informer. See INFORMER, COMMON.

Common in gross. Common vested in a person or corporation; not annexed to land.

Common intendment. Common understanding or meaning; natural sense; a simple, not strained construction.

Common intent. See INTENT, COMMON.

Common jour en plee de terre. Common day in plea of land.

Common in the soil. Liberty of mining or quarrying.

Common jury. See JURY, COMMON.

Common labor. Manual labor.

Common law. See LAW, COMMON.

Common law copyright. See COPYRIGHT, COMMON LAW.

Common law marriage. See MARRIAGE, COMMON LAW.

Common law lawyer. A lawyer learned in the common law.

Common learning. Familiar doctrine or law.

Common nuisance. See NUISANCE, COMMON.

Common of digging. The right to take for one's own use, soil in the land of another.

Common of estovers. The right to take wood necessary for use or repairs.

Common of fowling. The right to take wild fowl from the land of another.

Common of pasture. The right of feeding one's beasts on another's land, in common with the owner, or with other persons.

Common of piscary. The right to fish in another's waters.

Common of schaack (or shack). Same as COMMON DE SCHAACK.

Common of turbary. The right to dig turf on another's land.

Common place. Common pleas.

Common pleas. Civil cases. Pleas between subjects as opposed to crown pleas. See COURT OF COMMON PLEAS.

Common proceeding. See PROCEEDING COMMON.

Common prostitute. See PROSTITUTE, COMMON.

Common pur cause de vicinage. Same as COMMON BECAUSE OF VICINAGE.

Common recovery. A feigned recovery. See RECOVERY, COMMON.

Common right. See RIGHT, COMMON.

Common sans nombre. Common without stint. The right to common an indefinite number of cattle.

Common schools. See SCHOOLS, COMMON.

Common scold. A quarrelsome woman; one by habitually scolding and contending with her neighbors, becomes a public nuisance.

Common seal. One used by a corporation.

Common sergeant. An officer with judicial power who assisted the recorder at "Old Bailey" in disposing of criminal cases.

Common socage. See SOCAGE, COMMON.

Common stock. See STOCK, COMMON.

Common, tenancy in. The status of tenants in common. See COPARCENARY.

Common traverse. See TRAVERSE, COMMON.

Common vouchee. The person who is vouched to warranty in a common recovery. See RECOVERY, COMMON.

Common wall. Same as WALL, PARTY.

Common weal. The public welfare; the common good.

Commonable. Something over which a right of common may be exercised.

Commonable beasts. Beasts which are an aid to agriculture either by working, producing food, or manuring the ground.

Commonage. The right of common.

Commonalty. The barons and tenants in capite were anciently so styled. The people, not holding office. The middle class.

Commonance. Commoners collectively who have a right of common in a field.

Commoner. One enjoying a right of common. A member of the English House of Commons. An English subject who is not a peer.

Commons. Land set apart for the public, or over which people have rights of common of pasture. The freeholders of England not peers of the realm.

Commons, House of. The popular branch of the English and the Canadian Parliaments. Prior to 1868, the popular branch of the North Carolina Legislature.

Commonty. In Scotch law, land possessed in common.

Commonwealth. The people as a whole. The State.

Commorant. Dwelling; temporarily abiding. One who thus dwells. See COMMORANCY.

Commorantia. Commorancy; a sojourning.

Commorancy. The dwelling in any place as an inhabitant, which usually consists in usually lying there; a temporary residence.

Commorientes. Persons dying at the same place and time, as in an accident.

Commorth. A contribution gathered at marriages and first masses of young priests.

Commote. In Wales, a half cantred, half hundred, or fifty villages. A lordship of one or more manors.

Commotion, civil. An insurrection with or without acts sufficient to amount to a rebellion.

Communal, land. Land held by the ancient Irish tribes and divided annually.

Communance. The commoners or tenants who had the right of common in an open field.

Communante. Commonalty.

Communante des biens. Commonalty or community of goods, acquets or gains.

Communare. To common; to enjoy the right of common.

Commune. Commonalty; people. A self-governing town. In old French law, a municipal corporation. The committee of the people in the French revolution of 1793. The commonalty.

Commune concilium. The common council (of a corporation).

Commune bonum. A common good; a public advantage or benefit; a matter of mutual or general benefit.

Commune concilium regni Angliæ. The common council of the King and the people assembled in Parliament.

Commune forum. The common forum or place of justice. Applied to the seat of the principal courts, especially those that are fixed.

Commune hospitium. A common inn or tavern.

Commune nocumentum. A common nuisance; a public nuisance.

Commune piscarium. A common fishery; a right of fishing without restriction.

Commune placitum. A common plea, or action; an action of debt.

Commune vinculum. A common bond. Applied to the common stock of consanguinity, and the feudal bond of fealty between lord and tenant.

Communes plees. Common pleas.

Communes reipublicæ sponsiones. The common obligations of the State. The common obligation of inhabitants to observe the laws of a kingdom or State.

Communi custodia. An ancient writ allowed to the lord against a stranger who entered lands of a deceased tenant by knight's service and took his eldest son under age as ward.

Communi dividundo. In Civil law, an action to divide property held in common.

Communi lege. Of, from, or by, the common law.

Communia. Common; common to several. Common things. Communities. Towns enfranchised by the crown about the twelfth century and made free corporations by charters of community.

Communia ex causa vicinitatis. Common because of vicinage. Applied where the tenants are of two adjoining manors or inhabitants of contiguous townships.

Communia pasturæ. Common of pasture.

Communia pertinens. Common appendant.

Communia piscariæ. Common of piscary, or fishery.

Communia placita. Common pleas, causes, suits, or actions. In old English law, civil actions between subject and subject—as distinguished from pleas of the crown.

Communia placita non tenenda in scaccario. A writ to the treasurer and barons of Exchequer forbidding them to hear pleas in that court between common persons.

Communia præcepta. Common precepts, or regulations.

Communia sine numero. Common without number. In old English law, used in connection with the number of cattle which may be turned on a common.

Communia turbariæ. Common of turbary. A right to digging turf upon the land of another in common with others.

Communiam piscariæ. A common of fishery.

Communibus annis. In o r d i n a r y years; on the annual average.

Communicantes. Commoners.

Communicare. To common.

Communicatio. Communication, consultation, information, conference.

Communication. Information given by one person to another.

Communication, confidential. Information given or obtained by persons occupying positions of trust toward each other.

Communication, privileged. Communications which the law will not require one to disclose or which in law of libel is not a publication, or which defendant had a right to make.

Communings. In Scotch law, preliminaries to a contract.

Communio bonorum. Communion or community of goods.

Communio proximorum. Undivided land.

Communion of goods. In Scotch law, the right of married persons to personal property owned by them.

Communis. Common, ordinary, general.

Communis Bancus. Common Bench.

Communis barrectator. A common barretor or barrector. (A single act does not constitute the offence. There must be several acts of barretry, and the proof must show at least three instances of offending).

Communis error. A common error (of opinion or practice).

Communis opinio. Common opinion; general professional opinion.

Communis paries. A common or party wall.

Communis patria. The common country.

Communis rixatrix. A common scold.

Communis scriptura. A common writing. A writing common to both parties; a chirograph.

Communis stirpes. A common stock; the common stock or root of descent; a common ancestor.

Communis strata. A common street. The common street.

Communis strata via. The common paved way.

Communis terminus. A common termination, or limitation.

Communism. A system of government in which there is a community of property.

Communitas. A community, company, or society. A community living in the same place, under the same laws and who enjoy common rights.

Communitas regni. The ordinary people. Knights under the degree of baron.

Communitas regni Angliæ. The general assembly of the kingdom of England. An old name for the English Parliament.

Communitive justice. See JUSTICE, COMMUNITIVE.

Community. Mutuality. A mutual interest in property acquired during marriage by husband and wife, in Louisiana, Texas and California. In Civil law, a corporation or body politic. People living together and enjoying equal rights.

Community, conventional. A mutual interest in after-acquired lands created by express stipulation in the contract of marriage.

Community, legal. A community in property between husband and wife which is implied by or arises by operation of law.

Community of the kingdom. Commonalty (which see).

Community property. Property acquired by married persons during marriage.

Commutatio mercium. An interchange or mutual change of goods or property between nations or individuals.

Commutation. The act of commuting. Change, substitution. The substitution of one penalty or punishment for another after conviction of the party subject to it. The giving, exchanging one thing in satisfaction of another. See COMMUTE.

Commutation of homestead entry. The buying of land entered under the U. S. homestead law after residence and cultivation for a statutory period.

Commutation of punishment. Substituting a less for a greater punishment. Changing one punishment for another.

Commutation of tithes. Their conversion into a money payment.

Commutation ticket. A ticket for transportation permitting repeated trips at a less sum than the aggregate of all the trips.

Commutative contract. See CONTRACT, COMMUTATIVE.

Commute. To put one thing in place of another. To take that which is less in lieu of something greater. To pay in money in place of in gross or in kind. To make one payment for being transported several times instead of paying for each trip. In U. S. public land law, to acquire by purchase, land entered under the homestead law before the settler would otherwise obtain title.

Compact. A contract; a mutual agreement.

Compact, original. The implied contract entered into by the members of a community by which they surrender natural rights in return for protection and legal rights.

Companage. All kinds of food other than bread and drink.

Companagium. Companage; any meat or other edible to be eaten with bread.

Companion of the Garter. A Knight of the Garter. See GARTER.

Companions. In French law, those who are employed on the same vessel.

Company. A word supposed to indicate the existence of another partner whose name is not publicly made known. A corporation. Two or more persons associated together in trade whether incorporated or not.

Company, boom. A company organized to construct booms, improve streams, and boom, drive and raft logs.

Company, deposit. See DEPOSIT COMPANY.

Company, express. See EXPRESS COMPANY.

Company, joint stock. See JOINT STOCK COMPANY.

Company, stock. See STOCK COMPANY.

Comparatio literarum. Comparison of handwritings; a mode of proving a handwriting or signature by comparison, in order to ascertain whether both were written by the same person.

Comparative jurisprudence. See JURISPRUDENCE, COMPARATIVE.

Comparebit. He shall appear.

Comparentia. Appearance.

Comparere. To appear; to be present.

Comparet. He appears.

Comparison of handwriting. See HANDWRITING, COMPARISON OF.

Comparitio. Appearance.

Comparuerit. He may have appeared.

Comparuisset. They might, could, would or should have appeared.

Compascuum. Relating or belonging to commonage.

Compascuus. Suitable for or pertaining to common pasturage; the right of common pasture; belonging to commonage.

Compass. An instrument used in navigation containing a magnetic needle which always points North. To grasp. To procure. To obtain.

Compassing. Imagining. See IMAG-
INING.

Compatibility. Such relationship between two offices that one person can hold
and perform the duties of both.

Compearance. In Scotch law, the appearance of a defendant.

Compellativum. An adversary or accuser.

Compendia. Abridgements.

Compendium. An abridgement.

Compensacion. In Spanish law, the
extinguishment of one debt by another.

Compensatio. In Civil law, a set off
or compensation.

Compensatio criminis. A weighing
or balancing of crime; a setting off; equal-
izing of one crime against another. A plea
of recrimination in a suit for divorce.

Compensation. A cross-demand or
counter claim; a demand equalized by settling of another demand to reduce its amount
or totally extinguish it. That which is
given for something else. Something paid
for service, injury, or privation.

Compensation, just. Compensation
equal to the service or loss.

Compensationis gratia. Gratuitous
compensation. Same as TO-BOOT.

Compensatory. Serving to satisfy.

Competency. The condition of being
competent under the law. Qualification.
Authority. Admissability. See EVIDENCE,
COMPETENT; also CREDIBILITY.

Compertorium. A judicial i n q u e s t
made by delegates or commissioners, to find
out and relate the truth of a cause.

Comperuit ad diem. (He appeared
at the day). A plea in an action on a bail
bond stating that the defendant did appear
on the day specified in the bond.

Compesture. To manure. To till.

Competent. Legal; legally qualified.

Competent witness. See WITNESS,
COMPETENT.

Competere. To be proper, available.

Competit actio. An action lies.

Compilation. A work made up of se-
lections from different authors.

Compile. To take from other authors
or scources and arrange in a new form.

Competition. In Scotch practice, the
contest among creditors.

Complainant. One who charges another with crime or wrong. One who brings
a suit in equity.

Complaint. A charge made in legal
form and manner. The statement of a cause
of action.

Complete citizen. See CITIZEN, COM-
PLETE.

Complice. An accomplice.

Componere lites. To settle, compromise lawsuits.

Compos. Having control of.

Compos libertatis. Having the power
or possession of liberty.

Compos mentis. Sound in mind. A
man in such a state of mind as to be qualified legally to sign a will, deed, etc.

Compos patriæ. Partaking, partici-
pating, or sharing in one's country.

Compos sui. Having control over one's
self; having the use of one's limbs, or the
power of bodily motion.

Compositio mensurarum. The composition or ordinance of weights and measures. The title of an ancient ordinance
mentioned in stat. 23 Hen. VIII. c. 4. The
stat. 51 Hen. III. establishing a standard
of weights and measures.

Compositio ulnarum et petticarum.
The statute of ells and perches. The title
of an English statute establishing a standard
of measures.

Composition. An agreement, compromise. Money paid in compensation for
crimes committed. An agreement with the
owner of lands, that such lands shall for the
future be discharged from payment of

tithes, because of land or real recompense given the parson in lieu thereof. An agreement of a number of creditors of an insolvent debtor to accept less than their entire demand. An amicable arrangement of a lawsuit. A statute or ordinance. A compounding or putting together. That composed of parts. A chemical combination.

Composition in bankruptcy. An agreement by creditors to accept part in satisfaction of the whole of a debt.

Composition in insolvency. Same as COMPOSITION IN BANKRUPTCY.

Composition of matter. In Patent law, a combination of materials. The process of combining materials.

Composition, real. An agreement made between the parson and landowner, with consent of the ordinary and patron, that certain lands shall be discharged of tithes for some real recompense given in lieu thereof.

Compostum. Compost or dung laid on lands.

Compotarius. A party accounting.

Compotus. An account.

Compound. Composed of two or more elements. To make a compromise or settlement. To give or accept pay for an offence or injury. To agree for a consideration to refrain from prosecution. To add interest and principal together. To take part in satisfaction of the whole.

Compound interest. Same as INTEREST, COMPOUND.

Compound larceny. See LARCENY, COMPOUND.

Compounder, amicable. One who makes a composition.

Compounding a debt. Settling or discharging a debt for less than the sum due.

Compounding a felony. Agreeing for a valuable consideration not to prosecute one charged with a felony. Assisting a felony.

Compra y venta. In Spanish law, buying and selling.

Comprint. A surreptitious printing of another's book.

Comprivigni. Those having but one parent who is the parent of both.

Compromisarius. In Civil law, an arbitrator.

Compromise. An adjustment; a compact in which concessions are made on each side. To adjust a dispute by mutual concessions; a promise of two or more to a dispute to refer the matter to arbitrators. To make an end to.

Compte. A count. An earl. One who had both judicial and military jurisdiction over a defined district.

Compte arrete. An account in writing acknowledged correct by one against whom it is made.

Comptroller. Same as CONTROLLER.

Comptrollers of the Hanaper. Former officers of the Court of Chancery.

Compulsion. Duress. Coercion by mandate of law.

Compulsory. That done under duress. That required by law.

Compulsory arbitration. See ARBITRATION COMPULSORY.

Compulsory assignment. See ASSIGNMENT COMPULSORY.

Compulsory pilotage. See PILOTAGE, COMPULSORY.

Compurgator. One who by oath testified to another's innocence. See COMPURGATORES.

Compurgatores. In old English law, the eleven persons who swore with the defendant, in a trial by wager of law that he was not guilty, or did not owe the plaintiff anything; the twelve persons who swore with the defendant that he was not guilty, in the trial of a clerk for felony. This act was termed compurgation.

Compurgation. See COMPURGATORES.

Computare. To compute; to account.

Computasset, insimul. See INSIMUL COMPUTASSET.

Computatio temporis. A computing or reckoning of time; computation of time; the account and construction of time by rule of law.

Computation. The true account and construction of time. See COMPUTATIO TEMPORIS.

Computo. To sum up, to reckon, to compute. A writ to compel a bailiff, guardian, receiver or accountant to yield up his account.

Computus. An account; a reckoning up.

Comtroller. Same as CONTROLLER.

Comune. Common.

Comunement. Commonly.

Comyn. Common.

Con. Same as Cum.

Con buena fe. In Spanish law, with good faith ; in good faith.

Conceal. To hide, secrete, keep from view. To withhold information. In Insurance law, for an insured to withhold a fact material to a risk.

Concealed Weapons. See WEAPONS, CONCEALED.

Concealers. Those who concealed crimes. Officers who·sought for lands concealed from the King in England. (See CONCELATORES.

Concealment. The intentional suppression of a material fact by one party to a contract.

Concedere. To grant.

Concedo. I grant.

Concelata. Concealed.

Concelamentum. Concealment.

Concelatores. In old English law, detectors or discoverers of concealed lands. Persons appointed by letters patent (called letters of concealment) to discover lands, which were suspected of being concealed, or withheld from the crown. (Lord Coke called them turbidum hominum genus—a troublesome, disturbant sort of men).

Concelo. To conceal.

Concelamentum. Concealment.

Conceptio in factum. In Civil law, a formula in conformity with fact.

Conceptio in jus. In Civil law, a formula in conformity with law.

Conception. The vitalization of the ovule or egg in the womb of the female by contact with the generative fluid of the male.

Concern. Interest. Business. An establishment.

Concerning. Relating to.

Concerns. Affairs.

Concessi. I have granted.

Concessimus. We have granted ; a term used in conveyance, importing a joint covenant on the part of the grantors.

Concessio. A grant ; one of the Common law forms of transferring or conveying the property of incorporeal hereditaments or things which cannot pass by delivery.

Concession. The conveyance of territory from one sovereignty to another.

Concessisse. To have granted or yielded up.

Concessit. Granted, allowed, agreed, concurred. He has granted.

Concessit solvere. (He has granted and agreed to pay). An action in England of debt upon a simple contract.

Concessor. A grantor.

Concessum. Granted, allowed, conceded. A term indicating the assent of the court to a doctrine laid down in the argument of a cause.

Concessus. A grantee.

Concessus per literas patentes. A grantee by letters patent ; a patentee.

Concilium. A court; a council. A time and place of meeting. Argument ; the sitting of a court to hear argument. The legislative body in the government of a city or borough. An advisory body selected to aid the executive. The counsel in a cause or matter.

Concilium continuum. The perpetual council.

Concilium militare. The military council.

Concilium ordinarium. A judicial committee of the Aula Regis.

Concilium Regis. An English tribunal during the reign of Edw. I. and Edw. II., to which cases of unusual difficulty were referred.

Concilium regis privatum. The King's private council.

Concilium secretum regis. The King's secret council.

Concinnator. An arranger, disposer. A maker, contriver, author, inventor.

Concio. A meeting, assembly that is called together. A place for speaking, a tribune, rostrum. A council.

Concionator. A common council man; a freeman called to a (legislative) hall or assembly.

Concionatores. Plural of concionator.

Concipere. To conceive; to express in words; to frame or draw a legal instrument.

Conclude. To determine, finish, shut up or close. To stop or bar a man to plead or claim any other thing. To bar or shut out; to shut up a party to a position which he has taken.

Conclude to the country. See COUN-TRY, CONCLUDE TO THE.

Conclusion. The end of a plea; a bar. The ending. An inference.

Conclusion to the country. The tender of issue to be tried by jury, at the end of a plea of traverse.

Conclusive. Beyond question.

Conclusive presumption. See PRE-SUMPTION, CONCLUSIVE.

Concord. An agreement, accord. An agreement between the parties to a fine of lands in which the deforciant acknowledges the right of the complainant.

Concordat. A compact between two governments. An agreement between a sovereign and the Pope. A compromise by creditors with a bankrupt.

Concordes. Agreed—as a jury upon their verdict. Agreed or unanimous.

Concordia. An agreement; concord; accord. The agreement of a jury. An agreement between two or more persons, upon a trespass committed, by way of amends or satisfaction for it. An agreement between the parties to a fine of lands, how and in what manner the land should pass. (Fines were anciently called concords, and final concords).

Concordia Discordantium Canonum. The Harmony of the Discordant Canons. The Decretum Gratiani. A compilation by Gratian, an Italian monk, in about the year 1150, of the Canons or Ecclesiastical Constitutions.

Concordia finalis. A final concord.

Concords. Ancient name for fine of lands. See CONCORDIA.

Concords, final. Same as CONCORDS.

Concourse. In Scotch law, concurrence of criminal and civil actions based on the same facts.

Concubari. A pen or place where cattle lie.

Concubeant. Lying together.

Concubinage. An exception against a woman who sues for dower. In Civil law, a species of marriage authorized by law. A natural marriage; cohabitation as man and wife without marriage.

Concubinatus. In English law, concubinage; the cohabitation of a man with a woman under the character of a wife, to whom he is not married.

Concubine. A woman not married to a man who lives with him as his wife.

Concubinus. Same as CONCUBINATUS.

Concur. To go together. To agree. To have the same opinion.

Concurator. A co-curator.

Concurrence. Co-equal right, privilege or authority. Agreement in mind.

Concurrens. Concurrent; running together.

Concurrentes. Plural of concurrens.

Concurrent. Having equal authority, legality, or operation.

Concurrent action. Same as CONCURRENT REMEDY.

Concurrent conditions. See CONDITIONS, CONCURRENT.

Concurrent jurisdiction. The same power to exercise authority, whether legislative, executive or judicial.

Concurrent possession. Possession with another.

Concurrent promises. See PROMISES, CONCURRENT.

Concurrent remedy. One which will give the person injured relief equally with another, as trespass and case in certain instances.

Concurrent rights. Equal rights.

Concurrent titles. The same titles.

Concurrent writ. See WRIT, CONCURRENT.

Concurring opinion. See OPINION, CONCURRING.

Concursus. In Civil law, a collision.

Concursus actionum. A concurrence of actions.

Concursus creditorum. A conflict among creditors.

Concussio. Concussion.

Concussion. In Civil law, extortion by threats of violence.

Condedit. A plea to a libel in Ecclesiastical law, in which it is set up that deceased made the disputed will and was of sound mind.

Condemn. To find guilty; to doom to punishment; to censure; to blame. To declare illegal. To sentence. To forfeit. To confiscate. To declare to be a prize of war, or not seaworthy. To declare necessary for public use. To determine property will not satisfy a judgment in seven years.

(13)

Condemnation. A sentence or judgment which condemns some one to do, to give, to pay or suffer something, or which declares that his claim or pretensions are unfounded.

Condemnation money. Money which the law requires one to pay.

Condere. To make, establish.

Conders. Those who signal to fishermen the direction shoals of herring pass.

Condescendence. In Scotch law, a statement setting forth the grounds on which a plaintiff rests his right of recovery.

Condictio. An action in personam.

Condictio certi. In the Civil law, an action upon a promise to do a thing where the promise is certain.

Condictio ex lege. In Civil law, an action where the law provided no form of action, though gave a remedy.

Condictio furtivæ. An action of theft (for theft committed).

Condictio indebitati. In Civil law, an action to recover that given or paid by mistake of fact or law.

Condictio ob turpem causam. An action to recover back things given on account of a base or dishonorable cause.

Condictio rei furtivæ. In Civil law, an action to recover a thing stolen.

Condictio sine causa. In Civil law, an action to recover a thing parted with without consideration.

Condidit. (He made); a plea, in a suit attacking a will, that the testator made it and was of sound mind.

Conditio. A condition.

Conditio affirmativa. An affirmative condition, one which consists in doing a positive thing.

Conditio copulativa. A copulative condition. See CONDITION, COPULATIVE.

Conditio derisoria. A derisive (or derisory) condition. A ridiculous condition.

Conditio disjunctiva. A disjunctive condition ; one requiring one of several things to happen.

Conditio expressa. A condition expressed.

Conditio extraordinaria. A condition out of the common order.

Conditio illicita. An illicit or unlawful condition.

Conditio impossibilis. An impossible condition.

Conditio negativa. A negative or denying condition.

Conditio possibilis. A possible condition.

Conditio præcedens. A condition precedent; a preceding condition.

Conditio si non nupserit. A condition if he (or she) shall not have married.

Conditio viduitatis. A condition of widowhood. A condition restraining marriage of the testator's widow, is legal but not valid as to any other woman.

Condition. A restraint annexed to a thing which if performed the p e r s o n s performing obtain advantage, otherwise loss. That which may or may not happen. A term upon which a grant is made. A restriction upon acts.

Condition, affirmative. That which requires something to be done.

Condition, casual. One depending on chance.

Condition, collateral. That which is annexed to a collateral act, or incidental to another condition.

Condition, compulsory. One absolutely requiring some special thing to be done.

Condition, copulative. One requiring all of several things to happen.

Condition, disjunctive. One requiring only one of several things to happen.

Condition dissolving. Same as CONDITION RESOLUTORY.

Condition en fait. Condition in deed; condition in fact. A condition expressed in a deed in plain words or legal terms.

Condition en ley. Condition in law. One implied by law, without any words used by the party.

Condition, expressed. A condition created by express words. One expressed in the deed by which it is created.

Condition, implied. One implied from the nature of the estate. One implied by law.

Condition in deed. A condition expressed in a deed in terms.

Condition in law. One implied by law as annexed to a grant.

Condition, inherent. One which descends to the heir with the land.

Condition, insensible. One impossible or contradictory to the main condition.

Condition, mixed. One which depends on the will of the party with some other, or some other event.

Condition, negative. That which requires something not to be none.

Condition, positive. Same as CONDITION AFFIRMATIVE.

Condition, potestative. One which depends on the will of the party.

Condition, precedent. One which happens before the main act. One preceding the accruing of an estate, right or liability.

Condition, repugnant. Same as CONDITION INSENSIBLE.

Condition, resolutory. A condition which is intended to destroy or revoke a principal obligation should an event happen or not happen.

Condition, restrictive. Same as CONDITION NEGATIVE.

Condition, single. Same as CONDITION COMPULSORY.

Condition, subsequent. One which happens after the main act.

Condition, suspensive. One which makes the operation of a contract dependent upon the happening of some event.

Conditional. Depending upon a condition.

Conditional alienation. See ALIENATION, CONDITIONAL.

Conditional creditor. See CREDITOR, CONDITIONAL.

Conditional delivery. See DELIVERY, CONDITIONAL.

Conditional devise. See DEVISE, CONDITIONAL.

Conditional fee. One limited to descend to a particular class of heirs ; changed by the Statute de Donis, into fee-tail.

Conditional guaranty. See GUARANTY, CONDITIONAL.

Conditional legacy. See LEGACY, CONDITIONAL.

Conditional liability. See LIABILITY, CONDITIONAL.

Conditional limitation. See LIMITATION, CONDITIONAL.

Conditional obligation. See OBLIGATION, CONDITIONAL.

Conditional pardon. See PARDON, CONDITIONAL.

Conditional sale. See SALE, CONDITIONAL.

Conditional stipulation. See STIPULATION, CONDITIONAL.

Conditions, concurrent. Conditions dependent on each other and to be performed at the same time.

Conditions, consistent. Those not inconsistent with the subject-matter.

Conditions, covert. Same as CONDITIONS, IMPLIED.

Conditions, illegal. See ILLEGAL CONDITIONS.

Conditions, impossible. Those incapable of being performed under the circumstances.

Conditions, lawful. Those allowed by law.

Conditions of sale. The terms upon which a sale will be made, as to the manner of paying for the article bought.

Conditions, possible. Those capable of being performed.

Conditions, unlawful. Those prohibited by law or against public policy.

Conditions, void. Conditions which are either prohibited by law, not in accordance with law, or against public policy.

Condominia. In Civil law, limited or joint ownerships.

Condonacion. In Spanish law, the remission of a debt.

Condonation. Forgiveness. In cases of divorce, the forgiveness, either express or implied from actions, of a breach of marital duty, on condition that the fault shall not be repeated.

Condone. To expressly or impliedly forgive.

Condono. To forgive, to remit.

Conduct. The act of carrying on.

Conduct book. A book containing the record of seamen's conduct in the U. S. Navy.

Conduct, disorderly. See DISORDERLY CONDUCT.

Conduct money. The tax levied by Chas. I. to pay travelling expenses of the army. Money paid a witness for his travelling expenses and maintenance.

Conductitii. Hired persons, servants, domestics.

Conductio. A hiring, farming, hire, rent.

Conductor. A hirer, lessee, bailee.

Conductor militum. A presser of soldiers.

Conductor operarum. The hirer of labor; the conductor of works, operations.

Conductum. Anything hired, especially a house, dwelling, etc.

Conductus. Hired.

Cone and key. Accounts and keys. Applied to a woman of fourteen or fifteen, who at that age among the Saxons might take the cone and key of a house.

Cone et keye. Same as CONE AND KEY.

Conege. Same as CONGE.

Coneu. Acknowledged; known.

Coney. A rabbit. See CONEY BURROWS.

Coney burrows. Places where coneys or rabbits haunt and breed. (Commoners of England were prohibited from digging up these in a common).

Confarreatio. The religious patrician form of marriage among the Romans. This was their most solemn form of marriage.

Confarreation. Same as CONFARREATIO.

Confeccion. The execution of an instrument writing.

Confectio. The making or execution of a charter, deed, or other instrument writing.

Confederacy. A combination between two or more persons to do any hurt or damage to another, or to do an unlawful act. A union by league or mutual contract; federal compact. Conspiracy. The charge in a bill of equity of a confederacy between the defendant and other persons to injure the complainant.

Confederate bonds. See BONDS, CONFEDERATE.

Confederate money. See MONEY, CONFEDERATE.

Confederate States of America. The eleven Southern States that seceded in 1860–1861. They were South Carolina, Mississippi, Florida, Alabama, Georgia, Louisiana, Texas, Virginia, Arkansas, Tennessee and North Carolina. This confederacy was dissolved in 1865 after the war with the U. S. Government.

Confederation. An agreement. Confederacy.

Confederation, Articles of. See ARTICLES OF CONFEDERATION.

Confederation of Southern States. Same as CONFEDERATE STATES OF AMERICA.

Conference. A meeting of counsel for discussion of some special matter. An official consultation. A meeting of two committees, one from each branch of a legislature, to adjust matters in controversy between them as to the form or substance of a bill.

Confessing error. A plea admitting the correctness of an assignment of error.

Confessio. A confession.

Confessio criminis. An acknowledgement, confession of crime.

Confessio juris. A confession of law.

Confession. An admission of guilt. An admission that the plaintiff's action is good.

Confession and avoidance. Pleas which admit the facts alleged in the declaration, but aver new facts to avoid the legal effect of what is admitted.

Confession, direct. One made in open direct terms.

Confession, extra-judicial. Confession made out of court or before other than a magistrate with jurisdiction to hear the same.

Confession, incidental. One made in connection with the confession of some other fact or matter.

Confession, indirect. One implied from acts.

Confession, judicial. One made before a court or a magistrate with jurisdiction to hear the same.

Confession, naked. A confession without evidence to support it.

Confession of action. A plea admitting the cause of action to be true either in whole or part.

Confession of judgment. An admission of the jurisdiction of the court, the truth of the plaintiff's cause of action and assent to judgment being entered. In Criminal law, a plea of guilty.

Confession, plenary. A complete confession.

Confession, voluntary. One not incited by hope or fear.

Confessional. Relating to a confession to a priest. In old English law it was not privileged communication, but in some of the U. S. it has been made so by statute.

Confesso, bill taken pro. See PRO CONFESSO, BILL TAKEN.

Confessor. A priest of the Christian church who hears confessions in confidence from members of the church.

Confessiones juris. Confessions of law.

Confidence. The trust one reposes in another.

Confidential communication. See COMMUNICATION, CONFIDENTIAL.

Confidential relation. The relation which exists between those who transact matters for another, as attorney and client, agent and principal.

Confinement. Imprisonment.

Confirm. To complete that which was incomplete. To ratify that done without authority.

Confirmare. To confirm; to make strong or firm.

Confirmatio. A confirmation.

Confirmatio chartarum. Confirmation of the charters. After Magna Charta and after Charta de Foresta English Kings were required to confirm these charters. The title of the statute passed 25 Edw. I., A. D. 1297, directing Magna Charta to be allowed as the Common law.

Confirmatio crescens. A confirmation which enlarges a rightful estate.

Confirmatio diminuens. A confirmation which releases part of the services whereby the estate is held.

Confirmatio perficiens. A confirmation which makes a bad or defeasible title valid or a conditional estate absolute.

Confirmation. The conveyance of an estate in lands to another who has the possession or an estate therein. The strengthening of an estate. An assent to an estate already created. Affirmation. The sanction of a court.

Confirmation of the Charters. See CONFIRMATIO CHARTARUM.

Confirmee. The grantee in a confirmation deed.

Confirmor. The grantor in a confirmation deed.

Confiscare. To confiscate.

Confiscate. To forfeit. To condemn. To convert. To transfer to the fisc or treasury, for the use of the State.

Confiscation. The act of confiscating.

Confiscation Acts. Acts of U. S. Congress of August 6, 1861, and July 17, 1862, making the property of rebels the subject of capture and prize.

Confisk. Same as CONFISCATE.

Confitens reus. An accused who confesses his guilt.

Conflict. To oppose.

Conflict of laws. The opposition to each other of laws on the same subject.

Conflictus legum. A conflict of laws.

Conformity. Correspondence in form. In England, adherence to the established church.

Confrairie. A fraternity, brotherhood or society.

Confreres. Brethren in a religious house.

Confront. To bring to one's view.

Confrontation. Bringing a respondent into court (in matrimonial suits) to be identified by the witnesses.

Confronted. Brought before one for inspection and examination.

Confusio. In Civil law, the mixture of property in liquid form belonging to different persons. Being liquid, even though metallic it cannot afterwards be separated. See COMMIXTIO.

Confusion. A mingling; disorder. The mingling of the goods of two or more persons, so that the several portions can no longer be distinguished.

Confusion of boundaries. The conflict of boundaries of land. The branch of equity which adjusts disputed or uncertain boundaries.

Confusion of debts. The existence of two adverse rights to the same thing in the same person.

Confusion of goods. Such an intermingling of goods that one cannot be distinguished from the other. See CONFUSION.

Confusion of rights. In Civil law, the unity in one person of different titles to the same property. See MERGER.

Confusion of titles. The meeting of two titles to the same thing in the same person.

Confusion, property by. See CONFUSION.

Conge. Leave, license, or permission. In French law, a species of passport. Permission to navigate; a clearance.

Conge d'accorder. Leave to accord, or agree with the plaintiff; used in a fine of lands.

Conge d'emparler. Leave to imparl (or emparl).

Conge d'elire. Leave to elect or choose. The King's license to a dean and chapter to choose a bishop.

Conge d'eslire. Leave to elect or choose. The King's license for the selection of a dean or bishop.

Congeable. Licensed, lawful; done with permission.

Congildo. Same as GILDO.

Congildones. Fellow members of a gild.

Congregation. A gathering of persons for religious purposes.

Congress. A coming together. An assembly of representatives. The Federal legislature of the U. S. A meeting of representatives of different nations for the settlement of affairs in which they are interested. Sexual intercourse.

Congress, Continental. The Congress held by the American Colonies, except Georgia, from Sept. 5, 1774, to Oct. 26, 1774. Also a Congress held by the thirteen colonies from May 10, 1775, to Dec. 12, 1776. Also a body which met from Dec. 20, 1776, to March 1, 1781. See CONGRESS, FEDERAL.

Congress, Federal. The Congress which met under the Articles of Confederation from 1781 to 1789.

Congress, number of. To get the number of Congress subtract 1789 from the year of the first session, divide by two and add one.

Congress, session of. A meeting of Congress.

Congress, U. S. The Senate and House of Representatives of the Federal Government of the U. S., and law-making power, under the present Constitution. It first met March 4, 1789. It consists of representatives elected by the people of certain districts within States only, and Senators elected by the legislature of States. The term comprises a long and a short session. See LONG SESSION.

Congressus. A personal examination of a husband charged by his wife with being sexually impotent.

Conguis. An ancient measure of nine pints.

Congy. Same as CONGE.

Coningeria. A warren of conies or rabbits.

Conjectio. In Civil law, presumption.

Conjecto causæ. In Civil law, a statement of the case.

Conjecture. Supposition; surmise.

Conjoints. United; connected; associated. Persons married to each other.

Con-judex. An associate judge.

Conjugal. Belonging to marriage; connubial.

Conjugal rights. Rights belonging to the marriage state. See SUBTRACTION, also ADHERENCE.

Conjugialis. Conjugal; belonging to marriage, connubial.

Conjugium. Marriage.

Conjunct. In Scotch law, joint.

Conjunct persons. Persons related.

Conjuncta. In Civil law, things joined together.

Conjunctim. Jointly.

Conjunctim et devisim. Jointly and severally.

Conjunctim tenentes. Tenants jointly; joint tenants; joint holders.

Conjunctim tenens. A tenant jointly.

Conjunctio. In Civil law, connection of words.

Conjuctio a n i m o r u m. (Union of minds). Consent of the parties under such circumstances as by law required.

Conjunctive. Connective.

Conjunctive obligation. See OBLIGATION, CONJUNCTIVE.

Conjuctus. A connection, conjunction. In Scotch law, conjunct, joint. (Applied to rights).

Conjurati. Conspirators.

Conjuration. Swearing together ; an agreeing; a confirmation under oath; a combination under oath to do public harm ; a conspiracy.

Conjurator. One who swears with or is sworn with others ; one bound by oath with others; a compurgator.

Conjurare. Where several affirm a thing by oath.

Conjuratus. Same as CONJURATOR.

Connecting. That which is connected or capable of being connected.

Connection. Union. Combination. Relationship. Contact. Sexual intercourse.

Connivance. Actual consent or wilful indifference to the commission of a wrong.

Connive. To intentionally forbear to see a fault or other act; voluntary oversight.

Conniventia. Connivance.

Connoissement. A bill of lading; otherwise called police de chargement.

Connubium. In Roman law, matrimony between citizens, as distinguished from the marriage of slaves, &c. A lawful marriage.

Conociamento. In Spanish law, a recognizance.

Conocimiento. In Spanish law, a bill of lading.

Conpossessio. In Civil law, a joint possession.

Conquærere. To acquire.

Conquæstor. Conqueror.

Conquæstus. Acquisition or purchase; any means of acquiring an estate out of the course of inheritance; conquest.

Conquerentes. Plaintiffs; parties complaining.

Conquerer. To gain, acquire.

Conquereur. The conqueror or first purchaser of an estate.

Conqueror. To complain at or of a thing. The first purchaser of an estate.

Conqueror, William the. The Duke of Normandy, who conquered the Saxons in 1066, and established himself as King of England. He introduced the trial by battel and the feudal system and established a judicial system, though confirming to the Saxons many laws and customs.

Conquest. In Feudal law, acquiring property by any other means than inheritance. In Scotch law, the acquisition of property by donation or purchase. The property thus acquired. Property obtained after marriage.

Conquest, Norman. See NORMAN CONQUEST.

Conquestor. Conqueror; one of the titles given William the Conqueror.

Conquestus. Conquest; acquisition.

Conquets. In French law, the acquisitions of man and wife during marriage.

Conquisition. Acquisition; any means of acquiring an estate out of the common course of inheritance.

Conquisitor. A purchaser, acquirer, or conqueror.

Conquistador. A Spanish conqueror of America.

Consacramentales. Same as COMPURGATORES and CONJURATORES.

Consangu'neal. Of the same blood or ancestor.

Consanguinei. Blood relations.

Consanguineo. Sprung from the same blood. A cousin.

Consanguineos. Same as CONSANGUINEO.

Consanguineus. Related by blood.

Consanguineus, frater. A half brother on the father's side.

Consanguinitas. Connection of blood; kindred or relation by blood. See AFFINITAS.

Consanguinitas, collateral. Same as CONSANGUINITY, COLLATERAL.

Consanguinitas, lineal. Same as CONSANGUINITY, LINEAL.

Consanguinity. The relation existing between those who come from a common ancestor. See AFFINITY.

Consanguinity, collateral. The relation existing between those not descending one from the other, but from a common ancestor; as brother and sister, uncle and nephew, cousins, &c.

Consanguinity, lineal. The relation which exists between those who are descended one from the other; and in which each generation counts as a degree, as father and son.

Conscience, courts of. See COURTS OF CONSCIENCE.

Conscience, liberty of. See LIBERTY OF CONSCIENCE.

Conscience of the court. The mind of the judge.

Conscience, rights of. The right to hold any religious opinion; or engage in any religious practice not in violation of law.

Conscientia rei alieni. In Scotch law, the knowledge that property held by one belongs to another.

Conseil de famille. A council or meeting of the family.

Consil d'etat. A council of State.

Conscill. In old English and French law, counsel.

Consciller. A counsellor.

Conscionable. In accordance with law.

Conscious. Capable of distinguishing between right and wrong.

Conscription. Compulsory enrollment in the military service.

Consensu. Unanimously. With general consent. According to the general wish.

Consensual. Created by consent. In Civil law, while a contract of sale is created by consent, a contract for the loan of an article does not exist until the article is delivered.

Consensus et concubitus. Consent and lying together. Applied to a marriage by those who went to Scotland to be married in order to escape the formalities of the English law.

Consent. To agree; to comply; to assent. An agreement to what is proposed.

Consent, age of. The age under which seduction is punishable as rape.

Consent, express. That expressly given either in spoken or written words.

Consent, implied. That implied from acts.

Consent, rule. A term used in the former fictitious action of ejectment to denote the consent by a defendant to a confession of lease, entry and ouster, and thus leaving the title the only issue to be determined.

Consent to marriage, age of. Age when a male or female arrives at puberty (which see).

Consequences. That which results from an act.

Consequential. Flowing from a cause; resulting from an act.

Consequential damages. See DAMAGES, CONSEQUENTIAL.

Consequents. In Scotch law, implied powers.

Conservator. A keeper, protector, preserver or defender. An arbitrator or umpire. In Connecticut, a guardian.

Conservator induciarum et salvorum regis conductuum. Conservator of truces and safe conducts of the King.

Conservator of the peace. One whose duty is to see that the peace is not broken.

Conservator of the truce and safe conducts. Same as CONSERVATOR TRUCIS.

Conservator trucis. An official charged with supervision over and jurisdiction to hear and determine offences against safe conducts of the King upon the seas, except in the Cinque Ports.

Conservator vel custos pacis. Conservator or custodian of the peace.

Conservatores pacis. Conservators, keepers, or preservers of the peace. See CUSTODES PACIS.

Conservatoris. Same as CONSERVATOR.

Consideratio. The judgment of a court.

Consideratio curiæ. The consideration of the court. The judgment of the court given after consideration and reflection.

Consideration. The price for which an undertaking is promised and without which it is not legal. Compensation.

Consideration, adequate. A consideration equal to that for which it is given.

Consideration, continuing. Consideration comprised of acts extending over a period of time.

Consideration, executed. A consideration performed or paid.

Consideration, executory. A consideration to be given in the future.

Consideration, express. Consideration stated in terms in an instrument writing.

Consideration, further. See FURTHER CONSIDERATION.

Consideration, good. One based on blood relationship. One good in law even though not valuable.

Consideration, gratuitous. One not based upon anything which makes it valid.

Consideration, immoral. A consideration against good morals.

Consideration, implied. That implied by law.

Consideration, legal. One good in law.

Consideration, meritorious. One founded on natural love and affection.

Consideration, moral. One believed to be a duty, though not enforceable in law.

Consideration, past. Something paid or done before the promise is given.

Consideration, valuable. Money or the equivalent of money.

Consideration, want of. See WANT OF CONSIDERATION.

Consideration, concurrent. Where the acts which comprise it are to be performed at the same time on both sides.

Consideration, equitable. Those founded on a moral duty though not enforceable in law.

Considerations, illegal. Those against public policy.

Considerations, impossible. Those incapable of being performed.

Consideratum est per curiam. It is considered by the court. The familar and proper words of a judgment.

Consideratur. It is considered.

Considered. Determined by a court. Adjudged.

Consign. To transfer in trust; to transmit goods. In Civil law, to deposit an article under order of court for the benefit of a creditor.

Consignatio. The payment of money into the hands of a third party, when the creditor refuses to accept of it.

Consignatory. One into whose hands money is paid when the creditor refuses to accept it.

Consignee. One to whom articles are consigned. See CONSIGN.

Consignment. Arrticles deposited or the act of depositing articles to be transported.

Consignor. One who consigns goods to another. See CONSIGN.

Consilia. Counsel; advice.

Consilarii. Counsel; counsellors.

Consiliarius. A counsellor, or councilor.

Consiliarius in lege. A counsellor in the law.

Consiliarius vel advocatus. A counsellor and advocate.

Consiliarius vel narrator. A counselor or countor.

Consilium. A considering together. Time allowed an accused to make his defence. Day appointed to argue a demurrer. An advice.

Consimili casu. In a like case. A writ of entry for a reversioner to recover land alienated by a tenant for life or by courtesy for a greater estate than he had. See IN CONSIMILI CASU.

Consisting of. Words excluding all but what is specified.

Consistor. An ancient magistrate.

Consistorial actions. See ACTIONS, CONSISTORIAL.

Consistory. A tribunal of which the bishop's chancellor was judge.

Consobrini. Cousin germans. See COUSIN-GERMAN.

Consolato del mare. The consulate of the sea. The title of a collection of European Sea-law, now generally considered the most ancient extant.

Consolidate. To make into one. To place under one control.

Consolidated annuities. Different English funds consolidated for the payment of the national debt.

Consolidated fund. See FUND CONSOLIDATED.

Consolidatio fructus et proprietatis. Same as CONSOLIDATIO.

Consolidation. Combining or uniting. A uniting of possession, occupancy, or profit of lands with the property.

Consolidation of actions. The trial of several actions at one and the same time, or a direction that the judgment of one shall be applied to all of several involving the same issue.

Consolidation of associations. The merging of two or more corporations organized for the same purpose, into one.

Consolidation of corporations. See CONSOLIDATION OF ASSOCIATIONS.

Consolidation rule. An order requiring one who has instituted several suits against the same defendant to consolidate them if proper pleading permit.

Consols. Abbreviation of Consolidated Annuities (which see).

Consort A companion.

Consortes. Owners of an undivided inheritance.

Consortship. Companionship. A vessel that keeps with another on a voyage. A contract by the owners of wrecking vessels to share money obtained by salvage without regard to which earned the same.

Consortium. Society, companionship. Union of chances. Conjugal fellowship.

Conspiracy. Originally an agreement of two or more to have a third indicted. A combination or agreement of two or more persons to accomplish an unlawful purpose, or a lawful purpose by unlawful means.

Conspiratione. An old writ against conspirators.

Conspirators. Persons guilty of conspiracy.

Constable. Anciently an officer of the highest dignity in England, though at first a superintendent of the King's stables. Now, a conservator of the peace and server of processes for justices of the peace.

Constable, High. The chief constable.

Constable, Lord High. An ancient officer in England with jurisdiction over matters in chivalry. The office was forfeited in 1521, but has been occasionally conferred since.

Constable of a castle. A castellain.

Constable of England. An officer having charge of the peace of the kingdom in the matter of war and deeds of arms.

Constable, petty. One subordinate to a High Constable. One charged with keeping the peace and serving the process of justices of the peace.

Constable of Scotland. An ancient officer who represented the King in his absence as commander of the army and also had jurisdiction of offences committed within four miles of the King, of Parliament, or other meetings held in the interest of the government.

Constable, special. One appointed for a particular purpose or for a special occasion.

Constablewick. The district of a constable.

Constabularius. A constable.

Constabulary. Relating to constables. Constables as a body.

Constabulery. The district of a constable.

Constat. It is certain. It appears. In England, a certificate that a matter appears of record. A certified copy under the Great Seal of the enrollment of letters patent.

Constat, non. See NON CONSTAT.

Constate. To establish. To constitute. To ordain.

Constating instruments. See INSTRUMENTS, CONSTATING.

Constituent. One represented by another. A client. A principal. One possessing political rights.

Constituere. To constitute, establish, appoint or ordain.

Constituimus. We constitute.

Constitute. To make. To establish by authority. To give power to. To appoint.

Constituted authorities. See AUTHORITIES, CONSTITUTED.

Constituting authorities. See AUTHORITIES, CONSTITUTING.

Constitutio. A settlement. An amount paid according to agreement. A statute. A provision of a statute. In Civil law, an imperial ordinance which is merely the will of the Emperor.

Constitutio dotis. Establishment of dower.

Constitution. An act, statute, or ordinance; an establishment. A provision of a statute. Establishment. Creation. The fundamental laws of a State or nation; the form of government. A sum paid according to agreement.

Constitution, U. S. The instrument by which the Federal Government is established and powers delegated to it by the States. It went into effect March 4, 1789. It contains seven articles and fifteen amendments. (See Appendix at the end of this work).

Constitutiones. Laws of the Roman Emperor, which he had power to enact as the fountain of justice.

Constitutional. In accordance with the Constitution.

Constitutional convention. A convention called to frame a new or amend an existing constitution.

Constitutional government. See GOVERNMENT, CONSTITUTIONAL.

Constitutions. Imperial ordinances. Papal laws.

Constitutions of Clarendon. The sixteen articles adopted at the assise of Clarendon. Ten of these were condemned by Pope Alexander as hostile to the church; six were tolerated as less evil. Henry II. had these adopted to settle the points in controversy between him and Becket. See ASSISE OF CLARENDON.

Constitutions of the forest. See LAWS, FOREST.

Constitutor. In Civil law, one who agrees to pay the debt of another.

Constitutum. In Civil law, an agreement to pay an existing debt.

Constraint. Restraint. In Scotch law, duress.

Constringas. Same as DISTRINGAS.

Construct. To put together. To erect.

Construction. The act of interpreting. Determining the sense and application as to the case or subject-matter in question. Interpreting so as to obtain the intention of the parties or makers.

Construction, Court of. See COURT OF CONSTRUCTION.

Construction, liberal. A construction which goes beyond the mere letter and enlarges or restrains the meaning to carry out the intent of the makers of an instrument writing or law.

Construction, literal. Same as CONSTRUCTION, STRICT.

Construction, strict. A construction which confines the meaning to that expressed. See CONSTRUCTION, LIBERAL.

Constructionist, strict. One who construes the U. S. Constitution in a way that limits the power of the Federal Government to powers expressly delegated by the States.

Constructive. Inferred or implied, not actual. Assumed as being within the intent of an instrument writing, document or law.

Constructive annexation. One implied by law.

Constructive assent. Assent implied from acts as distinguished from that expressed.

Constructive breaking and entering. See BREAKING AND ENTERING, CONSTRUCTIVE.

Constructive, conversion. See CONVERSION, CONSTRUCTIVE.

Constructive fraud. See FRAUD, CONSTRUCTIVE.

Constructive loss. See LOSS, CONSTRUCTIVE.

Constructive malice. See MALICE, CONSTRUCTIVE.

Constructive notice. See NOTICE, CONSTRUCTIVE.

Constructive possession. See POSSESSION CONSTRUCTIVE.

Constructive service. See SERVICE, CONSTRUCTIVE.

Constructive taking. See TAKING, CONSTRUCTIVE.

Constructive total loss. In Marine insurance, a loss which entitles the insured to claim the whole amount of the insurance, on giving notice to the insurers that all right to anything saved has been relinquished, and the subject-matter abandoned.

Constructive treason. See TREASON, CONSTRUCTIVE.

Constructive trust. See TRUST, CONSTRUCTIVE.

Constructure. The right to materials belonging to another which one has used in his house, on payment of compensation to the original owner.

Construe. To obtain the meaning of an instrument or statute by arrangement and inference.

Consuetudinarius. A ritual or book containing the rights and forms of divine offices, or the customs of abbeys and monasteries.

Consuetudinary law. Customary or traditional law.

Consuetudines. Customs.

Consuetudines et assisa de Foresta. The customs and assise of the forest.

Consuetudines feudorum. The customs or customary laws of fiefs.

Consuetudinibus et servitiis. Of customs and services. A writ allowed a lord who was deprived by a tenant of rent or services.

Consuetudo. Custom. A custom; a usage; a customary law; an unwritten law originating, established by usage. A local usage not annexed to any person.

Consuetudo Anglicana. The custom of England. The old English law as distinguished from the Roman or Civil law.

Consuetudo curiæ. The custom or practice of a court.

Consuetudo de gavelet. A rent or service withheld or detained. See GAVELET.

Consuetudo et lex Angliæ. The custom and law of England.

Consuetudo feudi. The custom of the fief. The principal source of law in the Book of Fiefs.

Consuetudo mercatorum. The custom of merchants.

Consul. In Rome, chief officers, two of whom were yearly chosen to govern the city. In England, the word originally signified an earl. A person sent by one country to another to guard the interests of merchants.

Consul, Deputy. One who acts as assistant to a consul.

Consul-General. A consul having supervision of the other consuls in the country to which he is accredited.

Consul-General, Agent and. See AGENT AND CONSUL-GENERAL.

Consul-General, Deputy. One who is an assistant to the Consul-General.

Consul-General, Vice. One who acts in absence of a Consul-General and also has other duties relating to the office.

Consul-General, Vice and Deputy. An assistant or deputy to a Consul-General, who also acts as Consul-General in the latter's absence.

Consul, Vice. One who acts in the place of a consul during the latter's absence.

Consul, Vice and Deputy. One who performs the duties of a vice consul and also a deputy consul.

Consular agent. See AGENT, CONSULAR.

Consular officer. See OFFICER, CONSULAR.

Consulate general. The place where a Consul-General resides.

Consultation. A special conference to determine some question.

Consultation, Writ of. See WRIT OF CONSULTATION.

Consulti periti. Lawyers.

Consulto. In Civil law, with design, with intent.

Consultory response. The opinion of a court on a special case.

Consummate. To make perfect. Lacking nothing.

Consummation. Completion; perfection. In Marriage law, sexual intercourse. See MARRIAGE.

Consumption. Destruction by use.

Contagious. Transmitting by contact.

Contained. Being within; included in.

Contamus. We count; we declare.

Contango. A commission to extend the time of the delivery of or payment for stocks.

Conte. In old English law, an earl. A county; a county court. An account. Narratio.

Conteckours. Disturbers of the peace.

Contek. A dispute. A disturbance; opposition.

Contemner. One who contemns; one who has committed contempt of court.

Contemplation. The act of considering a fact with the expectation that it will come to pass.

Contemplation of bankruptcy. See BANKRUPTCY, CONTEMPLATION OF.

Contemplation of Insolvency. Same as BANKRUPTCY, CONTEMPLATION OF.

Contemporanea expositio. Same as CONTEMPORANEOUS EXPOSITION.

Contemporaneous. Occurring or existing at or near the same time.

Contemporaneous exposition. A construction after taking into consideration the time and circumstances, or a construction made soon after a statute was enacted or an instrument writing executed.

Contempt. Disregard of the orders or authority of a court or legislative body. Wilful disrespect.

Contempt, constructive. Failure to obey orders of court to be performed without the presence of the court.

Contempt, criminal. Contempt committed in the presence of the court.

Contempt of court. Same as CONTEMPT.

Contemptibiliter. Contemptuously. Contempt.

Contenement. A thing held together by another thing; that which is connected with a tenement or thing holden. A man's standing by reason of his estate. That which is necessary to maintain a certain standing.

Contenementum. Contenement (which see).

Contentious. Litigious. Proceedings in ecclesiastical courts upon matters in dispute, as distinguished from its voluntary jurisdiction, probate, etc., where there is no dispute.

Contentious business. Applied in a Probate court, where there is opposition to probate or administration. See NON CONTENTIOUS BUSINESS.

Contentious jurisdiction. See JURISDICTION, CONTENTIOUS.

Contentment. Same as CONTENEMENT.

Contents. A sum promised to be paid, in a note, bill, or bond. That which a thing contains.

Contents. Those in the English House of Lords who vote for the passage of a bill. See NON-CONTENTS.

Contents, non. Same as NOT CONTENTS.

Contents, not. See NOT-CONTENTS.

Contents, table of. See TABLE OF CONTENTS.

Contents, unknown. An acknowledgement in a bill of lading limited to the package being in good order so far as outside appearance indicates.

Contentus. Contained.

Conter. To count.

Conterminous. Adjoining; having the the same boundary. Co-terminous.

Contesimatio. The punishing of every hundredth man.

Contest. To dispute. To dispute a right claimed by another. To resist. The style of a proceeding in U. S. public land law in which a right is disputed. A controversy.

Contestable. Capable of being contested.

Contestant. One who disputes a right claimed by another. A litigant.

Contestatio. Contestation.

Contestatio l i t i s. Contestation of suits.

Contestation. The act of contesting. Attestation. Joint testimony of witnesses.

Contestation of suit. The process o joining an issue upon pleading.

Contested election. See ELECTION, CONTESTED.

Context. Words immediately preceding or following the words under consideration in a statute or instrument writing.

Contiguous. In close contact. Touching. Lying next to.

Continens. In Roman law, holding together, as building with a common wall between them.

Continental Congress. See CONGRESS, CONTINENTAL.

Continentia. In Roman law, held together by a common wall, as buildings.

Contingency. An uncertainty. An event that may or may not come to pass.

Contingency with a double aspect. Two contingencies so arranged that one is the substitute for the other should one fail though neither is in derogation of the other.

Contingent. That which may or may not exist.

Contingent fee. See FEE, CONTINGENT.

Contingent interest in personalty. An interest in personal property which does not vest in possession unless the person having the same live until the happening of an event.

Contingent liability. Same as LIABILITY, CONDITIONAL.

Contingent remainder. See REMAINDER, CONTINGENT.

Contingent use. One which may or may not vest.

Continual claim. See CLAIM CONTINUAL.

Continuance. A postponement.

Continuando. By continuing; in continuing. A word used in a declaration of trespass, where the plaintiff could recover damages for several trespasses in the same action.

Continuation. A continuance; an adjournment. The adjournment. The adjournment of the proceedings in a cause from one term or day to another.

Continuing. Prolonging the condition of. Existing without interruption. Remaining in the same place or condition.

Continuing breach. See BREACH, CONTINUING.

Continuing consideration. See CONSIDERATION, CONTINUING.

Continuing guarantee. See GUARANTEE, CONTINUING.

Continuous. Not broken. Not interrupted. Remaining the same.

Continuous adverse use. Adverse use without interruption.

Continuous, non. See NON CONTINUOUS.

Continuous voyage. See VOYAGE, CONTINUOUS.

Continuum clameum. Continual claim. See same.

Contra. Contrary ; against ; otherwise than; opposite to; toward.

Contra formam collationis. Contrary to the form of the collations. A writ to recover lands which had been given in perpetual alms to any of the houses of religion, and aliened.

Contra formam doni. Against the form of the grant.

Contra formam feoffamenti. Contrary to the form of the feoffment. A writ issued where a man, before the statute of quia emptores terrarum, (18 Edw. I.,) en feoffed another by deed to do certain service; and the feoffer or his heir distrained him to do other services than than those set out in the deed. The tenant was allowed this writ to prohibit the distress.

Contra formam statuti. Against the form of the statute. Technical words in indictments and declarations on penal statutes.

Contra formam statuti in tali casu edito et proviso. Against the form of the statute in such case made and provided. The usual conclusion of an indictment for a statutory offense.

Contra jus belli. Against the law of war.

Contra omnes gentes. Against all persons. (Words used in old covenants of warranty).

Contra pacem. Against the peace. A breach of the peace.

Contraband. Contrary to a ban or public proclamation. Things by law forbidden to be sold or transported.

Contraband of war. Articles that are prohibited by the laws of war for a neutral to furnish either of two belligerents. A fugitive slave who escaped from a rebel master and took refuge within the Union lines during the war between the United States.

Contracausator. A criminal or one prosecuted for a crime.

Contract. An agreement between two or more persons for a consideration to do or not do a certain act.

Contract, absolute. An agreement to perform without regard to what may occur.

Contract, accessory. One which promises the performance in another contract.

Contract, aleatory. An uncertain contract; one the performance of which depends on an uncertain event, as a contract of insurance.

Contract, ante-nupitial. A contract made before marriage.

Contract, bilateral. A contract wherein the promise of one is consideration for the promise of the other.

Contract, certain. One dependent on the will of the party, or one which owing to circumstances can only be performed as agreed.

Contract, conditional. A contract in which performance depends on a condition.

Contract, commutative. A contract where the payment or performance on one side is equivalent to that on the other.

Contract, consensual. One complete by the mere agreement of the parties. One which can be dissolved by mutual consent.

Contract de facto. One which purports to pass property from one person to another.

Contract, dependent. A contract which depends on some act to be done by another.

Contract, divisible. A contract in which it is provided that the consideration may be apportioned on one side to agree with that given on the other.

Contract, entire. A contract requiring everything to be done on one side before consideration is due from the other.

Contract, essence of a. The stipulation in a contract without the performance of which the contract cannot be carried out in accordance with the intent of the parties.

Contract, executed. One already performed.

Contract, executory. One which requires something to be done in the future.

Contract, express. One formally stated in terms whether written or verbal.

Contract, fiduciary. A contract by which one delivers a thing to another to be returned when wanted.

Contract, gaming. Same as CONTRACT, WAGERING.

Contract, gratutious. A contract without consideration. If, however, the promisee suffer damage or forbear to do something because of a gratutious promise, the promisor is bound though no benefit accrue to him.

Contract, hazarduous. One where the performance depends on some uncertain event. See CONTRACT, ALEATORY.

Contract, illegal. A contract to do that which is against public policy.

Contract, implied. One implied from acts and circumstances.

Contract, impossible. A contract in which performance by one party at least is impossible.

Contract, indemnity. A contract by which one person agrees to hold another harmless from a claim or liability for any loss or damage therefrom.

Contract, independent. One in which the acts do not depend one on the other.

Contract, joint. One in which two or more are jointly bound or are to be benefitted jointly.

Contract, literal. In Civil law, one arising from something written.

Contract, marine. A contract relating to commerce or navigation upon the sea or navigable waters.

Contract, maritime. Same as CONTRACT, MARINE.

Contract, marriage. A contract made in contemplation of marriage. See MARRIAGE.

Contract, mixed. A contract where one party confers a benefit on the other of more value than that which he requires in return.

Contract, nexal. See NEXUM.

Contract, nude. One without consideration.

Contract, obligation of a. See OBLIGATION OF A CONTRACT.

Contract of affreightment. The contract for the hire of a ship.

Contract of beneficence. One by which only one of the parties is benefitted, as a contract of mandate.

Contract of benevolence. Same as CONTRACT OF BENEFICENCE.

Contract of bottomry. See BOTTOMRY; also BOTTOMRY BOND.

Contract of location. A contract for personal services or use of a chattel.

Contract of mandate. A contract by which a bailee agrees to perform without compensation, some service with regard to property committed to him.

Contract of mutual interest. One which is made for the mutual benefit of both parties.

(14)

Contract of sale. A contract in which one party agrees to sell and the other to buy.

Contract, onerous. A contract where a burden is imposed on a gift, for which the gift is not an equivalent, or where the consideration on one side is manifestly unequal to that on the other.

Contract, option. See OPTION CONTRACT.

Contract, oral. One not in writing.

Contract, parol. A verbal or written contract not under seal.

Contract, personal. One relating to personalty or personal actions.

Contract, pignorative. In the Civil law, a contract created by the pledge of property.

Contract, pre. A previous contract which prevents the carrying out of another.

Contract, principal. One which is independent of any other. A contract relating to or containing the principal object of the agreement.

Contract, quasi. That which is in the nature of a contract.

Contract, real. One relating to realty. In Civil law, one which arose from something done.

Contract, reciprocal. A mutual contract.

Contract, separable. One capable of being divided in the matter of consideration.

Contract, simple. Same as CONTRACT, PAROL.

Contract, special. One containing particular provisions, or relating to some particular matter connected with another contract, or in addition thereto. A specialty.

Contract, sub. A contract to perform all or part of that which another has contracted to do.

Contract, unilateral. A contract where the agreement is made in express terms by one party only.

Contract upon credit. One where the work is to be performed or article delivered and paid for in the future.

Contract, verbal. Same as CONTRACT, PAROL. In Civil law, one arising from something said.

Contract, void. One which is unlawful or illegal of itself, as a contract against public policy or prohibited by law.

Contract, voidable. One which can be avoided if the parties desire, but can be made valid on subsequent ratification, as a contract to which a minor is a party, which the latter can rectify on coming of age and thus make valid.

Contract, wagering. An agreement providing that the parties thereto are to gain or lose by the happening of some uncertain event in which they are not interested. Such agreements are against public policy and void.

Contraction. The act of becoming less. The shortening of words by leaving out one or more letters or syllables.

Contractor. One who contracts to do anything. One who makes it a business to undertake to perform and complete specific work for a lump sum, superintend the same and employ his own assistants.

Contractor, independent. One who contracts to complete work but in accordance with his own method, and without supervision or control of his employer.

Contracts, innominate. In Roman law, those not included within the nominate contracts, but which, when one party had performed they could be enforced, as permutatio (exchange) and transactio (compromise).

Contracts, named. Same as CONTRACTS, NOMINATE.

Contracts, nominate. In Civil law, contracts of a particular form and name and which arose in one of four ways either from something due, written, said or agreed to.

Contracts of record. Those evidenced by matter of record.

Contracts, pooling. See POOLING CONTRACTS.

Contracts, unnamed. Same as CONTRACTS, INNOMINATE.

Contractual. Arising from a contract.

Contractus. A contract. A drawing together. The entering upon or beginning an affair.

Contractus bonæ fidei. In Roman law, contracts of good faith. Contracts not determined by law, but, the discretion of the judge, and to which equitable defences could be made.

Contractus civiles. In Roman law, civil contracts. They could be enforced or sued upon in law without the aid of the prætor.

Contractus prætorii. Contracts which could not be enforced or sued upon in law without the aid of the prætor.

Contractus stricti juris. In Roman law, contracts determined in accordance with law only and to which no equitable defence could be made.

Contradico. To oppose, to refute, to contradict.

Contradict. To prove that the statement of a witness is incorrect or false.

Contraescritura. In Spanish law, a counter letter.

Contra-facere. To counterfeit, to imitate.

Contra-facio. A counterfeiting.

Contrafactio sigilli regis. Counterfeiting the King's seal.

Contrafaction. Counterfeiting.

Contra-juris. Contrary to law, unlawful.

Contra-ligatio. Counter-obligation, counter-binding.

Contra-mandare. To command against; to countermand. To make an order contrary to a former order.

Contramandatio. Countermanding.

Contramandatio placiti. A countermanding of a plea. The respiting of a defendant, or giving him further time to answer; a sort of imparlance.

Contra-mandatum. A countermand. An order made contrary to a former one; the revocation of a thing done or directed to be done before; the countermanding of a writ, pleading, notice, etc.; the revocation of a lease, a will, etc.

Contra-placitum. A counter-plea.

Contra-positio. A counter-position; a setting opposite. A plea or answer.

Contrarients. Name applied to the barons who took part against Ed. II., of England.

Contrarotulator. An officer who took notes of the accounts, rolls, receipts, etc., of other officers as a check upon fraud or error or to discover the same if it existed. The keeper of a counter-roll. An officer who has the inspection and control of the accounts of others. One who keeps a duplicate register of accounts.

Contrarotulator custumarum. Controller of the customs.

Contrarotulator hospitii domini regis. Controller of the King's household.

Contrarotulator Pipæ. Controller of the Pipe (which see).

Contra-rotulus. A counter-roll. A roll kept by an officer as a check upon another officer's roll.

Contrary. In violation of; not in accordance with.

Contra-tallia. A counter-talley.

Contratenere. To withhold.

Contravene. To oppose. To violate. To transgress. To be inconsistent with. To nullify.

Contravening equity. See EQUITY, CONTRAVENING.

Contravention. Opposition; obstruction. Violation of an obligation. In Scotch law, anything done by an heir of entail counteracting the intentions of the entail, which by the deed is declared a ground for depriving him of the entail. A disregard of the direction contained in letters of law burrows.

Contravention, action of. In Scotch law, an action brought for failing to regard letters of law burrows.

Contre. Against.

Contrectare. To treat. In Civil law, to hold of. To meddle with.

Contrectatio. Meddling with. Handling. Removing in such a manner that if not returned the removal would be larceny.

Contribules. Kindred; cousins.

Contribution. That given by one as his share. Average. General average.

Contributione facienda. A writ to compel contribution. See BREVE DE CONTRIBUTIONE FACIENDA.

Contributive. Aiding a result.

Contributor. One who makes, or is liable to contribution.

Contributory. Contributive. Casually sharing in some act. A shareholder in a joint stock company who is required to pay his contributive share of its debts, on its being wound up

Contributory negligence. See NEGLIGENCE, CONTRIBUTORY.

Controfacere. To counterfeit.

Controfacta. A counterfeit.

Controfactum. Counterfeit.

Controfactura. A counterfeiting.

Control. To exercise governing influence over. Regulation. Directing or governing influence.

Controller. An officer whose duties relate to the examination and verification of public accounts; also written comptroller.

Controller of the Currency. An officer of the U. S. Treasury having the enforcement of law relating to the national banks.

Controller of the Hamper. An officer of chancery who on receiving records from the Clerk of the Hamper, entered them of record.

Controller of the Household. An English officer who has charge of the accounts of the King's household.

Controller of the Pell. A clerk of the Chamberlain of the Exchequer who keeps his accounts.

Controller of the Pipe. An officer of the English Exchequer who sends out summons to levy the farms and debts of the Pipe. The Chancellor of the Exchequer. See PIPE.

Controller of the Treasury. An officer of the United States Treasury, whose duty is to examine and adjust public accounts, countersign warrants and direct legal proceedings for the collection of debts due the government. His decision is final and binding within the scope of his authority.

Controlment. The checking of the account of another. Keeping a duplicate account of an officer.

Controver. A false newsmonger.

Controversia. Controversy. A dispute; a suit at law or in equity; a civil action or proceeding.

Controversies, cases and. See CASES AND CONTROVERSIES.

Controversy. A dispute, contention; a suit at law or in equity; a civil action or proceeding.

Controvert. To oppose; to dispute; to deny.

Controverted. A term applied in England to a contest over an election before a court or legislative body. See ELECTION, CONTESTED.

Contubernium. In Roman law, the marriage of slaves.

Contumace capiendo. Same as BREVE DE CONTUMACE CAPIENDO.

Contumacy. Refusal to obey the order of a court or tribunal having power to issue orders.

Contumacy, actual. A refusal in open court to obey an order of court.

Contumacy, presumed. Failing to appear on being cited.

Contumax. One who refuses to appear and answer an accusation.

Contusion. A bruise without breaking the skin.

Contutor. A co-tutor; a co-guardian.

Conusance. Cognizance or jurisdiction; conusance of pleas.

Conusance, claim of. See CLAIM OF CONUSANCE.

Conusance of pleas. A privilege which a town or city has to hold pleas.

Conusanci. Cognizance.

Conusans. Acknowledgment.

Conusant. Knowing, understanding; privy to. See COGNIZANT.

Conusee. Same as COGNIZEE.

Conusor. Same as COGNIZOR.

Conustre. To acknowledge.

Convalescere. To gain strength; to become valid.

Conveer. To convey; to transfer.

Convenable. Suitable, agreeable, fitting, convenient.

Convencio. A covenant or agreement. (An old form of conventio).

Convene. To call or summon together. To summon to appear, as by judicial authority. To convoke. To assemble for some public purpose, or to take concerted action. To sue.

Convenient. Reasonable. Proper.

Conveniently. By reasonable exertion.

Convenio. To covenant; to agree.

Convenire. To sue; to covenant; to prosecute.

Convenit. He agrees; it agrees.

Conventicle. A private meeting for the exercise of religion. Illegal meetings of the non-conformists in England.

Conventiculum. An assembly, meeting, association. A place of assembly.

Conventio. A covenant; an agreement by deed in writing. In Canon law, the act of calling the parties. The act of summoning.

Conventio duplicata. An agreement in two parts; a duplicate agreement.

Convention. An irregular meeting of a Parliament or Congress of its own motion. A compact between nations. An agreement between military commanders in time of war. A treaty. A body of persons elected by the people or appointed by an official to meet at some specified time for a specified purpose. In Civil law, a mutual agreement.

Conventional. Agreed. Resulting from custom. Created by a person, not by law.

Conventional community. See COMMUNITY, CONVENTIONAL.

Conventional estates. Those created by the acts of the parties, as distinguished from those created by operation of law.

Conventional life estate. See LIFE ESTATE, CONVENTIONAL.

Conventione. A writ of covenant.

Conventions. Compacts between foreign countries regarding the arrest and extradition of fugitives.

Conventuals. Religious persons united in a convent.

Conventus. A meeting; a company; a corporation. A judicial assembly; a court of justice. A compact, convention, agreement. A convent.

Conventus juridicus. A Roman court with civil jurisdiction.

Conventus magnatum vel procerum. An assemblage of the great men or nobles. One of the ancient names of the English Parliament.

Conversantes. Conversant; acquainted; commorant.

Conversation. Intimate association. Sexual intercourse.

Conversation, criminal. See CRIMINAL CONVERSATION.

Conversion. Changing from one state, position, form or substance to another. Wrongful appropriation to one's own use of the goods of another.

Conversion, constructive. A conversion of goods implied by law from the acts of the party.

Conversion, direct. An actual unauthorized appropriation of the property of another to one's own use or for the use of one other than the rightful owner.

Conversion, equitable. See EQUITABLE CONVERSION.

Conversion, qualified. A conversion directed to be made by the testator for some specified or particular purpose.

Conversion, trover and. The form of an action for damages for the value of a thing wrongfully converted by another to his use. See TROVER.

Conversos. Converted Jews.

Convey. To transfer.

Conveyance. The act of transferring an estate by instrument writing. A deed which passes land from one person to another.. A vehicle of transportation. The act of transporting.

Conveyance, absolute. One which is complete and leaves nothing to be done.

Conveyance, adverse. One of two or more conveyances transferring conflicting rights.

Conveyance, derivative. One which enlarges, transfers, restrains, confirms, or extinguishes another, as release, confirmation, surrender, assignment, defeasance.

Conveyance, fraudulent. A conveyance tinged with fraud. A conveyance made to defraud creditors.

Conveyance, mesne. One between two others and of the same interest.

Conveyance of a vessel. The conveyance by deed of the title to a vessel.

Conveyance of record. A transfer by judicial records.

Conveyance, ordinary. One made by persons in the transfer of property as distinguished from one made by order of court or authority of law.

Conveyance, original. One which creates an estate or by which it arises, as feoffment, grant, gift, lease, exchange, or partition.

Conveyance, primary. Same as CONVEYANCE, ORIGINAL.

Conveyance, private. A vehicle used for private use.

Conveyance, public. A vehicle used for the conveyance of the public in general.

Conveyance, re. See RECONVEYANCE.

Conveyance, secondary. Same as CONVEYANCE, DERIVATIVE.

Conveyance, tortious. At one time, one which conveyed a larger interest than the grantor had, and caused a forfeiture.

Conveyance, voluntary. A conveyance without a valuable consideration.

Conveyancer. One who draws instruments writing and transacts other business relating to land, as a business.

Conveyances at Common law. Feoffment, gift, grant, lease, exchange, partition, release, confirmation, surrender, assignment, defeasance.

Conveyancing. The business of a conveyancer. The law relating to title particularly title to land.

Conveyances, innocent. In English law, such conveyances as a leasehold tenant can make without forfeiting his term. These were lease and release, bargain and sale, and where there was a life tenancy, covenant to stand seized.

Conveyances in pais. Conveyance on the land.

Convicium. In civil law, the declaration in public that a person mentioned has been guilty of an act against good morals.

Convict. To find guilty. One found guilty of an offence by a jury, or upon his own confession.

Convicted. Adjudged guilty of a crime by a competent tribunal.

Conviction. The finding guilty by a jury. The judgment by a court that the accused is guilty.

Conviction, abiding. See ABIDING CONVICTION.

Conviction, former. A plea that the defendant has been once convicted of the same offence.

Convince. To satisfy with proof.

Convinco. To convict of crime; to condemn in a civil action; to find guilty.

Convivium. A living together. A service requiring the tenant to provide meat and drink for his lord once or oftener in the year.

Convocation. A convoking, calling, or assembling together. An assembly of representatives of the clergy.

Convoy. A protecting or protected vessel. A force going with property to protect the same, particularly with vessels at sea.

Convoy, right of. Exemption of a convoy from search by belligerents.

Co-obligor. One bound with another in an obligation.

Cool blood. The absence of anger.

Cooling time. The time required for a person under the influence of passion or excitement to become calm and cool.

Co-operative. Operating together.

Co-operative association. Same as ASSOCIATION, CO-OPERATIVE.

Co-operative society. Same as ASSOCIATION, CO-OPERATIVE.

Co-operative store. A store established by a co-operative association at which the members can obtain goods at little more than cost and receive profits, if any, in proportion to their stock.

Coopertio. The branches of a tree cut down.

Coopertio arborum. The bark and wood of fallen trees.

Coopertum. A shelter for wild beasts in a forest.

Coopertura. A thicket.

Coopertus. Covered, covered over.

Co-optation. Mutual chance. Selection. The act of selecting one to fill a vacant membership.

Co-ordinate. Of the same order, rank or authority.

Co-ordinate jurisdiction. See JURISDICTION, CO-ORDINATE.

Copable. Guilty.

Co-parcenary. Joint inheritance; an inheritance by co-parceners. The estate inherited by co-parceners.

Co-parceners (or Parcenors). Co-heirs; such as have equal portion in the inheritance of an ancestor.

Co-parceny. Equal share of co-parcenors.

Co-particeps. A co-parcener.

Co-participes. Co-parceners.

Co-partner. A joint partner; sharer.

Co-partnership. Joint partnership. See PARTNERSHIP.

Co-partnery. In Scotch law, a contract of co-partnership.

Cope. A custom or tribute anciently due the King or lord out of the lead mines in some parts of England. The covering of a house. A hill. The upper garment of a priest.

Copeman. Same as CHAPMAN.

Copesman. Same as CHAPMAN.

Copesmate. A merchant.

Copia. A copy. Copious ; abundant. Opportunity of access to a wife for copulation.

Copia libelli. The copy of a libel.

Copia libelli deliberanda. A writ directing an ecclesiastical judge to furnish a copy of a libel.

Copia peritorum. Abundance of skillful lawyers.

Copia vera. A true copy.

Coppa. A cock of grass, hay, or corn, divided into titheable portions. The laying up of corn in copes or heaps.

Copper-plate. A sheet of copper from which engravings are printed.

Coppice. Young wood closely cut or lopped.

Coppire. To cover.

Coppire domum. To cope a house; or to lay on the roof and covering on top of it.

Copula. That which joins together, or binds fast; a band, rope, line, tie. A bond, a connection. Carnal connection.

Copulæ. Same as COPULA.

Copulate. To have sexual intercourse. To unite.

Copulation. Sexual intercourse.

Copulative. Tending to connect or unite.

Copy. The transcript of an original writing.

Copy, attested. See ATTESTED COPY.

Copy, certified. A copy certified by the proper officer as a true copy of the original writing of which he has the custody.

Copy, examined. One compared with the original or a certified copy.

Copy, exemplified. A copy certified by a competent court as a true copy of the original.

Copy, office. See OFFICE COPY.

Copyhold. A base tenure held at the will of the lord; anciently a tenure held in villeinage, which has been so held out of memory. The only evidence of title is the copy of the rolls made by the steward of the lord's court.

Copyhold Commissioners. In England and Wales, tithe commissioners part of whose duty was carrying the provisions of the copyhold acts into execution.

Copyhold, privileged. See PRIVILEGED COPYHOLD.

Copyholder. One who holds land by tenure of copyhold.

Copyholds, enfranchisement of. See ENFRANCHISEMENT OF COPYHOLDS.

Copyright. An exclusive right of making copies of a certain literary or other production within the copyright statute for a certain period of time. In U. S. the right is granted for 28 years with a renewal of 14 years.

Copyright, Common Law. Probably did not exist, as very few could write, printing was not known, and courts of equity were not introduced until long after the Common law was established.

Copyright, International. An arrangement by which copyright in one nation carries protection of the work copyrighted to such other nations as are parties to the arrangement.

Cora. A hill.

Coraage. An ancient and extraordinary impost which was payable in corn.

Coraagium. A tribute of a certain measure of corn.

Coracle. A small, ancient, fishing boat made of wicker work covered with leather.

Coram. Before. In presence of.

Coram Domino Rege. Before our lord the King.

Coram Ipso Rege. Before the King himself. The original name of the Court of King's Bench in which the King once sat in person.

Coram nobis. Before us (before the Court of King's Bench). The name of a writ of error on judgments of the Court of King's (or Queen's) Bench.

Coram non judice. Before one who has no jurisdiction. A cause determined by a court without jurisdiction; proceedings in a competent court which are void for irregularity.

Coram paribus. Before the peers or freeholders ; before whom instruments writing were once acknowledged or executed.

Coram paribus vicineto. Before the peers (freeholders) of the neighborhood.

Coram vobis. Before you (the Common Pleas). A writ of error on judgments of the Court of Common Pleas, or other courts than the King's or Queen's Bench.

Corbel. A niche in the wall where an image is placed.

Corbel stone. Stone laid for the front and outside of corbels.

Cord. A quantity of wood eight feet long, four feet wide and four feet high. 128 cubic feet.

Cordage. All material from which ropes are made; ropes belonging to a ship's rigging.

Cordon sanitaire. A sanitary line. A line of troops or impediments to prevent the spreading of pestilence.

Cordubanarius. A shoemaker. A cordwainer.

Co-respondent. One summoned to answer with another in an Admiralty, Ecclesiastical, Divorce, or Probate Court. One made defendant in a divorce proceeding with the husband or wife and with whom he or she is charged with having committed adultery.

Coretes. Pools; ponds.

Corium forisfacere. To forfeit one's skin. To be whipped.

Corium perdere. Same as CORIUM FORISFACERE.

Corium redinere. To compound for a whipping.

Corn. In England, wheat, barley, rye and oats collectively. In Scotland, oats; in United States, maize or Indian corn, either shelled or in the ear.

Corn laws. See LAWS, CORN.

Corn rents. Rents payable in part with wheat or barley.

Cornage. A tenure the service of which required the blowing of a horn on the invasion of the Scots. See CORNAGIUM.

Cornagium. Cornage. Also a tribute of money paid in lieu of cornage.

Cornare. To blow in the horn.

Corner. An angle made by two boundary lines. To buy up a commodity in order to control the market and fix its price. The condition of the market caused by such condition. See FORESTALLING.

Corodio habendo. A writ to exact a corody of an abbey or religious house.

Corodio habere. Same as CORODIO HABENDO.

Corodium. A corody or corrody. A right of sustenance; or a right to receive certain allotments of victual and provision, drink, money, clothing, lodging and such like for one's maintenance.

Corody. An allowance of sustenance. Money, food, or clothing due from a religious house to the crown for the sustenance of a servant or the King residing there.

Corona. A garland, wreath, or crown. (In old English, corane, coroun).

Corona mala. The clergy who abused their character.

Coronam Regis. The King's Crown.

Coronare. To make one a priest.

Coronare filium. To make one's son a priest. (Originally denied tenants by villeinage).

Coronation. The ceremony of crowning a monarch.

Coronation oath. See OATH, CORONATION.

Coronation roll. The roll upon which the official record of the coronation is engrossed.

Coronator. A coroner.

Coronatore eligendo. A writ to the sheriff to call an election of a new coroner. See BREVE DE CORONATORE ELIGENDO.

Coronatore exonerando. A writ for the discharge of a coroner. See BREVE DE CORONATORE EXONERANDO.

Corone. A word applied to all matters concerning the crown.

Coroner. Anciently an officer to enquire into certain matters which concerned the coronam regis, as sudden deaths, shipwrecks, treasure trove. They were also conservators of the peace. In the United States their duties are to enquire into the cause of sudden deaths, and serve writs where the sheriff is not qualified so to do.

Coroner's inquest. See INQUEST, CORONER'S.

Corpora. Bodies, etc.

Corpora corporata. Bodies corporate.

Corpora juris civilis. Same as CORPUS JURIS CIVILIS.

Corporal. Relating to the body.

Corporal imbecility. See IMBECILITY, CORPORAL.

Corporal oath. An oath where the witness lays his right hand on the New Testament.

Corporal punishment. See PUNISHMENT, CORPORAL.

Corporal touch. Actual bodily contact.

Corporale sacramentum. Corporal oath. See same.

Corporales res. Corporeal things; substantial things.

Corporalis. Corporeal (which see).

Corporate. Concerning a corporation; considered as one; belonging to one.

Corporate body. A corporation.

Corporate county. See COUNTY, CORPORATE.

Corporate existence. The period of time for which a corporation is created. As to when it begins depends on the law which creates it.

Corporate laws. Laws relating to corporations.

Corporate name. The name given a corporation on its creation.

Corporate member. A member of a corporation who has a right to vote as distinguished from one who is merely an honorary member.

Corporate purpose. A purpose in keeping with the object for which it was created.

Corporate rights. Such rights as are expressly conferred upon a corporation, or those necessary to enable it to carry out its object.

Corporate seal. See SEAL, CORPORATE.

Corporation. A body politic. An artificial person or being, endowed by law with the capacity of succession, existing only in contemplation of law, and possessing no powers not conferred by law. In U. S. Bankrupt Law of 1898, corporation includes limited or other partnership associations organized under laws making the capital subscribed alone responsible for the debts of the association.

Corporation Act. Stat. 13 Charles 2, stat. 2, c. 1, requiring all government officers to be ineligible to hold office in a corporate town unless within a year previous they had received the sacrament of the Lord's Supper, according to the Church of England.

Corporation aggregate. A collection of individuals united in one legal being.

Corporation authorities. In the State of Illinois, municipal officers either elected or appointed.

Corporation, business. One engaged in any character of legal enterprise. See CORPORATION, COMMERCIAL.

Corporation, charitable. Same as CORPORATIONS, ELEEMOSYNARY.

Corporation, commercial. One chartered to engage in commerce.

Corporation, consolidated. A corporation formed of two others and enjoying the rights of each.

Corporation, dissolution of. See DISSOLUTION OF CORPORATION.

Corporation, district steam. In New York, one incorporated to furnish steam power, or heat.

Corporation, domestic. One exercising its powers within the jurisdiction of the governmnnt which created it.

Corporation, ecclesiastical. Same as CORPORATION, SPIRITUAL.

Corporation, foreign. One created by another state or government. See CORPORATION, DOMESTIC.

Corporation, manufacturing. A corporation engaged in or created for the purpose of manufacturing some article.

Corporation, moneyed. One with power to do a banking, lending, or insurance business.

Corporation, municipal. A public corporation created to carry out objects of the government proper. (The act creating it or its charter is not a contract but creates merely a revocable agency).

Corporation national. A corporation created by the Congress of the United States, or under a Federal law.

Corporation, navigation. One incorporated to transact business through the navigation of waters.

Corporation, non stock. Any corporation not a stock corporation.

Corporation, open. One in which all the citizens or incorporators cast a vote for the election of officers.

Corporation, political. Same as Cor-poration Public.

Corporation, private. A corporation created for other than the interest of the government or the administration of political power.

Corporation, public. One created for the public benefit and to carry out the affairs of the State.

Corporation, quasi public. One which is incorporated partially for the benefit and convenience of the public; as a railroad, bridge, turnpike, ferry and similar corporations.

Corporation, quasi. One exercising powers of a corporate character, but which was not created a corporation by law.

Corporation, reviving a. Extending the time of its existence after the period for which it was incorporated has expired.

Corporation, sole. A corporation consisting of one person only and his successors, the mention of whom is necessary, in order that they may succeed to rights or duties conferred upon the present representative of the corporation.

Corporation, spiritual. That composed of some minister or officer of a religious organization.

Corporation, stock. One whose capital is divided into shares on which dividends are authorized to be paid.

Corporation, temporal. That composed of mayors, commonalty, etc.

Corporation, trading. One engaged in buying or selling of real or personal property.

Corporation, water. One incorporated to accumulate, store, conduct, furnish or supply water for domestic, manufacturing, or municipal purposes.

Corporations by prescription. In England, corporations which have exercised the privilege of such beyond the memory of man to the contrary.

Corporations, civil. Business as distinguished from charitable corporations.

Corporations, close. Where a few and not all of the members have the election of officers.

Corporations, eleemosynary. Those created for the distribution of alms for relief of the poor, sick, or impotent.

Corporations, homestead. Corporations organized to acquire tracts of land, divide the same into lots, and distribute these among the stockholders.

Corporations, law. Those which are civil or eleemosynary, but not ecclesiastical.

Corporations, lay. Such as exist for business purposes, or other than religious purposes.

Corporations, open. Where all the members vote on the election of officers.

Corporations, transportation. Corporations engaged in the transportation of persons or things, as telegraph, gas, electric light, pipe, water, line, navigation, railroad.

Corporator. An organizer or first stockholder of a corporation. A stockholder in a corporation.

Corporeal. Relating to or affecting the body. Bodily; personal. Having a body. That which may be touched or handled, as houses, lands, &c. See Incorporeal.

Corporeal hereditament. See He-reditament, Corporeal.

Corporeal property. Such as can be seen and handled.

Corps de garde. A body of men who watched in a guard-room.

Corps diplomatique. A diplomatic body. The embassadors of all nations, acting under the diplomas from their respective governments, under which they derive their official characters.

Corps politique. A body politic.

Corpse. The dead body of a human being.

Corpus. A body. Any object composed of materials perceptible by the senses; body ; substance.

Corpus Christi Day. A feast in honor of the Sacrament, instituted in England in 1264.

Corpus comitatus. The body of a county, the inhabitants of citizens of a whole county as distinguished from a part of the county or a part of its citizens.

Corpus corporatum. A body having been formed; a body corporated; a corporation.

Corpus cui jus inest. A body to which a right is appurtenant or inherent.

Corpus cum causa. The body with the cause. A writ out of chancery to remove both the body and the record.

Corpus delicti. The substance of the fault. The subject of the crime or its visible effect.

Corpus juris. A body of law; the body of the law.

Corpus Juris Anglici. A body of English law.

Corpus Juris Canonici. The body of the Roman Canon Law. It comprised Gratian's decree (decretum Gratiani) Gregory's decrees (decretales Gregorii noni) the sixth decretal, the Clementine Constitutions and the Extravagants of John. XXIII. and his successors.

Corpus Juris Civilis. The body of the Civil (Roman) law, comprising the Pandects in 50 books, the Institutes, the Codex Repetitæ Prælectionis, the Novellæ or Novellæ Constitutiones. The Codex Prælectionis was a revised edition of the Codex Justinianeus. The Latin translation of the Novellæ, which were originally in Greek, is termed the Volumen Authenticum. What is termed Decima Collatio, is not part of the Corpus Juris Civilis.

Corpus omnis Romani juris. The body of the whole Roman law.

Corpus pro corpore. Body for body. A phrase to express the liability of manucaptors.

Correction. Punishment by one having authority over the one punished.

Correction, House of. See HOUSE OF CORRECTION.

Corrector of the Staple. A clerk who wrote and recorded bargains for merchants in the staple. See STAPLE.

Corredium. A corody. See CORODY and CORODIUM.

Corregidor. In Spanish law, an officer having limited civil and criminal jurisdiction.

Correi. In Civil law, two persons obligated by the same instrument.

Correi credendi. Joint creditors.

Correi debendi. Joint debtors.

Correlative obligations. Involving or implying each other.

Correspondence. Communication by letters. The letters forming the correspondence.

Corroborate. To support. To confirm. To strengthen.

Corroboration, bond of. See BOND OF CORROBORATION.

Corrodium. A corody. See CORODY and CORODIUM.

Corrody. Same as CORODY.

Corrupt. To make bad. To taint. To take away legal privileges. To pervert. Tainted. Perverted. Practices dishonesty.

Corruptio. Corruption, violation or defilement of the person.

Corruptio corporis. A corruption of the body.

Corruptio sanguinariæ. Corruption of blood.

Corruption. That prohibited by law. Taint. Defect. An official act resulting to the benefit of the officer doing it, which is not consistent with a proper administration of the office.

Corruption de sanke. Corruption of blood.

Corruption of blood. The effect of attainder. A condition by which one is deprived of the right to inherit, hold, or transmit property. If a noble, he and all his posterity are rendered base and ignoble. It was part of a sentence in England on being convicted of treason or felony. The U. S. Constitution confines corruption of blood for treason, to life of person attainted. See ATTAINDER.

Corruptive. Corruptly.

Cors. Body.

Corselet. A small body. The name of an ancient armor used to cover the trunk of a pikeman.

Corse-present. A mortuary present. A customary gift, usually the best or second best beast, given to the minister of a parish upon the death of a parisher; so called because it was brought to the church with the corpse at the time of the burial.

Corsned. The morsel of execration; the mouthful of execration. Ordeal bread among the Saxons. It was cursed or blessed by a priest and an accused compelled to swallow it; if it choked him he was guilty, otherwise he was innocent.

Corsned bread. See CORSNED.

Cort. Short.

Cortarium. Same as CORTULARIUM.

Cortes. The National Legislature of Spain or Portugal and consists of an upper house and chamber of deputies.

Cortex. Bark; the bark of trees. The outer covering of anything as distinguished from the inner substance. The letter of an instrument as distinguished from the spirit.

Cortis. A court in front of a house.

Cortularium. A yard or court adjoining a farm; a curtilage.

Corus. A heaped measure of corn, said to be eight bushels.

Corus tritici. Same as CORUS.

Corvee. In French law, labor exacted without compensation from inhabitants of towns and districts.

Corvee seigneuriale. In French law, services due from a tenant to the lord.

Cosa juzgada. In Spanish law, a matter adjudged.

Cosbering. The right of a lord and his retainers to eat and sleep at the house of a tenant.

Cosduna. A custom or tribute.

Cosen. To cheat.

Cosenage. Kindred; cousinship. A writ to oust a stranger who abates the heir on the death of a collateral ancestor, or the grandfather's grandfather.

Cosening. Doing deceitfully; cheating.

Coshering. A feudal perogative or practice for the lords to entertain themselves and their followers at their tenant's houses.

Co-servant. Same as SERVANT, FELLOW.

Cosin. A collateral relative by blood, as a brother, sister, uncle.

Cosinage. Same as COSENAGE.

Cosinage de consanguineo. The relationship of blood. Collateral relationship or kindred by blood; consanguinity.

Cosmus. Clean.

Cost. All which is paid for an article up to the time it is sold.

Cost, actual. The actual price paid as distinguished from the market price.

Cost bond. See BOND, COST.

Cost-book. A book in which persons engaged in a mining enterprise enter their agreement, their receipts, expenses and other details relating to the matter.

Cost-book mining companies. Associations of two or more persons joined together to work a mine and share the expenses and profits in proportions agreed upon. Their agreement, expenses, profits, &c., are entered in a book termed a cost-book.

Cost, freight and insurance. Words meaning cost of an article with commission and cost of premium of insurance and the freight.

Cost price. The price paid for a thing when bought.

Costages. Costs.

Costard. An apple.

Costera. Sea coast.

Costes. Costages; costs.

Co-stipulator. One who joins in a promise with another.

Costs. Expenses of litigation. The sum allowed the successful party to a cause in addition to what he recovered for the expenses of litigation. It was not allowed as costs by Common law, but before Statute of Gloucester, 6 Edw. I. cap. 1, was included in damages obtained or taxed by the justices in Eyre. After Statute of Gloucester, juries taxed the costs and judges some times allowed additional costs, termed costs de incremento (which see). In England, money due a lawyer for professional tervices.

Costs, accrued. Costs up to a certain point in a cause that would be allowed with the judgment if allowed to go to judgment.

Costs, accruing. Costs becoming but not yet due. Those which become due and are created after judgment.

Costs de incremento. Costs of increase (additional costs). The costs adjudged by the court in civil actions, in addition to the damages and nominal costs found by the jury. See COSTS.

Costs, double. In U. S. double costs vary. In some States common costs and one-half more; in other States double the single costs. At one time in England, common costs and one-half more.

Costs, bill of. See BILL OF COSTS.

Costs, carry. To have the right to costs annexed to it, as a judgment.

Costs, certificate of. A certificate from the judge that a party is entitled to costs.

Costs, double. See DOUBLE COSTS.

Costs, increase of. See INCREASE OF COSTS.

Costs of prosecution. Costs incurred by the plaintiff in carrying on a prosecution.

Costs of suit. Costs allowed a party to a cause by the court. Costs incurred in carrying on a suit.

Costs of the day. Costs of suit for a particular day, or preparing for a particular day of trial.

Costs of the term. Costs incurred in holding court for a term.

Costs, final. Same as COSTS.

Costs, interlocutory. Such as are allowed on matters interlocutory.

Costs, security for. Security given by a plaintiff that he will pay all the costs if not successful in his suit.

Costs, taxation of. The adjustment and allowance of costs by one charged with that duty.

Costs, treble. In U. S. in some States common costs and three-fourths more ; in in others three times the single costs. At one time in England, common costs and a half and quarter.

Costumbre. In Spanish law, a custom; an unwritten law.

Co-surety. A fellow surety.

Cosyn. Same as COSIN.

Cot. A cottage.

Cotagium. A cottage; a small house or cot.

Cotarii. Cottagers.

Cotarius. A cottager or tenant who held a free socage tenure. Also same as COTERELLUS.

Cotellus. A small house or homestead.

Coterelli. Outlawed peasants; robbers.

Coterellus. Servile tenants. One who held by a villein tenure which allowed the lord to dispose of his person, issue and goods. See COTARIUS.

Coteria. A cot, home, or home-stall.

Co-terminous. Having the same limits or common boundary lines.

Coteswold. A place where there is no wood. Sheep-cotes ; a place where sheep feed on hills.

Cotgare. Refuse or tangled wool.

Cotland. Land held by a cottager whether by socage or villein tenure.

Cotsethla. The cottage belonging to a small farm.

Cotsethland. Some as COTLAND.

Cotsethus. A cottager by servile tenure.

Cotseti. Cottagers.

Cotsetle. The cottage belonging to a small farm.

Cotsetus. Same as COTSETHUS.

Cottage. Anciently a small house in England prohibited without at least four acres of land. (Subsequently this land requirement was repealed).

Cottagium. Same as COTTAGE.

Cotter tenancy. See TANANCY, COTTER.

Cotuca. Coat armor.

Cotuchaus. Boors; husbandmen.

Coture. An inclosure.

Co-tutor. A fellow tutor.

Couchant. Lying down.

Couchant and levant. Lying down and rising up; applied to animals which trespass on land for one night or more.

Coucher. A factor who lives abroad to buy wines. A book in which corporations register their acts.

Council. An advisory body. An ordinance-making power of a city.

Council, cabinet. See CABINET COUNCIL.

Council, common. See COMMON COUNCIL.

Council, ecumenical. A council of the Roman Catholic Church made up of the members from all parts of the world. See COUNCIL, GENERAL.

Council, executive. The council of a governor.

Council, general. A council of the Roman Catholic Church made up of members from most, but not every part of the world. The English Parliament. See COUNCIL, ECUMENICAL.

Council, family. See FAMILY COUNCIL.

Council, Legislative. The upper house of the legislature of a U. S. Territory.

Council of the North. A court established by Henry VIII., in 1537, to dispense justice in the Northern counties of England. Because of its harshness it was abolished by the same act which did away with the Star Chamber. See COURT OF THE STAR CHAMBER.

Council, order in. See ORDER IN COUNCIL.

Counsel. A pleader. A counsellor. An advocate. Advice. Purpose. Design, Information.

Counsel, leading. See LEADING COUNSEL.

Counsellor. An officer of a court whose occupation is giving advice and pleading the causes of others in a court of justice. See ATTORNEY; BARRISTER; PROCTOR; SOLICITOR.

Counsellor-at-law. An attorney-at-law. There is no difference between an attorney-at-law and a counsellor-at-law except in a few States which make such distinction. In U. S. Supreme Court, there is no distinction.

Count. A statement of plaintiff's case in court; a declaration, particularly in a real action. A particular part, distinguished by section or division of a declaration, containing a distinct statement of a cause of action. A particular charge in an indictment. A Norman governor of a county. See COMES.

Countee. He who had charge of a county. A count. (Anciently in England, a count was the highest title held by a subject).

Countenance. Credit or estimation. See CHARACTER; also REPUTATION.

Counter. Same as COUNTOR.

Counter affidavit. See AFFIDAVIT, COUNTER.

Counter bond. See BOND, COUNTER.

Counter brief statement. See STATE-MENT, COUNTER BRIEF.

Counter-claim. See CLAIM, COUNTER.

Counter-deed. A secret deed which alters or invalidates one previously given.

Counter demand. See DEMAND, COUNTER.

Counter letter. See LETTER, COUNTER,

Counter mark. Marks on packages previously marked. Marks placed upon packages by several persons to indicate that they shall not be opened except in the presence of the several owners.

Counter rolls. The rolls kept by sheriffs of appeals, inquests, &c.

Counter security. See SECURITY, COUNTER.

Counterfeit. False; not genuine. To make a false semblance of that which is true. Something made fraudulently or illegally in imitation of the genuine or legal.

Counterfeit coin. Coin manufactured or altered without legal authority, whether equal or not in market value to the lawful coin.

Counterfeiter. One who makes counterfeit money.

Counter-feasance. The act of forging.

Countermand. To make void by a subsequent order.

Countermand, actual. Where the .power is made void by writing in express words.

Countermand, implied. Where the power is made void by some act which prevents the other being executed.

Counterpart. A duplicate of the original.

Counter-plea. See PLEA, COUNTER.

Counters. See COUNTOR.

Counter-security. Security given to one who has become security for another.

Countersign. A military watchword. An official signature, as to a certificate, &c. To sign against another. To sign in addition to another or in attestation of the other's signature.

Counters, sergeant. Barristers at law of a superior degree.

Counterstock. The part of a tally kept by a debtor. See TALLY.

Countervail. To oppose with equal power. To compensate for. Power sufficient to counteract an effect.

Countervailing equity. One opposing another with equal importance or right to consideration.

Countez. Count. Count these. A direction at one time given a crier by the clerk of a court to count the jury after they were sworn.

Counties corporate. Cities or towns which possess the government within their limits.

Counties palatine. The counties of Chester, Durham and Lancaster, in England, which at one time had royal rights of government vested in the Earl of Chester, Bishop of Durham and Duke of Lancaster, respectively.

Countor. Anciently, a lawyer employed to conduct a cause in court. A debtor's prison. A bench on which goods are exposed for sale. One who counts or calculates.

Countour. Same as COUNTOR.

Country. A place. The territory under the jurisdiction of a government. The inhabitants of a territory, or division of a territory, competent to be jurors.

Countrefacon. In French law, the printing or publication of a copyrighted work without authority.

Country, conclude to the. To offer an issue to be tried by a jury.

Country, God and my. Answer of an accused when arraigned at common law and asked how he would be tried.

Country, puts himself upon the. Submits to the verdict of a jury. The conclusion of the defendant in certain pleas when he desires the issue he raises tried.

Country rock. The walls of a vein of mineral. All rock on the sides of a lode. Rock in a mineral district not containing mineral.

Counts, common. Statements of a cause of action framed in different forms so as to agree with possible variation in the proof.

Counts, money. Common counts for money had and received, paid, lent, or due.

Counts, special. Counts stating the particular facts relating to the case.

County. Shire. A portion or circuit of the whole territory into which a State or nation is divided for the more convenient administration of justice and other public affairs.

County, body of. The people or territory of a county.

County bridge. A bridge erected and kept in repair at county expense.

County Commissioner. An officer charged with the management of certain affairs of a county, usually the finances, public regulations and public property.

County, corporate. A city or town given a county government of its own by royal franchise.

County Court. See COURT, COUNTY.

County, foreign. A county other than that in which an act is done or a question raised.

County Palatine. See COUNTIES PALATINE.

County, power of the. The posse comitatus (which see).

County purpose. Purpose in accordance with the object of its organization.

County rates. Rates of taxation imposed in counties for public improvements.

County seat. The town or city of a county in which county business is transacted and courts are held.

County sessions. Sessions of the peace held every quarter in each county, in England.

(15)

County Supervisor. See SUPERVISOR, COUNTY.

County warrant. See WARRANT, CITY.

Coup. The effect of force or violence. A stroke, blow, deed, act, action; aim, move, charge, thrust; trick, event.

Coup d'assurance. Same as SEMONCE.

Coup d'essai. A first essay or trial; an attempt.

Coup d'etat. A stroke of policy in public affairs. An extraordinary and violent measure taken by a government, when the safety of the state is, or is supposed to be in danger.

Coup de grace. A stroke of mercy; the finishing blow.

Coup de main. A stroke of the hand, a sudden blow, a bold stroke; a sudden attack; a surprise; a bold enterprise.

Coup de maitre. A master stroke; a masterly move.

Coup d'œil. A peep; a quick glance of the eye.

Coup de pied. A stroke of the foot; a kick.

Coup de soleil. A stroke of the sun; generally, any affection produced by the sun.

Coup de vent. A stroke of the wind; a cyclone or hurricane.

Coup de theatre. An unforseen event (in a play); an unexpected event. Claptrap.

Coup de malheur. Unlucky hit.

Coupable. Guilty.

Coupe. Fault, blame.

Coupled. Related or associated together. Connected with. Annexed to.

Coupled with an interest. See INTEREST, COUPLED WITH AN.

Coupon. A certificate representing interest due at a time certain attached to a bond, to be cut off and presented for payment when due. A detachable part of a ticket or instrument writing representing something connected therewith.

Coupon bond. A bond to which interest coupons are attached.

Coupon stamp. A government revenue stamp with a coupon attached, used on intoxicating liquors.

Coupon tickets. Complete tickets fastened together, issued by carriers of passengers to be detached and given up in payment of fare.

Coups-de-grace. The final blows, usually against a vital part, on one who was being broken on the wheel. See BROKEN ON THE WHEEL.

Cour de Cassation. The Court of Cassation. In French law, the supreme judicial tribunal and court of final resort in France; established in 1790, under the name of the Tribunal de Cassation It received its present name in 1804.

Couredium. Same as CORODIUM.

Courier. A special messenger of haste.

Couracier. One who raced horses.

Courcher. Same as COUCHER.

Course. Manner of procedure. Direction.

Course, of. See OF COURSE.

Course of an action. Progression of a legal proceeding.

Course of a voyage. The route pursued from port to port.

Course of business. The usual custom in business or a particular line of business.

Course of law. See DUE COURSE OF LAW.

Course of trade. Same as COURSE OF BUSINESS.

Court. The King's palace. A place where justice is administered in accordance with legal forms and principles. In U. S. Bankrupt law, court includes referee in bankruptcy. The judge, judges, or the judge and jury when court is in session.

Court, Appellate. A court having jurisdiction to hear causes on appeal and writ of error.

Court, Archdeacon's. A minor ecclesiastical court with appeal to the bishop.

Court, Audience. A similar but inferior court to the Court of Arches; an appeal from which lay to the Pope.

Court, Arches. The most ancient court belonging to the Archbishop of Canterbury for debating spiritual causes.

Court, Bail. See COURT, PRACTICE (or BAIL).

Court, Baron. A court which was an incident to every manor, of which the freeholders were the judges.

Court, Bas. An inferior court not of record, as a Court Baron.

Court below. One from which an appeal is taken or to which a writ of error is directed.

Court, Bishop's. An ecclesiastical court presided over by the bishop's chancellor and held in each diocese. The proceedings were according to the Civil and Canon law.

Court, Central Criminal. The English court which superseded the " Old Bailey."

Court, Circuit. One having sessions at different places within a certain circuit.

Court, Circuit of the United States. Originally held by one of the Justices of the Supreme Court on circuit; but now by a circuit judge with whom a Supreme Court Justice sits. Its jurisdiction is fixed by statute.

Court, Civil. One which had jurisdiction of civil causes as distinguished from criminal.

Court, Civil Bill. An Irish court with jurisdiction similar to that of the English county courts.

Court, Commissary. In Scotch law, a former consistorial court with jurisdiction over domestic relations. A sheriff's court with jurisdiction of probate matters.

Court, County. A court which among the Saxons was presided over by an alderman or earl and a bishop; one judged by the Common, the other by Ecclesiastical law. Subsequently it became a sheriff's court. More recently, in England, a court for the trial of small causes. In the U. S., it is a statutory court, the duties of which are different in different States. In some cases it has criminal and appellate jurisdiction.

Court, Criminal. One with jurisdiction to hear and determine criminal charges.

Court, Crown. The English court in which cases on behalf of the crown are prosecuted.

Court, Customary. A court baron which heard matters relating to customary tenants and copyholders; the lord or his steward was the judge.

Court, Diocesan. Same as COURT OF CONSISTORY.

Court, District. A court of original jurisdiction in several of the U. S. having territorial jurisdiction within a defined district. Matters of which it has jurisdiction with the extent of its district are fixed by statute.

Court, District of United States. Inferior Federal court having civil, criminal, admiralty or prize jurisdiction and presided over by one judge.

Court, divided. A court in which there are judges who do not agree with the decision rendered by the majority.

Court, Ecclesiastical. Courts held to determine matters that concern religious doctrine.

Court for the correction of errors. A court for the correction of errors of law and equity.

Court, Foreign. A manor court.

Court, Forty Days. Court of attachment in forests. See WOODMOTE.

Court, full. See FULL COURT.

Court, General. The court or assembly of the public. A legislature. The name of the legislature of New Hampshire and Massachusetts.

Court hand. The style of handwriting in which records were recorded in England from an early period.

Court, High Commission. An ecclesiastical court of extensive jurisdiction established during reign of Elizabeth and abolished during reign of Charles I.

Court, House of Lords. The Supreme Court of England, having appellate jurisdiction over common law courts and chancery, now over Court of Appeal. Original jurisdiction in impeachment only. The Lord High Chancellor is the presiding judge.

Court, Instance. See INSTANCE, COURT.

Court, Judicial Committee of the Privy Council. A committee in England having jurisdiction over certain colonial causes, and appellate from the Courts of Admiralty and Commissioners of Lunacy.

Court, Justiciary. The highest criminal court of Scotland.

Court, King's. A body composed of men of importance anciently attendant on the King of England. It was the successor of the Aula Regis. It had the jurisdiction and also appellate jurisdiction from Popular Courts. In 12th century another King's Court was created with five judges. In 1179 the justiciars went on circuit, also acted in presence of King as the Bench. The first and larger King's Court had appellate jurisdiction over smaller King's Court. From the first came the Privy Council, from the second, the King's Bench.

Court, Knight's. A court baron.

Court, Lady. The court of the lady of a manor.

Court, Land. A court at one time existing at St. Louis, Mo., with jurisdiction of controversies over land and of matters of partition and dower.

Court, Landed Estates. An Irish court having jurisdiction over title to land.

Court lands. Domain or lands kept for the lord's family. See INLAND.

Court, Last. See LAST COURT.

Court, Lawless. See LAWLESS COURT.

Court, Leet. An ancient English court of record held once a year within a particular hundred before the steward for the cognizance of pleas of the crown.

Court, Levy. See LEVY COURT.

Court, Lord Mayor's. The highest court of record in London with law and equity jurisdiction over personal and mixed actions within the city without limit as to the amount. Theoretically the Mayor presides, but in reality the Recorder is the judge.

Court, Magistrate's. A local court in some U. S. cities for the trial of small causes.

Court, Marine. A New York city court having, among other matters, jurisdiction over claims for services at sea.

Court, Maritime. A court of Admiralty.

Court, Market. An ancient court in the market for the trial of misdemeanors committed in the market.

Court, Marshal's. Same as COURT, PALACE.

Court Martial. A military tribunal created by statute for punishment of soldiers, according to what is termed martial law.

Court-martial. To try by court-martial.

Court, Memorial. Same as COURT BARON.

Court, Michaelmas Head. In Scotland, a meeting to revise the roll of freeholders.

Court, Military. Same as COURT OF CHIVALRY.

Court, Moot. See MOOT.

Court, Municipal. A city court.

Court, Nisi Prius. An ordinary court for the trial of civil cases by a jury of the county and a single judge. The name of a one time Philadelphia court.

Court not of record. Originally, a court which did not have jurisdiction above forty shillings and did not enroll its proceedings nor proceed according to the Common law. (To-day, in the United States, it is an undetermined question as to what is a court not of record). See COURT OF RECORD.

Court of Admiralty. An ancient English court for the settlement of matters both civil and criminal which happened at sea or foreign ports, of which the Admiral was judge. In the United States, jurisdiction over these matters is vested in the U. S. District Courts.

Court of Ancient Demense. See COURTS OF ANCIENT DEMENSE.

Court of Appeals. In the United States an appellate court the jurisdiction of which differs in different States.

Court of Appeals in cases of capture. A court having appellate jurisdiction in prize cases, established by the Confederate Congress prior to the adoption of the U. S. Constitution.

Court of Appeals of U. S., Circuit. A Federal court of appellate jurisdiction next below Supreme Court. Its jurisdiction is fixed by statute. Created March 3, 1891.

Court of Arbitration, Chamber of Commerce. A board of Arbitrators of the New York Chamber of Commerce for the settlement of disputes between members.

Court of Arches. See COURT, ARCHES.

Court of Assistants. A New England colonial Supreme Court.

Court of Attachment. The Woodmote of the forest; also called the Forty Days Court.

Court of Augmentations. A court established by 27 Henry VIII., c. 27, for protecting the King's interests as to suppressed monasteries. Dissolved in the reign of Mary.

Court of Earmote. Same as COURT OF BERGHMOTE.

Court of Berghmote. A court not of record which administered justice among the miners of the Peak, in Derbyshire, England.

Court of Cassation. See COUR DE CASSATION.

Court of Chancery. In England, the court of the Lord High Chancellor. Its ordinary jurisdiction consisted in issuing royal writs. Its extraordinary jurisdiction was what is known as equity. A term applied to some U. S. Courts of equity jurisdiction.

Court of Chivalry (or Military Court). An ancient English court presided over by the Lord High Constable and the Earl Marshal, which determined contracts relating to war and deeds of arms for which the common law had not provided.

Court of Claims. A court for the consideration and determination of claims against the U. S. Government.

Court of Common Bench. Same as COURT OF COMMON PLEAS.

Court of Common Pleas. (Communis Bancus). Derived from old King's Bench. It had exclusive jurisdiction of real actions and universal, and for a time exclusive, jurisdiction of personal actions between subjects. It was composed of four puisne and one chief justice. In modern times, a Common law court of record, having original jurisdiction of matters civil and criminal. Generally of statutory jurisdiction.

Court of Consistory. An ecclesiastical court held by each bishop with appeal to the archbishop.

Court of Construction. A court which is called upon to construe a will, as distinguished from one which has merely to decide whether it be valid or not, as a Probate Court.

Court of County Commissioners. A court of record held in Alabama counties composed of the Probate judge and four commissioners.

Court of County Sessions. Same as COURT OF QUARTER SESSIONS.

Court of Delegates. The highest appellate court in ecclessiastical matters after the abolishment in England of appeals to Rome.

Court of Dusty Feet. Same as the COURT OF PIEPOWDERS.

Court of Equity. A court having jurisdiction to exercise equity powers as distinguished from a court of law. Equity powers are such only as cannot be exercised by a court of law. Strictly a court of equity has no jurisdiction of any matter in which a remedy can be obtained in a court of law. See EQUITY; also LAW.

Court of Error. The court of Exchequer Chamber and House of Lords. A court having appellate jurisdiction in law, equity, or admiralty.

Court of Errors and Appeals. The highest appellate court in New Jersey.

Court of Exchequer. In England, originally the royal treasury, to keep accounts, collect revenues, &c. Afterwards had two sides: Receipt side, which managed revenues, and plea side, which had jurisdiction of personal actions between subjects. Until 1842, it had both Equity and Common law side when the equity jurisdiction was transferred to chancery. The Judges were four puisne barons and a chief baron.

Court of Exchequer Chamber. An intermediate Court of Appeal between Superior Courts of Common law and House of Lords. When on appeal from one court, judges of the other two courts sit.

Court of Faculties. An archbishop's court.

Court of First Instance. Court of primary jurisdiction.

Court of General Jurisdiction. One having jurisdiction to hear and determine various causes, both civil and criminal.

Court of General Sessions. A court of general criminal jurisdiction.

Court of Great Session. A superior court of Wales.

Court of Green Cloth. A court within the King's (or Queen's) household having charge of the King's Court and keeping the peace therein. It was held in the counting house, at a board covered with green cloth, from which it takes its name.

Court of High Commission. An ecclesiastical and admiralty court of appellate jurisdiction established under Henry VIII.

Court of Hustings. A court held in London before the mayor and aldermen and having jurisdiction of pleas of lands within that city. A court of local jurisdiction peculiar to some Virginia cities.

Court of Impeachment. A court for the trial of government officials. In England, it is the House of Lords; in U. S. in the case of Federal government officials the Senate. A trial of the President is presided over by the Chief Justice of the Supreme Court. In the State governments, each State has its own tribunal.

Court of Inquiry. A tribunal for investigating matters pertaining to the military or naval service.

Court of Justice Seat. The principal forest court. See JUSTICE SEAT.

Court of Justiciary. A Scotch court with original and appellate criminal jurisdiction over civil cases arising in any part of Scotland.

Court of King's (or Queen's) Bench. It in theory followed the King's person; in fact sat at Westminster. It was the highest court of Common law in England. It had four puisne and one chief justice and took cognizance of criminal cases on Crown side and civil cases on plea side. See COURT, KING'S.

Court of Last Resort. One from which there is no appeal.

Court of Law. One having jurisdiction of actions and suits at law as distinguished from a court of equity. See EQUITY; also LAW.

Court of Limited Jurisdiction. One the jurisdiction of which is limited to specified cases.

Court of Magistrates and Freeholders. A former South Carolina criminal court for the trial of slaves and free negroes.

Court of Marches. A court on the marches of Wales having limited jurisdiction.

Court of Marshalsea. Same as COURT, PALACE.

Court of Ordinary. In some of the United States a court having jurisdiction of probate matters.

Court of Original Jurisdiction. A court which has jurisdiction to hear and determine a cause in the first instance as distinguished from an appellate court.

Court of Oyer and Terminer. An English court of two or more judges of assize held twice a year in each county to hear and determine criminal causes. In United States, a court for the trial of felonies.

Court of Passage. An English court having jurisdiction of matters within the borough of Liverpool and also admiralty matters.

Court of Peculiars. A branch of the Arches Court, to which appeal lay.

Court of Pedlars. Same as the COURT OF PIEPOWDERS.

Court of Piepoudre. Same as COURT OF PIEPOWDERS.

Court of Piepowders. A court of record anciently held at fairs to do justice between buyer and seller.

Court of Private Land Claims. A court created by act of U. S. Congress, March 3, 1891, with jurisdiction over claims for lands in the territory acquired from Mexico, based on Mexican title.

Court of Quarter Sessions. A court held quarterly. An inferior criminal court held four times a year in each county.

Court of Record. A court which enrolls its proceedings, which are according to the Common law, and has functions independent of the person of the judge who holds it. (This definition is open to criticism. As to what is or is not a Court of Record in the U. S. is to-day an undetermined question. In England, the power to fine and imprison made a court one of record). See COURT NOT OF RECORD.

Court of Regard. An official examination of mastiffs held in England every three years for the purpose of lawing them. See EXPEDITATE.

Court of Requests. An English court for hearing causes brought before the King by petition. An English court for the recovery of small claims.

Court of Review. One whose principal function is passing upon final decisions of other courts.

Court of Session. The highest civil tribunal in Scotland.

Court of Sessions. Courts of criminal jurisdiction in several of the United States.

Court of Shepway. In old English law, a court of which the lord warden of the cinque port was judge.

Court of Special Jurisdiction. Same as COURT OF LIMITED JURISDICTION.

Court of St. Martin Le Grand. An ancient, but local, London Court so called from the church of that name.

Court of Star Chamber. A tyrannical English tribunal which usurped jurisdiction and created offences and punishments not known to any statute or the common law. It consisted of several lords and two common law judges, and acted without a jury. It had a statutory jurisdiction which was limited by stat. 3 Henry VII., c. 1, to matters therein specified. It was abolished in 1640.

Court of Survey. An English court having jurisdiction of appeals by masters or owners from orders detaining their ships because unsafe.

Court of Swainmote. See SWAINMOTE.

Court of Swanimote. See SWAINMOTE.

Court of Teind. In Scotch law, a court having jurisdiction of tithes, stipends and parish boundaries. It was composed of five judges.

Court of the Chief Justice in Eyre. Same as COURT OF JUSTICE SEAT.

Court of the Coroner. A court of inquiry and of record presided over by the coroner, to enquire into the cause of a sudden death. An inquest of office.

Court of the Duchy of Lancaster. A court held by the Chancellor of the Duchy of Lancaster with equitable jurisdiction over lands held in that duchy of the King.

Court of the General Quarter Sessions of the Peace. A criminal court in New Jersey. A county criminal court in England.

Court of the King's House. A court for the trial of offences in or within two hundred feet of the King's houses.

Court of the Steward and Marshal. Same as COURT, PALACE.

Court of the Trailbaston. A court established by Edw. I., with jurisdiction over certain criminal offences, and presided over by Justices of Trailbaston (which see).

Court of the Two Universities. See COURTS, UNIVERSITY.

Court of Wards and Liveries. A court founded by Henry VIII., to enquire into matters arising from tenures in chivalry, as concerning wardship, marriage and lands of the King's tenants in capite. Abolished 12 Car. II. c. 24.

Court, Old Bailey. See OLD BAILEY.

Court, Open. One in session. One open to orderly spectators.

Court, Orphans'. A court having jurisdiction over the estates of deceased persons and the guardianship of orphans.

Court, Palace. A court held by the steward and marshal of the King's household having jurisdiction of personal actions which arose within twelve miles of the royal palace at Whitehall, excluding London. A court of the Marshalsea.

Court, Parish. A local court in a Louisiana parish.

Court, Pentice. A court held by the sheriff of Chester, in a place there commonly called the pentice (a pent house or open shed covered with boards).

Court, Police. A city court for the trial of small offences.

Court, Policy of Assurance. A court created during the reign of Elizabeth to determine causes between merchants relating to policy of insurance.

Court, Practice (or Bail). Auxiliary to the King's Bench, presided over by puisne judges in rotation.

Court, Prerogative. Originally in England, an ecclesiastical court having cognizance of all testamentary causes. In New Jersey, a court held by the chancellor sitting as ordinary to determine appeals from the Orphans' Court.

Court, Prize. One having jurisdiction over prize cases. In U. S. the Federal District Court.

Court, Probate. A court having jurisdiction of the proof of wills, of guardianship, and the settlement of estates.

Court Provincial. An English Ecclesiastical court.

Court, Registers. A Pennsylvania court with probate jurisdiction.

Court, Rolls. The rolls of a manor.

Court, Superior. A court in some of the United States between the inferior and Supreme Courts, the jurisdiction of which is fixed by statute.

Court, Supreme. In some States of the United States, the court of last resort.

Court, Supreme of District of Columbia. An inferior court, of both civil and criminal jurisdiction with both local and Federal jurisdiction.

Court, Supreme of Judicature. In England, a consolidation of the High Court of Chancery, King's Bench, Common Pleas, Exchequer, High Court of Admiralty, Court of Probate and Divorce Court.

Court, Supreme of the United States. Court of last resort in Federal matters.

Court, Surrogate. An Orphans' or Probate Court.

Court, Thegnmen's. A Saxon court only open to tenants in capite or Thegns.

Court, Trial. A court which tries a cause as distinguished from an appellate court.

Courtesy. Same as CURTESY.

Courtesy of England. Same as CURTESY.

Courts, Appellate. In U. S. Bankrupt law of 1898, means Circuit Court of Appeals, the Supreme Courts of the Territories, and the Supreme Court of the U. S.

Courts, Borough. In England, courts of record, held by charter, prescription, or act of Parliament, in a borough, the Recorder of which is usually the judge.

Courts, Burlaw. In Scotch law, courts composed of neighbors selected to determine a matter in controversy between two neighbors.

Courts, Clerk of. See CLERK OF COURTS.

Courts, Consular. The Courts held in a foreign country by the consul of another country stationed there, for the trial of causes to which citizens of the same country as the consul are parties.

Courts, Diocesan. The consistorial courts of a diocese exercising jurisdiction in ecclesiastical matters.

Courts, Domestic. Those which have jurisdiction over the territory in which the person referring to them is resident.

Courts, Ecclesiastical. In England, these were the Archdeacon's Courts; Consistory Courts ; Court of Arches ; Court of Peculiars ; Prerogative Courts of the two Archbishops; Courts of Faculties; Courts of Delegates.

Courts, Hafne. Courts anciently held in English seaport towns.

Courts, Ferding. Ancient Gothic courts of inferior jurisdiction ; there were four in each jurisdiction.

Courts, Foreign. Courts of a foreign State or country.

Courts, Forest. Courts established to carry out provisions of Forest laws; they were courts of attachment, of regard, of justice seat and of sweinmote.

Courts, Haven. Same as COURTS, HAFNE.

Courts, Honour. Courts held within honours which decided disputes concerning precedency and honour.

Courts, Hundred. Inferior courts in a county held by the steward with freeholders as judges.

Courts, Inferior. Those from which an appeal may be taken or to which a writ of error may be directed.

Courts, Local. Courts whose jurisdiction is confined to a certain territory. In the United States, the State as distinguished from the Federal Courts.

Courts, Mineral. Ancient courts for administration of justice among tin miners in England. See COURTS STANNERY.

Courts-martial, Naval. A tribunal for the trial of naval officers charged with violation of the regulations of the navy.

Courts, Naval. Courts held to enquire into naval matters. A board in the English navy authorized to enquire into various matters relating to the conduct of officers and sailors.

Courts of Ancient Demesne. Courts anciently held by a bailiff appointed by the King, where tenants of the King's demesnes alone could be impleaded.

Courts of Conscience. Same as COURT OF REQUESTS. Courts for the recovery of small debts, in England.

Courts of Bankruptcy. In the United States, under the Act of Congress, approved July 1st, 1898, the District courts of the U. S. in the several States, the Supreme Court of the District of Columbia, the District Courts of the several Territories, and the United States Courts in the Indian Territory, and the District of Alaska. Their jurisdiction is specified in the act above mentioned.

Courts of Pedis Pulverizati. Courts of Piepowders.

Courts of the Cinque Ports. Courts at one time held in the English Cinque Ports before the Mayor and Aldermen.

Courts of the United States. The courts established by the Constitution and by Congress. These comprise the Senate, when sitting as a court of impeachment; the Supreme Court; the Circuit Court of Appeals; the Circuit Courts; District Courts; Court of Claims, and the Legislative Courts in the Territories and District of Columbia.

Courts, Ordinary's. The Court of Consistory and Archbishop's Court.

Courts, Popular. Local Saxon courts, as county and hundred courts.

Courts, Royal. The King's courts.

Courts, Stannery. Courts in Devonshire and Cornwall, England, for the administration of justice among the tin miners. They were courts of record and were held before the Lord Warden by virtue of various acts and grants of Parliament.

Courts, Superior of Common Law. In England, King's Bench, Common Pleas, Exchequer.

Courts, Superior of Equity. In England, Court of Chancery; Master of the Rolls; three Vice-Chancellor's Courts; two courts of Lord Justices of Appeal; Court of Appeal in Chancery.

Courts, Territorial. Courts created by Congress for the Territories.

Courts, University. Courts in the Universities of Oxford and Cambridge, England, having jurisdiction of personal actions arising within the university; also criminal courts with jurisdiction over offences committed within the same universities. They were established by Henry III.

Courts, Vice-Admiralty. Tribunals in British colonial possessions with admiralty jurisdiction.

Cousin. One collaterally related from a common ancestor, not a brother or sister. A noble of the King's Council. A fellow sovereign.

Cousinage. Same as COSENAGE.

Cousin-german. In Canon law, a first or full cousin.

Coustum. Custom, toll, tribute.

Coustumier. A book of customs and usages in the old law of France.

Couth. Know, knowing.

Couthutlaugh. One who receives and conceals an outlaw.

Coutome. Custom.

Couvenable. Convenient or suitable.

Couverture. In French law, a deposit placed with a broker to indemnify the broker against possible loss in making purchases for his principal. See COVERTURE.

Covenable. Same as COUVENABLE.

Covenant. A mutual agreement made by deed, signed, sealed and delivered, or inferred by law from certain words. A form of express contract contained in a deed, to do a direct act, or to omit one.

Covenant, absolute. An unconditional covenant.

Covenant, affirmative. A covenant to do a thing.

Covenant against incumbrances. A covenant that there are no incumbrances upon an estate.

Covenant, alternative. A covenant reserving the right of electing which of certain things to do.

Covenant, assertory. See ASSERTORY COVENANT.

Covenant, auxiliary. A covenant pertaining to and performed with another.

Covenant, collateral. One relating to a conveyance, but not directly connected with it.

Covenant, concurrent. One to be done with another.

Covenant, declaratory. One declaring or directing a use.

Covenant, dependent. A covenant which is dependent upon the performance of another covenant.

Covenant, disjunctive. One which allows an election as to the performance of one or more things.

Covenant en fait. Covenant in fact or deed.

Covenant, executed. One already done.

Covenant, executory. One to be done in the future.

Covenant, express. One stated in express terms.

Covenant for further assurance. A covenant by a seller of real estate to perform all acts which may be necessary to perfect the title of the land granted.

Covenant for quiet enjoyment. See COVENANT OF QUIET ENJOYMENT.

Covenant, general. One relating to lands in general, not any particular land.

Covenant, implied. One implied from the facts by law.

Covenant in deed. Same as COVENANT IN FACT.

Covenant in fact. That which is expressly agreed between the parties in specified terms.

Covenant in gross. Same as COVENANT, COLLATERAL.

Covenant in law. That which the law intends to be done though not expressed in words, or which the law infers from certain words.

Covenant, independent. One which is not dependent or conditioned upon any other.

Covenant, inherent. One which is directly connected with the property.

Covenant, intransitive. One limited to the covenantor.

Covenant, joint. A covenant which binds the covenantors jointly.

Covenant, joint and several. One which binds the covenantors both singly and jointly.

Covenant, negative. A covenant not to do a thing.

Covenant not to sue. A covenant not to attempt to enforce a right of action.

Covenant, obligatory. A covenant which is binding upon the party himself.

Covenant of quiet enjoyment. A covenant that the grantee or lessee shall be allowed to enjoy the land without interruption.

Covenant of non-claim. A covenant by a seller not to claim any title in land.

Covenant of right to convey. An assurance that the covenantor has title and right to convey the land in question.

Covenant of seisin. An assurance by the covenantor that he has the estate he pretends to convey.

Covenant of warranty. A covenant that the grantor and his heirs will warrant and defend and if necessary make good the title granted.

Covenant, personal. A covenant to be performed in person or where some particular person is to have the benefit. One which binds the covenantor personally and is not binding upon the real estate.

Covenant, principal. One which relates directly to the matter of contract as distinguished from auxiliary covenants.

Covenant, real. A covenant by which one agrees to convey real property. A covenant which binds the heirs. A covenant which runs with the land.

Covenant running with land. A covenant which is so annexed to land that it cannot be separated by a transfer of the title. A covenant that each succeeding assignee or heir is bound to observe or is entitled to the benefit of.

Covenant, Solemn League and. A seditious conspiracy originated in Scotland and declared illegal by English statute during reign of Charles II.

Covenant, special. One relating to particular lands as opposed to Covenant, General.

Covenant, specific. Same as COVENANT, SPECIAL.

Covenant to convey. An agreement under seal to convey a certain estate on certain conditions.

Covenant to stand seized to uses. A covenant by which a man bound himself and his heirs to stand seized of certain lands to the use of another or others.

Covenant, transitive. Covenant which passes to the representatives of the covenantor.

Covenant, writ of. A writ directing a sheriff to notify the defendant to keep his covenant or show cause why.

Covenantee. One to whom a covenant is made.

Covenantor. One who makes a covenant.

Covenants for title. Covenants which guarantee complete title and full and uninterrupted enjoyment of the estate conveyed Covenants of seizin, a right to convey, for further assurance, of quiet enjoyment, of warranty, and against incumbrances.

Covenants, illegal. Those in violation of law or against public policy.

Covenants in gross. Such as do not run with the land.

Covenants, mutual. Covenants which are consideration for each other.

Covenants, performed. The style of a plea to an action of covenant.

Covenants, several. Covenants which bind the covenantors severally.

Covenants, usual. See USUAL COVENANTS.

Coventry Act. Stat. 22 and 23 Car. II., c. 1, providing for the punishment of assaults with intent to disfigure or maim. The act was passed because of an assault upon Sir John Coventry.

Cover et key. Cone and key.

Covert. Under cover, authority, protection; sheltered. A thicket where game is wont to hide. A flock of feathered animals, as quail, pheasants, &c.

Covert baron. A married woman. Under the authority or protection of a husband.

Covert de baron. Same as COVERT BARON.

Covert feme. A married woman living with her husband.

Covert-way. A level space around an ancient fortification.

Coverture. A state of being covered or protected; a state of subjection or dependence. That condition of a woman wherein her existence is suspended and incorporated in that of her husband.

Covin. A secret contrivance between two or more persons to defraud and prejudice another of his rights.

Covina. Covin.

Covinous. Fraudulent.

Cowardice. Lack of courage in the performance of a dangerous duty.

Cowdash. In Scotch law, a young cow of two years.

Cr. Abbreviation of criminal; also of crown and credit.

Craft. A guild. A trade. All kinds of sailing vessels.

Craiera. A small sailing vessel; a smack.

Crail. An engine anciently used to catch fish.

Cranage. A license to use a crane for profit; also the toll paid, the money taken for such work.

Cranagium. Cranage.

Crane. A machine for raising weights.

Crannock. An ancient measure of corn.

Crass. Same as CRASSUS.

Crassa ignorantia. Gross ignorance.

Crassa infortunia. A great misfortune, misadventure.

Crassa negligentia. Great or gross negligence. The want of that care which every man of common sense, under the circumstances, takes of his own property.

Crassa piscis. Large fish.

Crassa turba. A gross or great turmoil, great disturbance.

Crassus. Solid, thick, dense, fat, gross, etc.

Crastino. On the day after. A title formerly given to the return days of writs, days in bank, or appearance days in Courts at Westminster.

Crastino Sancti Vincentii. The day after the feast of St. Vincent, the Martyr, or 22nd of January, being the date of the statute of Omerton, 20 Henry III.

Crate. A frame work used in transportation of manufactured articles, vegetables, or small animals. To put in a crate. The amount held by a crate.

Crater. The area within which a submarine mine or torpedo is destructive.

Crates. An iron gate in front of a prison used by Romans.

Cravant. Same as CRAVEN.

Cravare. To impeach.

Crave. To request. To demand.

Craven. (To beg). One who, in the duellum or battel, being defeated and has begged of his antagonist that his life be spared. See BATTEL, WAGER OF.

Cravent. Same as CRAVEN.

Creamer. A foreign merchant. One who keeps a stall in a market or fair.

Creamus. We create or constitute.

Creamus, erigimus, fundamus, incorporamus. We create, erect, found and incorporate. (Words used in incorporating a college).

Creance. Credence, trust, credit, confidence. In French law, a book-debt, a claim, a debt.

Creance courante. Outstanding debt.

Creance exigible. Outstanding debt due, payable.

Creance privilegiee. Privileged debt.

Creancer. Same as CREANSOR.

Creanci. Belief; faith.

Creancier. One who trusts or gives credit. In French law, a creditor, a debtee. A covenantee, obligee.

Creansor. One that trusts another with any debt, gives any credit, be it for money, wares, or other things.

Creansour. Same as CREANSOR.

Creast. A carving on a wainscot. Devices set over coats of arms.

Create. To cause to exist.

Creche. A drinking cup.

Credentials. The letters which introduce the representative of one country to another and define the capacity in which he comes. A certificate showing one entitled to the authority claimed by him.

Credible. Entitled to belief.

Credible witness. See WITNESS, CREDIBLE.

Credibility. Condition of being worthy of belief or competent to be heard as a witness.

Credit. Belief in the statements of a person. Confidence in one's ability to meet obligations. The condition of being trusted. That which is due. Ability to obtain property on one's good reputation.

Credit, bill of. See BILL OF CREDIT.

Credit Foncier. A French financial institution which lends money on agricultural lands and takes repayment in terminable annuities. An institution which lends money on real estate.

Credit, general. The general opinion of one's testimony as a witness. Reputation for being worthy of confidence generally.

Credit, letter of. See LETTER OF CREDIT.

Credit, Mobilier. An institution incorporated in France, in 1852, to carry on financial enterprises. A company incorporated in Pennsylvania which undertook the construction of the Union Pacific Railroad in 1863 and failed amid scandal.

Credit paper. See PAPER, CREDIT.

Credit, particular. Credit as a witness in some particular case.

Credit, personal. See PERSONAL CREDIT.

Credit, public. See PUBLIC CREDIT.

Credit stopping notice. See NOTICE, CREDIT STOPPING.

Creditor. One who has a money claim against another. One to whom another is indebted. In U. S. Bankrupt law of 1898, anyone, or his agent, attorney, or proxy, who owns a demand or claim provable in bankruptcy.

Creditor, bond. See BOND CREDITOR.

Creditor, Catholic. See CATHOLIC CREDITOR.

Creditor, conditional. In Civil law, one having a future right of action.

Credit, domestic. One a resident within the same jurisdiction as the debtor.

Creditor, execution. See EXECUTION CREDITOR.

Creditor, existing. One who becomes such after the debtor has made a fraudulent conveyance of property and before such conveyance has been set aside.

Creditor, foreign. One not a resident within the same jurisdiction as the debtor.

Creditor, insecured. One whose debt is not secured by lien or other security.

Creditor, judgment. One who has obtained a judgment against his debtor.

Creditor, junior. A subsequent creditor to another. One whose lien is subject to that of another.

Creditor, lien. One who has a lien of record.

Creditor, petitioning. The creditor who files a petition against an insolvent or bankrupt.

Creditor, preferred. A creditor entitled to be paid before others.

Creditor, prior. One whose debt is superior to that of another or others.

Creditor, secondary. One whose claim stands second in priority of liens.

Creditor, secured. One whose debt is secured by a lien on property or some form of security.

Creditor, subsequent. One whose claim arose or is to be satisfied after that of another.

Creditors at large. Same as CREDITORS, GENERAL.

Creditors, joint. Two or more creditors to whom the same debt is due.

Creditor's bill. See BILL, CREDITOR'S.

Creditors, general. Those whose claims are second to preferred creditors.

Credits. All which is due one as distinguished from that which is due from him. All claims and demands due a person over and above what he owes.

Credits, mutual. Credits allowed to both parties to an account.

Creek. That part of a harbor where anything is landed from the sea; a small arm of the sea; a small river.

Crementum comitatus. The increase of the county. Applied to the sheriff's return as to the King's rents above the vicontiel rents.

Creo. To make or create for any jurisdiction or office; to choose, to elect. To create, to constitute, or appoint as a guardian.

Crepare oculum. To put out an eye. In Saxon law, the punishment was fifty shillings.

Crepusculum. Dusk or twilight. See BURGLARY.

Cressant. Growing.

Cresser. To grow.

Crest. Same as CREAST.

Cretain de eau. The overflowing of water.

Cretinus. A sudden torrent.

Cretio. Cretion. In Roman law, the time within which the heir had to declare his intention to accept the inheritance. See DAYS OF CRETION.

Cretion. Same as CRETIO.

Crew. The officers and seamen on a ship. Those employed to work on a ship during a voyage.

Crew list. A list of a ship's crew; it is a necessary ship's paper.

Cri. Cry; hue and cry.

Cribler. To argue.

Crie. A proclamation.

Crie de pais. The cry of the country; hue and cry.

Crier. To proclaim; to make proclamation. An officer of a court whose duty it is to make proclamations, call parties, jurors and witnesses, and to perform various incidental services.

Crieur. A crier (which see).

Criez la peez. Rehearse the concord, or peace. (Formerly used in proceedings for levying fines. The justice directed the reading aloud of the concord or agreement between the parties as to the lands intended to be conveyed).

Crim. con. An abbreviation of criminal conversation (which see).

Crime. A violation of law which subjects the doer to punishment. See MISDEMEANOR.

Crime against nature. Sodomy.

Crime at Common Law. One which was an offence at Common law.

Crime, capital. See CAPITAL CRIME.

Crime, high. A mere expression meaning nothing more than a crime.

Crime, nominate. A crime having a legal or particular name.

Crime, infamous. One which renders one convicted of it infamous. A crime to which infamous punishment is affixed. See INFAMOUS PUNISHMENT.

Crime, statutory. An act made a crime by statute.

Crimen. A crime; a fault. A judicial decision, verdict, judgment. A charge, accusation, reproach, especially when unfounded; a calumny, slander.

Crimen affere. To bring a charge, etc.

Crimen falsi. The crime of falsifying; forgery and offences affecting the administration of justice. (The term has also been held to include perjury and subornation of perjury).

Crimen flagrans. A crime in its very heat. During the commission of a crime.

Crimen furti. The crime of theft.

Crimen imponere. To impute or prefer a crime or offence.

Crimen incendii. The crime of burning. It included arson, also the burning of a man, beast, or other chattel.

Crimen innominatum. The nameless crime. Buggery.

Crimen læsæ majestatis. In Roman law, high treason. The crime of injuring or violating majesty. (Employed by ancient writers to express any offence affecting the King's person or dignity).

Crimen paris gradus. A crime of equal grade.

Crimen raptus. The crime of rape.

Crimen repetundarum. The crime of extorting money. In Scotch law, the crime of accepting a bribe to prevent punishment.

Crimen roberiæ. The crime of robbery.

Crimen stellionatus. The crime of imposition, deceit or cheating.

Crimes, quasi. See QUASI CRIMES.

Crimina paris gradus. Crimes of equal grade.

Criminal. One guilty of a crime. Relating to crime; guilty of crime.

Criminal action. Prosecutions by indictment or information, of one accused of a criminal offence.

Criminal cases. Prosecution for violation of penal statutes.

Criminal classes. Those who habitually violate law.

Criminal contempt. See CONTEMPT, CRIMINAL.

Criminal conversation. Adultery. The style of an action for damages.

Criminal information. An accusation of a criminal offence presented by a prosecuting officer on oath.

Criminal intent. See INTENT, CRIMINAL.

Criminal law. See LAW, CRIMINAL.

Criminal lawyer. One skilled in the practice of criminal law.

Criminal letter. See LETTER, CRIMINAL.

Criminal libel. See LIBEL, CRIMINAL.

Criminal negligence. See NEGLIGENCE, CRIMINAL.

Criminal procedure. See PROCEDURE, CRIMINAL.

Criminal process. See PROCESS, CRIMINAL.

Criminal prosecution. A proceeding for the purpose of determining the guilt or innocence of one charged with a crime.

Criminal responsibility. See RESPONSIBILITY, CRIMINAL.

Criminal side. The criminal jurisdiction of a court having both civil and criminal jurisdiction.

Criminaliter. Criminally, as distinguished from civiliter, or civilly.

Criminate. To prove guilty of a crime.

Crimine flagrante. See FLAGRANTE CRIMINE.

Crimp. One who robs sailors while pretending to provide for them.

Cro. A Scotch weregild.

Crocards. Same as CROCKARDS.

Crocia. A pastoral staff carried by bishops as an ensign of their office. The disposal of a bishopric or abbey.

Crociarius. The cross bearer.

Crockards. Base coin prohibited from being brought into England by 27 Edw. I. st. 3.

Croft. A small piece of land adjoining a dwelling house and enclosed for any particular purpose.

Crofta. A croft.

Croftum. A croft.

Croftus. A croft.

Croisses. Same as CROYSES.

Croiteir. One who holds a croft.

Crok. Curling the hair.

Croo. Same as CRO.

Crop. The product of a harvest.

Crop, away going. See AWAY GOING CROP.

Crop, Growing. See GROWING CROP.

Crop, Outstanding. One not gathered.

Crop time. The period of the year when crops are planted or gathered.

Cropper. One who cultivates land in return for a portion of the crop.

Crospicis. A whale.

Cross. To go over. To intersect. Counter. Opposing. Two lines intersecting each other made in lieu of a signature by one who cannot write.

Cross-action. An action brought by a defendant against the plaintiff who is suing him, for a cause arising out of the same controversy.

Cross-appeal. An appeal made by one party to a cause when the other party has also appealed.

Cross-bill. See BILL, CROSS.

Cross-claim. A claim by one against another who has previously asserted a claim.

Cross-complaint. In California practice a complaint which a defendant is allowed to file with his answer if there be any relief he desires the court to afford him in and about the subject-matter of the plaintiff's suit.

Cross-demand. See DEMAND, CROSS.

Cross-error. Errors assigned by a party when the other side has also assigned error.

Cross-examination. See EXAMINATION, CROSS.

Cross-remainders. See REMAINDER, CROSS.

Crossing. Going over. The intersection of two railroad tracks or a road and a railroad track.

Cross-roads. Roads that cross each other.

Cross-rule. Rule obtained by a party when the other side also obtained a rule.

Cross-walk. A walk crossing a street, or alley, railroad track, canal or river.

Croy. Marsh land.

Croyses. Pilgrims; Crusaders during the reigns of Henry II., Richard I., and Henry III. and Edw. I. of England. See CRUCE SIGNATI.

Crown. The sovereign in a kingdom. The government of a kingdom.

Crown case. A case involving a crime against the English Government. A case on behalf of the crown.

Crown Court. See COURT, CROWN.

Crown debt. One due to the English Government.

Crown lands. Lands belonging to the crown by inheritance.

Crown law. English public and criminal law.

Crown office. An office in England belonging to the Court of King's Bench, where informations were exhibited for crimes and misdemeanors.

Crown paper. In England, a list of pending criminal cases.

Crown pleas. In England, criminal cases. Pleas between a government and its subject for violation of law.

Crown side. The criminal side of the King's or Queen's Bench.

Crowner. In Scotch law, a coroner.

Cruce signati. Signed or marked with the cross. (Applied to the pilgrims of the Holy Land (Crusaders) because they wore the sign of the cross upon their garments. See CROYSES.

Cruel and unusual punishment. See PUNISHMENT, CRUEL AND UNUSUAL.

Cruelty. A malicious act causing physical pain or reasonable fear of such pain. (As to what constitutes must be determined by the facts in the case).

Cruelty, extreme. Such cruelty as causes serious pain or reasonable fear that severe bodily harm will result therefrom.

Cruelty to animals. The causing of unnecessary pain to a dumb beast.

Cruelty to children. The infliction of severe punishment.

Cruise. A voyage.

Crusaders. See CROYSES.

Crustum. A garment of purple mixed with other colors.

Crux. A cross; the badge of the old Crusaders.

Cry. To proclaim. To announce.

Cry de pais. The cry of the country. Hue and cry raised in the absence of a constable on the commission of a felony.

Cryer. An auctioneer. One who proclaims.

Crypta. A chapel underground.

Cucking-stool. A ducking stool, etc. See CASTIGATORIUM.

Cuckold. The husband of an adulteress. A man whose wife is false to his bed. A man who knows his wife's infidelity and submits to it.

Cude. A face cloth used in baptizing children.

Cueillette, a. See A CUEILLETTE.

Cui ante divortium. To whom, before divorce. A writ of entry for a woman divorced from her husband, to recover her lands, etc., from him to whom her husband had conveyed them during the marriage.

Cui in vita. To which, or whom in the life. A writ of entry for a widow to recover lands which her husband aliened during his lifetime and in which she had an estate.

(16)

Cuicumque. Whoever; whatsoever; every one.

Cul. An abbreviation of culpabilis.

Cul. prit. (Guilty, ready). Words anciently used by the clerk of a court in answer to the plea of non culpabilis (not guilty) by an accused, in order to join issue with him. Cul. was abbreviation of culpabilis (guilty) and prit being an expression to indicate that issue was joined and the government was ready for trial.

Cul-de-sac. Applied to a way having an apparent passage, but closed at the end. A street or lane which you may enter at one end but find without egress at the other. A blind alley. A blind canyon.

Culagium. Docking a ship for repairs.

Cullers. Same as KEBBARS.

Culpa. Crime, failure, fault, neglect.

Culpa in abstracto. Neglect or fault in the abstract (absolute fault or neglect).

Culpa in concreto. Neglect or fault in the concrete See DILIGENTIA IN CONCRETO.

Culpabilis. Worthy of blame; culpable; criminal; guilty.

Culpable. Deserving of censure.

Culpable homicide. See HOMICIDE, CULPABLE.

Culpabilis de homicidio. Guilty of homicide.

Culprit. An accused; a legal teste to denote a person who is accused of a crime, or is supposed to be guilty of a crime. The word was derived from Cul prit., which see.

Culrach. In Scotch law, a pledge given in replevying a man from one court to another.

Cultivation. Preparing ground for raising crops. Raising crops.

Cultivators. Those who cultivate the soil.

Cultura. A parcel of arable land; a "wong."

Culvert. An artificial, covered passage way through a bank or under a road, canal, or bridge.

Culvertage. A term for the lands of a vassal forfeited to the lord.

Culverd. A coward; cowardice.

Culward. Same as CULVERD.

Cum. When; whereas. With; together with; in connection with. Complete.

Cum beneficio inventarii. With the benefit of an inventory. In Scotch law, a term applied when an heir is doubtful whether his ancestor's estate will be sufficient to satisfy the debts, thus keeping himself free from responsibility beyond the value of the estate.

Cum copula. With connection.

Cum fossa et furca. With pit and gallows. In ancient charters, an expression used in inventory conferring the rights of trying capital offences and of inflicting capital punishments.

Cum herezeldis. With the best things that move. In Scotch law, horses, cows, belonging to a deceased tenant, due by custom on his death to his landlord. An acknowledgement of vassalage.

Cum nota. With a critical or distinguishing mark. In Scotch law, the testimony of persons otherwise inadmissible but admitted as evidence cum nota, which is to be considered with regard to credit and belief

Cum onere. With the charge.

Cum talli filia mea, etc.,tenendum sibi, et hæredibus suis de carne talis uxoris. With this my daughter, etc., to hold to him and the heirs of the body of such wife. Words used in ancient settlements of land.

Cum testamento annexo. With the will annexed.

Cumulative. Additional. Of the same kind.

Cumulative remedy. See REMEDY, CUMULATIVE.

Cumulative sentences. See SENTENCES, CUMULATIVE.

Cumulative voting. See VOTING, CUMULATIVE.

Cuna. Coin.

Cuna cervisiæ. A tub of ale.

Cunagium. Coinage.

Cuneare. To coin.

Cuneata. Coined.

Cuneator. A coiner.

Cuneatus. Coined.

Cuneus. The iron die with which metallic money is coined. The money itself, so coined; coin. The place of coinage; a mint.

Cuntey-cuntey. A jury trial.

Cur. For what reason; wherefore, why, to what purpose.

Cur. adv. vult. An abbreviation of Curia advisari vult—the court will advise, or the court will be advised. See CURIA ADVISARI VULT.

Cura animarum. Cure of souls.

Curable. Capable of being rectified or remedied.

Curagulus. One who takes care of a thing.

Curate. A temporary minister in the English Church.

Curatio. In Civil law, the obligation of managing the estate of one under a legal disability.

Curative. Intended to cure a defect.

Curative, statute. See STATUTE CURATIVE.

Curator. The committee of the estate. In Scotch law, a guardian. One appointed to protect the person of an infant or minor, and the estate if any exist. SEE TUTOR.

Curator ad bona. A guardian of the goods or property.

Curator ad hoc. A guardian for this (purpose); a special guardian.

Curator ad litem. A guardian for (or in) the suit. In the Civil law, a guardian appointed to prosecute or defend a suit for one who is under some legal disability.

Curator bonis. A guardian of the goods or property.

Curator civitatis. A guardian of the community or city.

Curator in litem. Same as CURATOR AD LITEM.

Curator, interim. In England, a curator appointed to take charge of the estate of a convicted felon until an administrator is appointed.

Curator reipublicæ. A guardian of the republic.

Curatores viarum. Surveyors or guardians of the public roads.

Curatorship. The office of a curator.

Curatrix. A female guardian.

Curee. Charged with; having the care of.

Cure of souls. The duties of a clergyman in caring for the spiritual affairs of a parish.

Cured by verdict. Put in a condition where it cannot be objected to. Applied to a defect which could have been objected to in pleading, but which cannot be after verdict.

Curfa. A beating; a stroke.

Curfeu. Same as CURFEW.

Curfew. Cover fire. A bell which was rung at eight o'clock in the evening in the time of William the Conqueror, by which every one was commanded to cover over his fire, put out his light, and retire to rest. The origin of the regulation is said to have been to prevent meetings of Saxons to plot against the Normans. (Abolished by Henry I.) In Scotland the bell was at one time rung at nine o'clock, at another time at ten o'clock,

Curge. Runs.

Curia. A court; the place or household of a sovereign; the residence of a nobleman; a manor; the hall of a manor; the court of a manor; a lord's court, as being held in his manor; a judicial tribunal or court held in the sovereign's palace; the civil or secular power as distinguished from the church; a judicial tribunal; a court of justice, whether of special or general jurisdiction; a court yard or inclosed piece of ground; a close.

Curia Admiralitatis. The Court of Admiralty.

Curia advisari vult. The court will be advised. Phrase to denote that, after hearing argument, the court will take time to examine and consider, or consult together, before giving judgment.

Curia Banci Regis. The Court of King's Bench.

Curia baronis. A court baron.

Curia baronium. A court baron.

Curia Cameræ Stellatæ. Court of Star Chamber (which see).

Curia cancellariæ. Court of Chancery (which see).

Curia centuriæ. Court of the hundred. See COURTS, HUNDRED.

Curia Christianitatis. A court Christian, or ecclesiastical court.

Curia claudenda. Closing a court. A writ to compel one to make a fence or wall about a court or close.

Curia comitatus. The court of the county; the county court. A court of high antiquity, incident to the jurisdiction of the sheriff.

Curia Communium Placitum. The Court of Common Pleas.

Curia cursus aquæ. An old English court held to regulate the passage of boats on the river Thames.

Curia de Arcubus. Court of Arches.

Curia de Banco nostro. The Court of our Bench (of the King's Bench).

Curia domini. The lord's court; the court or meeting of the lord. The place where tenants of the lord met at the time of holding court.

Curia franci plegii. A court or meeting of frank pledge.

Curia hundredi. Hundred court; a court of the hundred. A large court baron, held for inhabitants of a particular hundred.

Curia legitime affirmata. Court lawfully opened. In Scotch law, a phrase used in records to denote that the court opened in due form.

Curia magna. The great court. One of the ancient names of Parliament. The King's court, Aula Regis.

Curia Majoris. The Mayor's court.

Curia militum. An ancient court held in the Isle of Wight at Carisbrook Castle.

Curia nostra de Banco. Our court of the Bench (the Common Bench).

Curia Palatii. The Palace Court.

Curia penticiarum. Court Pentice (which see).

Curia personæ. A parsonage house or manse.

Curia pedis pulverizati. The Court of Piepowders or Piepoudre.

Curia publica. A public court of law; an open court.

Curia Regia. The Queen's Court.

Curia Regis. The King's Court. The supreme court of judicature of the kingdom, established by the Normans. An ancient name of Parliament. The King's council, composed of earls, barons and the great men of the realm.

Curia visus franci plegii. A meeting or view of frank pledge.

Curiales. Of or relating to a curia. Belonging to the same curia, district or division of the people.

Curialitas. In Scotch law, courtesy; curiality; the estate by curtesy.

Curialitas Anglicana. Curtesy of England. See CURTESY.

Curiality. In Scotch law, curtesy. The authority of a court.

Curnock. A measure of four bushels.

Currat quatuor pedibus. It runs upon four feet; "it runs upon all fours." See ALL FOURS.

Currax. Running fast, quick, swift.

Currency. Legal money. That which is in use as money; anything used as a medium of exchange. The state of being in circulation as money.

Currency, fractional. Pieces of money or notes less than the unit of value. In U. S., pieces less than a dollar.

Currency, national. In U. S. that issued by the Federal government and by authority of Federal law.

Currency, paper. Paper money issued by authority of law.

Currency, postal. See POSTAL CURRENCY.

Current. Existing at the present time. Passing as money.

Current funds. See FUNDS, CURRENT.

Current money. The money in circulation.

Current notes. Bank notes redeemable in legal money.

Current price. See PRICE, CURRENT.

Current value. The market value.

Currere. To move quickly; to run; to hasten; to fly. To elapse, as time, with the effect of limitation.

Curriculum. The year. A class of subjects set apart in a college for study during a certain period.

Curriculus. The course of a year.

Curriers. Persons who dress leather.

Currus. A chariot or carriage.

Cursitor. A clerk in Chancery whose duty was to make out all original writs.

Cursitor Baron. An Exchequer Court officer appointed by letters patent.

Curso. A ridge.

Cursones terræ. Ridges of land.

Cursoriæ. Swift sailing ships.

Cursus. Of or relating to a course; running.

Cursus aquæ. A course of water.

Cursus carbonum. A seam of coal.

Cursus curiæ. The course or practice of a court.

Curtesia. Curtesy.

Curtesie d'Engleterre. Curtesy of England.

Curtesy. An estate to which a man is entitled, on the death of his wife, in the lands or tenements of which she was seized in fee-simple or fee-tail, during the marriage, provided he had issue by her, born alive, during the marriage, and capable of inheriting her estate. See CÆSARIAN OPERATION.

Curtesy, initiate. See INITIATE CURTESY.

Curtesy of England. Same as CURTESY.

Curteyn. The name of Edward the Confessor's sword which was the first sword carried before an English King at coronation.

Curtilage. A garden, yard, court-yard or piece of ground about a dwelling and the out buildings, as distinguished from ground lying in open fields.

Curtiles terræ. Court lands; a court yard. See COURT LANDS.

Curtillum. A space or area within the court or enclosure of a dwelling house.

Curtis. A cage, inclosure, or inclosed place. An area or space about a house. The King's mansions, not castles nor places of defence.

Curtus. Same as CURTIS.

Custages. Costs; expenses of judicial proceedings.

Custagium. Same as CUSTAGES.

Custantia. Same as CUSTAGES.

Custode admittendo. A writ for admitting a guardian.

Custode amovendo. A writ to remove a guardian.

Custodes. Keepers, guardian.

Custodes Libertatis Angliæ Auctoritate Parliamenti. The guardians or keepers of the liberty of England by the authority of Parliament. The style of writs and proceedings in England from the execution of Chas. II. to the beginning of Cromwell's Protectorate.

Custodes morum. The custodians, guardians of morals or conduct.

Custodes or conservatores pacis. The keepers or conservators of the peace.

Custodes pacis. Guardians of the peace. Conservatores of the peace anciently chosen by the freeholders in full county court before the sheriff. The predecessor of the justice of the peace.

Custodes placitorum coronæ. Keepers of the pleas of the crown (criminal actions or proceedings in which the crown was the prosecutor).

Custodes placitorum in plenu comitatu. The keepers of pleas in full county court.

Custodia. Custody; watch; guard; care.

Custodia castri. Guard of a castle; castle-guard.

Custodia comitatus. The wardship of a county.

Custodia legis. In custody of the law; legal custody.

Custodia pupillorum. Wardship; or guardianship of infants under the age of puberty.

Custodiam comitatum. Guard, custody of wardship of the county.

Custodiam lease. A grant or lease from the crown by which lands were demised or committed to some person to hold as custodee or lessee.

Custodian. A grant for life. A keeper. A curator.

Custodiarium. A watch-house; watchman's tent.

Custody. Keeping; ward or guard; the duty of keeping guard; wardship or guardship. Imprisonment; detention.

Custody of the law. In custody by virtue of a legal process.

Custody of property. The keeping of property by one who is charged with or assumes responsibility for its safety.

Custom. A right or unwritten law established by long usage and consent. A duty payable by a vendor or importer.

Custom, general. That which is general to the whole country.

Custom House. An office where goods are entered for import or export.

Custom House Broker. An agent who attends to the entrance and clearance of goods and vessels for others.

Custom, local. Same as CUSTOM, PARTICULAR.

Custom of merchants. A system of customs or rules relative to bills of exchange, partnership, and all other mercantile matters. Law Merchant.

Custom, Particular. That which belongs to a particular place.

Custon, special. Same as CUSTOM PARTICULAR.

Customary. According to custom; established by custom; held by custom. A written or printed statement of laws and customs.

Customary court. See COURT, CUSTOMARY.

Customary dispatch. See DISPATCH, CUSTOMARY.

Customary estate. An estate existing by the custom of a manor, evidenced by copy of court roll.

Customary freehold. A copyhold tenure, resembling freehold, not held at the will of the lord.

Customary incidents. See INCIDENTS, CUSTOMARY.

Customary services. Those due by custom or prescription.

Customary tenants. Those holding by custom of the manor. Copyholders belong to this class.

Custome. Custom.

Customer. One who deals at a store or shop.

Customs. Taxes on imports and exports.

Customs and services. Those which tenants owe their lords through being annexed to the tenure by which they hold lands.

Customs and services, writ of. See WRIT OF CUSTOMS AND SERVICES.

Customs duty. Same as CUSTOMS.

Customs of London. Particular customs which became established in London, England, through long usage.

Customs Union. A union of several nations for imposing and collecting custom duties in common.

Custos. A keeper, protector, custodian; a guardian; a magistrate; the warden of a city.

Custos brevium. Keeper of the writs. The chief clerk belonging to the Courts of King's Bench and Common Pleas, charged with receiving and keeping writs returned into the court, and records of nisi prius.

Custos brevium domini regis de banco. Keeper of the writs of the lord the King to the bench; keeper of the King's writs to the bench. The chief clerk in the Court of Common Pleas charged with receiving and keeping all writs returned into that court, and also the records thereof.

Custos ferarum. A game-keeper; the custodian of the game.

Custos forestæ. Keeper of the forest; chief warden of the forest. An officer charged with the government of all things relating to the forest and all officers belonging to the same.

Custos horrei regii. Keeper of the royal granary.

Custos limitis. A conservator of the limits or marches.

Custos magni sigilli. Keeper of the great seal. A high state officer, the holder and keeper of the great seal of England.

Custos maris. Warden or guardian of the sea. Warden of the fleet. The title applied to a high naval officer among the Saxons and after the conquest.

Custos morum. The guardian of morality. Applied to judges generally.

Custos placitorum coronæ. Keeper of the pleas of the crown. Officers said to have sat with the sheriff in the County Court.

Custos privati sigilli. Keeper of the privy seal. The English officer of state who keeps the seal used in making out grants before they are sealed with the great seal (magno sigillo).

Custos rotulorum. Keeper or master of the rolls. A civil officer in the county appointed under the common law to maintain the public peace, and who acted as justice of the quorum in the county where appointed.

Custos spiritualium. Keeper of the spiritualities. One having spiritual and ecclesiastical jurisdiction over a diocese during the vacancy of the sea.

Custos temporalium. Keeper of the temporalities. One to whom the custody of a vacant see or abbey was committed by the King and who was to render his account of the same to the escheator.

Custos terræ. A keeper of land.

Custuma. Cost, toll, duties or tariff imposts; customs.

Custuma antiqua. Ancient custom.

Custuma antiqua et magna. Ancient and great customs, imposts.

Custuma antiqua sive magna. Ancient or great customs. Certain duties or customs payable under English statute by merchants, on wool, sheepskins, or welfels and leather exported.

Custuma parva et nova. Small and new customs, duties, imposts. Usually called alien's duty.

Custumarii tenentes. Customary tenants.

Custus. Cost, charge; costs, charges; expenses.

Cut. A separation of anything by an edged tool or blade. An impression or print from a block or plate. In U. S. copyright, only pictorial illustrations or works connected with the fine arts and not prints or labels used for any other articles of manufacture.

Cut purse. A pickpocket.

Cuth. Know, knowing.

Cuthred. A shrewd counsellor.

Cutter of the tallies. One who cut the sum paid on the tallies or sticks. See TALLY.

Cutts. Flat-bottom boats anciently used to transport horses.

Cuve (or Keeve). A tub for brewing.

Cy. Here; so, as.

Cy pres. As near; as near as; as near as can be. The power of the English Chancellor to apply a charity to objects different from those intended by the donor. The power to appoint a specific object of a general gift to charity. The power of a court of equity to substitute for a particular charity which has failed, another of the same kind, as nearly as may be. The doctrine of interpreting written instruments so as to carry out the intention of the makers as nearly as possible.

Cycle. A period of 30 years in the Mohammedan calendar. It comprises 19 years of 354 days and 11 years with 355 days.

Cymbric peoples. The Welsh, Cornish and low Britons or Brezoneks. They were a branch of the Celtæ or Keltoi.

Cymeter. A cemetery; a burial place.

Cynebote. Same as CENEGILD.

Cynsour de burse. A cut-purse; a pickpocket.

Cyrce. A Saxon church.

Cyric. Same as CYRCE.

Cyricbrice. The crime or act of church-breach or breaking into a church. Interruption of church services.

Cyricsceat. A tribute due the church.

Cyrograffe. A chirograph.

Cyrographarius. A cyrographer.

Cyrographer. Anciently an officer of the Bancus, or Court of Common Bench.

Cyrographum. The name of a deed or charter among the Saxons.

Czar. An absolute monarch. The Emperor of Russia.

Czarina. The Empress of Russia.

Czarowitz. The eldest son of a Czar.

D.

D. As an abbreviation D. stands for Decimus, Deus, Divus, Dominus, Decurio, Doctor, District; and when used between two names in the style of a suit in ejectment, as Jones d. Smith vs. Doe, means Demissione. Before the dates of letters, D. signifies Dabam and also Dies. Some Civilians in citing the Digests, use D. the initial letter of the words Digesta or Digestum. In Roman notation it stands for five hundred.

D. B. E. De bene esse.

D. B. N. De bonis non.

D. C. District Court. District of Columbia.

D. C. L. Doctor of Civil or (Canon) law.

D. D. Divinitatis Doctor—Doctor of Divinity. Also, Dono dedit, has presented or given.

D. E. R. I. C. An abbreviation of De ea re ita censuere, concerning that matter have so ordered. (The initial letters of this phrase were employed in recording the decrees of the Roman Senate).

D. G. Dei Gratia—by the grace of God.

D. J. District Judge.

D. M. Doctor of Music.

D. N. Dominus Noster.

D. P. Doctor of Philosophy. Also Domus Procerum—The House of Lords.

D. S. Dal Segno—from the sign.

D. S. B. Debitum sine brevi. Debi sans breve.

D. T. Doctor Theologiæ, or Divinity.

D. V. Deo Volente—God willing.

D'accord. Agreed; in time; in accordtance.

Da. Yes.

Dabis? Will you give? A Roman form of making a stipulaticn.

Dabo. I will give. Answer to Dabis (which see).

Dacion. In Spanish law, the actual delivery of an object in carrying out a contract.

Dag. A gun; a hand gun.

Dagenham. Breach.

Dagge. Same as DAG.

Dagus. The chief table in a monastery.

Dailia. Same as DALUS.

Dailus. Same as DALUS.

Daily. Every day. Every day except legal holidays.

Dais. The cloth which covered the King's table. A platform or raised floor.

Daker. Ten hides.

Dale and sale. Fictitious names of places used by old English law writers in illustration.

Dalmatica. A garment with large open sleeves.

Dalus. A certain measure of land. A ditch.

Dam. A confinement or boundary. To confine water by building an obstruction to its flow. A structure to prevent the flow of water and control it in a body.

Damage. Hurt, loss, injury.

Damage-cleer. An ancient fee due the prothonotary of the Common Pleas, King's Bench, and Exchequer, where damages were recovered exceeding five marks.

Damage, collision and. See COLLISION AND DAMAGE.

Damage faisant. Same as DAMAGE FEASANT.

Damage feasant. Doing damage. (Applied to beasts which have broken into a field and are damaging the crops).

Damage, special. See DAMAGES, SPECIAL.

Damaged goods. Dutiable goods which have been injured on a voyage or while in a bonded warehouse.

Damages. Any injury to a person or his estate. The amount claimed or recompense for an injury.

Damages, abridgement of. See ABRIDGEMENT OF DAMAGES.

Damages, actual. Damage for actual loss or injury.

Damages, assessment of. Determining the amount of damages to which a person is entitled.

Damages, civil. Damages for injuries to one's civil rights, or rights as a member of a family.

Damages, compensatory. Damages which compensate for the actual loss.

Damages, constructive. Such as are implied in law.

Damages, contingent. Contemplated damages from an event which may or may not happen.

Damages, continuing. Damages which result from and continue during a continuing act.

Damages consequential. Damages which are the indirect consequences of an act, usually through the agency of a second act.

Damages, direct. Such as are the immediate result of an act without the agency of a second act.

Damages, double. Damages with an increase made by the court.

Damages, excessive. Damages in excess of the wrong or injury.

Damages, exemplary. Damages given by way of punishment for fraud, malice, or oppression.

Damages, general. Such as of necessity result from the injury.

Damages, immediate. Direct damages.

Damages, inadequate. Damages manifestly less than the injury or wrong.

Damages, increased. Same as DAMAGES, DOUBLE.

Damages, indirect. Damages which result indirectly from an act.

Damages, intervening. Damages to the appellee caused by delay in the determination of an appeal.

Damages, lay. To state the damages claimed.

Damages, liquidated. A sum agreed upon by the parties as compensation for a breach of contract.

Damages, measure of. See MEASURE OF DAMAGES.

Damages, nominal. A small sum awarded, where technical wrong has been done, but no loss or injury sustained.

Damages, prospective. Damages for a loss which will almost certainly occur.

Damages, punitive. Same as DAMAGES EXEMPLARY.

Damages, remote. Damages which indirectly result from an act through agencies far removed from the first act.

Damages, resulting. Damages resulting from an act, but through another agency or act.

Damages, sounding in. See SOUNDING IN DAMAGES.

Damages, special. Those which are specified in the declaration.

Damages, speculative. Prospective damages, where there is more than a faint doubt as to an injury being sustained.

Damages, substantial. Compensatory damages. (Opposed to nominal).

Damages, ultra. Damages claimed in addition to those paid into court by defendant.

Damages, unliquidated. Damages not fixed either by the parties or by the court.

Damages, vindictive. Same as DAMAGES EXEMPLARY.

Damaiouse. Causing damage or loss, as distinguished from torcenouse.

Dame. The legal title of the wife of a baronet or knight.

Dames de la halle. Dames of the market house; market women.

Damissella. A miss.

Damna. Damages, inclusive of costs of suit. Damages exclusive of costs.

Damna Clericorum. The compensation of clerks. A fee which the prevailing party in the Court of King's Bench and Common Pleas anciently had to pay the chief officer of the court before execution issued.

Damna in duplo. Double damages.

Damnabilis. Worthy of condemnation; damnable.

Damnabiliter. Culpably.

Damnanda res. A condemned estate or thing.

Damnare. To condemn.

Damnatus. Condemned; prohibited by law; unlawful.

Damnatus coitus. An unlawful connection.

Damner. To condemn.

Damner a la mort. To condemn to death.

Damni injuriæ actio. An action for injurious damages.

Damnificatus. Injured.

Damnify. To injure or damage any person; to cause a person loss.

Damno fatali. By fatal damage, that which could not have been foreseen or prevented.

Damnosa. Hurtful.

Damnosa hæreditas. A disadvantageous inheritance; a losing p r o p e r t y. Property of a bankrupt which would cost creditors more to keep than it would earn as a leasehold.

Damnosus. That which produces loss, as distinguished from injuriosus, that which works a wrong.

Damnum. Damage, loss, hurt, injury.

Damnum absque injuria. A damage which is not actionable at law; a loss arising from an act other than one tortious, and for which no damages can be obtained.

Damnum an injuria. Damage and injury.

Damnum corpori datum. Damage done the body.

Damnum cum injuria. A loss with injury; damages with legal wrong.

Damnum emergens. Damage brought forth; positive damage.

Damnum et injuria. A loss and an injury; a damage and a legal wrong.

Damnum et injuriam. Loss and injury; damage and legal wrong.

Damnum et intercesse. The loss and damage sustained.

Damnum facientes. Doing damage. Damage feasant.

Damnum fatale. A fatal loss. A loss beyond human control.

Damnum infectum. In Roman law, threatened damages. See QUASI DELICT.

Damnum injuriosum. Injurious damage; unlawful damage. A loss or damage for which an action lies.

Damnum rei amissæ. In Civil law, a loss caused by a payment through ignorance of law.

Damnum sine injuria. A damage or loss without injury. Damage without legal wrong.

Damnum triplum. Treble damages. In certain cases treble damages allowed by statute. Usually the jury find the single amount of the damages, and the court, on motion, orders that amount to be trebled.

Dampnare. To condemn.

Dampner. To condemn.

Dampner a la mort. To condemn to death.

Dampnum. Same as DAMNUM.

Dan. A title anciently applied to the better men of England.

Danegeld. A tribute of one shilling laid upon every hide of land in England, and paid to the Danes. A tax to maintain a force to drive Danish pirates from British seas. It existed a right of the crown to the time of Stephen.

Danegelt. Same as DANEGELD.

Danelage. Dane custom or law; the law of the Danes by which they governed part of England.

Danger. The condition of being exposed to injury or loss.

Danger, apparent. See APPARENT DANGER.

Danger de la terre. Danger of the land; land risks.

Dangeria. A license fee paid by forest tenants to be allowed to plow and sow in time of mast feeding.

Dangerous. That which is likely to cause great injury or death.

Dangerous weapon. See WEAPON, DANGEROUS.

Dangers of navigation. The ordinary dangers to which a vessel is liable on a voyage.

Dangers of the river. Accidents incident to river navigation such as a skillful pilot cannot avoid despite usual vigilance.

Dangers of the sea. Unusual dangers, as violent tempests and their incidents.

Danism. The act of lending money at usurious interest.

Dano. In Spanish law, damages. The injury one suffers from the fault of another.

Dans. Within. In.

Dapifer. Originally a domestic officer, afterwards the head bailiff of a manor.

Dapifer regis. Steward of the King's household.

Dar. An oak tree.

Dardus. A dart.

Dare. To give; to cause a thing to be effectually his who receives it. In Civil law, to transfer property.

Dare ad remanentiam. To give forever (applied to a remainder).

Dare judicium. To give judgment; to decide the cause.

Darraign Same as DERAIGN.

Darrein. The last.

Darrein continuance. The last continuance.

Darrein presentment. The last presentment. An ancient writ allowed when a stranger deforced the patron in the presentation of a clerk to a void benefice, directing the sheriff to summon a jury to determine who was the last patron.

Darrein seisin. An old plea for the tenant in a writ of right.

Darreine. The last.

Darreyne. The last.

Darreyne volunte. The last will.

Dartmouth College case. The case of Dartmouth College vs. Woodward, 4 Wheaton, 518, decided by the United States Supreme Court.

Dat'. Given.

Data. The date, the day when given. The date of a writ, called in modern practice the teste; the time when it was issued. The date when a grant, deed, charter, etc., was executed. Things granted, admitted; grounds of inference.

Date. Specified time. See DATA.

Date certaine. In French law, a deed has a date certaine (date fixed) when registered.

Date, false. One intentionally false.

Date of a deed. The date of its delivery.

Date of bankruptcy. See BANKRUPTCY, DATE OF.

Datif. Same as DATIVE.

Datio. In Civil law, the act of giving.

Datio contrahendi animo. A transfer to create an obligation or receive an equivalent.

Datio in solutum. A giving in payment. A giving as satisfaction.

Datio solvendi animo. A transfer made to discharge a debt.

Datio tutoris. The appointment of a tutor, when not provided for in the will.

Dation. In Civil law, a gift. A giving of something to which the recipient is entitled.

Dation en paiement. In French law, a giving by a debtor and acceptance by the creditor of something in lieu of money, as satisfaction for a debt.

Dative. In one's gift; that which may be disposed of at will. Appointed by public authority. Removable at pleasure.

Dativus. Dative.

Dativus casus. The giving case, the dative.

Datum. Given, dated, executed; a date.

Datus. A giving. Date of giving. The day of the giving.

Dauphin. The former title of the eldest son of a French King.

Davata terræ dawach. Scotch expression for a portion of land.

Day. The time between the rising and setting of the sun, called artificial day; the time from noon to noon or from midnight to midnight, called the natural day; twenty-four hours, beginning and ending at midnight, called the civil day. The period a face can be distinguished without artificial or moon light, before which breaking and entering is not burglary. Among the Hebrews and Greeks, the day began at sunset; the Romans began it at midnight; the Babylonians at sunrise; the Umbrians at noon; sailors and astromomers reckon it from noon to noon.

Day, appearance. The day a party is bound to appear in court.

Day, artificial. See DAY.

Day book. A merchant's book in which accounts of the day are entered.

Day, entire. During the twenty-four hours beginning and ending at midnight.

Day, general affirmance. See AFFIRMANCE DAY, GENERAL.

Day in court. The day on which a person is heard in his own behalf.

Day, judicial. A day when court is in session. A legal day. Dies legitimus.

Day, juridical. Same as DAY, JUDICIAL.

Day, lawful. A day when an act if performed is binding; not a legal holiday.

Day, motion. See MOTION DAY.

Day, order of the. See ORDER OF THE DAY.

Day, peremptory. The day set for a hearing with the understanding that there is to be no further continuance.

Day, return. See RETURN DAY.

Day, quarter. See QUARTER DAY.

Day rule. A release for one day. See DAY WRIT.

Day, solar. From the rising to the setting of the sun. See DIES SOLARIS.

Day, without. Indefinite. See SINE DIE.

Day writ (or rule). An order permitting a prisoner to go without prison for one day.

Dayer. The meeting of laborers to give an account of their daily work and receive wages for it.

Dayeria. The daily yield of cows, or profit made from their milk.

Daylight. That part of a day before sunrise and after sunset in which the features of a man are recognizable without artificial light or moonlight.

Daytime. That part of a natural day during which a man's features can be recognized without the aid of artificial light or moonlight.

Days, anniversary. See ANNIVERSARY DAYS.

Days common. Same as DAYS IN BANK.

Days in bank. In England, days in the Common Bench on which writs were returnable.

Days of cretion. In the Civil law, days within which an heir must decide upon accepting and entering upon an inheritance. See CRETION.

Days of the King's peace. Same as NON TERMINOUS.

Days of grace. The time allowed within which to pay a note, bill or insurance premium after it is due. In the first two it is usually three days; in the latter, thirty days.

Days, Seal. In English law, days for motions in chancery, so called because such motions were required to be sealed.

Day's work. The work of one day. Work payable by the day not by the entire job.

Daysman. An arbitrator.

Daywere of land. As much as can be plowed in one day's work.

De. In the titles of statutes, writs, and the general formulæ of court proceedings, the most prevalent and frequently occurring signification of de, is: Of, from, about, concerning, respecting, in relation to. See WRITS UNDER BREVE DE, &c.

De admensuratione dotis. A writ of admeasurement of dower.

De admensuratione pasturæ. A writ of admeasurement of pasture.

De advisamento consilii nostri. By under or with the advice of our council. (An expression used in the old writs of summons to Parliament).

De æquitate. In equity.

De æstimato. In Roman law, the sale of property guaranteed by a third person who had agreed to find a purchaser, at a fixed price.

De ætate probanda. A writ to summon a jury to enquire whether or not the heir to an estate be of age.

De afforest. To discharge from the forest law.

De aleatoribus. About gamesters. A title in the Pandects.

De allocatione facienda. A writ for making allowance.

De alto et basso. Of high and low. An expression used in ancient times to express the absolute submission of all differences, high and low, to arbitration.

De anno bisextili. Of the bisextile or leap year. The title of a statute passed 21 Henry III, by which the justices of the bench were directed that the additional day should, together with that which went before, he reckoned only as one.

De annua pensione. Writ of annual pension.

De annuo redditu. A writ for recovering an annuity.

De apostata capiendo. A writ for taking an apostate.

De arbitratione facta. Of arbitration had. A writ used when it was desired to bring an action for a cause which had been determined by arbitration.

De arte et parte. Of art and part. In Scotch criminal law, contriver and partner. An accessory before and after the fact; an aider and abettor in the commission of a crime.

De asportatis religiosorum. Of or concerning the taking away of (the property of) religious persons.

De assisa proroganda. A writ for proroguing an assise.

De attornato recipiendo. A writ to receive an attorney.

De audiendo et terminando. A writ for hearing and determining.

De advisamento et consensu consilii nostri consessimus. By the advice and consent of our council we have granted or conceded. The common form of the King's grants.

De averiis retornando. For returning the beasts or cattle, applied to pledges given in the old action of replevin.

De avo. Of ayle or aiel. See AYLE.

De avo et de tritavo. From grandfather and great grandfather's great grandfather.

De Banco. Of the bench. A term applied to the justices of the Court of Common Pleas or Bench.

De bene esse. Of well being. To be of good form. Of good precaution; of contingent or possible utility or effect; of conditional or permissive validity; to pass as a matter of form; to be allowed as of present formal sufficiency, with reference to some matter or question in the future; to be valid for the present, but subject to some further future proceeding, etc. (The testimony of a witness de bene esse is taken subject to the contingency of his being able to attend court at the trial. A jury may render a verdict subject to the opinion of the court, and this, strictly is a proceeding de bene esse).

De bien et de mal. Same as DE BONO ET MALO.

De bigamis. Concerning men twice married. Statute 4, Edw. I. st. 3.

De bonis asportatis. For goods taken away; for carrying away goods. The technical term for the action of trespass for wrongfully taking and carrying away goods.

De bonis non. Abbreviation of de bonis non administratis.

De bonis non administratis. Of the goods unadministered. Where an administrator dies or is removed before the administration is completed and a new one is appointed, the latter is termed an administrator de bonis non.

De bonis non amovendis. For not removing goods; for preventing the removal of goods.

De bonis propriis. Of his own goods. A judgment against an executor or administrator personally as distinguished from one to be satisfied from the estate of the deceased.

De bonis testatoris, or intestati. Of the goods of the testator, or intestate. A judgment against the estate of a deceased as distinguished from one against the executor or administrator personally.

De bonis testatoris ac si. From the goods of the testator if he have any, and if not, from those of the executor. The form of a judgment when an executor is to be responsible in case the testator's estate is not sufficient, or where the executor pleads falsely on any matter as a release.

De bono et malo. For good and evil. A phrase by which a party accused or appealed, put himself upon a jury. It was also the name of a special writ. See WRIT DE BONO ET MALO.

De cætero. Henceforth, henceforward, hereafter, in future.

De capitalibus dominis feodi. Of the chief lords of the fee. A phrase used in ancient grants to denote the tenure by which the estate granted was to be held.

Dé capite minutis. Of those who have lost their status. A title in the Pandects.

De certificando. A writ for certifying.

De champertia. The purchase of an interest in a thing with a view to maintaining litigation in and about it.

De char et de sank. Of flesh and blood. Words used at the time of Edw. II. in claiming one as a villein.

De chimino. A writ to enforce a right of way.

De cibariis utendis. Of or concerning victuals to be used. The title of statute, 10 Edw. III., st. 3, to restrain the expense of entertainments.

De claro die. By daylight.

De clero. Concerning the clergy. The title of stat. 25 Edw. III., st. 3, on the subject of presentations, indictments of spiritual persons, etc.

De cognitionibus certificare. To certify (to give a certificate of acknowledgments).

De combustione. Of house burning. An ancient form of appeal.

De communi consilio regni. By the common council (the Parliament of England). Anciently applied to the enactment of statutes.

De communi dividundo. For dividing a thing held in common. A Civil law action.

De comon droit. Of common right. By the common law.

De confes. In French church law, persons who died without confession.

De conjunctim feoffatis. Concerning persons jointly enfeoffed. Title of stat. 34 Edw. I. enacted to prevent delay caused by a tenant pleading in certain causes that another was seized jointly with him.

De consanguineo. Of kindred by blood; of cosinage. A writ. Same as Co-SINAGE.

De consilio. Of counsel. Concerning advice to commit an offence.

De consilio curiæ. By advice of court.

De corpore comitatus. From the body of the county, as distinguished from a particular locality.

De coste. From or on the side; collateral.

De cursu. Of course; as a matter of course.

De doneranda pro rata portionis. For discharging according to the rate of portion. A writ allowed when one is distrained for rent that ought to be paid by others proportionably with him.

De debitore in partes secundo. Of cutting a debtor in pieces. In Roman law, a law of the twelve tables of uncertain meaning. Some contend that it permitted the actual cutting of a debtor to pieces by his creditors; others, that it merely meant the division of his estate.

De die in diem. From day to day.

De disseisina super disseisinam. Of disseisin upon disseisin. One intrusion upon another.

De Diversis Regulis Juris Antiqui. Of Divers Rules of the Ancient Law. The last title of book L, in the collection of the Digests.

De donis. In relation to gifts or grants. The title of stat. Westm. II. (13 Edw. I.) See STATUTE DE DONIS CONDITIONALIBUS.

De donis conditionalibus. Concerning conditional gifts. The title of the first chapter of the statute commonly called "Statute de Donis."

De dono malo. Of or based upon fraud.

De esse in peregrinatione. Of being on a journey. A species of essoin.

De essendo quietam de theolonio. Of being quit of toll. A writ to prevent those exempted from paying toll from being molested for not paying the same.

De essono de malo lecti. Of essoin of infirmity or illness (in) bed.

De ester a droit. To stand to the right; to meet an accusation.

De eu et trene. Of water and whip of three cords. A term applied to a bond woman or female villein who could be corporally punished.

De excusationibus. Concerning excuses. Title 27 of the Pandects.

De expensis civium et burgentium. For the expenses of the citizens and burgesses. An old writ to raise sufficient to pay each of these two shillings per diem.

De expensis militum. Of or concerning the expenses of knights. A writ directing the sheriff to levy a tax to pay the expenses of a knight of the shire attending Parliament.

De facto. Of fact; from; arising out of, or founded on fact; in fact; in point of fact; in deed, actually, really, Of fact or act. Actually, but without right, as distinguished from de jure.

De facto contract. See CONTRACT DE FACTO.

De faire echelle. In French law, a license in a policy of marine insurance to stop and trade at intermediate points on a voyage.

De falso moneta. Of false money. Title of the stat. 27 Edw. I. Providing that importers of certain coins should forfeit lives and goods.

De feodo. Of fee; in fee. Applied in old statutes to officers named therein.

De fide privata bello. Of private faith in war. (A doctrine applied where one of two hostile parties sends a flag of truce to the other, or sailors are shipwrecked).

De fideli administratione. Of faithful administration. In Scotch law, an oath to faithfully discharge the duties of an office.

De finibus levatis. Concerning fines levied. A stat. of 27 Edw. I. providing that all fines should be levied in open court.

De frangentibus prisonam. Concerning those that break prison. Stat. 1 Edw. II., providing that thereafter prison-breaking should not be punished with loss of life or limb.

De furto. Of theft. A criminal appeal formerly made use of in England.

De gestu et fama. Of behavior and reputation. An ancient writ in cases of impeachment of a person's conduct and reputation.

De gremio mittere. To send from the bosom. Applied to the sending of a person as a delegate from a conventual church, or other body of persons, as distinguished from a latere legere, to send as ambassador from the side.

De hereditatibus mulierum. Concerning the inheritances of women. A title of the Voconian Law, restricting the right of women to inherit.

De haut et de bas. From high and low. Applied to the unlimited power of taxation which a ·lord had over his villein.

De homine replegiando. For replevying a man. A writ to replevy a man out of prison or out of restraint on giving security to the sheriff for his appearance when wanted to answer a charge.

De iis qui ponendi sunt in assisis. Of those who are to be put on assises. Title of stat. 21 Edw. I., defining the qualifications of jurors.

De incendio, ruina, naufragio, rate, nave expugnata. Of the burning, ruin of buildings, shipwreck, in respect to a boat or raft, or concerning a ship being taken by force.

De incremento. Of increase; of addition. See COSTS DE INCREMENTO.

De infirmitate. Of infirmity; sickness. The principal essoin for not appearing in court. See DE MALO LECTI.

De infirmitate reseantisæ. Same as DE MALO LECTI.

De infirmitate veniendi. Of infirmity in coming. Same as DE MALO VENIENDI.

De injuria absque residuo causæ. As to the injury or wrong, without the residue of the cause. A replication in which a part of a plea is admitted.

De injuria sua propria, absque tali causa. Of his own particular wrong without such cause or excuse. Replication in the form of a traverse by the plaintiff in reply to the plea of non assault demesne of the defendant in action of trespass.

De inofficioso testamento. Concerning an inofficious testament. A title of the Civil law.

De integro. Anew, afresh; a second time.

De jactura evitanda. For avoiding a loss. Applied to a defendant. See DE LUCRO CAPTANDO.

De Judaismo. Concerning Judaism. Statute 18 Edw. I, prohibiting usury.

De judicato solvendo. For payment of the amount adjudged. In Admiralty law, applied to bail to the action, or special bail.

De judiciis. Of judicial proceedings. In the Civil law, the title of the second part, including the fifth to the eleventh books inclusive of the Digests.

De judicio sisti. For appearing in court. In Admiralty law, applied to bail for a defendant's appearance.

De jure. Of right by law; growing out of right; rightful; lawful. The opposite of de facto. By or at law, according to law; founded on fact.

De jure immunitatis. In respect to the right of exemption from public duties, obligations, etc.

De jure maris. Of the law of the sea.

De jure maris, et branchiorum ejusdem. Of the law of the sea, and the branches of the same.

De jure maritimo. Of or concerning maritime law.

De jure naturæ. Of the law of nature; by the law of nature.

De jure successionis. By right of succession.

De la plus beale (or belle). Of the most fair. Applied to a species of dower, which was assigned out of the husband's tenements.

De latere. From the side. Collaterally. Collaterals.

De laudibus legum Angliæ. Upon the merits of the laws of England. The title of a treatise by Sir John Fortescue.

De legatis et fidei commissis. Of legacies and trusts. A title of the Pandects.

De Lege Rhodia de Jactu. Of the Rhodian Laws of Jettison. A title in the civil law.

De Legibus et Consuetudinibus Angliæ. Concerning the laws and customs of England. The title of the work by Bracton.

De libellis famosis. Of or concerning a defamatory publication. A scandalous libel; an infamous publication.

De libera falda. Writ of freehold.

De lucro captando. For gain or profit. Applied to a plaintiff. See DE JACTURA EVITANDA.

De lunatico inquirendo. For inquiring about a lunatic or lunacy. A commission to enquire into the condition of a person's mind, and whether the party be a lunatic or not.

De mal de lyt. Same as DE MALO LECTI.

De malefactoribus in parcis. Of or concerning malefactors in parks. The title of statute 21 Edw. I., ch. 2.

De malo lecti. Of infirmity or illness of or in bed. One of the principal essoins or excuses for default of appearance in court.

De malo veniendi. An essoin of illness or misfortune in coming.

De malo villæ. Of illness in a town. An excuse made by a party who had appeared in court, but was, before any answer to the suit, taken ill in the town where the court sat, and was unable to attend.

De medietate advocationis. Of a moiety of advowson. A writ of right.

De medietate linguæ. Of a moiety of the languages; half of one language, half of another. A term to denote a jury composed of one-half natives or denizens and one-half aliens. It was given by English statute in reign of Edw. III for benefit of merchants, where one party to a cause was an alien, and afterwards, but in same reign, extended to criminal causes.

De melioribus damnis. Of better (greater) damages. The election by a plaintiff against which of several defendants he will take judgment where the damages have been separately assessed.

De mercatoribus. Of merchants or traders; relating to merchants. See ACTON BURNEL.

De militibus. Of or concerning knights. The title of a statute in 1 Edw. II.

De modo decimandi. Of a modus of tithing. Applied to a prescription to have a special manner of tithing.

De moneta. Concerning money. Stat. 20 Edw. I., stat. 4. Also the stat. 20 Edw. I., st. 5.

De nautico fœnore. Of nautical interest; concerning maritime interest, usury or bottomry. A title in the civil law.

De non alienando. For not alienating; against alienating. Applied to a clause prohibiting alienations of the property.

De non decimando. Of not paying tithes. Applied to an exemption from tithes, or compensation in lieu thereof. In England the King enjoyed this exemption.

De non residentia clerici regis. A writ excusing one in the King's service being a resident.

De novi operis nunciatione. Concerning the prohibition of a new work. A title in the civil law.

De novo. Anew; from the first.

De novo damus. We give of new. In Scotch law, a charter in which there is a clause of novodamus joined to the dispositive clause.

De officio. Of office. Officially. In the discharge of official duty.

De officio coronatoris. Concerning the office of coroner. The title of the statute 4 Edw. I.

De pace et plagis fracta contra pacem. Of (breach) of the peace and for wounds inflicted against the peace. An old criminal appeal which lay in cases of assault, wounding and breach of the peace.

De pace et roberia. Of the breach (breach of peace) and a robbery. An old criminal appeal which lay in cases of robbery and breach of the peace.

De pace et imprisonamento. Of the peace (breach of peace) and imprisonment. An old appeal in cases of imprisonment and breach of the peace.

De parco fracto. See PARCO FRACTO.

De partitione faciendo. For division to be made.

De passagio simplici. Of simple passage. One of the essoigns of ultra mare.

De peregrinatio et passagio generali. Of pilgrimage and general passage. One of the essoigns de ultra mare.

De pipa vina carianda. For carrying a pipe of wine. Applied to a writ of trespass for carrying, etc., so carelessly that it was stove and the contents lost.

De plagis et mahemio. Of wounds and mayhem. A criminal appeal formerly in use in cases of wounds and maiming.

De plano. On level ground (not on the tribunal). Clearly, manifestly. (A phrase used in the stat. de Bigamis, 4 Edw. I.) By covin or collusion. In Scotch law, forthwith; straightway; immediately.

De pœnis. Of penalties, punishments. A title in the civil law.

De prærogativa regis. Of or concerning the prerogative of the King. Statute 17 Edw. III., st. 1, defining the prerogative of the crown.

De proavo. See BEFAYLE.

De protectionibus. Of or concerning protections. Statute 33 Edw. I. relating to the privileges given by writs of protection.

De quibus sur disseisin. An old writ of entry.

De quota litis. For or concerning a proportional part of the suit. A contract in respect to a claim difficult to recover, to give a part, for services in recovering the whole.

De rapto virginum. Of the ravishment of virgins. An old appeal in cases of rape.

De recto. Writ of right.

De recto patens. Writ of right patent.

De regulis juris antiqui. Of or concerning the ancient rules of law. A title in the Civil law.

De religiosis. Of or concerning religious persons. Statute 7 Edw. I.

De retorno habendo. For having a return. Applied to the judgment for the defendant in an action of replevin, awarding him a return of the property replevied; and to the writ issued thereon. Also to the pledges to return.

De scaccario. Of or concerning the exchequer. Stat. 51 Hen. III.

De scandalis magnatum. Of the defamation of great men. Title of many old statutes: Westm. 1; 3 Edw. I., c. 34; 2 Rich. II., c. 5; 12 Rich. II., c. 11.

De sententia judice appellare. To appeal from the sentence of a judge.

De servitio regis. Of or in the King's service. An essoin for a defendant's nonappearance in court.

De son tort, executor. One who performs in the capacity of an executor without authority.

De stapulis. Of staples. Stat. 27 Edw. III., st. 2.

De statuto. Founded upon statute. Applied to writs.

De tallagio non concedendo. Of not granting talliage or subsidy. Stat. 34 Edw. I., st. 4.

De termino Hilarii. Of Hilary term. One of the four terms of the English Courts of Common Law; so called from the festival day (St. Hilary's day), which immediately preceded its commencement. It formerly began on the 23rd of January, and ended on the 12th of February, but afterwards begun on the 11th and ended on the 31st of January in each year.

De termino Paschæ. Of the term of Easter. One of the four terms of the English Courts of Common Law; so called from the festival day (Easter) which immediately preceded its commencement. It begun on the 15th day of April, and ended on the 8th day of May each year.

De termino Sancto Michaelis. Of the term of St. Michael (Michaelmas Term). One of the four terms of the English Courts of Common Law; so called from the festival (St. Michael's day) which immediately preceded its commencement, It begun on the 2nd and ended on the 25th day of November.

De termino Trinitatis. Of Trinity term. One of the four terms of the English Courts of Common Law; so called from the festival day (the Holy Trinity), which immediately preceded its commencement. It begun on the 22nd day of May, and ended on the 12th day of June.

De terra sancta. Of the Holy Land. An essoin for default of appearance in court, because the party had gone to the Holy Land.

De testamentis. Of testaments. A Title of the Digest.

De transmare. See DE ULTRA MARE.

De ultra mare (or De transmare). Of or beyond the sea. An essoin that the party was detained in parts beyond the seas.

De una parte. See DEED DE UNA PARTE.

De ventre inspiciendo. See WRIT DE VENTRE INSPICIENDO.

De verborum significatione. Of the signification of words. A title in the Pandects defining words and phrases of the Civil law.

De viceneto. From the vicinage or country.

De warrantia custodiæ. A writ allowed a purchaser of lands in knight's service against a grantor who warranted the land free of wardship, when wardship was claimed in connection with the land.

De warrantia diei. Of warranty of day; warranty from default of the day. A writ to prevent default being taken against one absent in the King's service.

De wrecko. Of wreck.

De viridi et venantione. Of vert and venison. A term in the old Forest law.

Dead freight. The amount paid by a charterer for the part of a vessel which he does not use, after contracting for it.

Dead ground. In mining, ground through which work has to be done in order to reach ore.

Dead head. One other than an employee allowed to travel on a public conveyance without paying fare. One allowed to send telegraph messages without paying toll.

Dead letter. When applied to a law implies one which has been long unused or which is not enforced.

Dead letters. See LETTERS, DEAD.

Dead line. The line in military regulations across which a prisoner is not allowed to go without being fired upon.

Dead lode. See LODE, DEAD.

Dead man's part. According to the custom of London and York, England, that part of a decedent's personal effects which went to the administrator.

Dead pledge. A pledge of land or goods. A mortgage.

Dead rent. See RENT, DEAD.

Dead use. See USE, DEAD.

Deadly. See WEAPON, DEADLY.

Deadly weapon. See WEAPON, DEADLY.

Deadly feud. A term applied among the Saxons where a murderer did not make satisfaction and the murdered man's relatives took up the quarrel for revenge. It was sanctioned by law.

Dead's part. In Scotch law, such personal effects as remained beyond the shares of the widow and children, which could be disposed of by will.

Deaf, dumb and blind. One in this condition is regarded in law the same as an idiot.

Deafforest. To exempt from Forest law.

Deafforested. Exempted from Forest laws.

Deal. A low meadow by a river. A secret bargain or understanding for the benefit of the parties to it.

De-albo. To whiten over. Applied to the converting of base money, in which rents were paid, into silver or white money.

Dealbore firmam. To whiten rent or farm. See DE-ALBO.

Dealer. One who buys, sells, or exchanges as a business.

Dealings. Business transactions.

Dean. A term derived from the Latin words Decanus and Decem, and the old French Deien. Originally a Roman Catholic ecclesiastic presiding over ten canons or prebendaries. The head of a capitulum or chapter, which, with the dean, was the bishop's council. Originally a dean was chosen by the chapter with permission of the king and confirmed and installed by the bishop. After the time of Henry VIII. they were appointed by letters-patent without being elected or confirmed. Under old

English law a dean was appointed as head of a chapter, and was a check on the bishop in the matter of grants, which would not bind the bishop's successor without the consent of the dean and chapter, the latter acting like a corporation, through a common seal. The head of a theological, medical or law school. In Oxford and Cambridge University one who superintends the discipline. The head of any constituted body, who acts as its executive or organ. The presiding officer of a society of lawyers. See DECANUS.

Dean and Chapter. A spiritual corporation, the council of a bishop.

Dean of the Arches. Presiding judge of the Court of Arches.

Deans in the universities. Officers appointed to enforce discipline and regulate the behavior of the students in Oxford and Cambridge Universities.

Deans, Lay. Deans not in church orders but with certain jurisdiction, as was the dean of the Court of Arches.

Deans of Chapters. Deans of cathedral or collegiate churches, or church endowed for a society or corporation.

Deans of Peculiars. Deans with care of souls, also those having certain jurisdiction only, as the dean or presiding officer of the Court of Arches.

Deans, rural. Originally deans over certain divisions of a diocese. Afterwards deputies of the bishop in matters of probate and administration.

Deanery. The office or house of a dean.

Deanery, rural. The territorial jurisdiction of an archbishop or dean.

Deanship. The office of a dean; deanery.

Death. Cessation of natural, political, or civil life. Cessation of operation or existence.

Death bed. In Scotch law, sickness which ends in death.

Death bed deed. See DEED, DEATH BED.

Death by the hands of justice. Legal execution.

Death, civil. The deprivation of legal rights.

Death, natural. Cessation of life. Physical death as distinguished from civil death. Death from natural causes or disease and not from violence.

Death, penalty. Capital punishment.

Death sentence. One directing the taking away of life.

Death-warrant. An order for the execution of one sentenced to death.

Deathsman. A public executioner.

Death's part. Same as DEAD MAN'S PART.

Debar. To disbar.

Debas. Downwards; below.

Debased coin. Coin reduced in value or impaired in credit.

Debauch. To entice or corrupt. To seduce. To have sexual intercourse with.

Debent. They owe.

Debenture. A bond to pay a charge or sum due. A bond of an English company. A Custom House certificate that an importer is entitled to a drawback. An acknowledgement of a debt. A government payment order.

Debenture bond. See DEBENTURE.

Debenture stock. A stock of money borrowed by a corporation for the payment of which all or a part of its property is liable.

Debet. He owes.

Debet et detinet. He owes and detains. Words employed in an action of debt.

Debet et solet. He ought and has been used (to do). Words in a writ meaning that the plaintiff sues for a thing withheld, for the first time.

Debit. To set down as a debt. The amount so set down.

Debit sans breve. Same as DEBITUM SINE BREVI.

Debita. Debts.

Debita fundi. Debts affecting the ground; debts secured upon land.

Debita laicorum. Debts of the laity ; debts recoverable in the Civil Courts.

Debitor. A debtor.

Debitor capitalis. See CAPITALIS DEBITOR.

Debitor in solido. A debtor for the whole.

Debitoris. A debtor.

Debitorum. Debts.

Debitrix. A female debtor.

Debitum. A thing due or owing; a debt.

Debitum fructuum. A debt upon the fruits. (Tithes are said to be a lien upon the fruits; not upon the ground).

Debitum fundi. A debt of or affecting the land; a debt which is a charge upon real estate.

Debitum in presenti. A debt owing at the present time.

Debitum in presenti, solvendum in futuro. A debt contracted or owing at the present time, to be paid in the future.

Debitum recuperatum. A debt recovered.

Debitum sine brevi. Debt without writ. A term applied where action was begun by bill and not by original writ. A debt for which judgment has been confessed.

Debitum solvendum in futuro. A debt to be paid in the future.

Debitum solvendum in presenti. A debt to be paid at the present time.

Debitum subesse. A debt due. That the debt was legally due.

Debt. A sum of money due by express agreement. What one man owes to another.

Debt, active. One which bears interest.

Debt, action of. See ACTION OF DEBT.

Debt, ancestral. One contracted by an ancestor and binding upon the heir.

Debt, antecedent. A prior debt. A debt entitled to payment before another.

Debt, bill of. A written acknowledgment of a debt, stating amount, place and date of payment.

Debt, book. A debt created by goods sold and delivered and work performed, evidenced by an entry in an original book.

Debt by simple contract. A debt based on a verbal or implied agreement, or one·written but not under seal.

Debt by specialty. A debt acknowledged by writing under seal.

Debt, contingent. In Scotch law, one which will become due only on the happening of an event.

Debt, desperate. One not to be recovered.

Debt, doubtful. A debt, the payment of which is uncertain.

Debt, ex mutuo. One which arose out of a loan of goods to be returned in kind.

Debt, extinguishment of a. See EXTINGUISHMENT OF A DEBT.

Debt, floating. A debt due at different times and in different amounts.

Debt, funded. Outstanding debts converted into bonds.

Debt, future. In Scotch law, a debt which will not come due until a future day.

Debt, fraudulent. A debt created with the aid of fraud.

Debt, hypothecary. A debt which is a lien on property.

Debt, judgment. A debt established by a judgment.

Debt, liquid. One due immediately and without condition.

Debt, liquidated. See LIQUIDATED DEBT.

Debt, national. A debt due from a nation to its creditors.

Debt of record. A judgment or recognizance of debt.

Debt, passive. One not bearing interest.

Debt, preferred. One having priority of payment.

Debt, privileged. Same as DEBT, PREFERRED.

Debt, proof of. See PROOF OF DEBT.

Debt, public. The debt of a nation, State, or political division.

Debtee. A creditor.

Debtor. One who owes a sum of money.

Debtor, absconding. See ABSCONDING DEBTOR.

Debtor-executor. One who is the executor or administrator of his deceased debtor.

Debtor, joint. One of two or more who owe a debt jointly.

Debts, legal. See LEGAL DEBTS.

Debts, mutual. Debts due by each of two persons to the other.

Debt, pure. In Scotch law, a debt already due.

Debt, simple contract. A debt based on unsealed notes or verbal promises.

Debt, specialty. A debt owing because of an instrument writing under seal.

Debuit. He owed.

Debuit reparare. He ought to repair.

Deca. On this side; from this.

Decagram. In the Metric system, 0.353 ounces avoirdupois.

Decaliter. In Metric system, a measure of capacity equal to 9.08 quarts dry or 2.64 gallons liquid measure.

Decameter. In Metric system, a measure of length equal to 3.937 inches.

Decanatus. A deanery. A company of ten persons.

Decana. Same as DECANATUS.

Decania. The office, jurisdiction, territory or command of a decanus or dean.

Decanus. A chief of ten; one set over ten persons. A dean. An ancient officer of the church, now grown out of use; otherwise called bishop's dean. A bishop's deputy, appointed to inspect the conduct of the parochial clergy, with certain authority over them. In Roman law, an officer who had command of ten soldiers. The chief of the corpse-bearers. See DEAN.

Decanus in majori ecclesia. Dean of a cathedral church, presiding over ten canons or prebendaries. An ecclesiastical dignitary who presided over the chapter of a cathedral, and is next in rank to a bishop. See DEAN.

Decanus monasticus. Dean of a monastery; an officer over ten monks.

Decanus et capitulum. A dean and a chapter. It was a spiritual corporation. See DEAN.

Decanus friborgi. Dean of a friborg; a tithing man.

Decanus militaris. A military officer having command of ten soldiers.

Decanus ruralis. A rural dean.

Decapitation. Cutting off the head.

Decaproti. A later name for the Decem prima (which see).

Decea. Same as DECA.

Decease. Death. To die.

Decedent. A deceased whose estate is unsettled. A dying person. A deceased person.

Deceit. Arts used to deceive or defraud. An old common bench writ to recover land lost in a real action by default of the tenant, through collusion. An original writ to recover damages for forgery, collusion or fraud.

Deceit, action of. See DECEIT; also DECEIT, WRIT OF.

Deceit, writ of. An original or judicial writ for one who was injured by deceit.

Decem. Ten.

Decem prima. The ten chief aldermen, in the municipia and colonies, afterwards called decaproti.

Decem tales. Ten such (ten tales jurors). (When a full jury was not present at a trial a writ apponere decem tales is issued to supply the deficiency).

Decemviri. The ten men appointed to compose the twelve tables of the laws for the Romans.

Decemviri litibus judicandis. In Roman law, ten assistants to the prætor when he decided questions of law.

Decenna. A tithing; decennary; the precinct of a frank-pledge, consisting of ten freeholders with their families.

Decennaries. The division of persons by ten.

Decennarii. Members of a decennary. See DECCENNA, also DECENNARY.

Decennarius. A freeholder in a decennary. One who had a half virgate of land.

Decennary. A town consisting of ten families of freeholders. See DECENNA.

Decennier. One of the freeholders who made up a tithing.

Decennium. A period of ten years.

Deception. Fraud, cheat, craft; collusion used to deceive and defraud others.

Decern. In Scotch law, to decree.

Decessus. A going away, departure. Withdrawal, retirement. Decease, death.

Decet. It is fit, becoming.

Decha. Same as DECA.

Decide. To come to a decision. To render judgment. To determine.

Decido. To decide; to determine. To fall to; to remain to; to escheat.

Decies tantum. Ten times as much. A writ against an embracer or a juror who took money for giving his verdict.

Decigram. In Metric system, 1.543 grains avoirdupois.

Deciliter. In Metric system, a measure of capacity equal to 6.1022 cubic inches dry or 0.845 gills liquid measure.

Decima. The tenth part; tithe. A tithe, as a tax on landholders in the provinces. See DECIMÆ.

Decima collatio. A collection of laws found in some editions of the Corpus Juris Civilis comprising the Books of Fiefs, the Constitutions of Conrade the Third and the Emperor Frederick. See CORPUS JURIS CIVILIS.

Decimæ. Tenths. The tenth part of the annual profit of the livings of ecclesiastical benefices, formerly claimed of the English clergy by the Papal see, and afterward made a part of the royal revenue.

Decimæ garbales. Corn tithes.

Decimæ rectoriæ. Parsonage tithes.

Decimatio. Decimation.

Decimation. The punishing by lot, by the Romans, of every tenth soldier for any violation of duty.

Decimeter. In Metric system, a measure of length equal to 3.937 inches.

Deciners. Those who had charge of friborgs or views of frank-pledge for maintenance of the King's peace.

Decision. The determination of a question by judge or other person.

Decision, extra judicial. A decision on a question beyond the issue or jurisdiction of the court.

Decision, judicial. See JUDICIAL DECISIONS.

Decision, rules of. Rules of law. In U. S. Federal Courts, the laws of a State where they do not conflict with the Federal law; at one time the laws as they existed when the judiciary act of 1798 went into effect.

Decisive oath. See OATH, DECISIVE.

Decisory oath. See OATH, DECISORY.

Decisum. Decided. A decision.

Declamation. Proclamation.

Declarant. One who declares a thing affirmatively.

Declaration. A statement. That which is declared. A plaintiff's allegation of the facts which constitute his cause of action or demand. The formal pleading at old English law which followed the declaration were the defendant's answer, then the plaintiff's replication, then defendant's rejoinder, then plaintiff's surrejoinder, then defendant's rebutter, then plaintiff's surrebutter.

Declaration, dying. The declaration of one who believes he will die; admissible in evidence under certain circumstances.

Declaration in chief. A declaration of the principal ground of action.

Declaration, Mecklenburg. The draft of the Declaration of Independence of the American Colonies, made at western North Carolina, May 20th, 1775, and sent to the Continental Congress at Philadelphia.

Declaration of Independence. The declaration of the Colonial Congress of July 4th, 1776, setting forth the grievances of the American colonies and declaring their independence of Great Britain.

Declaration of intention. The declaration of an alien that he intends to become a citizen of the U. S.

Declaration of Paris. An agreement by the leading powers arrived at in the International Convention held at Paris in 1856, that they would adhere to certain rules in time of war. These were, a blockade must be effective to be binding; privateering will not be authorized; neutral flag protects any goods not contraband ; neutral goods in enemy's ship will not be confiscated if not contraband.

Declaration of rights. Same as RIGHTS, BILL OF.

Declaration of trust. A declaration in writing acknowledging a trust.

Declaration of war. A proclamation by a nation that war exists between itself and another nation.

Declarator. In Scotch law, an action to judicially ascertain and declare a right.

Declarator of trust. In Scotch law, an action against a trustee who holds property by title which on its face is for his own benefit.

Declaratory. Making clear. Explanatory.

Declaratory action. See ACTION, DECLARATORY.

Declaratory decree. One which simply declares the rights of the parties without making any order.

Declaratory judgment. See JUDGMENT, DECLARATORY.

Declaratory part of a law. See LAW, DECLARATORY PART OF A.

Declaratory statement. In the U. S. Public Land law, a declaration in writing that the subscriber intends to purchase a certain piece of public land under the pre-emption law.

Declaratory statement, soldier's. In the U. S. Public Land law, a declaration by a soldier or sailor that he intends to make homestead entry of a certain piece of land within six months.

Declaratory statutes. Those which declare the existing law.

Declare. To prepare, file and serve a declaration. To proclaim. To state before witnesses. To announce. To interpret. To define. To assert.

Declare the use. In a fine of lands, to execute a deed after the fine specifying to whose use the fine should inure.

Declination. In Scotch law, a plea to the jurisdiction.

Declinatoires. In French law, pleas to the jurisdiction and lis pendens.

Declinatory plea. The plea of sanctuary, or benefit of clergy.

Declinature. Same as DECLINATION.

Decline. To object to.

Decoctor. In Roman law, one who squanders public moneys. A bankrupt. A spendthrift.

Decollat. Beheaded.

Decollatio. Decollation.

Decollation. The act of punishing by beheading.

Deconfes. Those who died without making confession.

De-consuetudo. Disuse, disuetude.

Decoration Day. See HOLIDAY, LEGAL.

Decouper. To cut down; to cut off.

Decoy. That which is used to induce one to commit a crime or disclose his guilt.

Decoy letter. See LETTER, DECOY.

Decree. The judgment of a Court of Equity or Admiralty. The title of first division of the Canon law.

Decree, dative. In Scotch law, a court order appointing an administrator.

Decree, declaratory. See DECLARATORY DECREE.

Decree, execution of. The carrying out of a decree.

Decree, final. A decree which terminates a cause.

Decree, foreign. See FOREIGN DECREE.

Decree in absence. In Scotch law, a decree where the defendant makes default or refuses to answer.

Decree, interlocutory. One which disposes of some plea or issue in a cause not the main question.

Decree, Macedonian. In Roman law, a decree of the Senate providing that no action should be maintained to recover a loan made to children under paternal authority.

Decree, nisi. One which will be made absolute on motion unless some reason to prevent intervenes.

Decree of Constitution. In Scotch law, a decree necessary to determine a debt or vest title in a creditor.

Decree of forthcoming. In Scotch law, a decree following an arrestment directing a debt to be paid or the property of the debtor delivered to the creditor.

Decree of locality. In Scotch law, a tiend court order fixing or modifying a stipend.

Decree of modification. In Scotch law, a tiend court order fixing or modifying a stipend.

Decree of registration. In Scotch law, a procedure which gives a creditor an immediate execution.

Decree pro confesso. A decree rendered when the defendant is in default, that the averments in a bill in equity be taken as confessed, and the plaintiff be allowed to proceed ex parte.

Decrees, remedial. See REMEDIAL DECREES.

Decreet. In Scotch law, the final judgment or sentence of court by which the question at issue between the parties is decided.

Decreet absolvitor. In Scotch law, a decree acquitting a defendant or dismissing a claim.

Decreet arbitral. In Scotch law, the award of arbitrators. The form of promulgating such award.

Decreet cognitionis causa. A decree for the sake of jurisdiction or judicially investigating. In Scotch law, a decree entered when an heir, whose lands the creditor has endeavored to make liable for the ancestor's debt, appears and renounces the succession.

Decreet condemnator. A decree in favor of the plaintiff.

Decreet of valuation of Teinds. In Scotch law, a decree of the Court of Session as to the extent or value of tithes.

Decrementum. A decreasing.

Decrementum lunæ. A decrease of the moon.

Decrementum maris. Decrease of the sea; receding of the sea from the land.

Decreta. Decrees.

Decretal order. A Chancery order, in the nature of a decree, made on motion.

Decretales. Decretals. The title of the second of the two great divisions of the Corpus Juris Canonici. See DECRETALS.

Decretales Bonifacii octavi. Decretals of Boniface the VIII. See SEXTUS DECRETALIUM.

Decretales Gregorii noni. Decretals of Gregory the ninth. A collection on Canon law, collated from the decretal rescripts, or epistles of the Popes, published by Pope Gregory IX., A. D. 1234.

Decretalia. Decretals.

Decretalis. Belonging to or depending on a decree, decretal.

Decretals. A volume of the Canon law, containing the decrees of the Popes, or a digest of the Canons. Letters of the Pope determining some question of Canon law.

Decretio. A decision, decree.

Decreto. In Spanish law, an o r d e r issued by authority of the Sovereign relating to church matters.

Decretorius. Belonging to a decision; decisive.

Decretum. A species of imperial constitution, being a judgment or s e n t e n c e given by the Emperor upon hearing of a cause, in his capacity as a judge. An ecclesiastical law, in contradistinction to a secular law.

Decretum Gratiani. Gratian's decree, or decretum. See CONCORDIA DISCORDANTIUM CANONUM.

Decrowning. Depriving of a crown.

Decry. To cry down. To destroy the credit of.

Decuria. A tithing or decennary, otherwise called decenna, decania, and decinia.

Decuriæ. In old European law, marks made upon trees to show the boundary lines.

Decuriare. To bring to order.

Decurio. The head or chief of a decuria; a decurion.

Decurion. One of the chief men or senators in the provincial towns having the entire management of the same.

Decurionatus. The office of a decurion.

Dedbana. A homicide or manslaughter.

Dedeins. Within.

Dedens. Within.

Dedi. I have given. A word anciently used in charters of feoffment, and deeds of gift and grant.

Dedi, concessi, barganizavi et feoffavi. I have given, granted, bargained and enfeoffed. The operative words of conveyance in ancient charters of feoffment, and deeds of gift and grant.

Dedi et concessi. I have given and granted.

Dedicate. To set apart private property for public use.

Dedication. Consecration. Appropriation to a certain use or uses. Giving for the use of the public.

Dedication, express. A dedication made by express words either in a deed or by declaration in some public form.

Dedication, implied. A dedication implied from the acts of the owner.

Dedicere. To deny.

Dedicit. He denies.

Dedicta. Denied.

Dedictum. Denied.

Dedimus. (We have given). An abbreviation of Dedimus Potestatem (which see).

Dedimus et concessimus. We have given and granted. Words used in old grants where there were more than one grantor, or where the King made the grant.

Dedimus potestatem. We have given power or authority. A writ giving authority to perform some judicial or other act. A commission to take testimony.

Dedimus potestatem de attornato faciendo (recipiendo). We have given the power of making (receiving) an attor-

Decollat. Beheaded.

Decollatio. Decollation.

Decollation. The act of punishing by beheading.

Deconfes. Those who died without making confession.

De-consuetudo. Disuse, disuetude.

Decoration Day. See HOLIDAY, LEGAL.

Decouper. To cut down; to cut off.

Decoy. That which is used to induce one to commit a crime or disclose his guilt.

Decoy letter. See LETTER, DECOY.

Decree. The judgment of a Court of Equity or Admiralty. The title of first division of the Canon law.

Decree, dative. In Scotch law, a court order appointing an administrator.

Decree, declaratory. See DECLARATORY DECREE.

Decree, execution of. The carrying out of a decree.

Decree, final. A decree which terminates a cause.

Decree, foreign. See FOREIGN DECREE.

Decree in absence. In Scotch law, a decree where the defendant makes default or refuses to answer.

Decree, interlocutory. One which disposes of some plea or issue in a cause not the main question.

Decree, Macedonian. In Roman law, a decree of the Senate providing that no action should be maintained to recover a loan made to children under paternal authority.

Decree, nisi. One which will be made absolute on motion unless some reason to prevent intervenes.

Decree of Constitution. In Scotch law, a decree necessary to determine a debt or vest title in a creditor.

Decree of forthcoming. In Scotch law, a decree following an arrestment directing a debt to be paid or the property of the debtor delivered to the creditor.

Decree of locality. In Scotch law, a tiend court order fixing or modifying a stipend.

Decree of modification. In Scotch law, a tiend court order fixing or modifying a stipend.

Decree of registration. In Scotch law, a procedure which gives a creditor an immediate execution.

Decree pro confesso. A decree rendered when the defendant is in default, that the averments in a bill in equity be taken as confessed, and the plaintiff be allowed to proceed ex parte.

Decrees, remedial. See REMEDIAL DECREES.

Decreet. In Scotch law, the final judgment or sentence of court by which the question at issue between the parties is decided.

Decreet absolvitor. In Scotch law, a decree acquitting a defendant or dismissing a claim.

Decreet arbitral. In Scotch law, the award of arbitrators. The form of promulgating such award.

Decreet cognitionis causa. A decree for the sake of jurisdiction or judicially investigating. In Scotch law, a decree entered when an heir, whose lands the creditor has endeavored to make liable for the ancestor's debt, appears and renounces the succession.

Decreet condemnator. A decree in favor of the plaintiff.

Decreet of valuation of Teinds. In Scotch law, a decree of the Court of Session as to the extent or value of tithes.

Decrementum. A decreasing.

Decrementum lunæ. A decrease of the moon.

Decrementum maris. Decrease of the sea; receding of the sea from the land.

Decreta. Decrees.

Decretal order. A Chancery order, in the nature of a decree, made on motion.

Deed of grant. Originally a deed conveying an incorporeal hereditament; now applied to a deed conveying anything corporeal or incorporeal.

Deed of inspectorship. See INSPECTORSHIP, DEED OF.

Deed of partition. A deed by those holding property jointly, in common or coparceny, which has the effect of vesting in each a separate and distinct portion of the property.

Deed of release. An instrument writing under seal by which a right or interest is relinquished.

Deed of settlement. See SETTLEMENT, DEED OF.

Deed of trust. A deed that creates a trust.

Deed, onerous. In Scotch law, a deed for a valuable consideration.

Deed, poll. A deed signed and sealed by but one person. A deed not indented, as distinguished from a duplicate deed.

Deed, privileged. In Scotch law, an instrument writing or document which the law permitted to be drawn in different form, under certain circumstances, from that which the law required.

Deed, Quit claim. A deed conveying the interest of the grantor at the time it is delivered. It vests such an estate as firmly as any other kind of deed.

Deed, title. A deed conveying a title, or a sealed evidence of title.

Deed to declare uses. Same as DEED TO LEAD USES.

Deed to lead uses. A deed executed before and showing the object of a fine or common recovery.

Deeds, execution of. The signing, sealing, delivery and acceptance in accordance with law.

Deeds, gratuitous. Deeds made without consideration which was binding.

Deeds, registry of. See REGISTRY OF DEEDS.

Deeds under the Statute of Uses. Deeds that by the Statute of Uses conveyed an interest in lands without entry or livery of seisin, as lease and release, bargain and sale.

Deem. To adjudge. To decide. To sentence; to condemn.

Deem meet. See MEET, DEEM.

Deemster. A judge on the Isle of Man, selected from the inhabitants, who decided controversies without process or charge.

Deer fold. A park for deer.

Deer hayes. Nets for catching deer.

Defalcatio. Deduction, abatement; a cutting off. Defalcation (which see).

Defalcation. A fraudulent appropriation of money held in trust. Deduction of a claim by deducting a counter claim. The amount deducted or cut off. A deficiency caused by breach of trust.

Defalta. Default, omission, neglect, failure.

Defamatio. Defamation.

Defamation. The act of injuring a person's reputation, fame, or character, either by spoken or written words.

Defamator. A defamer.

Defamatory. Tending to cause injury to one's reputation.

Defamer. One who is guilty of the offence of defamation.

Defames. Infamous.

Default. Omission of what ought to be done. To allow judgment to be taken because of some neglect.

Default, judgment by. See JUDGMENT BY DEFAULT.

Defaulted. Neglected or omitted to perform a legal duty.

Defaulter. One who neglects to account for money placed in his charge.

Defeasance. To defeat or undo. A collateral deed providing that the other deed is to be void upon the happening of certain conditions. A condition in a bond which when performed defeats the latter.

Defeasible. Capable of defeating, destroying, or impairing.

Defeat. To make void; to annul; to deprive of. Making void.

Defeazance. Same as DEFEASANCE.

Defect. Absence of that necessary to make complete.

Defect, latent. See LATENT DEFECT.

Defects, apparent. Those which can be seen on inspection.

Defectum sanguinis. Defect, deficiency, failure of blood.

Defectus. Defeat, deficiency, imperfection; failure, default; want.

Defence. Same as DEFENSE.

Defend. To prohibit; to forbid; to deny. To claim, vindicate, or prosecute at law. To guard, to protect, support, maintain.

Defendant. One who is sued or charged with a crime. The party against whom an action, either civil or criminal, is instituted.

Defendant, above. The defendant in an appellate court.

Defendant below. The defendant in the trial or inferior court, as distinguished from the one styled the defendant in the appellate court. See DEFENDANT ABOVE.

Defendant, co. One made defendant with another.

Defendant in error. One defendant above in a cause taken up on writ of error.

Defendant, material. One in equity from whom relief is requested or who has an interest adverse to the plaintiff.

Defendant, nominal. One in name only, not having a substantial interest adverse to plaintiff.

Defendaunt. Defending; the party defending; the defendant.

Defendemus. We will defend. A word used in ancient grants binding the grantor and his heirs to defend the grantee against servitudes other than those mentioned.

Defender. To deny. To defend, to appear for a defendant. To prohibit or forbid; to keep or protect. In Scotch law, the person against whom an action is brought.

Defender of the Faith. A title conferred upon Henry VIII. of England by the Pope for writing against Martin Luther in behalf of the Church of Rome. Catholicus was applied to the King of Spain, and Christianissimus to the French King.

Defendere. To defend or deny.

Defendere se per corpus suum. To offer to fight as a trial or appeal. See BATTEL.

Defendere unica manu. To wage law. To deny upon oath.

Defendour. The defendant.

Defendre. Same as DEFENDERE.

Defeneration. The act of lending money at usurious interest.

Defensa. A park or place fenced in for deer, and defended for a property, and peculiar for that purpose.

Defense. The act of resisting force. Opposition. Denial. Denying that a charge or complaint is true, sufficient, or valid. That done in resisting force, or offered to defeat a charge or complaint. Justification. A protection.

Defense, affidavit of. See AFFIDAVIT OF DEFENSE.

Defense au fond en droit. A defense from the foundation or ground in right. A demurrer.

Defense au fond en fait. A defense from the foundation or ground in fact or deed. The general issue.

Defense, dilatory. One not intended to meet the issue raised, but to delay, dismiss, or obstruct the prosecution.

Defense en droit. Same as DEFENSE AU FOND EN DROIT.

Defense, equitable. One resting upon equitable grounds.

Defense, full. A defense, at one time made by the defendant in stating in his plea that he defends the wrong and injury when and wherever it shall behoove him and the damages and whatever else he ought to defend, &c. See DEFENSE, HALF.

Defense, general. A denial in general terms of the statements in the complaint.

Defense, good. Same as DEFENSE, SUFFICIENT.

Defense, half. A defense made in Common law pleading by the defendant simply stating in his plea that he "defends the wrong and injury and says," &c., instead of the words used in full defense. The distinction between full defense and half defense has long been abolished. See DEFENSE, FULL.

Defense, legal. A defense based on law as opposed to equity; or a defense good in law.

Defense, month. Same as FENCH MONTH.

Defense, no. No right or justification which can be set up in answer to a claim.

Defense, peremptory. A plea that the plaintiff never had the right or if he did he has it no longer.

Defense, self. Defense of one's own person or property.

Defense, sham. A pretended defense existing neither in fact or law.

Defense, special. A defense in which special facts or law are set up.

Defense, statement of. See STATEMENT OF DEFENSE.

Defense, sufficient. One good in law.

Defense, valid. Same as DEFENSE, SUFFICIENT.

Defensio. A defending, defense.

Defensio ripariæ. Prohibition to use a river; exclusive appropriation to the use of the King.

Defensiones. Defenses.

Defensiva. A lord of the Marches, who was a defender of his county.

Defensive alliance. See ALLIANCE, DEFENSIVE.

Defensive allegation. The plea of a defendant, in an ecclesiastical court, which states the facts relied upon, and to which he prays the plaintiff's answer under oath.

Defensive war. See WAR, DEFENSIVE.

Defenso. That part of an open field allotted for corn and hay and upon which there was no common or feeding. A wood enclosed to prevent the undergrowth being injured by cattle.

Defensor. In old English law, one accused in an appeal; a defendant. One who warrants the title of another in a real action. An officer having charge of the temporalities of a parish church. A church advocate. In Civil law, one who appeared for another in an action in court. In Roman law, a magistrate with jurisdiction of matters of guardianship and the estates of minors.

Defensor civitatis. Defender of a city. A Roman officer charged with the defense of the people, the acts of judges, officers and money lenders. He also had charge of public records and had judicial jurisdiction in certain matters.

Defensor Fidei. Defender of the Faith (which see).

Defensum. An enclosure or any fenced ground. A state of prohibition against the use of a thing.

Defer. To postpone.

Deferred. Postponed.

Deferred annuity. See ANNUITY, DEFERRED.

Deferred payments. Payments postponed, or not made when due.

Deferred stock. See STOCK, DEFERRED.

Deficiency. That which is wanting.

Deficiency bill. See BILL, DEFIC-IENCY.

Deficit. A deficiency in amount.

Define. To clearly bring out the limits of. To explain. To interpret. To declare what constitutes (as to define a crime).

Definite. Certain. Fixed. Precise. Bounded. Defined.

Definite failure of issue. See FAILURE OF ISSUE, DEFINITE.

Definitio. A boundary. A prescribing; a limiting; a definition; an explanation.

Definition. The act of stating what a thing is. The act of defining. A description of a thing by its substance or properties.

Definitive. Determinate. Exact. Bringing to an end. Conclusive. Final.

Definitive sentence. The final judgment of an ecclesiastical court.

Defloration. Seduction. The act which deprives a female of her virginity.

Deforce. To unlawfully keep a freehold from another.

Deforceare. To deforce.

Deforcement. A keeping out by force or wrong. A wrongful withholding of lands or tenements from the right owner. It includes an abatement, an intrusion, a disseisin, or a discontinuance, or any other wrong by which one having a right to the freehold is kept out of possession.

Deforceor. One who overcomes and casts out by force.

Deforciamentum. Deforcement (which see).

Deforcians. A deforciant.

Deforciant. One who overcomes and casts out by force.

Deforciare. To deforce. To withhold lands or tenements from the right owner. To deforce another, or keep him out of his freehold.

Deforciation. A distress, distraint, or seizure of goods in satisfaction of a debt.

Deforciator. A deforceor. One who deforces another or keeps him out of his freehold.

Defortians. A deforciant.

Defortiari. To deforce.

Defossion. Burial alive.

Defraud. To deprive of something by fraud. To deceive.

Defraudacion. In Spanish law, avoiding the payment of a tax.

Defraudation. The act of depriving by fraud.

Defuer. To run away.

Defunct. Deceased; a deceased person; the deceased.

Defunctus. Defunct, deceased; a deceased person; the deceased.

Defustare. To beat with a club or stick.

Degaster. To waste.

Degradation. Deprivation of rank or dignity; a reducing from a higher to a lower rank or degree. The depriving a peer of his nobility, a knight or baron of his dignity. An ecclesiastical censure, whereby a clergyman is divested of his holy orders and ecclesiastical distinctions.

Degradation, solemn. Where the party degraded is stripped of those ornaments and rights which are the ensigns of his degree.

Degradation, summary. Ecclesiastical censure by word only.

Degradations. In French law, waste.

Degrade. To lessen in reputation or character. To lower in standing or grade.

Degree. The relationship between one person and the next in line of ascent or descent. A grade of crime.

Degree of relationship. The distance of persons, one from another, in the line of ascent or descent.

Deguerpys. Abandoned.

De-hinc. From this place forth; from here, hence. From this time forth, henceforth. Hereupon, afterward, next, then.

Dehors. Without, out of, foreign to, irrelevant, unconnected with. A word used in pleading.

Dei judicium. The judgment of God. Trial by ordeal.

Deien. Old French for Dean (which see).

Deins. Within.

Deinz. Within.

Deis. The high table of a monastery.

Dejacion. In Spanish law, surrender; release; abandonment; surrender of property to creditors or insurers.

Dejeration. Making oath.

Dejecter. To cast off, out, away ; to throw down.

Dejicio. To drive out; to put out of possession; to eject. To dispossess.

De-juro. To take an oath, to swear.

Del bien estre. Of well being. De bene esse.

Del credere. Of belief, trust or warranty. An agreement by which, in consideration of a larger commission or premium, an agent or factor guarantees the payment of the price for which he sells the goods of his principal on credit.

Delaissement. In French law, abandonment.

Delantal. Outlawed.

Delantale. Outlawed.

Delate. In Scotch law, to accuse ; to charge.

Delatio. An accusation, denunciation. An information.

Delator. An accuser; an informer.

Delatura. An accusation, information. The reward of an informer.

Delay. Putting off. A temporary stay.

Delectus. Selection; choice.

(18).

Delectus personæ. The choice of a person An election or choice of the person who becomes tenant. The right of a partner to determine what person shall be introduced into the firm as a new partner.

Delectus personarum. Choice of persons. See DELECTUS PERSONÆ.

Delegata. Empowered; given authority.

Delegate. To empower. To give authority. One appointed to act for another. A representative of a U. S. territory in Congress. He can talk but not vote.

Delegation. The act of making a delegate. An assignment of a debt. In Civil law, the substituting one debtor for another by the agreement of all three parties. See NOVATION.

Delegation of authority. See AUTHORITY, DELEGATION OF.

Delegatus. One chosen to represent or act for another.

Delestage. In French law, discharging ballast from a ship.

Delete. In Scotch law, to erase ; to strike out.

Deletion. In Scotch law, erasure.

Delf. A quarry or mine. Earthenware; counterfeit chinaware.

Deliberate. To weigh facts without haste. To premeditate after cooling time. To examine and discuss without haste.

Deliberabitur. He shall or will be delivered.

Deliberatio seysinæ. Delivery of seisin. A ceremony in the ancient conveyance by feoffment, without which there could be no investiture, and without which the feoffee had but a mere estate at will. Livery of seisin.

Deliberation. The act of weighing reasons for or against a proposition. Examination and discussion of a proposition. In Criminal law, premeditation after cooling time.

Deliberative body. See BODY, DELIBERATIVE.

Deliberatur. He is delivered.

Delict. A misdemeanor, fault, crime. A wrong or injury inflicted with or without intent. In Civil law, the act of causing injury to another by malice.

Delict, quasi. Same as QUASI TORT.

Delicta. Faults, offences, crime.

Delicto pari. See PARI DELICTO.

Delictorum. Faults, offences, crimes.

Delictum. A crime or offence; a violation of law constituting a crime or misdemeanor for which one may be punished.

Delictum par. See PAR DELICTUM.

Delictum, propter. See PROPTER DELICTUM.

Delimit. To mark out the limits of a district or country.

Delimitation. The act of determining or marking the limits or boundaries of a locality, district, or territory.

Delinquent. In Civil law, one convicted of a crime or violation of duty.

Delito. In Spanish law, a crime or violation of a duty.

Delirium. A temporary insanity. As to whether a condition be a delirium must be determined by the facts in each case.

Delirium tremens. Trembling delirium. A violent delirium; an affection resulting from excessive indulgence of strong liquors, opium or tobacco.

Delit. A violation of a penal law. A small offense. See DELICT.

Delit, quasi. An act of injury, which though from inexcusable negligence, is without malice.

Deliveraunce. The verdict of a juror.

Deliveraunce de gaol. Goal (jail) delivery.

Delivery. The act by which possession is transferred. Release. (Delivery is one of the requisites to the validity of a deed or pardon). See ACCEPTANCE.

Delivery, absolute. A delivery without qualification or condition.

Delivery, actual. Delivery in fact.

Delivery bond. See BOND, DELIVERY.

Delivery, conditional. A delivery coupled with a condition which prevents title vesting until it is fulfilled or comes to pass.

Delivery order. See ORDER, DELIVERY.

Delivery, symbolic. See SYMBOLIC DELIVERY.

Delivery, symbolical. Same as SYMBOLIC DELIVERY (which see).

Delve. To dig.

Dem. For demise; on the demise of.

Demain. Same as DEMESNE.

Demaine. Same as DEMESNE.

Demand. To request payment, or restoration of a right, or performance of an obligation. A claim.

Demand, counter. Same as DEMAND, CROSS.

Demand, cross. One set up against another. A set-off.

Demand in reconvention. Same as RECONVENTION.

Demand, liquidated. See LIQUIDATED DEMAND.

Demand note. See NOTE, DEMAND.

Demand, on. See ON DEMAND.

Demand, personal. See PERSONAL DEMAND.

Demand, stale. See STALE.

Demanda. A demand (which see).

Demandant. He that sues or complains in action real for title to lands.

Demandare. To demand. To order or award; to direct a sentence to be carried into effect. To give in charge, as to a jury.

Demander. To demand; to enquire or ask. To call a party in court.

Demand-in-law. An entry on land, distress for rent, &c., without words or writing.

Demandress. A female demandant.

Demandum. A demand; a claim. A thing or amount claimed to be due.

Demanium. Domain; demesne.

Demease. Death.

Demeigne. Demesne.

Demembration. In Scotch law, cutting off a limb maliciously.

Demens. One demented; one who has lost his mind.

Dementers. In the meantime; meanwhile.

Dementia. Insanity arising from weakness or loss of mind. Mental derangement. As to what comes within must be determined by the facts in each particular case.

Dementia naturalis. Idiocy; natural or permanent madness.

Dementia, senile. Decay of the mind from old age.

Dementiers. Same as DEMENTERS.

Demesne. Own; one's own. Lands of which a man had proper dominion or ownership, as distinguished from the land which another held of him in service.

Demesne as of fee. See SEIZED IN HIS DEMESNE AS OF FEE.

Demesne land. That held by the lord or King for his own use.

Demesnial. Relating to demesne.

Demesne lands of the crown. Lands originally reserved for the crown or which came to it from various sources.

Demeure. Same as DEMURRER.

Demeurer. Same as DEMURRER.

Demeyne. Demesne.

Demeynes. Demesne lands.

Demidietas. A half. A moiety.

Demi-mark. An old English coin worth six shillings and eightpence.

Demi-monde. (Literally, half-world). Disreputable female society; abandoned women.

Deminutio. In Civil law, a loss, deprivation, or taking away.

Deminutio, capitis. See CAPITIS DEMINUTIO.

Demi-rep. A woman of questionable chastity.

Demi-official. With partial authority of office.

Demi-sangue. Half-blood. Blood on the father's or mother's side only.

Demi-vill. One of the smallest of the ancient divisions of England, comprising only five freemen, with their families and servants.

Demise. A word creating a covenant or warranty of title. A conveyance of an estate in fee, for life or for years. Death.

Demise and redemise. Mutual leases of the same land or something connected with it.

Demise of the crown. Death of the King, which causes the transfer of the property of the crown to his successor.

Demisi. I have demised, or leased.

Demissio. A demise, lease, or transfer.

Demission. A bringing down. Lowering. A relinquishment. The laying down of an office.

Demissionary. Relating to the demise of an estate.

Demissione. On the demise.

Demissory. In Scotch law, relating to the laying down of an office.

Demittere. To send away or part with. To transfer; to demise or lease.

Demittere per balium. To discharge by or on bail.

Demitto. To send down.

Demiurge. One of a class of ancient magistrates in Peloponesian States.

Demobilization. Disbanding of military forces.

Democracy. Government by the people.

Democracy, pure. A government in which officials or representatives are elected directly by the people, and not selected by representatives of the people.

Democratic. Relating to the democracy, or to a democratic party.

Democratic Republic. See REPUBLIC, DEMOCRATIC.

Demolior. To demolish; to throw down or overthrow.

Demolitio. A demolishing.

Demolition. In French law, annulment.

Demollire. To demolish.

Demonetization. The act of withdrawing from use as money. The act of divesting of its character as money.

Demonetize. To destroy, withdraw, or divest of its character as money.

Demonstratio. Demonstration.

Demonstration. Proof beyond doubt. Designation. Description.

Demonstrative. Pointing out; designating.

Demonstrative legacy. One paid out of a specified fund.

Demorage. Same as DEMORAGIUM.

Demoragium. Demurrage.

Demorari. To demur; to wait; to stay.

Demoratur. He demurs; he abides.

Demourier. Same as DEMOROR.

Dempster. In old Scotch law, an officer of the court whose duty it was to pronounce the sentence or doom of the court.

Demur. To stop, pause, abide, rest in law or judgment. To object for legal insufficiency.

Demurer. Same as DEMURRER.

Demurrable. That which can be demurred to.

Demurrage. The stoppage, stay, detention of a vessel by the freighter beyond the time allowed by the charter-party for the loading or unloading, or for sailing. The allowance, payment, compensation made for such detention or delay.

Demurrant. One who demurs.

Demurrer. An exception by one of the parties to an action, to the pleading of the opposite party, as not being sufficient in point of law to sustain the claim made. In criminal law, a plea admitting that while the fact alleged may be true it is not sufficient in law to constitute an offense.

Demurrer, book. See BOOK DEMURRER.

Demurrer, general. One which excepts generally to a pleading without alleging any particular cause.

Demurrer in equity. A plea as to whether the bill shall be answered because of insufficient equity therein.

Demurrer in law. A plea which admits the facts but questions their sufficiency.

Demurrer, joinder in. See JOINDER IN DEMURRER.

Demurrer, parol. See PAROL DEMURRER.

Demurrer, speaking. A demurrer in equity which alleges new matter.

Demurrer, special. One which states the cause of objection.

Demurrer to the evidence. A plea that the evidence is insufficient to maintain the case.

Demurrer to the interrogatory. The reason given for not answering an interrogatory.

Demy. Half.

Demy-sangue. Half-blood.

Demy-sanke. Half-blood.

Den. A valley, vale or dale. A hollow or low place among woods.

Den and strond. A license for ships or vessels to land.

Dena. A valley or den; a hollow in woody grounds. A measure of wood land.

Dena terræ. A hollow between two hills; a coppice.

Denarata. The value or worth of a penny.

Denarata reditus. A penny rent.

Denariata. An acre rented for a penny. The price in pence. As much land as is worth a penny per annum.

Denariatus. A penny's worth.

Denarii. Pennies; pence. Money in general.

Denarii de caritate. Customary tributes paid cathedrals.

Denarius. An ancient English penny, originally a Roman silver coin, at one time it was gold and later copper.

Denarius Dei. God's penny or earnest money, so called because anciently earnest money was given to the church or the poor and was not part of the consideration, but only used as a token or pledge passing between parties to contracts, to bind the contract. See ARRHA.

Denarius Petri. Peter's pence.

Denarius tertius comitatus. Among the Saxons, a third of the fines of the county courts, and which belonged to the earl.

Denbera. A swinecomb or place where hogs are fed.

Dene. Same as DEN.

Denelege. Same as DANELEGE.

Denegatio justitiæ. A denial of justice.

Dener. A penny.

Dener appromptes. Money borrowed.

Dener Seint Pere. Saint Peter's money; Peter's pence.

Dengleterre. Of England.

Denial. Declaring a statement to be untrue. A traverse of a statement by the other side.

Denial, general. A denial in general terms.

Denier. A penny.

Denier a Dieu. Money from God; God's penny. In French law, a sum of money which one party gives to another in consideration of a contract. Either party may annul the contract within twenty-four hours, the one by demanding, and the other by returning the money given.

Denier d'adieu. Money of farewell; a gratuity. A gratuity given on hiring anything.

Denier de Saint Pierre. Saint Peter's penny; Peter's pence. See DENARIUS DEI.

Denization. The act of making one a denizen.

Denizen. An adopted or naturalized citizen. A stranger admitted to reside in a foreign country. A dweller; an inhabitant.

Denonbrement. A statement of a fief, its creation, description and the rights thereto belonging.

Denomination. Description, title.

Denumeration. In civil law, the act of paying at the time for a purchase.

Denouncement. A proceeding in Mexican law, similar to inquest of office.

Denshiring. Burning stubble, &c., to improve land.

Denuncia. In Spanish and Mexican law, certain judicial proceedings in the denunciation of a mine. A proceeding for the pre-emption of abandoned or unoccupied lands.

Denuncia de obra nueva. In Spanish law, a proceeding to prevent or restrain the prosecution of a new work, on the ground that it may damage the plaintiff.

Denunciation. In the Civil law, the act informing a public prosecuting officer, that a crime has been committed. In old English law, a public notice or summons. In Scotch law, the announcement that a person is a rebel.

Denunciator. Anciently, a police officer; police inspector.

Denuncio. To intimate, announce, declare.

Denuntiatio. Same as DENUNCIATION.

Denuntio. Same as DENUNCIO.

Deodand. (A thing given to God). Anything which caused or occasioned death. Anything which causes the death of a reasonable creature. Deodands were forfeited to the crown, to be applied to pious uses, and distributed in alms.

Deodandum. Deodand (which see).

Deodend. Same as DEODAND.

Deor hedge. The hedge about a deer park.

Depart. To abandon one ground taken in pleading for another. To leave a place. To leave one port for another.

Departer. To divide.

Departi. Divided.

Departier. To divide.

Departison. Division, partition.

Departire. To forsake, abandon; to separate, divide; to part. To leave a port; to be out of port.

Department. One of the branches of a government, charged with certain duties of government. A division of the executive department of the U. S. Government. A division of territory.

Department, Executive. One of the subordinate branches of the Federal Government of the U. S. charged with executing the law. It is subordinate to Congress, but while the President cannot pardon one sentenced by Congress, nor refuse to obey Congress, he can pardon one sentenced by the judiciary and refuse to obey its orders. See CONGRESS, U. S.; also JUDICIARY.

Department, Interior. An executive department of the U. S. Government having charge of the public lands, patents, pensions, Indian affairs, geological survey, census, and a bureau of education. It was organized March 3, 1849.

Department, Navy. A branch of the Executive Department of the U. S. Government charged with the administration of naval affairs. It was organized April 30, 1789.

Department of Agriculture. The branch of the Executive Department of the U. S. Government charged with the collection and dissemination of information relating to agricultural subjects. It was created Feb. 9, 1889.

Department of Justice. The branch of the Executive Department of the U. S. Government which acts as legal counsel for the government. An Attorney General was first provided for by act of Sept. 24, 1789. The present department was created by act of June 22, 1870.

Department of Labor. A department established by Act of Congress approved June 13, 1888, to obtain and disseminate various information in which both capital and labor are interested.

Department, Postoffice. A branch of the Executive Department of the U. S. Government charged with the care, transportation and delivery of the mail. It was established by acts of Sept. 22, 1789; Feb. 20, 1789; May 8, 1794; March, 1799, and April 30, 1810.

Department, State. A branch of the Executive Department of the U. S. Government charged with conducting foreign affairs and having custody of the Great Seal and Acts of Congress. It was organized Sept. 15, 1789. Prior to that it was termed the Department of Foreign Affairs.

Department, Treasury. A branch of the Executive Department of the U. S. Government charged with the collection, custody and distribution of the public revenues. It was established Sept. 2, 1789.

Department, War. A branch of the Executive Department of the U. S. Government charged with the administration of military affairs. It was organized August 7, 1789.

Departure. Going away from. Separating from. Deviation from a course. Varying from a case or line of defence.

Departure in despite of court. Departure from the court-room and failure to answer after having once made appearance, in despite (contempt) of court.

Departure from the State. The leaving and remaining away from a State to prevent service of process.

Departy. Divided.

Depasture. To put cattle out to graze.

Depeculation. Stealing public funds.

Dependency. A territory apart from but dependent upon and governed by a sovereign power.

Dependent. Depending upon something else for completeness or validity. A person supported by another.

Dependent contract. See CONTRACT, DEPENDENT.

Dependent covenant. See COVENANT, DEPENDENT.

Dependent, promise. See PROMISE, DEPENDENT.

Depending. Pending; undetermined.

Depesas. Land reserved in Spanish-American town for common or pasturage.

Depone. To testify in writing. To give testimony.

Deponent. One who deposes.

Deponer. In Scotch law, a deponent.

Depopulatio agrorum. Destroying, ravaging, laying waste a country.

Depopulation. A laying waste, marauding, pillaging. The act of dispeopling.

Depopulatores agrorum. Those who depopulated towns and villages.

Deportation. Exile; abjuration of the realm; outlawry. In Roman law, loss of civil rights and perpetual banishment. See RELEGATION.

Depose. To make oath in writing. To state under oath. To deprive of position.

Deposer. A deponent.

Deposit. To give to the care of another, to be taken care of and returned without pay. That given to the care of another. See CONTRACT OF MANDATE.

Deposit account. An account of money placed with a bank, not to be withdrawn except after notice as agreed upon.

Deposit, certificate of. A written statement by a bank that money has been deposited there by a person named.

Deposit company. A company which makes a business of renting fire and burglar-proof boxes for the deposit of valuables.

Deposit, conventional. A deposit sequestration by consent of the parties.

Deposit, general. The deposit of an article to be returned in kind.

Deposit, gratuitous. One in which the depositary receives no compensation other than the custody of the thing deposited.

Deposit in lieu of bail. A deposit of money or valuables as security for appearances.

Deposit, involuntary. One arising without the consent or knowledge of another, as articles thrown upon a person's land by a flood, or wreck.

Deposit, irregular. A deposit with another of a sum of money by one not believing it safe in his own custody to be returned in kind when demanded.

Deposit, judicial. A deposit sequestration by order of court.

Deposit, naked. See NAKED DEPOSIT.

Deposit, necessary. A deposit of property made necessary by the circumstances, as in case of fire, shipwreck.

Deposit of title deeds. The deposit of title deeds as security for a loan.

Deposit, quasi. A deposit arising by the finding of property belonging to another.

Deposit, sequestration. A deposit with a third person until ownership is decided.

Deposit, simple. In the Civil law, one made by persons having a common interest.

Deposit, special. A deposit to be returned in specie.

Deposit, voluntary. In Civil law, one arising from the consent of the parties only.

Depositarius. A trustee; a depositary.

Depositary. One who receives a deposit. See DEPOSITORY.

Depositary for hire. One who receives anything to be taken care of for a consideration.

Depositio. A deposition (which see).

Deposition. The testimony of a witness in writing. The act of giving testimony under oath; a matter related on oath. Depriving a person of some honor or office.

Depositiones testium. Depositions of the witnesses.

Deposito. In Spanish law, the depositing an object with another with agreement that it be returned when requested.

Depository. A place where things are deposited. A storehouse. See DEPOSITARY.

Depositum. A bailment of goods, deposited by one man with another to keep for the use of the bailor without reward and to be returned when demanded.

Depot. A depository. A warehouse for storage of goods or military stores. The rooms at a railway station for passengers or freight. The railway station and necessary grounds. See STATION.

Deprave. To vilify. To indicate contempt for.

Depredation. In French law, pillage of a decedent's estate.

Deprivatio. Deprivation; loss, want, bereavement.

Deprivation. A taking away. The taking from a clergyman his benefice, either by sentence of court, or in pursuance of statutes which declare the same void for some neglect, or crime.

Deprive. To take away from.

Depuis. Since.

Deputare. To appoint, fix or designate. To appoint or designate for a particular purpose.

Deputatus. A deputy.

Depute sheriff. See SHERIFF, DEPUTE.

Deputise. To authorize as one's agent or deputy.

Deputy. One who is deputed to act for another; one who exercises an office, in the name of his principal. An assistant to an officer.

Deputy consul. See CONSUL, DEPUTY.

Deputy, general. One authorized to do general acts usual to an office or calling.

Deputy lieutenant. See LIEUTENANT, DEPUTY.

Deputy sheriff. See SHERIFF, DEPUTY.

Deputy, special. One appointed to perform a special act.

Deraign. To displace. To forsake. To prove; to justify. A defective summons.

Deraigner. To deraign; to prove; to clear one's self.

Derainer. Same as DERAIGNER.

Derationare. To deraign; to prove. To disprove or refute the assertion of an adverse party. To deny or refuse. To put out of place or order; to turn one out of his order; to degrade.

Derchief. Again, moreover.

Derechief. Again, moreover.

Derecho. In Spanish law, right of law.

Derecho comun. A term for Common law, which means in Spain the Civil law.

Derechos. Rights.

Dereigner. To deraign; to prove; to clear one's self.

Dereiner. Same as DEREIGNER.

Derelict. Forsaken, abandoned, cast away. Personal property abandoned by the owner. Land uncovered by the receding of water. Property abandoned at sea with no expectation of recovering the same.

Derelict lands. Those suddenly left by the receding of the sea (when the sea or water recedes below the usual water mark). See DERELICTION.

Dereliction. An abandoning. The gaining of land from the water; as when the sea shrinks back below the usual water mark. See DERELICT.

Derelictum. Same as DERELICT.

Derelictus. Abandoned, forsaken, neglected, etc. Deserted or abandoned, as a vessel voluntarily deserted at sea.

Derener. To deraign; to prove; to clear one's self.

Dereyn. Same as DERAIGN.

Dereyner. Same as DERENER and DERAIGNER.

Derichief. Again, moreover.

Derivative. Derived from another. That which originates from something else.

Derivative acquisition. See ACQUISITION, DERIVATIVE.

Derivative conveyances. See CONVEYANCES, DERIVATIVE.

Derivative possession. See POSSESSION DERIVATIVE.

Derivative title. See TITLE, DERIVATIVE.

Derived. Obtained by transmission from another.

Dernier. Latest, final; highest, greatest, utmost; lowest, vilest, meanest.

Derniere. Same as DERNIER.

Derobare. To steal, to pilfer.

Derogate. To impair; to lessen.

Derogation. Limiting in effect or application. Impairing in effect. Detraction. A change in a contract for sale of stock by decreasing the amount.

Derogatory-clause. A clause inserted in a will, with a condition that any subsequent will shall be invalid unless this clause be inserted.

Des absentees. A Parliament held in Dublin, May 10th, 8 Hen. VIII. See ABSENTEES.

Desafuero. In Spanish law, an act in violation of law or custom.

Desamortizacion. In Mexican law, to take property from a corporation.

Desblemy. Unblemished.

Descend. To go down. To be transmitted from ancestor to heir. To be transmitted by operation of law.

Descendant. One descended from the person or stock spoken of.

Descender. To descend.

Descender, writ of foremedon in. See WRIT OF FORMEDON IN DESCENDER.

Descendit. To descend or proceed from any person or thing.

Descensus. A descent. Succession by law to an estate in lands.

Descent. Passing downward. The title by which a person obtains a freehold on the death of an ancestor. Hereditary succession. Means of acquiring an estate as distinguished from purchase. Birth, extraction. See ASCENT.

Descent by distaff. Descent from the mother.

Descent, canons of. See CANONS OF DESCENT.

Descent, cast. In old English law, where the heir of a disseisor took the estate by inheritance which defeated an entry by the rightful owner and compelled him to bring action.

Descent, immediate. Descent direct from ancestor to heir.

Descent in a collateral line. Descent through an ancestor and down from him through collaterals.

Descent, lineal. Descent in a direct line as father to son, grandfather to grandson; not uncle to nephew, &c.

Descent, root of. See ROOT OF DESCENT.

Descent, stock of. See STOCK OF DESCENT.

Descriptio. Description, designation, delineation.

Descriptio personæ. Description of the person. Description of office or agency.

Description. Designation, delineation.

Desert. To leave; forsake.

Desertion. Abandonment of a duty. Continued cessation of matrimonial cohabitation without cause.

Deserving. Worthy. Meritorious.

Deservio. To zealously serve, be devoted to, subject to.

Derervire. To serve (as a feudal tenant did his lord).

Desfontaines. The name of the oldest law writer on the law of France. It was on the French law of custom and published in 1253.

Desgarnys. Unwarned. Unprovided, unfurnished.

Deshonora. In Spanish law, injury, slander, dishonor.

Desicut. Whereas; inasmuch as; since.

Design. Intent. Purpose. A conception of the mind in practical form.

Designatio. Designation.

Designatio personæ. Designation of the person.

Designation. Appointment; direction; specification ; describing. A disposition, arrangement.

Deslinde. In Spanish law, the act of determining the limits of an estate or district.

Desmaintenant. From henceforth ; from the present moment; even now; forthwith.

Desmemoriados. In Spanish law, persons who have lost memory.

Desore. From now; from this time.

Desorenavant. Same as DESORE EN AVANT.

Desorenaunt. Same as DESORE EN AVANT.

Desormes. From henceforth ; hereafter.

Desoubes. Under.

Desoubs. Under.

Desouth. Under, below.

Despacheurs. In Maritime law, those appointed to determine average.

Despatch. To transact or e x e c u t e promptly. Prompt performance of work. A message sent in haste by special means.

Desperate. Impossible of collection, worthless; applied to debts and claims.

Desperate debt. See DEBT, DESPERATE.

Despite. Contempt.

Despitus. A contemptible person. Contempt.

Despitz. Contempts.

Despoil. To deprive one of something by violence or robbery.

Despojar. In Mexican law, an action to recover personal property of which one has been deprived by fraud or violence.

Desponsation. The act of bringing about an agreement to marry.

Desposorio. In Spanish law, the agreement to marry.

Despot. A sovereign. A master. A tyrant.

Despotism. Abuse of power.

Despotize. To act as a despot.

Desrenable. Unreasonable.

Dessaisissement. In French law, the depriving a bankrupt of his property.

Dessus. Above.

Destination. The act of appointing. The place to which a course or voyage is taken. In Scotch law, the nomination by the owner of property.

Destruction. A pulling down, waste, extinction. Oppression against law by color of any usurpation of authority.

Destroy. To so injure as to be unfit for use. To so mutilate or change as to be unrecognizable or undistinguishable.

Destruere. To destroy.

Destruo. To destroy, weaken, ruin.

Desubito. To weary with continual barking and then bite.

Desuetude. Discontinuance of use or enforcement.

Desus. Above.

Detachiare. To take into custody another's goods by legal writ.

Detail. To select for a special purpose. Any single part of anything. A mode of statement giving the smallest particulars. A minor part.

Detain. To hold in custody. To withhold.

Detainder. Same as DETINUE.

Detainer. One who detains or withholds. The wrongful detention of another's goods, though received lawfully. A writ. See DETAINER, WRIT OF.

Detainer, forcible entry and. An entry and detention of real property by force.

Detainer, forcible. A forcible holding of possession of another's land.

Detainer, writ of. An ancient writ commencing a personal action against one in prison.

Detainment. In Marine insurance, the effect of superior force on a vessel at sea.

Detention. The wrongful withholding of personal property from another. Restraint of one's person. The state of being detained or having property withheld.

Detenue. Detention.

Determinable. Likely to end.

Determinable fee. Same as FEE, QUALIFIED.

Determinable freeholds. See FREEHOLDS DETERMINABLE.

Determinate. Determined. Fixed. Specific.

Determination. Termination, ceasing, coming to an end.

Determine. To end. To ascertain. To decide.

Detestatio. In Civil law, a notice given before witnesses.

Detinet. He detains; he keeps. The term has given name to the mode of declaring in certain actions of debt, as against executors and administrators.

Detinet, replevin. See REPLEVIN, DETINET.

Detinue. A form of an action to recover the specific possession of a personal chattel or its value, and damages for its detention, wrongfully detained from another, where the original taking was lawful. It is classed an action ex contractu.

Detinue of goods in frank marriage. An old writ allowed a divorced wife to recover goods given with her when married.

Detinuit. He has detained; he kept back, withheld.

Detinuit, replevin. See REPLEVIN, DETINUIT.

Detractare. To draw off or drag away; to draw along.

Detractari. To be torn or drawn apart by wild horses.

Detunicari. To lay open to the world.

Deunees. Same as DEUNX.

Deunx. In Roman law, a division of an As of eleven unciae.

Deuterogamy. A second marriage. A marriage after the death of a wife or husband.

Devadiatus. Where an offender is without sureties.

Devant. Before.

Devastation. A laying waste; squandering. The waste of the property of a deceased person by his executor or administrator.

Devastationis. Same as DEVASTATION.

Devastaverunt. They have wasted. See DEVASTAVIT.

Devastavit. He has wasted. The mismanagement and wasting of a deceased person's property by his executor or administrator or one holding it as a trustee. A return made by a sheriff (after a return of nulla bona) to a fi. fa. against an executor signifying that he has wasted the goods of the testator; upon which return the plaintiff may have execution immediately against the executor or administrator personally. A suggestion on the record, of waste by an executor or administrator, made on the part of a plaintiff, as the foundation of a new writ fieri facias de bonis propriis, or of an action of debt.

Devastavit by direct abuse. That caused by the wrongful appropriation of the assets of the estate.

Devastavit by mal-administration. That caused by the payment of claims not due or out of order, or legacies before debts, &c.

Devastavit by neglect. That caused by neglect to collect moneys due or to sell perishable or other goods at the proper time.

Devaunt. Before.

Devenerunt. They have come or fallen to. A writ directing the escheator to enquire by the oaths of good and lawful men what lands and tenements escheated to the King by the death of a tenant.

Devenio. I become.

Devenit. It comes or falls. (Distinguished from descendit).

Develop. To uncover to light. To bring to perfection.

Dever. To owe.

Devers. Against; towards.

Devest. To take away. To deprive of, as a title, estate or possessions. In Feudal law, to take away an investiture; to deprive of possession of a fee or feud.

Devestio. To devest.

Deviation. An unnecessary departure from the course of a voyage.

Device. An instrument or mechanical contrivance constructed for a special purpose.

Device, gambling. See GAMBLING DEVICE.

Devier. To die.

Devil on the neck. An ancient contrivance to gradually or suddenly break the back. It was used as a means to extort confessions.

Devil's advocate. See ADVOCATE, DEVIL'S.

Devisa. A devise; a giving by will.

Devisable. Capable of being devised.

Devisamentum. A devise, of real property See DEVISE.

Devisare. To devise.

Devisatio. Same as DIVISAMENTUM.

Devisavit vel non. (Did he devise or not)? An issue directed from a court of equity to a court of law, to try by a jury the validity of a will upon some alleged fact, such as incapacity on the part of the testator, fraud, etc.

Devise. A boundary; a dividing line or space separating lands. An instrument writing signed, declared and witnessed, making a gift of lands or other real estate, to take effect on the death of the donor. A testamentary disposition of lands or other real property, as distinguished from a bequest of personal property. See WILL; also TESTAMENT.

Devise, conditional. One which depends on some uncertain event.

Devise, contingent. Same as DEVISE, CONDITIONAL.

Devise, executory. A devise of real property by will which does not vest in the devisee at the death of the devisor, but only on the happening of some event after the latter's death. This is contrary to the rule of conveyances of real property, and it differs from a contingent remainder, as the latter must have an estate to support it. If there be such a supporting estate in a devise, it is a contingent remainder, and not an executory devise. See ESTATE, SUPPORTING.

Devise, lapsed. Same as LAPSED LEGACY.

Devise, specific. A devise of a specific piece of property.

Devise, vested. One which vests at the death of the devisor as distinguished from a contingent or executory devise.

Devisee. The person who r e c e i v e s lands or other real property by will.

Devisee, residuary. See RESIDUARY DEVISEE.

Devisor. One who wills lands to another. The maker of a will of lands or real estate. One who makes a devise. See TESTATOR.

Devoir. Duty.

Devoires. Duties or customs.

Devolution. The act of transferring or transmitting to another. The forfeiture, in ecclesiastical law, of a right by non user, as a right of presentation.

Devolve. To cause to pass to another. To pass from one to another.

Devorce. Divorce.

Devyer. To die.

Dewanny, adawlut. The civil courts of justice in India.

Dewarrante. When a warren is broken up and turned into common.

Dextans. In Roman law, ten unciæ. See UNCIÆ.

Dextram dare. " To give the right hand." An expression meaning to close a bargain.

Dextrarios. Saddle horses.

Dextrarius. One at the right hand of another.

Dextras dare. To shake hands as an indication of friendly feeling. To confide oneself to the power of another.

Di colonna. In Italian law, a contract between the owner, master and sailors of a vessel, to share the profits of the voyage. In New England, the whaling voyages are regulated by a similar agreement.

Diæta. Same as DIETA.

Diaconate. The office of a deacon.

Diaconus. A deacon.

Dialogues de scaccario. Dialogues of the Exchequer. The title of an ancient treatise on the Court of Exchequer.

Diarium. As much as will do for the day. A daily allowance, food or pay.

Diasperatus. Stained with m a n y colors.

Diatim. Daily ; every day ; from day to day.

Dica. A tally by number of cuts, marks or notches, for accounts. See TALLY.

Dicast. A Greek citizen with functions of a judge and juryman, who sat in a dicastery.

Dicastery. An ancient Athenian law court. One of the bodies of Grecian citizens who represented the people as a jury. The number varied, sometimes reaching 500 in an important matter.

Dickar. Ten hides of leather or ten bars of iron.

Dict. Said; a saying.

Dicta. A saying or remark.

Dicta, obiter. See OBITER DICTA.

Dictate. To command. To d i r e c t. To prescribe. To declare to another for the latter to put in writing.

Dictation. The act of pronouncing that which is to be written by another.

Dictator. One who dictates. One who has absolute powers of government.

Dictionary. A book containing the words of a language or words common to a science, arranged in alphabetical order, with the definition of such words. (A dictionary is limited to words and definitions).

Dictionary clause. The clause in a statute which defines words or terms used therein.

Dictores. Arbitrators.

Dictum. A saying. The verdict of a jury. An extra judicial opinion aside from the point in question.

Dictum de Kenilworth. The declaration or edict of Kenilworth. An award between Henry VIII. of England and his barons in the fifty-first year of his reign.

Dictum gratis. A gratuitous remark. A remark not necessary and not material.

Dictum, alias. See ALIAS DICTUS.

Die without issue. See DYING WITHOUT ISSUE.

Diei. A day. See DIES.

Diei dictio. In Roman law, a notice by a magistrate that he intends, on a day mentioned, to impeach a citizen before the public for a crime.

Diem clausit extremum. (He has closed his last day). A writ directing the escheators to ascertain the lands of which a tenant in capite died seized and restore them to the King.

Dies. A day. The civil day of twenty-four hours. (See DAY).

Dies a quo. (The day from which). In Civil law, the day from which a transaction begins.

Dies ad quem. The day to which. In the civil law, the concluding day.

Dies amoris. A day of love. A day of grace, a day granted by the court to a party, as a matter of favor, out of the usual course of proceedings.

Dies artificialis. An artificial day from the rising to the setting of the sun. See DAY.

Dies bi-sextus (or bissextus). A bis-sextile day; an intercalary day.

Dies cedit. The day begins. In Civil law, a phrase indicating that an interest has vested.

Dies civilis. The civil day (from midnight to midnight).

Dies clara. Daylight.

Dies claris. Daylight.

Dies communes in banco. Common days in banc. Days for appearance of parties in the courts ; also return days, originally peculiar to the Court of Common Bench.

Dies concilii. Same as DIES CONSILII.

Dies consilii. The day of imparlance. Also a day appointed to argue a demurrer. A day to hear the counsel of both parties in court.

Dies continui. The successive or following days; consecutive days.

Dies cretionis. Days of cretion (which see).

Dies datus. The day of the date. A day given; the day appointed for a hearing. A return day; a day of respite to a defendant.

Dies datus in banco. A day given in the bench (the Court of Common Pleas).

Dies datus partibus. A day given to the parties. Continuance given to the parties.

Dies datus prece partium. A day given at the request of the parties.

Dies dominicus. The Lord's day; Sunday.

Dies excrescens. The added day ; the day in leap year.

Dies fasti. A court day ; a day on which courts could be held, and on which judgments could be pronounced.

Dies fasti et nefasti. Lucky and unlucky days (business days and holidays).

Dies feriales. Ferial days; holidays. Working days, or week days as distinguished from Sunday.

Dies gratiæ. A day of grace, favor, courtesy.

Dies in banco. A day (or days) in banc ; a day in the Court of Common Bench. Days in which the court sits.

Dies in curia. A day in court.

Dies in judicio. A day when proceedings were had in court.

Dies intercisi. Divided days. In Roman law, days on which courts were open but a part of the day.

Dies Juridici. Plural of Dies Juridicus.

Dies juridicus. A juridical or court day.

Dies justi. Days of grace.

Dies legitimus. A lawful or law day ; a term day. An appearance day in term.

Dies lunæ. The day of the moon (called Monday).

Dies marchiæ. A day of the march; of the limits, confines, borders. Anciently a day when English and Scotch met annually on the marches, or borders, to adjust differences between them and renew the compact of peace.

Dies naturalis. A natural day. See DAY.

Dies nefasti. In Roman law, days on which the courts were closed, days on which no public business was transacted. See DIES NON JURIDICUS.

Dies non. An abbreviation of Dies non juridicus (which see).

Dies non juridicus. A day not juridical; not a court day. Applied to the days on which no legal proceedings can take place.

Dies pacis. Days of peace. All days in the year were anciently either days of peace of the King or of the church.

Dies solis. The day of the sun; Sunday.

Dies solaris. A solar day. A period which elapses between the appearance of the sun upon the same meridian, hence twenty-four hours. Sometimes also applied to the period when the sun is visible. In modern science, the interval between two moons.

Dies utiles. Available days; days on which an act might be done.

Dies votorum. The wedding day.

Diet. In Scotch law and practice, the sitting of a court. A day appointed for the trial of a criminal cause. An appearance day. A criminal cause as prepared for trial. A legislative assembly.

Dieta. A day's expenses; a day's work; a day's journey.

Dietæ computatæ. Day's journeys computed or reckoned. Journey's accounts.

Diets of compearance. In Scotch law, days on which persons were summoned to appear in court.

Dieu et mon droit. God and my right. motto of the Kings of England; it was first adopted by Richard I.

Dieu et son acte. God and his act; the act of God. An act beyond human foresight and control. (A legal excuse for the non-performance of a contract).

Diffacere. To destroy.

Diffamatio. A publishing, promulgating. Defamation or slander.

Diffamationis. Same as DIFFAMATIO.

Difference of person. Diversity of person (which see).

Differential. Different; unequal.

Differential duties. Unequal duties on the imports of different countries.

Diffidare. In Feudal law, to renounce one's fealty, faith, allegiance. To put out of allegiance; to outlaw. To proclaim hostilities; to declare war; to defy.

-Diffiducariare. Same as DIFFIDARE.

Difforciare. To keep from one.

Difforciare rectum. To take away or deny justice.

Digama. Same as DIGAMY.

Digamy. Marrying the second time after the first wife's death.

Digest. The book of Pandects of the Civil law. Distribution of subjects into classes in an abridged form. A reproduction of the points decided in legal cases in the form of an index. A body or system of laws; a code; a system.

Digesta. The Digests of Justinian. See DIGEST.

Digging. Excavating.

Dignitaries. Those who possess honorable stations, exalted rank, especially ecclesiastical rank.

Dignitarii. Dignitaries (which see).

Dignitas. An honor; a title, station, or distinction of honor. A dignity.

Dignitas primogeniti. The privilege of the eldest.

Dignitas ecclesiasticalis. An honorary office in the church.

Dignity. In old English law, honor and authority. A species of incorporeal hereditament, in which a person could have a property.

Dignity, ecclesiastical. An honorary office in the church.

Dijudication. Judicial determination.

Dike. Eruptive material in a fissure of a rock. See VEIN; also LODE.

Diker. Same as DAKER.

Dilacion. In Spanish law, time granted within which to answer or produce evidence.

Dilapidatio. Dilapidation (which see).

Dilapidation. The taking apart of the stones of a building. The pulling down, in whole or in part of a building; the permitting to fall into decay or partial ruin; neglect of necessary repairs of a building. Waste committed or permitted on the lands or buildings of a church.

Dilatio. Time allowed to do a judicial act; the putting off, deferring of a cause.

Dilationes in lege sunt odiosæ. Delays in the law are odious.

Dilato. To spread out, to dilate; to enlarge, amplify, extend.

Dilatoria exceptio. A dilatory exception or plea; a plea for delay. See EXCEPTIO DILATORIA.

Dilatorius. That which delays or puts off; dilatory. Anciently applied to a plea by which action was delayed.

Dilatory. Tending to cause delay.

Dilatory defense. See DEFENSE, DILATORY.

Dilatory pleas. Such as are put in for delay. See EXCEPTIO DILATORIA.

Diligence. Care and attention required by law in certain cases. In Scotch law, a subpœna for the attendance of a witness; also a process of execution for debt.

Diligence against the heritage. In Scotch law, a writ of execution against the real estate of a debtor.

Diligence against the person. A writ of execution against the person of the debtor.

Diligence against witnesses. A writ to compel the attendance of witnesses.

Diligence due. Such diligence as is reasonable under the circumstances. See CARE.

Diligence, great. That care which unusually careful persons exercise in their own affairs.

Diligence, incident. In Scotch law, a writ for summoning or examining witnesses.

Diligence, ordinary. Such care and attention as an ordinary man exercises with his own affairs.

Diligence, second. In Scotch law, a second writ issued on refusal or neglect to regard the first.

Diligence, slight. That degree of care which careless persons usually take in their own affairs.

Diligence, summary. A writ issued in a summary manner.

Diligence to examine havers. In Scotch law, a writ to obtain the testimony or a discovery of those having the custody of articles or documents.

Diligenter. Diligently, attentively, carefully, earnestly.

Diligentia. Diligence, carefulness, attention.

Diligentissimus. The utmost diligence; superlative diligence.

Diligiatus. One who is outlawed; an outlaw.

Dilligrout. Pottage made for the King's table on coronation day. The finding of which was a service by which lands were held in sergeanty.

Dillonques. From thence; after that time.

Dilucidus. Clear ; clear in mind ; rational.

Dime. A U. S. silver coin valued at one-tenth of a dollar.

Dimidia. In the Civil law, half.

Dimidia acra. Half an acre.

Dimidia marca. Half a mark; a demi-mark.

Dimidia pars. A half part; one-half.

Dimidia villa. Half a vill; a demi-vill.

Dimidietas. A moiety or one-half.

Dimidius. Half. An undivided half of a thing.

Dimidium. Same as DIMIDIUS.

Dimidium unius acræ. Half an acre.

Dimidium unius liberatæ. Half a pound.

Diminutio capitis. See CAPITIS DIMINUTIO.

Diminution. Decrease, abatement; a taking away; loss, deprivation. An allegation that part of the record is omitted.

Diminution, alleging. See ALLEGING DIMINUTION.

Diminution of the record. See RECORD, DIMINUTION OF.

Dimisi. I have demised, let go, given up.

Dimisi, concessi, et ad firmam tradidi. I have demised, granted, and to farm let. Old words of operation in a lease.

Dimissio. A demise or release.

Dimissionis. A demise or release.

Dimisit. He has demised.

Dimissor. A lessor.

Dimissoris. A lessor.

Dimissoriæ litteræ. Letters dimissory. See DIMISSORY LETTERS.

Dimissory letters. Letters directing the ordination of a candidate for church orders in another than his own diocese. A notice sent to a higher court or judge. See LETTERS MISSIVE.

Dimittere per plegios. To discharge on pledge.

(19)

Dimitto. To dismiss, part with, send away. To let go, release from custody. To demise.

Dinarchy. A government of two.

Dinero. In Spanish law, money.

Dinero contado. In Spanish law, money counted.

Dingley Bill. The Tariff Act of Congress, approved July 24, 1897, entitled "An act to provide revenue for the government and to encourage the industries of the U. S."

Diocesan. Belonging to a diocese.

Diocese. The territorial extent of a bishop's jurisdiction. Several form a province or circuit of an archbishop's jurisdiction.

Diocesis. A diocese.

Dioichia. The diocese of a bishop.

Diploma. A letter folded double. An instrument given by colleges, societies, etc., on commencement of any degrees. A license granted to a clergyman or a physician, to practice a profession, &c. In the civil law, a royal charter ; letters-patent granted by a prince or sovereign.

Diplomacy. The method of carrying on negotiations between nations. The acts comprising the negotiations. Skill in obtaining a desired end without friction.

Diplomat. The person who represents a nation in conducting negotiations with another nation.

Diplomatic agent. Same as DIPLOMAT.

Diplomatic corps. The whole body of diplomatic persons credited to a country.

Diplomatics. The science governing the deciphering of diplomas and documents, wills, deeds, &c., and information as to their authenticity, date, meaning, &c.

Diplomatist. Same as DIPLOMAT.

Dipsomania. Thirst mania; rage for drink. Often applied to habitual drunkenness and to delirium tremens.

Dipsomaniac. One afflicted with an uncontrollable desire for intoxicating liquor.

Diptycha. Tablets used by the Romans for writing purposes. They were made of metal, wood and other substances and folded like a book of two leaves.

Dirationare. To deraign; to prove. To disprove; to acquit one's self by proof.

Direct. Clear in meaning. Without circumlocution.

Direct admission. See ADMISSION, DIRECT.

Direct coercion. See COERCION, DIRECT.

Direct contempt. Same as CRIMINAL CONTEMPT.

Direct evidence. The opposite of circumstantial evidence.

Direct examination. See EXAMINATION, DIRECT.

Direct index. See INDEX, DIRECT.

Direct interest. See INTEREST, DIRECT.

Direct interrogatories. See INTERROGATORIES, DIRECT.

Direct line. From father to son.

Direct tax. See TAX, DIRECT.

Direction. The exposition of the law given to a jury by a judge in the case.

Directions, further. See FURTHER DIRECTIONS.

Director of the Mint. An officer charged with the management of the U, S. Mint.

Director of the Census. An officer charged with supervision and direction of the twelfth census for the United States.

Directors. Anciently the same as Condors or Balkers. The managers of the business of a corporation.

Directors, board of. The directors of a corporation as a body.

Directory. Giving instruction how a thing should be done; expressive of mere direction or instruction and not involving invalidation if disregarded. A board of directors. A list of the names and addresses of persons inhabiting a city, with their occupations.

Directory law. Same as DIRECTORY STATUTE.

Directory statute. One which directs that an act should be done in a certain manner, but does not invalidate if done otherwise.

Directory trust. See TRUST, DIRECTORY.

Diribitores. In Roman law, persons who distributed ballots to the voters.

Dirigo. I direct or guide; I lead. (The motto of the State of Maine).

Diriment impediments. Those impediments which make a marriage void from the beginning even though entered into.

Disabilitas. Disability (which see).

Disability. Legal incapacity. Any cause which prevents one from performing a duty.

Disability, absolute. One annexed to a person and to his heirs or successors.

Disability, canonical. In marriage, one which makes a marriage voidable, but not void.

Disability, civil. Incapacity created by law. In marriage, one which makes a marriage or act void.

Disability, general. One which incapacitates to perform legal acts of a general nature.

Disability, legal. A disability placed by law, because of age, condition, &c.

Disability, personal. One which is annexed to a particular person only.

Disability, physical. An infirmity of body or mind.

Disability, special. A disability which incapacitates to perform a particular act or function.

Disable. To make legally incapable.

Disabling. Making legally incapable. Restraining or destroying.

Disabling statute. See STATUTE, DISABLING.

Disadvocare. To deny or refuse to acknowledge.

Disaffirm. To set aside. To reverse. To refuse to confirm.

Disaffirmance. A reversal. A repudiation.

Disafforest. To clear off a forest.

Disagreement. A failure to agree. The refusal to accept an estate, lease, pardon, legacy, &c. Without the express agreement the law presumes acceptance.

Disalt. To disable a person.

Disappropriation. The act of putting out of possession of church property.

Disavow. To refuse to acknowledge as binding. To repudiate the act of an agent as beyond his authority.

Disbar. To take away the privilege of attorney at law.

Disbocation. A conversion of woodland into pasture or arable; an assarting.

Disbocatis. Same as DISBOCATION.

Disbursement. The act of paying out money. The money so paid out.

Discarcare. Discharging or unloading a ship.

Discargare. To discharge or unload.

Discarcatio. Same as DISCARCARE.

Disceit. Deceit.

Discent. Descent.

Disceptatio causæ. The argument of a cause by the advocates of both sides.

Discharge. To free of a charge, duty, or obligation. To free from imprisonment. To vacate. To dismiss. To satisfy. A written evidence of such action. In U. S. Bankrupt law of 1898, the release of a bankrupt from all his debts as allowed by that act.

Discharge, charge and. See CHARGE AND DISCHARGE.

Discharge, lawful. See LAWFUL DISCHARGE.

Disclaimer. A plea denying or renouncing a title or claim (where false it was anciently a civil crime). The relinquishment, renunciation, waiver, refusal of an estate, right or interest. The refusal to act as executor. In Patent law, the renunciation of a claim to a part of a title or specification of a patent.

Disclamation. In Scotch law, denial that land is held of another.

Disclamium. A disclaimer (which see).

Disc'ose. To make known.

Discommon. To change from a common to private or reserved land. To deprive of the privilege of using a common. In English Universities to deprive a tradesman of the privilege of trading with students.

Discontinuance. An interruption or breaking off. The keeping out of the true owner of an estate by one who got possession lawfully.

Discontinuance of an estate. See ESTATE, CONTINUANCE OF.

Discontinuance of plea. The answering in a plea of but a part.

Discontinuance of process. Where the proceedings are not continued within the time required.

Discontinuous servitude. One made up of repeated acts, such as drawing water, &c.

Disconvenable. Not convenient; not proper or fit.

Discooperta. Same as DISCOVERT.

Discount. Anything deducted or counted off.

Discount broker. See BROKER, DISCOUNT.

Discovert. Unprotected, uncovered. A woman not married, either spinster or widow.

Discoverture. Condition of being exempt from the disabilities or without the protections of marriage.

Discovery. Act of finding; disclosure. The act of revealing any matter by a defendant in his answer in equity.

Discredit. To injure the credit of. To depreciate the credibility or testimony of a person.

Discrepancy. A disagreement between things expected to agree.

Discretion. The ability to decide with judgment. The separating right from wrong. Independent judgment governed by reason and law. The ability to decide between good and evil, between what is lawful and unlawful.

Discretion, age of. The age at which a person becomes liable to a criminal penalty or is capable of transacting his own affairs.

Discretion, at. See AT DISCRETION.

• **Discretion, judicial.** The discretion of a judge exercised with due regard for legal principles.

Discretionary. Unrestrained except by discretion.

Discriminating. Differential. Establishing inequality.

Discrimination. The act of treating differently.

Discuss. In Scotch law, to exhaust proceedings against a debtor, before proceeding against a surety. In French Canadian law, to sell by legal process for the payment of debt.

Discussion. Arguments for and against a matter. In Scotch law, the right of the sureties to defer payment of a debt for which they are bound, until the creditor has failed to collect from the principal debtor, by action. Fixing the order in which heirs are liable for the debts of the ancestor. See DISCUSS.

Disease. Such a departure from the normal action of the functions of a living being as affects the health or continuance of life.

Disencumber. To relieve of an incumbrance.

Disenfranchise. Same as DISFRANCHISE.

Disentail. To bar an estate tail. To break an entail.

Disentailing assurance. Same as DISENTAILING DEED.

Disentailing deed. In England, an enrolled deed made in pursuance of 3 and 4 Wm. IV., c. 74, by which a tenant in tail could convey his estate absolutely.

Disfranchise. To deprive of the rights and privileges of a free citizen.

Disfranchisement. The act of depriving one of a privilege. To deprive one of a right to vote or any privilege given by a government or corporation of which one is a member.

Disgage. To deliver from pledge or pawn. To redeem.

Disgrace. To lower in the estimation of the public.

Disgrading. Depriving of a dignity.

Disguise. To change the appearance to make recognition difficult. That which alters the appearance so as to render it difficult of recognition.

Dishabilitas. Disability.

Disherison. A disinheriting. An injury done to one who has the inheritance; particularly to a remainder-man or reversioner.

Disheritor. One who disinherits another or puts him out of his inheritance.

Dishonor. To fail or refuse to pay a note of bill or exchange at maturity. The act of so doing.

Disincarcerate. To set free from confinement.

Disinherison. Same as DISHERISON.

Disinherit. To declare in a testament, will, or devise, that a natural heir shall not inherit any part of the ancestral estate.

Disinheritance. The act of depriving another of an inheritance.

Disinterested. Not having any interest in the matter referred to or in controversy.

Disinterested witness. See WITNESS, DISINTERESTED.

Disjuncta. Things separated.

Disjunctim. In Civil law, separately, severally.

Disjunction. Separation. Separately; severally.

Disjunctive. That which separates or disconnects.

Disjunctive allegation. See ALLEGATION, DISJUNCTIVE.

Disjunctive term. See TERM, DISJUNCTIVE.

Dismes. Tithes. Tenths. Fomerly applied to the ten cent pieces of the U. S. See DISNIES.

Dismiss. To reject without hearing. To send away.

Dismortgage. To satisfy a mortgage. To redeem.

Disnies. Tithes or tenths of produce anciently due the clergy in England.

Disnies, perpetual. The tenth of the spiritual living due the King.

Disorder. That which disturbs t h e peace. Violation of law. Disease.

Disorderly behavior. See BEHAVIOR, DISORDERLY.

Disorderly conduct. Same as BEHAVIOR, DISORDERLY.

Disorderly house. One within which acts in violation of law are habitually committed.

Disorderly person. One who violates law by disturbing the peace.

Disparagacion. An unequal alliance or unsuitable connection in marriage. The matching an heir or ward in marriage, under his or her degree or condition, or against the rules of decency.

Disparagare. To connect unequally; to match unsuitably.

Disparagatio. Same as DISPARAGACION.

Disparagation. See DISPARAGACION.

Disparage. To degrade one by connecting in marriage with another of inferior rank or station.

Disparagement. Inequality in rank. An injury by being unsuitably connected in marriage, as where an heir or ward is wedded to one beneath his or her degree.

Disparager. Same as DISPARAGARE.

Disparagium. Inequality in b l o o d, honor, dignity. Disparagement.

Dispark. To convert a park into private property or a reservation.

Dispatch. See DESPATCH.

Dispatch, customary. In accordance with the usual custom.

Dispauper. To take away the right to sue as a pauper after it has been granted.

Dispensation. (An ecclesiastical term). An exemption from some rule, law, or service. A license.

Dispensator. A household superintendent; a manager, steward; a manager of the public treasury; a cashier, treasurer.

Displace. To disrate. To remove from a place of honor or profit. To take the place of.

Dispersonare. To disparage.

Displace. To disrate. To remove from a place of honor or profit. To take the place of.

Displacement. The weight of water displaced by a body floating in it.

Dispone. In Scotch law, to grant or convey to another.

Disponee. A grantee.

Disponer. In Scotch law, a grantor.

Dispono. To dispose of, grant, convey; to arrange or set in order; to direct or regulate.

Dispose. To convey ownership by any method. To determine.

Disposing mind. The capacity to dispose of property by will, testament, or devise.

Disposition. In Scotch law, a unilateral deed by which a property right is transferred.

Disposition, final. See FINAL DISPOSITION.

Disposition, power of. See POWER OF DISPOSITION.

Dispositive clause. The clause in a will or grant which disposes of the subject-matter.

Dispositive fact. See FACT, DISPOSITIVE.

Dispossess. To put out of possession.

Dispossession. The act of putting or keeping one out of possession.

Disprove. To refute; to show to be illegal.

Dispungo. To examine, revise, settle, balance an account.

Dispunishable. Not answerable. Not punishable.

Disputable presumption. See PRESUMPTION, DISPUTABLE.

Disputatio fori. In Civil law, argument before a court.

Dispute. To question the legality of. A controversy. A contest of words.

Dispute in dispute. The subject-matter of a suit.

Disputo. To cast up, calculate a sum by going over its items; to estimate, compute.

Disqualify. To incapacitate. To make incompetent.

Disrate. To lower in rate or rank.

Disrationare. To prove; to deraign; to establish or make good a claim, charge, or accusation.

Disrationatio. Deraignment or proof; the making good a claim or charge.

Dissasina. In Scotch law, disseisin. Dispossession.

Dissection. The act of cutting in pieces for examination.

Disseise. To unlawfully oust from possession of a freehold estate.

Disseisee. One who is disseised of an estate.

Disseisin. In old English law, deprivation or turning out of seisin wrongfully; the wrongful turning the tenant out of his tenure, and usurping his place and feudal relation; a wrongful ouster of him who is seized of an estate or freehold.

Disseisin, actual. Turning out of possession when the person disseised was in actual possession at the time he was disseised.

Disseisin by election. Disseisin where the freeholder allowed himself to be disseised.

Disseisin by force. More properly deforcement (which see).

Disseisin, single. Disseisin without force.

Disseisine. Same as DISSEISIN.

Disseisitor. A disseisor.

Disseisitus. A disseisee.

Disseisitrix. A female disseisor.

Disseisor. One who has disseised another of his freehold.

Disseisoress. A female disseisor.

Disseisour. A disseisor; he who disseises; one who puts another out of possession or seisin of the freehold.

Dissent. To refuse approval. A declaration of disagreement.

Dissenters. Those who separated from their church. See NON-CONFORMISTS.

Dissenting opinion. See OPINION, DISSENTING.

Disseysin. Same as DISSEISIN.

Disseysina. Same as DISSEISIN.

Disseysinam. Disseisin.

Disseysitor. A disseisor.

Disseysitus. A disseisee.

Dissignare. To break a seal.

Dissolution. A dissolving; breaking up; destroying. The annulling of a contract by relieving the parties of its provisions. The act of rendering a legal proceeding void or changing its character. The extinction of a corporation.

Dissolution of a corporation. The extinguishment of its existence in the manner prescribed by law.

Dissolve. To loosen asunder, separate, destroy. To discharge what one owes. To annul; to set free from obligation.

Dissolvo. To dissolve (which see).

Dissuade. To persuade or advise one not to do an act.

Distaff, descent by. See DESCENT BY DISTAFF.

Distilled spirits. Spirits produced by distillation.

Distillers. Those who distill or manufacture alcoholic liquors.

Distillery. An establishment where alcoholic liquors or spirits are made by distillation.

Distilling. A quasi public business of manufacturing alcoholic spirits.

Distincte et aperte. Distinctly and openly. Words used in old writs of error stating how return shall be made.

Distinguish. To note points of difference. To point out difference between principles and their application.

Distracted. Deranged mentally.

Distractio. In Civil law, the sale of a thing pledged. The appropriation of a thing held in trust.

Distrahere. To draw apart. To divorce. To sell. To dissolve.

Distrahere controversias. To settle a controversy.

Distrahere matrimonium. To dissolve matrimony.

Distrain. To levy a distress. See DISTRESS.

Distrainder. The act of distraining.

Distrainer. Same as DISTRAINOR.

Distrainor. One who distrains.

Distraint. The act of distraining.

Distreindre. To draw or take away from; to distrain.

Distress. To take personal property as a pledge for something due, or a satisfaction for wrong committed. To take the goods of a defendant to compel appearance in court. The act of such taking. In Scotch law, a pledge of goods given to the sheriff by persons attending a fair as security for their good behavior.

Distress, grand. See GRAND DISTRESS.

Distress infinite. A distress which has no bounds with regard to its quantity. A distress made again and again to compel one to perform some obligation; the things distrained could not be sold but were restored on the person performing the obligation or satisfying the debt. The process directing the sheriff to make such distress.

Distress warrant. See WARRANT, DISTRESS.

Distresse. Same as DISTRESS.

Distreyndre. To draw or take away from; to distrain.

Distributee. One who receives part of the estate of an intestate.

Distribution. A sum paid creditors of a bankrupt. Division of personal property among a number of persons.

Distribution, statutes of. Statutes which direct how the estate of an intestate shall be distributed.

Distibutive. Received or due under a distribution.

Distributive finding of the issue. Where part is found for the plaintiff, and part for the defendant.

Distributive justice. See JUSTICE, DISTRIBUTIVE.

District. The power of coercion or distress. The jurisdiction of a feudal lord. A district within which distraint might be made or other authority exercised. Any portion of a State, territory, or municipality. A circuit, a province, a territory, within which the power of distraining, or other coercive authority might be exercised. In Colonial Massachusetts, part of a town.

District Attorney. A United States Federal or a State attorney who represents the Government or the State (as the case may be), in a particular district.

District Clerk. Clerk of the U. S. or a State district court.

District, election. A division of territory for convenience in conducting an election and counting the votes cast.

District Judge. The judge of a district. The judge of a U. S. or a State district court.

District of Columbia. The seat of the United States Government. It originally comprised 100 square miles and was obtained by cession from both Maryland and Virginia, and lay on both sides of the Potomac. The present area is seventy square miles, ten of which are under water. The other thirty square miles were ceded back to Virginia, on July 11, 1846.

District parishes. Divisions of church jurisdiction.

Districtio. A distress.

Distriction. A distress, distraint, or distraining. The right of distress. A thing, chattel, or animal distrained. A district or territory within which the power of distraining might be exercised. A compulsory proceeding. See DISTRESS; also DISTRICT.

Districtione Saccarii. The name of a statute 51 Henry III., relating to distress for the King's debt.

Districtus. District (which see).

Distringas. You restrain, detain, distrain, hinder. A writ commanding a sheriff to distrain for a debt or appearance. A Chancery process to compel the appearance of a corporation in certain cases. An execution in detinue and assise of nuisance.

Distringas juratores. A writ to enforce the attendance of jurors.

Distringas nuper vice comitem. (That you distrain the late sheriff). A writ to distrain the goods of a former sheriff for neglect or non-performance of duty while in office.

Distringas vicecomitem. A writ to the coroner to distrain the goods of a sheriff who neglects to execute a writ of venditioni exponas.

Distringere. Same as DISTRINGO.

Distringo. To draw asunder, to stretch out. To detain a person anywhere, to hinder; to occupy, to engage; to distrain; to coerce or compel. To bind fast or strain hard.

Distructionist. One who believes in the destruction of existing institutions.

Disturbance. Interference with the enjoyment of an incorporeal right, easement, &c. Breach of the peace.

Disturbance of common. The hindering or annoyance of one in the lawful enjoyment of a right of common.

Disturbance of franchise. Wrongfully interfering with one in the enjoyment of a franchise.

Disturbance of patronage. Obstructing the presentation of a clerk to a benefice.

Disturbance of tenure. Causing a tenant to leave a tenancy by persuasion, threats, or force.

Disturbance of ways. Obstructing a right of way so as to prevent the use of the same by one entitled to it.

Disturber. One who commits a disturbance. A bishop who neglects or refuses without reason to admit a clerk on presentation.

Disuse. To cease to use. Cessation from use.

Dit. Said; a word, decree.

Dites ouster. Say over; the form of awarding a respondeas ouster.

Dittay. In Scotch law, the matter or charge against an accused person.

Ditz. Same as DIT.

Diurna pensitatio. Daily expenses or expenditures.

Diurnum lumen. Daylight. See DAY.

Diurnus. Of or belonging to the day; daily; by day, of the day.

Divers. Several, sundry, various.

Diversion. The act of turning aside from a course.

Diversitas. Diversity, difference, unlikeness.

Diversitatis. Same as DIVERSITAS.

Diversities des courts. Diversity of the courts. A treatise on the courts and their jurisdiction, written in French, and printed in 1525 and again in 1534. The author is unknown though thought to be Fitzherbert.

Diversity. The state of being different.

Diversity of person. Difference of person. A plea that there is a mistake as to identity. See IDENTITY OF PERSON.

Diversity of the courts. See DIVERSITIES DES COURTS.

Diversorium. A lodging or inn.

Diversory. Tending to divert. An inn by the wayside.

Dives costs. (The rich man's costs). The ordinary costs as distinguished from those paid by a person suing in forma pauperis.

Divest. Same as DEVEST.

Divestitive fact. See FACT, DIVESTITIVE.

Divide. To part into different pieces; to disunite; to separate; to deal out.

Divided per capita. See CAPITA, DIVIDED PER.

Divided per stirpes. See STIRPES, DIVIDED PER.

Dividend. A share of part allotted in the division of a thing; the profits of a corporation divided among shareholders; the interest paid on public funds as expressed in stocks or bonds; the division of a bankrupt's or insolvent's effects among creditors. A part of a deed or indenture executed in two parts.

Dividend, preferred. A dividend paid on a certain interest before any is paid on another interest in the same enterprise or corporation.

Dividend, preferential. Same as DIVIDEND, PREFERRED.

Dividend warrant. See WARRANT, DIVIDEND.

Dividenda. A part of an indenture executed in two parts.

Divine service, tenure by. See TENURE BY DIVINE SERVICE.

Divisa. A division or partition; a devise. An award or decree. Boundaries; which divide a parish or farm. Anciently, a will or testament of goods or chattels. A will of real estate as distinguished from a bequest of personal property.

Divise. Distinctly, separately.

Divisible. That which can be divided.

Divisim. Severally, separately.

Division. The act of separating into parts. A part. Disagreement. Separation. A separation into affirmative and negative parts.

Division, Ecclesiastical. See ECCLESIASTICAL DIVISION.

Division of opinion. Such a disagreement by judges as prevents a decision being rendered by a majority.

Division wall. Same as WALL, PARTY.

Divisiores. The persons, among the Romans who divided money among the people at elections.

Divisum imperium. A divided empire or jurisdiction. Alternate jurisdiction. Jurisdiction, exercised by courts of equity and law over the same subject.

Divorce. A legal separation of a man and woman who are married.

Divorce a mensa et thoro. A divorce from table and bed or suspension of the marriage relation. Commonly expressed from bed and board.

Divorce a vinculo matrimonii. A divorce from the bond of marriage. An absolute dissolution of the marriage tie. Under old English law there were many causes for divorce a vinculo matrimonii, among which were pre-contract, fear, impotence or frigidity, affinity and consanguinity.

Divorce causa consanguinitatis. Divorce by reason of consanguinity or relationship.

Divorce causa frigitatis. Divorce by reason or on account of coldness, frigidity.

Divorce, foreign. See FOREIGN DIVORCE.

Divorce, limited. See LIMITED DIVORCE.

Divortium. A point of separation, place where a road divides in two; a fork in a road. Divorce.

Divortium a vinculo. A separation from the bond.

Dixie. A term applied to the Southern part of the U. S. below Mason and Dixon's line.

Dixieme. Tenth. An old French tax on incomes.

Do. I give or grant. The most ancient term of grant or conveyance.

Do, dico, addico. I give, I say, I adjudge. In the Civil law, words used by the Prætor to express the execution of his civil jurisdiction.

Do law. To make law. See FACERE LEGEM.

Do, lego. I give, I bequeath; or I give and bequeath. Formal words in making a bequest or legacy.

Do ut des. I give that you may give. A civil law form of entering into an innominate contract.

Do ut facias. I give that you may do. A Civil law form of entering into a class of contract in which one agreed to give something if the other did something.

Doarium. Dower.

Doceo. To show, set forth, make out a case by proper statements.

Dock. A place for building and laying up ships. A space between two adjoining piers. An artificial basin for vessels. The place where a prisoner is put when in court for trial. To decrease. To rescind.

Dock an account. To deduct from an account.

Dock an entail. To destroy, cut off, or bar an entail.

Dock charges. Same as RENT, DOCK.

Dock dues. Same as RENT, DOCK.

Dock rent. See RENT, DOCK.

Dock warrant. A certificate from a dock owner that certain specified goods are deliverable to a person therein named or his assigns.

Dockage. A charge for the use of a dock.

Docket. To enter in a docket. To enter a proceeding in a docket. A book kept by a court clerk for the entry of the title of causes and the proceedings therein.

Docket, appearance. See APPEARANCE DOCKET.

Docket fee. See FEE, DOCKET.

Docket, judgment. A book containing a statement of the judgments of a court.

Docket, trial. A calendar of the causes to be tried at a term.

Dockmasters. Officers charged with mooring vessels in positions that will cause the least inconvenience to commerce.

Doctor. A teacher, instructor. A learned man. A physician.

Doctor and Student. A dialogue in book form in which the principles of Common law are discussed. It was written by St. Germain during the reign of Henry VIII.

Doctor of Civil Law. An honorary title sometimes conferred upon persons by institutions of learning.

Doctor of Laws. An honorary title conferred upon persons by some institutions of learning for various reasons.

Doctor of Medicine. One who is licensed or permitted by law to practice medicine.

Doctoris. Doctor.

Doctors' Commons. Buildings near St. Paul's churchyard, London, England, where the Ecclesiastical and Admiralty Courts used to be held.

Doctrine. A principle, precept, tenet. A particular view of a subject. That which is set forth for acceptance.

Doctrine, Monroe. See MONROE DOCTRINE.

Doctrine of election. See ELECTION, DOCTRINE OF.

Doctrine of relation. See RELATION, DOCTRINE OF.

Document. A record, writing, precept; written instructions or directions; an evidence of right or title. In U. S. Bankrupt law of 1898, any book, deed or instrument writing.

Document, ancient. One more than thirty years old.

Document, executive. A document of or relating to executive business.

Document, foreign. One executed in or from another jurisdiction.

Document, judicial. One made by a court.

Document, legislative. A document or record of or relating to legislative action.

Document, private. A document relating to the business of an individual.

Document, public. Any public record or instrument writing made by public authority.

Documentary. Relating to a document or instrument writing.

Documents of title. Those which show a right of ownership.

Documents. In Civil law, evidence introduced in accordance with law, particularly of witnesses. See DOCUMENT.

Documentum. Document (which see).

Dodrans. In Roman law, nine unciæ.

Doe and Roe. (John Doe and Richard Roe). Fictitious names used when the names of defendants were not known. Also used as names of fictitious bail for the appearance of plaintiff or defendant when such bail was required.

Doe, John. See DOE AND ROE.

Doed-bana. In Saxon law, one who actually kills a man.

Doer. In Scotch law, an agent or attorney.

Dog-draw. Trailing or drawing after a deer with a dog.

Dog Latin. Latin of the illiterate; that is, sentences made up of Latin words put together in English form.

Dogger men. Fishermen on dogger ships.

Dogget. Same as DOCKET.

Dogma. A philosophic opinion; tenet, doctrine. In the Civil law, an ordinance of the Senate. A principle of doctrine asserted or taught without sufficient evidence.

Dogmata. Plural of Dogma.

Doient. They ought.

Doigne. I give. Given.

Doing. A word in old grants reserving services.

Doit. He or it ought; he owes.

Doitkin. An ancient and base English coin.

Dol. Evil or malicious design ; deceit ; fraud.

Dole. Saxon for portion. In Scotch law, criminal intent.

Doles. Portions. Also same as DEAL (which see).

Dolefish. A share or portion of fish.

Dolg. A wound.

Dolg-bote. A recompense for a wound.

Doli capaces. Capacity to commit a crime. Used in connection with the liability of infants to punishment for crimes.

Doli capax. Same as DOLI CAPACES.

Doli incapax. Incapacity to commit a crime. Incapable of doing wrong.

Doli prati. Narrow strips between plowed furrows.

Dolium. A ton.

Dollar. A piece of money valued differently in different and even in the same countries. The word does not stand for any particular value, but simply a piece of money. In U. S. and Canada, it is the monetary unit and equal to a hundred cents, or in Canada 4 s. 1½ d. In U. S. a silver coin composed of 371.25 grains of silver and 41.25 grains of alloy. A gold piece of 25.8 grains 9-10 fine. A legal tender note.

Dollar, Hard. Spanish dollar coined previous to 1772 in Mexico.

Dollar, Pillar. Those coined in Mexico after 1772; the best known coin in the western world up to 1800.

Dollar, Spanish. At the time of the adoption of the Constitution it was a Spanish silver piece of eight which varied in weight from 368 to 386 grains of pure silver of 10¾ out of 12 fine. See DOLLAR, HARD and DOLLAR, PILLAR.

Dollar, Standard. The standard dollar of the U. S. as established by the coinage act of Feb. 28, 1878, known as the Bland-Allison Act.

Dollar, Trade. A silver dollar of 420 grains, not a legal tender; formerly coined by the U. S. for trade with Eastern Asia.

Dollar, U. S. See DOLLAR.

Dolo. In Spanish law, wicked design.

Dolose. Craftily, deceitfully, fraudulently.

Dolus. A device, trick, artifice. A fraudulent address or false pretense used to deceive some one.

Dolus bonus. That degree of artifice which one may lawfully use to advance his own interest or in self-defense against an attack of an enemy, or for other justifiable purpose.

Dolus malus. The intentional endeavor to injure another by a criminal device, fraudulent delusion or other unlawful means.

Dom. Proc. An abbreviation of Domus Procerum, or Domo Procerum. The House of Lords in England.

Domain. Territory over which dominion is exercised. Absolute ownership of land. The exercise of jurisdiction.

Domain, Eminent. The right to take private property for public use.

Domain, National. Land owned by the government.

Domain, Public. Public lands.

Domain, Royal. Crown lands.

Domanium. Absolute ownership; paramount ownership; domain. An estate of an individual; that which one possesses in his own right.

Dombec. Dome-book (which see).

Dombeck. Dome-book (which see).

Domboc. Dome-book (which see).

Dome. A judgment, sentence or decree. An oath. The oath of one swearing homage.

Dome-book. A lost work, compiled by King Alfred of England and supposed to contain the local customs of the different provinces of the Kingdom, the principal maxims of the Common law, the penalties for misdemeanors and the forms of judicial proceedings.

Domesche. Domestic.

Domesday. The title of a book alleged to have been written in the time of St. Edward the Confessor. Lombard and Camden assert that this book was made in the time of William the Conqueror, A. D. 1086–1087. It describes the lands in England, their value, and who held them during the reign of King Edward and also of King William. It is styled respectively, The Decisive Record of Judgment; The Survey of England; The Tax Book of England ; The King's Roll and The Book of Winchester.

Domesday Book. Domesday (which see).

Domesmen. Judges.

Domestic. Pertaining to one's own home, State or country. Relating to the jurisdiction of the county, State or political division spoken of. A household servant.

Domestic administrator. See AD-MINISTRATOR.

Domestic animals. See ANIMALS, DOMESTIC.

Domestic, assignment. See ASSIGN-MENT, DOMESTIC.

Domestic attachment. One against a resident.

Domestic factor. See FACTOR, DO-MESTIC.

Domestic bill of exchange. See BILL OF EXCHANGE, DOMESTIC.

Domestic commerce. See COMMERCE, DOMESTIC.

Domestic manufactures. See MAN-UFACTURES, DOMESTIC.

Domesticus. A judge's assistant. An assessor. A steward. A servant.

Domicella. A damsel.

Domicelli. The better class of servants in monasteries.

Domicellus. A word anciently applied in France to a King's natural son; also to a nobleman's eldest son.

Domicile. To domiciliate. That place where a man has a fixed and permanent home and principal establishment, and to which, whenever he is absent, he has the intention of returning. The relation created by law between a person and a locality.

Domicile by birth. The place of birth.

Domicile by choice. That voluntarily acquired by a party.

Domicile by operation of law. That which is consequential, as that of the wife acquired from marriage.

Domicile, necessary. That which exists by operation of law.

Domicile of origin. The place of birth.

Domiciled. Established or resident in a place.

Domiciliary. Relating to one's domicile.

Domiciliary visit. A visit to a private dwelling by legal authority and for some legal purpose.

Domiciliate. To establish in a place of residence.

Domicilium. Domicile.

Domicilium matrimonii. A domicile acquired by marriage, as by a wife.

Domicilium necessarium. A necessary domicile. One adopted through attention to public duty; or at the domicile of a husband or father.

Domicilium originis vel nativitatis. The home of a family or nativity, the home of the parents; the domicile of nativity.

Domicilium voluntarium. A voluntary domicile; a domicile of one's own free will.

Domigerium. In old English law, power over another.

Domina. (Dame). Mistress of a family; or of domestics. A lady of a manor. An honorable woman, who anciently, in her own right of inheritance, held a barony.

Dominant. Governing; controlling.

Dominant estate. See ESTATE, DOM-INANT.

Dominant tenement. See TENEMENT, DOMINANT.

Dominatio. Rule, dominion; the act of dominating.

Dominationes. Possessions of land.

Domini. Proprietors, lords, or sovereigns.

Dominia. Plural of Dominium.

Dominica curtis. The Lord's Court.

Dominica dies. The Lord's day; Sunday.

Dominica Palmarum. Palm Sunday; the Sunday next before Easter.

Dominica potestas. The master's power.

Dominicain. Palm Sunday.

Dominical. That which denotes the Lord's days.

Dominicales. That part of a manor which the lord preserves to himself and his family.

Dominicide. The crime of killing one's lord or master.

Dominicum. Domain, demesne. Ownership of land. That portion of a lord's lands retained in his own possession as distinguished from that which was granted out to tenants. That in which one had a free tenement or freehold.

Dominicum antiquum. Ancient demesne.

Dominicum bannum. The lord's ban; the sovereign's edict.

Dominicus. Of or belonging to the king or lord.

Dominion. Complete control. Full title. Same as DOMINIUM (which see).

Dominion, foreign. See FOREIGN, DOMINION.

Dominion, remote. Title which vests on the purchase of a thing.

Dominium. Ownership; right of property, and the right of possession or use. The right of property which the lord had in the fee of his tenant. The estate of a feoffee to uses. A lordship. Sovereignty.

Dominium directum. Right of ownership; the right of a lord, as distinguished from that of his tenant. The title of the King in all the lands of the kingdom, they being held either mediately or immediately of him. Allodial property.

Dominium directum et absolutum. The direct and absolute dominion. Applied to property of which one is seized absolutely.

Dominium directum et utile. The direct ownership and use; the union of the title and exclusive use.

Dominium eminens. Eminent domain. The right claimed by the people of a State, in and to all lands within the jurisdiction of the State. See ALLODIUM.

Dominium plenum. Full ownership.

Dominium utile. The right to use the soil; the right of a tenant to its use and profits.

Dominus. In the Civil and Feudal law, lord, master, owner, proprietor: one who has the control or property of a thing. In Admiralty practice, a client.

Dominus capitalis. A chief lord; the king.

Dominus fundi. The owner of land or ground.

Dominus ligius. Liege lord or sovereign.

Dominus litis. Master or controller of a suit. An advocate, who, after the death of his client, carried on a suit for the executor. In Admiralty practice, one defending a suit in behalf of the real party.

Dominus Magnus Admirallus Angliæ. The Lord High Admiral of England.

Dominus medius. A mesne or intermediate lord.

Dominus navis. In Civil law, the owner of a vessel.

Dominus negotiorum. The controller of the business. The manager of another's affairs.

Dominus pro tempore. The owner for the time; the temporary owner.

Dominus rex. The lord the King. The sovereign lord.

Dominus soli. Lord of the soil.

Domitæ naturæ. Of a tame, domestic nature. Applied to tame and domestic animals. See FERÆ NATURÆ.

Dommages interets. In French law, damages.

Domo procerum. In the House of Lords. (Abbreviated D. P. and Dom. Proc.)

Domo reparanda. To cause repair in a house. A writ allowed where one feared a neighbor's house would fall and cause injury.

Domus. One's native place, or home. A family, or race. A dwelling; a habitation.

Domus capitularis. A chapter house; the chapter house.

Domus competens. A competent, or suitable house.

Domus conversorum. The house of the converted. A house built by Henry III., of England, for converted Jews.

Domus Dei. The house of God. Applied to hospitals and religious houses.

Domus mansionalis. A mansion house; a dwelling house.

Domus mansionalis Dei. The mansion house of God.

Domus procerum. The House of Lords.

Domus religiosa. A religious house.

Don. A gift.

Dona. Donations, gifts, presents.

Dona, supreme. Same as SUPREME DONA.

Donare. To give.

Donarium. Dower.

Donatarius. A donee.

Donatary. Same as DONATORY.

Donate. To give without consideration.

Donatio. A gift or donation of lands or chattels.

Donatio ante nuptias. (A gift before marriage). A gift by a bridegroom to a bride as security for the dos she was to bring.

Donatio feudi. The donation, or grant of a fee.

Donatio inter vivos. A gift between living persons. A contract by which one divests himself of title to property and vests it in another.

Donatio mortis causa. A donation (gift) made in view or in consideration of death, to be kept by the donee if death take place.

Donatio propter nuptias. A gift in consideration of marriage. In Roman law, a gift to a woman by her husband made after marriage as security for the dos she has brought.

Donatio stricta. A precise or peculiar gift.

Donation. The act of donating. The thing given.

Donationes velatæ. Veiled or concealed gifts. The term is applied to deeds granted by a wife to third parties in trust for her husband's use.

Donative. A benefice given or which can be given by a patron to a man without presentation by the ordinary. A benefice free from church jurisdiction in the matter of presentation.

Donative advowson. See ADVOWSON, DONATIVE.

Donator. A donor or giver; the party who makes a donation or gift.

Donatorius. One to whom a gift is made. A donee.

Donatory. In Scotch law, one to whom escheated property is, on certain conditions, made over by the crown.

Donatricis. Same as DONATRIX.

Donatrix. She who gives. A female donor.

Dono. Then.

Done. A gift. In old law, given.

Donec. Given. Until; a word of limitation in old conveyances.

Donee. In old English law, one to whom lands are donated; one to whom lands or tenements are given in tail. One to whom a gift or donation is made. The party executing a power ; otherwise called appointor; in New York, called the grantee.

Doneresse. A female donor.

Donis. Gift.

Donis, statute de. See STATUTE DE DONIS.

Donneur d'aval. In French law, one who guarantees the payment of commercial paper other than by endorsing it.

Donor. One by whom lands were given to another; the party who makes a donation. One who gives, donates lands or tenements to another in tail. The party conferring a power. In New York, called the grantor.

Donque. Then.

Donques. Then.

Dont. Whereof, whence, whereby.

Donum. A gift, present.

Donum gratuitum. A free gift.

Doom. Same as DOME.

Doomsday. Domesday (which see).

Doomster. Same as DEMPSTER.

Dorce. The back.

Doresnavant. From henceforth.

Dormant. Sleeping; suspended; not in exercise ; not apparent; not known. Applied to a partner. Also applied to an execution, when it is delivered to the sheriff with directions to levy and not to sell.

Dormant claim. One in abeyance, not enforced.

Dormant execution. See EXECUTION, DORMANT.

Dormant judgment. See JUDGMENT, DORMANT.

Dormant partners. Those who do not take any active part, but share in the profits or losses of a business.

Dors. The back.

Dorse. The back.

Dorsum. The back of a man or beast. The back of anything.

Dorsus. Same as DORSUM.

Dorture. The common sleeping room of a convent or monastery.

Dos. A marriage portion; dowry.

Dos adventitia. An adventitious dowry or marriage portion. In the Roman law, a dowry or portion given by another person than a parent.

Dos rationalibus. A reasonable marriage portion.

Dossale. Tapestry.

Dossier. In French law, the brief of an advocate. A package of papers relating to a public matter or subject of investigation or litigation.

Dot. Dowry or marriage portion; independent settlement.

Dotage. Feeble mental condition resulting from old age.

Dotal. Relating to the dowry or portion of a woman.

Dotal property. See PROPERTY, DOTAL.

Dotalitium. In Canon and Feudal law, dower.

Dotation. Endowment. The act of giving a dowry or portion.

Dotarium. Dower.

Dotatus. Well or richly endowed, gifted, provided.

Dote. In Spanish law, the marriage portion of a wife. The property which the wife gives to the husband on account of marriage, or for the purpose of supporting the matrimonial expenses. To be feeble from age. To be silly. A marriage portion.

Dote assignando. For assigning dower. A writ to the escheator to assign dower to the widow of a deceased tenant of the King.

Dote unde nihil habet. In old English law, a writ allowed a widow to whom no dower had been assigned.

Dotis administratio. Admeasurement of dower.

Dotissa. A dowager.

Dotkin. Same as DOITKIN.

Douarium. Dower.

Double. Two-fold. Twice as much. Relating to or on behalf of two. Containing two or more.

Double adultery. See ADULTERY, DOUBLE.

Double arrest. See ARREST, DOUBLE.

Double avail of marriage. In Scotch law, twice the ordinary value of marriage.

Double bond. In Scotch law, a bond with a penalty.

Double complaint. Same as DOUBLE QUARREL.

Double costs. See COSTS, DOUBLE.

Double damages. Twice the amount of damages assessed by the jury.

Double Eagle. A U. S. gold coin valued at twenty dollars.

Double entente. Double meaning; a play on words.

Double entendre. A double meaning. An ambiguous expression to which two meanings may be attached.

Double fine of lands. See FINE OF LANDS, DOUBLE.

Double insurance. See INSURANCE, DOUBLE.

Double ordeal. Same as Simple Ordeal, except that the criminal carried hot weights of two pounds.

Double plea. One in which two separate matters are alleged in bar where one is sufficient.

Double possibility. See POSSIBILITY, DOUBLE.

Double quarrel. A complaint to the archbishop against an ordinary for refusing to do justice in an ecclesiastical matter.

(20)

Double recovery. See RECOVERY, DOUBLE.

Double rent. See RENT, DOUBLE.

Double use. See USE, DOUBLE.

Double value. Twice the value.

Double voucher. Where the estate was first conveyed to a person called the tenant to the præcipe, he vouched the real tenant, who in turn vouched the common vouchee. See COMMON RECOVERY.

Double waste. See WASTE, DOUBLE.

Doubles. Letters-patent.

Doubt. Lack of certainty.

Doubt, reasonable. See REASONABLE DOUBT.

Doubtful. Uncertain; admitting of doubt.

Doubtful title. See TITLE, DOUBTFUL.

Doun. A gift.

Dount. From whence.

Dow. To give or endow.

Dowable. Entitled to dower. Subject to dower.

Dowager. A widow endowed or having a jointure. A widow who either enjoys a dower from her deceased husband, or who has property of her own brought by her to her husband on marriage, and settled on herself after his decease. A title given in England to a widow, to distinguish her from the wife of the husband's heir bearing the same name. A title applied chiefly to the widows of princes, dukes, and other personages of rank and title.

Dowager, Queen. The widow of a King.

Dowarie. Dower.

Dower. A widow's life interest in a third part of the lands and tenements of which her deceased husband was seized during the marriage. By Gavelkind, it was half; in some places in England it was the whole; but in no case was it more than a life interest.

Dower ad ostium ecclesiæ. Dower at the church door or porch. In old English law, the naming by the husband of particular lands as dower for his wife, not more than a third, which she could enter upon on his death without other assignment. It was anciently conferred by the husband himself at the church door or porch. It is supposed to have been derived from the donatio propter nuptias of the Civil law. It has been abolished.

Dower, assignment of. The assigning of dower to the widow of a deceased.

Dower, assignment of by common right. An assignment by metes and bounds upon legal process.

Dower, assignment of against common right. An assignment by deed to which the widow is a consenting party.

Dower by custom. Dower according to the particular custom of the place.

Dower by the Common law. A third part of the husband's land.

Dower de la plus belle. Dower of the fairest part. Where the wife was endowed with the best lands.

Dower, establishment of. See ESTABLISHMENT OF DOWER.

Dower ex assensu patris. Dower by the assent of the father. Where certain lands were set apart for the wife's dower, with the consent of the husband's father, and put in writing as soon as the son was married. On his death she could claim no other dower.

Dower, profectitious. That given by a father or mother, or another relative, in a contract for the marriage of a daughter.

Dower unde nihil habet. (Dower whereof she has nothing). A writ allowed a widow to whom no dower had been assigned.

Dower, writ of. A real action against a tenant who had deprived a widow of part of her dower.

Dower, writ of right of. Same as DOWER, WRIT OF.

Dowl and deal. A division; portion.

Dowle. Stones. The stones which divide fields.

Dowress. A tenant in dower; a woman entitled to dower.

Dowry. A portion or property given with a woman to her husband in marriage. If in lands it was called maritagium. If in personal property, it was called marriage portion.

Doz. Abbreviation for twelve.

Dozein. A territory or jurisdiction.

Dozen peers. The twelve peers assigned at the instance of the barons in the reign of Henry III. to be conservators of the kingdom.

Dozime. Twelve.

Dozine. Twelve.

Doziners. Same as DECINERS.

Drachma. A groat. An Athenian coin of silver valued at 7¾ pence English money.

Draco regis. The military colors of England.

Draconian laws. See LAWS, DRACONIAN.

Draft. An order drawn by one person or party on another for the payment of money to a third person. A rough copy of a legal document. To outline in writing; to compose or draw up a first form of.

Draftsmen. One who prepares pleadings in equity. One who writes wills.

Draftsman, equity. See EQUITY DRAFTSMAN.

Dragoman. An interpreter at the Turkish and other Eastern courts.

Drags. Rafts.

Drain. A ditch. A channel on or under ground which carries off water. To rid land of water by means of a drain or drains.

Drainage. The act of draining. That which is drained off.

Dram. A drink which intoxicates.

Dram shop. A place where intoxicating liquors are sold to be drunk on the premises.

Drana. A drain or water course.

Drapery. A word signifying the manufacture of woolen cloth.

Draw. To remove from a fund or deposit. To take the names of from among others, as a jury. To write out in proper form. To earn, as money draws interest. To drag.

Drawback. A rebate.

Drawbridge. A bridge which can be drawn out of the way of vessels passing on a stream of water.

Drawee. The person upon whom a bill of exchange or order for the payment of money is drawn.

Drawer. The person who draws a bill of exchange or order for the payment of money.

Drawing to execution. The act of taking to a place of execution, a criminal condemned to death.

Draw-latches. Thieves and robbers.

Drayage. The charges for moving articles on a drag or truck.

Drecca. Same as DRANA.

Dred Scott Case. Dred Scott vs. Sandford (19 How. 393).

Dredge. A floating machine for deepening canals, rivers and other waters. To deepen waters with a dredge.

Dredgermen. Oystermen.

Dreit-dreit. A double right, as of possession and property.

Drenches. Tenants in capite. Those put out of and subsequently restored to their estates by William the Conqueror.

Drengage. The tenure by which drenchers or drenges held their lands.

Drenges. Same as DRENCHES.

Drift. A driving.

Drift-land. A rent paid annually by tenants for driving cattle through a manor.

Drift of the forest. Periodical examinations of what cattle were in the forest and whether they were commonable or not.

Driftstuff. Material which drifts on the water without known owner. See SEA MANURE.

Drift-way. A way, road, or path used for driving cattle. A by-road.

Drinclean. Same as DRINKLEAN.

Drinklean. A contribution by Saxon tenants to provide ale to entertain the lord or his steward.

Drip. A species of servitude. See AQUÆ IMMITTENDÆ.

Drofdene. A grove where cattle were kept.

Drofland. A toll for driving cattle through a manor to fairs or markets.

Drofman. A keeper of cattle in a drofdene.

Droit. Right, justice, equity, law.

Droit, civil. An individual right not dependent on citizenship.

Droit close. An old writ allowed tenants in ancient demesne against their lord.

Droit d'accession. Right of accession. In French law, that right of property which is acquired by making a new species out of the material of another.

Droit d'aubaigne. The right of escheat to the French Crown of the property of an alien deceased.

Droit d'aubaine. Same as DROIT D'AUBAIGNE.

Droit d'aubenage. Same as DROIT D'AUBAIGNE.

Droit de bris. The right to the fragments, from shipwreck. In old French law, a right which French lords claimed to persons and property shipwrecked, cast upon the shore.

Droit d'execution. The right of a broker in French law, to sell securities bought for his principal if the latter does not accept the same. Also to sell securities deposited with him to secure him against loss in buying for his principal.

Droit de garde. Right of ward.

Droit de gite. Right of home, or board or lodging. In French Feudal law, the duty of one holding lands within the royal domain, to supply board and lodging to the King, and to his followers, while on a journey.

Droit de greffe. A right concerning the register or clerk's office. In old French law, the right to sell various offices connected with the custody of judicial records or official acts.

Droit de maitrise. A right of or concerning mastership. In old French law, a sum payable to the crown by an apprentice on becoming a master workman.

Droit de detractione. The right of withdrawal.

Droit de pescher. The right to fish; a right of fishing.

Droit de prise. A right of prize. In French Feudal law, the duty of supplying the King on credit, during a certain period, such articles of domestic consumption as he might require.

Droit de quint. The right of a fifth or fifth part. In French Feudal law, a relief payable by a noble vassal to the King on a change in the ownership of his fief.

Droit de retraite. The right of withdrawal.

Droit de suite. In French law, the right to follow property of a debt.

Droit de viduite. The right of widowhood. In French law, tenancy by curtesy.

Droit des gens. The law of nations.

Droit-droit. A two-fold or double right. A right of possession united with right of property. See DREIT-DREIT.

Droit ecrit. (The written law). The corpus juris civilis.

Droit international. International law.

Droit naturel. Natural law.

Droit of admiralty. A ship taken in war by a subject. A vessel of the enemy taken in port at the starting of a war. See DROITS OF ADMIRALTY.

Droit patent. A patent right.

Droits, admiralty. See DROITS OF ADMIRALTY.

Droits civils. In French law, private rights of those residing in France, whether citizens or aliens.

Droits of admiralty. Proceeds from wrecks, ships and goods taken from pirates or from the enemy in time of war, claimed by a government.

Droitural. Relating to a right of property as distinguished from a right of possession.

Droiture. Right, justice.

Droiture, common. Common right of justice.

Dromones. Men of war; large ships.

Dromos. Same as DROMONES.

Dromunda. Same as DROMONES.

Drove-road. A cattle drive.

Drove stance. In Scotch law, a resting place on a cattle drive.

Drovers. Those who bought cattle in one place and sold them in another. They were required by English statute to be married and licensed.

Drown. To merge.

Dru. A thick wood in a valley.

Drug. Any substance used as an ingredient in chemical compositions, or as medicine.

Druggeria. A druggist's shop.

Druggist. One who deals in drugs. See APOTHECARY.

Drumheads. Dressed wolf skins.

Drummer. A travelling agent who takes orders for goods to be delivered by his principal.

Drungarius. A military commander.

Drungus. A band of soldiers.

Drunk. Under the influence of intoxicating liquor to such an extent as to have lost the normal control of one's bodily and mental faculties.

Drunkard. One who habitually becomes drunk.

Drunkenness. The condition which results from excessive drinking of intoxicating liquors.

Dry blows. Blows without causing blood to flow.

Dry exchange. An ancient term for usury.

Dry multures. In Scotch law, corn paid to a mill whether the one who pays grind or not.

Dry rent. A reserved rent without a clause of distress.

Dry trust. See TRUST, DRY.

Drycræft. Witchcraft.

Dryftland. Same as DRIFTLAND.

Duarchy. A government by two.

Dubitans. Doubting.

Dubitante. Doubting.

Dubitatur. It is doubted.

Dubitare. To doubt.

Dubitavit. Doubted.

Ducatus. A duchy. The territory or jurisdiction of a duke.

Duces et milites limitanei. Commanders and soldiers upon the frontiers.

Duces tecum. That you bring with you. A writ of subpœna commanding a person other than a party to the cause to appear at a day certain and bring with him books, instrument writings, or other things the court desires to view.

Duces tecum licet languidus. You bring with you, although sick. An obsolete writ to the sheriff to bring his prisoner though sick.

Duchy of Lancaster. Lands at one time owned by the Dukes of Lancaster in England. These included the county of Lancaster, the Savoy, in London, and other land.

Ducking stool. See CASTIGATORIUM; CATHEDRA STERCORIS; also CUCKING STOOL.

Duco. To take; to carry off a person to prison, to punishment, etc. To calculate.

Ducroire. In French law, guaranty.

Due. Owing and demandable. Lawful. Sufficient.

Due-bill. A written acknowledgment of debt without a promise to pay.

Due care. See CARE, DUE.

Due course of law. Regular legal procedure.

Due notice. See NOTICE, DUE.

Due process of law. Proceedings according to the established rules and principles of the jurisprudence of the country.

Due return. See RETURN, DUE.

Duel. Anciently the trial by battle, or a fight for the trial of the truth. A fight between two persons in accordance with certain rules.

Duellum. The judicial combat, or trial by battle.

Dues. Tributes.

Duke. Among the Romans, one who led their armies. A governor of a province. In England, next in rank below a prince; first created 11 Edw. III., with the Black Prince as first Duke of Cornwall. See DUX.

Duke of Exeter's Daughter. A rack in the tower of London, named after the Duke of Exeter, minister to Henry VI.

Dulocracy. A government where servants and slaves have so many privileges that they domineer.

Duly. Legally. According to law. In regular form or manner.

Dum. While, while that. So long as, if so be that, provided that, if only.

Dum fuit in prisona. (While he was in prison). An ancient writ to recover lands which a man had aliened under duress.

Dum fuit infra ætatem. (While he was under age). An old writ to recover lands aliened when an infant.

Dum fuit non compos mentis. A writ to recover lands aliened while one was of unsound mind.

Dum sola. Whole, sole, or unmarried.

Dumb-barge. A barge without oars or sails.

Dumb bidding. A reserved price secretly fixed, so that an article put up for sale at auction will not be sold for less.

Dummodo. Provided that; so that; so long; if only.

Dun. To beset, or ask as a debtor for payment. An urgent demand for payment of a debt. One who demands payment. A low hill.

Duna. Earth thrown up in a bank.

Dungeon. An underground place of confinement.

Dunio. A base English coin of small value.

Dunnage. Pieces of wood placed against the bottom and sides of a vessel to prevent the goods being injured by leakage.

Dunsetts. Those who dwell on hills.

Dunum. A hill.

Duo. Two.

Duodecim. Twelve.

Duodecim Tabulæ. The Twelve Tables.

Duodecim Tabularum Fragmenta. The Fragments of the Twelve Tables.

Duodecima manus. The twelfth hand. The oath of twelve men.

Duodecimvirale judicium. The trial by twelve men, or by jury.

Duodena. A dozen. A jury of twelve men.

Duodena manu. Twelve hands; twelve witnesses to purge a criminal of an offense.

Duodena panis. A dozen (loaves) of bread.

Dupla. In Civil law, double the price of a thing.

Duplex ordalium. Same as DOUBLE ORDEAL.

Duplex placitum. A double plea. A plea of several matters. A plea containing an averment or denial of several facts, constituting distinct points or defenses. A plea containing several distinct answers to the plaintiff's declaration.

Duplex querele. A double complaint, or a double quarrel. See DOUBLE QUARREL.

Duplex valor maritagii. Double the value of marriage. In Scotch law, the double avail of marriage.

Duplicate. Originally second letters-patent for the same thing. A copy of any writing or record. A transcript. The discharge of an insolvent debtor.

Duplicate originals. Two originals.

Duplicate will. See WILL, DUPLICATE.

Duplicatio. Doubling. In the Civil law, the defendant's answer to the plaintiff's replication. See DECLARATION.

Duplicationis. Same as DUPLICATIO.

Duplicatum jus. Double right.

Duplicity. Stating two or more grounds to sustain a single demand. Joining two or more offenses in one count.

Duply. In Scotch law, a defendant's rejoinder.

Dupondius. Two pounds.

Durante. During. A word of limitation.

Durante absentia. During absence. An administration granted until the return of the executor who is out of the country,

Durante bene placito. During our good pleasure. Form of the royal writ appointing sheriffs. (Judges of the Superior Courts of England were formerly appointed for a like term).

Durante minore ætate. During minor age ; during minority. An administration granted until an infant executor arrives at the age of seventeen.

Duration. Extent of time.

Durden. A thicket in a valley.

Duress. That state in which a person is induced by the restraint of his liberty, or menace of bodily harm, detention or injury of his goods, to do some legal act or commit a wrong.

Duress of imprisonment. See IM-PRISONMENT, DURESS OF.

Duress per minas. Duress by threats and menaces. Compulsion by threats causing fear of loss of life, or else fear of mayhem, or loss of limb.

Duresse. Same as DURESS.

Duressor. One who subjects another to duress.

Durham. An English county Palatine, the jurisdiction of which was vested in the crown during reign of Wm. IV.

During. Throughout the continuance of. Within the time of.

Duritia. Duress.

Durslegi. Same as DURSLEY.

Dursley. Blows without wounding or bloodshed,

Duscens. (French). Two hundred.

Dustuck. A permit under the seal of the East India Company, exempting goods from duties in Hindostan.

Dutch auction. Offering a thing for sale at auction above its value and gradually lowering the price until some one buys it.

Dutch standard. See STANDARD, DUTCH.

Duties. Obligations one is bound to discharge. Customs.

Duty. Whatever one is bound to perform; obligation; obedience; service; tax; custom; toll.

Duty, aliens'. See CUSTUMA PARVA ET NOVA.

Duty, ad valorem. A duty assessed at a percentage upon its value as invoiced by the importer.

Duty of the flag. See FLAG, DUTY OF THE.

Duty, specific. A custom duty upon imports charged upon the quantity, weight, or number, and not upon the value.

Duty, succession. Same as TAX, SUCCESSION.

Duty, ascertained. A duty paid on an estimate as to the amount due.

Duumviri. A Roman board or court consisting of two persons; magistrates elected in pairs to fill any office, or perform any duty.

Duumviri municipales. The highest board of magistrates in the municipia.

Duumviri navales. An extraordinary board created for the purpose of equipping fleets.

Duumviri perduellionis. An extraordinary criminal court. The duumviri.

Dux. A leader, commander, general-in-chief. A military governor of a province. A military officer having charge of the borders or frontiers of the empire.

Dux facti. The leader, commander of the fact.

Duz. One who leads.

Dwell. To live in a place.

Dwelling. See DWELLING HOUSE.

Dwelling house. A house used as a domicile and such buildings as are used in connection with it.

Dwelling place. A place where one dwells with no intention of removing.

Dwined. Consumed.

Dy. Just.

Dyent. They say.

Dyers. Those who dye cloth and other articles.

Dyet. Same as DIET.

Dying declaration. See DECLARATION, DYING.

Dying without issue. At Common law, where issue failed at any time before or after the ancestor's death. In modern times, applied to those dying without issue at the time of death.

Dyke-reed. An officer who had care of dykes and drains.

Dyke-reve. Same as DYKE-REED.

Dynasty. A succession of rulers of the same family.

Dynian. To make a din, to clamor.

Dyreno. A harvest song.

Dyrenum. A song.

Dysnomy. The making of bad laws.

Dyvour. An obsolete Scotch term for bankrupt.

Dyvour's habit. In Scotch law, a dress which debtors set free on cessio bonorum, or bankrupts who had been engaged in illicit trade, were required to wear. See DYVOUR.

E.

E. A contraction of et (and). An abbreviation of ex, Exchequer, English, Edward, Equity, East, Eastern, Easter, Ecclesiastical.

E converso. On the contrary.

E. G. Abbreviation of Exempli gratia.

Ea. The water. The river. Between high and low water mark at the mouth of a river.

Each. Every one of a number.

Eadem. The same way; the same. Of, from, by, at; in the same.

Eadling. Same as ADELING.

Eagle. A U. S. gold coin valued at ten dollars.

Eahalus. An ale house.

Ealder. An elder; a chief.

Ealderman. An alderman. A very ancient title applied to a great variety of offices.

Ealding. Same as EALDER.

Ealdor-biscop. An archbishop.

Ealdorburg. Saxon for the chief city.

Ealdorman. Same as EALDERMAN.

Ealehus. Saxon for ale house.

Ealhorda. The privilege of selling ale and beer.

Eane. Water.

Ear grass. Grass on the ground between the mowing and the Feast of the Annunciation (March 25).

Ear mark. A mark for identification.

Earl. A title of nobility of great antiquity; a rank between a marquis and viscount; a mere personal dignity independent of land. A European pipe fish.

Earl Marshal of England. An officer in England who at one time was head of the Court of Chivalry, Court of Honor, the Herald's office and the Marshalsea Court. See COMES MARISCALLUS.

Earldom. The office, jurisdiction or dignity of an earl.

Earl's penny. Earnest money; a corruption of arles penny, an English and Scotch term for earnest money.

Earmark. A mark for identification.

Earnest. Money advanced in a bargain. Money paid as part consideration on the completion of the agreement. See ARRHA; also DENARIUS DEI.

Earnest money. See EARNEST.

Earnings. That which is earned. That obtained by labor or the operation of an enterprise.

Earnings, gross. Receipts without deduction of expenses.

Earnings, net. Receipts after the deduction of expenditures.

Earnings, separate. Earnings of a married woman or minor which either is allowed to own.

Earnings, surplus. Earnings exceeding in amount the capital, expenses and charges.

Earth. Soil as distinguished from solid rock.

Ear-witness. One who testifies as to what he has heard.

Easement. A right, distinct from ownership, to use in some way the land of another without compensation.

Easement, affirmative. A right, in the land of another, which authorizes that which injures it; as a right of way, or right of water.

Easement, apparent. One where the means of enjoying it depends upon some artificial or natural formation. (As the right of support to a building, by an adjoining one).

Easement, appendant. Where the easement is to be used or enjoyed in connection with other land.

Easement, appurtenant. Same as EASEMENT, APPENDANT.

Easement, continuous. One which can be enjoyed without any action on the part of the owner of the right, as easement of light, air, &c.

Easement, discontinuous. One which requires some action on the part of the owner in order to enjoy the right, as right to a way to obtain water, &c.

Easement, negative. Where the servient tenant is restrained from exercising some right to the prejudice of the one holding the easement. (As the obstruction of light or air, or support of land or building).

Easement, non-apparent. One enjoyed at intervals, as a right of way.

Easement, non-continuous. Same as EASEMENT, DISCONTINUOUS.

Easement of convenience. One which enables the owner of it to prosecute his business with increase of facilities or comfort.

Easement of drip. See AQUÆ IMMITTENDÆ.

Easement of necessity. One without which the dominant tenant would be unable to enjoy some privilege, or carry on his business.

Easement, private. One held by one or more individuals, as distinguished from one held by the public.

Easement, public. One which is enjoyed by the people generally.

Easement, quasi. A positive obligation.

East Greenwich. A royal manor in Kent, England.

East India Company. An English corporation styled " The United Company of Merchants of England, trading in and from the East Indies;" first created in 1600, dissolved, and revived in 1693, reorganized in 1708.

Easter. A feast held by the Christians in memory of the resurrection of Jesus Christ. It is celebrated on the Sunday after the fourteenth day of the Paschal moon, which confines Easter to some time between March 21 and April 25.

Easter dues. In England, money required to be paid the parish clergy at Easter as personal tithes, and recoverable at law.

Easter offerings. Same as EASTER DUES.

Easter term. The term in English courts beginning on April 1 and ending May 8. See DE TERMINO PASCHÆ.

Easterling. A native of the East. In England, applied to a person or vessel trading from the Hanse towns of the Baltic. An old English silver penny so called because said to have been first coined by Richard II. in the East. See STERLING.

Easterlingus. Same as EASTERLING.

Eastintus. An east coast, east street, or east side of a river.

Eastland. A name anciently applied to the ports of the Baltic Sea.

Eastland Company. A company created in England in 1579, and given exclusive trade into certain European countries.

Eat. He may or can go.

Eat inde sine die. He may go thence without day. Words used on the acquittal of a defendant.

Eating house. A place where food is sold to casual guests to be eaten upon the premises.

Eaton Code. See CODE, EATON.

Eau. Water.

Eaves. That part of a roof which projects beyond the sides of a house to carry off the water.

Eavesdroppers. In old English law, those who stood under the walls or windows by night or day to hear news, and to carry it to others. An offense punishable in the Court Leet by fine.

Eavesdropping. See EAVESDROPPERS.

Eawe. Water.

Ebb. The reflux of the tide. Waste. To flow back towards the sea; to decay; to decline.

Ebb and flow. Recession and rise. A term meaning the limit of admiralty jurisdiction. See EBB.

Ebba. Ebb.

Ebba et fluctus. Ebb and flow of the tide.

Ebdomadarius. An ancient officer appointed weekly to supervise service in cathedrals.

Ebdomadary. Same as EBDOMADARIUS.

Eberemord. Aberemurder; open killing.

Eberemors. Aberemurder (which see).

Eberemorth. Aberemurder (which see).

Eberemurder. Same as EBEREMORD. See ABEREMURDER.

Ebriamen. Intoxicating liquor.

Ebriaminis. Same as EBRIAMEN.

Ebrietas. Drunkenness, ebriety.

Ebrietatis. Same as EBRIETAS.

Ebriosus. An habitual drunkard.

Ecce. Behold; see !

Ecclesia. A place of religious worship; a church; a parsonage. A living or benefice; an advowson or right of presentation. The assembly or legislature of ancient Greek States, in which every freeman had a voice.

Ecclesia commenda. See COMMENDA.

Ecclesiæ guardiani. Guardians, overseers or keepers of the church; church wardens.

Ecclesiæ sculptura. The image of a church.

Ecclesiarch. The ruler of a church.

Ecclesiastic. A clergyman.

Ecclesiastical. Relating to the church; not civil or secular.

Ecclesiastical authorities. In England, the clergy and others having authority in the church.

Ecclesiastical corporations. Those created for the furtherance of religion.

Ecclesiastical commissioners. See COMMISSIONERS, ECCLESIASTICAL.

Ecclesiastical Courts. See COURTS, ECCLESIASTICAL.

Ecclesiastical division. The division of a territory into provinces, dioceses, archdeaconries, deaneries and parishes; one of such divisions.

Ecclesiastical jurisdiction. That exercised by the church.

Ecclesiastical law. See LAW, ECCLESIASTICAL.

Ecclesiastics. Clergymen.

Ecdicus. The solicitor of a community. The attorney, proctor or advocate of a corporation; a recorder.

Echantillon. In French law, one of the two parts of a wooden tally. A counter-stock (which see).

Echevin. In French law, an officer corresponding to an alderman or burgess.

Echouement. In French law, stranding; the striking or running aground on a bank by a vessel. See COLLISION.

Economite. A member of a sect in the U. S. and Germany holding property in common.

Ecrivain. In French law, the clerk of a ship.

Ecumenical. Universal; general.

Edderbreche. Hedge breaking.

Edestia. Buildings.

Edia. Aid or help. Ease.

Edico. To declare or make known a decree or ordinance.

Edict. A command or ordinance; a decree; a proclamation. A law established by an Emperor or King of his own accord. In Scotch law, an ecclesiastical notification to show cause why an ordination should not take place.

Edict, Kenilworth. See KENILWORTH, EDICT.

Edict of Nantes. The order of Henry IV. of France granting to Protestants, in 1598, freedom of conscience. It was revoked by Louis XIV. in 1685.

Edict of Theodoric. See CODES BARBARIAN.

Edict, Perpetual. In Roman law, a general edict. An edict published with a view to being permanent. Also the Edictum Perpetuum (which see).

Edictal citation. See CITATION, EDICTAL.

Edicts of Justinian. Local laws of Justinian relating to the police, found in editions of the Corpus Juris Civilis.

Edictum. In Roman law, an edict.

Edictum perpetuum. The perpetual edict. In Roman law, a compilation of law in 50 books by Julian, taken from the prætor's edicts and parts of the Jus Honorarium.

Edilingi. The highest of the three ranks among the Saxons. See FRILINGI; also LAZZI.

Editor. One who superintends the selection, preparation, or arrangement of articles for publication. One who publishes a magazine or newspaper.

Editus. Put forth; published or promulgated; passed as a law. Brought forth or born, as a child.

Education. That which is learned. Moral, physical and mental instruction. The entire acquirement of a person both as to knowledge, habits, manners, &c.

E'e. Abbreviation of Estre; also Este.

Eel-fares. Broods of eels.

Ees. Bees.

Effect. That which results from some agency or cause.

Effects. That belonging to a person or estate which can be turned into money.

Effectum. An effect.

Effendi. A Turkish title of respect.

Effeir. In Scotch law, quality, state, condition. Fitting, becoming, corresponding with.

Effigy. A representation of a person's body.

Efflux. That which flows forth. The ending of the term of a lease as stipulated in the same.

Effluxion. Efflux. Abortion during the first week or at an early stage of gestation.

Effluxion of time. The natural expiration of a period of time agreed upon and not the expiration of the term by the act of the parties or unexpected event.

Efforcialiter. Forcibly.

Effraction. A breach made by force.

Effractor. A burglar.

Effractorum. Same as EFFRACTORES.

Effusio sanguinis. The shedding of blood. A mulct or fine for the same granted by English Kings to many lords of manors.

Efters. Ways; walks; hedges.

Egaltie. Equality.

Egalite. Equality; uniformity.

Egetter. To eject.

Egettement. Ejectment.

Egglise. A church; church.

Eglise. Same as EGGLISE.

Ego. I, myself.

Egress. Going forth from. An issue, exit.

Egressus. A going forth; an issue, exit.

Egyptians. Formerly a name in England for Gypsies. See GYPSIES.

Eia. An island.

Eide. Aid; relief.

Eight hour law. A law which provides that eight hours shall constitute a day's work.

Eign. The eldest or first born.

Eigne. Same as EIGN.

Eignesse. Eldership. Esnecy. The privilege of an elder sister of choosing first on a partition of lands held in coparcenary.

Eik. In Scotch law, an addition.

Eik to a reversion. In Scotch law, an additional loan to a mortgagor who is the reversioner of the mortgaged estate.

Eik to a testament. An addition to an executor's inventory.

Einecia. Eldership. The right or privilege of the first born.

Einetia. Same as EINECIA.

Einetius. The eldest or first born. The part or share of eldest sister.

Eins. In, into.

Einz. Same as EINS.

Einzelhofe. Isolated farms; farmsteads; farms.

Eirant. Errant; wandering.

Eire. A journey, circuit. The court of the justices in eyre. See EYRE.

Eirenarcha. A term applied to a justice of the peace.

Eisne. The eldest.

Eisnetia. The part or share of the eldest.

Eit. Has.

Either. One or the other. Any. Each.

Eject. To cast, thrust or drive out; to expel; to put or turn out of possession.

Ejecta. A woman deflowered; an outcast woman.

Ejectio. A casting or throwing out. Dispossession.

Ejection. A turning out of possession.

Ejectione custodiæ. Ejectment of ward (which see).

Ejectione firmæ. Ejectment of farm (which see).

Ejectment. A writ or action for recovering the possession of real property, and damages.

Ejectment of farm. The name of a writ or action of trespass in ejectment which lay where lands or tenements were let for a term of years, and afterwards the lessor, reversioner or remainderman, or any stranger, ejected or ousted the lessor of his term, firme or farm.

Ejectment of ward. The name of a writ, first mentioned in Stat. Wesminister II., which anciently lay against him who turned out a guardian from any land during the minority of the heir.

Ejector, casual. See CASUAL EJECTOR.

Ejectum. Cast, thrust, or driven out. That which is thrown out of a vessel into the sea, in order to be saved from loss by shipwreck; or from a house to prevent being destroyed by fire. Wreck; jetsom.

Ejectus. Cast out, ejected, expelled. A whoremonger.

Ejercitoria. In Spanish law, an action against a ship's owner for supplies or repairs ordered by the master. See ACTIO EXERCITORIA.

Ejicere. Same as EJICIO.

Ejicio. To cast, thrust, or drive out; to eject. To throw or cast out; to eject or dispossess.

Ejidos. In Spanish law, lands used in common by the inhabitants of a town or city for pasture or other purposes.

Ejurare. To abjure.

Ejuration. Resigning or renouncing one's place.

Ejus. Of him or that; from or by him or that.

Ejusdem generis. Of the same kind.

Elaborata. Same as ELABORATUS.

Elaboratus. Property acquired by labor.

Elaboro. To labor, exert one's self, take pains; to work out, elaborate a thing.

Elargatio. An enlargement.

Elargationis. Same as ELARGATIO.

Elder brethren. The members of Trinity House. See TRINITY HOUSE.

Elder title. See TITLE, ELDER.

Eldest. That of the longest duration. The first born or created.

Elect. To choose. To select by ballot.

Elected. Selected by vote.

Election. Act or power of choosing; choice; the ceremony of a public choice. The choice of a representative, officer, &c. The obligation to choose between two rights or claims. The right of selecting one of several forms of action for the redress of injury or enforcement of a right. The choice by a public prosecutor on which of two or more charges he will prosecute an accused.

Election, contested. In U. S. an election contested for illegality in a court or before a legislature. In England, an election where two or more are candidates for the same office. See CONTROVERTED.

Election district. See DISTRICT, ELECTION.

Election, doctrine of. The doctrine governing the selection or rejection of one of two or more rights or claims presented to a person by one who manifests the intention that he or she should enjoy both.

Election, general. An election for officials throughout a State as distinguished from those of a particular locality.

Election, primary. The district election at which delegates, who are subsequently to attend a convention and nominate a candidate, are selected.

Election, special. One called to elect an official for a particular office.

Election, judges of. See JUDGES OF ELECTION.

Election, primer. See PRIMER ELECTION.

Election, regular. Same as ELECTION GENERAL.

Elective. Relating to choice by vote. Depending upon election.

Elective judiciary. See JUDICIARY, ELECTIVE.

Elector. One who enjoys the right of voting at a public election. One who exercises such right. In U. S., one who elects the President and Vice-President. One of the princes in Europe who between the 12th century and 1806, elected the Emperor of the Holy Roman Empire.

Electoral. Consisting of electors. Relating to electors.

Electors, Presidential. Persons selected by the people of the different States to select a President and Vice-President of the United States.

Electoral College. See COLLEGE, ELECTORAL.

Electoral Commission. A commission created by the U. S. Congress on January 29, 1877, to decide questions relating to the election of President at the election of November, 1876, and at which Hayes and Tilden were the candidates. The commission was composed of fifteen members of which five were Justices of the Supreme Court, and ten members of the U. S. Senate. The commission decided, among other matters, that the regular election returns of a State must be accepted as correct and the commission could not go behind them.

Electrocution. The act of killing by electric shock.

Electus. Picked, selected.

Eleemosyna. Alms, pity, mercy.

Eleemosyna aratria. Same as ELEE-MOSYNA REGIS.

Eleemosyna carucarum. Same as ELEEMOSYMNA REGIS.

Eleemosnyna Regis. A penny to support the poor, anciently paid for every plow, by order of the Saxon King Aethelred.

Eleemosynæ. The possessions belonging to the church.

Eleemosynaria. The place where the common alms were deposited, and thence by the eleemosynarius distributed to the poor.

Eleemosynarius. An almoner, or distributor of alms. An officer in the King's house, called the King's almoner, or almner.

Eleemosynary. One who subsists on charity. Relating to charity; intended for the distribution of charity. Given in charity or alms; founded by charity. Supported by charity.

Eleemosynary corporations. Those constituted for the perpetual distribution of free alms or bounty; they include colleges and academies.

Eleganter. Accurately, judiciously, with discrimination.

Elegit. He has chosen. A judicial writ given by the Statute of Westminster (II., 13 Edw. I., c. 18) directing the sheriff to seize all the defendant's goods and chattels (except oxen and beasts of the plow). If the same were insufficient, then the moiety of the defendant's lands, etc., for damages recovered. The goods are then delivered to the plaintiff, who retains them until the whole debt and damages have been paid. During that period he is called tenant by elegit.

Elements. The force in nature of air or water.

Elf-arrows. Flint arrowheads.

Elidere. To defeat an opponent's pleading.

Eligibility. The quality of being eligible. Fitness; suitableness.

Eligible. Qualified for selection or to hold. Capable of being chosen for, or of holding office.

Elimination. The act of turning out of a house or banishing.

Elinguation. Cutting out the tongue; an ancient punishment.

Elisors. Electors or choosers. Two court clerks or other persons appointed by court to select a jury where the sheriff and coroner are challenged for partiality.

Elke. A species of yew of which bows were anciently made.

Ell. A measure of length of differing in different countries. In England, it is 45 inches.

Elocatio. A lease or letting.

Elogium. In Civil law, a will or testament; a clause in a will, especially one which disinherits. A judicial statement or record in criminal cases.

Eloign. To remove or send at a distance.

Eloigne. Same as ELOIGN.

Eloigner. He who makes an eloignment. To eloign; to remove or carry to a distance. To take one's self away; to go away; to elope, as a wife from her husband.

Eloignment. Same as ELOIGNMENT OF GOODS.

Eloignment of goods. The removal of goods out of the county so they could not be distrained.

Eloine. Same as ELOIGN.

Elongata. Eloigned; carried away to a distance. A return of a sheriff in replevin that the cattle cannot be found or are removed beyond his jurisdiction; upon which the party replevying had a writ of capias in withernam.

Elongatus. Eloigned; carried to a distance. The sheriff's return to a writ de homine replegiando, signifying that the party or person had been conveyed out of the sheriff's jurisdiction; upon which a capias in withernam issued, to imprison the defendant himself, without bail or mainprize till he produced the party.

Elongavit. He has eloigned, carried away.

Elopement. The act of a married woman in leaving her husband and living with another man.

Elsewhere. At another place. Otherwhere.

Eluviones. Spring tides.

Ely, Isle of. A territory on the east coast of England which possessed certain privileges by royal franchise, though not a county Palatine.

Emanare. To issue or award.

Emanavit. It issued.

Emancipation. A liberating, setting free.

Emancipation, filial. See FILIAL EMANCIPATION.

Emancipation Proclamation. The proclamation issued by President Lincoln on January 1st, 1863, which declared the slaves in certain parts of the United States should be free.

Emancipare. To liberate, set free; to emancipate.

Emancipo. Same as EMANCIPARE.

Embargo. A hindrance or restraint. A prohibition by public authority, and for a limited time of departure of a ship from a port.

Embargo, civil. An embargo upon the ships belonging to the subjects of the nation which imposes it.

Embargo, hostile. One upon the ships of an enemy.

Embassador. Same as AMBASSADOR.

Embassage. An embassador's commission, An embassador's establishment.

Embassy. Same as EMBASSAGE.

Ember Weeks. Weeks containing Embring Days (which see).

Embezzlement. The act of appropriating to one's self that which is received in trust for another. It was not an offense at Common law, but has been made so by statutory enactments both in England and the United States. As to what is included in the term depends in many cases upon statute.

Emblavance de bled. Corn sprung up above ground.

Emblements. Yearly profit of land from crops produced by annual planting and culture, but not grass, fruit, or such as are the natural produce or profit from permanent roots in the earth.

Embler. To show. To steal.

Embler de gentz. Stealing from the people.

Embraceor. Same as EMBRACER.

Embracer. One who endeavors to corrupt or influence a jury. See EMBRASOUR.

Embracery. Endeavoring to corrupt or influence a jury.

Embrasour. An embracer; one who attempts to influence a jury corruptly to one side.

Embring Days. Certain fast days in the church when people sat in ashes or put them on their heads.

Embroidery. Ornamental work done on cloth, canvas or leather; anciently forfeited and burnt in England if imported.

Emenda. Amends.

Emendals. In emendals, was an ancient expression meaning money to one's credit.

Emendare. To make amends for committing a wrong.

Emendatio. Amendment, correction. The power of amending and correcting abuses according to certain rules and measures. A pecuniary satisfaction for an injury.

Emendatio panni. The power to examine cloth to see if it were of proper measurement.

Emendatio panis et cervisiæ. Correction of bread and beer. The assizing of bread and beer (the power of supervising and correcting the weights and measures of them).

Emerald. The green color in the coats of armor of English noblemen. See VERT.

Emerge. To arise.

Emergent year. The first year of an epoch. The year from which time is computed, as the beginning of the Christian era.

Emergency. An unexpected condition demanding immediate action.

Emergo. To emerge, to arise, to happen.

Emigrant. One who leaves his country for another.

Emigration. The act of removing from one country to another. See IMMIGRATION.

Eminence. An honorary title given Cardinals.

Eminent domain. See DOMAIN, EMINENT.

Emissary. One who goes upon a mission as agent of another.

Emit. To issue. To send out. To discharge.

Emolument. Advantage, gain or profit obtained through the holding of an office, aside from the regular compensation.

Empalement. Thrusting a sharp stick up the anus. An ancient species of Roman punishment.

Empanel. Entering in writing the names of a jury. To make out a list of persons for jury duty.

Emparl. To speak together. See IMPARLANCE.

Emparlance. Same as IMPARLANCE.

Emparler. To imparl, or emparl; to speak together.

Emparnours. Those who undertook suits for others.

Emperor. A ruler. A title anciently given victorious generals; at one time held by Saxon Kings.

Empeschement. Impeachment.

Empeschement de wast. Impeachment of waste.

Emphyteusis. In Civil law, perpetual lease of lands in return for an annual rent and improvements being made on the property.

Emphyteuta. In Civil law, a tenant under emphyteusis.

Emphyteuticus. In Civil law, held under or based on an emphyteusis.

Empire. The territory or jurisdiction of an Emperor. A nation composed of what was previously several separate countries but which have been brought by conquest, compact, or colonization under one government at the head at which is an Emperor. Extensive dominion or influence.

Empiric. A pretended or ignorant physican; a quack. A practioner not properly qualified.

Emplazamiento. In Spanish law, a summons or citation.

Emplead. To accuse.

Employ. To secure the services of. To use. To apply. To occupy. To hire.

Employe. One who is employed.

Employed. Retain the services of. Engaged to perform services.

Employee. Same as EMPLOYE.

Employer. One who employs another.

Employer's liability insurance. See INSURANCE, EMPLOYER'S LIABILITY.

Employment. Occupation. Service.

Emporium. A place of extensive commerce or trade.

Empower. To authorize legally. To confer authority upon.

Emprestito. In Spanish law, a thing lent at the request of the borrower.

Emprimechief. First of all.

Emprisoner. To imprison.

Emprisonment. Imprisonment.

Emprompt. Borrowed; borrowing.

Emprompter. To borrow.

Empti actio. An action of purchase; an action for a thing purchased.

Emptio. In Civil law, a purchase. The act of purchasing.

Emptio bonorum. In Roman law, a forced and public sale of the property of an insolvent by which the purchaser assumed, to a certain extent, the liabilities.

Emptio et venditio. Purchase and sale.

Emption. Same as EMPTIO.

Emptor. A purchaser. A court purveyor.

Emptrix. In Civil law, a female purchaser.

Empty. To remove the contents of. Deprived of the contents.

En. In; into.

En apres. Hereafter; moreover.

En arere. In time past.

En autre droit. In the right of another.

En banke. In the bench.

En brevet. In French law, a term applied to an instrument recorded by a notary who drew it.

En commandite. In French law, in partnership, in which the acting partners are responsible without limitation, and the dormant ones to the extent of their shares only. It is sometimes called Societe en commandite. Also, a partnership in which some furnish money, and others labor in place of capital.

En commandite, societe. See EN COMMANDITE.

En declaration de simulation. A Louisiana form of action brought to have a contract declared void and to restore the title which passed or was incumbered, as it was before the contract was made.

En demeure. In default. Not paying an obligation when it becomes due.

(21)

En dernier ressort. In the last resort; without appeal.

En gros. At large. In substance.

En juicio. Judicially.

En mort meyne. In mortmain.

En owel main. In equal hand.

En pais. See PAIS, EN.

En recouvrement. In French law, an endorsement merely conferring authority to a person to collect the amount of a bill without transferring ownership.

En vente sa mere. In its mother's womb.

Enabling. Giving power to do a thing.

Enabling power. See POWER, ENABLING.

Enabling statute. See STATUTE, ENABLING.

Enach. The satisfaction for an offence or crime.

Enact. To perform; to establish; to decree.

Enajenacion. In Spanish law, pledge, mortgage, emphyteusis or creation of a servitude in an estate or any transfer of property.

Enbler. To sow.

Enbrever. To write down briefly.

Encænia. Same as ENCENIA.

Encaustum. Ink.

Encaustuno. Ink.

Enceinte. Pregnant. Being with child.

Encenia. A festival in memory of a church dedication. An annual commemoration at Oxford College, England, in honor of its founders. An ancient Jewish festival celebrating the reconstruction of the temple.

Enchaz et rechaz. In chase and out chase; the right of driving cattle to and from a common.

Enchemin. On the way.

Encheson. Occasion, cause, reason.

Enchesson. Same as ENCHESON.

Enclamer. To claim.

Enclose. In Scotch law, to confine a jury after a case is given them for verdict.

Enclosure. Land surrounded by a fence or that which prevents the entrance of cattle.

Encomienda. In Spanish law, a royal grant of colonial territory. A grant of privileges to the military.

Encourage. To incite. To instigate.

Encroach. To invade the possessions or rights of another. To infringe To take more than one's right.

Encroachment. Invasion upon the rights or possessions of another. Trespass.

Encumber. Same as INCUMBER.

Encumbrance. Any lien, claim, interest, or liability upon land.

Encumbrancer. One who holds a legal claim against property.

End. To put an end to. The extremity of that which has length.

Endeavor. To attempt.

Endenizen. Same as ENDENZIE.

Endenzie. To free. To enfranchise.

Enditer. To endict.

Enditement. Same as INDICTMENT.

Endorse. Same as INDORSE.

Endorser. One who endorses. To indorse.

Endorsement. Same as INDORSE-MENT.

Endosser. Same as ENDORSER.

Endow. To give the rights of dower. To confer something upon.

Endowment. The giving or assuring of dower to or upon a woman. The setting out or severing of a sufficient part or portion to a vicar for his perpetual maintenance, when the benefice is appropriated. Property, fund, or revenue permanently appropriated to any object.

Endowment de la plus belle. See DOWER DE LA PLUS BELLE.

Enemy. One at war with another.

Enemy, alien. See ALIEN ENEMY.

Enemy, public. A foreigner at war with a government. A pirate.

Eneyus. The eldest born.

Enfaunt. An infant (child).

Enfeoff. To give, convey a fee or fief.

Enfeoffment. The act of creating investiture; the act of investing with any dignity or possession. The deed or charter by which a person is invested with the possession of lands.

Enforce. To cause to have force and effect. To compel obedience to.

Enfranchise. To make free; to admit a person to a society; to make a denizen, or a citizen; to confer a power to vote.

Enfranchisement. The act of enfranchising. See ENFRANCHISE.

Enfranchisement of copyholds. Converting copyholds into freehold tenure. It was done by a conveyance or release from the lord.

Enfraunchir. To make free; to enfranchise; to confer a liberty or privilege.

Engagement. An obligation, promise, or agreement.

Engager. To pledge.

Engetter. To eject; to cast or throw out; to dispossess.

Enghein. Same as ENGIN.

Engin. Deceit; fraud; ill design.

Engine. A device for catching or killing game or fish. A machine for doing work. A means to accomplish something.

Engineer. One who manages an engine. One who practices engineering.

Englecery. Englishery; the fact of being an Englishman. Proof that a person killed by an Englishman was not a Dane; or in later times, a Norman, by which proof a town was exempt from fine.

Englecherie. Same as ENGLECERY.

Englechire. Same as ENGLECERY.

Englescherie. Same as ENGLECERY.

Engleschery. Same as ENGLECERY.

Engleshire. Same as ENGLECERY.

Engleterre. England.

Engleys. English.

English. Pertaining to the English peoples. The natives, the language, or t h e people of England.

English Justinian. Edw. I. of England; so called because of the perfection reached in the English jurisprudence during his reign.

Englishery. Being an Anglo-Saxon, as distinguished from a Dane, Norman, or Irishman. Same as ENGLECERY.

Englishmen. Natives or citizens of England. Anciently, one whose father or mother was known to be a native of England.

Engraving. In U. S. Copyright l a w same as a '' cut.''

Engross. To copy in a large, fair hand. To make the indenture of a fine. To copy a paper for the purpose of filing. To get into one's possession. The buying up a commodity in large quantities with intent to sell it at an unreasonably enhanced price.

Engrosser. One who writes a document, law or instrument writing, in a large plain hand. One who buys provisions in large quantities to enhance the price of same.

Engyn. Same as ENGIN.

Enhance. To raise the price or value of. See FORESTALLING.

Enicia pars. Same ENITIA PARS.

Enitia pars. The part or share of the eldest.

Enitius. The eldest-born.

Enjoin. To prohibit by special order or judgment. To direct one to do or not to do a thing.

Enjoyment. The act of deriving beneficial use or possession.

Enjoyment, adverse. Enjoyment adverse to the owner of the land.

Enjoyment, beneficial. See BENEFICIAL ENJOYMENT.

Enjoyment, quiet. Enjoyment without interruption.

Enjoyndre. To enjoin.

Enke. Ink.

Enlarge. Same as ENLARGER.

Enlarge an order. To extend the time within which it must be complied with.

Enlarge a rule. Same as ENLARGE AN ORDER.

Enlarger. To enlarge; to extend, add to, make more comprehensive.

Enlargement. Same as ENLARGER L'ESTATE.

Enlarger l'estate. The enlarging of an estate. As if there be a tenant for life or years, remainder to another in fee, and he in remainder releases all his rights to the particular tenant and his heirs, this gives him the estate in fee.

Enlarging statute. See S T A T U T E, ENLARGING.

Enlistment. A voluntary agreement to serve in the army or navy.

Enormia. Wrongs; unlawful or wrongful acts.

Enormis. Enormous; excessive; immoderate.

Enparler. To speak or talk together; to imparl.

Enpleet. Implead (which see).

Enprisoner. To imprison.

Enprompter. To borrow.

Enprouer. To improve.

Enquest. Inquest, inquisition, or inquiry; the inquisition of a jury. A jury.

Enquete. In Canon law, an inquiry to obtain testimony to be used at a trial.

Enquiry. See INQUIRY.

Enquiry, writ of. See WRIT OF ENQUIRY.

Enroll. To put in or on a roll. To write, transcribe or enter on a roll of parchment or other material. To enter on record —as a decree in chancery. To record—as a deed.

Enrollment. When applied to a vessel, a statement showing the national character of one engaged in coasting trade.

Enrollment of vessels. See ENROLLMENT.

Enrouler. To enroll; to put or write on a roll.

Enroulment. An entering on a roll, or on record.

Ens. In, within. A thing. Being, existence.

Ens legis. A being of the law.

Enseal. To seal.

Ensealing. Sealing.

Ensemble. Together.

Ensement. Also; in a similar manner.

Ensenses. Instructed.

Enserver. To subject to a servitude or service.

Ensi. Same as ENSY.

Ensient. Same as ENCIENTE.

Ensiency. The condition of being with child.

Ensienture. Same as ENSIENCY.

Ensy. Thus; so; in like manner.

Entail. To create an estate tail. A fee entailed, that is, abridged, curtailed, limited to certain heirs. See TAIL.

Entail, quasi. See QUASI ENTAIL.

Entailed. Settled in strict settlement or in tail. See STRICT SETTLEMENT; also TAIL.

Entailed money. See MONEY, ENTAILED.

Entaille. Entail (which see).

Entencion. A count or declaration.

Entendement. Understanding.

Entendre. To understand. To intend.

Entente. Understanding, also same as ENTENCION.

Entente cordial. A cordial understanding. An evidence of good will exchanged by the chief persons of two States; or armies.

Enter. In; within; among. To enroll or inscribe among the records.

Enterceur. A person who claims goods in the hands of a third person.

Enterlesse. Omitted; left out.

Enterpleader. Same as INTERPLEADER.

Enterprise, gift. See GIFT ENTERPRISE.

Entice. To persuade by promise of pleasure or advantage.

Entiertie. See ENTIRETY.

Entire. Complete; undivided; whole.

Entire contract. A contract requiring everything to be done on the one side before consideration is due from the other.

Entire day. See DAY, ENTIRE.

Entire interest. See INTEREST, ENTIRE.

Entire tenancy. The whole possession in one man. See SEVERAL TENANCY.

Entirely. Wholly; completely.

Entireties, tenancy by. See TENANCY BY ENTIRETIES.

Entirety. The whole; entire; in contradistinction to a part or moiety.

Entirety, estate in. See ESTATE IN ENTIRETY.

Entitle. To bestow a name upon. To confer a claim or right upon.

Entre. In, within, between.

Entrebat. An interloper.

Entrega. In Spanish law, delivery.

Entrelignure. Interlining.

Entrepot. A warehouse or magazine for the deposit of goods.

Entries, book. See BOOK ENTRIES.

Entry. The putting a proceeding on record in legal terms, language and order. The act of going in or upon the premises of another with felonious intent. The taking possession of lands and possessions by one who has title of entry. In United States of Public Land Law, the filing of necessary papers and paying of fees under the Homestead, Desert Land, Timber Culture Laws, &c. The act by which an importer brings goods into a country. Depositing for copyright, the necessary title or designs.

Entry, ad communem legem. A writ for a reversioner against one in possession, where tenant for life or courtesy or life of another, aliens and dies.

Entry, ad terminum qui preteriit. A writ against tenant for years who held over his term. See AD TERMINUM QUI PRETERIIT.

Entry and detainer, forcible. See DETAINER, FORCIBLE ENTRY AND.

Entry for marriage in speech. The writ of entry causa matrimonii præloquuti.

Entry, forcible. One made with force without legal authority.

Entry in casu consimili. See CASU CONSIMILI.

Entry in casu proviso. See CASU PROVISO.

Entry on the roll. The former custom of entering oral and afterwards other pleadings and proceedings in a cause, on a roll called the issue roll.

Entry, original. The first entry relating to money due upon a sale or contract.

Entry, right of. A right which a man has to enter and take possession of land without invoking the aid of the law.

Entry, short. The entry by a bank, of a bill of exchange received for collection, without crediting the amount of the bill to the owner; the credit not being made until the actual collection.

Entry, sine assensu capituli. A writ where the bishop or other churchman aliened church lands without the assent of the Chapter or Convent. See SINE ASSENSU CAPITULI.

Entry, title of. Where entry was necessary before an action to recover could be brought.

Entry, writ of. See WRIT OF ENTRY.

Enumeration. The act of naming separately. The act of obtaining the number by counting.

Enumerators. Those persons who are appointed to take the census.

Enure. To take place or be available. To operate to the benefit of.

Enveer. To send.

Envers. Against.

Envoy. One sent on an errand. One charged with a mission. A diplomatic representative ranking next below an ambassador.

Eo. In so much, for as much, by as much. For the reason. There; therefore; on that account; for that reason.

Eod. Abbreviation for Eodem.

Eo instanti. At that instant; at the very moment, immediately.

Eodem. To the same place; to the same thing; to this. By the same, in the same, etc. By the said.

Eoder. A hedge.

Eoderbrice. Hedge breaking.

Eorl. An earl (which see).

Eorle. An earl (which see).

Eorum. Of or from the same; of these; of such a sort, character or quality.

Eoryl. An earl.

Eoth. Saxon for oath.

Ephemeris. A day-book, diary.

Epimenia. Expenses, gifts.

Epiqueya. In Spanish law, equity.

Episcopacy. In Church law, the office of a bishop. Government by a bishop.

Episcopalia. Synodals, pentecostals, and other customary payments from the clergy to their diocesan bishops; formerly collected by the rural deans.

Episcopus. An overseer, superintendent. In Civil law, a superintendent. One who inspected and supervised provisions. A bishop.

Epistola. A letter or epistle. A charter.

Epistolæ. In Civil law, rescripts. Answers of Emperors and juris-consulti on questions submitted to them.

Epoch. A point of time from which the succeeding years are reckoned. The event which marks the time reckoned from. A period of history.

Epoch, Gregorian. See GREGORIAN EPOCH.

Equal. Of the same degree. Impartial. Just. Having the same right.

Equal protection. See PROTECTION, EQUAL.

Equality. The state of being equal.

Equally. Equal in quantity, quality, or degree.

Equerry. An officer subordinate to the Master of Horse.

Eques. A knight.

Eques auratus. A knight; so called from the gilt spurs he wore.

Equiculus. A Roman instrument of torture for securing confessions.

Equilocus. An equal.

Equitable. Impartial. Relating to the principles of right as laid down by courts of equity. Relating to the rules and remedies of equity courts as distinguished from common law courts. Within the jurisdiction of a court of equity.

Equitable assets. Assets which a creditor can reach through a court of equity only.

Equitable assignment. One which though not good at law, is enforceable in equity. (As rights of action, expectancies, &c.)

Equitable conversion. A change in the nature of property in contemplation of law, to effect some purpose; such as the intention of the party or parties.

Equitable defense. Same as EQUITABLE PLEA.

Equitable estate. An estate cognizable only in courts of equity, as the estate of one for whose use lands are held by another.

Equitable estoppel. See ESTOPPEL, EQUITABLE.

Equitable execution. See EXECUTION, EQUITABLE.

Equitable interest. See INTEREST, EQUITABLE.

Equitable levy. See LEVY, EQUITABLE.

Equitable mortgage. See MORTGAGE, EQUITABLE.

Equitable owner. See OWNER, EQUITABLE.

Equitable plea A plea or defense to a legal action in a case resting on equitable grounds, and where an injunction would be granted in equity.

Equitable remedy. See REMEDY, EQUITABLE.

Equitable right. See RIGHT, EQUITABLE.

Equitable seisin. See SEISIN, EQUITABLE.

Equitable title. See TITLE, EQUITABLE.

Equitable value. See VALUE, EQUITABLE.

Equitable waste. Such a destruction or injury as cannot be remedied at law.

Equitatura. In old English law, traveling furniture, or riding equipments, including horses, horse harness, etc.

Equites aurati. Knights of the gilt spurs; so called from the gilt spurs they wore; and equites because they always served on horseback.

Equites Garterii. Knights of the (order of) the Garter.

Equity. The sense of an equity judge as to what is right confined within certain principles established by decisions of the Courts of Equity in England and the United States.

Equity, better. Superior from an equity point of view.

Equity, bill in. See BILL IN EQUITY.

Equity, contravening. An equitable right opposed to that claimed or sought to be enforced.

Equity, countervailing. As well-founded as another equitable claim.

Equity, Court of. See COURT OF EQUITY.

Equity draftsman. One who draws equity pleadings.

Equity, equal. Equal in importance or foundation.

Equity jurisprudence. See JURIS-PRUDENCE, EQUITY.

Equity, natural. See NATURAL EQUITY.

Equity of a statute. The interpretation of a statute according to reason and the spirit of it. The doctrine that what is within the mischief is entitled to the remedy of a statute even though not mentioned therein.

Equity of redemption. See REDEMPTION, EQUITY OF.

Equity, paramount. A right superior in equity to another with which it is in conflict.

Equity, secret. An equitable claim, notice of which has been withheld from the public or one interested.

Equity side. See SIDE, EQUITY.

Equity to a settlement (or wife's equity). The right which a wife has to have a part of her equitable estate settled upon herself and children.

Equity, wife's. See EQUITY TO A SETTLEMENT.

Equivalent. That which is equal. Equal in effect. That which is operated on the same principle or performs the same things in the same way.

Equivocal. Susceptible of being understood in more than one way.

Equuleus. A rack for extorting a confession.

Equus co-opertus. Anciently applied to a horse equipped with saddle and furniture.

Erabilis. A maple tree. See ARABILIS.

Erasure. Obliteration. Act of erasing. (A material erasure invalidates an instrument).

Erastians. The followers of Erastus who contended in England, during Selden's time, that the State and not the Church, should punish offenses against religion.

Erbe. Something worked out or elaborated. An inheritance. That which a man acquired by his own labor.

Erciscundæ, judicium familiæ. See JUDICIUM FAMILIÆ ERCISCUNDÆ.

Erciscundus. In Civil law, to be divided.

Ercisere. To divide.

Erect. To construct. To establish.

Erection. The act of construction or establishment.

Ereximus. We have erected. A word formerly used by the King in creating a new office.

Erer. To plow.

Ergalabi. In Civil law, contractors.

Ergo. Proceeding from, in consequence of; on account, because of. Consequently, accordingly, therefore, then.

Eriach. In Brehon law, a recompense which a murderer was obliged to pay to the relatives of the man he had murdered. See WERE.

Erigimus. We erect. (Words used in granting a charter).

Erminage street. One of the four great highways made by the Romans in England; it began at St. David's in West Wales and extended into Southampton.

Ermine. At one time the state robe of a judge; so called because lined within the white fur of the Armenian rat (mustela erminea).

Ern. A secret place. To glean grain.

Ernde. Harvest.

Ernden. To cut or mow corn.

Ernes. Scattered ears of corn left on the ground after binding.

Erotic mania. Abnormal sexual desire.

Erosion. The eating away of soil or rocks by the ocean or waters of a stream or lake. See SUBMERGENCE.

Errant. Wandering; itinerant. Justices of the circuit. Bailiffs.

Erraticum. A stray, a waif; a wandering beast.

Erratum. Error.

Erroneous. Contrary to law.

Erroneous judgment. See JUDGMENT, ERRONEOUS.

Erronice. Erroneously ; through mistake.

Error. A mistake in law or fact. That which is contrary to law.

Error, assignment of. The allegation of an error committed by the court below. The paper on which it is stated.

Error, clerical. A mistake in writing, either in spelling, punctuation, or in properly writing out the intention of the parties to an instrument.

Error, common. See COMMON ERROR.

Error, confessing. See CONFESSING ERROR.

Error de persona. An error in the identity of a person.

Error, defendant in. See DEFENDANT IN ERROR.

Error in fact. A fact not shown by the record which makes void the judgment.

Error in law. Any illegal defect not cured by verdict, which appears on the face of the record.

Error, joinder of. See JOINDER OF ERROR.

Error, no. A form of judgment of an upper court when no error is found.

Error nominis. An error in name. See ERROR DE PERSONA.

Error of fact. Failure to know that a fact does or does not exist.

Error of law. Ignorance of the legal effect of a fact.

Error, special. Error alleged by defendant in error regarding some matter outside the issue raised by the errors assigned by plaintiff in error.

Error, specification of. Same as ERROR, ASSIGNMENT OF.

Error, writ of. See WRIT OF ERROR.

Errore lapsus. An error through mistake.

Errors, court of. See COURT OF ERRORS.

Errors, excepted. A phrase attached to an account as excuse for any possible mistakes.

Erse. See GADHELIC PEOPLES.

Erthmiotum. An ancient meeting of the neighbors to compromise differences among themselves.

Esbrancatura. Cutting off branches in a forest.

Escæta. An escheat.

Escætas quercum. Escheats of oaks (whatever fell or dropped from trees).

Escætor. The escheator.

Escaldare. To scald.

Escaldare porcos. To scald swine. A tenure in sergeanty during the reign of King John of England.

Escambio. An ancient license in England to exchange money with a foreign country.

Escambium. Exchange ; an equivalent.

Escambium ad valentiam. Recompense, compensation to the value.

Escape. Removing oneself from legal custody.

Escape, actual. Bodily freedom without authority.

Escape, constructive. Temporary freedom by permission of the custodian, but without authority.

Escape, negligent. An escape made through the negligence of one having a prisoner in custody.

Escape, voluntary. Where the prisoner escapes by the express consent of his keeper.

Escape warrant. An old English warrant directed to every sheriff in England to arrest an escaped debtor and detain him until he satisfy the debt due.

Escapio quietus. An ancient exemption from punishment for allowing beasts within forbidden forest land.

Escapium. An escape (which see).

Esceppa. An ancient measure of corn.

Eschæta. An escheat. The falling of a material object—as a tree; the limbs of a tree felled or cut down.

Eschambium. Exchange.

Eschaunge. Exchange.

Eschaunge a la vaillaunce. Exchange for or to the value.

Eschaper. To escape.

Eschapium. Chance, accident; a casual opportunity.

Escheat. A falling or happening. If a tenant died without heirs of his blood, or if his blood was corrupted and stained by commission of treason or felony, the land fell back to the chief lord of the fee. The falling back, in the nature of forfeiture of lands and tenements to a lord, King or State.

Escheat, writ of. An ancient writ granted a lord to recover possession of lands escheated to him.

Escheator. A officer of record who enquired and held inquests as to what had escheated to the King; (originally done without a jury).

Escheator-General. A former officer of Pennsylvania whose duties were those of an escheator.

Escheator of the Jews. An ancient officer whose duty was to enquire into forfeiture of Jews' property.

Eschecoum. A jury or inquisition.

Eschier. To fall; to escheat.

Eschipare. To build; to equip.

Eschoir. Same as ESCHIER.

Eschuer. To eschew.

Escoce. Scotland.

Escosse. Scotland.

Escot. Same as SCOT and LOT.

Escoter. To pay.

Escribano. In Spanish law, an official with authority to attest to judicial acts and contracts.

Escrier. To proclaim.

Escript. A written instrument.

Escrit. Same as ESCRIPT.

Escritura. In Spanish law, an instrument writing attested by an escribano or other person of authority.

Escroquerie. Fraud.

Escrow. A deed placed in the hands of a third person to be delivered in the future upon the performance of a condition certain.

Escrowl. An escrow. A scroll.

Escu. A shield or buckler.

Escuage. (Service of the shield). A knight service which required the tenant to follow his lord into war at his own expense. Later, a pecuniary compensation in lieu of knight service given to the lord by the tenant.

Escurare. To clean; to scour.

Esglise. The law of churches. Law relating to churches.

Eschætria. The office of escheator.

Esketores. Destroyers of other men's lands or fortunes.

Eskepper. To ship.

Eskippa. Shipped.

Eskippamentum. Ship furniture or tackle.

Eskippare. To ship.

Eskipper. To ship.

Eskipped. Shipped.

Eskippeson. Passage by sea.

Eslier. To choose. See ELISOR.

Esliors. Electors or choosers. See ELISORS.

Eslisors. Electors or choosers. See ELISORS.

Esloigner. To eloign; to adjourn.

Esne. A hireling. A serf.

Esnecy. Privilege of the eldest. A right allowed the eldest coparcener to make first choice of the inheritance.

Espera. The time fixed by authority within which acts are to be performed.

Esperons. Gilt spurs.

Espervarius. Sparrow-hawk.

Espiguranancia. The sealer of the King's writs. See SPIGURNEL.

Esplees. Full products and profits of land.

Espousailles. Espousals.

Espousal de præsenti. Marriage.

Espousals. A mutual promise between a man and woman to marry.

Esprit des lois. The spirit of the laws.

Espurio. In Spanish law, a bastard of unknown father.

Esquire. One who attended a knight in war and carried his shield or armor. A title of dignity next above gentleman and below knight. An honorary title anciently usurped by barristers. A title by virtue of office; as justices of the peace, and others who bear any office of trust under the crown.

Essart. See ESSARTUM.

Essarter. To clear land.

Essartum. Essart or assart; woodland turned into tillage by uprooting the trees, and removing the underwood.

Esse. To be, being.

Essence. The distinctive quality of a thing. That stipulation in an agreement without the performance of which the contract cannot be carried out.

Essence of a contract. See CONTRACT, ESSENCE OF A.

Essendi. Being, of being.

Essendi (or de essendo) quietum de theolonio. Of being quit of toll. An ancient writ to be relieved of paying toll.

Essendum. Same as ESSENDI.

Essentialia negotii. The essential parts of a transaction.

Essingæ. Anciently applied to the Kings of Kent, England; derived from Ese, the surname of King Ochta.

Essoign. Same as ESSOIN.

Essoign Day. The first day of the term, or day for receiving essoins.

Essoin. An excuse or reason for not appearing in court. An extension of time within which to answer.

Essoin Day. Same as ESSOIGN DAY.

Essoin de infirmitate. Ill in bed.

Essoin de mal de lit. Ill in bed.

Essoin de mal de venue. That he had met with an accident in coming.

Essoin de malo lecti. Ill in bed.

Essoin de malo veniendi. That he had met with an accident in coming.

Essoin de malo villæ. Sick in a village.

Essoin de outre mer. Absent beyond the sea.

Essoin de service del roy. Absent on the King's service.

Essoin de servitio regis. Absent on the King's service.

Essoin de terra sancta. Absent in Palestine (or the Holy Land).

Essoin de terre seynte. Same as ESSOIN DE TERRA SANCTA.

Essoin de ultra mare. Absent beyond the sea.

Essoin roll. The roll on which essoins were entered.

Essoine. Same as ESSOIN.

Essoinare. To essoin, to present an excuse in court.

Essoinatus. A person essoigned, or for whom an essoign was present.

Essoniator. An essoiner; one who presents an excuse for another.

Essonio. I essoin; I offer an excuse or reason.

Essonium. An essoin; an excuse for not appearing in court.

Est. Is, it is, there is. He, she or it is.

Establish. To create. To found permanently. To fix firmly. To make. To settle. To ordain. To institute.

Establishment. A statute. An ordinance.

Establishment of dower. The settlement of dower made by a husband to his wife on marriage.

Establissement. Same as ESTABLISHMENT.

Estache. A bridge or dam of stone or timber.

Estadal. In Spanish-American law, sixteen square yards.

Estadia. In Spanish law, delay in delivering a cargo.

Estandard. A standard; an ensign.

Estanques. Weirs in rivers.

Estate. The condition or circumstances in which the owner stands with regard to his property. The interest which the owner has in his lands, tenements and hereditaments. The property itself in which one has an interest.

Estate, abatement of an. Same as ABATEMENT OF A FREEHOLD.

Estate ad remanentiam. Estate in fee-simple.

Estate ad sufferance. Where a tenant is allowed to hold over after his term.

Estate at will. One which may be ended at the will of the lessor.

Estate, base. One held by a base service.

Estate by courtesy. That which a man has in the lands of his deceased wife.

Estate by dower. That which a widow has in the lands of her deceased husband.

Estate by elegit. An estate obtained and held by writ of elegit.

Estate contingent. When the right of enjoyment is to accrue, on an event which is dubious and uncertain. See CONTINGENT REMAINDER.

Estate conventional life. See LIFE ESTATE, CONVENTIONAL.

Estate, customary. See CUSTOMARY ESTATE.

Estate, derivative. One derived from or carved out of another. See ESTATE, ORIGINAL.

Estate, discontinuance of an. The termination of an estate-tail, by the tenant in tail granting a greater estate than he had. Such an alienation by a tenant in tail or one seized in the right of another, as prevents the issue in tail or successor from entering.

Estate, dominant. Same as TENEMENT, DOMINANT.

Estate, equitable. See EQUITABLE ESTATE.

Estate executed. One which is to pass in præsenti without any after act.

Estate executory. Where an estate in fee is to be afterwards executed by entry, livery, or some other proceeding.

Estate, fast. Real estate.

Estate for life. That which one has for his own life or the life of another.

Estate for years. A chattel interest in lands for a certain period whether one year or a thousand.

Estate from year to year. A lease for a year which unless terminated arises new by implication for another year.

Estate in common. Where there is a unity of possession, but need not be a unity of interest, of title, or of time. See JOINT TENANCY.

Estate in condition implied. Where a condition is expressed in the deed or grant.

Estate in coparcenary. An estate held by two or more male or female persons as heirs. At common law, an estate held by female heirs; by particular custom it might be held by males.

Estate in entirety. One held by a husband and wife, which anciently could only be created by deed or devise ; but in United States, where not prohibited by statute, may be created by operation of law, by devise, or statute. It is neither common, coparcenary, nor j o i n t - t e n a n c y, though the survivor takes the whole.

Estate in expectancy. Remainders and reversions.

Estate in fee simple. An estate to a man and his heirs forever.

Estate in gremio legis. An estate in the keeping of the law, as an estate in abeyance.

Estate in joint-tenancy. Where there is a unity of interest, unity of title, unity of time, and unity of possession; where one dies the entire estate vests in the survivor or survivors.

Estate in possession. See POSSESSION, ESTATE IN.

Estate in remainder. An estate to take effect after the expiration of a preceding estate.

Estate in reversion. An estate to revert to the grantor after the expiration of a particular estate, granted out of it.

Estate in severalty. An estate held in one's own right and not with another.

Estate in statute merchant. An estate held by a creditor until the profits or rents from it discharge the debt; entered into before a chief magistrate of a town by virtue 13 Edw. I.

Estate in statute staple. Same as Estate in Statute Merchant except that the arrangement was entered into before the mayor of a staple.

Estate in vadio. In pledge, or gage.

Estate, intestate's. See INTESTATE'S ESTATE.

Estate, landed. An interest in lands.

Estate legal. One held by legal title; not equitable.

Estate, limited. An estate limited as to the time for which it is to be enjoyed.

Estate of joint tenancy. See ESTATE IN JOINT TENANCY.

Estate, original. The first 'of several estates in the same land.

Estate, particular. A contingent interest or term of years granted out of another estate. The estate which precedes a remainder or reversion.

Estate per autre vie. An estate for the life of another.

Estate, present. One enjoyed at the present time as distinguished from one to be enjoyed in the future.

Estate, quality of. See QUALITY OF ESTATE.

Estate, que. See QUE ESTATE.

Estate, ratable. An estate subject to taxation.

Estate, real. An interest in land. Land and whatever is attached permanently by man or nature.

Estate, residuary. That part of the estate of a testator which remains after debts and legacies have been satisfied.

Estate, separate. The estate which belongs to a married woman and over which her husband has no right. The estate of one of two persons as distinguished from that in which they are jointly interested.

Estate, servient. Same as TENEMENT, SERVIENT.

Estate, stipendiary. One granted in return for services.

Estate, supporting. An interest in land which is to be enjoyed until another estate vests by the happening of some event.

In a grant of an estate to a person for life and then to another in fee, the first would be the supporting estate.

Estate tail. An estate limited to particular heirs with a condition that if the donee died without the particular issue the estate reverted. On birth of issue the donee could alienate and bar both the issue and the reversioner, or could incumber it, or it could be forfeited for treason. It was customary for the donee to alienate and repurchase and thus obtain a fee-simple absolute. To prevent this, the Statute de Donis was passed. See STATUTE DE DONIS; also TALTARUM'S CASE.

Estate tail, general. Where lands are given to one and his heirs begotten; that is, by all his heirs, whether by one or more marriages.

Estate tail, improper. Same as ESTATE TAIL, QUASI.

Estate tail, quasi. An estate granted by a tenant for life to a man and his heirs. It is so termed because a tenant for life cannot grant such an estate, as it is greater than he holds.

Estate tail, special. Where the gift is limited to certain heirs of the donor.

Estate, the fourth. A term applied to the Press. See ESTATES, THE THREE.

Estate upon condition. An estate which is to vest only upon the happening or not happening of an uncertain event.

Estate upon condition expressed. Where the condition is expressed in the deed or grant.

Estate upon condition implied. An estate with an implied condition annexed.

Estate, vested. A fixed interest that is not subject to any condition or contingency.

Estates absolute. Estates in fee-simple.

Estates in gage. Those held in pledge as vifgage, or vivum vadium, and mortgage.

Estates less than freehold. Estates for years, at will, by sufferance.

Estates limited. Limited by conditions or qualifications, as qualified, or base fees, and fees conditional, or fee tail.

Estates not of inheritance. Estates less than freehold.

Estates of freehold. Those which could not be conveyed without livery of seisin, as of inheritance, and for life.

Estates of inheritance. Those which are vested in a person and his heirs.

Estates of the realm. In England, the Lords Spiritual, the Lords Temporal and the Commons. See ESTATES, THE THREE.

Estates other than freehold, or less than freehold. Estates upon condition, mortgage.

Estates, personal. Interests in goods or chattels.

Estates, the three. The Lords Spiritual, Lords Temporal, and Commons of England.

Estates vested in interest. Where there is a present fixed right of a future enjoyment.

Estates vested in possession. Where there exists a right of present enjoyment.

Estates, volatile. Same as PRÆDIA VOLANTIA.

Este. Summer. Been.

Estendard. A standard carried in war.

Estendart. Same as ESTENDARD.

Estende. To extend.

Ester in judgment. To appear as a party in court.

Esterling. An English silver penny. See EASTERLING.

Estimate. A calculation. A rough valuation. An appraisement.

Estimatio, capitis. See CAPITIS ESTIMATIO.

Esto. Be it.

Estop. To stop, bar, impede; to prevent, preclude. To stop or obstruct.

Estoppel. A bar to an action arising from one's own act; or by matter of record, or where one is forbidden by law to speak against his own deed.

Estoppel by deed. A bar arising from one's own act.

Estoppel by matter of record. A bar arising from some matter on record.

Estoppel, collateral. The determination of a question collaterally by a court having general jurisdiction of the matter.

Estoppel, equitable. Such an estoppel as a court of equity imposed upon one because of his acts, as where he has made misrepresentations or concealed facts.

Estoppel in pais. Estoppel in the country. A bar by acts of notoriety in the country.

Estoveria. Estovers (which see).

Estoveria de communi. Estovers of common.

Estoverium. Same as ESTOVERS.

Estoveris habendis. See BREVE DE ESTOVERIS HABENDIS.

Estoverium ardendi. Estovers of firewood; fire-bote.

Estovers. Any kind of sustenance. That sustenance a man who committed felony anciently had out of his lands and goods for the sustenance of himself and family while imprisoned. A wife's alimony. An allowance out of an estate for one's nourishment, maintenance, support.

Estovers, common of. See COMMON OF ESTOVERS.

Estray. Anything out of its place. A domestic animal that has escaped from its owner and strays about.

Estraye. Same as ESTRAY.

Estrayeur. Same as ESTRAY.

Estre. To be.

Estreat. A true copy of some original record usually applied to record of fines, amerciaments, etc., to be levied. To take from the court records. To levy by virtue of an estreat.

Estreciatus. A word anciently applied to roads.

Estreite. Straitened.

Estrepament pendente lite. Estrepement or waste during the pendency of the suit.

Estrepe. To strip; waste; to lay bare.

Estrepement. Any impairment or injury made by a tenant for life upon lands or woods to the damage of the reversioner. Making lands barren by continual plowing. The name of two writs to prevent the tenant making waste during suit and to prevent waste until a demandant after judgment gets into possession.

Estuary. The part of a tide river near its mouth. An arm of the sea.

Estrepement, Writ of. See ESTREPEMENT.

Et. And. And indeed, and moreover, and that too. As, than. When, and then. Now, but. And in fact, and indeed, and truly, and so. And so too, and also; too, also, likewise.

Et adjournatur. And it is adjourned.

Et alius. And another.

Et cos saints. And these holy things (i. e. gospels). The conclusion of the ancient form of an oath.

Et sequitur. And follows.

Et ux. Abbreviation of Et Uxor.

Et uxor. And wife.

Etheling. Same as ATHELING.

Ethics, legal. The principles which govern the conduct of a lawyer in his professional capacity.

Etiam. And also, and furthermore; also, likewise, besides.

Euangelies. The evangelists.

Eunomy. Equal laws.

Eureka. I have found it. (Motto of California).

Evagation. A wandering about; a roaming.

Evasion. Escape (from prison or custody). An endeavor to evade telling the truth or escape punishment of the law.

Evasive. Tending to evade.

Evectio. A warrant or privilege to travel by the public post.

Evenings. The delivery at evening of a certain portion of the crop to the tenant who cuts it.

Event. That which happens. The result of anything. Termination.

Eventus. An event.

Everwyk. York.

Every. Each. Each of the whole.

Evesche. A bishop's diocese.

Evesdroppers. Those who stand under the walls or windows by night or day to hear news, and to carry to others, to make strife and debate among their neighbors. (An offence punishable in the Court Leet by fine).

Evesque. A bishop.

Evict. In Civil law, to legally dispossess of land. To recover possession of land by judgment. See OUSTER.

Evicted. Dispossessed.

Eviction. The recovery of lands, etc., by form of law. The compelling a tenant to abandon the demised premises by rendering them unfit for occupation, as by a nuisance.

Evictum perpetuum. A perpetual eviction, or ouster of possession.

Evidence. Testimony of witnesses, writings, records, or articles. All the means by which any alleged matter of fact, the truth of which is submitted to investigation, is attempted to be established or disproved.

Evidence, adminicular. Evidence in support of other evidence.

Evidence, admissible. That which can be introduced under the rules of evidence.

Evidence, best. The evidence most likely to establish a fact. Primary evidence. Original evidence.

Evidence, circumstantial. Evidence made up of facts which, when taken together, are supposed to establish the fact in issue.

Evidence, collateral. Indirect or subordinate evidence. Supporting evidence tending to prove the same facts as other evidence, but not directly proving it.

Evidence, competent. That which the law permits to be introduced to prove or disprove a fact. Evidence relevant and material to the issue.

Evidence, conclusive. Such evidence as conclusively establishes the truth of a fact.

Evidence, corroborative. Evidence to support a fact in addition to, though of different character, from that already given.

Evidence, cumulative. Evidence merely additional and of the same kind as other evidence.

Evidence, demonstrative. That which establishes a fact beyond doubt.

Evidence, direct. Evidence directly to the point in issue.

Evidence, documentary. That in the form of documents and instruments writing.

Evidence, extra-judicial. Evidence obtained by persons in making a private inquiry.

Evidence, extrinsic. Evidence outside of a document or instrument writing.

Evidence, fabricated. Evidence manufactured for the purposes of the case, which is either entire falsehood or such a mixture of truth and falsehood as to be deceiving in effect.

Evidence, finding against. See FINDING AGAINST EVIDENCE.

Evidence, hearsay. Evidence composed of facts learned only from another.

Evidence, immaterial. Evidence not affecting the issue.

Evidence, incompetent. Evidence not material or relevant to the issue.

Evidence, inconclusive. Evidence which may be rebutted.

Evidence, indicative. A suggestion of the existence of evidence which may be secured if effort be made to obtain it.

Evidence, indirect. Evidence from which the facts or issue may be presumed to exist.

Evidence, indispensable. Evidence without which a fact cannot be established.

Evidence, instruments of. Persons or things by which facts are laid before a court or other tribunal.

Evidence, intrinsic. The evidence of a document alone without explanatory evidence.

Evidence, irrelevant. Evidence not pertinent or bearing upon the issue.

Evidence, judicial. Evidence presented in an inquiry by a court or other competent tribunal. See EVIDENCE, EXTRA-JUDICIAL.

Evidence, material. That which tends to prove or disprove the fact in issue.

Evidence, mathematical. That which establishes a fact with certainty.

Evidence, newly discovered. Evidence discovered after judgment or verdict.

Evidence of debt. Instruments writing or securities promising the payment of money, or showing the existence of a debt.

Evidence of title. A grant, deed or will, document, or judgment establishing the title to property in a person.

Evidence, original. Same as EVIDENCE PRIMARY.

Evidence, parol. Evidence composed of testimony and not in writing. Applied to evidence other than that of an instrument writing itself, the meaning of which is in dispute.

Evidence, partial. Evidence of a fact not directly connected with the fact in issue, but which may be through other evidence.

Evidence, positive. Same as EVIDENCE, DIRECT.

Evidence, preappointed. Evidence required by law to establish a fact.

Evidence, presumptive. Circumstances from which other circumstances may or may not be presumed.

Evidence, prima facie. Evidence deemed sufficient to establish a fact in the absence of any other in rebuttal.

Evidence, primary. First in importance, as a writing would be primary evidence of its contents, and a copy, secondary evidence.

Evidence, probable. Presumptive evidence.

Evidence, rebutting. That produced to rebut or avoid the effect of a presumption of fact or law. Evidence introduced to destroy the effect of prior evidence.

Evidence, relevant. Evidence material to the issue.

Evidence, satisfactory. Evidence which satisfied the tribunal before whom it was produced. (This is the only true test of whether evidence be satisfactory or not).

Evidence, secondary. Evidence inferior in degree to what would be best evidence if the latter were obtainable (as the instrument writing itself would be best evidence to prove an agreement, but in its absence testimony as to its contents would be secondary).

Evidence, State's. The evidence introduced by the State in a criminal cause. The evidence of one guilty of a crime who offers himself as a witness against his accomplice.

Evidence, substantive. Evidence for the proof of a fact as distinguished from that introduced to impeach, contradict, or corroborate a witness.

Evidence, substitutionary. That which is substituted for original or the best evidence, as the testimony of persons as to the contents of an instrument writing instead of the instrument itself.

Evidence, sufficient. Same as EVIDENCE, SATISFACTORY.

Evidenced. Made clear. Established.

Evidences. Those instruments writing which establish a title or fact, as deeds, are evidences of title; promissory notes, of indebtedness, &c.

Evident. Apparent. Clear.

Evidentia. Evidence.

Evidentia documenta. Evidence in the form of documents and instruments writing.

Evidentia testimonia. Evidence in the form of the testimony of witnesses.

Evidential. Relating to evidence.

Evidentiary. Same as EVIDENTIAL.

Evidents. In Scotch law, title deeds.

Evocation. In French law, removing a cause from an inferior to a superior court.

Ew. Marriage. (A Saxon term).

Ewa. In old German and Saxon law, law.

Ewage. Same as AQUAGE.

Ewbrice. In Saxon law, marriage breach. Adultery.

Ewry. The linen closet of a royal household.

Ex (or **E**). Out of, from. Excepting, without. Reserving.

Ex assensu patris. By the consent of the father. A gift or dower to the wife by the husband, during the life of his father, out of his father's land.

Ex assensu suo. With his assent. Words in judgment by default for damages.

Ex cathedra. From the pulpit, chair, or bench; from high authority. (Applied to the Pope's decisions).

Ex causa. By title.

Ex certa scientia. Of certain knowledge. Words used in ancient patents indicating that the King had full knowledge of the same.

Ex commodato. Out of loan. A right of action arising from a loan.

Ex comparatione scriptorum. By comparison of writings.

Ex continenti. In Civil law, without delay.

Ex contractu. See ACTION, EX CONTRACTU.

Ex curia. Out of court.

Ex debito justitiæ. From a debt of justice. As a matter of right. See EX GRATIA.

Ex defectu sanguinis. From failure of blood.

Ex delicto. See ACTION, EX DELICTO.

Ex demissione. Upon the demise.

Ex dolo malo. Out of fraud or deceit.

Ex emptio. Out of purchase. Based on purchase.

Ex eo. With the condition of stipulation.

Ex gr. Abbreviation of Exempli Gratia, (which see).

Ex gratia. As matter of grace. That granted as a favor as distinguished from that granted as a right.

Ex gravi querela. From grievous complaint. An old writ for a devisee who was kept out of lands by the heir.

Ex industria. Intentionally.

Ex lege. By law.

Ex locato. From lease or letting. A Civil and old English law term applied to actions arising from locatum.

Ex maleficio. In Civil law, same as Ex Delicto as distinguished from Ex Contractu.

Ex mero motu. Of his own accord. Applied to letters issued voluntarily by the King, or orders issued by a court of its own motion.

Ex mora. From the delay. From default.

Ex more. In accordance with custom.

Ex mutuo. Out of loan. Applied to a debt or action which arose out of something lent.

(22)

Ex necessitate rei. From the necessity of the thing.

Ex officio. From office.

Ex officio information. A criminal information filed by the English Attorney-General by virtue of his office, in criminal matters affecting the crown.

Ex officio oath. See OATH, EX OFFICIO.

Ex parte. From one part; from o n e side; at the instance of one party or side only.

Ex parte application. One made in the absence of the opposite party; one made by a person not a party.

Ex parte injunction. See INJUNCTION, EX PARTE.

Ex parte materna. On the mother's side. From the line of the mother.

Ex parte paterna. On the father's side; from the father's line.

Ex post facto law. See LAW, EX POST FACTO.

Ex provisione hominis. By the provision of man. By the act of man as distinguished from the operation of law.

Ex rel. Abbreviation of Ex Relatione.

Ex relatione. From or on the relation. Applied to a proceeding by the State, but at the instigation or information of an individual. The term is also used by reporters of court decisions in reporting decisions they only know of through another. See RELATION; also RELATOR.

Ex stipulatu actio. See ACTIO EX STIPULATU.

Exactimissa diligentia. Exact diligence; the most careful diligence.

Exaction. A demand. A wrong done by an officer, or by one pretending to have authority, in demanding or taking any reward or fee for that matter, cause, or thing, which is not allowed by law. See EXTORTION.

Exactor. One who collected taxes and other public moneys.

Exactor Regis. The King's collector of taxes. (Sometimes applied to the sheriff).

Exadoniare. To manumit.

Exagoga. An exportation of goods.

Exaltare. To elevate. To raise.

Examen. A trial; examination.

Examen computi. The balance of an account.

Examination. Investigation. Hearing. Perusal. Inquiry by interrogation.

Examination, ante mortem. An examination made of a person before death.

Examination, cross. Interrogation of a witness regarding matters stated in the direct examination.

Examination de bene esse. An examination before trial and without a court, of a witness whose testimony is material, and whose failure to attend is feared.

Examination, direct. The first examination other than that to test competency of a witness. See EXAMINATION, VOIR DIRE.

Examination in chief. Same as EXAMINATION, DIRECT.

Examination of a bankrupt. Inquiry as to his property.

Examination of a married woman. An examination to learn if an act on her part was performed without coercion.

Examination of an accused. Inquiry as to whether he should or should not be held for further action.

Examination of a National Bank. Examination by a Federal officer to see whether the bank is or is not complying with the law.

Examination of an invention. Examination as to whether the same is patentable under the law.

Examination of a title. An examination of the records to determine t h e soundness of a title.

Examination, post mortem. An examination made after death.

Examination, private. The interrogation of a person separate and apart from others.

Examination, re. Another examination either at the same or another hearing.

Examination, re-cross. A cross examination made after a redirect examination.

Examination, redirect. A direct examination made after cross-examination.

Examination, separate. Examination of a witness apart from others.

Examination, voir dire. An examination to test competency of a witness or juror.

Examined. Inspected. Investigated. Enquired of by interrogation.

Examined copy. See COPY, EXAMINED.

Examiner. One charged with the examination of any matter.

Examiner, special. A person appointed to take testimony in a particular suit. A person charged with the examination of a particular question, as to whether an invention be patentable; or to determine claims for public land.

Examiner in Chancery. A person appointed to take testimony in Chancery causes.

Examiners. Lawyers appointed by a court to examine applicants for admission to the bar.

Examiners of Patents. Officials in the United States Patent Office whose duty is to examine and pass upon applications for patents.

Examiners of Land Cases. Officials in the United States Land Office who examine and decide contests over public lands.

Examining. Questioning in order to obtain facts. Investigating.

Exannual roll. An ancient roll containing the sheriff's accounts, illeviable fines and bad debts, which was annually examined to see what of it could be collected.

Exarta. Possessions of land.

Excadentiæ. Escheats.

Escamb. In Scotch law, to exchange.

Excambiare. To exchange.

Excambiator. An exchanger, broker.

Excambiatores. Plural of Excambiator.

Excambion. Exchange. In Scotch law, exchange of land.

Excambium. Exchange, a recompense. A mutual grant of equal interests in land, the one in exchange or consideration of the other. Exchange of money.

Excelsior. "More elevated." (Motto of the State of New York).

Exceptant. One who accepts.

Exceptio. An exception. A defence; a plea. An exclusion.

Exceptio ad breve prosternendum. A plea in abatement.

Exceptio dilatoria. A dilatory exception or plea. Pleas to the jurisdiction, pleas in suspension, and pleas in abatement.

Exceptio doli mali. A plea of fraud.

Exceptio in factum. In the Civil law, an exception on the fact. A plea based on the facts of the case.

Exceptio jurisjurandi. In Civil law, an exception of oath. A plea that the creditor had brought suit notwithstanding an oath by the debtor, made at the instance of the creditor, that the former owed him nothing.

Exceptio metus. In Civil law, a plea of fear or duress.

Exceptio pacti conventi. In Civil law, a plea that the plaintiff had contracted not to bring suit.

Exceptio pecuniæ non numeratæ. In Civil law, an exception of money not paid. A plea that the money sued for had never been received by defendant.

Exceptio peremptoria. A peremptory plea; a plea in bar.

Exceptio rei adjudicatæ. A plea that the matter has been previously adjudged.

Exceptio temporis. In Civil law, an exception of time. A plea that the action had not been brought within the time required by law.

Exception. A denial of a matter pleaded in bar; that which is alleged against the sufficiency of an answer; an objection; a saving clause. See BILL OF EXCEPTIONS.

Exception, note on. See NOTE ON EXCEPTION.

Exception to bail. An objection on the ground that it is insufficient.

Exceptions, bill of. See BILL OF EXCEPTIONS.

Exceptions, declinatory. Pleas which decline the jurisdiction of the court. See DECLINATURE.

Exceptions, dilatory. Pleas tending to delay the action.

Exceptions, peremptory. Those raised with a view to having the action dismissed.

Exceptis. Excepted; excepting.

Exceptor. A party who excepted, or put in a plea.

Excerpt. To take out. Citation. Extract.

Excerpta. Extracts; abridged notices taken from a work.

Excerpts. Extracts.

Excess. That which is greater than a given amount, limit, measure, power, or jurisdiction.

Excessive. Unreasonable in amount.

Excessive bail. See BAIL, EXCESSIVE.

Excessus. Excess, transgression, violation of engagements.

Exchange. Exchanging money of one country for that of another. Giving one thing for another. Compensation due the warrantee if the land be taken from him because of the title being defective.

Exchange, bill of. See BILL OF EXCHANGE.

Exchange broker. See BROKER, EXCHANGE.

Exchange, deed of. A Common law conveyance for transfer of interests of the same nature.

Exchange, foreign. Drafts drawn in one State or country and payable in another.

Exchange of lands. The exchange of an equal estate or interest in lands.

Exchange, rate of. See RATE OF EXCHANGE.

Exchange, stock. See STOCK EXCHANGE.

Exchangers. Those who return money by bills of exchange; those who exchange money of one country for that of another.

Exchequer. An ancient court of record introduced in England by William the Conqueror, where all matters concerning the revenue and rights of the crown were heard, and where the revenues were received. Among the ancient Normans, an assemby of justices to correct the errors of inferior justices; now merged in the Queen's Bench. An English court where the public revenue is received and paid, and all causes relating to the revenue tried.

Exchequer-bill. A bill of credit issued by the authority of the British Parliament.

Exchequer Chamber, Court of. Originally created 31 Edw. III., to determine causes upon writs of error from Common law side of Exchequer.

Excise. An inland tax levied upon commodities of home consumption. To levy a tax or excise.

Excise laws. See LAWS, EXCISE.

Exciseman. An inspector of excised goods.

Exclusa. A sluice; a structure for carrying off water. The payment by a tenant for a sluice.

Exclusagium. A sluice or sluisage. See EXCLUSA.

Exclusive. Independent of others. Existing alone.

Exclusive privilege. A monopoly. In Scotch law, a privilege granted certain incorporated trades or burgs of exercising a trade and prohibiting those not a member of either from exercising it within a locality.

Excommenge. Excommunicated.

Excommengement. Excommunication.

Excommunication. An ecclesiastical interdict or censure, by which a person was cut off from communion with his church. There was lesser and greater excommunication; the lesser was an ecclesiastical censure which excluded the party from participation in the sacraments; the greater excluded him also from the company of all Christians.

Excommunication, the greater. See EXCOMMUNICATION.

Excommunication, the lesser. See EXCOMMUNICATION.

Excommunicato capiendo. A writ directing the sheriff to apprehend one who would not submit to the sentence of the Spiritual Court.

Excommunicato deliberando. A writ to deliver an excommunicated person from prison.

Excommunicato recapiendo (or recipiendo). A writ to retake one unlawfully delivered from prison when imprisoned for not obeying the sentence of the Spiritual Court.

Excriminate. To exculpate. To free of crime.

Excubiæ. A watch; a guard; keeping watch.

Exculpation, letters of. See LETTERS OF EXCULPATION.

Excusable. Justifiable. Worthy of excuse. Without malice.

Excusable homicide. See HOMICIDE, EXCUSABLE.

Excusatio. In Civil law, an excuse which relieves of a duty or obligation.

Excusator. An excuser; one who offered the excuse of another in court.

Excuse. To free of fault or blame. That given as the reason for doing or not doing a thing.

Excuss. To seize and detain by law.

Exeat. Leave given a priest by a bishop to go beyond his diocese.

Exeat, ne. See NE EXEAT.

Execute. To make legal by fulfillment. To complete. To kill by authority of law.

Executed. Accomplished; finished; effected; now in force; past. Killed by authority.

Executed consideration. See CONSIDERATION, EXECUTED.

Executed estate. See ESTATE, EXECUTED.

Executed fine. See FINE, EXECUTED.

Executed remainder. Same as REMAINDER, VESTED.

Executed trust. See TRUST, EXECUTED.

Executed use. See USE, EXECUTED.

Executed writ. See WRIT, EXECUTED.

Executio. Administration. Carrying out whatever is required to be done regarding a matter. An execution.

Executio bonorum. Administration of goods.

Execution. The act or mode of putting the sentence of the law in force. A writ directing the satisfaction of a judgment. The final process in an action. The acts of signing, sealing and delivering a deed or instrument writing, or of signing and declaring a will.

Execution-attachment. A seizure of goods to satisfy a judgment.

Execution creditor. One who has obtained an execution to satisfy a judgment.

Execution, dormant. An execution issued but purposely unserved for some reason.

Execution, equitable. The taking charge by a court, through a receiver, of property of an equitable nature.

Execution, final. That which turns the defendant's goods into money or puts them into the hands of the plaintiff in satisfaction of the judgment.

Execution, mandamus. A writ to enforce the satisfaction of a judgment against a public corporation.

Execution of decree. See DECREE, EXECUTION OF.

Execution of deeds. See DEEDS, EXECUTION OF.

Execution of statutes. A power said to have been possessed by the Star Chamber.

Execution of wills. See EXECUTION.

Execution paree. In French law, a right by which a creditor can seize and sell the property of a debtor and satisfy his debt from the proceeds. It is given by the debtor before a notary and is similar to a warrant of attorney or confession of judgment.

Execution quousque. That which only tends to a satisfaction of the debt; as a capias ad satisfaciendum.

Execution, writ of. A writ directing an officer to satisfy a judgment of a court.

Executione faciendi. A writ commanding execution of a judgment.

Executione facienda in withernam. See BREVE DE EXECUTIONE FACIENDA IN WITHERNAM.

Executione judicii. See BREVE DE EXECUTIONE JUDICII.

Executioner. One who executes those condemned to death.

Executive. One who superintends the enforcement of law. The person or power that executes the laws and administers the government. Relating to the enforcement of law.

Executive authority. See AUTHORITY, EXECUTIVE.

Executive, chief. See CHIEF EXECUTIVE.

Executive department. See DEPARTMENT, EXECUTIVE.

Executive officer. See OFFICER, EXECUTIVE.

Executive power. The power or authority given or exercised by the executive department of a government as distinguished from the judicial and law making.

Executor. A person appointed or authorized to execute or perform a duty or trust. One who carried judgments into effect.

Executor a lege constitutus. An executor appointed by law.

Executor a testatore constitutus. An executor appointed by a testator.

Executor ab episcopo constitutus. An executor appointed by the bishop.

Executor, acting. One who actually performs the duties of the office.

Executor dativus. An executor who is given or appointed.

Executor debtor. See DEBTOR, EXECUTOR.

Executor de son tort. An executor of his own wrong; one who acts illegally under a will.

Executor, general. One not limited in power to specific acts.

Executor, instituted. One who has the preference over another, of executing the will of the testator.

Executor, joint. One who is executor jointly with another.

Executor, limited. See LIMITED EXECUTOR.

Executor, rightful. The legal executor.

Executor, sole. The only executor.

Executor, special. One limited as to time, place, or duties.

Executor, substituted. One who is to be substituted for an instituted executor should the latter not serve.

Executor testamentarius. A testamentary executor.

Executor testamenti. Executor of a will.

Executor to the tenor. One who, though not executor, is charged in a will with duties which an executor is required to perform.

Executor lucratus. An executor having assets of a testator who during his lifetime had become liable for interfering with the property of another.

Executory. To be completed; future; unfinished.

Executory bequest. See BEQUEST, EXECUTORY.

Executory consideration. See CONSIDERATION, EXECUTORY.

Executory devise. See DEVISE, EXECUTORY.

Executory estate. See ESTATE, EXECUTORY.

Executory fine. See FINE, EXECUTORY.

Executory interest. See INTEREST, EXECUTORY.

Executory limitation. See LIMITATION, EXECUTORY.

Executory proceeding. See PROCEEDING, EXECUTORY.

Executory process. See PROCESS, EXECUTORY.

Executory trust. See TRUST, EXECUTORY.

Executory use. See USE, EXECUTORY.

Executour. An executor.

Executress. A female executor.

Executrix. A female executor.

Executry. In Scotch law, all the personal property of a deceased subject to administration.

Exemplary damages. See DAMAGES, EXEMPLARY.

Exempli gratia. By way of example; therefore; for instance. (Abbreviated Ex. Gr. or E. G.)

Exemplification. A certified transcript (under seal) of a record. The term applies strictly to matters of record.

Exemplificatione. A writ for the exemplification of a record.

Exemplified copy. See COPY, EXEMPLIFIED.

Exemplum. An example.

Exempt. Not subject to the operation of law. The person so relieved.

Exemption. A privilege of being free from a service or appearance, or operation of law; property exempt from operation of law.

Exemption laws. See LAWS, EXEMPTION.

Exempts. Persons not bound by law; those exempted from certain services or duties.

Exennium. A gift; a New Year's gift.

Exequatur. (Let him execute or perform his office). The official recognition of a consul or commercial agent, issued by the government to which he is accredited, authorizing him to exercise his powers in the country. An official permission given by the executive of a government. A regium placet. In French law, permission and authority to execute a judgment.

Exercise. To put in practice. To perform or execute.

Exercitalis. A soldier. A vassal.

Exercitor. One entitled to the earnings of a vessel.

Exercitor maris. One who fits out and equips a vessel whether he be the absolute or qualified owner, or even a mere agent. A managing owner; a "ship's husband."

Exercitor navis. In Roman law, the charterer or temporary owner of a ship.

Exercitorial power. See POWER, EXERCITORIAL.

Exercitory actio. In Civil law, an action which lay against the employer of a vessel for the contracts made by the master.

Exercituale. A heriot; a payment or tribute in arms or military accoutrements.

Exercitualis. Heriettum.

Exercitus. An army; an armed force. A collection of thirty-five men and upwards. An assembly of forty-two men; also of four men.

Ex-ere. To issue as a writ.

Exeter Domesday. A record in Exeter Cathedral, England, containing a description of Western England.

Exeure aliquem beneficio legis. To deprive one of the benefit and protection of the law.

Exfestucare. To deliver or surrender an estate to another.

Exfrediare. To break the peace.

Exhæredere. To exheredate.

Exhæredatio. In Civil law, an old English law, a disinheriting.

Exhæredation. Disherison; an injury done to one who has the inheritance, particularly to a remainder-man or reversioner.

Exhæres. In Civil law, one who is disinherited.

Exhenium. Same as EXENNIUM.

Exheredate. To disinherit; to exclude from inheriting.

Exheredation. Same as EXHÆREDATION.

Exhibere. To present a thing for inspection and examination. To personally appear and defend an action.

Exhibit. An instrument writing proved by a witness; to expose for inspection. Any article or writing introduced in evidence and identified by a witness. To offer for inspection. To present publicly. To file of record.

Exhibitant. One who makes the complaint in articles of the peace.

Exhibitio. Sustenance, maintenance. An allowance for meat and drink.

Exhibitio billæ. The exhibition of the bill. The commencement of the suit.

Exhibition. In Scotch law, an action to compel the production of a writing. An allowance to a vicar for meat and drink; also for maintaining pupils in a university.

Exhibitus. An exhibit.

Exhinc. Hereupon, after this, then.

Exigence. Need; requirement; demand.

Exigency. The state of requiring immediate remedy. Requirement.

Exigendarius. An exigendary.

Exigendary. In old English law, one who made out exigents; an exigenter.

Exigent. An extendi facias. A writ directing the sheriff to call a person five county court days charging him to appear on pain of outlawry. It lays in personal and criminal actions. See EXTENDI FACIAS.

Exigent list. A list of causes for hearing.

Exigenter. An officer of the Common Pleas who made out exigents and proclamations in the process of outlawry.

Exigi facias. You cause to be demanded. Another name of the writ of exigent. See EXIGENT.

Exile. Banishment; one driven from his country. A species of waste committed by manumitting or ejecting tenants, or so excessive in itself as to have the effect of driving them away.

Exile, voluntary. The voluntary leaving of one's country; one who voluntarily leaves his country.

Exilium. Same as EXILE.

Ex-interest. Without interest.

Ex-ire. To issue, as a writ.

Existens. Being, remaining.

Existimatio. In Civil law, a citizen's reputation as such. The award of an arbitrator.

Existimo. To judge, consider, suppose, think, esteem.

Exist. To be. To have actual existence. To be in force.

Exit. Issued. It goes forth. It has been issued. Issuance, as of a writ.

Exitus. Issue of offspring; a child or children. Issues; the rents or profits of land. An issue in pleading. A custom on goods imported.

Exitus termini. The end of a term.

Ex-legalitas. Outlawry. One who is prosecuted as an outlaw.

Ex-legare. To outlaw.

Ex-lex. Beyond the law, bound by no law, lawless. An outlaw.

Ex-officio oath. See OATH, EX-OF-FICIO.

Exoine. In French law, the written reason why one fails to appear after summons.

Ex-onerare. To free from a burden; to disburden, unload, discharge.

Exoneration. In Scotch law, a discharge, or a deed, by which a person is disburdened. The act of relieving one of a charge or burden.

Exoneratione sectæ. A writ to exempt the King's ward from a suit at court. See SUIT OF COURT.

Exoneratione sectæ ad curiam baron. A writ allowed the guardian of the King's ward to prevent the ward being distrained for not doing suit in court; also allowed tenants in ancient demesne; also parsons. See SUIT OF COURT.

Exoneretur. Let him be discharged. An entry made upon a bail-piece, where the bail are discharged either by the surrender of their principal, or for other cause.

Exordium. The opening part of an oration or speech.

Exp. Exparte.

Expansion. The act of increasing in amount, size, jurisdiction, or authority.

Expansionist. One who advocates expansion. One who advocates the increase n the extent of a nation's territory.

Exparte. See EX PARTE.

Expatriation. The renouncing or abjuration of one's native allegiance; the voluntary act of removing, forsaking one's native country and becoming the citizen or subject of another.

Expectancy. A right to something in the future.

Expectant. Having relation to or dependent upon.

Expectant fee. See FEE, EXPECTANT.

Expectant heir. See HEIR, EXPECT-ANT.

Expectation of life. The length one may be expected to live.

Expede. In Scotch law, to expedite.

Expeditare. Same as EXPEDITATE.

Expediment. The whole of a person's goods or chattels.

Expeditatæ arbores. Trees uprooted or cut down to the roots.

Expeditate. To cut off the ball and claws of dogs' fore-feet to prevent them running game in the forest; otherwise called lawing of dogs.

Expeditation. The act of expeditating. See EXPEDITATE.

Expeditio. An expedition.

Expeditio brevis. The service of a writ.

Expenditores. Persons in England who disbursed the money collected for the repairs of sewers. The steward who supervised the repairs of the banks and water courses in Romney Marsh, England.

Expenditure. Payment of money.

Expensæ litis. Costs of suit allowed plaintiff or defendant.

Expense. The laying out of money for a required purpose.

Expenses. Money laid out for a required purpose.

Expensis militum non levandis. A writ to prohibit the sheriff levying upon tenants in ancient demesne for knights of the shire.

Experimenta. A trial, proof, experiment.

Experimentum crucis. The experiment of the cross (eliciting truth by torture).

Expers criminis. Not guilty.

Expert. Tried, proven, known by experience. A person having skill, experience in certain professions, or peculiar knowledge on certain subjects; a skilled laborer, artisan or artist.

Expilare. In Civil law, to rob.

Expilatio. In Civil law, the act of wrongfully appropriating goods belonging to a succession.

Expilation. Robbery; waste.

Expilator. In Civil law, a robber.

Expiration. Coming to an end; termination.

Expiry of the legal. In Scotch law, the termination of the term within which a thing may be redeemed which has been taken by judgment.

Explecia. Esplees ; the rents a n d profits of land. (So called, because the estate is made complete and perfect by reaping the explees, i. e. the fruit, profit and commodity thereof).

Explees. The rents or profits of an estate. Same as ESPLEES.

Expleta. Rents and profits of an estate. See EXPLECIA.

Expletia. Same as EXPLECIA.

Explicatio. In Civil law, same as the surrejoinder in Common law pleading.

Expose. To exhibit. To show.

Expositio. Interpretation.

Explorator. A scout; a huntsman.

Explosion. Rapid combustion and a sudden breaking apart.

Expoliatores. Robbers.

Export. To send away from a country.

Exportation. Banishment, deportation The shipping of native commodities out of one country to another.

Exports. Things sent from one country to another.

Expose. To publicly exhibit. A document giving reasons for an act. To place in an unprotected situation.

Expositio. Interpretation. Explanation.

Expositio contentiosa. A disputatious, obstinate exposition or interpretation.

Exposition. An explanation or interpretation; a public exhibition; a commentary; an analysis; that part of a dramatic composition which unfolds the plot.

Exposition de part. In French law, the abandonment of a helpless child.

Ex post facto. From or by an after act. See LAW, EX POST FACTO.

Exposure, indecent. See INDECENT EXPOSURE.

Exposure of person. An intentional exposure of the private parts.

Express abrogation. See ABROGATION, EXPRESS.

Express. To set forth. To tell. To send by an express company. Set forth in unmistakable terms. Not left to inference.

Express admission. See ADMISSION, EXPRESS.

Express affirmance. See AFFIRMANCE, EXPRESS.

Express appeal. See APPEAL, EXPRESS.

Express assent. See ASSENT, EXPRESS.

Express assumpsit. See ASSUMPSIT, EXPRESS.

Express authority. See AUTHORITY, EXPRESS.

Express color. See COLOR, EXPRESS.

Express Company. A corporation engaged in the business of transporting money and packages for hire.

Express consent. See CONSENT, EX PRESS.

Express consideration. See CONSIDERATION, EXPRESS.

Express malice. See MALICE, EXPRESS.

Express promise. See PROMISE, EXPRESS.

Expressage. The charge for carrying anything by express. The things carried by express.

Expressio. Expression. Definitely set forth.

Expressio falsi. A false statement.

Expromissio. In Civil law, the act by which a new debtor assumes the obligations of a former one, who is thereby released.

Expromissor. In Civil law, one who becomes obligated for the debt of another, thereby releasing him.

Expropriate. To surrender claim to. To take from the private owner for public use. To exclude from rights, privileges or property.

Expropriation. The act or result of expropriating. The exclusion of the small owner or wage earner from the ownership of land and other property through their centralization in the hands of monopolists.

Expulsion. The act of depriving of privileges in a society, community, or corporation.

Expunge. To erase, efface, or destroy.

Exsilium. Same as EXILE (which see).

Ex-solvo. To discharge, pay a debt or obligation.

Extend. To extend. To appraise at a yearly value lands or tenements of one who has forfeited a recognizance. To seize under a writ of extent. See EXTENDI FACIAS.

Extended. See EXTEND.

Extendere. To appraise or value; to extend to the full value.

Extendi facias. You cause to be extended (appraised) to the full value. The name of an execution, commonly called an extent, to value lands or tenements to the utmost extent where one has forfeited a bond, and the debtor is to take the lands and satisfy his debt out of the yearly rent. The estimate of the value of lands and tenements by the inquest on a writ Extendi Facias.

Extensio. An extent. See EXTENDI FACIAS.

Extension. The continuance of that which exists.

Extensores. Extenders or appraisers. The name applied to certain officers appointed to appraise and divide or apportion lands.

Extent. An execution upon debts due the crown or upon recognizance executed before a statute merchant or staple. In Scotch law, the value of lands; also the rents and profits. See EXTENDI FACIAS.

Extent in aid. A writ against one indebted to a crown debtor.

Extent in chief. One issued at suit of the crown.

Extent, writ of. Same as EXTENDI FACIAS.

Extenta. An extent (which see).

Extenta manerii. The extent or survey of the manor.

Extentio. An extending, surveying or laying out of lands.

Extenuation. The act of representing less deserving of blame than the facts indicate.

Exterus. A foreigner or alien; one born abroad.

Extentionis. Same as EXTENTIO.

Exterritoriality. The right of exemption from the laws of a country within which one is temporarily residing.

Extinct. Destroyed. Extinguished.

Extinguish. To cause to end. To satisfy. To destroy.

Extinguishment. Extinction of a less estate in a greater. Consolidation of one right with another. The payment of a debt. The destruction of a right.

Extinguishment of a debt. Satisfaction of a debt. Destroying a debt.

Extinguishment of common. See COMMON, EXTINGUISHMENT OF.

Extinguishment of copyhold. The uniting of a freehold with a copyhold interest.

Extinguishment of rent. Destroying rent by the person paying the same getting title to the land.

Extinguishment of ways. Destroying a right of way by purchase.

Extirpamentum. Same as ESTREPEMENT.

Extirpatione. A judicial writ against one who maliciously injured any thing on lands, after a judgment against him for them.

Extirpationes. Possessions of lands.

Extocare. To grub lands and make cultivatable.

Extorsively. A word used in indictments for extortion; as extorsively taking.

Extorted promise. A promise that is made involuntarily without the concurrence of the will.

Extortion. Illegal exaction; oppression under color of right. A taking of more than is due, by color or pretense of right.

Extortionis. Same as EXTORTION.

Extra. Over and above; without; beyond; out of; except.

Extra judicial. Out of the regular order of judicial procedure, beyond the jurisdiction or limits of judicial authority; out of or beyond the matter to be adjudged.

Extra judicial cautionry. See CAUTIONRY, EXTRA JUDICIAL.

Extra judicial oath. See OATH, EXTRA JUDICIAL.

Extra judicium. Extra judicial; out of court.

Extra jus. Beyond the law.

Extra legem. Out of the law's protection.

Extra quatuor maria. Beyond the four seas (out of the kingdom of England). In the U. S. it signifies out of the State or out of the United States.

Extra regnum. Out of the kingdom.

Extra viam. Out of the road.

Extra-dotal. Not a part of dowry.

Extra-dotal property. See PROPERTY, EXTRA-DOTAL.

Extra-familiatus. Put out of a family.

Extra-hazardous. Unusually risky.

Extra-official. Beyond the authority of the office.

Extra-parochial. Not within the bounds or limits of any parish. Any thing exempt from the duties of a parish.

Extra-territorial. Without the territory. Exempt from territorial jurisdiction. Not subject to the laws where one resides. Pertaining to things beyond the national territory.

Extra-territoriality. The privilege of not being subject to the laws of a foreign country. (Neither sovereigns nor direct representatives of sovereigns are subject to the laws of a nation they enter by express or implied invitation. A warship is included in this principle).

Extra-territorium. Outside of the territorial limits.

Extra-vagantes. The name given to the Constitutions of the Popes posterior to the Clementines; they were said to be outside of the Canon law.

Extract. Excerpt. A quotation. In Scotch law, a certified copy of an instrument writing that is of public record.

Extracta curiæ. The profits from the fees, dues and fines of a court.

Extracta Scaccarii (or **de Scaccario**). Estreats of the Exchequer. Profits arising from amercements.

Extractor of the Court of Session. In Scotland, an officer of the High Court of Justice.

Extracts. Estreats.

Extractum de libris actorum Adjornalis. Extracts from the book of minutes of Adjornal.

Extractum ex Curia Justitiæ Extracts from the minutes of the Court of Justice.

Extradition. Delivery, by one nation or State to another, of fugitives from justice, in pursuance of law or treaty.

Extradition, foreign. The surrender by one country of a fugitive who has fled to it from another country.

Extradition, international. Same as EXTRADITION, FOREIGN.

Extradition, State. The surrender by one State of a fugitive from another.

Extrahere. To estreat.

Extrahura. An estray, a wandering beast.

Extraneous. Not relating to a subject.

Extraneus. A stranger; a person not known; a foreigner. In Roman law, an heir born outside the family of the testator.

Extraordinary. Beyond the ordinary. Unusual. Used for an exceptional purpose.

Extraordinary remedy. See REMEDY, EXTRAORDINARY.

Extraxit. Estreated.

Extreme cruelty. See CRUELTY, EXTREME.

Extremis. Same as IN EXTREMIS.

Extremus. The extreme.

Extrinsic. External; not contained in; from outside sources. In Scotch law, irrelevant.

Extum. Thence; from then.

Extumæ. Relics in churches and tombs.

Ex-tunc. From, then, from thence, from that time, thereafter.

Exuere patriam. To throw off or renounce one's country or native allegiance to expatriate one's self.

Exulare. To banish.

Exuperare. To overcome; to apprehend or take.

Ey. An island. Water; a watery place.

Eyde. Aid.

Eyder. To aid, help.

Eye witness. One who gives evidence as to facts seen by himself.

Eyer. Same as EYRE.

Eyery. A repository for hawks' eggs.

Eygne. Eldest.

Eyott. A little island.

Eyre. A journey. The journey or circuit of the King's justices. The court of the justices itinerant, or justices in eyre.

Eyre, Chapters of the. See CHAPTERS OF THE EYRE.

Eyrer. To go about.

Ez arts. At arts, of arts.

F.

F. The letter branded on felons who took benefit of clergy. Also anciently branded on the ear or face of those guilty of falsity or fighting. See BENEFIT OF CLERGY.

F. F. Fieri facias (which see).

F. J. First judge or justice.

F. O. B. (Free on board). A term frequently inserted in contracts for the sale of goods, meaning that the goods will be placed on the vehicle of transportation free of charge.

Fabric lands. Lands given toward the repair and rebuilding of churches.

Fabricare. To forge or create falsely.

Fabricated evidence. See EVIDENCE, FABRICATED.

Fabricate. Same as FABRICARE.

Fabricated fact. See FACT, FABRICATED.

Fabula. In old European law, a contract. A contract of marriage. A will.

Fac. See FACERE.

Fac simile. An exact copy.

Fac simile probate. See PROBATE, FAC SIMILE.

Face. Appearance. As it is stated. Phase. Aspect. View. Amount stated in an evidence of indebtedness or record.

Facere. To do; to make.

Facere legem. To make law.

Facias. You cause, or cause to be made.

Faciendo. Doing, paying.

Facies. View; appearance.

Facile. In Scotch law, easily persuaded.

Facilities. A term applied to certain notes made payable two years after the war of 1812, which were issued by some of the Connecticut banks. Applied to railroads, means everything necessary for the convenience of passengers and the safety and prompt transportation of freight.

Facility. In Scotch law, easiness to be influenced through mental infirmity.

Facio ut des. I do that you may give. A civil law form of contract by which the one agrees to perform in consideration of a specific sum or a sum to be determined by law.

Facio ut facias. I do that you may do. A civil law form of contract by which one agrees to perform for the other in consideration that other does something for him.

Facit. He does. He acts.

Fact. A thing done; reality. Any act or deed done or event which happens. An event. A true statement. The statement of a thing done or which has happened or which exists.

Fact, after the. See ACCESSARY AFTER THE FACT.

Fact, before the. See ACCESSARY BEFORE THE FACT.

Fact, collateral. One not directly connected with the fact in issue.

Fact, dispositive. Such a fact as originates, transfers, or extinguishes a right.

Fact, divestitive. A fact which brings about the termination of a right.

Fact, fabricated. A false fact so presented that, while false, it has the appearance of truth.

Fact, immaterial. See IMMATERIAL FACT.

Fact, in. Actually. In a matter of fact, as distinguished from In Law.

Fact, infirmative. A fact which tends to weaken or destroy the presumption drawn from evidence of guilt.

Fact, investitive. A fact by which a right is invested or arises in a person.

Fact, investive. Same as FACT, INVESTITIVE.

Fact, material. A fact material to the determination of the issue.

Fact, minor. An incidental, collateral, or subordinate fact.

Fact, physical. One having physical existence, as something which can be seen, felt, or heard, as distinguished from an inference or that conceived by the mind.

Fact, principal. A fact which is the object of inquiry or principal issue in a cause.

Fact, probative. A fact which proves another fact.

Fact, psychological. A fact which can be mentally conceived only.

Fact, relative. A fact incidental to another. A fact relating to another fact.

Fact, simulated. That which is given the appearance of a fact in order to deceive.

Fact, special issue of. See ISSUE OF FACT, SPECIAL.

Fact, translative. A fact which brings about the transfer of a right from one to another.

Fact, ultimate. A fact in issue as distinguished from a fact probative.

Fact, verbal. That which is said about an act as explanatory of it.

Facta. Deeds. Actions.

Facta armorum. Tournaments. Feats of arms.

Facter. Same as FACTOR.

Factio testamenti. In the Civil law, the capacity to make a will.

Factio passiva. The capacity to take by will.

Facto. In fact. Where anything is actually done.

Factor. An agent who buys or sells goods on commission.

Facto armorum regalium. The King's armorer.

Factor, domestic. One who lives in the same country as his principal.

Factor, foreign. One who lives in a foreign country from his principal.

Factorage. Wages, commission, or allowance made a factor.

Factorize. To garnish. In parts of New England, to notify a debtor by judicial writ not to pay a creditor but to pay the money to the petitioner who is that creditor's creditor.

Factorizing process. See PROCESS, FACTORIZING.

Factors' acts. Statutes in England and United States relating to factors and dealings with them.

Factory. A building in which goods are manufactured.

Factory acts. Statutes relating to the employees in factories.

Factory price. See PRICE, FACTORY.

Factum. A thing done. A deed. In old law, a portion. In French law, a brief statement of the issue of a contest, and the ground of a plaintiff's action and the defendant's defense.

Factum probandum. The fact to be proved. The issue to be determined.

Factum probans. A proving fact. One of a series of facts comprising circumstantial evidence.

Factum simplex. A simple deed.

Facultates in plurali. Wealth; means; abilities.

Faculties. The financial resources of a husband estimated by his earnings, income, fixed property and ability to earn, in determining the amount of alimony he should pay.

Faculties, Court of. See COURT OF THE FACULTIES.

Faculty. A license. A privilege granted one to do that which by law he ought not to do. Instructors in an educational institution or one of its departments. In Scotch law, power.

Faculty of advocates. See ADVOCATES, FACULTY OF.

Faderfium. A gift from a woman's father or brother given to her upon marriage.

Fæder-feoh. An ancient term for the portion brought by a wife at her marriage.

Fæstingman. Same as FESTINGMAN.

Fag. A knot in cloth.

Fag end. The end of a piece of cloth, linen or muslin where the weaver worked in the worst part of the material.

Faggot. A badge representing a faggot worn on the sleeve by persons who had abjured heresy.

Faggot vote. In England, the vote of those who have property conveyed to them merely to qualify them to vote.

Faida. In Saxon law, malice or deadly feud. See DEADLY FEUD.

Fail. To neglect to do or accomplish because of circumstances over which one has no control.

Failing circumstances. Circumstances which lead to failure. The condition of one about to fail.

Failing of record. Failure of a person to produce a record he has pleaded.

Faillite. In French law, bankruptcy.

Failure. Becoming bankrupt or failing to succeed in business. Wanting. Deficiency. Defect. Default. Neglect.

Failure of consideration. Absence of consideration.

Failure of evidence. Absence of necessary evidence.

Failure of issue. Lack of an heir who can take an estate.

Failure of issue, definite. Absence of a legal heir at a time or event set by deed or will.

Failure of issue, indefinite. The time when the issue becomes extinct whatever that time may be.

Failure of justice. Defeat of justice.

Failure of record. Failure to produce a record or failure of the record to sustain an allegation.

Failure of title. Absence of title.

Failure of trust. Absence of facts or operation of law necessary to carry the object into effect.

Faint action. Same as ACTION FEIGNED.

Faint pleader. A false or collusory manner of pleading.

Fair. Equal, just, reasonable, equitable. Anciently, a large market for the sale of all articles of necessity. A place for the exhibition of agricultural products, and machinery.

Fair play men. In about 1769, one of a tribunal of three elected by the squatter inhabitants of a tract of land in Pennsylvania lying between Lycoming and Pine Creeks, to decide disputes as to boundaries.

Fair abridgement. In Copyright law, such an abridgement as is not an appropriation of the author's language or arrangement. As to what comes within this term the facts in each case alone can determine.

Fair criticism. Such a criticism as does not indicate a malicious intention to injure the reputation of the author of that criticised. As to whether a criticism is or is not malicious or injurious the facts in each case must determine.

Fair knowledge and skill. A reasonable degree of knowledge or skill.

Fair pleader. Same as BEAU PLEADER (which see).

Fair preponderance. A preponderance apparent on fair consideration of evidence.

Fair sale. A sale made with justice to all parties interested.

Fair value. A reasonable equivalent. That which a thing is reasonably worth.

Faire. To make; to do.

Fairly. Reasonably. Justly.

Fairly merchantable. Medium in quality. Neither good nor bad.

Faisant. Doing.

Fait. A thing done; an act. A deed of writing lawfully executed.

Fait enrolle. A deed of bargain and sale.

Fait juridique. In French law, a juridical fact. One of the elements of an obligation.

Faith. Credit; confidence; trust. Belief. Intent. In Scotch law, an oath; a pledge.

Faith and credit. See FULL FAITH AND CREDIT.

Faith, Articles of. See ARTICLES OF FAITH.

Faith, bad. With fraudulent intent, or wilful ignorance.

Faith, full. See FULL FAITH AND CREDIT.

Faith, good. Legal intent. Without fraudulent intent, or knowledge of fraud.

Faithful. Legal. With diligence. Without unnecessary delay. With h o n e s t y . (Applied to the faithful performance of an act).

Faithfully. According to law.

Faitours. Evil doers. Tramps.

Faker. One who vends wares upon the street. One who represents the spurious as genuine; also called a fakir (which see).

Fakir. A religious beggar among Mohammedans. A faker.

Falang. A jacket.

(23)

Falcare. To mow.

Falcare prata. To cut down grass in meadows reserved for hay.

Falcata. Newly-mown grass.

Falcatio. A mowing.

Falcator. A servile tenant who mowed the lord's grass.

Falcatura. One day's mowing of grass.

Falcatura una. One mowing of the grass.

Falcidia. In Spanish law, the Falcidian portion.

Falcidian law. See LAW, FALCIDIAN.

Falcidian portion. The portion referred to in the Falcidian law, which a testator could not will away. See LAW, FALCIDIAN.

Fald. A sheep-fold.

Fald fee. Same as FALDFEY.

Falda. In Spanish law, the slope of a hill.

Faldæ. Same as FALDAGE.

Faldæ cursus. A sheep-walk.

Faldage. The privilege of setting up a movable sheep-fold in order to manure the land.

Faldagii. Same as FALDAGE.

Faldata. In old English law, a fold of sheep.

Faldfey. A fee paid by customary tenants for the liberty of folding sheep upon their own land.

Faldistor. Same as FALDISTORY.

Faldistory. In Ecclesiastical law, the bishop's seat.

Faldsoca. Same as FALDAGE.

Faldstool. A folding seat.

Faldworth. In old English law, one old enough to be a decennier. A person of age.

Faleræ. The tackle of a cart.

Falesia. A large rock by the seashore.

Falkland. Same as FOLCLAND.

Fall. In Scotch law, to lose. To lose or forfeit a right.

Fall of land. In England, six ells square.

Fall. To merge. To be transmitted. To be assigned.

Fallo. In Spanish law, a final decree in a cause.

Fallonia. Felony.

Fallow. Same as FALLOW LAND.

Fallow-land. Land plowed up some time previous to planting that it may improve.

Falsa. False; deceptive.

Falsa demonstratio. In Civil law, erroneous description of a person or thing.

Falsa moneta. In Civil law, false money.

Falsare. To counterfeit.

Falsarius. A counterfeiter.

False Illegal. Wrongful. Fraudulent. Counterfeit. Not in accordance with fact. Contrary to truth.

False action. A feigned action. Where the words of the writ were false.

False arrest. See ARREST, FALSE.

False claim. In old English Forest law, a claim for more than is due.

False date. See DATE, FALSE.

False form. Where proceedings are not in proper form.

False imprisonment. See IMPRISONMENT, FALSE.

False judgment. One contrary to law. A writ where false judgment was given in an inferior court not of record.

False Latin. A Latin or other word in lieu of one which the law required to convey a certain meaning. (While law proceedings were in Latin, in England, a bad Latin word if significant, would not make void; but if the word were not Latin and was material, it made the indictment, declaration, or fine void.

False news. The spreading of false statements to cause discord between the King and nobility. (It was an offense at Common law and by English statute).

False oath. See OATH, FALSE.

False plea. See PLEA, FALSE.

False pretence. See PRETENCE, FALSE.

False prophecy. The foretelling of things to come which caused or was likely to cause a breach of the peace, punishable at Common law and English statute.

False representation. See REPRESENTATION, FALSE; also MISREPRESENTATION, FALSE.

False return. A false return to a writ of mandamus or other writ to show cause.

False swearing. See SWEARING, FALSE.

False token. A piece of counterfeit money. A false document or sign indicating a fact which does not exist.

False verdict. One contrary to law or the evidence.

False weights and measures. Those which do not agree with the standard established by law.

Falsedad. In Spanish law; falsehood; fraud; deception.

Falsehood. A material statement known to be false by the person who makes it and made to gain some advantage or in answer to a material question which the interrogator had authority to ask. Forgery.

Falsi, crimen. See CRIMEN FALSI.

Falsification. A term applied to an item in a debt which is false in whole or in part. See SURCHARGE.

Falsify. To prove a recovery, verdict, record or other thing false. To disprove (in equity) an item in an account. To interlineate, obliterate, change or otherwise tamper with a document after execution. To represent falsely.

Falsifying a record. Changing a record by interlineations, erasures or otherwise.

Falsifying judgments. Reversing judgments.

Falsing. In Scotch law, making false; forgery.

Falsing of dooms. In Scotch law, the reversal of a decree.

Falso retorno brevium. In old English law, a writ against a sheriff for false return of writs.

Falsonarius. One guilty of forgery or counterfeiting.

Falsum. In Civil law, a counterfeit or any kind of falsification.

Falsus. False; erroneous; deceptive.

Fama. Fame; report; rumor.

Famacide. A slanderer.

Fame. Reputation.

Fame, good. Favorable reputation.

Fame, ill. Bad repute.

Familia. In Roman law, a family. A portion of land sufficient to support one family. A hide. A manse.

Familia erciscunda actio. An action for dividing a way or matter of inheritance.

Familiæ emptor. In Roman law, an imaginary purchaser of an inheritance sold per æs et libram in making a will in accordance with the twelve tables.

Familiæ erciscundæ. In Roman law, an action for partition of an inheritance.

Familian. Slaves.

Familiares regis. Persons of the King's household. Anciently applied to the six clerks of Chancery.

Family. Servants. Those who live in one house under the direction of one. A man, wife, and children. Persons springing from a common ancestor.

Family arrangement. An agreement for the disposal or partition of property in a manner different from that provided by law.

Family Bible. A Bible in which the dates of births, deaths, and marriages are kept.

Family council. The meeting of the relatives of one legally incompetent, to enquire into his affairs.

Family, head of. A father, or in his absence a mother, or in some cases a person of age.

Family meeting. In Louisiana, a meeting of at least five relatives or friends of a minor, called by order of court to advise under oath as to the proper management of his affairs and property.

Family physician. A physician who is the usual attendant on a family in sickness.

Family use. For the ordinary use of a family.

Famosi libelli. Libellous books. Libels.

Famosus. Slanderous. In old English law, that which was injurious to reputation.

Famosus defamator. A libeller.

Famosus libellus. A slanderous book or writing.

Fanal. In French law, a light-house. The lamp in a light-house. A high light on the stern of a ship.

Fanaticism. Intemperate zeal. See FANATICS.

Fanatics. Persons supposing themselves inspired. A general name for dissenters from the Church of England. Those actuated by extravagant zeal.

Fanatio. The fence-months in Forest laws, being fifteen days before and fifteen days after midsummer when female deer fawned.

Fanega. In Spanish law, a measure of land in some parts of Spanish-America, being 6400 square yards.

Fang. The act of seizing or clutching. Prey; spoil. (A thief taken with the fang, is one having the stolen property on his person).

Farandman. A traveller or merchant stranger.

Fardel of land. Fourth part of a yard land. According to some authorities an eighth part.

Fardella. A bundle.

Farding-deal. Fourth part of an acre.

Fare. A voyage or passage by water. Money paid for the transportation of the person. Tax for water. Compensation for water.

Farinagium. Toll of meal or flour.

Farinarium. A mill.

Faristel. Stopping of way.

Farley. Same as FARLEU.

Farleu. Money paid in lieu of a heriot. The best goods payable on the death of a tenant.

Farlingarii. Whoremongers and adulterers.

Farm. A large tract of land used for raising provisions. The rent of lands leased. Provisions. A term of years in lands. A system of renting or selling the right to collect revenues in a district. The district thus let out. The income from farm lands.

Farm bolt. A farm.

Farm, fee. See FEE-FARM.

Farm let. Formerly, words used in a lease to create a term for years. To rent for a share of the crops.

Farm out. To rent. To lease for a portion of the profits.

Farmer. One whose occupation is to work a farm for what it will produce. One who rents the right to collect public revenue.

Farmer-general. In France, a farmer of public revenue before the Revolution of 1789.

Farmstead. A farm.

Farrago libelli. A book on miscellaneous subjects not properly arranged or associated together.

Farrier. One who makes a business of shoeing horses.

Farthing. A coin valued at a fourth part of a Saxon or English penny.

Farthing of gold. An ancient English coin valued at one-fourth of a noble.

Farthing of land. Same as FARDING DEAL.

Farundel of land. Same as FARDING DEAL.

Farvand. Passage by water; voyage.

Faryndon Inn. An old name for Serjeant's Inn, Chancery Lane, England.

Fas. Right. Justice. The Divine law.

Fasiculus. A bundle or package. A group.

Fasius. A faggot of wood.

Fast days. Days of fasting anciently fixed by statute.

Fast estate. See ESTATE, FAST.

Fastermans. Saxon pledges; bondsmen.

Fasti. Lawful.

Fasting-men. Same as FASTERMANS.

Fatua mulier. A whore.

Fatuitas. Idiocy. Without reason.

Fatuity. Idiocy; imbecility.

Fatum. In Civil law, fate. An event that could not be prevented.

Fatuous person. In Scotch law, one without reason.

Fatuum judicium. A foolish judgment.

Fatuus. An idiot.

Faubourg. In Louisiana, a suburban district or part of a city.

Fauces terræ. Headlands enclosing an arm of the sea.

Faucher. To forge.

Fault. An illegal act. A neglect of duty. A defect.

Fault, gross. Lack of such care as a careless man usually takes of his own affairs.

Fault, ordinary. Lack of such care as an ordinary man usually takes of his affairs.

Fault, slight. The lack of the care which very careful people take of their own affairs.

Faults, with all. With slight defects.

Fausenerie. Forgery.

Fausetum. A faucet. A musical pipe. A flute.

Fausse. False; counterfeit.

Fautor. In Spanish law, a supporter. An abettor.

Faux. In French law, a fraudulent alteration or suppression of truth.

Fauxer. Same as FAUCHER.

Favor. Partiality. Preference. A desire to benefit.

Favor, challenge for. See CHALLENGE FOR FAVOR.

Fazenda. Same as HACIENDA.

Feal. Faithful.

Feal and divot. In Scotch law, a right of turbary.

Feal homager. Faithful subject.

Fealtie. Fealty.

Fealty. The oath taken by a tenant to perform obedience and service. That which every tenant owed his lord or which the lords owed the ruler.

Fealty, oath of. The oath taken on the admission of a tenant, except those in frankalmoigne.

Fear. An emotion caused by threatened injury.

Fear, to put in. See TO PUT IN FEAR.

Fearme. Food; a feast. Also means same as FERM.

Feasance. A doing.

Feasance, gratuitous. A voluntary service.

Feasant. Doing or making.

Feasor. Doer; maker.

Feasors del estatute. Makers of the statute.

Feasts. Anciently, anniversary times of feasting and thanksgivings fixed by statute.

Fecial law. See LAW, FECIAL.

Feciales. In Roman law, priests who acted as ambassadors and were charged with conducting relation with other nations or peoples, particularly in making declarations of war and treaties of peace.

Federal. Relating to a compact between independent States. Relating to a government organized by independent sovereignties; as the Federal Government of the U. S.

Federal Anti-Trust Law. See ANTI-TRUST LAW.

Federal Congress. See CONGRESS, FEDERAL.

Federal Government. See GOVERNMENT, FEDERAL.

Federal question. See QUESTION, FEDERAL.

Federalist. A publication circulated in 1787 to 1789, in which was printed the personal opinions of Madison, Jay and Hamilton, upon the proposed Federal Constitution.

Fee. A freehold estate held of a lord on condition of some service. An estate of inheritance in land. An estate granted to a man and his heirs. A recompense given officials or professional men for labor. A gratuity given a servant or other person.

Fee and life rent. In Scotch law, a term used in grants or conveyances to two persons where it was intended that one should have a life estate and the survivor should have the fee; or, life estate to the parent and fee to the heir.

Fee, base. Same as FEE, QUALIFIED.

Fee bill. A statement of the charges for various orders, writs, &c., in a cause.

Fee, conditional. See CONDITIONAL FEE.

Fee, contingent. A reward payable upon an uncertain event or success.

Fee, determinable. Same as FEE, QUALIFIED.

Fee docket. A fee taxable in costs of record.

Fee, expectant. One which depends upon some expected event.

Fee farm. Land held in fee at a rent without services. Land held at a perpetual rent.

Fee farm rent. Rent reserved in grants of fee farms.

Fee, knight's. See KNIGHT'S FEE.

Fee, limited. See LIMITED FEE.

Fee, qualified. One having a qualification which determines the estate when the qualification is at an end, though it may never end.

Fee, quasi. A fee acquired wrongfully.

Fee-simple. An unlimited estate in land. An absolute inheritance.

Fee-simple conditional. An ancient estate where land was granted to a man and a limited class of heirs, changed by the statute de donis into estates tail.

Fee-tail. A fee descendible to a certain class of heirs only, as the heirs of his body.

Fee, toleration. See TOLERATION FEE.

Feed. To supply with that which strengthens or supports.

Fefellit. He has deceived or betrayed.

Fegangi. A thief caught with the stolen goods on his person.

Fehm, Holy. Same a VEHMGERICHT.

Fehmgerichte. Same as VEHMGE-RICHT.

Feigned action. See ACTION, FEIGNED.

Feigned issue. See ISSUE, FEIGNED.

Feigned recovery. Same as RECOVERY, COMMON.

Felagus. A companion bound for the good behavior of others of the same decennary.

Feld. A field. Wild or not cultivated.

Feldgemeinschaft. A community of land.

Fele. Faithful.

Fele homager. Faithful subjects.

Fellow-heir. A co-heir. One who is heir with another to the same inheritance.

Fellow servant. See SERVANT, FELLOW.

Felo. A felon.

Felo de se. A felon of himself. A suicide.

Felon. One who has committed or been convicted of felony.

Felonia. Felony.

Felonice. Feloniously; a technical word in old indictments for felony for which no other word could be used.

Felonious. Showing intent to commit a felony. Done with criminal purpose.

Felonious homicide. See HOMICIDE, FELONIOUS.

Felons escries. Notorious felons.

Felon's goods. The goods of felons and fugitives from justice forfeited to the King.

Feloniously. In a felonious manner. A technical word in indictments for felony equivalent to felonice (which see).

Felony. Anciently, an offense for which the convict forfeited his fee and goods. One having an infamous punishment affixed.

Felony Act. The act of 33 and 34 Victoria, c. 23, which abolishes forfeiture for felony and allows the appointment of an interim curator and administrator of the felon's property.

Felony, compounding a. Agreeing for a consideration not to prosecute one who has committed a felony.

Feme. A woman. A wife.

Feme covert. A woman married. See COVERTURE.

Feme sole. A spinster. A woman not married.

Feme sole trader. A married woman permitted to trade as if unmarried.

Femicide. The killing of a woman. One who kills a woman.

Femme. Same as FEME.

Femme de fait. A wife de facto.

Fenatio. In Forest law, the fawning of deer. The season of fawning.

Fence. An enclosure for land. A receiver of stolen goods. A place where stolen goods are received and kept. In Scotch law, the act of opening a court and warning all persons from disturbing its proceedings.

Fence month. In English Forest laws, the month when female deer fawn, being fifteen days before and fifteen days after midsummer.

Fence, partition. A fence erected on the legal line between the lands of two persons.

Feneration. Adding to money by lending it for interest. Usury.

Fengeld. An ancient tax exacted for repelling enemies.

Fenian. A hero. One of an ancient Irish tribe said to have furnished the military force for the King of Ireland. One of a society organized in New York in 1857 to overthrow England and establish a republic in Ireland.

Fens. Low marshy grounds.

Feod. A fee.

Feod land. Land held as fee or reward.

Feodal. Belonging to a feud or fee.

Feodal actions. See ACTIONS, FEODAL.

Feodal system. Same as FEUDAL SYSTEM.

Feodality. Fealty.

Feodarum. Same as FEUDARUM CONSUETUDINES.

Feodarum consuetudines. The customs of feuds. The style of an ancient work on feudal customs compiled in the twelfth century.

Feodary. An officer of the Court of Wards who was to be present at the finding of office of lands to give evidence as to the value and tenure, to survey and rate lands of a ward after office found, assign dower to widows of the King, and receive rents of ward lands. (Abolished by 12 Car. 2 cap. 24).

Feodatory. The tenant who held his estate by feodal service.

Feodi firmi. Fee farm.

Feodi firmarius. One who leases a fee farm.

Feodum. An estate in fee.

Feodum antiquum. Same as FEUDUM ANTIQUUM.

Feodum laicum. A lay fee.

Feodum militare. A knight's fee.

Feodum nobile. Same as FEUDUM NOBILE.

Feodum novum. Same as FEUDUM NOVUM.

Feodum simplex. A fee simple.

Feodum talliatum. An entailed estate.

Feoff. To give lands to one by delivery of possession.

Feoffamentum. A feoffment.

Feoffare. To enfeoff. To bestow a fee upon.

Feoffator. A feoffor.

Feoffatus. A feoffee.

Feoffavit. He enfeoffed.

Feoffee. One to whom a feoffment is made.

Feoffee to uses. One who is granted an estate for the use or benefit of another.

Feoffment. The conveyance of a fee by livery of seizin. The deed or charter of such conveyance.

Feoffment to uses. A grant to one for the use of another.

Feoffer. The grantor of a feud.

Feoh. A stipend. A fee. A reward.

Feonatio. In Forest law, the fawning season of deer.

Feorman. To feed or yield victuals.

Feorme. Provisions. Rent. A farm. A lease.

Feormfultum. An Anglo-Saxon tax to maintain the King while travelling through the kingdom.

Feræ bestiæ. Wild beasts.

Feræ campestres. Beasts of the chase. (Buck, doe, fox, marten and roe).

Feræ naturæ. Of a wild nature. Animals not usually tamed. See DOMITÆ NATURÆ.

Feræ silvestres. Beasts of forests. (Hart, hind, boar and wolf).

Fercosta. In old Scotch law, a small boat.

Ferdella terræ. A fardel land.

Ferdfare. A call to military service.

Ferdingus. A freeman of a lower class.

Ferdwite. In Saxon law exemption for murder by a soldier. A fine on those who refused to perform military duty.

Feria. In old English law, a week day; a holiday; a fair.

Feriæ. In Roman law, holidays.

Feriæ privatæ. In Roman law, private holidays or those observed by individuals for private reasons.

Feriæ publicæ. In Roman law, public holidays, or those observed by the public generally and which were dies nefasti.

Ferial. Relating to week days or holidays.

Ferial days. Working days. Holidays as distinguished from Sunday.

Ferita. A wound.

Ferling. The fourth of a penny. The fourth of a ward in a borough.

Ferlingata terræ. A fourth part of a yard land.

Ferlingus. A furlong.

Ferm. A house and land leased. A farm. A rent. A lease.

Fermary. A hospital.

Ferme. Same as FERM.

Fermer. A lessee. A farmer. One who holds a right to the profit of anything.

Fermier. In French law, one who has the right to public revenue in any district.

Fermisona. The winter season of killing deer.

Fermor. Same as FERMER.

Fermory. A place where the poor were anciently received and fed.

Fernigo. Ground where fern grew.

Ferramentum. The iron tools or instruments of a mill.

Ferrandus. Iron-grey.

Ferrator. A farrier.

Ferri. In Civil law, to be carried on a person. See PORTARI.

Ferriage. The transportation on a ferry. The price paid for such transportation.

Ferrifodina. An iron mine.

Ferruere. The shoeing of horses.

Ferrum. In old English law, iron.

Ferruminatio. Same as ADFERRUMINATIO.

Ferrura. Iron. A horse shoe.

Ferry. A license or grant to have a boat upon a river for conveying passengers or articles from one shore to the other. The place where the ferryboats land. The boats.

Ferry franchise. A right to transport persons, merchandise, animals, &c., across water and charge toll or fare for the same.

Ferryman. One who enjoys a right to transport persons across water and charge toll for the same.

Ferspeken. To speak suddenly.

Fesaunt. Doing.

Fesour. A doer.

Festa in cappis. Holy days on which the choir wore capes.

Festingman. A surety. A frank-pledge.

Festingpenny. Earnest money given servants when hired.

Festinum remedium. A speedy remedy.

Festnian. To confirm. To fasten.

Festuca. In law of the Franks, a rod or stick used as a pledge of good faith or as a symbol in conveying interest in land.

Festum. A feast.

Festum Stultorum. The feast of fools.

Fet. Done. Made.

Fet assavoir. The appendix to Fleta. See FLETA.

Fetiales. See COLLEGIUM FECIALUM.

Fetters. Irons placed on a prisoner's hands or feet to prevent his doing injury or escaping.

Feu. A hearth; a fireplace. A fee. Land held by an agricultural service, or rent in grain or money. To rent in feu. In Scotch law, a tenure where grain or money are paid in lieu of military service.

Feu annuales. In Scotch law, the annual payment of one holding by feu.

Feu duty. The annual compensation for the use of land.

Feu et lieu. Hearth and home. In old French-Canadian law, actual settlement on land by a tenant.

Feu holding. In Scotch law, a tenure in which grain or money is paid in lieu of military service.

Feuage. A tax on chimneys and fireplaces.

Feuar. One holding lands in feu.

Feud. Same as FEOD.

Feud, deadly. See DEADLY FEUD.

Feud, improper. See IMPROPER FEUD.

Feuda. Feuds or fees.

Feudal. Having the quality of a feud. See FEODAL. Held of another. See ALLODIAL.

Feudal law. See LAW, FEUDAL.

Feudal possession. Seisin.

Feudal system. The system of fiefs. A system originated in Europe in about the eighth century by the peoples who over-turned the Romans, and introduced in England by William the Conqueror. The underlying principle was that all lands were held either mediately or immediately of the King. Originally these lands were granted to retainers at will ; then for years, and for life, and finally forever ; subject, however to certain or uncertain services and burdens.

Feudal tenures. The tenures by which land was held under the feudal system. See TENURE.

Feudalism. The feudal system.

Feudalize. To conform to feudalism.

Feudary. One who held land by a feudal tenure. An officer of the English Court of Wards.

Feudataries. Those to whom the King granted fiefs. See FEUDATORY.

Feudatary. One to whom the King granted a fief. Same as FEUDATORY.

Feudatory. The grantee of land under the feudal system. A tenant.

Feudbote. A compensation for engaging in a deadly feud.

Feude. Hostility or conflict between persons or families in revenge for injuries.

Feudis antiquis. By fees of ancestry.

Feudist. One subject to feudal law. One learned in Feudal law.

Feudo. In Spanish law, feud or fee.

Feudorum Libri. The Book of Feuds, published about the year 1152.

Feuds, Honourary. See HONOURARY FEUDS.

Feuds, proper. Feuds which were held by military service alone.

Feudum. A fee, feod, feud, fief. Land granted to be held as a benefice.

Feudum antiquum. A feud which descended to a vassal from an ancestor. One which had been in the family for generations.

Feudum apertum. An open fee. A fee upon which the lord might enter and take for failure of issue or wrong on the part of the tenant.

Feudum avitum. A fee derived from the grandfather.

Feudum de camera. A fee or fief from the chamber or coffer. A pecuniary stipend as aid to a vassal by his lord.

Feudum de cavena. Ancient feasts given by the King to his companions.

Feudum de soldatæ. A gratuitous pension or reward.

Feudum francum. A free feud or one free from the tallaige or other subsidies of the vulgar feud.

Feudum gastaldiæ. A salary for acting as agent and transacting the King's business.

Feudum Gerardiæ. A sum paid out of the King's exchequer for the defense of a castle.

Feudum habitationis. L i b e r t y of dwelling in a house belonging to the lord.

Feudum hauberticum. A fee held on military service of appearing armed when summoned.

Feudum improprium. A fee of later origin than the original military fee. A derivative fee.

Feudum individuum. A fee which could descend only to the eldest son.

Feudum laicum. A lay fee, not held by spiritual service.

Feudum ligium. A liege fee held directly of the King.

Feudum maternum. A fee descended from the mother.

Feudum mercedis. A fee to a lawyer for being an advocate or defender of the lord.

Feudum militare. A military fee.

Feudum militis. A knight's fee.

Feudum nobile. A fee in return for which the tenant did guard and owed fealty and homage.

Feudum novum. A new fee; one acquired by the man himself.

Feudum novum ut antiquum. A new fee held with the incidents and qualifications of an old one.

Feudum paternum. A fee which paternal ancestors had held for four generations. A fee which could only descend to heirs on paternal side; one which could be held by males only.

Feudum proprium. A proper fief; an original, purely military fee.

Feudum simplex. Fee-simple.

Feudum talliatum. Fee-tail.

Fey. Faith; a deed.

Feyn. A fine.

Feyre. A fair.

Fi. fa. Fieri Facias (which see).

Fiancer. To pledge one's faith.

Fianza. In Spanish law, a surety or guarantor. The obligation of a surety.

Fiar. The proprietor; the owner of the fee. In Scotch law, one whose property is charged with a life rent.

Fiar price. The price of grain fixed in different counties of Scotland by the sheriff and jury. This is the price when no other is agreed upon.

Fiat. Let it be done. An order or warrant of a magistrate or judge directing the doing of some act. An authority to do an act.

Fiat justitia. Let justice be done. Words written by the King in granting a writ of error on petition for the same.

Fiaunt. Warrant. An order. A command.

Fictio. A fiction. In Roman law, a fiction of law.

Fictio juris. A fiction of law (which see).

Fiction. That which is pretended. The acceptance as true of that which is in reality false or has no existence. Done for a just purpose, as that which is not done legally is not done.

Fiction of law. A legal assumption that something is true, which may in fact be false.

Fictitious action. See ACTION, FICTITIOUS.

Fictitious party. See PARTY, FICTITIOUS.

Fictitious person. See PERSON, FICTITIOUS.

Fidei-commissa. In Civil law, trusts.

Fidei commissarius. In Civil law, a trustee; a factor.

Fidei-commissum. In Civil law, a trust.

Fide-jubere. In Civil law, to order upon one's own credit. To pledge one's self; to become surety for another.

Fide-jussio. Being surety.

Fide-jussor. In Roman law, a surety whose heirs were bound. In Admiralty law, a bail.

Fidelis. Faithful. Trustworthy.

Fidelitas. Fidelity; fealty.

Fidem mentiri. When a tenant does not keep the fealty he has sworn.

Fidepromissor. In Roman law, a surety who could not bind himself nor his heirs by the word spondeo, because not a Roman citizen.

Fides. Good faith.

Fides nuptialis contractus. A promise (or obligation) of a marriage contract.

Fiducia. In Roman law, an agreement to restore property transferred to one.

Fiducial. In the nature of a trust.

Fiduciarius tutor. In Roman law, the elder brother of one emancipated, but whose father had died before he was fourteen years of age.

Fiduciary. Relating to a trust.

Fiduciary contract. See CONTRACT, FIDUCIARY.

Fief. A fee; a manor; a possession held of a superior.

Fief de haubert. Same as HAWBERK.

Fief d'haubert. A fee held by knight service.

Fiefs. Fees granted by the King. See ARRIERE FIEFS.

Fief-tenant. The holder of a fief.

Fiel. In Spanish law, one in whose hands a thing is deposited by authority or pending a controversy over the ownership. A receiver.

Field. A tract of land either cultivated or used as pasture for stock.

Field ale. An ancient custom of bailiffs drinking in the field.

Field codes. See CODES, FIELD.

Fieldad. In Spanish law, sequestration.

Fierding Courts. See COURTS, FERDING.

Fieri. To be made. To be done.

Fieri facias. (Abbreviated fi. fa.) That you cause to be made. A writ of execution for the seizure and appropriation of property of a defendant to satisfy the amount of a claim.

Fieri facias de bonis ecclesiasticis. A writ directed to the bishop where the defendant was a beneficed clerk commanding him to satisfy the sum mentioned from the goods of the defendant within his diocese. It was issued only after a sheriff had returned nulla bona to a fieri facias.

Fieri facias de bonis testatoris. A writ on a judgment against an executor when sued for what was due by the testator.

Fieri facias de bonis propriis. A writ for the seizure of the goods of an executor, where devastavit has prevented satisfaction of a judgment from goods of the testator.

Fieri feci. I have caused to be made or levied. The return of a sheriff to a fi. fa., that he has satisfied the judgment.

Fifteenth Amendment. The fifteenth amendment to the U. S. Constitution.

Fifteenths. An ancient tax or aid imposed on cities and towns in England of one-fifteenth of their assessed personal property.

Fitewite. A fine for fighting or disturbing the peace.

Filace. A file.

Filacers. Officers in the Common Pleas and other Superior Courts who filed and issued writs.

Filare. To file.

Filazers. Same as FILACERS.

Filctale. Anciently, an entertainment given by bailiffs of hundreds at which they extorted money from their guests.

File. A string or wire upon which writs were strung for safe keeping and reference. To present to court in the regular way. To leave a paper with an office for record and safe keeping. To endorse a paper as so received and put in its proper place. A record of a court.

File, on. In the custody of the proper officer.

Fileinjaid. An ancient term for villein in Brittany.

Files. Legal papers kept in the custody of an official charged with that duty.

Filial. Relating to a son or daughter.

Filial emancipation. Reaching the age of majority or freedom from parental authority.

Filiate. To determine who is the father of a bastard.

Filiation. In Civil law, the relation of a son to his father. The adjudging a bastard to be the child of some man.

Filiation, order of. See ORDER OF FILIATION.

Filicetum. In old English law, a place where ferns grow.

Filii nobilium. Noblemen's sons.

Filing. In U. S. Public Land law, a declaratory statement filed with the Register of the Land Office. See DECLARATORY STATEMENT.

Filious. A godson.

Filius. A son. A child.

Filius familias. In Civil law, the son of a family. A son not emancipated.

Filius mulieratus. A mulier; a lawful son. The first son of a married woman who had previously had a bastard by the same man before marriage.

Filius nullius. (The child of nobody). A bastard.

Filius populi. A son of the people; a natural child. A bastard.

Filizers. Same as FILACERS.

Filicetum. A ferny ground.

Filiolus. A godson.

Filkdale. Same as FIELD ALE.

Fill. To so occupy that no space remains. To hold, as an office. To put up in package or mix or compound, as a prescription. To comply with the terms of.

Fils. A son.

Filum. A thread.

Filum aquæ. The thread of the water. The water line or edge. The middle line of a stream.

Filum forestæ. The line or boundary of the forest.

Filum viæ. The middle line of a street.

Fin. End. Limit. The time of limit.

Fin de non recevoir. In French law, a plea contending that the plaintiff's action is not well brought because the right, though once subsisting has been destroyed by lapse of time or some other cause.

Final. Complete. Finishing.

Final balance. See BALANCE, FINAL.

Final concords. Same as CONCORDS.

Final costs. Same as COSTS.

Final decision. One from which there is no appeal or for which no writ of error will lie.

Final decree. A decree which puts an end to the action by declaring that the plaintiff is or is not entitled to recover. A decree which determines the particular case.

Final disposition. A disposition which leaves nothing further to be done. In an award a disposition that leaves no matter undetermined.

Final hearing. See HEARING, FINAL.

Final judgment. The determination by a court of the issue before it in an action at law.

Final passage. The passage of a bill before a legislative body after all the preliminaries have been carried out.

Final process. See PROCESS, FINAL.

Final proof. Proof made by one taking up land under Public Land laws of the United States, that the law has been complied with and the applicant is qualified.

Final recovery. The final determination of a cause by a court. The verdict in a cause as distinguished from the judgment.

Final sentence. A sentence which determines the issue as distinguished from an interlocutory sentence.

Final settlement. See SETTLEMENT, FINAL.

Finalis concordia. A final concord. A fine of lands.

Finances. Funds on hand. Pecuniary resources. Revenue.

Financier. Originally one who received or farmed revenue. To manage or conduct financial matters. One skilled in financial affairs or operations.

Find. To discover. To obtain lawfully that which has no known owner. To determine. To terminate.

Finders. Anciently searchers or persons employed to see what if any goods were smuggled.

Finding. The verdict of a jury. The decision of an arbitrator, referee, or judge.

Finding against evidence. A finding not warranted by the evidence.

Finding, general. A verdict or decision in general terms upon all the issues.

Finding, special. A finding upon a particular fact or issue.

Fine. Money paid as punishment. To adjudge it to be paid. A price for a privilege. A feoffment of record. A final agreement between landlord and tenant or vassal and lord, concerning tenure and rent of lands. A fee paid by the tenant to the lord in addition to the rent.

Fine, abstract of. See FINE, FOOT OF; also FINE, NOTE OF.

Fine and recovery act. Statute 3 and 4 Wm. IV. c, 74, abolishing fines and recovering.

Fine annullando levato de tenemento quod fuit de antiquo dominico. A writ for disallowing a fine of lands in ancient demesne to prejudice the lord.

Fine capiendo pro terris. A writ to remit an imprisonment and have lands and goods returned to one convicted of a crime, imprisoned, and whose lands were forfeited.

Fine, common. A small sum of money which was anciently paid to the lord toward the support of the Court Leet. See CERT MONEY.

Fine, concord of a. In a fine of lands an acknowledgement made by the cognizor that the lands were the property of the cognizee.

Fine, executed. A feoffment of record. A fine of land upon the acknowledgment which the cognizee has by gifts.

Fine, executory. A fine of lands upon acknowledgment of right only. Also a fine by acknowledgment of a grant de novo, but of no precedent right. Also a fine upon gift, grant and render.

Fine, foot of. An abstract containing the whole matter of a fine of lands engrossed and delivered to the cognizor and cognizee.

Fine for alienation. A price paid by a tenant in chivalry for permission to alien his lands.

Fine for endowment. An ancient fine payable by a widow to the lord, without paying which, she could not receive her dower.

Fine force.   Absolute necessity.

Fine, freedom.   See FREEDOM FINE.

Fine non capiendo pro pulchre placitando.   A writ to inhibit officers of courts from taking fines for fair pleading.

Fine, note of.   An abstract of the writ of covenant and concord in a fine of lands.

Fine of lands.   A conveyance of lands by acknowledgment of record.   An old proceeding by which one, termed the cognizee, sued out a præcipe on an alleged covenant made by the one holding the land, called the cognizor, to convey the land to him, the cognizee.   On the court granting a leave to agree, an acknowledgement was made by the cognizor in open court, or before commissioners, that the land was the property of the cognizee.   The record constituted a conveyance and barred an estate tail by excluding the issue.

Fine of lands, double.   Where something is granted back to the cognizor.   Also where the land is situated in two or more counties.

Fine, post.   Three-twentieths the annual value of land due the King on the granting of a licentia concordia in a fine of lands.

Fine, primer.   One-tenth the annual value of land due the King on suing out a writ of præcipe in a fine of lands.

Fine pro redisseisina capienda.   A writ for the release on payment of a fine of one imprisoned for redisseisin.

Fine roll.   In old English law, a roll containing the list of the fines due the King.

Fine, single.   A simple and single conveyance of land by fine.

Fine sur cognizance de droit come ceo que il a de son done.   A fine upon acknowledgment of the right of the cognizee as that which he hath of the gift of the cognizor.   In a fine of lands the acknowledgment in court by the deforciant that he has previously made a gift or feoffment to the plaintiff.

Fine sur cognizance de droit tantum.   A fine of lands upon acknowledgment of right merely and not that a gift had been made.   It was used to pass a reversion.

Fine sur concessit.   A fine upon concessit.   A fine of lands in which the cognizor without acknowledging a previous right granted an estate de novo to determine the dispute.

Fine sur done grant et render.   A double fine of land in which the cognizee granted back to the cognizor or another some other estate in the land.

Finem facere.   Same as FINIRE.

Fineness.   The quality of a coin as regards the quantity of pure metal which it contains; as distinguished from the alloy.

Fines le roy.   The King's fines or fines payable to the King for various offenses.

Fines to the King.   Money paid for original writs.

Finire.   To fine; to pay a fine on composition.

Finis.   An end; a limit; a fine.

Finitio.   Death.

Finium regendorum actio.   In Civil law, action for regulating boundaries.

Finors.   Those who separated gold and silver from the ore.

Firdfare.   A going forth to military service.

Firdiringa.   Preparation to go into military service.

Firdsocne.   Exemption from military duty.

Firdwite.   A fine paid for refusing to do military service; a fine in lieu of military service.

Fire.   The evolution of heat and light by combustion.   To set on fire.   To excite. To discharge a firearm or cannon.

Fire and sword, Letters of.   See LETTERS OF FIRE AND SWORD.

Fire escape. A contrivance or apparatus on a building to enable the occupants to escape without injury in a case of fire.

Fire insurance. See INSURANCE, FIRE.

Fire ordeal. See ORDEAL, FIRE.

Fire policy. See POLICY, FIRE.

Fire proof. Proof against fire. Composed of incombustible material. Composed of material usually used in fire proof buildings, vaults, &c.

Firearm. A contrivance which can be carried on the person from which a deadly missile is thrown by some explosive.

Firebare. A light-house.

Firebote. An allowance of wood for a tenant's fire.

Fireworks. Any device of paper or pasteboard containing explosives which make a noise or produce colored lights.

Firkin. A capacity of nine gallons or 56 pounds avoirdupois.

Firlot. A Scotch measure of two gallons and a pint.

Firm. The persons composing a partnership. The name under which a partnership carries on its business.

Firm name. The name under which the business of partners is transacted.

Firma. Victuals, provisions, rent, farm.

Firma alba. White rent.

Firma feodi. A fee farm.

Firma noctis. A tribute anciently paid to entertain the King one night.

Firmam Regis. An ancient tribute toward the King's country place.

Firman. An oriental term for a passport or grant of privileges.

Firmaratio. The right of a tenant to his lands.

Firmarium. An infirmary.

Firmarius. A farmer. A fermor.

Fermarius, vel proprietarius. The farmer or proprietor.

Firmatio. Doe season. Supplying with food.

Firme. A farm.

Firmitas. An assurance of some privilege by deed or charter.

Firmura. Liberty to scour and repair a mill dam and carry away the soil.

First. That which precedes all others.

First class. The best of its kind.

First fruits. The first year's profits of a spiritual living, due anciently to the Pope.

First impression, a case of. One raising a new point of law.

First purchaser. See PURCHASER, FIRST.

Firthe. Same as FRITH.

Fisc. The treasury of a prince or State.

Fiscal. Of or pertaining to the treasury or public finances. A financial secretary or minister. In Spain and Portugal, the Attorney-General. In Scotland, a public prosecutor. State or royal revenue.

Fiscal action of a government. The act of levying and collecting taxes and disbursing the same.

Fiscal agent. See AGENT, FISCAL.

Fiscal judge. See JUDGE, FISCAL.

Fiscal lands. See LANDS, FISCAL.

Fiscal year. See YEAR, FISCAL.

Fiscalia. Moneys for the treasury.

Fiscalinus. Same as HOMO FOSCALIS.

Fiscalis. Of or relating to the public treasury.

Fiscus. A money basket or purse. The wreath of the Emperor. See ÆRARIUM.

Fish. To catch or try to catch fish. An animal habitually living in the water.

Fish, broad. To fish beyond the three-mile limits within which fishing by foreign vessels is prohibited by the treaty of 1818 between the U. S. and Great Britain. See FISHERY OFF-SHORE.

Fish Commissioner. An officer of the U. S. Government, whose duty is to preserve and increase food fishes throughout the United States. Some States have similar officials.

Fish laws. Laws regulating the catching of fish.

Fish, royal. Whale, porpoise and sturgeon.

Fisheries Commission. A commission appointed by virtue of a treaty with Great Britain in 1871 relating to the right of fishing on the Atlantic coast.

Fishery. A place where fish were usually sought and caught. A privilege of catching fish.

Fishery, coast. Within the three-mile limit. See FISH, BROAD.

Fishery, common. The right of fishing in public waters. See FISHERY, COMMON OF.

Fishery, common of. The privilege of fishing in another's waters.

Fishery, free. An exclusive right to fish in public waters.

Fishery laws. See LAWS, FISHERY.

Fishery, off-shore. Outside the three-mile limit. See FISH, BROAD.

Fishery, in-shore. Within the three-mile limit. See FISHERY, COAST.

Fishery, separate. Same as FISHERY, SEVERAL.

Fishery, several. The exclusive right of fishing which belongs to or is obtained from the owner of the soil.

Fishes, food. Fish usually eaten as food.

Fishgarth. A dam or weir in a river for taking fish.

Fishing bill. See BILL, FISHING.

Fishing-banks. A place of shoal water in the sea used as a fishing ground.

Fisk. In Scotch law, the right of the crown to the movable estate of a rebel. The revenue of the crown.

Fistuca. A staff. A rod by which livery of seizin was made in conveyance by feoffment.

Fistula. In Civil law, a pipe for conveying water.

Fit. In proper condition or shape. Suitable.

Fitz. A son.

Fitzherbert. A law writer, author of a grand abridgement of the Year Books and of the new Natura Brevium (F. N. B.), a treatise on writs existing during the reign of Henry VIII.

Five-Mile Act. An English statute of 1665, 17 Chas. II., c. 2, prohibiting the non-conformist ministers from coming within five miles of a place where they had preached since the Act of Oblivion of 1660.

Fix. To prescribe; to determine; to settle; to adjust. To render certain. To show one to be liable. To transform a possible into a definite liability. To corruptly procure the verdict of, as to "fix a jury."

Fixing bail. See BAIL, FIXING.

Fixture. A chattel so fastened to the land or building as to become in law a part of it.

Flaco. A place covered with standing water.

Flag. An emblem of nationality.

Flag, duty of the. The one time duty required by England of foreign vessels, of striking the flag and lowering the topsail on meeting a British ship in British waters.

Flag, law of the. See LAW OF THE FLAG.

Flagellat. In old Scotch law, whipped.

Flagrans. Flaming up. In the act.

Flagrans crimen. A crime being committed.

Flagrant necessity. A necessity which makes lawful what would otherwise be an unlawful act.

Flagrante bello. During actual war.

Flagrante crimine. A crime in its heat—while being committed.

Flagrante delicto. In the very act. Same as FLAGRANTE DELIT.

Flagrante delit. In French law, a crime which has been or is being committed. In the very act.

Flat. A flat place in a stream or arm of the sea, at times covered with water. A flat place on a mountain top. A series of rooms on one floor arranged for housekeeping.

Flavianum jus. In Roman law, the style of a book published by Cneius Flavius containing the forms of actions.

Flecta. A fleet, or feathered arrow.

Fledwit. A fine paid by an outlaw for pardon. A discharge from amercement when an outlaw delivered himself up of his own accord.

Fleduite. In old English law, an exemption from punishment of an outlaw who delivered himself up. A privilege of determining and fining for beating and striking. A sum required of a fugitive for the King's pardon.

Fledwite. Same as FLEDWIT.

Flee. To run away from.

Flee from justice. To withdraw oneself from the jurisdiction of a court to avoid its process.

"Flee to the wall." To use every means to get away from an assailant before killing him.

Fleet. A London prison. A place of running water where it meets the flow of the tide. A number of ships travelling or anchored near each other.

Fleet books. Records of marriages in Fleet Prison between 1686 and 1754.

Flem. An outlaw; a fugitive.

Flemene frit. Same as FLEMENES FRINTHE.

Flemenes frinthe. Receiving a fugitive or outlaw.

Flemenswite. A fine imposed on an outlaw.

Flemeswite. Same as FLEMENSWITE.

Flet. Same as FLETH.

Fleta. An ancient law book founded on Bracton and supposed to have been written by a lawyer confined in Fleet Prison during reign Edward I. In old English law, an estuary.

(24)

Fleth. Land. A house.

Flichwite. In Saxon law, a fine for engaging in brawls.

Fliedwite. Same as FLEDWIT.

Flighers. Masts for ships.

Flight. The act of withdrawing one's self from the jurisdiction of a court after committing a crime or making one's self liable to process.

Flightwite. Same as FLEDWIT.

Float. A certificate authorizing the occupation of land. A Mexican grant of quantity.

Floatable stream. A stream upon which logs, &c., can be floated.

Floating capital. Capital retained to meet current expenses.

Floating debt. See DEBT, FLOATING.

Floating security. Same as SECURITY, SHIFTING.

Floatsam. Same as FLOTSAM.

Flodemark. Same as FLOOD MARK.

Flogging. Whipping.

Flood. A flowing of water over land not usually overflowed.

Flood mark. High-water mark.

Floor. The horizontal part of the interior of a building upon which persons walk. The place in a hall where members have their seats as distinguished from the gallery and the presiding officer's platform.

Floor of the court. The part where a person stands who appears in court. The part between the first row of counsel and the judge.

Florence. An ancient English gold coin. A fiftieth part of a pound weight of gold each valued at six shillings.

Florentine Pandects. Applied to a copy of the Pandects alleged to have been discovered at Amalphi, in Italy, about 1137 and deposited at Florence.

Florin. A coin about equal in value to two English shillings, originally made at Florence, Italy.

Flota navium. A fleet of ships.

Flotages. Articles which float on rivers by accident. The commissions of water bailiffs.

Flotsam. Goods floating on the water lost from a wreck. See JETSAM AND LIGAN.

Flotsan. Same as FLOTSAM.

Floude marke. Flood mark; high-water mark.

Flowing lands. Damming or obstructing a stream or body of water so the natural drainage is prevented and the lands overflowed with water.

Fluctus. Flood; flood-tide.

Flumen. In Roman law, the right to direct rain water from a roof on to the land of another.

Flumineæ volucres. Wild fowl; water fowl.

Fluvius. A river; a public river. Flood tide.

Fluxus. Flow.

Fly for it. Words formerly used in England in a criminal trial after a verdict of not guilty.

Flying switch. The switching of cars on a railroad while in motion and after the locomotive which gave them the impetus has been uncoupled and passed ahead on the main track.

Flyma. A fugitive from justice.

Flyman-frymth. Same as FLEMENES FRINTHE.

Flymena frynthe. Same as FLEMENES FRINTHE.

Focage. House bote. Fire bote.

Focal. In old English law, firewood or the right of taking it.

Focale. In old English law, firewood.

Fodder. A prerogative of a prince to be provided with food for his men and horses in the time of war or while on expeditions. Food for horses and cattle.

Fodertorium. Provision or fodder to be given to the King's purveyor.

Foderum. Fodder.

Fodina. A mine.

Fœdal. Relating to a feod; of the nature of a feod. Concerning the relation between lord and tenant.

Fœdero. To establish by treaty or league.

Fœdus. Leagued together; allied. A treaty or league.

Fœlnisse. An offence; felony.

Fœmina viro cooperta. A married woman.

Fœneration. Lending money at interest.

Fœnus nauticum. Marine interest. A high rate paid on ship loans.

Fœsa. Grass; herbage.

Fœticide. Destroying a fœtus.

Fœtus. A child in the womb.

Fœtura. In Civil law, the produce of animals and property which enured to the owner thereof.

Fog. Watery vapor suspended near the earth.

Fogage. Same as FOGAGIUM.

Fogagium. A rank grass not eaten in summer.

Foi. In French feudal law, fealty.

Foinesum. In old English law, the fawning of deer.

Foirfault. In old Scotch law, to forfeit.

Foirthocht. In old Scotch law, forethought.

Fois. Time. Times.

Foiterers. Vagabonds.

Folc. The people.

Folcgemote. Same as FOLCMOTE.

Folc-land. Land held without charter or writing. Land of the vulgar (common) people. Terra Vulgi. Copyhold lands.

Folcmote. A County Court. An assembly of the people.

Folc-right. Composition of differences. The Common law.

Foldage. Same as FALDAGE.

Fold-course. Same as FALDAGE.

Fold-soke. In Feudal law, a tenure requiring the tenant to allow his sheep to lie in the lord's fold that the latter might get the manure.

Folgare. To follow or serve.

Folgarii. Menial servants.

Folgere. In old English law, a freeman without dwelling of his own who was the retainer of another, for whom he performed certain services.

Folgeres. Followers or servants. See FOLGERE.

Folgers. Followers or servants. See FOLGERES.

Folgoth. Official dignity.

Folio. A leaf. A page of seventy-two words; in chancery, ninety words; in U. S., one hundred words.

Folk-land. Same as FOLC-LAND.

Folk-moot. Same as FOLK-GEMOTE.

Fondong. Same as FURST.

Fonds perdus. In French law, the repayment of a sum by paying an instalment of it with the interest.

Fonsadera. In Spanish law, a tribute or loan to pay expenses of a war.

Fontana. A fountain. A spring.

Fool. An idiot.

Food. That usually fed man or beast to sustain normal life and health.

Fooretooth. Striking out the foreteeth in mayhem.

Foot. A measure of length of twelve inches. The end; conclusion.

Foot of a fine. See FINE, FOOT OF.

Foot-geld. A fine for not expeditating dogs in a forest. See EXPEDITATE.

For. Out; without. On account of; in behalf of, as agent for. For cause. Because of some legal disability. In French law, a tribunal.

For collection. See COLLECTION, FOR.

For that. Because. Words used in introducing the allegations in a declaration.

For that whereas. Words in a declaration in actions, other than trespass, in introducing the recital of the cause of action, and meaning, for that, in view of the circumstances.

For use. See USE, FOR.

For value. See VALUE, FOR.

For want of novelty. For not being new or original.

For whom it may concern. For all persons who may be interested.

Forage. Hay and straw for horses in an army.

Foragium. Straw when the corn (wheat or barley) is thrashed out.

Foraneus. A foreigner.

Forathe. One who could swear for another. (Saxon).

Forbalca. A strip of unploughed land lying next the highway.

Forbalk. Same as FORBALCA.

Forbannitus. Banished, outlawed.

Forbarre. To bar out.

Forbarrer. Same as FORBARRE.

Forbatudo. In old European law, the one who struck the first blow.

Forbatudus. The aggressor slain in combat.

Forbearance. Refraining from claiming a right.

Force. Unlawful violence.

Force, actual. Where actual violence is used.

Force and arms. Violence.

Force and fear. Duress.

Force, consequential. Same as FORCE, MEDIATE.

Force, compound. Where a crime accompanies it, as entering a house with force and then killing or assaulting its inmates.

Force, direct. A forcible act itself.

Force, immediate. Same as FORCE DIRECT.

Force, implied. That which is implied in law from an act.

Force, irresistible. Force by human agency, such as an army or navy, &c., as distinguished from the force of wind, water, fire or other accident.

Force, majeure. Superior force.

Force, mediate. That which results from or is a consequence of an act of force, but not directly so.

Force of, by. By virtue of.

Force, simple. Force committed without any other crime accompanying it, as entering a house with force.

Force wool. To clip off the hairy part of the sheep's wool.

Forced. Unnatural.

Forced heirs. See HEIRS, FORCED.

Forced sale. See SALE, FORCED.

Forcelet. A fortress.

Forcerium. A strong box to keep deeds, documents, &c., in.

Forces. The military and naval strength of a country.

Forcheapum. Pre-emption; forestalling the market.

Forcible detainer. See DETAINER, FORCIBLE.

Forcible entry. See ENTRY, FORCIBLE.

Forrible entry and detainer. See DETAINER, FORCIBLE ENTRY AND.

Forcible marriage. Marriage against the will of one or both of the parties.

Forcibly. With force. Against the consent.

Forclorrer. To foreclose.

Ford. A shallow place in a river.

Forda. A shallow place in a stream made by damming the water above it. A ford.

Fordal. A piece of land extending into lands of another.

Fordanno. Same as FORBATUDO.

Fordiko. The grass growing on the banks of ditches.

Fordol. A portion of land extending into other boundaries.

Fore. Out. Before. Prior. Former. At or near the forward part.

Forecheapum. Same as FORCHEAPUM.

Foreclose. To bar. To shut out. To destroy the equity of redemption in a mortgage.

Foreclose a mortgage. See MORTGAGE, FORECLOSE A.

Foreclosed. Shut out. Barred the equity of redemption.

Foreclosure. Shutting up; barring out. The proceeding in equity which bars the equity of redemption of a pledgor or mortgagor. Forfeiting the mortgagor's title. The enforcement of a mechanic's lien.

Forefang. A previous taking. The taking of provisions in a market before the King's purveyors were served. Rescuing stolen cattle; the reward for such rescue.

Forefault. In Scotch law, to forfeit; to lose.

Forefeng. Same as FOREFANG.

Foregift. A premium for a lease.

Foregoers. The King's purveyors. Those who went before to provide for the King's household.

Fore-hand rent. That payable in advance.

Foreign. Of another country. Of another State. Of a different jurisdiction.

Foreign administration. See ADMINISTRATION, FOREIGN.

Foreign answer. An answer which could not be tried in the country in which it was made.

Foreign apposer. See FOREIGN OPPOSER.

Foreign assignment. See ASSIGNMENT, FOREIGN.

Foreign attachment. See ATTACHMENT, FOREIGN.

Foreign bill. A bill of exchange drawn or payable in a foreign country.

Foreign charity. A charity established by one who is domiciled in a foreign State or county.

Foreign coins. Coins of a foreign country.

Foreign commerce. See COMMERCE, FOREIGN.

Foreign corporation. See CORPORATION, FOREIGN.

Foreign county. Another county from that then spoken of.

Foreign creditor. One domiciled in another State or county than the debtor.

Foreign decree. The decree of a foreign court.

Foreign divorce. A divorce obtained in another State or country from that in which the marriage was entered into.

Foreign document. A record or paper from, or instrument executed in, a foreign State or county.

Foreign dominion. A possession of a nation acquired from a foreign nation.

Foreign Enlistment Act. Statute 59 Geo. III., c. 69, prohibiting Englishmen enlisting in the service of a foreign country as sailors or soldiers.

Foreign exchange. See EXCHANGE, FOREIGN.

Foreign extradition. See EXTRADITION, FOREIGN.

Foreign factor. See FACTOR, FOREIGN.

Foreign minister. See MINISTER, FOREIGN.

Foreign judgment. The judgment of a foreign court or tribunal.

Foreign jurisdiction. See JURISDICTION, FOREIGN.

Foreign jury. See JURY, FOREIGN.

Foreign laws. See LAWS, FOREIGN.

Foreign matter. A matter under consideration or determined in another county.

Foreign office. See OFFICE, FOREIGN.

Foreign opposer. An English officer in chancery who makes a charge to all sheriffs for the greenwax, fines, issues, recognizances, etc.

Foreign plea. A plea showing some other court in which the matter should be tried.

Foreign port. See PORT, FOREIGN.

Foreign service. Knight service where a mesne lord held of another beyond his own land. Services performed by a tenant to other than his own lord. Serving as a soldier under a foreign government.

Foreign State. See STATE, FOREIGN.

Foreign trade. The trade with foreign countries.

Foreign vessel. See VESSEL, FOREIGN.

Foreign voucher. Where a tenant vouched one living out of the jurisdiction of the court to defend the right against the demandant.

Foreign voyage. See VOYAGE, FOREIGN.

Foreign waters. Waters subject to a foreign jurisdiction.

Foreigner. One not a citizen of the State or country in which he resides or is mentioned.

Foreigner, transient. See TRANSIENT FOREIGNER.

Foreigners. Aliens.

Forejudge. To deprive of something by judgment. To banish. To expel. To judge before hearing the evidence.

Forejudged. See FOREJUDGE.

Forejudger. A judgment depriving one of something. Banishment. Expulsion.

Foreman. The organ and presiding officer of a jury. An overseer; chief man.

Forensic. Belonging to courts of judicature.

Forensis. In Civil law, relating to or connected with a court.

Forensis homo. An advocate before a court.

Forera. Forehand.

Foresaid. In Scotch law, same as aforesaid.

Foreschoke. Forsaken. Lands and tenements seised by a lord for want of services performed by the tenant, and held a year and a day, and not recovered by the tenant.

Foreshore. That part of the shore between low-water mark and the average high-water mark.

Forest. A tract of land belonging to the King reserved for wild beasts and having certain laws and courts of its own. A wooded tract of land.

Forest, Chief Warden of. See CHIEF WARDEN OF THE FOREST.

Forest laws. Laws relating to the government of the forest and covert, vert and venison.

Forest reserve. A tract of land reserved (in U. S.) as a forest to protect and preserve the headwaters of streams.

Forestage. A duty paid to the King's foresters.

Forestagium. Duty payable to the King's foresters.

Forestall. To obstruct a highway. To buy up provisions in order to enhance their price. See FORESTALLING.

Forestallan. Forestalling.

Forestaller. Obstruction or hindrance of any character. One guilty of forestalling the market.

Forestalling. Intercepting the highway. Buying up provisions on the way to market to sell at a higher price. A conspiracy to enhance the value of provisions.

Forestarius. A forester.

Forester, riding. An officer who led the King when hunting.

Foresters. Officials who watched over the forest.

Forethought. See MALICE, AFORETHOUGHT.

Forethought felony. Murder after premeditation and deliberation.

Forever. For all time. Until changed by law.

Forfang. Same as FOREFANG.

Forfeit. To surrender or lose because of some crime, breach of duty, or obligation. The thing thus surrendered or lost. The clause of forfeiture in a contract.

Forfeitable. Admitting of forfeiture.

Forfeitable, non. Not subject to forfeiture.

Forfeiture. A penalty for crime, breach of duty, or obligation. The thing forfeited.

Forfeiture de terre. A forfeiture of land.

Forfeiture of a bond. Failure to perform the conditions on which it was to become null and void.

Forefeiture of marriage. Compelling a ward in chivalry to pay the lord the amount the latter could have received from one who desired to marry the ward. Compelling him to pay double the amount when he refused an equal match and married before majority without the guardian's consent.

Forfeiture of silk. In England, the forfeiture of such silk as was imported and allowed to lie at the docks at a time when its importation was prohibited.

Forfeitures abolition act. In England, the felony act of 1870 abolishing forfeiture for felony.

Forgablum. A quit rent.

Forgavel. A quit rent or rent reserved in money.

Forge. To falsely make or alter a written instrument to another's injury. To imitate another's signature for a fradulent purpose.

Forger. A person guilty of forgery.

Forgery. The making or altering of any written or printed instrument for fraudulent purposes, or to prejudice another's right.

Forherda. In old English law, a headland or foreland.

Fori disputationes. Arguments in the Law Courts.

Forinsecum manerium. That part of a manor which was without the liberty of the town.

Forinsecum servitium. The payment of extraordinary aid. See INTRINSECUM SERVITIUM.

Forinsecus. Outward. External. Outlawed.

Foris. Abroad. Without.

Forisbanitus. Banished.

Forisfacere. To forfeit. To violate law.

Forisfacta, bona. Forfeited goods.

Forisfactum. Forfeited.

Forisfactura. A forfeiture.

Forisfactura plena. A forfeiture of all a man's property. The property forfeited.

Forisfactus. A criminal. One who forfeited life because of crime.

Forisfactus servus. A freedman who forfeited freedom because of crime.

Forisfamiliare. In old English law, the acceptance by a son of part of the father's lands during the latter's lifetime in lieu of what he would have gotten after his father's death.

Forisfamiliated. In old English law, provided for. Given his portion.

Forisfamiliation. See FORISFAMILIARE.

Forisfamiliatus. In old English law, put out of a family. Emancipated.

Forisjudicatio. Forejudgment. Forejudger.

Forisjudicatus. Forejudged. Banished.

Forisjurare. To foreswear. To renounce.

Forisjurare parentilam. To go from under parental authority.

Forisjurare, provinciam. To abjure the country.

Forjurer. Same as FORISJURARE.

Forjurer royalme. To abjure the realm.

Forland. Lands extending further or lying before the rest. A promontory.

Forler-land. Land in the ancient bishopric of Hereford, England, once granted or leased so that the successor might have it for his present revenue.

Form. According to established method.

Form, false. See FALSE FORM.

Form of action. The formula, prescribed method, or model, after which an action was shaped to distinguish it from action of another character.

Forma. Form. The fixed form of judicial proceedings or actions.

Forma essentialis. A substantial form.

Forma et figura judicii. The form and manner of the judgment.

Forma pauperis. See IN FORMA PAUPERIS.

Formal. In accordance with established form. Relating to form as distinguished from substance.

Formaliter. Formally; in form.

Formalities. Settled method or practices. In England, the robes of magistrates.

Formality. In accordance with established form.

Formata. Canonical letters.

Formata brevia. See BREVIA FORMATA.

Formed action. One for which a set form of words is prescribed. See ACTIO NOMINATA.

Formedon. An ancient writ of right for a tenant in tail.

Foremedon in descender. A writ of foremedon when brought by the heir against his ancestor's alienee or disseisor.

Formedon in the remainder. A writ of formedon when brought by a remainder-man.

Formedon in the reverter. A writ of formedon when brought by the donor or his heirs.

Formella. An ancient English weight of seventy pounds.

Former acquittal. See ACQUITTAL, FORMER.

Former adjudication. See ADJUDICATION, FORMER.

Former recovery. Former judgment.

Formido periculi. Fear of danger.

Forms of actions. The technical forms in which actions were required to be brought in England from a very early period. The original writs which defined these forms were preserved in chancery in a book called Register of Writs; it was first printed and published during the reign of Henry VIII. and styled Registrum Brevium.

Formula. The settled form of words required in pleading and practice. In Civil law, an action.

Formulæ. In Roman law, the procedure for the disposition of actions sent by the magistrates to the judge who proceeded in accordance therewith, unless justice required it to be departed from.

Formularies. The collection of forms of judicial procedure used among the early peoples of Europe.

Formulary. A book containing stated forms. A form; a precedent.

Fornagium. The fee paid by a tenant for the privilege of baking in the lord's or his own oven.

Fornication. Act of copulation by unmarried persons.

Fornix. Fornication. A brothel.

Fornix et cætera. Fornication and the rest. Fornication and bastardy.

Forno. In Spanish law, an oven.

Foro. The court of jurisdiction. In Spanish law, the place where causes are heard and determined.

Foro domestico. In the court at home; in the domestic court.

Foro ecclesiæ. In the spiritual court.

Foros. In Spanish law, emphyteutic rents.

Forprise. An exception or reservation. An exaction.

Forprised. See FORPRISE.

Forschel. A narrow piece of land lying next a highway.

Forses. Waterfalls.

Forspeaker. An attorney or advocate. In old English law, a prolocutor.

Forspeca. Same as FORSPEAKER.

Forspeeca. Same as FORSPEAKER.

Forsque. Only; but.

Forstal. Same as FORESTALL.

Forswear. To swear falsely. To renounce by oath. To reject. To repudiate. To abjure.

Forsworn. Perjured.

Fort. A fortification which is a defense in itself and has a ditch, parapet, stockade, or some similar obstruction to attack.

Fortalice. A fortress.

Fortalitium. In old Scotch law, a castle; a fortress.

Fortaxed. Wrongly or e x c e s s i v e l y taxed.

Fortesque, John. A judge during the reign of Henry VI., of England, and the author of De Laudibus Legum Angliæ.

Fortelace. Same as FORTALICE.

Forte et dure. See PEINE FORTE ET DURE.

Forthcoming. Coming forth w h e n required or due.

Forthcoming bond. See BOND, FORTHCOMING.

Forthwith. Immediately; without delay. Within a reasonable time, taking into consideration the nature of the act required.

Fortia. Force; power; dominion; jurisdiction.

Fortia frisca. Fresh force.

Fortility. In old English law, a fortified place.

Fortin. A small fort. A fort in a field.

Fortior. Stronger.

Fortiori. See A FORTIORI.

Fortis. Strong.

Fortis et sana. Strong and sound; applied to a vessel.

Fortlet. A small fort.

Fortret. A small fort.

Fortuit. Accidental.

Fortuitment. By chance.

Fortuitous. Accidental.

Fortuitous collision. In Maritime law, accidental collision.

Fortuitous event. In Civil law, an event, other than irresistible force, which could not be prevented.

Fortuna. Treasure-trove.

Fortune-teller. One who pretends to be able to reveal future events.

Fortunium. In old English law, a tournament.

Forty-days-court. The court of attachment of the forest or woodmote.

Forum. A court. A jurisdiction. A tribunal. In Roman law, an open paved space in Rome where business was transacted and judges sat. The right to have a matter decided by a court.

Forum actus. The forum of the place where the thing was done.

Forum conscientiæ. The tribunal of conscience. A Court of Equity.

Forum contentiosum. A court of justice. A place where litigation is carried on.

Forum contractus. The forum where the contract was made.

Forum domesticum. A domestic jurisdiction.

Forum domicilii. The forum of the domicile.

Forum ecclesiasticum. A spiritual court.

Forum judicium. A code established for the Visigothic Kingdom, in Spain, in the seventh century.

Forum ligeantiæ rei. The forum of allegiance of the defendant.

Forum litis motæ. The forum where the suit happens to be brought.

Forum originis. The forum of a persons nativity.

Forum regium. The King's court.

Forum rei. The forum where the property is.

Forum rei gestæ. The forum of the place where the act was done.

Forum rei sitæ. The court where the thing in controversy is situated.

Forum sæculare. The secular court.

Forum seculare. The secular court.

Foruth. A long slip of ground.

Forwarder. One who receives and forwards merchandise for others for a compensation, though not interested in the means of transportation.

Forwarding merchant. A forwarder.

Forwards and backwards. In Marine insurance, a phrase meaning not only a ship's course from a port to its destination and back, but from one port to another in the course of that voyage.

Fossa. A dike or ditch. A grave. A ditch where women convicted of felony were formerly drowned.

Fossage. Same as FOSSAGIUM.

Fossagium. In old English law, contribution for the maintenance of ditches.

Fossatorum operatio. Work done by tenants in repairing ditches.

Fossatum. A ditch. A place enclosed by a ditch. Obligations of citizens to repair city ditches.

Fosse. Same as FOSSA.

Fosseway. One of the four highways built by the Romans, in England.

Fostering. Placing a child with another to nourish and rear.

Foster-land. Land given in return for food.

Fosterlean. A nupital gift. A stipend for the maintenance of the wife. Compensation for rearing a child. The jointure of a wife.

Fother. An ancient English weight of about a ton.

Foujdarry adawlut. The criminal courts of justice in India.

Found. Met. Come upon. (A corporation doing business in a foreign State or country is "found" there). To establish; to create.

Found office. See OFFICE, FOUND.

Foundation. The founding or establishing of a college or hospital.

Founder. One who creates or establishes an institution or organization. One who melts and pours metal into a mold.

Founderosa. Out of repair.

Founder's shares. In England, shares issued in payment of something assigned or transferred to a corporation, but which do not represent the capital and do not share in profits until after a certain dividend has been paid on the capital stock.

Foundling. An abandoned child whose parents are unknown.

Foundling hospitals. Institutions established and existing for the care of foundlings.

Four corners. All parts of an instrument; the whole. That shown on its face. (Applied to a deed).

Four orders. See ORDERS, FOUR.

Four seas. The four seas around England.

Four seas, within the. Within the jurisdiction of England.

Fourcher. (To divide or fork). A putting off of an action, used where two persons are defendants and they enter appearance separately to delay the consideration of the cause.

Fourcher by essoin. Same as FOURCHER.

Fourching. The act of retarding legal proceedings.

Fourierism. A socialistic system advocated by F. C. M. Fourier.

Fourteenth Amendment. The fourteenth amendment to the U. S. Constitution.

Fovea. A grave.

Fowls of warren. Fowls protected by English game laws; they comprised partridges, rails, quails, woodcock, pheasants, mallards and heron.

Fox's Libel Act. Statute 52 Geo. III. c. 60. It provided that juries could find a general verdict of guilty or not guilty of libel and did not confine them to the mere question of publication.

Foy. Fidelity. Faith. Oath.

Fractio. A division. Breaking. A payment. A separate part.

Fraction. Same as FRACTIO.

Fractional currency. See CURRENCY, FRACTIONAL.

Fractional quarter section. See QUARTER SECTION, FRACTIONAL.

Fractitium. Arable land.

Fractura navium. Wreck of shipping at sea.

Frais. Expense; cost.

Frais d'un proces. Costs of suit.

Frais de justice. In French law, costs incurred as incident to the action.

Frais jusqu' a bord. In French law, expenses to the board. Free on board (which see).

Frampole fences. Ancient hedge fences built or grown by tenants of the Manor of Writtle in Essex county, England.

Franc. Free. A French silver coin valued at 19.3 cents and the monetary unit of the Latin Union.

Franc tenancier. In French law, a freeholder.

Franc-aleu (or alleu). Allodial land.

Franchiare. To enfranchise.

Franchilanus. A freeman.

Franchise. A liberty. A right. A privilege. A privilege or redemption granted by a king or government.

Franchise, ferry. See FERRY FRANCHISE.

Francia. France.

Francigena. A foreigner. A Frenchman. An alien.

Franclaine. A gentleman; a freeholder; a freeman.

Franclein. Same as FRANCLAINE.

Francling. Same as FRANCLAINE.

Francus. Free. A freeman.

Francus bancus. Free bench (which see).

Francus banque. Free bench (which see).

Francus homo. A free man.

Francus plegius. A frank pledge.

Francus plegiws. Same as FRANCUS PLEGIUS.

Francus tenens. A freeholder.

Frangere clausum. To break close.

Frank. Free. A French gold coin. The signature or mail matter of one holding the franking privilege.

Frank chase. Free chase.

Frank fee. Lands in fee-simple. Lands held without other service than homage. Lands held by the lord of the manor, not in ancient demesne of the crown.

Frank ferme. An ancient socage tenure changed by a new feoffment from knight's service.

Frank law. Legal rights. The rights and privileges of a citizen to be a juror, witness, &c.

Frank marriage. An estate in tail special given to one who married the donor's female relative, to them and to their heirs and free of service except fealty, until the fourth generation of their descendants.

Frank pledge. A tithing or decennary. The pledge of all the members to answer for or produce an offender. A pledge of good behavior required of all freemen on arriving at fourteen years of age.

Frank pledge, view of. See VIEW OF FRANK PLEDGE.

Frank tenant. A freeholder.

Frank tenement. Freehold.

Frankalmoign. Free alms. A tenure by which religious corporations held land. It was free of service except bridge-bote, burgh-bote and fyrd.

Frank-bank. Same as FREE-BENCH.

Frankfold. A privilege of a lord to have his tenant's sheep on his lands to manure them.

Franking privilege. The privilege of sending matter through the mail without stamping or paying for the same.

Frankleyn. Same as FRANCLAINE.

Frankleyne. Same as FRANCLAINE.

Franklin. Same as FRANKLEYN.

Frassetum. A wood.

Frater. A brother.

Frater consanguineus. A brother by the father's side.

Frateria. A fraternity of religious persons.

Fraternity. A body of persons associated together for a common purpose.

Frater uterinus. A brother by the mother's side.

Frater nutricius. A bastard brother.

Fratres conjurati. Sworn brothers or companions. Those sworn to defend the King.

Fratres poes. A class of friars.

Fratres uterini. Brothers on t h e mother's side.

Fratriage. Same as FRATRIAGIUM.

Fratriagium. A younger brother's inheritance.

Fratricide. One who kills his brother. The act of killing a brother.

Fraud. Deceit, which may be either suppression of the truth or suggestion of falsehood.

Fraud, actual. Fraud actually committed. An act done with intent to defraud, as distinguished from constructive or implied fraud.

Fraud, constructive. Same as FRAUD, IMPLIED.

Fraud, implied. Fraud implied by law from the facts.

Fraud in fact. Same as FRAUD, ACTUAL.

Fraud in law. Same as FRAUD, IMPLIED.

Fraud, positive. Same as FRAUD, ACTUAL.

Fraudare. In Civil law, to defraud.

Frauds, Statute of. See STATUTE OF FRAUDS.

Fraudulent. Characterized or based on fraud.

Fraudulent conveyance. A conveyance made in fraud of a previous purchaser or to defeat a creditor or creditors.

Fraudulent conveyances, Statute of. See STATUTE OF FRAUDS.

Fraudulent possession. See POSSESSION, FRAUDULENT.

Fraudulent sale. See SALE FRAUDULENT.

Fraudulently. With intention to defraud.

Fraudum facere legi. To commit a fraud in the law.

Fraunc. Frank.

Fraunche. Frank.

Fraunchise. A franchise.

Fraunk. Same as FRANK.

Fraunk ferme. Same as FRANK FERME.

Fraunk homo. A freeman.

Fraunke. Frank.

Fraus. Fraud. Deceit. Cheating.

Fraus dans locum contractui. A fraud without which the contract would not have taken place. A fraud practiced in order to obtain a contract.

Fraus legis. In Civil law, fraud of law.

Fraxinetum. Ash wood.

Fray. See AFFRAY.

Frea. A female ward.

Freborhesheofed. In Saxon law, the chief of a friborgh or decennary. A chief pledge.

Frectare. To freight.

Frectum. Freight.

Freda. A term among the Franks answering to Wite, of the Saxons.

Fredgisle. A pledge of peace.

Frednite. An ancient liberty to hold courts and make amerciaments.

Fredstole. Sanctuaries.

Fredum. An ancient composition made by a criminal to be freed of prosecution, one-third of which went to the King.

Free. Not subject to arbitrary r u l e . Living under a government of the people. Being of age. Emancipated. Without cost. Certain. Limited to the possessor as distinguished from that held in common.

Free alms. Frankalmoign.

Free-bench. Dower in copyhold lands usually a third or fourth part to be held while the widow lived single and chaste (dum sola et casta vixerit).

Free-board. Same as FREEBORD.

Free boot. To rob as a freebooter.

Free born. Not born in slavery.

Free borough. Not responsible for the conduct of themselves or others.

Free borough men. Those who did not engage to be surety for the good conduct of others.

Free bridge. See BRIDGE, FREE.

Free chapel. A chapel established by the King or by grant of the King and not subject to the jurisdiction of the ordinary.

Free city. One having an independent government.

Free course. In Admiralty law, the course of a vessel when the wind is most favorable to it.

Free entry, egress and regress. The right to go and come over land when necessary.

Free fishery. The exclusive right to fish in a public navigable river.

Free fold. Frank fold.

Free lage. Legal status of a freeman. Franchise.

Free law. Civil rights.

Free list. Goods not subject to tariff charges. A list of people not charged for a privilege.

Free love. The doctrine of unrestrained choice in sexual relations.

Free marriage. Same as FRANK MARRIAGE.

Free milling. Easily worked or reduced, applied to ore.

Free on board. See F. O. B.

Free pledge. Frank pledge (which see).

Free port. One open to the ships of all nations; one where no duties are charged on articles of commerce.

Free services. Such as a soldier or freeman performed, not base, uncertain or villeinous.

Free ships. Ships of a neutral nation in time of war. In U. S., ships which though foreign built may be registered in U. S. when owned by a citizen. A piratical vessel.

Free socage. See SOCAGE, FREE.

Free sockage lands. Lands held under certain rents and free services.

Free socmen. Tenants in free socage.

Free States. Before Civil War in U. S. States where slavery did not exist.

Free tenure. Freehold. Tenure by free service.

Free trade. Commerce without the imposition of duty.

Free warren. The exclusive right of killing game of warren within certain limits.

Freebooter. A pirate.

Freebooty. Pillage by freebooters.

Freebord. Ground claimed "more or less" beyond the line, anciently two feet and a half.

Freeborough men. Certain men who did not engage as frank pledge.

Freedman. One who was a slave but has secured his freedom.

Freedom. The condition of being free from restraints other than those prescribed by equal laws.

Freedom fine. Money paid on being admitted into an incorporated trade.

Freedom of speech. The right to state the truth and express an opinion.

Freedom of the press. See PRESS, FREEDOM OF THE.

Freedom of the city. In English law, not being subject to the jurisdiction of the county organization and having the privilege of self-government and taxation under a grant from the crown.

Freehold. Such an estate as a freeman might accept; (an estate of life or inheritance, not a leasehold). An estate in free socage, not copyhold or villeinage.

Freehold, determinable. An estate for life which may be determined upon the happening of a condition if the same come to pass before the death of the grantee.

Freehold in deed. The possession of lands in fee or for life.

Freehold in law. The right to lands or tenements before entry or seizure.

Freeholder. An actual owner of land. The owner of a freehold estate.

Freeholder, Chosen. In State of New Jersey, an officer who manages the business of a county.

Freeholder, resident. One residing within the district referred to and owns a freehold there.

Freely. Without compulsion or coercion.

Freeman. In old English law, a freeholder, not a villein. One enjoying civil rights. An inhabitant of a city.

Freemen's roll. A list of persons in England and Colonial U. S., admitted as burgesses by the Municipal Corporation Act.

Freewiller. During the Colonial period in Maryland, an immigrant who sold his labor for a term of years.

Freewoman. One not a slave.

Freight. The price paid for transporting goods. Goods transported.

Freight, dead. See DEAD FREIGHT.

Freightage. A cargo. The price paid for carrying goods. The carrying of freight.

Freighter. One who loads a vessel for hire. One who transports freight for others. A vessel engaged in carrying freight.

Freigraf. See VEHMGERICHT.

Freischoffen. Justices of the Vehmgericht.

Frelinghuysen-Zavala Treaty. A proposed treaty dated December 1, 1884, between the United States and Nicaragua providing for the construction of a ship canal across the territory of the latter country to connect the Atlantic and Pacific Oceans. It was rejected by the Senate, the vote reconsidered, but the treaty was never ratified.

Frempul. Profitable.

French, Norman. See NORMAN, FRENCH.

French spoliation claims. See SPOLIATION CLAIMS, FRENCH.

Frenchman. Anciently in England, every stranger.

Frendlesman. An outlaw.

Frendwit. A fine for harboring an outlawed friend. An exemption from the penalty for forfang.

Frendwite. Same as FRENDWIT.

Freneticus. A madman.

Frentike. Frantic. A madman.

Freoborgh. A frank pledge.

Freoling. A freeman born.

Freomortel. An immunity for committing manslaughter.

Frequent. Often; habitually.

Frere. A brother.

Frere eyne. Elder brother.

Frere puisne. Younger brother.

Fresca. Fresh water; land floods.

Fresh disseisin. Recent disseisin. Disseisin within fifteen days which a man could legally overcome by force.

Fresh fine. A fine of lands levied within a year.

Fresh force. Deforcement committed within forty days past.

Fresh pursuit. An immediate pursuit.

Fresh suit. See SUIT, FRESH.

Freshet. An overflowing of a river.

Fret. In French law, freight.

Freteur. In French law, freighter. A ship owner who lets it out to a merchant.

Freth. Same as FRITH.

Fretter. In French law, to freight a ship. To let a ship.

Fretum. A straight.

Fretum Britanicum. The strait between England and France.

Fretum Brittannicum. The straits between Dover and Calais.

Frettum. In old English law, the freight or money paid for carrying freight.

Friar. One of a religious order. These were divided into Grey Friars, Minors or Franciscans, Augustines, Black Friars or Dominicans, and Carmelites or White Friars.

Friborgh. A frank pledge.

Friburg. Same as FRIBORGH.

Fribusculum. In Civil law, a temporary separation of husband and wife caused by a quarrel.

Fridhburgus. A pledge by which chiefs or lords bound themselves for their dependents' good behavior.

Fridstall. A place of peace. A sanctuary.

Fridstoll. Same as FRIDSTALL.

Fridwite. In old English law, a fine for deserting the army.

Friend, alien. Same as ALIEN AMY.

Friend, next. See NEXT FRIEND.

Friend of the court. A bystander who suggests fact or law to the court to assist it in its determination of a cause.

Friendless man. Saxon expression for an outlaw.

Friendly societies. English benevolent societies among tradesmen.

Friendly suit. A suit in equity by the creditor against an executor or administrator to compel an equal distribution of the assets. It is really brought for the executor to compel the creditors to accept an equal share of the assets. A suit to obtain a judicial determination of a question at issue between two or more parties.

Frier. An order of religious persons.

Frier-observant. A branch of Franciscan friers.

Frigidity. Impotence. Coldness.

Frilazin. One freed from bondage.

Friling. A freeman born.

Frilingi. The second of the three ranks among the Saxons. They were born freemen, that is, not subject to any servitude. See EDILINGI; also LAZZI.

Fripperer. A second-hand clothes dealer, or broker.

Fripper. Same as FRIPPERER.

Frisca disseisin. Fresh disseisin.

Frisca fortia. Fresh force.

Friscus. Fresh uncultivated ground.

Frith. In old English law, a wood; a plain between woods; a lawn; an arm of the sea; the mouth of a tidal river. To protect; to enclose. A coppice; a game park; a game forest; a small field enclosed from a common. Civil or legal security. Peace.

Frithborg. Same as FRIBORGH.

Frithbote. A fine for breaking the peace.

Frithbrech. The breaking of the peace.

Frithburg. A frank pledge or surety.

Frithgar. The Saxon year of jubilee or meeting for peace and friendship.

Frithgeard. Same as FRITHSPLOT.

Frithgilda. A fraternity. A gild hall.

Frithman. A member of a frithgild.

Frithsoca. A sanctuary.

Frithsocne. Jurisdiction of, or a right to preserve the peace.

Fritsoen. A sanctuary.

Frithsoke. Surety of defense. A jurisdiction for preserving the peace.

Frithsoken. Same as FRITHSOKE.

Frithsplot. Same as FRITHSOCA.

Frithstoll. Same as FRIDSTOLL.

Frithstool. Same as FRIDSTOLL.

Frithstow. Same as FRIDSTOLL.

Frivolous. Insufficient in law and made for delay.

Frodmortel. Same as FREEMORTEL.

Front foot. A foot on the highway, street, or water front. When applied to lots means a foot front and the entire depth of that foot as distinguished from square foot.

Frontage. The extent of front on a street, or water

Frontager. One owning property fronting a street, seashore, &c. One who resides on the frontier of a country.

Frozen snake. A term applied to a person who is ungrateful.

Fructuarius. In Civil law, one entitled to usufruct.

Fructus. Fruit. Fruits. Profit; increase. The right of using that which springs from anything.

Fructus civiles. Revenues and recompenses, rents, profits.

Fructus industriales. The fruits of industry, as distinguished from fructus naturales.

Fructus legis. The fruits of the law (execution).

Fructus naturales. Natural fruits. See FRUITS, NATURAL.

Fructus pendentes. Hanging fruits not severed from the land.

Fructus perceptio. The rightful taking of the produce of property by a person not the owner of the property.

Fructus rei alienæ. The fruits of another's property.

Fructus separati. Fruits severed from the land.

Fructus stantes. Standing fruits.

Fruges. In Civil law, that produced from vines, underwood, chalk-pits, quarries, grains and vegetables of the bean family.

Fruit. Profit. Product. Enjoyment.

Fruit, fallen. That produced from a possession, but detached so as to be enjoyed by itself.

Fruits, artificial. Produced by man or through artificial agencies, as the fruits of money or industry.

Fruits, first. See FIRST FRUITS.

Fruits, natural. Those produced by nature; as the natural products of the soil, or increase of animals.

Fruits of crime. That acquired through crime.

Frumentum. In Civil law, grain.

Frumgyld. The first payment made to the kindred of a person slain toward the recompense for his murder.

Frumstal. The chief seat or mansion house.

Frumstoll. Same as FRUMSTAL.

Frusca terra. Waste and desert land.

Frussura. A breaking or plowing of land.

Frussura terræ. Newly-broken land.

Frussuro domorum. House-breaking.

Frustra. In vain, to no purpose.

Frustura. A breaking down. Plowing or breaking up.

Frustrum terræ. A small piece of land.

Frutectum. A place where shrubs grow.

Frutos. In Spanish law, profits, fruits.

Fryderinga. Going forth to war. The fitting out of an expedition.

Frymith. In English law, harboring a person.

Frythe. Same as FRITH.

Fuage. A tax on chimneys.

Fuel. Wood, turf, coal, anything used to make heat.

Fuer. To fly. Flight.

Fuero. In Spanish law, a law; a code; a custom; a grant of privileges; a charter; a donation; a declaration of a magistrate. A judicial tribunal; its jurisdiction.

Fuero de Castilla. In Spanish law, the law and customs of the Castillians.

Fuero de correos y caminos. In Spanish law, a tribunal charged with the postal service.

Fuero de guerra. In Spanish law, a tribunal having charge of those doing military service.

Fuero de marino. In Spanish law, a tribunal charged with naval affairs.

Fuero juzgo. In Spanish law, the forum judicium.

Fuero municipal. In Spanish law, municipal laws.

Fuero real. A code of Spanish law promulgated in 1255.

Fuero Viego. A compilation of Spanish law, published about 992.

Fuga catallorum. A drove of cattle.

Fugacia. A chase.

Fugacio. Hunting; a privilege to hunt.

Fugam fecit. He has made flight (on which the goods of a felon were forfeited).

Fugator. In old English law, a privilege of hunting. A driver.

Fugatores carrucarum. Wagoners who drove oxen without goading.

Fugatio. A privilege to hunt.

Fugitate. In Scotch law, to outlaw.

Fugitation. In Scotch law, the act of declaring a criminal who does not appear, to be a fugitive. Outlawry.

Fugitation. Outlawry. A sentence of outlawry.

Fugitive. One who leaves a jurisdiction to escape prosecution, or service of process, or punishment.

Fugitive from justice. One who removes himself from the jurisdiction within which he has committed a crime.

Fugitive slave. A slave who fled from his owner.

Fugitive Slave Law. United States statutes of 1793 and 1850. They provided for the return of escaping slaves to their owners in the States from which they had escaped.

Fugitives' goods. Same as BONA FUGITIVORUM.

Fugitives over sea. Anciently, those who left England without the King's license. The penalty was forfeiture of goods, and forfeiture of vessels carrying the fugitives.

Fugitivus. In Civil law, a fugitive.

Fulfrea. Entirely free.

Full. Complete; entire; perfect; without defect.

Full age. Majority. At Common law, twenty-one years; Civil law, twenty-five.

Full answer. One sufficient in law.

Full blood. Descent from both of two parents or married ancestors.

Full court. A court in banc with all the judges present.

Full defense. See DEFENSE, FULL.

Full faith and credit. Acceptance of as legal.

Full, in. See IN FULL.

Full life. Life in fact and law. Legal capacity.

Full price. A reasonable price.

Full proof. In Civil law, proof by two witnesses or a public document. Proof beyond reasonable doubt.

Full right. Title with possession.

Full wages. Wages up to the end of a period of contract. Wages for a full day, week or month, or period engaged for, as the case may be. The full amount usually paid for the particular work done, as distinguished from reduced wages.

Fullum aquæ. A stream of water coming from a mill.

Fully. Completely; sufficiently; without defect.

Fumadoes. Pilchards, smoked and salted.

Fumage. Manure. A payment or tax for having a chimney. See FUAGE.

Function. Any specified power belonging to an agent. That done under such power. One's duty or office.

Functionary. A public officer. An officer of a corporation.

Functus. One who has performed. Discharged.

Functus officio. One who has served his term of office or whose authority has ceased.

Fund. A collection of money for a specific purpose. To capitalize. To convert into a fund.

(25)

Fund, blended. See BLENDED FUND.

Fund, borough. See BOROUGH FUND.

Fund, consolidated. An English fund for the payment of the public debt.

Fund, general. All the assets of a State.

Fund holder. One having the custody of a fund or funds.

Fund, sinking. Money set apart to pay a public debt.

Fund, suitor's fee. See SUITOR'S FEE FUND.

Fundamental law. See LAW, FUNDA-MENTAL.

Fundamus. (We found or establish). Words used in charters for founding a college.

Fundatio. A founding.

Fundation. An estate. Land. A giving of revenues or fund.

Fundator. A founder.

Fundator perficiens. The endower or founder.

Funded debt. A debt for which a fund has been set apart.

Fundi patrimoniales. Lands of inheritance.

Funding system. A system of finance by which floating debts are changed into a permanent loan.

Funditores. Pioneers.

Fundo annexa. Annexed to the soil.

Funds. Available money. Money lent to a government. Money on hand in the Government Treasury.

Funds, current. See CURRENT FUNDS.

Funds, no. No assets; no money on deposit.

Funds, public. Public money or securities.

Fundus. A piece of land. A farm. An estate. One who has the principal decision or approval of a thing.

Fundus adscriptus. An estate bound to or burdened with a duty.

Funeral expenses. Expenses attending the burial of a dead body.

Fungible. Consumable ; measurable. That which may be replaced in kind.

Fungible, res. In Civil law, things of a kind as distinguished from specific things.

Fur. A thief. The coat of animals.

Fur manifestus. A thief caught in the act.

Furandi animus. An intention to steal.

Furca. A gallows. A whipping post. A fork-shaped yoke for criminals.

Furca et flagellum. Gallows and whip. A servile tenure whereby the tenant's life and limbs were at the disposal of the lord.

Furca et fossa. Gallows and pit. An ancient privilege of jurisdiction to punish felons, by hanging men and drowning women.

Furcare ad tassum. To pitch corn with a fork in loading a wagon.

Furche. A gallows.

Furigeldum. A mulct for theft.

Furiosity. In Scotch law, madness as distinguished from idiocy.

Furiosus. A lunatic.

Furlingus. A furlong. A furrow a furlong in length.

Furlong. A measure of length ; an eighth of a mile. An eighth of an acre. A piece of land of more or less but unknown acreage.

Furlough. Leave of absence.

Furnage. Same as FURNAGIUM.

Furnagium. See FORNAGIUM.

Furnarius. A baker.

Furniare. To bake.

Furniture. Equipment. Outfit. Household chattels.

Furniture, household. Such articles as are commonly used for ornament or convenience by a family keeping house.

Furniture of a ship. A ship's masts, tackle, rigging, apparel and provisions and such other articles as are necessary for a voyage.

Furnival's Inn. A former inn of Chancery, in England.

Furnum. A bake house; an oven.

Furor uterinus. Same as ANDROMANIA.

Furst. Same as FURST AND FONDUNG.

Furst and fondung. In old English law, time to take advice.

Furta. In old English law, a right to try and punish thieves and felons within a certain territory.

Further. Additional.

Further advance (or charge). A second loan to a mortgagor by the mortgagee, either with or without additional security.

Further assurance. A covenant that the grantor will execute any further deeds which may be necessary to complete title.

Further consideration. Consideration postponed until after further examination.

Further hearing. See HEARING, FURTHER.

Further directions. A hearing after a master in chancery had made his report in pursuance to a decree.

Further maintenance of action, plea to. See PLEA TO A FURTHER MAINTENANCE OF ACTION.

Furtive. In old English law, by stealth.

Furtum. Theft.

Furtum conceptum. In Roman law, a theft discovered by finding the stolen property on a person searched.

Furtum grave. Aggravated theft, punishable with death.

Furtum manifestum. Open theft. Bacberend.

Furtum oblatum. In Civil law, offered theft. Theft discovered. The stolen article on one to whom it has been offered.

Fust. Same as FUZ.

Fusticks. Dyewoods.

Futhwite. Same as FITHWITE.

Fustigatio. In old English law, beating with sticks and clubs, an ancient punishment of malefactors.

Fustis. A staff delivered as a symbol of land.

Future. Such as may be, or occur hereafter. The time yet to come. Any security or article sold or bought upon an agreement for future delivery.

Future assurance. See ASSURANCE, FUTURE.

Future debt. See DEBT, FUTURE.

Future use. See USE, FUTURE.

Futures. Anything sold or bought upon a contract of future delivery.

Futuri. Persons not yet in being.

Futyf. A fugitive from justice.

Fuz. A Celtic word for wood or forest.

Fyhtwite. A fine for homicide.

Fyke. A net for catching fish.

Fyle. In Scotch law, to defile. To declare an accused guilty.

Fylit. In Scotch law, found guilty.

Fyrd. A military contribution. An army.

Fyrderinga. Going out to war. An expedition. An offense for not going on an expedition with the King when summoned.

Fyrdung. Same as FYRDERINGA.

Fyrdwite. In old English law, a fine for not properly responding to the call for military service.

Fyrthing. Same as FYRDERINGA.

Fyrthwite. Same as FYRDWITE.

G.

G. In law French, often used for W. as garranty for warranty, &c.

G. S. General Statutes.

Gabel. Anciently, a tax on salt. A tax; a rent; duty; impost.

Gabel-end. The triangular end of a house or building.

Gabella. Same as GABEL.

Gablatores. Those who paid gabel.

Gablum. A rent. A tax. The gable of a house.

Gabula. Same as GABLUM.

Gabulum. Same as GABLUM.

Gabulus denariorum. Rent paid in money.

Gadhelic peoples. The Irish, Erse and Manx. A branch of the Celtæ.

Gadsen purchase. The purchase, for ten million dollars, from Mexico in 1853, of what is now part of New Mexico and Arizona. It was negotiated by James Gadsen. The territory acquired by the purchase.

Gafol. Same as GAVEL.

Gafol gild. The payment of tribute or custom. The payment of rent. Usury. See GAFOL; also GAVEL.

Gafol land. Land liable to taxation. Land rented.

Gaful-land. Same as GAFOLD-LAND.

Gage. A pawn, security or pledge. In old English law, to pledge. To pawn; to give as security. In French law, the contract of pledge and the article pledged.

Gage deliverance. A bond for the delivery or return of cattle distrained.

Gage, estates in. See ESTATES IN GAGE.

Gager. To find security. To wage. Also same as GAGE (which see).

Gage de deliverance. Same as GAGE DELIVERANCE.

Gager deliverance. Same as GAGE DELIVERANCE.

Gager del ley. Wager of law. See LAW, WAGER OF.

Gaignage. Same as GAINAGE.

Gain. Profit. To acquire. To get. Increase. Addition. The profit obtained by cultivating land.

Gainage. Profit on tilled land. The land itself. Farm tools. Wainage.

Gainer. A socman occupying arable land held at the will of the lord, the tenant receiving no reward but the profit from the land.

Gainery. Profit from tillage. Beasts used in cultivating.

Gainor. Same as GAINER.

Gainure. Tillage.

Gajum. A dense wood.

Gale. In England, rent, tribute, tax, annuity. A right to open a mine or quarry in consideration of a rental or royalty.

Galea. A galley or fast ship.

Galenes. In old Scotch law, compensation for killing.

Gales. Wales.

Galleti. Welshmen.

Galli-halfpence. A Genoese coin anciently prohibited in England by statute.

Gallimawfry. Meals served galley-slaves.

Galloches. An ancient shoe worn by the Gauls; now, a rubber and cloth overshoe.

Gallon. A liquid measure containing, in the U. S., 231 cubic inches. In Great Britain, 277.274.

Gallon, ale. A measure of capacity of 282 cubic inches.

Gallon, imperial. A gallon of 27 cubic inches.

Gallows. A framework upon which criminals are hanged.

Gamacta. A stroke.

Gamalis. A child born of parents betrothed or married.

Gamba. Military boots or defences for the legs.

Gamberia. Same as GAMBA.

Gambeyson. A coat anciently worn under armor.

Gamble. To play a game of chance for money.

Gambler. One who gambles as an occupation.

Gambler, common. One who keeps a place for gambling purposes.

Gambling. Risking money on a chance, or event, or contingency.

Gambling, contract. Same as CONTRACT, WAGERING.

Gambling, device. A device to determine which of those who risk their money on its actions wins or loses. Any device used in gambling.

Gambling house. A place w h e r e gambling is habitually carried on.

Gambling policy. See POLICY, GAMBLING.

Gambria. Same as GAMBA.

Game. Animals usually hunted for food or sport, generally specified by statute. A friendly contest for amusement, usually with some article or contrivance, as a ball or pack of cards, dice, &c.

Game-birds. Birds commonly hunted as game.

Game fish. Food fish requiring skill to capture and which fight against capture.

Game laws. Laws regulating the hunting of game or the catching of fish or both.

Game preserve. A tract of land where game is preserved and protected.

Game tenant. One who rents the privilege of hunting or fishing on a preserve or estate.

Gamekeeper. One who has the care or preservation of game.

Gaming. Playing some game of chance for money, or setting animals to fight or race for money. Gambling.

Gaming contract. See CONTRACT, GAMING.

Gaming house. Same as GAMBLING HOUSE.

Ganancial. In Spanish law, the property which husband and wife acquire during matrimony by a common title, or which they hold at the day of the marriage ; it is divisible between them on dissolution of the marriage.

Ganancias. In Spanish law, profits from ganancial property.

Gang days. Anciently, the days when the clergy, wardens, &c., of a church went in procession to survey the church lands and boundaries, &c.

Gangiatori. Anciently officers charged with the examination of weights and measures.

Gangtelope. An old military punishment by which the criminal ran between two rows of men receiving a blow from each. The word is pronounced gauntlet.

Gangue. The mineral accompanying the ore in a vein.

Gang-week. The time when the parish officers go over the bounds of the parish; rogation week.

Gantelope. Same as GANGTELOPE.

Gaol. A jail.

Gaol delivery. The emptying of a jail by trying the prisoners.

Gaol delivery, commission of. See COMMISSION OF GAOL DELIVERY.

Goal liberties. A district around a jail within which prisoners were allowed to go at large on giving security to return.

Goal limits. Same as GOAL LIBERTIES.

Goaler. One who has charge of a jail.

Garandia. A warranty.

Garantia. A warranty.

Garantie. A French term for warranty.

Garantum. A warranty.

Garathinx. An absolute gift.

Garaunt. Warrant. To Warrant.

Garauntor. One who warrants a thing.

Garb. Same as GARBA.

Garba. A bundle. A sheaf of corn, a handful.

Garba sagittarum. A sheaf of twenty-four arrows.

Garbaldo decimæ. Same as GARBALES DECIMÆ.

Garbales decimæ. In Scotch law, tithes of corn.

Garballes decimæ. Same as GARBALES DECIMÆ.

Garble. To sever dust and dross from drugs, spice, etc.

Garbler of spices. An ancient officer in London who had authority to enter any shop where drugs and spices were for sale and compel the cleansing of the same.

Garbling. Cleansing the good from the bad.

Garceones. Servants who follow an army.

Garceons. Same as GARCEONES.

Garcio. A groom or servant.

Garcio stolæ. A groom of the stole to the King.

Garde. Ward, custody, guardianship.

Gardebrache. An armour or vambrace for the arm.

Gardein. A guardian. A keeper.

Garden. A small piece of ground devoted to the raising of flowers or vegetables or both.

Garderobe. A wardrobe. A closet.

Gardia. Custody; wardship.

Gardianus. A guardian; a protector.

Gardianus ecclesiæ. A churchwarden.

Gardianus quinque portuum. Warden of the cinque ports.

Gardinum. In old English law, a garden.

Garene. A warren.

Garlanda. A coronet, chaplet or garland.

Garner. To warn; to summons; to garnish.

Garnestura. All necessary articles of war, including provisions for the defense of a town or castle.

Garnir. Same as GARNER.

Garnish. To warn. To warn a debtor not to pay money to a certain creditor but to answer plaintiff's suit and keep the goods until judgment. At one time in England, money paid by a prisoner, on entering prison, to his fellow prisoners.

Garnishee. A person warned not to deliver money or goods. One in whose hands money belonging to the defendant is attached.

Garnishment. A warning for one to appear in a cause to which he is not a party and give information to the court. A notice not to deliver goods or money to a defendant but to appear and answer the suit of the plaintiff.

Garnishing process. The writ containing the warning. See GARNISH.

Garnishor. One who warns The plaintiff in a garnishment proceeding. See GARNISH.

Garnistura. A furnishing or providing. Whatever is required to ornament a thing or fortify a camp or city.

Garrant. Warrant.

Garrantie. Warranty. Guarantee.

Garrena. A warren.

Garrote. An instrument for executing criminals in Spain and Portugal. It consists of an iron collar with a sharp point or blade in which the neck of the condemned is enclosed. By turning a crank the point or blade enters into the spine at the base of the brain.

Garson. A menial Irish servant.

Garsumme. A fine or amercement.

Garter. The ensign of a noble order of knights, instituted by Ed. III. in about 1348, called Knights of the Garter.

Garth. A yard. A small close. A dam or weir.

Garthmen. Men who take fish by means of a weir.

Garytour. In old Scotch law, a warder or one who keeps guard.

Gasachio. An adversary.

Gasindus. A house servant.

Gast. Waste.

Gastalders. Same as GASTALDUS.

Gastaldus. A governor of a country whose office was temporary. A bailiff; a steward.

Gastel. Wastel. In old English law, a fine wheat bread.

Gaster. To waste.

Gastine. Uncultivated or unused lands.

Gate. A right in land for the use or passage of cattle.

Gaudies. Double commons in English universities.

Gauge. To measure. The instrument by which measure is taken. The distance between the rails of a railroad.

Gauge, broad. A distance between railway tracks of more than 56½ inches. It was formerly five feet.

Gauge, narrow. A distance between railway tracks of less than standard guage, usually of twenty-four or thirty inches.

Gauge, standard. A distance between railroad tracks of four feet eight and one-half inches.

Gaugeator. A guager.

Gauger. An officer of the internal revenue service appointed to measure the contents of casks, barrels, &c., containing liquors and things subject to tax.

Gaugetum. Gauging.

Gavel. Custom, tribute, yearly revenue, tax rent. Rent paid periodically. An old Saxon and Welsh form of tenure by which the estate passed to all the sons equally; also the partition of such an estate. A fourth of a township. See RHANDIR.

Gavelbred. Rent payable in provisions.

Gavelcester. A certain measure of rent ale.

Gavelchester. Same as GAVELCESTER.

Gavelet. Rent. A process restricted to gavelkind tenure for the recovery of rent, whether there was distress on land or not, by stat. 10 Ed. II. extended to rent service generally where payment could not be obtained by distress. Under process the land was forfeited if not redeemed within a year and a day. See CESSAVIT.

Gavelet in London. A writ where the parties tenant and demandant appear by scire facias to show cause why the one should not have his tenement on payment of rent, and the other recover the lands on default thereof.

Gavelgeld. Payment of tribute or toll.

Gavelherte. In old English law, plowing done by a customary tenant.

Gaveling men. Tenants who paid a rent reserved in addition to customary duties.

Gavelkind. A socage tenure in Kent, England, where the land descends to all the sons or heirs together. Dower is given of half the land; the land may be aliened by heir at the age of fifteen; may be disposed of by will; does not escheat for felony.

Gaveller. In England, an officer having the management of mines and quarries in the Forest of Dean and Hundred of St. Barravels, and the granting of sales to free miners.

Gavelman. A tenant liable to tribute.

Gavelmed. The duty or work of mowing grass required by customary tenants.

Gavelrep. In old English law, the duty of reaping grain at the lord's command.

Gavelwerk. Work performed by tenant as tribute either by hand or with cart or carriage.

Gazette. An official report. A newspaper. A publication of the British Government in which are published the official acts of State and of the Queen.

Geaspecia. A grampus.

Gebocced. Saxon for conveyed.

Gebocian. A written conveyance. In Saxon law, to convey boc-land to.

Gebure. A ploughman or farmer.

Geburscript. Adjoining or neighboring district.

Geburus. A county inhabitant of the same village.

Geld. Money or tribute or fine.

Geldabilis. In old English law, taxable.

Geldable. Liable to pay tax or tribute.

Gelding. A castrated horse.

Geldum. Same as GELD.

Gemma. In Civil law, a gem.

Gemot. Same as GEMOTE.

Gemote. An assembly. A court.

Gen. Abbreviation of Generosus (which see).

Genealogia. Genealogy. A family or clan village.

Genealogy. A record of descent.

Genearch. The head of a family.

Geneath. The King's villein.

Gener. In Civil law, a son-in-law.

General. Relating to the whole of a kind. Widespread; prevalent; not restricted; usual; customary; common to the greater number; comprehensive.

General accountant. See ACCOUNTANT, GENERAL.

General affirmance day. See AFFIRMANCE DAY, GENERAL.

General agent. See AGENT, GENERAL.

General appearance. See APPEARANCE, GENERAL.

General appointment. See APPOINTMENT, GENERAL.

General assembly. See ASSEMBLY, GENERAL.

General assignment. See ASSIGNMENT, GENERAL.

General assumpsit. Where the contract on promise is implied by law.

General authority. See AUTHORITY, GENERAL.

General average. See AVERAGE, GENERAL.

General challenge. See CHALLENGE, GENERAL.

General character. See CHARACTER, GENERAL.

General charge. See CHARGE, GENERAL.

General council. See COUNCIL, GENERAL.

General credit. See CREDIT, GENERAL.

General custom. See CUSTOM, GENERAL.

General damages. See DAMAGES, GENERAL.

General defense. See DEFENSE, GENERAL.

General demurrer. See DEMURRER, GENERAL.

General denial. A denial in general terms.

General deposit. See DEPOSIT, GENERAL.

General deputy sheriff. See SHERIFF, GENERAL DEPUTY.

General election. See ELECTION, GENERAL.

General executor. See EXECUTOR, GENERAL.

General field. Several pieces of land fenced as one.

General finding. See FINDING, GENERAL.

General fund. See FUND, GENERAL.

General gaol delivery. See COMMISSION OF GENERAL GAOL DELIVERY.

General government. See GOVERNMENT, GENERAL.

General guarantee. See GUARANTEE, GENERAL.

General guardian. See GUARDIAN, GENERAL.

General imparlance. See IMPARLANCE, GENERAL.

General Inclosure Act. Statute 41, Geo. III, c. 109, consolidating a number of regulations relating to the inclosure of commons and waste lands.

General intent. See INTENT, GENERAL.

General issue. See ISSUE, GENERAL.

General issue of fact. See ISSUE OF FACT, GENERAL.

General jurisdiction. See JURISDICTION, GENERAL.

General Land Office. See LAND OFFICE, GENERAL.

General law. See LAW, GENERAL.

General legacy. See LEGACY, GENERAL.

General lien. See LIEN, GENERAL.

General malice. See MALICE, GENERAL.

General manager. See MANAGER, GENERAL.

General meeting. The meeting of all or nearly all of a class, as stockholders, creditors, &c.

General monition. See MONITION, GENERAL.

General occupant. See OCCUPANT, GENERAL.

General order. See ORDER, GENERAL.

General owner. See OWNER, GENERAL.

General pardon. See PARDON, GENERAL.

General partnership. See PARTNERSHIP, GENERAL.

General property. See PROPERTY, GENERAL.

General question. See QUESTION, GENERAL.

General restraint of trade. See RESTRAINT OF TRADE, GENERAL.

General retainer. See RETAINER, GENERAL.

General return day. A day for the return of all writs directed to a particular term.

General rules. General rules of court relating to practice, &c.

General sessions. See COURT OF GENERAL QUARTER SESSIONS OF THE PEACE.

General ship. See SHIP, GENERAL.

General, solicitor. See SOLICITOR-GENERAL.

General special imparlance. See IMPARLANCE, GENERAL SPECIAL.

General statute. See STATUTE, GENERAL.

General surveyor. See SURVEYOR, GENERAL.

General tail. See TAIL, GENERAL.

General tenancy. See TENANCY, GENERAL.

General term. See TERM, GENERAL.

General traverse. See TRAVERSE, GENERAL.

General usage. See USAGE, GENERAL.

General verdict. See VERDICT, GENERAL.

General warrant. See WARRANT, GENERAL.

General warranty. See WARRANTY, GENERAL.

General welfare. See WELFARE, GENERAL.

General words. Words intended to include any and all of a class.

Generale. The general provision for the religious.

Generalissimum, nomen. See NOMEN, COLLECTIVUM.

Generals, great. The furniture of a fishing vessel necessary for a voyage furnished by the owner. See GENERALS, SMALL.

Generals of orders. Chiefs of the orders of monks, friars and religious societies.

Generals, small. In New England, provisions, hooks, lines, and articles furnished by the crew of a fishing vessel, as distinguished from the things furnished by the owner of the vessel. See GENERALS, GREAT.

Generatio. The branch of a monastery.

Generation. A body of persons existing during the same period.

Generosa. Gentlewoman.

Generosi filius. The son of a gentleman.

Generosus. Gentleman. A man entitled to bear arms; one above the rank of yeoman.

Geneva award. The award, in 1872, of arbitrators, rendered in Geneva, Switzerland, to the effect that Great Britain should pay the U. S. $15,500,000 for injuries to U. S. commerce by the vessels Alabama, Florida and Shenandoah, which Great Britain allowed to be constructed in her ports by the Confederates.

Geniculum. A degree of consanguinity.

Gens. In Roman law, a tribe; a clan.

Gentes. People; folk.

Gentiles. In Roman law, the members of a gens.

Gentilhome. A gentleman.

Gentility. State of being a gentleman.

Gentleman. A man well born. All persons in England above yeomen. One who without title bears a coat of arms or whose ancestors were freemen. One made a gentleman by letters patent. In U. S., the word has no specific meaning, thieves, gamblers, dog-fighters, lawyers, preachers, judges, politicians, and men in all occupations and of any character are termed " Gentlemen " and " perfect gentlemen " by their respective friends. See YEOMAN.

Gentleman Usher of the Black Rod. See BLACK ROD.

Gentlewomen. An addition for the estate and degree of a woman in England. Does not exist in U. S. See LADY.

Gentoo law. See CODE, GENTOO.

Gentz. People, folk.

Genu. A knee; a knot.

Genuine. Belonging to the true stock. Having the characteristic represented.

Genuineness. The quality of being genuine.

Genus. The general stock as distinguished from the specific. A man's direct ancestors.

Geological survey. A bureau of the government at Washington, D. C., having charge of the survey of the forest reserves and the classification and examination of their geological structure, mineral resources and products of the public domain.

Geometrical pace. See PACE GEOMETRICAL.

Geoponics. Agriculture.

George Noble. A gold coin current during reign Henry VII. of England, value 6s. 8d.

Gerechtsbode. In old New York, a constable or court messenger.

Gerefa. A reeve. An officer.

Gerens. Bearing.

Gerens datum. Bearing date.

Gerere. To bear, to act, to behave.

Gerere pro hærede. To act as heir.

German. In descent, means the whole as distinguished from the half blood.

Germanus. Of the whole blood. Of the same stock.

Germen terræ. A sprout from the earth. A young tree.

Gerontocomi. In Roman law, officers who managed hospitals for the indigent and infirm.

Gerontocomium. In Civil law, a home for the aged.

Gerrymander. To alter the voting districts so that they are unfairly arranged for the benefit of a particular party or candidate. Supposed to have first been done by Eldridge Gerry, Governor of Massachusetts.

Gersoma. A price. A fine. Reward. Amercement.

Gersuma. Same as GERSOMA.

Gersumarius. Liable to be fined.

Gersume. In old English law, compensation. Expense. A fine.

Gesta (or Gestæ). Deeds; things done; transactions.

Gestation. The period of development of a fœtus, beginning at conception and ending at birth. It is usually 280 days.

Gestio. In Civil law, conduct; behavior.

Gestio, negotiorum. In Civil law, the transaction of the business of another in his absence and without authority, through friendship.

Gestio pro hærede. (Behavior as heir). In Scotch law, conduct which renders an heir liable for his ancestor's debts, such as receiving rents, taking possession of title deeds, &c.

Gestor. In Civil law, one who acts for another.

Gestu et fama. An ancient writ where a person's behavior was impeached.

Gestum. A deed, thing done; transaction.

Get a silk gown. See GOWN, GET A SILK.

Getæ. Goths.

Getter. To throw; bring; cast.

Gevillouris. In old Scotch law, gaolers.

Gewere. Possessions of lands.

Gewinda. The public convention of people to decide a cause.

Gewineda. Same as GEWINDA.

Gewitnessa. The giving of evidence.

Gewrite. Deeds, charters, or writings.

Gibbet. A gallows.

Gift. A gratuitous transfer of anything. A conveyance of land in tail. A voluntary transfer of personal property without consideration.

Gift enterprise. The creation of an estate tail. A business which offers gifts to secure trade. A scheme for the distribution of certain articles by chance among those who have taken shares in or toward the purchase of the same.

Gift, manual. See MANUAL GIFT.

Gift, onerous. One made subject to certain burdens placed upon the donee.

Gift, substitutional. See SUBSTITUTIONAL GIFT.

Gift-taken. Same as AGISTER.

Gifta aquæ. The stream of water to a mill.

Giftoman. The one who has a right to dispose of a woman in marriage.

Gigmills. Mills for filling and burling woolen cloth anciently prohibited in England by statute.

Gild. In Saxon law, a tax. A fine. A mulct. A corporation. A fraternity or society to which the members made contributions. A friborg. A decennary.

Gild, adulterine. See ADULTERINE GILD.

Gild rent. Payments to the crown by a gild or society.

Gilda mercatoria. See GUILDA MERCATORIA.

Gildable. In old English law, subject to tax or tribute.

Gildale. Where each of several persons at a carousal paid for his own share of what he consumed.

Gild-hall. Same as GUILD-HALL.

Gildo. In Saxon law, members of a gild.

Gill. A measure of one-fourth of a pint.

Gilour. A cheat; a deceiver.

Gipsy. A wandering race known in Western Europe since 1417 probably of Hindu origin. In England sometimes styled Egyptians.

Girantem. In Italy, a drawer of a bill of exchange.

Girth. In old English law, a measure equal to one yard.

Girth and sanctuary. In old Scotch law, a refuge given those who killed without premeditation.

Gisant. Lying.

Gisarms. A halbert or handaxe.

Gise. To use the pasture for the cattle of others.

Gisement. Same as AGISTMENT.

Giser. To lie.

Gisetaker. An agister. One who takes cattle to graze.

Gisle. A pledge.

Gislebert. An illustrious pledge.

Gist. The main ground of action.

Gist of action. The ground or foundation for which the action lies.

Gist takers. Same as AGISTERS.

Git. The foundation or ground; the point. Same as GIST.

Give. To transfer ownership or possession without compensation. To supply. To allow. To admit. To confer. To deliver. To announce. To communicate.

Give bail. To furnish bail or security for appearance.

Give color. See COLOR, GIVE.

Giver. One who makes a gift.

Giving in payment. In Louisiana, the receipt of property in satisfaction of a debt.

Giving time. Extending the time within which to pay a debt or discharge an obligation.

Gladio succinctus. Possessing jurisdiction over the county of which he is made earl. Said of one created earl.

Gladius. A sword. An emblem of defense. The emblem of the law's power to punish crimes. In Norman laws, supreme jurisdiction.

Glaive. A sword, lance or horseman's staff. One of the weapons allowed the contending parties in a trial by combat.

Glans. In Civil law, fruits of trees.

Glanvill (or Glanville). The author of De Legibus et Consuetudinibus Angliæ, written about 1181 and, with the exception of a first part of the Mirror of Justices, the oldest book of English law.

Glassmen. A term used in ancient English statutes to denote wandering rogues or vagrants.

Glavea. A hand-dart.

Gleaning. See GLEANING and LEASING.

Gleaning and Leasing. An ancient privilege in certain parts of England whereby the poor were allowed to enter and glean upon another's ground after harvest, without being guilty of trespass.

Gleba. A glebe church land. A portion in addition to the parsonage.

Gleba terræ. A clod of earth.

Glebæ ascriptitii. (Assigned to the land; annexed to the soil). See ASCRIPTITII GLEBÆ.

Glebariæ. Turf dug out of the ground.

Glebe. Revenue. Lands belonging to a parish church or benefice.

Gliscywa. A fraternity.

Glomerells. Commissioners appointed to determine differences between pupils of a school or university and the townsmen of the place.

Glos. In Civil law, a husband's sister.

Gloss. To explain by a comment on the margin. To interpret by remarks. A comment interpreting or explaining something in the text of a law or work.

Glossa. A gloss. An interpretation or explanation.

Glossæ interlineales. Interpretations or comments placed between the lines of the text.

Glossæ marginales. Glosses placed on the margins.

Glossary. A compilation of a class of words. A collection of glosses.

Glossator. In Civil law, one who made glosses or comments, also an ancient teacher of Roman law.

Glossemata. Words requiring interpretation or explanation.

Gloucester. The name of a statute made in 1278 in reign of Edward I. See STATUTE OF GLOUCESTER.

Glove silver. Money given servants with which to buy gloves. Also money given the court criers by barristers on circuit in England. Money given to a judge to buy gloves with. See GLOVES.

Gloves. The giving, by the sheriff, to the judge of assise, a pair of white gloves when there was no prisoner to be tried.

Glyn. A valley.

Go. To issue. To be dismissed by the Court. To rest.

Go bail. Become bondsman for.

Go to. To be transmitted to. Affect, as "go to" the competency.

Go to protest. To be protested for non-payment.

Go without day. To be permitted to go free without day set for appearance in court. The record of such permission.

Goat. In old English law, a contrivance to drain water from land.

God, act of. See ACT OF GOD.

God and my country. See COUNTRY, GOD AND MY.

God-gild. That offered to religion.

God-bote. A fine for spiritual offense.

Godi. An ancient Irish magistrate.

God's acre. A burying ground; a church yard.

God's penny. Earnest money.

Gogin-stole. Cucking stool.

Going concern. One continuing to exist though insolvent.

Going rate. The rate or price for freight for the time being.

Going through the bar. The calling on members of the bar present, by a judge, for any motion which they may desire to make.

Going to the country. Filing a plea with the conclusion "the said defendant puts himself upon the country."

Going witness. One about to leave a jurisdiction in which his testimony is wanted.

Gold certificate. See CERTIFICATE, GOLD.

Gold standard. See STANDARD, GOLD.

Golda. A mine.

Goldsmiths' notes. Bankers' notes.

Goldwit. A mulct in gold.

Goliardus. A jester.

Gomashtah. In Hindu law, an agent.

Gondobada lex. Same as LEX GONDOBADA.

Good. Legal. Genuine. Able to meet obligations.

Good abearing. A species of probation by which a man was bound to good behavior to refrain from acts against good morals as well as against the peace.

Good and lawful men. Those competent to serve on a jury.

Good and valid. Legal. Responsible. Sufficient.

Good and moral character. As to what constitutes, a court must determine when the question arises. Generally one who has not been convicted of a crime which is bad in itself, or of habitual violations of a crime merely made so by statute, is of good moral character though circumstances may change this definition.

Good behavior. Acting in accordance with good morals. Conformity to law.

Good character. See CHARACTER, GOOD.

Good consideration. One founded on natural affection, blood relationship. See CONSIDERATION.

Good country. In Scotch law, good men of the country. Competent jurors.

Good defense. Same as DEFENSE SUFFICIENT.

Good faith. See FAITH, GOOD.

Good fame. Favorable reputation.

Good ground. Good cause.

Good jury. One of which the members are selected from the list of special jurors.

Good repute. Of good reputation.

Good title. See TITLE, GOOD.

Good will. Established popularity of a business house.

Goodright. A name at one time applied to a fictitious plaintiff in ejectment.

Goods. Personal property. W a r e s. Merchandise.

Goods and chattels. Personal property as distinguished from lands.

Goods and merchandise. Articles bought and sold in trade.

Goods, household. See HOUSEHOLD GOODS.

Goods, lawful. See LAWFUL GOODS.

Goods, perishable. See PERISHABLE GOODS.

Goods, wares and merchandise. Articles usually the subject of trade and commerce. As to what comes within this designation as used in the Statute of Frauds, a court must determine in each particular case, wherein the question arises.

Goodtitle. A fictitious plaintiff in the old form of ejectment.

Goole. A breach in a sea bank or wall. A passage worn by the flux and reflux of the sea.

Gorce. Same as GORS.

Gore. A narrow strip of land.

Gors. A weir. A fish pool.

Gort. Same as GORS.

Gote. A ditch, sluice or gutter.

Gotti. Goths.

Government. The executive and legislative bodies of a State.

Government appraiser. See APPRAISER, GOVERNMENT.

Government, charter colony. See CHARTER COLONY GOVERNMENT.

Government, constitutional. A government which has certain restraints upon its agents as a protection for the people. These restraints may be in the form of a written constitution or only recognized customs or principles of right.

Government de facto. Government of fact only. One having unlawful possession of and claiming to exercise the authority of a legal government.

Government de jure. Government of right. A government in accordance with established law.

Government, federal. A government composed of, established by and for the interests of independent States.

Government, general. The U. S. Federal Government as distinguished from a State government.

Government, local. One confined to a particular locality.

Government, military. See MILITARY GOVERNMENT.

Government, municipal. Government of a political division of a State. City government.

Government, National. Same as GOVERNMENT, GENERAL.

Government Printing Office. In U. S., an office at Washington, D. C., charged with all business relating to public printing and binding.

Government, proprietary. See PROPRIETARY GOVERNMENT.

Government, republican form of. A form of government in which the people are the sovereigns.

Government, United States. The Federal Government established by the North American States.

Governor. The chief executive officer of a State, colony or district. One who exercises executive control over an institution. A device for regulating the speed of an engine, or motor, or flow of gas or liquid.

Governor-General. A governor who has deputy governors under him. A viceroy.

Gown, to get a silk. In England, to be raised from barrister to King's or Queen's counsel.

Grace. Favor. Toleration. Acts of Parliament for a general and free pardon. See DAYS OF GRACE.

Grace, act of. Act of favor, as a pardon.

Grace, days of. See DAYS OF GRACE.

Grace widow. A woman permitted to live apart from her husband by decree of court.

Gradatim. By degrees.

Grade. To classify by grades. To bring to a level. Degree Rank. With reference to surface, the inclination from the horizontal. The height or level of a street compared with surrounding land.

Graduate. One who receives a certificate of having completed a course in any institution or calling.

Gradus. In Civil law, a measure of space. A degree of consanguinity.

Gradus parentetæ. A pedigree.

Graffarius. A notary or graffer, or scrivener.

Graffer. A notary or scrivener.

Grafflo. A landgrave or earl.

Grafflum. A writing book, register of deeds and evidences.

Graflo. Same as GRAFFIO.

Graft. The equitable right of one holding a mortgage on property to which the mortgagor had bad title, to have his lien continued should the mortgagor subsequently get good title.

Grain. The twenty-fourth part of a pennyweight. Any kind of seed sown to procure food.

Grainage. An ancient duty of the twentieth part of salt imported by aliens.

Gram. The unit of mass or weight in the metric system, equal to 15.432 grains avoirdupois. See METRIC SYSTEM.

Grammatophylacium. In Civil law, a place where records were kept.

Gramme. Same as GRAM.

Granage. A former duty payable in London on salt brought into that city. It consisted of the twentieth part of the quantity imported.

Granatarius. In old English law, an officer having custody of a granary.

Grand. Great. Chief. Greater or greatest.

Grand assize. A jury of sixteen knights employed to try writs of right, formerly triable only by battel; introduced by Henry II.

Grand bill of sale. In maritime law, an instrument whereby a ship is transferred to the first purchaser; a written statement furnished an owner by a shipbuilder of all the dimensions of a vessel.

Grand cape. A writ or plea of land where the tenant makes default for the King to take the land. Same as CAPE MAGNUM, (which see).

Grand Coutumier de Normandie. A book, probably compiled since 1100, containing the ducal customs of Normandy.

Grand days. Certain holidays which were no days in ancient English courts.

Grand distress. A distress made when a person defaulted after being attached, which extended to all the person's goods and chattels in the county.

Grand distress, writ of. See WRIT OF GRAND DISTRESS.

Grand inquest. A grand jury.

Grand jury. See JURY, GRAND.

Grand larceny. See LARCENY, GRAND.

Grand serjeanty. An ancient tenure by military service. See SERJEANTY.

Grange. A barn, a granary. A farm. An isolated farm.

Grange cases. Cases decided by U. S. Supreme Court in 1876 and reported in vol. 94 of the Reports. The cases arose from statutes regulating tolls and charges of common carriers and others.

Grangearius. One having care of a grange.

Grangia. A farm house; a farm.

Grant. A gift. A conveyance. A conveyance without livery of seizin.

Grant and demise. Words implying a warranty of title and quiet enjoyment.

Grant, bargain and sell. Words of conveyance in a deed.

Grant of personal property. A transfer of personal property for a consideration, as distinguished from a gift, which is gratuitous. An assignment.

Grant, office. See OFFICE GRANT.

Grant, public. See PUBLIC GRANT.

Grant to uses. A grant with uses added.

Grantee. One who receives a grant.

Grantor. One who makes a grant.

Grantz. Grandees.

Granum crescens. Growing grain.

Grass-hearth. The turning up of earth with a plow. A service of one day's plowing.

Grass week. Ancient term in the Inns of Court and Chancery for Rogation Week.

Grass widow. A married woman who lives apart from her husband. See GRACE WIDOW.

Grasson. Same as GRASSUM.

Grassum. A sum paid in anticipation of rent. A fine paid for a lease. A customary fine due from a copyhold tenant on the death of the lord.

Gratiani, Decretum. See CONCORDIA DISCORDANTIUM CANONUM.

Gratian's Decree. See CONCORDIA DISCORDANTIUM CANONUM.

Gratification. A voluntary reward for services.

Gratis. Freely. Gratuitously.

Gratis dictum. A voluntary assertion.

Gratten. Stubble.

Gratuitous. Bestowed freely; made without consideration.

Gratuitous bailment. See BAILMENT, GRATUITOUS.

Gratuitous contract. See CONTRACT, GRATUITOUS.

Gratuitous deeds. Deeds made without consideration which is binding.

Gratuitous feasance. A voluntary service.

Gratuitous service. One voluntarily performed without reward.

Gratuity. That given voluntarily, without reward or consideration.

Grava. A little wood or grove.

Gravamen. Burden. Injury; grievance. That part of a charge which is most material. The special cause of action in a suit. In English Church law, a grievance by a lower house to an upper house of convocation.

Gravare et gravatio. An accusation or impeachment.

Gravatio. An accusation. An impeachment.

Grave. A place in which a dead body is buried.

Gravio. Same as GRAFFIO.

Gravis. Grievous.

Gravius. Chief magistrate.

Gray's Inn. See INNS OF COURT.

Grazier. A breeder or keeper of cattle.

Great care. See CARE, GREAT.

Great cattle. Beasts except sheep and yearlings.

Great charter. Magna Charta (which see).

Great Council. The ancient Council of the King of England and out of which grew Parliament.

Great law, the. See LAW, THE GREAT.

Great men. Temporal lords. Members of the House of Commons.

Great roll. The roll in the English Treasury containing the treasury accounts.

Great Seal. See SEAL, GREAT.

Great tithes. See TITHES, GREAT.

Great vassal. See VASSAL, GREAT.

Greater excommunication. See EXCOMMUNICATION.

Gree. Satisfaction; consent; g r a c e; agreement.

Green bag. The bag or satchel in which a lawyer formerly carried papers to and from court.

Green cloth. See COURT OF GREEN CLOTH.

Green cloth, board of. Same as COURT OF GREEN CLOTH.

Green silver. An ancient custom in the manor of Writtel, in Essex, England, by which tenants whose doors opened toward Greenburg were required to pay a yearly halfpenny as rent.

Greenback. A term applied to a U. S. Treasury note.

Greenhew. Same as VERT.

Greenhue. Same as GREENHEW.

Greenland Company. A corporation created in England, during the reign of William III, for catching seals in Greenland seas.

Greenwax. Estreats delivered to the sheriffs out of the Exchequer under a seal in greenwax, to be levied in the several counties.

Greek calends. See CALENDS, GREEK.

Greek kalends. Same as CALENDS, GREEK.

Greffe. A prothonotary's office.

Greffler. A register or prothonotary.

Gregorian Code. See CODE, GREGORIAN.

Gregorian epoch. The time from which the Gregorian calendar dates, i. e., from the year 1582.

Gremial. A resident at a university. An apron of an officiating bishop.

Gremio. In Spanish law, a guild.

Gremium. The breast. Protection; safe-keeping.

Grenville Act. State 10 Geo. III. c. 16, transferring jurisdiction over parliamentary elections from the whole house to committees.

Gresham's law. See LAW, GRESHAM'S.

Gressume. Grassum (which see).

Gretna Green Marriage. See MARRIAGE, GRETNA GREEN.

Greva. Aggrieved. The seashore.

Greve. Power. Authority. Also same as REEVE.

(26)

Grieve. Same as REEVE.

Grieved. Aggrieved.

Grievous. Causing grief, injury or destruction.

Grils. A small fish.

Grimgribber. Technical jargon.

Grith. Peace, protection.

Grithbreche. Breach of the peace.

Grithstole. A place of sanctuary.

Grocer. In old English law, an engrosser of merchandise.

Gronna. A pit or place where turfs for burning are dug.

Groom. An official of the King's household having specified duties. A stable servant.

Groom of the stole. An officer of the English royal household having charge of the King's wearing apparel.

Groom porter. A superintendent over the royal gaming tables.

Gros. Large. Substance.

Gross. Absolute. Entire. Not depending on another.

Gross adventure. In Maritime law, a bottomry loan, so called because the lender is liable to gross average.

Gross average. See AVERAGE, GROSS.

Gross bois. Timber.

Gross fault. See FAULT, GROSS.

Gross, in. In entirety. Independent of another.

Gross neglect. See NEGLIGENCE, GROSS.

Gross negligence. See NEGLIGENCE, GROSS.

Gross profit. See PROFIT, GROSS.

Gross receipts. Receipts without any reduction.

Gross weight. The whole weight out of which tare and tret are allowed.

Grosse avanture. In French law, same as GROSS ADVENTURE, which see.

Grosse bois. Timber.

Grossement. Largely.

Grossement enseint. Big with child. Pregnant.

Grossome. In old English law, a fine paid for a lease.

Grot. A den, cave, or hollow place in the ground. A woody place with springs of water.

Groth-halfpenny. An ancient tribute paid for every fat beast, ox, or unfruitful cattle.

Ground. Land ; earth ; soil.

Ground annual. In Scotch law, an annual ground rent. The term comprises feu rents and ground rents from city lots.

Ground, dead. See DEAD GROUND.

Ground, good. See GOOD GROUND.

Ground, landlord. One who grants land for years or in fee-simple in consideration of ground rent.

Ground of action. The ground upon which an action is based.

Ground rent. Rent paid on a building site lease. See FARM RENT.

Groundage. A custom or tribute paid for the standing of a ship in a port.

Growing crop. A crop growing at the time it is referred to.

Growme. An ancient engine to stretch woolen cloth after being woven.

Growth, half-penny. An old English rate for tithe of every fat unproductive beast.

Gruarii. The principal officers of the forest in general.

Guadagium. The price given for safe conduct through another person's lands.

Guadia. In old law, a pledge ; also a custom.

Guadaloupe Hidalgo, treaty of. A treaty between the U. S. and Mexico, dated May 30th, 1848, ending the war between the two countries and ceding in consideration of $15,000,000 what is now California,

Nevada and Utah, and part of Colorado, Wyoming, Arizona and New Mexico. See GADSEN PURCHASE.

Guage. To determine by measurement or other test.

Guagetum. Guaging by a guager.

Guager. One who guages. A person appointed to measure the quantity and proof of liquor in a cask. A revenue officer.

Guarantee. To assure against loss or damage. One to whom a guarantee is given.

Guarantee clause. The clause in the U. S. Constitution (section 4 of Article 4) which guarantees each State a Republican form of government.

Guarantee, continuing. One which extends to continuing acts, as a guarantee to be responsible for goods sold to a person from time to time.

Guarantee, general. One open to the acceptance of the public.

Guarantee, special. One open to the one to whom it is made.

Guaranteed. Warranted. Promised the performance, continuance, or maintenance of. Assured against loss or injury.

Guarantor. One who makes a guaranty.

Guaranty. An undertaking to be answerable for the debt or performance of another. The undertaking. A warranty; to warrant.

Guaranty, absolute. A guarantee without a condition.

Guaranty, conditional. One which does not become absolute until the happening of some event, or performance of some act.

Guaranty, continuing. A guaranty covering several successive future transactions which continue or renew the guaranty.

Guardage. The condition of being under the care and control of a guardian.

Guardia. Ward; guardianship.

Guardian. A keeper; a protector. One who has the custody or charge of any person or thing. One who has charge of those unable to guide themselves or their affairs.

Guardian ad interim. A guardian serving in the absence of the real guardian.

Guardian ad litem. A person appointed by a court to represent the interests of a minor in a suit at law.

Guardian by Common law. Same as GUARDIAN IN SOCAGE.

Guardian by custom. The next of blood in copyhold. In London, the Mayor and Alderman.

Guardian by deed or will. A guardian appointed by the will or deed of the father or mother.

Guardian by nature. The father, or if dead, the mother.

Guardian by Statute. A guardian appointed by will or deed by virtue of 12 Car. II., chap. 24.

Guardian de l'eglise. A church warden.

Guardian de l'estemary. The guardian of the Stannaries, in the county of Cornwall, England.

Guardian, domestic. One appointed from the same jurisdiction as that of the infant or minor.

Guardian for nurture. Guardian of the person only; usually the father o mother.

Guardian, foreign. One appointed in another jurisdiction from that of the infant or minor.

Guardian, general. One who has general power over the person and estate of an infant or minor.

Guardian in chivalry. Wardship of a lord. The superior lord, who, when the heir was under twenty-one if male, or fourteen if female, was entitled to the wardship and marriage of the heir and profits of the lands during that period.

Guardian in socage. In socage tenure the next of blood to whom the inheritance could not possibly descend or ascend; the guardianship existed until the heir was fourteen.

Guardian of the Cinque Ports. A magistrate of the ports or havens commonly called Cinque Ports, with jurisdiction equal to that of the Admiral of England.

Guardian of the estate. One legally appointed to take charge of and manage the estate of an infant or minor.

Guardian of the person. One legally appointed to care for the person of an infant or minor.

Guardian of the spiritualities. See CUSTOS SPIRITUALIUM.

Guardian of the temporalities. See CUSTOS TEMPORALIUM.

Guardian, special. A guardian appointed for some particular purpose.

Guardian, testamentary. One appointed by will.

Guardians of the peace. Those who have charge of keeping the peace.

Guardians of the poor. Those who administer the poor laws of a county.

Guardianship. The duty or office of a guardian. Protection. Care. The relation between guardian and ward.

Guardianus. A guardian. A keeper.

Guarentigio. In Spanish law, a written authority to a court to enforce performance of a contract.

Guarnimentum. In old law, provision of necessities.

Guarra. War.

Guastald. One having custody of the royal mansions.

Gubernator. A pilot or steersman of a ship.

Gubernatorial. Relating to a governor, or office of governor.

Guerpi. Abandoned; deserted.

Guerpy. Same as GUERPI.

Guerrilla party. A body of men not regularly connected with either of two belligerents, but who carry on an irregular warfare against one of them.

Guerra. War.

Guerre. War.

Guest. A lodger at an inn.

Guest-taker. An agister.

Guet. Watch.

Guet apons. An ambush.

Guia. In Spanish law, a narrow right of way.

Guidage. The fee paid a guide.

Guiders. Conders.

Guidon de la mer. A work on maritime law, of unknown authority supposed to have been written in Normandy about 1671.

Guild. A fraternity, each of which was bound to pay something toward the support of the company. It originated in the old Saxon associations of neighbors who bound themselves to make satisfaction for crimes committed by their members. A tribute, tax, or amercement.

Guildhall. The hall of a guild. A place where goods were offered for sale. The legislative hall of the city of London, England. The Stilyard in London.

Guild rents. Rents payable by a guild or fraternity to the crown.

Guilda mercatoria. A company of merchants incorporated. An ancient franchise granted merchants in E n g l a n d whereby they were authorized to hold pleas of lands, etc., within their own precinct.

Guilder. A gold or silver coin of Germany, Portugal, Poland and Holland, valued differently.

Guildhall sittings. The sittings for London City cases, held in the Guildhall.

Guildhelda teutonicorum. The fraternity of Easterling merchants in London. See STILYARD.

Guillotine. A machine with a heavy blade sliding between vertical posts used to behead criminals. It was named after Dr. J. I. Guillotin because he had advocated the abolition of the axe or sword. It was invented by Dr. Antoine Louis, though a similar machine had been previously used.

Guilt. The state of one who has made himself liable to punishment.

Guiltwit. Same as GYLTWITE.

Guilty. Liable to punishment for having committed a crime. A plea admitting a charge.

Guilty, not. See NOT GUILTY.

Guinea. The sum of £1., 1s., in English money. It was formerly the name of a coin issued during the reign of William IV.

Guisarmes. Same as GISARMS.

Gule of August. First of August.

Gules. A term used in heraldry for red.

Gun, affirming. Same as SEMONCE.

Gurgites. Wears.

Guti. Goths, Jutes.

Guttera. A gutter on the roof of a house.

Gwabr merched. Maid's fee. A payment made to the lord of the manor upon the marriage or incontinency of a tenant's daughter.

Gwayf. In old English law, waif, or a stolen article dropped by a thief in his flight.

Gwalstow. A place of execution.

Gwerra. Same as GEWERE.

Gylput. The name of an ancient court held every three weeks in the liberty or hundred of Pathbew, in the County of Warwick, England.

Gyltwite. A compensation or amend for trespass.

Gynæcocracy. Same as GYNARCY.

Gynarcy. Government by a woman. A government of which a woman is the sovereign.

Gypsy. Same as GIPSY.

Gyrovagi. Wandering monks.

Gyves. Fetters for the legs.

Gyvn. A Jew.

H.

H. As an initial denotes, Hilary, Habeas, Hoc, House, Henry (King).

H. A. Hoc Anno (this year).

H. B. House Bill.

H. C. House of Commons ; Habeas Corpus.

H. L. House of Lords.

H. R. House of Representatives. House Roll.

H. T. Hoc Titulo (this title).

H. V. Hoc Verbo or Hac Voce (this word).

Hab. fa. poss. Abbreviation of Habere facias possessionem.

Habe (or Have). A term sometimes used in the Codes of Theodosius and Justinian in place of Ave (hail).

Habeas corpora juratorum. "That you have the bodies of the jurors." A writ for the sheriff to compel the attendance of jurymen in the Common Pleas.

Habeas corpus. "That you have the body." The name applied to several writs to bring a person into court. The writ which is referred to merely as a writ of habeas corpus, is the habeas corpus ad subjiciendum.

Habeas Corpus Act. The 31 Charles II., chap. 2.

Habeas corpus ad deliberandum et recipiendum. A writ to remove an accused person from one county to the one in which the offense was committed.

Habeas corpus ad faciendum et recipiendum. That you have the body or doing and receiving. A writ to remove the cause as well as the defendant to the jurisdiction of a Superior Court.

Habeas corpus ad prosequendum. That you have the person for prosecuting. A writ to remove a prisoner to be prosecuted.

Habeas corpus ad respondendum. That you have the person for answering. A writ to remove a prisoner that he may be charged with a new action in a Superior Court.

Habeas corpus ad satisfaciendum. That you have the person for satisfaction. A writ to bring up a defendant to a Superior Court and charge him with the execution upon judgment obtained below.

Habeas corpus ad subjiciendum. A writ directed to a person detaining another, commanding him to produce the prisoner with the cause of his detention and to do, submit to, and receive whatsoever the judge or court shall consider in that behalf.

Habeas corpus ad testificandum. That you have the person for testifying. A writ to remove a prisoner so that he may testify before a court.

Habeas corpus cum causa. Same as HABEAS CORPUS AD FACIENDUM ET RECIPIENDUM.

Habendum. To be held. That part of a deed which defines the estate granted, containing the words of limitation.

Habendum et tenendum. To have and to hold; to be had and held.

Habentes homines. Rich men.

Habentia. Riches.

Habere. To have.

Habere facias possessionem. That you make him have possession. A writ of execution, for the successful plaintiff in ejectment to recover possession of the lands.

Habere facias seisinam. That you cause to have seisin. A writ to give the plaintiff in a real or mixed action possession of the freehold.

Habere facias visum. That you cause to have a view. A writ to cause the sheriff to take a view of the lands in question.

Habere licere. To allow to have. In Roman law, applied to the obligation of a seller to allow the buyer to have possession of the thing bought.

Habergeon. A helmet which covered head and shoulders.

Haberjecto. A cloth of mixed color mentioned in Magna Charta.

Habeto tibi res tuas. Have thy property to thyself. In Roman law, words used in divorcing a wife.

Habiliments of war. Armor, provisions, etc.

Habilis. Able; good; sound; suitable.

Habit. See HABITS.

Habit and repute. Held and reputed.

Habit and repute of marriage. Living in the manner and conducting themselves as married persons.

Habit in repute. In Scotch law, applied to the belief in the taking place of some act or the existence of some condition.

Habitable repair. Such repair as renders safe and comfortable.

Habitancy. The act of occupying a permanent abiding place.

Habitant. In French law, also Canadian law, a settler.

Habitatio. In Civil law, the right to dwell in the house of another. See HABITATION.

Habitation. Place of abode; residence; occupancy. In Civil law, the right to dwell in the house of another, but not to use the house for any other purpose.

Habits. Usual conduct.

Habitual. Characterized by repeated practice. Frequently.

Habitual criminal. One repeatedly convicted of crime.

Habitual drunkard. One so repeatedly drunk that a guardian is required to manage him and his affairs.

Habitually. By frequent practice.

Habitus. Habit; apparel; manners.

Hable. A seaport town. A harbor.

Hachia. An instrument for digging. A pick.

Hacienda. In Spanish law, the public domain. The wealth of the State. A large plantation or landed estate owned by an individual.

Hackney carriage. A public carriage used to transport persons for hire.

Hadbote. A recompense for violence to persons in holy orders.

Hadd. In Hindu law, a limit. A punishment fixed or limited by law.

Hade of land. A small quantity of land; a hide.

Haderunga. Partiality. Prejudice. Hatred.

Hadgonel. A tax or mulct.

Hæc est conventio. This is an agreement. Words anciently used in beginning written contracts.

Hæc est finalis concordia. This is the final agreement. Words anciently used in beginning the foot of a fine of lands.

Hæreda. An old Gothic court similar to the Court Leet.

Hærede abducto. An old writ allowed a lord whose ward had been abducted.

Hærede deliberando alteri qui habet custodiam terræ. A writ directing the sheriff to compel the delivery of a ward to his or her guardian, by reason of his land.

Hærede rapto. A writ against one who took from a guardian, his ward. See Ravishment de Gard.

Hæredes. In Civil law, heirs.

Hæredes extranei. Extraneous heirs; those not within the testator's power.

Hæredes necessarii. Necessary heirs. In Roman law, heirs who were compelled to take an inheritance, as slaves, who were given freedom and property by will.

Hæredes proximi. In Roman law, heirs; children of the deceased.

Hæredes remotiores. In Roman law, heirs not begotten, as grandchildren, &c.

Hæredes sui et necessarii. Own and necessary heirs. In Roman law, the direct descendants of the deceased, as distinguished from those made heirs by will.

Hæredifacti. Heirs made (by will or testament).

Hæredipeta. An inheritance seeker. The next heir to lands.

Hæreditament. That which may be inherited.

Hæreditamentum. Hereditament (which see).

Hæreditas. Inheritance.

Hæreditas damnosa. A burdensome inheritance.

Hæreditas jacens. A prostrate inheritance. An inheritance not yet accepted and entered upon by the heir.

Hæreditas luctuosa. A mournful inheritance, as of a parent to a child.

Hæreditas paterna. An inheritance from the father.

Hæres. Heir. In Roman law, an heir who represented the deceased and was bound to discharge the obligations of the deceased, therefore in a sense acting as his representative.

Hæres actu. An heir by appointment.

Hæres astrarius. An heir in possession.

Hæres de facto. An heir in fact, from the wrongful act of an ancestor.

Hæres designatus. An heir designated.

Hæres ex asse. In Civil law, only heir, or heir to the whole.

Hæres ex semisse. Heir to one half.

Hæres ex dodrante. Heir to three-fourths.

Hæres extraneus. In Civil law, a strange heir or one who was not under the control of the one from whom he inherits.

Hæres factus. An heir by will.

Hæres fidei commissarius. He for whose benefit an estate was given in trust for another.

Hæres fiduciarius. An heir in trust, or trustee.

Hæres jure representationis. An heir by right of representation.

Hæres legitimus. A legitimate heir.

Hæres natus. A born heir.

Hæres necessarius. In Civil law, a necessary heir. See HÆREDES NECESSARII.

Hæres proximus. The descendant of the deceased.

Hæres rectus. A right heir.

Hæres remotior. A more remote heir (not a descendant).

Hæres suus. A proper heir, a child or grandchild.

Hæres suus et necessarius. In Civil law, an heir by relationship and necessity.

Hæretare. In Old English law, to confer a hereditary right upon one.

Hæretico comburendo. Same as HERETICO COMBURENDO.

Hafne. A haven or port.

Hafne Courts. Same as COURTS, HAFNE.

Hag. A part of a wood from which the owner cut wood yearly.

Haga. A house in a city or borough. An enclosure or hedge.

Hagia. A hedge.

Hagne. In old English law, a small hand-gun.

Hagnebut. In old English law, a hand-gun larger than a hagne.

Haia. A hedge. An enclosed park.

Haiebote. Same as HAYBOTE.

Haill. In Scotch law, the whole.

Hailworkfolk. Same as HALYWERC-FOLK.

Haimhaldare. In old Scotch law, to secure the return home of one's goods.

Haimsecken. Same as HAIMSUCKEN.

Haimsucken. In Scotch law, assaulting a person in his own house by one who enters the same illegally. Burglary.

Hake. A dried and salted fish.

Haketon. An ancient military defensive coat.

Halceonii dies. Halcyon days.

Half blood. The relation between those having but one parent, who is the ancestor of both. One whose parents are of different races.

Half brother. A male who has the same mother and a different father, or the same father and a different mother from that of another person.

Half defense. See DEFENSE, HALF.

Half endeal. A half of anything.

Half mark. An English coin valued at six shillings and eight pence.

Half proof. In the Civil law, proof by only one witness ; or a private instrument.

Half seal. An old English chancery seal used on the commissions of delegates appointed on an appeal in ecclesiastical or admiralty causes.

Half tongue. A jury de medietate linguæ, which on the trial of a foreigner is composed of half of his countrymen, if he demand the same.

Half year. One hundred and eighty-two days.

Halfendeal. A moiety or one-half of a thing.

Half-kineg. In Saxon law, half king; also a title given the aldermen of all England.

Halifax inquest. See INQUEST, HALIFAX.

Haligemot. (Saxon). A meeting of tenants in the baron's hall, or of citizens in their public hall.

Halimas. In English law, the Feast of All Saints on November 1.

Halke. A hole.

Hall. A mansion house. A room devoted to assemblies or legislative bodies.

Hallage. Toll paid on goods sold in a hall. Anciently a toll on cloth taken to Blackwell Hall, in London, for sale.

Hallamshire. A part of the county of York in England.

Hallazco. In Spanish law, the act of finding and taking possession of an article previously without an owner.

Hallegemote. Same as HALLMOTE.

Halmote. The court baron among the Saxons.

Halsfang. Healfang (which see).

Halymote. An Ecclesiastical court. An old London court held on Sunday before St. Thomas' day, before Mayor and Sheriffs, to regulate the bakers.

Halywercfolk. People who held land on service to defend or repair a church, or sepulchre.

Ham. A home. A dwelling place. A small narrow meadow. A house. A small village.

Hama. In old English law, an engine for pulling down a house when on fire. A tract of land.

Hamallare. To summon.

Hambling. In Forest law, laming dogs by hocking, or cutting the tendons of the hock.

Hamburg Company. The first English Trading Company.

Hame. A house; a home.

Hamel. A hamlet.

Hameleta. A hamlet.

Hamefare. Breach of the peace in a house.

Hameling. Same as HAMBLING.

Hamesucken. Same as HAIMSUCKEN.

Hamlet. A small village. Part of a village or parish. The seat of a freeholder.

Hamleta. A hamlet.

Hamma. A close adjoining a house. A small meadow.

Hammer, sold under the. Sold at public auction.

Hamper. A receptacle for documents or valuables. A basket in which chancery writs, their returns and the fees were kept.

Hamsecken. Same as HAIMSUCKEN.

Hamsoca. Same as HAMSOCUE.

Hamsocua. Same as HAMSOCUE.

Hamsocue. The right to security and freedom from invasion in one's own house.

Hamsoken. Same as HAMSOCUE.

Hamsoone. The privilege of a man's house. A breach against a man's hospitality.

Hanaper. Same as HAMPER.

Hanaper, clerk of the. See CLERK OF THE HANAPER.

Hanaper office. One of the offices belonging to the Court of Chancery on the Common law side, so-called, which kept matters relating to private persons. Those relating to the crown matters were kept in Petty Bag.

Hanborows. Inferior pledges under a Headborough.

Hand. An employee. Handwriting. A signature. An oath. A linear measure of four inches.

Hand and seal. Signature and seal.

Hand down. To announce. To declare.

Hand down an opinion. In an Appellate Court, to deliver to the clerk to be transmitted to the court below.

Hand money. Earnest money.

Hand, strong. See STRONG HAND.

Hand, whip. The right hand.

Handbill. A small sheet of paper containing an advertisement.

Handborow. A hand pledge. The nine frank pledges of a decennary. See HEADBOROW.

Handfasting. Betrothal.

Handful. By early English statute, four inches.

Handgrith. Protection given by the King personally (with his own hand).

Hand-habend. Having in hand. A thief caught in the act with the stolen goods in his hand. See BACKBERINDE.

Hand-money. Earnest money.

Hands. Legal status. Authority. Force. Violence.

Hands, clean. Without justice or illegality.

Hands, comparison of. Comparison of handwriting.

Handsale. A sale confirmed by striking hands. The price paid in such a sale.

Handsel. Earnest money; handsale.

Handwriting. The form of letters and marks made by one in writing words.

Handwriting, comparison of. A method of producing evidence of a signature or writing being that of a person mentioned, by comparing it with some signature or writings proved to be that of the same party.

Handywarp. A kind of cloth mentioned in English statutes.

Hang. To be in process of settlement. To pend.

Hanging. The act of executing by suspending by the neck with a rope. Breaking the neck by allowing the person to suddenly fall through a trap, or be jerked upward at the end of a rope placed about the neck with a slip-knot. In practice, pending; undecided.

Hanging in chains. A former English practice of hanging a murderer's body upon a gibbet, in chains, after execution, near the place where the murder was committed.

Hangman. One who executes a condemned person by hanging.

Hangwit. Same as HANGWITE.

Hangwite. A fine for hanging a felon or thief without judgment, or allowing one to escape custody. The right of a lord to challenge the forfeiture of the goods of one who hanged himself within the lord's fee. Exemption from the fine for illegal hanging.

Hanig. A term for customary labor to be performed.

Hanper. Same as HAMPER.

Hanse. A confederacy of merchants or commercial towns. In France, of the Middle Ages, a gild of merchants. The Hanseatic League. An imposition upon merchandise.

Hanse towns. Towns which were members of the Hanseatic League.

Hanse towns, laws of. See LAW, HANSEATIC.

Hanseatic. Pertaining to a hanse or league of German towns.

Hanseatic League. A political commercial confederation of cities in Northern Germany, during the Middle Ages, for mutual protection and profit.

Hanseatic Laws. See LAWS, HANSEATIC.

Hansgrave. The chief of a corporation or company.

Hantelode. In old European a law, an attachment. An arrest.

Hap. To catch.

Happiness. The right to act in accordance with one's own desires without other restraint than the law of the land.

Haque. A small hand-gun anciently prohibited in England.

Haquebut. A harquebuss or hand-gun.

Haracium. Horses and mares kept for breeding.

Harbinger. Same as HERBENGER.

Harbor. A port or haven; a sheltered place for the protection of vessels against storms. To give shelter or protection to.

Harbour. Same as HARBOR.

Hard cases. Judicial decisions which, though not in accordance with legal principles, are made to relieve a case of hardship.

Hard labor. See LABOR, HARD.

Hard pan. A layer of rock or pieces of rock under loose soil.

Hardheidis. In old Scotch law, coins valued at half a penny.

Hardship. Injury. That which is hard to endure.

Hardwic. Same as HERDEWIC.

Hare. A beast of warren.

Hariot. Same as HERIOT.

Harlots. Same as PROSTITUTES.

Harmiscara. A fine.

Harnasca. In old law, defensive armor worn by a man.

Harness. Anciently all warlike instruments and armor. The tackle of a ship. The tackle used on a horse with which to draw a wagon or carriage.

Harniscara. A fine.

Haro. An outcry for felons and malefactors.

Harping-irons. Harpoons.

Harriot. Same as HERIOT.

Harron. Same as HARO.

Hart. A male deer of five or more years of age.

Hart, royal. A hart which has been hunted by a king or queen and escaped from the forest.

Harter Act. Act of U. S. Congress, February 13, 1893, exempting owners, agents and charterers of vessels from responsibility for damages or loss under certain conditions.

Harth penny. A penny tax on every hearth.

Harvest. To gather crops of grain or grass. The time when such crops are usually gathered.

Hasp and staple. Anciently, the form of an heir's entry into property held by burgage tenure, in Scotland.

Haspa. In old English law, a hasp on a door. It was sometimes used in livery of seisin.

Hasta. In Rome, a spear; it was the sign of an auction sale.

Hasta porci. A shield of brawn.

Hastæ subjicere. In Rome, to put under the spear. To offer at public auction. In Feudal law, the symbol used in investing one with the fee of land.

Hat money. Primage.

Hatches. Dams of clay and earth.

Hauber. A great lord.

Haubergeon. A coat of mail.

Haubert. A coat of mail.

Hauberticum feudum. Same as HAWBERK.

Haugh. A green spot in a valley.

Haul. To transport by drawing. The distance over which freight is transported by a railroad.

Hault. High.

Haur. Hatred.

Haustus. Drawing. The servitude of drawing water. The right to draw water from a well or stream and right of way so to do.

Haut. High.

Haut chemin. Highway.

Haut estret. High street. Highway.

Hauthoner. A man armed with a coat of mail.

Have. To possess actually. To be in bodily occupation of.

Haven. A sheltered place for ships. A harbor.

Haver. In Scotch law, the person holding a document who is called on to produce it in court.

Havers. In Scotch law, behavior; manners.

Haw. A small piece of land. A house.

Hawberk. A shirt of mail. One who anciently held lands in France by a service of finding a shirt of mail.

Hawbert. Same as HAWBERK.

Hawg. Same as HAUGH.

Hawgh. Same as HAUGH.

Hawkers. Itinerant tradesmen or peddlers; hucksters.

Hawking. Offering goods for sale by crying them aloud.

Hay. A hedge or enclosure. A net to take game. Dried or cured grass.

Haya. Same as HAY.

Hay-bote. A privilege of taking wood for making rakes, and forks for making hay, also to repair gates, fences, etc.

Haye. Same as HAY.

Hayward. An officer of the lord's court who kept the common cattle of a town and protected the hedges. A poundmaster.

Hazard. Peril; risk; danger. A game with dice, at one time prohibited in England.

Hazardors. Those who played the game of hazard.

Hazardous. Involving peril or risk.

Hazardous contract. See CONTRACT, HAZARDOUS.

Head. Chief; principal; the upper part.

Head courts. Scotch tribunals with certain civil and criminal jurisdiction at one time held by sheriffs, stewards and barons, annually.

Head money. In prize law, the amount paid each person on a ship as a bounty for sinking or destroying an enemy's ship.

Head of a family. See FAMILY, HEAD OF A.

Head silver. An ancient exaction for the support of the leet.

Headborough. A chief of the frank pledge or ten pledges in a borough. A kind of constable. See HANBOROWS.

Headborow. Same as HEADBOROUGH.

Headland. A strip of unplowed land left at the end of furrows or near a fence. A cliff projecting into the sea or a river.

Headnote. The note placed at the head of a published court decision. The syllabus.

Headpence. An ancient exaction by the sheriff of the inhabitants of Northumberland County, England. Abolished by 23 Hy. VI., c. 7.

Heafodweard. An old term applied in England to the service performed by a villein or a thane.

Healgemote. In Saxon law, an ecclesiastical court. A court baron.

Healsfang. A Saxon pillory, by which the head of the condemned was held between two boards.

Health. Physical condition. Freedom from sickness.

Health, bill of. See BILL OF HEALTH.

Health, Board of. A board of persons in a nation, State, or political division charged with the regulation of matters affecting the public health.

Health, clean bill of. A certificate that no contagious or infectious disease exists.

Health laws. See LAWS, SANITARY.

Health, National Board of. A board created by act of U. S. Congress, dated March 3, 1879, comprising eleven members, to obtain information relating to public health.

Health officer. See OFFICER, HEALTH.

Health, public. The general health of a community.

Healthy. Free from disease or ailment.

Hearing. A trial of an equity suit. The session of a court for passing upon evidence. An examination of testimony. A listening to an argument.

Hearing, final. The trial of the merits of an equity matter as distinguished from the interlocutory matters.

Hearing, further. Hearing after continuance.

Hearing, re. See RE-HEARING.

Hearsay. That which is heard from another.

Hearsay evidence. See EVIDENCE, HEARSAY.

Hearth money. An ancient tax on on every hearth.

Hearth silver. In English law, a composition paid for tithes.

Heat of passion. Violent anger. During the period when a person is in great anger.

Hearthfeste. Fixed to the house or hearth.

Hebbermen. Ancient poaching fishermen who fished at ebb tide.

Hebberthef. In Saxon law, the privilege within a certain district of trying a thief and taking his goods.

Hebbing-wears. Wears used by hebbermen for catching fish.

Hebdomad. A week.

Hebdomadius. One having charge of a choir in a church for a week.

Heccagium. Royalty or fee paid for privilege of using hecks.

Heck. An ancient device for catching fish.

Hectoliter. In Metric system a measure of capacity equal to 2 bushels, 3.35 pecks, or 26.42 gallons.

Hectare. In Metric system a measure of surface equal to 2.471 acres.

Hectogram. In Metric system, 3.527 ounces.

Hectometer. In Metric system a measure of length equal to 328 feet one inch.

Heda. A wharf or landing place.

Hedagium. Toll paid for landing goods at a heda or wharf.

Hedge parson. At one time in England, an illiterate parson.

Hedge priest. Formerly, an Irish priest ordained without having studied at a regular college, but in a hedge school. A hedge parson.

Hedge school. Formerly, in Ireland, a school kept in a hedge corner. An open air school.

Hedgebote. Privilege of taking enough wood to make hedges with.

Hegemony. Leadership. Political supremacy of a city or State.

Hegira. A flight. The Mahometan period of time beginning with the flight of Mahomet from Mecca, July 16, A. D. 622.

Hegumenos. The head of a Greek Church monastery.

Heifer. A young cow which has not had a calf.

Heir. Originally, one who took a fee to land by descent. Now, applied to one who takes any property by descent. (As between husband and wife, neither is the heir of the other).

Heir apparent. One who will be heir if he outlive the ancestor.

Heir, appearand. In Scotch law, an apparent heir.

Heir at Common Law. Same as HEIR AT LAW.

Heir at law. One to whom the law transmits the estate of a deceased.

Heir, beneficiary. In Civil law, one who accepts the succession under an inventory.

Heir by custom. Heir by some particular custom.

Heir by devise. One to whom lands are devised.

Heir by intestacy. Same as HEIR AT LAW.

Heir, collateral. See HEIRS, COLLATERAL.

Heir, conventional. In Civil law, one who takes the succession under some contract or settlement which entitles him to the same.

Heir expectant. One who expects to inherit property.

Heir, forced. One who cannot be deprived of an inheritance. In Lousiana, a person having reserved for him by law such an interest in a portion of an estate that he cannot be deprived of it by a donor without good cause.

Heir, general. Same as HEIR AT LAW.

Heir, institute. In Scotch law, the first person to whom an estate is given by destination or limitation.

Heir, irregular. One upon whom the estate is cast by law on there being failure of testamentary or blood heirs.

Heir, last. See LAST HEIR.

Heir, legal. In Civil law, one upon whom the succession is cast by law as distinguished from a conventional or testamentary heir.

Heir, male. In Scotch law, an heir institute who is the nearest male relation of the deceased.

Heir of conquest. In Scotch law, an heir of property or rights which the deceased did not acquire by inheritance.

Heir of line. In Scotch law, a blood relative who succeeds to property which deceased acquired by inheritance.

Heir of provision. In Scotch law, an heir because of a provision in a deed or other instrument writing.

Heir of tailzie. In Scotch law, one who inherits an estate which would not have passed to him by law.

Heir, presumptive. The person who would be heir if the ancestor died, but whose right may be defeated.

Heir, special. The heir in tail, who may or may not be heir general.

Heir, substitute. In Scotch law, one of several heirs technically described.

Heir substitute, in a bond. In Scotch law, one who is to be paid the amount mentioned in a bond on or after the death of a creditor.

Heir, testamentary. One made an heir by will.

Heir, unconditional. In Civil law, one who inherits without condition or without inventory either by express or tacit acceptance.

Heirdom. Succession by inheritance.

Heiress. A female heir.

Heirlooms. Chattels which go by custom to the heir with the real estate, and not to the executor or administrator.

Heirs. Words in a deed used when a fee is intended to be conveyed.

Heirs ab intestato. Heirs upon whom a succession is cast by operation of law.

Heirs, collateral. Collateral kindred who succeed next in absence of direct heirs.

Heirs of the body. Heirs begotten of a man's body who would inherit his property if he died intestate.

Heirship. The condition of an heir. The relationship between ancestor and heir.

Heirship movables. In Scotch law, those necessary articles connected with a house and land, such as furniture, farming utensils and stock, which did not go to the executor, but to the heir; the law deeming these to be part of the establishment.

Held. See HOLD.

Helier. A roofer.

Hell. A word applied to the place under the English Exchequer where debtors to the King were confined.

Hellsing. A brass coin among the Saxons equal to the English half-penny.

Helm. Thatch. Straw. A covering for the head in war. That part of a coat of arms which bears the crest. The handle of the rudder of a vessel.

Helmelborch. Same as HEMOLDBORH.

Helowe wall. The end wall that covers and defends the rest of the building.

Helsing. Same as HELLSING.

Hemoldborh. A title to possession.

Hence. Hereinafter. From this time. In the future. From this cause. Consequently.

Henchman. An attendant upon another.

Henedpenny. An ancient customary payment of money instead of hens at Christmas.

Heneward. An ancient duty to the king in Cambridgeshire, England.

Henfare. In old English law, a fine for fleeing or committing murder.

Hengen. An ancient English prison for those sentenced to hard labor.

Henghen. Same as HENGEN.

Hengwite. Same as HANGWITE.

Hengwyte. Same as HENGWITE.

Henricus vetus. Henry the Old. Applied to King Henry I.

Heordfæte. In Saxon law, one who had a dwelling. A householder.

Heordfeste. Same as HEORDFÆTE.

Heordpenny. Peterpence.

Heordwerck. In Saxon law, the service of herding.

Heorthpening. Same as HEORDPENNY.

Heptarchy. Government by seven persons. A group of seven governments. The seven kingdoms established in England by the Saxons, comprising Essex, Wessex, Sussex, Kent, East Anglia, Northumbria and Mercia.

Herald. An officer at arms of the King, whose duty was to denounce war, proclaim peace and carry martial messages, examine and judge gentlemen's coat of arms, act as marshal on public occasions, etc. The three chief heralds were called king at arms.

Heraldry. The office of heralds. An old practice of selling the right of precedence in the hearing of a cause.

Heralds' College. An English corporation, founded by Richard III., empowered to grant arms and preserve pedigrees, consisting of three kings at arms, six heralds and four pursuivants, together with the Earl Marshal of England.

Heraud. A herald.

Herbage. The privilege of feeding cattle in the ground of another or in the forest.

Herbagium. Herbage. The right of pasture.

Herbagium auterius. The first crop of grass or hay.

Herbagium terræ. The herbage of the land ; the crop.

Herbery. An inn.

Herbenger. An officer in the King's house who goes before and selects and allots lodgings for noblemen.

Herbergagium. Lodgings for guests.

Herbergare. Same as HERBIGARE.

Herbergatus. Spent in an inn.

Herbigare. To harbor. To entertain.

Herbinger. Same as HERBENGER.

Herbury. An inn.

Herce. A harrow. A candlestick made in the form of a harrow.

Hercia. Same as HERCE.

Herciare. To harrow.

Herciature. Harrowing.

Herciscere. To divide.

Herciscunda. In Civil law, to be divided.

Herdewic. Same as HERDEWICH.

Herdewich. A grange or place for cattle and husbandry.

Herdwerck. Herdman's work or customary services performed by shepherds, herdsmen and inferior tenants at the will of the lord.

Hereafter. In some future time. From now on.

Herebannum. A mulct for not going armed into the field, when called forth.

Herebote. The King's edict commanding his subjects into the field.

Hereby. By virtue of this.

Heredad. In Spanish law, a cultivated piece of land.

Heredad yacente. In Spanish law, an inheritance not yet taken possession of.

Heredero. In Spanish law, an heir.

Hereditagium. In Italy, that held by hereditary right.

Hereditament. That which may be inherited.

Hereditament, corporeal. Such as is visible, tangible and could be passed by livery of seisin.

Heriditament, incorporeal. That which lay only in grant and not capable of being handled or delivered by hand or feoffment. A right issuing out of a thing whether real or personal and concerning, annexed to or exercisable within the same.

Hereditary. Capable of passing, or that which must pass by inheritance.

Hereditary right of the crown. The right of inheriting the crown.

Hereditary revenue of the King. The revenue which a King is entitled to by reason of inheritance.

Herefare. A military expedition.

Heregeat. A heriot.

Heregeld. A tribute or tax levied for maintenance of an army.

Herein. In this connection, place, circumstance or particular.

Hereinafter. In an after part of this.

Hereinbefore. In a preceding part of this.

Herellus. A small fish.

Heremitorium. A place where hermits retired.

Heremones. Those who followed an army.

Herenach. An archdeacon.

Heres. In Civil law, an heir.

Hereschip. In old Scotch law, robbery.

Hereslita. A hired soldier who departs without license.

Heressa. Same as HERESLITA.

Heressiz. Same as HERESLITA.

Heresy. A false opinion repugnant to some essential or important point of doctrine.

Heretable jurisdictions. Grants of criminal jurisdiction bestowed on great families in Scotland. Abolished by 20 Geo. II., c. 50.

Hereteams. Same as HEREMONES.

Heretic. One who adheres to and is convicted of heresy.

Heretico comburendo. Burning a heretic. A writ out of chancery issuing only by special direction of the King in council, to burn one convicted of heresy and refusing to abjure it, or being guilty of it after having abjured it. Abolished by 29 Charles II., c. 9.

Heretoche. A baron. A leader of a military district or army among the Anglo-Saxons.

Heretochias. A leader or commander of military forces.

Heretochii. Plural of Heretoche.

Heretofore. Previous to the present time.

Heretum. A court or yard. An orchard.

Herezeld. In Scotch law, a gift to a lord by his tenant, as a mark of respect.

Herge. In Saxon law, those who joined in a band of thirty-five or more for robbery, &c.

Hergripa. Pulling by the hair.

Heri. Landholders ; proprietors.

Herigalds. A garment.

Heriot. A tribute to the lord for his better preparation for war. The best beast or chattel payable to the lord on the tenant's death.

Heriot service. A rent due upon a special reservation in a grant or lease upon the death of a tenant in fee-simple.

Heriot custom. A customary tribute of goods or chattels payable to the lord of the fee on the decease of a tenant for life.

Hence. Hereinafter. From this time. In the future. From this cause. Consequently.

Henchman. An attendant upon another.

Henedpenny. An ancient customary payment of money instead of hens at Christmas.

Heneward. An ancient duty to the king in Cambridgeshire, England.

Henfare. In old English law, a fine for fleeing or committing murder.

Hengen. An ancient English prison for those sentenced to hard labor.

Henghen. Same as HENGEN.

Hengwite. Same as HANGWITE.

Hengwyte. Same as HENGWITE.

Henricus vetus. Henry the Old. Applied to King Henry I.

Heordfæte. In Saxon law, one who had a dwelling. A householder.

Heordfeste. Same as HEORDFÆTE.

Heordpenny. Peterpence.

Heordwerck. In Saxon law, the service of herding.

Heorthpening. Same as HEORDPENNY.

Heptarchy. Government by seven persons. A group of seven governments. The seven kingdoms established in England by the Saxons, comprising Essex, Wessex, Sussex, Kent, East Anglia, Northumbria and Mercia.

Herald. An officer at arms of the King, whose duty was to denounce war, proclaim peace and carry martial messages, examine and judge gentlemen's coat of arms, act as marshal on public occasions, etc. The three chief heralds were called king at arms.

Heraldry. The office of heralds. An old practice of selling the right of precedence in the hearing of a cause.

Heralds' College. An English corporation, founded by Richard III., empowered to grant arms and preserve pedigrees, consisting of three kings at arms, six heralds and four pursuivants, together with the Earl Marshal of England.

Heraud. A herald.

Herbage. The privilege of feeding cattle in the ground of another or in the forest.

Herbagium. Herbage. The right of pasture.

Herbagium auterius. The first crop of grass or hay.

Herbagium terræ. The herbage of the land ; the crop.

Herbery. An inn.

Herbenger. An officer in the King's house who goes before and selects and allots lodgings for noblemen.

Herbergagium. Lodgings for guests.

Herbergare. Same as HERBIGARE.

Herbergatus. Spent in an inn.

Herbigare. To harbor. To entertain.

Herbinger. Same as HERBENGER.

Herbury. An inn.

Herce. A harrow. A candlestick made in the form of a harrow.

Hercia. Same as HERCE.

Herciare. To harrow.

Herciature. Harrowing.

Herciscere. To divide.

Herciscunda. In Civil law, to be divided.

Herdewic. Same as HERDEWICH.

Herdewich. A grange or place for cattle and husbandry.

Herdwerck. Herdman's work or customary services performed by shepherds, herdsmen and inferior tenants at the will of the lord.

Hereafter. In some future time. From now on.

Herebannum. A mulct for not going armed into the field, when called forth.

Herebote. The King's edict commanding his subjects into the field.

Hereby. By virtue of this.

Heredad. In Spanish law, a cultivated piece of land.

Heylode. A customary burden imposed upon inferior tenants for repairing the hedges.

Heymectus. A net for catching conies.

Hibernagium. Same as IBERNAGIUM.

Hidage. An extraordinary tax payable to the King on every hide of land. An exemption from hidage.

Hidalgo. In Spanish law, a noble.

Hidalgo, Guadaloupe. See GUADALOUPE HIDALGO, TREATY OF.

Hidalguia. In Spanish law, nobility by descent.

Hidare. Same as HIDAGE.

Hidden ambiguity. Same as AMBIGUITY LATENT.

Hidgild. Same as HIDEGID.

Hide. A plowland, or as much as could be plowed with one plow. From 60 to 120 acres. As much as would maintain a family. A mansion house.

Hide and gain. Arable land. See GAINAGE.

Hide lands. In Saxon law, the lands of or connected with a hide or dwelling house.

Hide of land. Sufficient land to maintain one family. The area of land which can be ploughed by one plough in a year.

Hidegild. Interpreted by the Saxons as a ransom to save one's hide or skin from beating.

Hidel. In old English, a sanctuary.

Hierarchy. Ecclesiastical rulers. Government by clergy.

High bailiff. An officer of a county court.

High Commission Court. See COURT, HIGH COMMISSION.

High Constable. The chief constable.

High crime. See CRIME, HIGH.

High Justice. See JUSTICE, HIGH.

High Justiciar. In Feudal law, one who exercised the right of high justice. See JUSTICE, HIGH.

High misdemeanor. See MISDEMEANOR, HIGH.

High sea. See SEA, HIGH.

High sheriff. A sheriff.

High treason. Treason to the King or State.

High water mark. See WATER MARK, HIGH.

High wood. Timber.

Highway. A passage, bridge, footpath, wagon-road, street, or water-way open to the public.

Highway acts. Statutes relating to the laying out and maintenance of highways.

Highway, common. One open to the public on equal terms.

Highway, public. Same as HIGHWAY, COMMON.

Highway robbery. See ROBBERY, HIGHWAY.

Highwaymen. Those who commit robbery upon the highway. See ROBBERY.

Higler. A peddler of provisions. A travelling huckster.

Higuela. In Spanish law, a receipt by an heir stating the property received under the inheritance.

Hijadalgo. Same as HIDALGO.

Hijra. Same as HEGIRA.

Hikenild street. Same as IKENILD STREET.

Hilary rules. A collection of forms and orders which modified the pleading and practice in the English Superior Courts of Common law established 1834.

Hilary Sittings. The term of English Court beginning January 11, and ending Wednesday before Easter. It succeeded Hilary Term.

Hilary Term. From the eleventh to the thirty-first of January, in the English Courts. See DE TERMINO HILARII.

Hilda. Same as HIDE.

Hinc inde. A Scotch law term meaning on either side. Reciprocally.

Hind. A farm servant.

Hindas. The wives of Hindeni Homines.

Hinder and delay. To attempt to defraud. To obstruct a creditor in obtaining satisfaction of his debt.

Hindeni homines. A society of men.

Hine. Same as HIND.

Hinefare. The departure of a servant from his master.

Hinegeld. A fine for an offense committed by a servant.

Hipoteca. In Spanish law, a mortgage of realty.

Hippocras. Liquor made of wine and honey.

Hirciscunda. A division of an inheritance among heirs.

Hire. To contract for the use of a thing or services for a specified use or time, for a consideration. Compensation for services of a person or the use of a thing.

Hireman. A subject. One who guards the King in his hall.

Hirer. One who hires a person or thing.

Hiring. A contracting for the possession of some article for a specified time or use for a consideration. The act of contracting for the service of another for a consideration.

Hirst. A small wood or forest.

His testibus. These witnesses. The attestation clause in deeds.

Hith. Same as HYTHE.

Hitherto. To this time.

Hiwisc. A hide of land.

Hlaf æta. In Saxon law, a servant fed at the expense of his master.

Hlaford. In Saxon law, a lord.

Hlafordsocna. In Saxon law, the lord's protection.

Hlafordswice. In Saxon law, treason to one's lord.

Hlasocna. In Saxon law, the protection of the law.

Hloth. A company or band from seven to thirty-five, united for unlawful purpose, such as riot.

Hlothbote. A mulct for being one of a hloth, or a rioter.

Hlothbote. Same as HLOTHBOTA.

Hoastmen. In old English law, a gild of sea-coal dealers.

Hoblers. Light horsemen or tenants bound to maintain a cavalry to give notice of an invasion. Those who used bows and arrows.

Hobilers. Same as HOBLERS.

Hoc. This.

Hoc voce. Under this word.

Hoccus saltis. A small salt fish.

Hoch. Same as HOGA.

Hockettor. An old or incapacitated knight. A basket carrier.

Hock Tuesday. The day the English mastered the Danes. Celebrated the second Tuesday after Easter.

Hock Tuesday money. A duty paid a landlord that his tenants and servants might solemnize Hock Tuesday.

Hocqueteur. Same as HOCKETTOR.

Hodge-podge. Same as HOTCHPOT.

Hodge-podge Act. A statute containing provisions relating to several subjects.

Hoga. A mountain or hill.

Hogaster. A young sheep.

Hogenhine. Same as AGENHINE.

Hogenhyne. Same as AGENHINE.

Hoggacius. A sheep of the second year. In Northern England young sheep were formerly called hogs.

Hoggus. Same as HOGIETUS.

Hogictus. A swine. A grown pig.

Hogium. Same as HOGA.

Hokeday. Same as HOCK TUESDAY.

Hoketide. Same as HOCK TUESDAY.

Hold. A holding or tenure as leasehold, freehold, copyhold. To decide to be. To possess. To occupy. To maintain. To believe. To conduct. To bind legally. To be in possession of.

Hold over. To remain in possession after the term.

Hold pleas. To hear and determine causes.

Holder. One who holds possession of anything. One who holds by lawful title.

Holdes. Bailiffs of a town or city. A general.

Holding. A farm. The tenure or nature of the right given to a grantee or tenant by a superior.

Holding, feu. See FEU HOLDING.

Holding over. Keeping possession of property after the expiration of a term without the lessor's consent.

Holiday. A day on which persons generally refrain from labor. See HOLIDAY, LEGAL.

Holiday, legal. One upon which public business is suspended by authority of law. One made a holiday by law, and on which persons are exempt from legal obligations. In U. S. Bankrupt law of 1898, Christmas, Fourth of July, Twenty-second of February and any day appointed by the President or Congress as a holiday.

Holiday, public. Same as HOLIDAY, LEGAL.

Holm. An island or fenny place. A hill or cliff.

Holmgang. The custom of ancient Northern nations of trial by battel ; the combat taking place on a holm or small island.

Holografo. In Spanish law, a holograph.

Holograph. A deed or will written entirely by the grantor or testator in his own hand.

Holographic. Relating to a holograph.

Holt. A wood.

Holy fehm. Same as VEHMGERICHT.

Holy office. A tribunal for the trial of heretics. An inquisition.

Holy Roman Emperor. Emperor of the Holy Roman Empire. He was selected by the Archbishops of Mayence, Treves and Cologne and the rulers of Saxony, Bohemia, Brandenburg and the Palatinate; afterwards electors from Bavaria, Hanover and Hesse Cassel were added.

Holy Roman Empire. Portions of the old Roman Empire of the West, together with the possessions of Charlemagne, the later being crowned Emperor in 800 by the Pope at Rome. The later Holy Roman Empire was established in 962 and ended in 1806 by Francis II. resigning as Emperor of it and assuming the crown of Austria. See HOLY ROMAN EMPEROR.

Homage. An acknowledgment by a tenant in knight's service that he was the lord's vassal subject only to the King.

Homage, ancestral. Where a man and his heirs had out of mind held their land of the lord by homage.

Homage, liege. Same as HOMAGE, LIGEANCE.

Homage, ligeance. Such as was due the King without any reservation, independent of tenure.

Homage jury. See JURY, HOMAGE.

Homage reddere. To renounce homage.

Homager. One who was bound to do homage to another.

Homagio respectuendo. A writ to the escheator commanding him to deliver seisin of lands to the heir of the King's tenant, notwithstanding his homage not done.

Homagium. Same as HOMAGE.

Homagium ligium. Unconditional homage due the sovereign as supreme lord without any reservation of the rights of others.

Homagium planum. In Feudal law, plain homage or fidelity without any other service.

Homagium reddere. Same as HOM-AGE REDDERE.

Homagium simplex. In Feudal law, simple homage with a reservation of the rights of other lords.

Hombre bueno. In Spanish law, a district judge. An arbitrator. A competent witness.

Home. A person's fixed abode. See DOMICILE.

Home port. See PORT, HOME.

Homehyne. Same as AGENHINE.

Homesoken. Same as HAMSOKEN.

Homestall. A mansion house.

Homestead. A home. A place exempted by statute to execution for debt or damages.

Homestead law. A Public Land law of the U. S. which permits a citizen or one who has declared his intention to be such, to make entry of 160 acres of public land. By living on and cultivating the land for five years, the entryman, if a citizen, can obtain a patent for the land certain proofs being first made and fees paid.

Homesteader. One who holds land under the Homestead Law of the U. S.

Homicidal. Relating to homicide. Tending to homicide.

Homicide. The killing of a man by a man.

Homicide by necessity. Homicide required by the circumstances without desire or negligence on the part of the one who kills; as the killing of one sentenced to death.

Homicide, culpable. A killing which is the result of negligence.

Homicide excusable. The killing of a man in self-defense or to preserve one's life.

Homicide, felonious. The killing of a man without justification or excuse. See MURDER.

Homicide in rixa. Homicide in a quarrel.

Homicide, justifiable. The execution of a legally convicted and s e n t e n c e d criminal in pursuance of law. Killing a man in defense of self, house or goods, where the assailant was attempting to commit a capital crime as burglary or arson.

Homicide se defendendo. Homicide in self-defense.

Homicidium. Homicide.

Homicidium ex justitia. Homicide required to carry out the sentence of the law.

Homicidium ex necessitate. Homicide required through necessity, as in defense of one's self or property.

Homicidium ex casu. Homicide by accident.

Homicidium ex voluntate. Voluntary homicide.

Homicidium per infortunium, per misadventure. Accidental homicide committed while doing a lawful act.

Hominatio. The doing of homage. The mustering of men.

Homine capto in withernamium. A writ to take him that had taken any bondman or bondwoman out of the country so that he or she could not be replevied according to law.

Homine eligendo ad custodiendam peciam sigilli pro mercatoribus editi. A writ directed to a corporation, for the choice of a new person to keep one part of the seal appointed for statute merchant, when a former is dead, according to the statute of Acton-Burnel.

Homine replegiando. A writ to replevy a man out of prison.

Homines. Men. Feudatory tenants who claimed a privilege of having their causes and persons tried only in the court of their lord.

Homines de fief. Feudal tenants.

Homines feodaux. Feudal tenants.

Homines ligii. Feudal tenants.

Hominium. Homage.

Homiplagium. Maiming a man.

Homme. A man. Men.

Homme levant et couchant. An old Norman law by which a tenant was compelled to reside on his lord's land and not live elsewhere.

Hommes de fief. Men of the fief. In Feudal law, feudal tenants.

Hommes feodaux. In Feudal law, feudal tenants.

Homo. A man. Men. It also includes women. A vassal.

Homo alta mente præditus. A man endowed with a lofty mind.

Homo casutus. One who served within a house.

Homo chartularius. A slave freed by charter.

Homo commendatus. One who placed himself under another for protection or maintenance.

Homo consiliarius. A counsellor.

Homo coronatus. One who had received the first tonsure.

Homo ecclesiasticus. The vassal of a church.

Homo exercitalis. A man of the army.

Homo feodalis. A tenant. One who held a fee.

Homo fiscalis. A vassal of the fisc or treasury.

Homo francus. A freeman.

Homo ingenuus. A freeman.

Homo liber. A freeman.

Homo ligius. A liege man. A King's vassal. A subject's vassal.

Homo novus. In Feudal law, a new tenant. One given a new fee.

Homo pertinens. In Feudal law, a bondman. One who was annexed to the soil.

Homo regius. A King's vassal.

Homo Romanus. A Roman.

Homo trium litterarum. A man of three letters, or the letters composing the word fur (thief).

Homologacion. In Spanish law, a consent implied by law from the failure of parties to object to an act.

Homologare. To confirm or approve.

Homologate. To say the like.

Homologation. Approbation; confirmation.

Homonymiæ. In Civil law, cases wherein the law was laid down or stated more than once.

Homsoken. Same as HAMSOCUE.

Homstale. A homestall. A mansion house.

Hond-habend. Hand-habend. Authority to adjudicate offenses in the lord's court.

Hondfangenethef. A thief taken with the thing stolen in his hand. See HAND-HABEND.

Honestus. Of good standing.

Honor. A barony. The seignory of a lord paramount. Several manors held by one baron. A jurisdiction and territory comprising lands, franchises and liberties held directly of the King. To accept a bill of exchange when presented or pay a note or bill when due.

Honor, act of. The acceptance or payment of a protested bill of exchange or note, by one not a party to it. The written evidence of such act when done in writing. See ACCEPTANCE SUPRA PROTEST.

Honorable, amende. See AMENDE HONORABLE.

Honorarium. An honorary or free gift, which cannot be exacted.

Honorarium jus. In Rome, the law of the prætors and edicts of the ædiles.

Honorary canons. In England, those without compensation or profit.

Honorary feuds. Titles of nobility descendible to the eldest son in exclusion of all others.

Honorary services. Those incident to the tenure of grand serjeanty and commonly annexed to an honor; those without emolument.

Honour. Same as HONOR.

Honour Courts. See COURTS, HONOUR.

Honourary feuds. See HONORARY FEUDS.

Honourary services. See HONORARY SERVICES.

Hontfongenethef. Same as HONDFANGENETHEF.

Hony. Evil; shame; disgrace.

Hoo. In old English law, a hill.

Hook. To steal.

Hookland. Land plowed and sown annually.

Hopcon. A valley.

Hope. A valley.

Hora auroræ. The morning bell.

Horæ judiciæ. Judiciary hours; hours in which the court sits.

Horca. In Spanish law, a gallows; hanging.

Horda. An old term for a cow with calf.

Hordera. A treasurer.

Hoderium. A hoard. A treasury. A repository.

Hordeum. Barley.

Hordeum palmale. Beer barley.

Hordeum quadragesimale. Common, as distinguished from beer barley.

Hore. Now.

Horn book. A book treating of the elementary principles of a science.

Horn book law. Elementary law.

Horn tenure. Same as CORNAGE.

Horn with horn. The promiscous feeding of horned cattle from several parishes upon the same common.

Horn under horn. Same as HORN WITH HORN.

Hornagium. Same as HORNEGELD.

Horn-beame pollengers. Trees not tithable, of about twenty years growth.

Hornegeld. A tax payable on horned beasts in a forest. To be exempt of such tax.

Horners. Dealers in horns of cattle.

Horning, letters of. See LETTERS OF HORNING.

Horreum. A granary. A storehouse.

Hors. Out; without; out of.

Hors de son fee. Out of his fee. A plea to an action for rent or services.

Hors de temp. Out of time.

Hors wealh. In old English law, a Briton having charge of the King's horses.

Hors weard. In old English law, a service to watch the lord's horses.

Horse bread. Coarse bread for horses.

Horstilers. Innkeepers.

Hortensian law. See LAW, HORTENSIAN.

Hortus. In Civil law, a garden.

Hospes. A guest. A host.

Hospes generalis. A great chamberlain.

Hospitallers. Knights of a religious order who built a hospital at Jerusalem where pilgrims were received. These knights were afterwards called Knight Templars, then Knights of Malta.

Hospitator. A host.

Hospitator communis. An innkeeper.

Hospitator magnus. The marshal of a camp.

Hospitalarius. An innkeeper.

Hospites. Host. Guest.

Hospitia. Inns.

Hospitia cancellariæ. Inns of Chancery.

Hospitia communia. Common inns.

Hospitia curiæ. Inns of court.

Hospiticide. The killing of a host or guest.

Hospitilaria. Same as HOSTILARIA.

Hospitium. Household.

Host. One who entertains a guest. An innkeeper. An army.

Hostage. A person given to an enemy as security for the performance of some agreement by another.

Hostelagium. In English law, the right of a lord to be entertained and lodged in the house of a tenant.

Hosteler. An innkeeper.

Hostelier. An innkeeper.

Hostellagium. See HOSTELAGIUM.

Hostels. The Inns of Court.

Hostes. Enemies.

Hostes humani generis. Enemies of the human race; pirates.

Hosterium. A hoe.

Hostilaria. The room in a religious house for the reception of strangers.

Hostilarius. A hospitaller.

Hostile. An enemy. A hostile Indian. Opposed to; antagonistic.

Hostile embargo. See EMBARGO, HOSTILE.

Hostile witness. See WITNESS, HOSTILE.

Hostility. Open war.

Hostility, permanent. The relation of one who is a citizen of a country at war with another, toward that other.

Hostility, temporary. The relation of one merely a resident of a country, during war, toward the other belligerent.

Hostis humani generis. An enemy of the human race. A pirate.

Hostlers. Innkeepers.

Hostman. An ancient merchant who dealt in sea-coal, at Newcastle on Tyne.

Hostricus. A goshawk.

Hot water ordeal. See ORDEAL.

Hotchpot. A confused mingling of divers things together. A blending or mixing of lands or money given in marriage with other lands or money falling by descent. The considering together of aggregated property belonging to two or more persons in order that each may receive an equal portion. Also spelled Hodge-podge; Hotchpotch.

Hotel. A large inn.

Hough. A valley.

Hour of a cause. In Scotch law, the time when a court meets.

Housage. A fee paid for housing goods.

House. A dwelling; a building.

House, ancient. See ANCIENT HOUSE.

House, disorderly. See DISORDERLY HOUSE.

House, mansion. A dwelling house.

House of Commons. One of the branches of the English Parliament. Its members are elected by the people. See HOUSE OF LORDS.

House of Correction. A place of detention for young offenders or for those convicted of minor offenses.

House of ill-fame. A house of prostitution. A bawdy house

House of Lords. One of the branches of the English Parliament. It is composed of lords spiritual and lords temporal.

House of Refuge. A public place for the instruction and confinement of uncontrollable children.

House of Representatives. The branch of the U. S. Congress to which the members are elected directly by the vote of the people of their respective districts. See SENATE.

House, public. A house allowed to exist by public authority, as a tavern, or for the sale of liquors.

Housebote. The privilege of taking necessary timber out of the lord's wood for repairing and support of a house.

Housebreaking. Actual breaking and entry into a house with the intent to commit a felony, whether the intent be executed or not. See BURGLAR.

Houseburning. Arson.

Household. Relating to a dwelling house. A family.

Household furniture. See FURNITURE, HOUSEHOLD.

Household goods. Articles of furniture for use in a house.

Household stuff. Generally, all articles used in ordinary housekeeping, but what comes within must be determined in each particular case.

Householder. The occupant of a house. The head of a family who occupies a house.

Housekeeper. One who is possession of a house as a dweller therein.

Hovel. A place where agricultural instruments are placed to be protected from rain and sun. A mean house.

How. A hill.

Howe. Same as HOW.

Hoy. A small coastwise vessel used to convey freight and passengers.

Hoyman. The master of a hoy.

Howgh. Same as HAWG.

Hredige. Readily. Quickly. In a short time.

Huba. A measure of land. A hide.

Hubæ. Farm lots.

Huckster. One who sells his wares by crying them aloud; a hawker.

Hucusque. An old term used in pleading, meaning "hitherto."

Hudefæst. Same as HEORDFÆTE.

Hudegeld. Same as HIDGILD.

Hudson's Bay Company. An English Company to whom was granted by Charles II, in 1670, the exclusive right to trade within Hudson's Straights, in North America.

Hue and cry. The Common law process of pursuing with horn and voice all felons. A written proclamation for the arrest of a felon escaped from prison.

Huebra. In Spanish law, a piece of land which two oxen can plow in a day.

Huis. A door.

Huisserium. A ship used in the transportation of horses.

Huissier. In French and Canadian law, a court officer who serves process and performs other minor duties similar to those of a constable.

Hulka. An old English term for a small vessel.

Hullus. A hill.

Humagium. A moist place.

Hundred. An ancient division of a shire. (The reason for the name has been always in doubt).

Hundred Court. A court not of record for the inhabitants of a hundred. It resembled that of a court baron, freemen being judges.

Hundred fetena. Inhabitants of a hundred.

Hundred gemote. Same as A HUNDRED COURT.

Hundred secta. In old English law, service at the Hundred Court.

Hundredarius. A chief of a hundred. The freeholders of a hundred.

Hundredary. The chief of a hundred.

Hundredes earldor. One who presided at a Hundred Court.

Hundredes man. Same as HUNDREDES EARLDOR.

Hundredor. Inhabitant of a hundred qualified to sit as juror. A bailiff of a hundred.

Hundred-lagh. The Hundred Court.

Hundred-penny. A tax levied on the inhabitants of a hundred.

Hundred-setena. Inhabitants of a hundred.

Hung. Failed to come to an agreement; applied to a jury.

Hunting. Pursuing, capturing, or killing wild animals.

Hurdereferst. A domestic servant.

Hurdle. A sled originally used to draw traitors to execution.

Hurst. A wood or grove.

Hurtardus. A ram. Wether. A sheep.

Hurto. In Spanish law, theft.

Hurtus. Same as HURTARDUS.

Hus and Haut. Hue and cry (which see).

Husband. A man who is legally married to a woman.

Husband and wife. Male and female joined in marriage and one person in law.

Husband de facto. A man who acts the part of a husband to a woman without being legally married to her.

Husband land. In old Scotch law, six acres.

Husband of a ship. See SHIP'S HUSBAND.

Husbandman. A farmer; agriculturist.

Husbandria. In old English law, husbandry.

Husbandry. Agriculture.

Husbrec. In Saxon law, burglary, housebreaking.

Husbrece. Same as HUSBREC.

Huscarle. A menial servant. A vassal.

Huscaus. Boots.

Husfastne. He who holds house and land; a householder.

Husgable. House rent. A tax on houses.

Husgablum. Same as HUSGABLE.

Hush money. Money paid to prevent the disclosure of a crime, or other information.

Husseling people. Church communicants.

Hustings. A London Mayoralty Court. A court in Virginia cities. The raised place from which candidates for English Parliament address the electors. Used similarly in some parts of the United States, notably Georgia.

Hutesium et clamor. Hue and cry.

Hutilan. Taxes.

Huy. A door.

Hybernagium. The time for sowing winter wheat.

Hydage. Same as HIDAGE.

Hyde. Same as HIDE.

Hydegild. Same as HIDEGELD.

Hyde lands. Plough lands.

Hydrometer. An instrument used to determine the density of fluids.

Hyems. In Civil law, winter.

Hypnotism. Artificial method of producing sleep or insensible condition.

Hypobolum. In Civil law, a legacy left a wife by her deceased husband in addition to her dower.

Hypothec. A mortgage of property, either real or personal, as security for debt where the debtor retains possession. In Scotch law, a landlord's lien on the crop and stock of his tenant for rent.

Hypotheca. A pledge or mortgage where the pledge remains with the debtor. To pawn.

Hypothecaria actio. In Civil law, an hypothecary action.

Hypothecarii creditores. In Civil law, hypothecary creditors, or those who lent money on pledge or mortgage.

Hypothecary action. An action for possession of property pledged as security for debt, where it is in the hands of the debtor, or for its sale.

Hypothecate. To deliver as security for a debt.

Hypothecation. A lien given by contract to a creditor on property without passing possession of the same. The act of pledging personal property as collateral security. In Maritime law, bottomry.

Hypothecation bond. A bottomry bond.

Hypothecation, conventional. One created by agreement.

Hypothecation, general. One by which the debtor hypothecates both present and future estates.

Hypothecation, legal. One which arises without either express or implied contract.

Hypothecation, special. Hypothecation of a particular property.

Hypothecation, tacit. One given by the law to protect the creditor, as a lien.

Hypothecator. Same as HYPOTHECARY.

Hypotheque. In French law, hypothecation. A mortgage on realty.

Hypothesis. A logical supposition.

Hypothetical. Based on hypothesis.

Hypothetical case. An imaginary state of facts, usually used to obtain the opinion of an expert.

Hypothetical question. A question consisting of a statement of assumed facts on which the opinion of the witness is asked.

Hypothetical yearly tenancy. An English system of rating the value of lands and tenements.

Hyrnes. In old English law, a parish.

Hyrst. Same as HURST.

Hysteromania. Same as ANDROMANIA.

Hysteropotmoi. A term applied to those who appeared after having been thought to be dead because of long absence and unknown whereabouts.

Hysterotomy. The Cæsarian operation.

Hythe. In old English law, a port; a haven; a wharf.

I.

I. As an abbreviation stands for Institutes, Irish, Internal.

I. C. C. Interstate Commerce Commission.

I-ctus. Abbreviation of Jurisconsultus.

I. E. Id est, that is.

I. O. U. Abbreviation of "I owe you," and used in a memorandum of indebtedness.

Ib. Abbreviation of IBIDEM.

Ibernagium. Season for sowing winter corn.

Ibi. Abbreviation of Ibidem.

Ibid. Abbreviation of Ibidem.

Ibidem. In the same place.

Icel. This. him. These. Those.

Iceluy. Same as ICEL.

Icelle. Same as ICEL.

Iceni. An ancient name in England for inhabitants of Suffolk, Norfolk, Cambridgeshire and Huntingdonshire.

Iceux. Same as ICEL.

Ich Dien. (I serve). The motto of the Prince of Wales. It was formerly motto of John, King of Bohemia, then of Edward the Black Prince, who killed John and took the motto to show his subjection to his (Edward's) father, King Edward III.

Icona. A representation of anything.

Ictus. In old English law, a blow or a bruise, as distinguished from a wound.

Ictus fulminis. A stroke of lightning.

Ictus orbis. A hurt without cutting the skin or shedding blood. See PLAGA.

Id. That.

Id est. That is.

Idem. The same.

Idem per idem. The same by the same; an illustration or proof.

Idem sonans. Sounding the same.

Identification. Proof of the identity of a person or thing. The act of identifying.

Identitate nominis. An ancient writ for one imprisoned by mistake for another of the same name, to enquire into his indentity.

Identity. Sameness.

Identity of person. An issue raised for a jury to determine, on a plea of diversity of person by one convicted or outlawed, whether the convict or outlaw is the identical person supposed to be.

Ideo. Therefore.

Ideo consideratum est. Therefore it is considered. Words formerly used in beginning the entry of a judgment when records were in Latin. Also the term used to indicate that part of the record.

Ideot. An old form of spelling Idiot (which see).

Ides. The eighth day after the Nones. See NONES.

Idiochira. In Civil law, an instrument writing executed privately.

Idiocy. Total absence of mind. A species of insanity commencing at birth. Want of understanding.

Idiot. One who has never had understanding. One who is deaf, dumb and blind.

Idiota. An idiot. In Civil law, an illiterate person. A man not holding public office.

Idiota inquirendo, de. A writ to enquire whether a person be or be not an idiot.

Idonea cautio. Sufficient security.

Idoneum se facere (Idoneare se). To purge one's self by oath of a crime of which one is accused.

Idoneus. Sufficient; competent; proper; responsible; above impeachment.

Idoneus homo. A man possessing honesty, knowledge and ability.

Idoneus testis. A good (or sufficient) witness.

Idonietas. In old English law, competency; fitness.

Idumanus fluvius. Blackwater, in Essex County, England.

If. Provided that. On condition that.

Ifungia. The finest white bread. Cocket bread.

Iglise. A church.

Ignis judicium. Purgation by fire. Fire ordeal.

Ignitegium. Curfew.

Ignominy. Disgrace; dishonor.

Ignoramus. We are ignorant. The words formerly used by a grand jury to indicate that the evidence before them on bill of indictment was not sufficient to warrant an indictment being found a true bill.

Ignorance. Want of knowledge.

Ignorance, essential. Ignorance of some fact connected with the subject-matter so intimately that it influences the parties to act in and about the same. See IGNORANCE NON-ESSENTIAL.

Ignorance involuntary. Ignorance which does not exist through neglect or fault.

Ignorance of fact. Not knowing a fact to exist.

Ignorance of law. Not knowing of the existence of a law.

Ignorance, non-essential. Ignorance of a fact not so connected with the subject-matter as to influence the parties to act in the same.

Ignorance, voluntary. Ignorance through failure to make reasonable exertion to obtain information

Ignorantia. Ignorance.

Ignorare. To be ignorant.

Ignoratio. Ignorance.

Ignoratio elenchi. Failure to observe an opponent's counter-position in an argument.

Ignorari. To have no knowledge of.

Ignore. To throw out a bill of indictment. To treat as if not in existence. To disregard.

Ikenild street. One of the four famous ways made by the Romans in England.

Il. It. He.

Ilet. A small island.

Ill. Evil. Bad. Erroneous.

Ill-fame. Evil repute.

Ill-fame, house of. See HOUSE OF ILL-FAME.

Ill-pleading. Bad pleading.

Illata et invecta. Articles brought to a house by a tenant for personal use.

Illegal. Unlawful; contrary to law. Void. Prohibited by law.

Illegal conditions. Those contrary to law, immoral, or repugnant. See CONDITION, REPUGNANT.

Illegal trade. Same as ILLICIT TRADE.

Illegality. The state of being illegal.

Illegitimacy. The condition of a bastard.

Illegitimate. Unlawful; spurious; born out of wedlock. See BASTARD.

Illeviable. A debt or duty which cannot or should not be levied.

Illicenciatus. In old English law, without license.

Illicit. Unlawful; illegal; prohibited by law.

Illicit trade. Illegal trade. Trade unlawful in a country to which a vessel is destined. Trade against public policy.

Illicite. Unlawfully; formerly a technical word required in indictments for charging an unlawful act.

Illicitum, collegium. See COLLEGIUM ILLICITUM.

Illickes. There.

Illiterate. Ignorant of writing.

Illocable. Not capable of being hired.

Illongues. There.

Illonques. There.

Illud. That.

Illuminare. To illuminate. To draw the initial letters and sometimes pictures, in gold and silver letters in MSS.

Illuminatores. Those who practice the art of illuminating. See ILLUMINARE.

Illunges. There.

Illusory appointment. See APPOINTMENT, ILLUSORY.

Imagine. To devise. To plan mentally.

Imagining. Compassing. (This word imagining, used in English statutes against treason, could only be presumed from some overt act). Imagining the death of the King could only be presumed from some overt act.

Imbargo. A stay or arrest of ships by public authority. Same as EMBARGO.

Imbasing. Debasing coin by increasing the proportion of alloy and reducing the quantity of precious metal.

Imbezzle. Same as EMBEZZLE.

Imbladare. Same as IMBLADER.

Imblader. To sow grain.

Imbracery. Same as EMBRACERY.

Imbrocus. A brook, gutter, or water passage.

Imitation, colorable. See COLORABLE IMITATION.

Immaterial. Not pertinent to the issue. Not important, necessary or essential.

Immaterial allegation. See ALLEGATION, IMMATERIAL.

Immaterial alteration. See ALTERATION, MATERIAL.

Immaterial averment. An averment which does not legally bear on the point at issue.

Immaterial fact. One not necessary to the determination of the issue.

Immaterial issue. See ISSUE, IMMATERIAL.

Immature. Too soon. Imperfect.

Immaturity. Before due. Before the termination. Before period for performance. Imperfection.

Immediate. Direct. Present. Near.

Immediate interest. See INTEREST, IMMEDIATE.

Immediate parties. See PARTIES, IMMEDIATE.

Immediate vassal. Same as VASSAL, IMMEDIATE.

Immediately. Direct; without any intervention. Within reasonable time.

Immemorial. Beyond the memory of man. Before the time of Richard I.; before the year 1189. See TIME, IMMEMORIAL.

Immemorial possession. See POSSESSION, IMMEMORIAL.

Immemorial usage. One which has existed out of legal memory.

Immeubles. In French law, immovables.

Immigration. The act of persons coming into a country with intent to remain there.

Immigration laws. See LAWS, IMMIGRATION.

Immiscere. In Civil law, to mix with. To join or meddle with.

Immittere. In Civil law, to let into. To let cattle on a common.

Immobilia. Immovables.

Immobilis. Immovable.

Immoral. Contrary to public policy. Illegal.

Immoral consideration. See CONSIDERATION, IMMORAL.

Immoral contracts. Agreements in which the consideration is against good morals or public policy.

Immovables. Things which cannot be taken from a place.

Immunities. Freedom from any penalty.

Immunity. Exemption from a penalty or obligation.

Impair. To injure. To lessen in quantity, quality, value, degree or power.

Impalare. To put in a pound.

Impanel. Same as EMPANEL.

Imparcare. To shut up.

Impargamentum. The right to impound cattle.

Imparl. To confer together. To be permitted to compromise a suit. To be allowed time to file a plea.

Imparlance. Time to plead. A continuance. A stay of execution.

Imparlance, general. Time to plead until next term without saving any exception to the defendant.

Imparlance, general special. An imparlance with a reservation of all exceptions, the effect of which is to allow the defendant to plead in abatement or to the jurisdiction, but he cannot plead tender, as the prayer for imparlance is an admission that he is not ready to pay.

Imparlance, special. Time to plead generally to some time in the same term, saving all exceptions to the writ or count and in abatement but not to the jurisdiction.

Imparsonee. A person inducted and in possession of a benefice.

Impartial. Not inclined to favor one as against another. Not prejudiced.

Impatronization. The act of placing in a benefice.

Impeach. To discredit. To call in question. To endeavor to show to be unworthy belief. To accuse. To sue. To call to account. See IMPEACHMENT.

Impeach collaterally. Same as ATTACK COLLATERALLY.

Impeachment. The act of showing or attempting to show a person to be unworthy of belief. The act of accusing or calling to account. In the United States the accusation by the House of Congress of a civil officer and trial before the Senate. The accusation must originate in the House, the trial is before the Senate.

Impeachment, articles of. The formal written charges against a public official.

Impeachment, collateral. See COLLATERAL IMPEACHMENT.

Impeachment, court of. See COURT OF IMPEACHMENT.

Impeachment of a witness. Producing proof to show the witness is unworthy of belief.

Impeachment of waste. A restraint from or accountability for waste or injury to land. A demand for waste committed.

Impechiare. To impeach. To accuse and prosecute.

Impede. To obstruct. To hinder.

Impediatus. Disabled by being expeditated. See EXPEDITATE.

Impediens. A defendant. A deforciant.

Impedimento. In Spanish law, a prohibition against entering into a marriage because of a certain status.

Impediments. Legal hindrances to making contracts; such as being under age, under coverture, non compos mentis, beyond sea, etc. In Civil law, bars to marriage.

Impediments, absolute. In Civil law, impediments which prevent the parties subject to them from marrying at all.

Impediments, diriment. See DIRIMENT IMPEDIMENTS.

Impediments, prohibitive. In Civil law, impediments which, while they do not render the marriage void, subject the parties to a penalty.

Impediments, relative. In Civil law, such as arise from the relation of the parties to each other.

Impedimentum dirimens. See DIRIMENT IMPEDIMENTS.

Impeditor. The disturber in quare impedit.

Impensæ. Expenses.

Imperative. Expressing command. Peremptory.

Imperator. One with supreme military command. A title applied to Roman Emperors and Anglo-Saxon Kings in England.

Imperfect obligation. See OBLIGATION, IMPERFECT.

Imperfect rights. See RIGHTS, IMPERFECT.

Imperfect trust. An executory trust. See TRUST, IMPERFECT.

Imperfect usufruct. See USUFRUCT, IMPERFECT.

Imperial. Relating to an empire. Tending toward an empire. Anything of more than usual size.

Imperial constitution. That which the Emperor has established by decree, edict, or letter.

Imperialism. Imperial character or spirit. Ambition to extend territorially. Desire to form an empire. The system of imperial government.

Imperialist. One who advocates or upholds imperialism.

Imperite. Unskillfully.

Imperitia. Unskillfulness.

Imperium. Supreme military command. Command without limitation. Power; authority.

Imperium, divisum. See DIVISUM IMPERIUM.

Imperium in imperio. One government within another. "A power behind the throne."

Impersonalitas. A term used when no particular person is intended.

Impertinence. Matter in pleading which is immaterial, prolix, or scandalous.

Impertinent. Irrelevant.

Impescare. In old English law, to impeach.

Impescatus. Impeached or accused.

Impetere. To accuse.

Impetitio. An accusation.

Impetitio v a s t i. Impeachment of waste.

Impetrare. In old English law, to obtain by petition.

Impetration. Obtaining anything by request. The pre-obtaining of a benefice from the Court of Rome which of right belonged to the King.

Impier. An umpire.

Impierment. Impairing or prejudicing.

Impignorata. Given in pledge.

Impignoration. The act of pledging.

Implacitare. To implead. To sue.

Implead. To sue or prosecute by course of law.

Impleaded. Sued. Prosecuted. Brought suit against two or more.

Implement, adjudication in. See ADJUDICATION IN IMPLEMENT.

Implements. Things necessary to a trade or profession. Household furniture.

Implicata. Small quantities of goods received on a ship for transportation on which the freight is to be paid whether the goods be lost or not on the voyage.

Implication. An inference of something not directly declared.

Implication, necessary. An implication so strong that the contrary cannot be supposed to be true.

Implied. A necessary inference of something not expressed.

Implied abrogation. See ABROGATION, IMPLIED.

Implied admission. See ADMISSION, IMPLIED.

Implied affirmance. See AFFIRMANCE, IMPLIED.

Implied assent. See ASSENT, IMPLIED.

Implied assumpsit. See ASSUMPSIT, IMPLIED.

Implied authority. See AUTHORITY, IMPLIED.

Implied coercion. See COERCION, IMPLIED.

Implied color. See COLOR, IMPLIED.

Implied consent. See CONSENT, IMPLIED.

Implied countermand. See COUNTERMAND, IMPLIED.

Implied malice. Same as MALICE, CONSTRUCTIVE.

Implied power. See POWER, IMPLIED.

Implied promise. See PROMISE, IMPLIED.

Implied repeal. See REPEAL, IMPLIED.

Implied trust. See TRUST, IMPLIED.

Implied use. See USE, IMPLIED.

Implied warranty. See WARRANTY, IMPLIED.

Imponere. To impose.

Import. To bring from a foreign country.

Imported. Borne or carried into a country.

Importation. The bringing of goods and merchandise into a country from a foreign country. A thing or person imported.

Importer. To carry away. One who imports.

Imports. Articles brought into a country.

Importunity. Frequent and earnest request.

Impose. To place upon. To levy. To exact. To subject. To pass off falsely, as true.

Impositio. Imposition.

Imposition. The act of imposing. That imposed legally; as a tax, toll or duty.

Impossible contract. See CONTRACT, IMPOSSIBLE.

Impossibilis. Impossible.

Impossibility. That which cannot be done under the circumstances.

Impossibility, legal. One created by law.

Imposuit commune ballium. Put in common bail.

Impost. A government tax or levy.

Imposters. Those who pretended a commission from heaven, punishable at common law by fine and imprisonment.

Impotence. Want of power. Lack of power to copulate or cause conception in a female. See CONCEPTION.

Impotency. Inability in a male to copulate or beget children.

Impotency, property by reason of. Qualified property during the time they remain there, in animals feræ naturæ, born on one's land.

Impotent. A word applied to a male who is incapable of copulation or power to reproduce his species.

Impotentiam. Same as IMPOTENCY, PROPERTY BY REASON OF.

Impound. To place in custody of a court of law. To put in a pound.

Imprescriptibility. The condition of property to which title cannot be acquired by prescription.

Imprescriptible. Incapable of being lost or acquired by usage or prescription.

Imprescriptible rights. See RIGHTS, IMPRESCRIPTIBLE.

Impress. To compel to enter the public service. To seize for public use.

Impression. Effect on a mind.

Impression, case of first. A case raising a new point of law.

Impressment. The act of impressing. SEE IMPRESS.

Imprest money. Money paid on enlisting soldiers or sailors. See IMPRESS.

Impretrabilis. Invaluable.

Imprimere. To imprint upon.

(28)

Imprimatur. Let it be printed. A license to publish.

Imprimery. An impression. The art of printing. A printing house.

Imprimis. In the first place; first of all.

Imprish. Those who defend or take the part of another.

Imprisii. Accomplices; adherents.

Imprison. To restrain of liberty.

Imprisonment. Confinement. Confinement without hard labor.

Imprisonment, duress of. Illegal confinement until the performance of an act.

Imprisonment, false. Confinement of a person without authority of law.

Imprisonment, unlawful. Same as IMPRISONMENT, FALSE.

Imprisonment, wrongous. See WRONGOUS IMPRISONMENT.

Impristi. Followers; adherents.

Improbare. To disapprove, disallow.

Improbation. In Scotch law, an action to annul an instrument by proving it false or forged.

Improbation reduction. See REDUCTION, IMPROBATION.

Improper. Not fit; unsuitable.

Improper estate tail. Same as ESTATE TAIL, QUASI.

Improper feud. A feud held otherwise than by military service.

Improper navigation. That done with a ship which interferes with or is contrary to the object of her voyage.

Impropriated. Granted to a layman or lay corporation.

Impropriation. The annexing a benefice to the use of a lay person or corporation. See APPROPRIATION.

Impropriator. A layman who has abtained control of church property or revenue.

Improve. To cultivate. To reclaim. To make better. In Scotch law, to disprove, invalidate, impeach.

Improved land. See LAND, IMPROVED.

Improved property. See PROPERTY, IMPROVED.

Improvement. Cultivation; reclamation; making better. In U. S. Public Land law, an act toward making land suitable for habitation and cultivation. The erection of buildings upon vacant land. The act of making better. Approvement (which see).

Improvement, under. Used to profitable advantage. A useful addition to a patentable thing.

Improvements. Internal c h a n g e s within a State or country which benefit the public at large.

Improviare. To improve land.

Improvidence. The quality of lacking foresight or thrift.

Improvident. Not fit to perform certain duties or manage one's own affairs.

Improvidently. Prematurely. Without reflection or foresight.

Impruamentum. Same as IMPRUIAMENTUM.

Impruiare. To improve land.

Impruiamentum. The improving of lands.

Impubes. In Roman law, a child under the age of puberty. A boy less than 14 or a girl less than 12.

Impudicity. Same as INCONTINENCE.

Impulse. Sudden motive or feeling.

Impunity. Freedom from punishment.

Imputatio. In Civil law, legal liability.

Imputation of payment. In Civil law, the application which a debtor makes of a payment to his creditor.

Impute. To charge or credit to one. To attribute. .

Imputed negligence. See NEGLIGENCE, IMPUTED.

In. Into; in possession.

In action. Recoverable by action. Not in possession.

In adversum. Against an adverse or unwilling party.

In æqua manu. Same as IN ÆQUALI MANU.

In æquali jure. In equal right.

In æquali manu. In equal hand; in the hand of a third person.

In alieno solio. In another's land.

In alio loco. In another place.

In amity. In friendship or peace.

In antea. Henceforth.

In aperta luce. In open daylight. In day time.

In apicibus juris. Among the subtleties or extreme doctrines of the law.

In arbitrium judicis. At the pleasure of the judge.

In arcta et salva custodia. In close and safe custody.

In aretro. In arrears.

In articulo. In a moment. Immediately.

In articulo mortis. In the moment of death. At the point of death.

In autre droit. In another's right.

In banco. In banc as distinguished from at nisi prius.

In Banco Regis. In the King's Bench.

In behalf of. In the interest of. At the request of.

In bonis. Among the goods.

In bonis defuncti. Among the goods of the deceased.

In borh and out borh. See INBOROW AND OUTBOROW.

In borow and out borow. See INBOROW AND OUTBOROW.

In bulk. See BULK, IN.

In camera. In chambers. In private.

In capita. In heads; to or among heads.

In capite. In chief. A tenure direct from the crown as feudal superior.

In casu consimili. In like case.

In casu proviso. In case provided.

In causa. In Scotch law, in the cause or on merits, as distinguished from In Initialibus (which see).

In chief. See CHIEF, IN.

In commendam. In commendation. In Louisiana, applied to a limited partnership like the commandite of French law.

In communi. In common.

In consideratione ejus. In his sight or view.

In consideratione inde. In consideration thereof.

In consideratione legis. In consideration or contemplation of law; in abeyance.

In consideratione præmisorum. In consideration of the premises.

In continenti. Immediately; without any interval.

In corpore. In body or substance.

In course of business. See BUSINESS, IN COURSE OF.

In crastino. On the morrow.

In crastino Animarum. On the morrow of All Souls.

In cujus rei testimonium. In testimony whereof.

In curia. In court.

In custodia legis. In custody of the law.

In delicto. In fault.

In diebus non juridicis. In days when there was no court; applied to a reason for not appearing.

In diem. For a day.

In dominico. In demesne.

In dominico suo ut de feodo. In his demesne as of fee.

In dorso. On the back.

In dorso recordi. On the back of the record.

In dubio. In doubt.

In duplo. In double.

In eadem causa. In the same state or condition.

In eire. In the ancient court of the judges in "eyre" who went the circuit of England.

In emultationem vicini. See ACTION EMULATIONEM VICINI.

In equilibrio. Equal; in even balance.

In equity. In a court of equity, as distinguished from a court of law.

In esse. In existence.

In evidence. Submitted and admitted as evidence.

In excambia. In exchange. Technical words in ancient deeds of exchange.

In exitu. In issue.

In extenso. Fully; at length.

In extremis. At the end. In the last moments of life.

In facie curiæ. In the face of the court.

In facie ecclesiæ. In the face of the church; a term anciently applied in England to conferring dower, and afterwards to marriages.

In faciendo. In doing.

In fact. See FACT, IN.

In favorem libertatis. In favor of liberty.

In favorem vitæ. In favor of life.

In feodare. To give a fee. To enfeoff.

In feoda. In fee.

In fieri. In being made. Inchoate. Pending.

In fine. At the end.

In forma pauperis. In the form (character) of a pauper.

In foro. In the forum or court.

In foro conscientiæ. Before the tribunal of conscience; applied to moral as distinguished from legal obligations.

In foro contentioso. In the tribunal or forum of litigation.

In foro ecclesiastico. In the ecclesiastical forum or court.

In foro sæculari. In the secular forum or court.

In fraudem creditorum. In fraud of creditors. With intent to defraud creditors.

In fraudem legis. In fraud of the law; contrary to law.

In full. In complete discharge of a demand. Without diminution.

In full life. Not dead, legally nor naturally.

In futuro. At a future time.

In generali passagio. In the general passage. On a journey to Jerusalem as a crusader. An old excuse for non-appearance in court.

In genere. In kind.

In gross. In the whole. Not connected with another.

In hac parte. In this behalf; on this part or side.

In hæc verba. In these words.

In iisdem terminis. In the same terms.

In individuo. In the identical, individual or specific form.

In infinitum. Indefinitely.

In initialibus. In the initiation. In Scotch law, applied to the preliminary examination of a witness as to his qualifications. See IN CAUSA.

In initio. At the beginning; in the beginning.

In itinere. In eyre. On a circuit. On a journey. In course of transportation.

In integrum. The original condition.

In invitum. Unwillingly.

In judgment. In a court of judgment.

In judicio. In Roman law, before a judex or judge, as distinguished from in jure (which see).

In jure. In Roman law, in law, or before a prætor, where the introductory procedure of a suit was conducted before it went before the judex or judge for trial. See IN JUDICIO.

In jure alterius. In another's right.

In jure proprio. In one's right.

In jus vocando. Summoning to court.

In jus vocare. To summon to court.

In kind. Of the same class or nature, not the specific article. If one deposit a bushel of wheat in specie the depositary could not use it and return other wheat; he must return the identical wheat deposited. If deposited in kind the depositary could use the wheat and return it in other wheat. The same applies to money deposited.

In law. Existing by operation of law. Implied by law. Within the contemplation of law.

In lecto mortali. On a death-bed.

In limine. In or at the beginning.

In litem. For a suit; to the suit.

In loco. In place; in the place or stead.

Inloco parentis. In the place of a parent.

In majorem cautelam. For greater security.

In malem partem. In a bad sense.

In medias res. In the middle of things.

In medio. Intermediate. In Scotch law, applied to a fund in controversy.

In mercy. A phrase denoting that the defendant was in mercy of the King (liable to amercement) for his delay; or that the plaintiff and his pledges were liable to amercement for false claim.

In misericordia. See MISERICORDIA.

In mitiori sensu. In a milder acceptation. A phrase applied to a doctrine of construing slanderous words, if possible, so that an action for slander could not be maintained.

In mortu manu. In the dead hand; in mortmain.

In modum assisæ. In the manner or form of an assize.

In mora. In default. In delay. Negligent in performing a duty.

In notis. In the notes.

In nubibus. In the clouds. In the custody of the law. In abeyance.

In nullius bonis. Among the goods of nobody.

In nullo est erratum. In nothing is there error; applied to a plea which denied error in the record and thus joined on the question of law.

In omnibus. In all things; on all points.

In ordinary. See ORDINARY, IN.

In pacato solio. In a country which is at peace.

In pace Dei et regis. In the peace of God and the King.

In pais. In the country. Done with legal proceedings. Not in writing.

In paper. A term applied to proceedings in a cause before being recorded on permanent records which were formerly on parchment.

In pari materia. See MATERIA IN PARI.

In patiendo. In suffering, permitting, or allowing.

In pectore judicis. In the breast of the judge; applied to a judgment.

In pejorem partem. In the worst part.

In perpetuam rei memoriam. For the perpetual memory or remembrance of a thing.

In perpetuum rei testimonium. In perpetual testimony of a matter.

In person. See PERSON, IN.

In personam. Relating to a particular person or persons as distinguished from all persons generally, or a thing. See IN REM.

In pios usos. For pious uses, or religious purposes.

In pleno lumine. In public; in the light of day.

In posse. In possibility; not in actual existence.

In potestate parentis. In the power of a parent.

In præmissorum fidem. In confirmation or attestation of the premises.

In præsenti. At the present.

In prender. In taking; applied to things incorporeal which a person was entitled to take for himself. See IN RENDER.

In presence of. In sight of.

In principio. At the beginning.

In promptu. In readiness; at hand.

In re. In the matter of.

In rebus. In things, cases, or matters.

In rem. Against a thing. Relating to persons at large and not a particular person or persons, or to things as distinguished from persons. See IN PERSONAM.

In render. In rendering. When a right existed by which the tenant was bound to offer, or to pay, or to leave on death to the lord.

In rerum natura. In the nature of things; applied to that existing as distinguished from that fictitious.

In scrinio judicio. Among the judges' writings; applied to that which, though in the judges' papers, is not embodied in the decree.

In scriptis. In writing.

In sea pay. In commission. Applied to a ship, means ready for sea service.

In separali. In several; in severalty.

In simili materia. In the same matter. Dealing with the same matter.

In simplici peregrinatione. In simple pilgrimage or absent on a private journey to Jerusalem; an excuse for not appearing in court.

In solido. In Civil law, for the whole; as a whole.

In solidum. For the whole.

In solio. In the soil or ground.

In solio alieno. In another's soil.

In solio proprio. In one's own ground.

In specie. In the identical shape or form. The identical article. Opposed to in kind (which see).

In statu quo. In the same situation as; in the same condition as.

In stirpes. According to stocks. See PER STIRPES.

In tantum. In so much; so much; so far; so greatly.

In terminis terminantibus. In terms of determination; exactly in point. In express terms.

In terrorem. In terror; as a threat.

In terrorem populi. To the terror of the people; technical words once necessary in indictments for riot.

In testimonium. In witness or in evidence thereof.

In totidem verbis. In just so many words.

In toto. In the whole; wholly; completely.

In trajectu. In the passage over; on the voyage over.

In vacuo. Without concomitants or coherence.

In vadio. In pledge; in gage.

In ventre. In the womb; conceived but not yet born.

In ventre sa mere. In the mother's womb.

In vinculis. In chains. In custody. A condition made unfortunate by circumstances.

Inadequate price. Same as INADEQUACY OF CONSIDERATION.

Inadmissable. Not admissable. That which cannot be received under the laws of evidence.

Inædificatio. In Civil law, building with materials belonging to another or on another's land.

Inalienable. Not transferable.

Inauguration. The ceremony in the United States of placing a Governor or President in office.

Inblaura. Profit or product of the ground.

Inborh. In Saxon law, security by the deposit of chattels.

Inbound common. A common marked out by boundaries but not enclosed.

Incapable. Incompetent; unfit.

Incapacity. Incompetence. Unfitness. Lack of qualification or jurisdiction.

Incapacity, legal. See LEGAL INCAPACITY.

Incastellare. To make serve as a castle.

Incaustuno. Ink.

Incendiary. One who burns a house maliciously; one guilty of the crime of arson.

Inception. The beginning; commencement.

Incertæ personæ. Uncertain or unknown persons, who cannot be known until an event has happened; as a posthumous heir.

Incertainty. Uncertainty.

Incest. Sexual intercourse between persons that the law prohibits from marrying.

Incestuosi. Incestuously begotten offspring.

Incestuous adultery. See ADULTERY, INCESTUOUS.

Incestuous bastard. See BASTARD, INCESTUOUS.

Inchartare. To give, grant or assure anything by instrument of writing.

Inborow and outborow. An office for observing the ingress and egress and allowing the passage of persons between England and Scotland.

Inch. A measure of length originally determined by laying three grains of barley end to end.

Inchoate. Begun, but not in full existence or operation.

Inchoate dower. A woman's interest in her husband's land during his life.

Incident. A thing necessarily depending upon, appertaining to or following another as principal.

Incidental. Collateral. A c c e s s o r y. Subordinate in importance.

Incidental admission. See ADMISSION, INCIDENTAL.

Incidents, annex. Things which are to be considered as incidental to other things.

Incidents, customary. Such as are established by custom.

Incidere. In Civil law, to fall into. To become liable to. To happen. To fall upon.

Incidere in legem. To become subject to punishment of law.

Incile. In Civil law, a trench; a ditch; a well.

Incipitur. It is begun. In old English law, the beginning of pleadings entered on the issue roll.

Incite. To urge or stimulate a person to commit a crime.

Incivile. Irregular. Against due course of law.

Incivism. Lack of attachment to a State or city. Lack of patriotism.

Inclamare. To cry out.

Inclaudare. To fetter a horse.

Inclausa. An enclosure near a house.

Inclose. To confine within.

Inclosed lands. See LANDS, ENCLOSED.

Inclosures. Land fenced or separated from other land. Fences, hedges, etc., which enclose land. Extinction of rights of common in land.

Include. To embrace ; to enclose ; to comprise.

Inclusio. Inclusion.

Inclusive. Embraced; included in.

Incola. An inhabitant of a place, not a native.

Income. That which one receives as the result of labor or earnings of capital.

Income, annual. See ANNUAL INCOME.

Income-tax. See TAX, INCOME.

Incommunicada. In Spanish law, not permitted to speak or to see any person. Prisoners are subjected to this condition on the alleged ground that they might attempt to corrupt witnesses against them if allowed to communicate with any one.

Incommunicatum. Same as INCOMMUNICADA.

Incommutable. Not capable of being substituted.

Incompatible. Incapable of existing together in harmony. Inconsistent.

Incompatibility. Inconsistency. The inability to exist together in harmony or agreement.

Incompetency. Legal capacity.

Incompetent. Not legally qualified.

Incompetent witness. See WITNESS, INCOMPETENT.

Inconclusive evidence. See EVIDENCE, INCONCLUSIVE.

Inconclusive presumptions. See PRESUMPTIONS, INCONCLUSIVE.

Inconsulto. In Civil law, without intention; without advice.

Incontinence. Indulgence in sexual intercourse illegally.

Incontinency. Lack of proper restraint over the sexual desire.

Incontinenti. Immediately.

Incontinently. Immediately.

Incopolitus. A proctor; a vicar.

Incorporalis. Incorporeal.

Incorporamus. We incorporate. Words used in England in the creation of an incorporation.

Incorporate. To form into a legal corporation.

Incorporation. The act of forming into a corporation. In Civil law, the joining of one domain to another.

Incorporation by reference. Making one instrument writing, or document, part of another by referring to it so as to adopt its provisions.

Incorporator. One who forms a corporation. One who is a charter member.

Incorpore. In body, in substance.

Incorporeal. Not appreciable by the senses. Not tangible.

Incorporeal chattels. Incorporeal rights incident to chattels, such as patent rights, copyrights, &c.

Incorporeal hereditament. Same as HEREDITAMENT, INCORPOREAL.

Incorporeal hereditament appendant. One annexed to the manor and passing by grant of the latter.

Incorporeal hereditament in gross. One disconnected with, and which can be granted separate from, the manor.

Incorporeal property. See PROPERTY, INCORPOREAL.

Incorrigible. Incapable of being corrected, or reformed.

Incorruptible. Not subject to criminal influence.

Increase. That which is added. That which is produced by land. The offspring of animals.

Increase, affidavit of. Affidavit that increased costs have been paid.

Increase, costs of. Formerly, in English law, the amount of costs assessed by a court above that allowed by the jury.

Increment. Increase or improvement.

Incrementa. Additions. Increase of land by the sea.

Incrementum. Increment. A piece of land enclosed from a common or improved.

Incriminate. To charge with a crime. To show to have been party to a crime.

Incroachment. An unlawful gain upon the right or possession of another.

Incrocare. To hang from a hook.

Inculpate. To involve in or connect with a crime.

Inculpatory. Tending or intending to prove guilt.

Incumbent. One holding a benefice. One who has qualified for an office after his appointment or election.

Incumber. To place a lien or obligation upon.

Incumbrance. A paramount claim or interest resting as a charge upon land.

Incumbrance, mesne. See MESNE INCUMBRANCE.

Incumbrancer. One who places an incumbrance upon an estate. One who holds a claim against an estate.

Incumbrances, covenant against. See COVENANT AGAINST INCUMBRANCES.

Incur. To bring upon one's self by some act.

Incurable. Not capable of being corrected or remedied.

Incurramentum. Being subject to a penalty, fine or amercement.

Incurri alieni. To be liable to another's legal censure or punishment.

Inde. Thence; thereof; therefrom; thereupon.

Indebitatus. Indebted.

Indebitatus assumpsit. See ASSUMPSIT.

Indebiti solutio. In Scotch law, a payment of that which is not due.

Indebitum. In Civil law, not owing.

Indebted. The condition of owing a debt. Owing.

Indebtedness. The condition of being in debt. The extent or amount of such debt.

Indecency. Want of decency; immodesty. (To commit any indecency, such as exposing the person in public, is a misdemeanor).

Indecency, public. See PUBLIC INDECENCY.

Indecent. Immodest. Impure. (As to what is, the facts in a case must determine).

Indecent assault. Taking indecent liberties with a female against her consent.

Indecent exposure. Intentional exposure of the naked body or privates, in a public place.

Indecent liberties. Causing a female to submit to exposure of her naked person or to having her naked body or limbs handled.

Indecent publications. Such publications as tend to debase the mind of the community; as to what comes within the term, a court must determine from the facts in each particular case.

Indecimable. That which by law ought not to pay tithe.

Indefeasable. That which cannot be defeated or made void.

Indefeasible. Same as INDEFEASABLE.

Indefeisible. Indefeasable.

Indefensus. One who is impleaded and refuses to make answer.

Indefinite failure of issue. See FAILURE OF ISSUE, INDEFINITE.

Indefinite payment. One not appropriated or recorded when made.

Indemnificatus. Indemnified.

Indemnify. To make good another's loss; to exempt from loss.

Indemnis. Without damage; without injury.

Indemnity. Compensation for loss.

Indemnity contract. See CONTRACT, INDEMNITY.

Indemnity lands. See LANDS, INDEMNITY.

Indemnitee. One whom another agrees to indemnify in case of loss.

Indemnitor. One who agrees to indemnify another against loss.

Indempnis. Same as INDEMNIS.

Indenization. The act of making a denizen or citizen.

Indent. To cut in a line like the teeth of a saw, or in a waving line.

Indent. An indented contract. An indenture. An indented certificate issued by the U. S. at the close of the Revolution for principal or interest due on the National Debt. In India an order for supplies.

Indenture. An instrument writing or deed between two or more persons as distinguished from one which but one person executes. Anciently, a deed or instrument writing by two or more made in duplicate, which duplicates were cut apart by a line like the teeth of a saw. See CARTA INDENTATA.

Indenture of a fine. Indentures reciting the whole proceeding of a fine of lands, executed and engrossed at the chirographic office and delivered to the cognizor and cognizee.

Indenture of apprenticeship. An instrument writing in two parts by which an apprenticeship is created.

Independence. Freedom from control by another.

Independence, Declaration of. See DECLARATION OF INDEPENDENCE.

Independence, political. Freedom from the political dictation of another power.

Independent. Not dependent on anything else to confer validity or completeness.

Independent contractor. See CONTRACTOR, INDEPENDENT.

Independent promise. See PROMISE, INDEPENDENT.

Indeterminate. Not determined, fixed or certain, not particularly designated.

Index. That part of a book which gives in alphabetical order, a brief summary of the contents.

Index ad sectam. Index of instruments delivered or made to a plaintiff in a cause.

Index, direct. An index of the names of the first parties to recorded instruments.

Index, indirect. An index which gives the names of the second parties to recorded instruments.

Index, reverse. Same as INDEX, INDIRECT.

Indfine. A division of an ancient Irish clan.

Indian. A member of one of the aboriginal races within the jurisdiction of the U. S., including Alaska.

Indian depredation acts. Various acts of the U. S. Congress providing indemnity for persons whose property was destroyed or injured by Indians.

Indian Country. That part of the U. S. to which the Indian title has not been extinguished.

Indian tribe. A distinct and separate body of the Indian race having its own laws and customs.

Indicare. In Civil law, to show; to discover; to accuse. To fix the price of.

Indicate. To point to. To convey direction to the mind.

Indicatif. An ancient writ for removing certain causes from the Court Christian to the Queen's Bench.

Indication. A fact from which a conclusion is drawn.

Indicative evidence. See EVIDENCE, INDICATIVE.

Indicavit. A writ of prohibition allowed a patron of a church whose clerk is sued in the spiritual court by another clerk for tithes, which amount to the fourth part of the profits of the advowson, to bring the action into a court of Common law.

Indicia. Signs; tokens; evidence; badges.

Indicium. Singular of Indicia.

Indict. To accuse of a crime. To find and present an indictment against.

Indictable. That which a Grand Jury can indict for.

Indictare. To indict.

Indicted. Charged by an indictment of a Grand Jury.

Indictee. In old English law, one who has been indicted.

Indictio. Indictment.

Indiction. The period of fifteen years. A method of computing time by which after every fifteen years a new indiction began, just as now after every hundred years a new century begins. It was used in both Rome and England. A proclamation. Declaration. Indictment.

Indictment. A written accusation in legal form, found to be true by a Grand Jury. In Scotch law, the process by which one is brought to trial by the Lord Advocate as distinguished from process by criminal letter. See TRUE BILL; also PRESENTMENT.

Indictment, joint. See JOINT INDICTMENT.

Indictor. One who indicts another for any offense.

Indifferent. Free from partiality or prejudice.

Indigena. Native; indigenous.

Indigent. Without sufficient means of support; or without means to accomplish or acquire something.

Indignity. An act which humiliates or debases.

Indirect evidence. See EVIDENCE, INDIRECT.

Indirect, index. See INDEX, INDIRECT.

Indirect tax. See TAX, INDIRECT.

Indistanter. Without delay.

Individual. Belonging to one person.

Individual liability. See LIABILITY, INDIVIDUAL.

Individuum. In Civil law, incapable of division.

Indivisible. Entire. Not admitting of division.

Indivisum. What two persons hold in common without partition.

Indolis. A studious young man. A youth.

Indomit. Boisterous and ungovernable.

Indorsat. In old Scotch law, indorsed.

Indorse. To write upon. To write one's name upon the back of a paper.

Indorsee. One to whom any commercial paper is endorsed.

Indorsee in due course. One who in good faith and for value obtains commercial paper properly indorsed or payable to bearer.

Indorsement. Anything written on the back of an instrument writing. Writing one's name on the back of a check, note or bill as payee, drawee or holder whereby the property in it is transferred.

Indorsement, accommodation. An endorsement to give credit to an instrument.

Indorsement, blank. An endorsement where the transferee is not named.

Indorsement, conditional. An endorsement by which the indorser becomes liable only on condition.

Indorsement in full. The adding of the name of the person to whom a check, note or bill is assigned.

Indorsement, irregular. An endorsement not in the usual place or in the usual manner.

Indorsement, qualified. One where the liability is limited, as an indorsement without recourse.

Indorsement, restrictive. One which limits negotiability to a special purpose or person.

Indorsement, special. Same as INDORSEMENT IN FULL.

Indorsement without recourse. Indorsement with the words "without recourse" which mean a conveyance of the title, but without incurring the liability for non-acceptance or non-payment.

Indorser. One who indorses by writing his name on a paper or negotiable instrument.

Indossans. An indorser.

Indossatarius. An indorsee.

Indowment. Same as ENDOWMENT.

Inducement. Anything that determines or disposes to a course or act. The preamble to the particular charges and allegations in pleading. A preamble or introduction.

Induciæ. A stopping or suspension of proceedings.

Induciæ legales. In Scotch law, the days between citation and appearance or between the issuance and return of a writ.

Inducias. A truce. Delay or indulgence.

Inductio. In Civil law, drawing a pen or stylus over writing to obliterate it.

Induction. Giving a parson possession of his church.

Indulto. In old Ecclesiastical law, a privilege granted by the Pope to do that prohibited by the Common law. In Spanish law, the right to remit punishment imposed upon a criminal.

Indulgence. Forbearance in the enforcement of a right.

Indument. Endowment.

Industriam. Reclaiming and making tame. Confining within one's power so they cannot escape (applied to wild animals).

Industriam, per. By industry, art or skill.

Inebriate. An habitual drunkard.

Ineligibility. Incapacity to be elected to or hold an office.

Ineligible. Not qualified to be chosen for or to hold an office.

Inevitable accident. See ACCIDENT, INEVITABLE.

Inewardus. A guard; a watchman.

Infalistatus. Exposed upon the sands of the seashore; an ancient punishment.

Infamia. Infamy.

Infamia facti. General bad character.

Infamia juris. Infamy resulting from conviction of a crime.

Infamis. In Roman law, one who was infamous, or who had lost his political rights.

Infamous. Notoriously wicked or unjust. Incompetent to be a witness or to vote. One convicted of an infamous crime.

Infamous crime. See CRIME, INFAMOUS.

Infamous punishment. In U. S., death or imprisonment in a State prison or Federal penitentiary.

Infamy. The legal status of a person convicted of an infamous crime.

Infancy. The condition of an infant. The period one is an infant. See INFANT.

Infancy, natural. Infancy which ends on a child reaching the seventh year. See INFANT.

Infangenetheof. Same as INFANGTHEF.

Infangenthef. Same as INFANGTHEF.

Infangthef. A privilege or liberty granted to lords of certain manors to judge any thief taken within their fee.

Infans. A child under the age of seven.

Infant. Technically a person under the age of seven years. Generally applied to one under twenty-one years of age. See MINOR.

Infantia. From birth until seven years of age

Infanticide. The killing of a child after it is born. See FŒTICIDE.

Infanzon. In Spanish law, a nobleman who exercises no other privileges than those which he has been conceded.

Infection. Taint of illegality.

Infectious. That transmitted by some means other than contact. See CONTAGIOUS.

Infeff. Same as ENFEOFF.

Infeft. To give seisin; to enfeoff.

Infeftment. The act of giving possession of inheritable property by symbol.

Infensare curiam. A court when it suggests to counsel something he has forgotten or is ignorant of.

Infeodatio. Enfeoffment.

Infeodation. Infeudation.

Infeodation of tithes. The granting of tithes to mere laymen.

Infeoff. Same as ENFEOFF.

Infeoffment. Same as ENFEOFFMENT.

Infer. To conclude from facts.

Inference. Conclusion from facts.

Inferential. Presumptive. Deducible by inference.

Inferior. Smaller. Lower. Subordinate.

Inferior Courts. See COURTS, INFERIOR.

Inferior officer. See OFFICER, INFERIOR.

Infeudare. To grant in fee; to enfeoff.

Infeudation. The granting or putting in possession of an estate in fee. The feudal relation. The granting of tithes to laymen.

Inficiari. In Civil law, to deny an allegation, charge, or liability, or refuse to pay a debt or restore a pledge.

Inficiatio. In Civil law, denial of a debt, liability, claim or allegation.

Infidel. One who does not believe in a God. One who does not accept as true, the beliefs of the Christian or other religion. One having no religion which binds him to tell the truth. A faithless vassal.

Infidelis. In old English law, an infidel. One who violated fealty.

Infidelitas. In Feudal law, failure to keep an oath of fealty.

Infiduciare. In old law, to pledge property.

Inflht. In Saxon law, an assault on one dwelling in the same house.

Infirm. Incomplete. Legally incomplete.

Infirmative. Having a tendency to weaken. Tending to make void.

Infirmative fact. See FACT, INFIRMATIVE.

Infirmative hypothesis. An hypothesis which assumes the innocence of defendant, and shows that the evidence of guilt is not inconsistent.

Infirmity. Weakness. Invalidity.

Influence, undue. See FRAUDULENT INFLUENCE.

Informal. Deficient in legal form.

Informality. An irregularity. Not in accordance with the usual method.

Informant. One who files an information on behalf of the State.

Information. A complaint exhibited against a person for a criminal offense. An accusation under oath presented by a prosecuting officer without action by a Grand Jury. A bill filed in a civil action to obtain redress for an injury to the State or those under its protection. A complaint to recover a penalty under a statute or ordinance. In Scotch law, a written argument submitted to a court.

Information, bill of. See BILL OF INFORMATION.

Information, criminal. See CRIMINAL INFORMATION.

Information, ex officio. See EX OFFICIO INFORMATION.

Information in the nature of a quo warranto. A proceeding for the trial of the right to a franchise or office.

Information of intrusion. A proceeding against intruders upon public lands of a State or Nation.

Informatus. Informed ; instructed.

Informatus non sum. Same as NON SUM INFORMATUS.

Informer. One who informs against others. One who brings an action for the recovery of a penalty, the amount recovered to be divided between the informer and the State. See QUI TAM.

Informer, common. Originally, one who made it a business to institute qui tam actions for his own profit. One who volunteered to give information of the criminal acts of others.

Infortiatum. One part of the Digests of the Civil law.

Infortunium. Misfortune. Misadventure.

Infortunium, homicide per. The unintentional killing of another by one doing a lawful act.

Infra. Below. Underneath. Within.

Infra ætatem. Under age.

Infra annos nubiles. Under marriageable years.

Infra annum luctus. Within the year of mourning.

Infra brachia. Within her arms ; applied to a murdered husband for whom alone a woman could have an appeal whether he was a husband de facto or de jure.

Infra civitatem. Within the State.

Infra corpus comitatus. Within the body of a county.

Infra dignitatem curiæ. Beneath the dignity of the court.

Infra hospitium. Within the inn. Under the care of the innkeeper.

Infra præsidia. Within the protection. Applied to a prize of war brought within the jurisdiction of the country of its captors.

Infraction. A violation. In French law, an act for which a punishment is affixed by law.

Infringement. Encroachment upon the right of another. The violation of another's rights.

Infringer. One who violates the rights of another.

Infugare. To put to flight.

Infula. A priest's garment. A cassock.

Inge. Meadows.

Ingenium. · Originally, any instrument used in war. A net. A hook. A machine.

Ingenui. In Roman law, those born free.

Ingenuitas. In Roman law, liberty given a slave by manumission.

Ingenuitas Regni. Barons and Lords of the King's council.

Ingenuus. A freeman. A yeoman.

Ingress. The right to enter. A term used in a lease signifying a free entry into.

Ingress, egress and regress. The right to enter, go upon, and return from.

Ingressu. A writ of entry. A præcipe quod reddat.

Ingressus. The relief which the heir at full age paid to the head lord for entering upon the fee or lands fallen by the death or forfeiture of the tenant. Entry. Ingress.

Ingressus et egressus. Freedom of entry and exit.

Ingrossator. An engrosser.

Ingrossator Magni Rotuli. Ancient name for Clerk of the Pipe.

Ingrosser. One who transcribes instruments, writes resolutions, etc. One who controls the supply of a commodity, as provisions. See INGROSSING.

Ingrossing. Obtaining control of large quantities of provisions with intent to sell them again at an enhanced price. The act of making a correct copy of an instrument or bill.

Ingrossing a fine. Making the indentures by the chirographer.

Inhabitancy. Residence.

Inhabitant. A dweller or householder in a place.

Inherent. Existing as an element of original quality.

Inherent condition. See CONDITION, INHERENT.

Inherent power. A power existing as an original quality, and not conferred by another.

Inheretrix. An heiress.

Inherit. To take property by operation of law.

Inheritable blood. Blood capable of transmitting an inheritance.

Inheritance. An estate which passes by operation of law upon the death of the ancestor.

Inheritance Act. An act regulating the inheritance of property. Particularly, in England, the statute 3 and 4 Wm. IV., c. 106.

Inheritance, collateral. One cast upon collateral heirs.

Inheritance, corporeal. That which may be touched and handled.

Inheritance, incorporeal. Rights issuing out of, annexed to, or exercised with corporeal inheritance.

Inheritance, several. Where two or more hold or inherit lands severally.

Inheritance, shifting. An inheritance which may shift from one heir by the birth of a nearer heir.

Inhibition. In Scotch law, a writ to forbid a judge proceeding further in a cause before him. A writ to prohibit a person from burdening a heritable estate with a debt.

Inhibition against a wife. A writ prohibiting persons having transactions with, or giving credit to a man's wife.

Inhoc. A corner of a common field cultivated.

Inhoke. Same as INHOC.

Inhonestus. In old English law, not in proper order.

Iniquity. In Scotch law, a decision by an inferior judge, contrary to law.

Iniquum. Unequal.

Initial. Relating to the beginning of anything. The opening. The first letter of a word or name.

Initialia testimonii. In Scotch law, the practice of examining a witness to discover his sentiments toward the parties, before taking his evidence. (Now obsolete).

Initiate. Begun.

Initiate curtesy. The interest of a husband during his wife's lifetime in her lands, after the birth of a child capable of inheriting.

Initiate tenant by courtesy. Same as INITIATE COURTESY.

Initiative. A beginning. The right to begin. The right to propose.

Initium. The beginning.

Injunction. A writ issued out of a court of equity forbidding a person to do or allow a certain act.

Injunction, common. One granted on default.

Injunction, ex parte. One granted at the instance of one party without the other having notice of the application.

Injunction, final. Same as INJUNCTION, PERPETUAL.

Injunction, interlocutory. Same as INJUNCTION, PRELIMINARY.

Injunction, mandatory. An injunction commanding or forbidding, or which forbids a thing to continue, which is equivalent to directing it to be discontinued or removed.

Injunction, permanent. Same as INJUNCTION, PERPETUAL.

Injunction, perpetual. One prohibiting the person forever from doing an act or continuing the existence of a thing.

Injunction, preliminary. One granted to restrain the person's action pending the determination of the suit. See RESTRAINING ORDER.

Injunction, preventive. An injunction commanding one to refrain from doing some act.

Injunction, provisional. Same as PRELIMINARY.

Injunction, pendente lite. Same as PRELIMINARY.

Injuria. Injury; legal wrong.

Injuria absque damno. Injury without damage. A wrong from which no damage results.

Injuriosus. That which works a wrong. See DAMNOSUS.

Injurious words. See WORDS, INJURIOUS.

Injury. A wrong or damage to a man's person or goods.

Injury, absolute. An injury to the rights possessed by one as a member of society.

Injury, civil. A wrong against one's individual rights.

Injury, irreparable. An injury which cannot be compensated for in damages.

Injury, malicious. See MALICIOUS INJURY.

Injury, personal. See PERSONAL INJURY.

Injury, private. Injury to one's civil or private rights.

Injury, public. An injury to the rights of the community as a community.

Injury, real. An injury to the person, dignity, or honor.

Injury, relative. An injury to the right one possesses by reason of his relation to the one immediately injured.

Injury, threatened. See THREATENED INJURY.

Injury to personal property. The taking and detention of property from the owner, or damage to the same.

Injury to real property. Any act which deprives the owner of the full enjoyment of the same or which makes it less useful or profitable.

Injury, verbal. Injury by slander or libel.

Injusta captio et injusta detentio. Unjust arrest and unjust detention.

Injustice. Denial of justice. An act contrary to equity.

Inlagare. To admit or restore to the benefit of the law.

Inlagary. Same as INLAGATION.

Inlagation. A restitution of one outlawed to the protection of the law.

Inlagh. He who was some frank-pledge and not outlawed. See UTLAGH.

Inlagatus. Same as INLAGH.

Inland. Lands enclosed and reserved for the lord's own use. Inlantal. See OUT-LAND.

Inland bills. See BILLS, INLAND.

Inland navigation. See NAVIGATION, INLAND.

Inland trade. See TRADE, INLAND.

Inlantal. Inland. See DELANTAL.

Inlantale. Same as INLANTAL.

Inlaughe. In old English law, under the law.

In-law. To restore to civil rights. To restore to the protection of the law.

Inleased. Intangled and snared. A word used in a champion's oath.

Inlegiare. See SE INLEGIARE.

Inligare. In old law, to league together.

Inmates. Anciently persons unable to maintain themselves who were admitted to dwell in the house of another. Suffering such to so dwell was at one time prohibited by English statute.

Inn. A place kept for the purpose of lodging and entertaining travellers.

Innamium. A pledge.

Innaturalitas. Unnatural usage.

Innavigable. Applied to a vessel unfit for navigation; or to a stream not capable of being navigated.

Inner barrister. In England, a barrister admitted within the bar. A Queen's counsel.

Inner house. In Scotland, the name given to the chambers in which the sittings of the First and Second Divisions of the Court of Sessions are held.

Inner temple. See INNS OF COURT.

Innings. Lands recovered from the sea by draining.

Innkeeper. A person who makes it his business to provide lodging and necessaries for persons, their attendants and horses.

Innocence. Freedom from guilt or taint.

Innocent. Not tortious.

Innocent agent. See AGENT, INNO-CENT.

Innocent conveyances. See CONVEY-ANCES, INNOCENT.

Innominate. Unnamed.

Innominate contracts. See CON-TRACTS, INNOMINATE.

Innonia. An inclosure.

Innotescimus. We make known. Words used in letters-patent. See VIDI-MUS.

Innovation. Changing one obligation for another, so as to make the second take the place of the first.

Innoxiare. To purge one of a fault and make him innocent.

Inns of Chancery. Formerly English preparatory colleges for students. They were Clifford's Inn, Clement's Inn, New Inn, Staple Inn, Barnard's Inn, Furnival's Inn, Strand Inn, Lyon's Inn, Thaives' Inn, and Serjeant's Inn.

Inns of Court. Associations in London with the privilege of admitting to the bar or conferring the degree of barrister. Inner and Middle Temple belonged originally to the Knights Templar, and Lincoln's Inn and Gray's Inn to the Earls Lincoln and Gray.

Innuendo. An explanatory phrase used in pleading, of some matter formerly expressed. In pleading it is generally stated in brackets thus; "he (meaning the plaintiff)'' or '' he foreswore himself (meaning he committed wilful perjury),'' but it must not enlarge what it explains.

Inofficiosum. Undutiful.

Inofficiosum testamentum. An unnatural will.

Inofficious testament. See TESTAMENT, INOFFICIOUS.

Inoficiocidad. In Spanish law, that which is contrary to a duty or obligation.

Inoperative. Lacking in operation. Incapable of being enforced. Ineffective.

Inoperationis causa. When pleadings were to cease. Term applied to such days used in an excuse for not appearing.

Inops consilii. Destitute of counsel.

Inordinatus. One who died intestate.

Inpensioner. A pensioned soldier who lives in a public institution.

Inpenny and outpenny. Money paid on the alienations of tenants, particular to some manors.

Inprisii. Adherents or accomplices.

Inquest. An inquiry into a special matter by a jury empanelled for that purpose. A proceeding for the determination of damages or values where no defense has been made.

Inquest, Coroner's. An inquiry by a coroner into the cause of a death.

Inquest, Grand. Grand Jury.

Inquest, Halifax. A summary punishment and trial; so called from an old custom in dealing with thieves in the parish of Halifax, England.

Inquest of office. An inquiry made by an officer of the King or State concerning any matter which entitles the King or State to lands, tenements, goods or chattels. The verdict is called ''office found.''

Inquest, sheriff's. See SHERIFF'S INQUEST.

Inquilinus. In Roman law, the hirer of a house. A tenant of a house in a city. See COLONUS.

(29)

Inquirendo. An authority given to enquire into something.

Inquirendo de lunatico. A writ to bring a person thought to be of unsound mind before a commission to enquire into his sanity.

Inquiry. The act of seeking information by questions. Investigation.

Inquiry, court of. See COURT OF INQUIRY.

Inquiry, writ of. SEE WRIT OF INQUIRY.

Inquisitio. In old English law, an inquisition.

Inquisitio patriæ. The inquisition of the country. A trial jury as distinguished from the grand assise.

Inquisitio post mortem. Inquest after death. An ancient inquest of office, made on behalf of the crown.

Inquisition. The return of a jury empanelled to enquire of a particular offense only. The jury making such inquiry. The act of inquiry. A tribunal for examination and punishment of heretics established by Pope Gregory IX, in 1235 ; suppressed in France, 1772 ; in Spain, 1834.

Inquisitor. In Ecclesiastical law, a person empowered to hear, determine and punish offenses against the church.

Inroll. Transcribe. To make a record of.

Inrollment. The entering or registering of any lawful act.

Insane. Mentally deranged. Those legally declared to be, and restrained because mentally deranged. A condition in which free mental action is destroyed.

Insanity. Mental disorder.

Insanity, emotional. Temporary insanity caused by extraordinary emotion or passion.

Insanity, moral. An insanity in which the person afflicted knows what is right but cannot choose it.

Insanity, temporary. That which exists for a short period only. Delirium.

Inscribere. In Civil law, to subscribe an accusation. To agree to submit to the same punishment which the one accused would suffer if convicted.

Inscriptio. A written instrument of grant.

Inscription. That which is written, printed, engraved, stamped or otherwise impressed. In Civil law, an agreement by an accuser to suffer the same punishment affixed to a crime of which he accuses another, if his accusation be not sustained.

Inscriptiones. Instruments writing by which anything is granted.

Insectator. A prosecutor or adversary at law.

Insensible. Not intelligible.

Inservire. To reduce persons to servitude.

Insetena. An inditch. (One dug within another for greater protection).

Insidiæ. A watch. A guard.

Insidiatores viarum. W a y l a y e r s . Words prohibited from being put in indictments by stat. 4 Hy. IV., c. 2.

Insignia. Ensigns or arms.

Insilarius. An evil counsellor.

Insilium. Evil advice or counsel.

Insimul. Together. Jointly.

Insimul computassent. A writ or action of account, which only lies for things uncertain. A count in a declaration in assumpsit which sets forth an account stated wherein the defendant was found indebted to the plaintiff so much as a consideration for the defendant's promise to pay the sum found in arrear.

Insimul tenuit. One species of the writ of foremedon brought against a stranger by a coparcener on the possession of the ancestor.

Insinuacion. In Spanish law, presenting a document to a judge for his official sanction, or attestation of its authenticity.

Insinuare. In Civil law, to put into. To file in court.

Insinuatio. Suggestion. In Roman law, registration among the public records.

Insinuation. Creeping into one's mind or favor covertly.

Insinuation of a will. The first production of it. Leaving it with the registrar for probate.

Insolvency. The condition of one who has not sufficient property for the payment of his debts.

Insolvency, act of. See ACT OF INSOLVENCY.

Insolvency, composition in. Same as COMPOSITION IN BANKRUPTCY.

Insolvent. Unable to pay the claims of creditors. Of or pertaining to insolvency or bankruptcy. A bankrupt. One whose property is taken by a court to be divided among his creditors. In U. S. Bankrupt law of 1898, the condition of a person whose known property will not at a fair valuation be sufficient in amount to pay his debts.

Insolvent laws. See LAWS, INSOLVENT.

Inspectator. A prosecutor.

Inspection. Official examinations by the proper parties.

Inspection laws. See LAWS, INSPECTION.

Inspection of documents or records. The right to inspect documents or records material to a cause either on record or in possession of the other side.

Inspection of the person. Examination of one alleging injuries in a suit for damages; or a defendant in a suit for divorce accused of being impotent.

Inspection, trial by. A trial so called, where the judge makes a decision without a jury, on his own examination; used in determining the age or competency of a person as a witness, etc.

Inspector. An officer appointed to examine or oversee any matter of public concern. An officer of police.

Inspector, General. In U. S. Army, a staff officer who has the inspection of troops as to their condition and needs.

Inspectorate. A district under an inspector. An administrative district in Greenland.

Inspectorship, deed of. A deed of property to creditors made by a debtor on the understanding that the latter is to manage the same under inspection for a specified time for the benefit of the creditors.

Inspeximus. We have inspected. The first word in English letters patent and charters which renewed a former grant. The renewal of a royal charter. A royal grant.

Installation. The ceremony of investing a person with any office or dignity.

Instalment. A settlement; establishing or placing in. A partial payment.

Instance. In Civil law, any civil action or judicial demand. In Scotch law, that which may be insisted on at one diet or course of probation. Anciently, evidence.

Instance, causes of. In English Ecclesiastical law, causes that proceed at the solicitation of some party.

Instance, Court of First. Court of primary jurisdiction.

Instance Court. See COURT, INSTANCE.

Instancia. In Spanish law, the prosecution of a cause from the initiation to final decision.

Instantia, Primera. In Spanish law, the institution of a suit before a competent tribunal.

Instancia, Secunda. In Spanish law, the prosecution of a suit before an appellate tribunal.

Instancia, Tercera. In Spanish law, the prosecution of a cause before an appellate tribunal which has once considered it, or before a still higher tribunal having jurisdiction to hear the same.

Instant. An indivisible moment of time. That which though indivisible, yet in law is divisible for some purpose.

Instanter. Instantly; presently.

Instantly. Without noticeable delay; immediately.

Instar. Likeness. Equivalent.

Instar dentium. Like teeth. (The word Indenture is supposed to be derived from Instar Dentium because an indenture is divided in two parts with edges like the teeth of a saw).

Instar omnium. Equal to all.

Instauramentum. Young beasts.

Instaurum. A stock of cattle. All stock and implements of husbandry on a farm.

Instaurum ecclesiæ. Books, vestments and utensils belonging to a church.

Instigation. The act of urging or inciting.

Instirpare. To plant. To establish.

Institor. In Civil law, a clerk; an agent.

Institoria actio. In Civil law, an action to compel performance of a contract made with an institor.

Institorial power. In Civil law, the charge of managing a shop or store given to a clerk, sometimes a slave.

Instituta. Institutes.

Institute. To begin. To nominate or appoint. A treatise or commentary. In Scotch law, the person to whom an estate is first given by limitation or destination.

Institutes. Commentaries upon law. An elementary treatise of the general principles of the Civil law, comprised in four books and promulgated under direction of Justinian. See INSTITUTES OF JUSTINIAN.

Institutes of Gaius. A work by Gaius, a Roman jurist, on the principles of Roman law. It is said to have been the foundation of Justinian's Institutes.

Institutes of Justinian. An elementary work on the Roman law compiled about A. D. 533, by Tribonian and others under directions of Justinian; it is part of the Corpus Juris Civilis.

Institutes of Lord Coke. Four volumes written by Lord Coke, on the law of England. The first is upon Littleton's Treatise on Tenures; the second, on old Acts of Parliament; the third, on Pleas of the Crown, and the fourth, on the Courts.

Institutio hæredis. In Roman law, the appointment of the hæres to carry out the provisions of a will.

Institution. The investiture of a clerk by a bishop ; the ceremony of ordaining him as a rector of a parish. The beginning of anything. A rule of conduct, or government. An organization for public purpose. In Civil law, the nomination by a testator of the one who is to be his heir.

Institution au droit Francois. An institution of French right.

Institutiones, the. One of the compilations made under the direction of Justinian, and part of the Corpus Juris Civilis.

Instruct. To give directions to. To convey information to. To inform as to the law. In Scotch law, to verify; to confirm; to prepare; to arrange in order.

Instruction. In French law, the preparation for a criminal prosecution by examination of the accused, obtaining of evidence, &c.

Instruction, binding. An instruction which directs the jury to give a certain verdict.

Instruction, peremptory. Same as INSTRUCTION, BINDING.

Instructions. Directions given an agent by a principal. Information of the law applicable to the facts in a cause, given by the judge to a jury. The statement of his cause of action, given by a client to his attorney.

Instrument. An instrument writing.

Instrument of saisine. See SAISINE, INSTRUMENT OF.

Instrument writing. A written document which is the evidence of some deed, contract, or obligation.

Instrumenta. Writings not under seal.

Instruments, constating. Instruments conferring power, or creating a corporation, board or commission.

Instrument, negotiable. Written securities which possess the quality of negotiability. Negotiable paper.

Instruments of evidence. See EVIDENCE, INSTRUMENTS OF.

Insufficiency. In an answer in equity, neglect to specifically reply to specific allegations. Failure to specify particularly.

Insufficient. Incompetent. Inadequate. Less than required by law.

Insula. An island. An isolated house.

Insultus. An assault.

Insuper. Moreover. Over and above. Applied in English Exchequer to charge upon one's account.

Insurance interest. An interest which exists by reason of another's life. Such an interest as can be insured by the one holding it. Such an interest as would occasion a loss to the holder on the death, destruction, or injury of the subject-matter.

Insurance. A contract whereby one person undertakes in consideration of the payment of certain specified sums at certain periods, to pay a certain sum on the happening of some event.

Insurance, accident. That form of insurance wherein injury or death from accident alone, makes the insurer liable for payment of the money agreed upon.

Insurance against birth of issue. An English system of insurance in which the insurer agrees to pay a sum if a child be born or come of age who will deprive the insured of an estate.

Insurance agent. One who acts as agent for an insurer in obtaining contracts of insurance.

Insurance broker. Same as INSURANCE AGENT.

Insurance, casualty. Insurance in which injury or destruction to property by accident alone makes the insurer responsible.

Insurance Company. A company whose business is to act as insurer.

Insurance Company, Mutual. One made up of persons insured, from whose contributions the losses are paid.

Insurance, credit. Insurance against loss by failure of creditors to meet their obligations with the insured.

Insurance, double. A second insurance upon the same subject with the same insured.

Insurance, employer's liability. An agreement to indemnify an employer for damage obtained against him by an employee for injuries sustained while in the service of the former.

Insurance, fidelity. Insurance against loss through dishonesty or negligence of an employee.

Insurance, fire. Insurance against loss or injury by fire.

Insurance, guaranty. Insurance in the nature of a guaranty against the unfaithfullness of employees.

Insurance, life. Generally, a contract by which the insurer, in consideration of a sum of money paid to him, agrees to pay on the death of a person mentioned, a sum of money to an estate or to a person or persons mentioned in the contract.

Insurance loss. A loss occasioned by the happening of the event upon which money was to be paid by an insurer.

Insurance, marine. Insurance against loss at sea or on navigable waters.

Insurance, over. Insurance above the value of property insured.

Insurance peril. Same as INSURANCE RISK.

Insurance policy. A written contract of insurance.

Insurance policy, running. Same as POLICY, OPEN.

Insurance, premium of. See PREMIUM OF INSURANCE.

Insurance, re. See RE-INSURANCE.

Insurance risk. The contingency insured against.

Insurance scrip. See SCRIP, INSURANCE.

Insurance, title. An insurance against loss by reason of a defect in the title of real estate, or incumbrances, or liens.

Insurance, tontine. See TONTINE; also TONTINE POLICY.

Insure. To agree to indemnify one for a loss or injury to property or to pay a sum in case of accident or death of a person.

Insured. One who contracts with an insurer for the payment of money on a certain contingency.

Insurer. One who insures another.

Insurgent. A party to an insurrection.

Insurrection. A revolt against political authority.

Intake. An enclosure made of waste lands. That which is taken in as parks from a farm.

Intakers. Thieves in north of England who received property stolen from Scotland.

Integer. Entire. Untouched.

Intemperate. In the habit of becoming drunk.

Intend. To set the mind upon as a purpose to be effected.

Intendant. One having charge of some public affair. In Spanish law, a district administrator or treasurer.

Intended to be recorded. A term sometimes used in referring to a deed or instrument writing not yet recorded.

Intendente. In Spanish law, an agent of the Minister of Finance.

Intendment. The true meaning.

Intendment of law. The understanding and true meaning of law.

Intent. The purpose with which one does an act. The presumption which the law draws from an act.

Intent, common. The usual meaning of words.

Intent, criminal. Malicious design.

Intent, general. An intent to do something but not in particular; as to violate law generally, but no particular law.

Intent, particular. Same as INTENT, SPECIFIC.

Intent, specific. An intent shown by the doing of some particular thing.

Intentio. A count; a charge. The plaintiff's demand. Purpose; intention.

Intentio cæca. A secret purpose.

Intention. The true meaning. The presumption. The intent.

Intentione. A writ against one who entered lands after the death of tenant in dower or for life, and holds out one in reversion or remainder.

Inter. Between; among.

Inter alia. Among other things.

Inter alios. Between others.

Inter apices juris. See APEX JURIS.

Inter canem et lupum. Between dog and wolf. Words anciently used to signify the crime being done in the twilight.

Inter cæteros. Among others. In Civil law, applied to clauses in a will which disinherited.

Inter partes. Between parties. A term applied to deeds and contracts wherein two parties each covenant or agree to perform.

Inter regalia. In English law, among the rights of the crown.

Inter se. Among themselves.

Inter sese. Among themselves.

Inter vivos. Between living parties. A term applied to gifts made while the parties are alive, as distinguished from a bequest.

Intercalare. In Civil law, to insert among others. To insert a day or month in a calendar.

Intercedere. In Civil law, to become bound for the debt of another.

Intercommon. See INTERCOMMON-INGS.

Interchangeably. By way of exchange. Applied to the signing by parties of duplicate copies of instrument writings and exchanging the same.

Intercommoning. Pasturing cattle in the common of two manors which adjoin each other. The act of proscribing those who have assisted or harbored outlaws.

Intercommoning, letters of. See LETTERS OF INTERCOMMONING.

Intercommune. To denounce for communicating with rebels.

Intercontinental Railway Commission. A commission organized to examine the routes, and furnish estimates of cost, &c., for an intercontinental railway to connect the U. S. with other republics on the American continent. Its headquarters are at Washington, D. C.

Intercourse. Communication, correspondence, or association.

Interdict. A prohibitive order. A process ordering or prohibiting something to be done. In Scotch law, a judicial injunction. An interdiction.

Interdicted of fire and water. Denied of fire and water; a part of an ancient sentence of banishment which prohibited anyone from receiving the banished one into his house or giving him fire or water.

Interdiction. A prohibition against entering into commercial relations with subjects of a foreign country. The restraint under which a person is placed by judicial decree with relation to his property, because of some legal incapacity. In Scotch law, restraint upon persons liable to be taken advantage of because of their weakness of mind or character.

Interdiction, judicial. In Scotch law, one made by order of court.

Interdiction, voluntary. In Scotch law, one made by deed of the party by which he covenants not to take any action regarding his property without the consent of certain persons mentioned in the deed.

Interdictum. In Civil law, an injunction.

Interdictum Salvianum. The Salvian edict. In Roman law, a process to obtain possession of goods pledged by a tenant for payment of rent.

Interesse. Interest either on money or in lands.

Interesse termini. Interest in a term. The right in land, which a lessee acquires, before entry, by virtue of a demise at common law.

Interest. Any estate, right or title in a thing. Concern. Payment for the use of money, or money so paid. Compensation due a creditor for the time money due remains unpaid.

Interest, absolute. An interest without condition. An interest so vested that the owner cannot be deprived of it without consent.

Interest, at. Applied to money which is lent.

Interest, beneficial. See BENEFICIAL INTEREST.

Interest, chattel. See CHATTEL INTEREST.

Interest, compound. Interest computed on principal and accrued interest.

Interest, conventional. Interest where the rate is agreed upon.

Interest, coupled with an. An agency or power in which the agent or donee has an interest in the business or estate.

Interest, direct. In practice a certain and not doubtful interest in the matter in controversy.

Interest, entire. All the interest without any diminution.

Interest, equitable. Such as can be enforced in equity.

Interest, ex. See EX-INTEREST.

Interest, executory. A future estate other than a remainder or reversion.

Interest, immediate. Direct, present, or close interest.

Interest in lands. See LANDS, INTEREST IN.

Interest, legal. The rate established by law where no rate has been agreed upon.

Interest, life. See LIFE INTEREST.

Interest, marine. Extra interest because of extra risk where money is advanced on a bottomry bond.

Interest, maritime. Same as INTEREST, MARINE.

Interest, of general. Of interest to a large portion of a community or State, though not all.

Interest, of public. Of interest to all persons of a community or State.

Interest, opposing. An interest which opposes any action or which might be injured by it if taken.

Interest or no interest. Applied to a policy of insurance which is to be operative whether the insured has or has not an insurable interest.

Interest policy. See POLICY, INTEREST.

Interest, rate of. The relative amount as compared with the principal, paid for the use of money.

Interest, reversionary. See REVERSIONARY INTEREST.

Interest, simple. That computed on the original principal only.

Interest, with. With interest added.

Interested witness. See WITNESS, INTERESTED.

Interference. The application for a patent covering in whole or part any pending application or unexpired patent. The contest which arises from such condition.

Interim. Meanwhile; in the meantime.

Interim committitur. In the meantime let him be committed. Applied to an order of court for the detention of a person pending some action which is taken with respect to him.

Interim curator. See CURATOR, INTERIM.

Interim factor. In Scotch law, an officer who takes charge of an estate until the election of a trustee.

Interim officer. See OFFICER, INTERIM.

Interim order. An order made pending a suit or appeal.

Interim receipt. A receipt for money paid on a proposed contract of insurance.

Interior Department. See DEPARTMENT, INTERIOR.

Interior, Secretary of. The chief official of the Interior Department in the United States. He is a subordinate executive official whose duties and pay are regulated by Congress.

Interlaqueare. To link together. Applied to writs issued to several parties for the same purpose.

Interlineation. The insertion of any matter in an instrument after it is executed or engrossed.

Interlocutio. Imparlance.

Interlocutor. In Scotch law, a judgment or decree in a suit.

Interlocutor of relevancy. In Scotch law, a decree as to the relevancy of an indictment or libel.

Interlocutory. Done during the pendency of a cause and not final.

Interlocutory costs. See COSTS, INTERLOCUTORY.

Interlocutory decree. One entered during the pendency of a suit, but which is not a final decree; usually a decree upon some question or motion necessary to be determined or acted upon before the final decree can be entered.

Interlocutory judgment. Same as INTERLOCUTORY DECREE, except that the term judgment is applied to law cases and decree to equity cases.

Interlocutory order. See ORDER, INTERLOCUTORY.

Interlocutory sentence. In Civil law, an interlocutory decree.

Interloper. One who interferes with the trade of another.

Intermediary. One who negotiates a matter between two persons. A broker.

Intern. To restrict a person within a certain territory as a political prisoner. See RECONCENTRADOS.

Internal improvements. See IMPROVEMENTS, INTERNAL.

Internal revenue. See REVENUE, INTERAL.

Internal revenue laws. See LAWS, INTERNAL REVENUE.

International. Pertaining to two or more Nations.

International arbitration. See ARBITRATION, INTERNATIONAL.

International copyright. See COPYRIGHT, INTERNATIONAL.

International extradition Same as EXTRADITION, FOREIGN.

International law. Same as LAW OF NATIONS.

International law, public. See LAW, PUBLIC INTERNATIONAL.

International law, private. See LAW, PRIVATE INTERNATIONAL.

International rules of navigation. Rules agreed to by Nations for the government of the movement of vessels when approaching each other.

Internuncio. A Papal minister to inferior courts.

Internuncius. A messenger between others.

Interplead. To become a party to a cause.

Interpleader, bill of. See BILL OF INTERPLEADER.

Interpolation. The act of questioning a member of a government. A demand for a statement from an official. Verbal interruption. In Civil law, the declaration by a person that he will not be bound by an agreement to which he is a party, beyond a certain time.

Interpolate. To insert words in an instrument after it has been completed. To alter. To corrupt by insertions.

Interpret. To explain. See CONSTRUE.

Interpretation. Construction. The act of expounding or obtaining the true meaning of anything. The sense given by the interpreter.

Interpretation, artful. Giving a meaning other than that known to be intended.

Interpretation, authentic. An interpretation by the author.

Interpretation clause. A section of a statute which defines the meaning of words occurring in other sections.

Interpretation, close. Taking words in their most narrow sense.

Interpretation, doctrinal. An interpretation made in accordance with technical rules.

Interpretation, extensive. Placing a liberal construction on words.

Interpretation, extravagant. Placing a meaning upon words far beyond what is the evident intention of those using them.

Interpretation, free. An interpretation not limited by any rules, but made in good faith.

Interpretation, limited. An interpretation which gives even a more restricted meaning than the usual rules would give.

Interpretation, predestined. An interpretation forced to meet a prejudiced view or desire.

Interpretation, restricted. Same as INTERPRETATION, LIMITED.

Interpretation, unrestricted. Same as INTERPRETATION FREE.

Interpretation, usual. One based on usage.

Interpreter. One who translates the testimony of witnesses from one language to another.

Interregnum. The suspension of authority through a change in the government.

Interrogation, suggestive. One which suggests the answered desired.

Interrogatoire. In French law, a paper containing the interrogatories made by a judge to an accused, and the answers thereto.

Interrogatory. A question reduced to writing and read to the witness.

Interrogatory, counter. Same as INTERROGATORY, CROSS.

Interrogatory, cross. A written question put to a witness as cross-examination of a direct interrogatory. A question put by the party adverse to the one calling the witness.

Interrogatory, direct. A written question propounded to a witness for the first time. A question put by the side calling the witness.

Interrogatory, fishing. One which seeks to draw out that which the interrogator is not entitled to know.

Interrogatory, suggestive. One which indicates the answer desired.

Interruption. An act which breaks in upon and prevents the continuance of any course of progress. In Scotch law, the claiming of a right by the true owner during an adverse possession.

Interruption, civil. An interruption owing to some judicial act.

Interruption, natural. An interruption in fact.

Interruptio. Interruption; interference.

Intersect. To cross.

Intersection. The point at which two streams, roads, &c., meet.

Interstate. Relating to intercourse between different States or citizens of States.

Interstate Commerce. See COMMERCE, INTERSTATE.

Interstate Commerce Act. See LAW, INTERSTATE COMMERCE.

Interstate Commerce Commission. See COMMISSION, INTERSTATE COMMERCE.

Interstate Commerce Commissioner. See COMMISSIONER, INTERSTATE COMMERCE.

Interstate Commerce Law. See LAW, INTERSTATE COMMERCE.

Interstate rendition. See RENDITION, INTERSTATE.

Intervene. To interpose in a law suit, so as to become a party.

Intervening damages. See DAMAGES, INTERVENING.

Intervenor. One who applies to be heard as a party to another suit.

Intervention. The act of admitting a third party to a suit to enable him to protect some interest which might otherwise be affected. Among nations the interference by one nation in the affairs of another on the ground of humanity.

Intestabilis. An incompetent witness.

Intestable. Incapable of making a will, testament, or devise.

Intestacy. The condition when one dies without leaving a will, testament or devise.

Intestate. One who dies leaving no will, or leaving a will and the executor nominated therein refuses to act, or leaving an illegal will. Not disposed of by testament, will, or devise.

Intestate succession. See SUCCESSION, INTESTATE.

Intestate's estate. The goods and chattels of persons dying intestate.

Intestato. In Civil law, intestate.

Intestatus. In old English law, an intestate.

Intimacy, criminal. Sexual intercourse between persons not married.

Intimation. In Civil law, a notice to one that a legal proceeding will be taken. In Scotch law, a written notice by an assignee of a right or claim, to the one against whom it is held.

Intimidation of voters. Such acts of persons as prevent another from freely exercising his right to vote at an election, through fear of injury.

Intoxicating liquors. See LIQUORS, INTOXICATING.

Intol and uttol. Toll or custom paid for things imported or exported.

Intra. Within.

Intra mænia. Same as INTRA MŒNIA.

Intra mœnia. Within the walls. Domestic.

Intra parietes. Between the walls. Among friends. Out of court. Without contest.

Intra quatuor maria. Within the four seas.

Intra vires. Within the powers.

Intra-territorial. Within the territory. Within the jurisdiction. See EXTRA-TERRITORIAL.

Intransigentes. Those who refuse to agree or compromise. Applied to Cuban insurgents.

Intrare. To enter.

Intrare mariscum. To drain low ground. See INNINGS.

Intrinsicum servitium. The ordinary duties within the lord's court. See FORINSECUM SERVITIUM.

Intrinsic value. See VALUE, IN-TRINSIC.

Introduction. That part of a document or writing which tends to explain what follows.

Intromission. In Scotch law, assuming authority over the property of another, legally or illegally. Dealing in the property which comes to one as agent of another.

Intromission, necessary. Such an intromission as the circumstances m a k e necessary to preserve the property, as assuming control of the property of a deceased wife or husband.

Intromission, vicious. In Scotch law, an unauthorized meddling with the affairs of another.

Intromittere. To intermeddle with.

Intronisation. In French Church law, the installation of a bishop.

Intruder. One who enters land and keeps the right heir or owner from possession or enters the State or King's land and takes the profits.

Intrusion. The unlawful entry of a stranger into lands or tenements void by the death of a tenant for life or years or before one in remainder or reversion. Compare with Abator.

Intrusion de gard. A writ where an infant entered lands and kept out the lord.

Intrusion, information of. See IN-FORMATION OF INTRUSION.

Intrusione. A writ against an intruder by him who has the fee.

Inundation. The act of overflowing. Overflow.

Inure. Same as ENURE.

Inurement. That which inures to the benefit of another, as service, improvements, use, &c.

Invadiare. To mortgage lands.

Invadiatio. A pledge. A gage.

Invadiatus. One who having been accused of some crime not fully proved is put sub debita fidejussione.

Invading a judge. Assaulting a judge.

Invalid. Illegal Legally, insufficient.

Invasion. Entrance into a country with hostile intent.

Invasiones. A title given certain lands during reign of King John of England.

Invecta et illata. Things brought and carried in. A tenant's furniture.

Inveniendo. Finding. A word used in reserving rent.

Invent. To create or produce that not previously known.

Inventio. In Civil law, finding. It was one of the modes of acquiring property through occupancy. In old English law, a thing found.

Invention. Discovery. Some mechanical device or process.

Invention, useful. Such invention as could be used beneficially by a community or which is useful in connection with another invention or process.

Inventiones. Money or goods found and not challenged by the owner. Originally they belonged to the finder, then to the State or King. Concealment of such goods or money was once punishable in England with death, subsequently with fine and imprisonment. See TREASURE TROVE.

Inventor. One who discovers or invents a new article or process.

Inventory. A list or schedule containing a true description of property with its appraised value.

Inventus. Found. Come upon; met.

Inveritare. To verify or make proof of a thing.

Invest. To clothe with office, authority or dignity. To clothe with title. To put in possession. To lay out money in real or personal property for an income. To lay siege to.

Investigation. A legislative inquiry. Inquiry by any legal means necessary to obtain information concerning a subject.

Investitive fact. See FACT, INVESTITIVE.

Investive fact. Same as FACT, INVESTITIVE.

Investiture. The delivery of the possession of lands in presence of witnesses. The ceremony of inducting an abbot or bishop into his office.

Investment. The act of investing. The article purchased, or the enterprise in which money is invested. Act of blockading. The act of clothing with authority.

Inviolable. Not to be violated, injured or disturbed. Exempt from prosecution or punishment.

Inviolability. The condition of being inviolable.

Inviolate. Same as INVIOLABLE.

Invitatoria et venitarium. Hymns to invite persons to church. Mentioned in ancient English statutes.

Invito. Unwilling.

Invito debitore. Against the debtor's will.

Invito domino. The owner being unwilling.

Invitus. Against the will.

Invocation. A demand or order of a court.

Invoice. A list of goods sent to a purchaser, factor, consignee. The goods so listed.

Invoice price. The original cost.

Invoke. To call for by judicial process.

Involuntary. Against one's will.

Involuntary bankruptcy. See BANKRUPTCY, INVOLUNTARY.

Involuntary ignorance. See IGNORANCE, INVOLUNTARY.

Involuntary manslaughter. See MANSLAUGHTER, INVOLUNTARY.

Involuntary nonsuit. See NONSUIT, INVOLUNTARY.

Involuntary servitude. Slavery of any character.

Ipse. He; himself; the same.

Ipse dixit. He himself said it. A bare assertion on the authority of the one making it.

Ipso facto. By the fact itself. A censure of excommunication in the Ecclesiastical court.

Ipso jure. By the law itself.

Ipsissimis verbis. In the very words.

Ire ad largum. To go at large; to escape.

Ire sine die. To go without day.

Irenarcha. In Roman law, a magistrate or conservator of the peace.

Ironage. A duty anciently imposed on merchants of the staple.

Irony. The use of words designed to convey a meaning opposite to the literal sense with a view to indicating contempt or to hold up to ridicule. In England, irony has been held to be libellous.

Irrebuttable. That which cannot be rebutted.

Irrecusable obligation. See OBLIGATION, IRRECUSABLE.

Irregular. Contrary to rule or the usual practice. Not general; exceptional. In violation of law.

Irregular deposit. See DEPOSIT, IRREGULAR.

Irregular judgment. See JUDGMENT, IRREGULAR.

Irregular process. See PROCESS, IRREGULAR.

Irregularity. Out of rule. A transgression of form in practice. An impediment to being installed in a church office.

Irregularity, legal. See LEGAL IRREGULARITY.

Irrelevancy. The quality of not being material to the issue.

Irrelevant. Not relevant. See RELEVANT.

Irrelevant evidence. See EVIDENCE, IRRELEVANT.

Irremovability. The condition of a pauper who cannot be removed from a place where he is in receipt of relief.

Irreparable. That which cannot be repaired. That which cannot be compensated for by damages.

Irreparable injury. See INJURY, IRREPARABLE.

Irreplegiabilis. Cannot be bailed.

Irrepleviable. Not to be obtained by replevin.

Irreplevisable. Same as IRREPLEVIABLE.

Irrepreviable. That which cannot or ought not to be replevied.

Irreprevisable. Same as IRREPLEVIABLE.

Irresistible. That which cannot be resisted or opposed.

Irresistible force. See FORCE, IRRESISTIBLE.

Irresponsible. Not able to meet just obligations or expectations.

Irrevocable. That which cannot be annulled. Beyond recall.

Irrigation. Watering land by artificial means, usually ditches.

Irritancy. In Scotch law, the coming to pass of that which makes an instrument writing containing an irritant clause, void.

Irritant. In Scotch law, conditionally making void.

Irritant clause. See CLAUSE, IRRITANT.

Irritus. Void. Invalid.

Irrogare. In Civil law, to impose. To inflict. To enact or ordain.

Irrotulatio. An enrollment. A record.

Irrotulamentum. Same as IRROTULATIO.

Irrotulare. To enrol.

Is. That one. The.

Is qui cognoscit. The cognizor in a fine of lands.

Is cui cognoscitur. The cognizee in a fine of lands.

Ish. In Scotch law, the period of the ending of a lease.

Ish and entry, clause of free. In Scotch law, exit and entry.

Issint. So. Thus. A Norman French term once used in pleading.

Issuable. Producing an issue.

Issuable plea. See PLEA, ISSUABLE.

Issuable terms. Terms during which issues are made.

Issue. Children. Descendents. Profits from fines and amercements. Profits from lands and tenements which a sheriff is directed to take by writ of distringas to compel an appearance in court, or out of which to satisfy costs. A point affirmed on one side and denied on the other. That which the parties agree to refer to trial. To put in circulation. That which is sent out or put in circulation.

Issue, actual. An actual affirmation on one side and denial on the other in a proceeding regularly brought to have determined a question of right between the parties.

Issue, collateral. An issue upon a matter incidental to the main question.

Issue, common. The issue raised by a plea of non est factum in an action of covenant.

Issue, feigned. One made up upon a supposed case to obtain a determination of a collateral question of fact.

Issue, formal. An issue raised in technical form.

Issue, general. Where the whole declaration, indictment or cause of action is denied without offering new matter. (An accused in the U. S. is entitled in a criminal matter to a trial by jury of the facts alleged against him. If he pleads guilty, he can be sentenced without a trial, because there is no question between him and the State for a jury to determine the truth of. But whenever there is such a question no one can be deprived of the right to have such question determined by a jury).

Issue, immaterial. An issue which if determined does not determine the whole merits of the cause.

Issue in fact. One in which the truth of a fact is affirmed on one side and denied on the other.

Issue, informal. An issue raised in other than in technical form.

Issue in law. A dispute as to a question of law usually raised by demurrer.

Issue, joinder in. See JOINDER OF ISSUE.

Issue, material. One necessary to a determination of the case.

Issue, matter in. The matter affirmed on one side and denied on the other.

Issue of body. Heirs of the body.

Issue of fact, general. Where it is left to the jury to determine whether the defendant has done as charged by the plaintiff.

Issue of fact, special. Where some special matter or material point, alleged by the defendant in his defense, is to be tried.

Issue, re. Another issue. A continuance of a patent.

Issue, real. An issue raised in an actual suit and in regular manner, as distinguished from a feigned issue.

Issue roll. See ROLL, ISSUE.

Issue, special. A single material point upon the determination of which the case rests.

Issue upon matter of fact. Where the plaintiff and defendant have agreed upon a point to be tried by jury.

Issue upon matter of law. Where there is a joinder in demurrer which is to be determined by the judge.

Issued, re. Issued again. Continued.

Issues. Profits from real estate. The goods and profits of land taken under a writ of distringras or distress infinite.

Issues on sheriffs. In old English law, fines on sheriffs for neglect of duty taken from the issues of their lands.

Istimrar. Perpetuity. A perpetual lease granted by a government in India.

Istimrardar. One who holds a perpetual lease in India.

Ita. So. Thus.

Ita est. So it is. In Civil law, words written by the register of a dead notary in making copies of the latter's official acts, in lieu of the notary's name.

Ita quod. So that.

Ita te Deus adjuvet. So help you God !

Item. Also. A single charge in an account.

Iter. Way. Right of way. Journey. Circuit of a judge. The route of a voyage.

Iteratio. Repetition. In Roman law, the liberation by one having the legal title to a slave, after his liberation by the equitable owner.

Itinera. Eyres. Circuits.

Itinerant. Travelling. Anciently applied to justices in England.

Itinerantes. Travelling in eyre.

Itinerary. A commentary on events happening during a journey. The route of a journey.

Iule. In old English law, Christmas.